Stephen R. Bradley

*Letters of a Revolutionary War
Patriot and Vermont Senator*

STEPHEN R. BRADLEY

Edited by Dorr Bradley Carpenter

Foreword by H. Nicholas Muller III

McFarland & Company, Inc., Publishers
Jefferson, North Carolina, and London

Frontispiece: Stephen Rowe Bradley, 1754–1830 (Michelle M. Powell).

LIBRARY OF CONGRESS CATALOGUING-IN-PUBLICATION DATA

Bradley, Stephen Row, 1754–1830.
[Correspondence.]
Stephen R. Bradley : letters of a Revolutionary War patriot and Vermont senator / Stephen R. Bradley ; edited by Dorr Bradley Carpenter ; foreword by H. Nicholas Muller III.
p.   cm.
Includes bibliographical references and index.

ISBN 978-0-7864-3358-2
softcover : 50# alkaline paper ∞

1. Bradley, Stephen Row, 1754–1830 — Correspondence. 2. Senators — United States — Correspondence. 3. United States — History — Revolution, 1775–1783 — Sources. 4. United States — History — 1783–1865 — Sources. 5. United States — Politics and government — 1775–1783 — Sources. 6. United States — Politics and government — 1783–1865 — Sources. 7. Vermont — History — To 1791 — Sources. 8. Vermont — Politics and government — To 1791 — Sources.
I. Carpenter, Dorr, 1928– II. Title.
E302.6.B8A4   2009   328.73092 — dc22   [B]   2008048596

British Library cataloguing data are available

©2009 Dorr Bradley Carpenter. All rights reserved

No part of this book may be reproduced or transmitted in any form or by any means, electronic or mechanical, including photocopying or recording, or by any information storage and retrieval system, without permission in writing from the publisher.

On the cover: Stephen R. Bradley portrait in watercolor by Michelle M. Powell; background ©2008 Shutterstock

Manufactured in the United States of America

*McFarland & Company, Inc., Publishers
Box 611, Jefferson, North Carolina 28640
www.mcfarlandpub.com*

Stephen R. Bradley

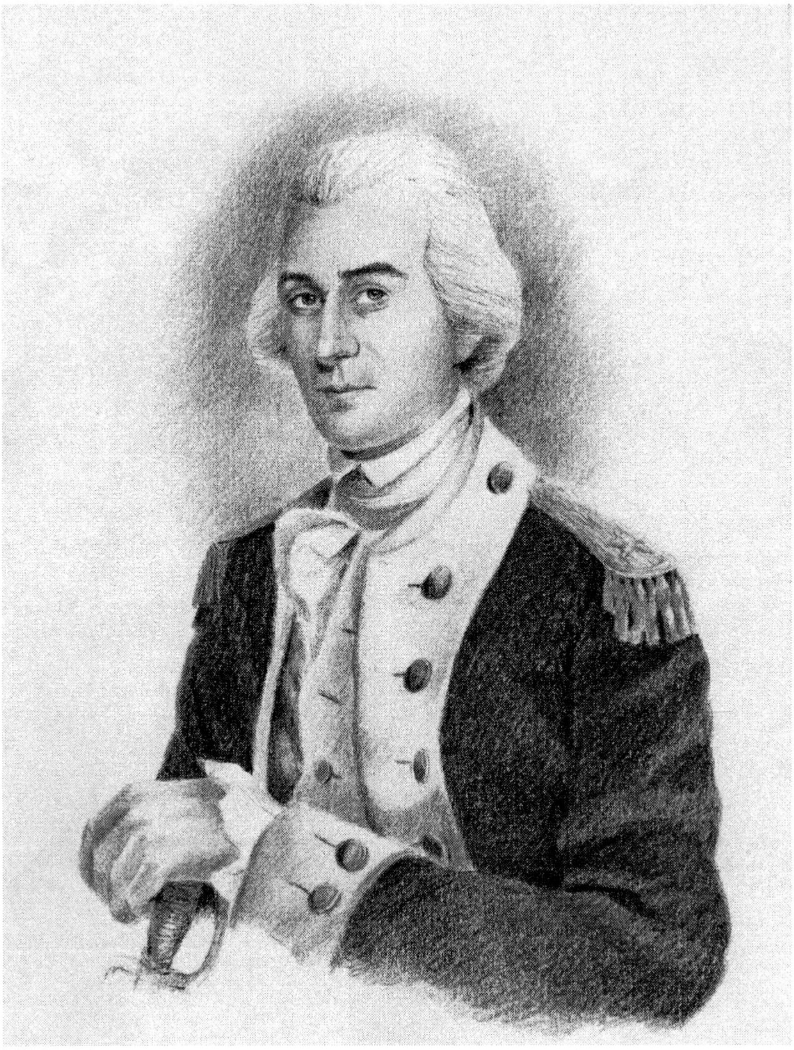

To the memory of

Eleanor Bradley,

Mrs. Benjamin Carpenter, Jr.,
and third great-granddaughter of Stephen R. Bradley

ACKNOWLEDGMENTS

Two names belong at the very beginning of this page. In fact, in the editor's opinion, without the professional work of transcribers Jeanne Kerr Cross and Anne Decker Cecere, the production of this volume would have been impossible. They took documents, some of which were almost illegible, and created easily read and comprehended material. Inexpressible gratitude is owed these two women by all those who gain a greater understanding of the life and times of Stephen Rowe Bradley through a study of these writings which their skills made available to the general public.

Numerous other individuals made unselfish contributions to this effort. A space in these acknowledgments can only begin to convey my appreciation for their time, knowledge, and encouragement.

Katherine B. Watters	Ellen McCallister Clark	Bryson Clevenger, Jr.
Noel Perrin	Donald Richie	John Buxton
Kenneth Jensan	David W. Ditmars	Barbara Wilanin
Jeffrey D. Marshall	Milton Gustenson	Keith Marshall Jones III
Gay Wilson	Benjamin Carpenter IV	Fredrick Ernst
Vera Graham	Benjamin Carpenter V	William Irwin
Jeffrey Flanery	Walter W. Campbell	Mark Mastromarino
Jane Morse	Kevin Hughes	Jack Robertson
Linda McCurdy	Elizabeth Carpenter	Barbara Oberg
Paul A. Carnhan	Barbara Lane	Michelle M. Powell
Betty K. Koed	Gregory Stanford	Sarah Hutcheon
Charles Perdue	Samuel B. Hand	Arthur Carpenter
John Rhodehamel	Heather Moore	

The Advisory Committee: John P. Kaminski, Ph.D.—History Department, University of Wisconsin; H. Nicholas Muller III, Ph.D. (Ret.)—History Department, University of Vermont; Theodore J. Crackel, Ph.D.—University of Virginia (editor-in-chief of "The Papers of George Washington")

Illustration Credits: All Bradley family pictures are from various family albums. All historical contemporary pictures are from the Library of Congress. The portrait of General Stephen R. Bradley is a watercolor by Michelle M. Powell. This project has been endorsed by the following organizations: New England Historic and Genealogical Society in Boston, Massachusetts; Vermont Council on the Humanities in Morrisville, Vermont; State of Vermont, Office of the Secretary of State, Montpelier, Vermont; Vermont Historical Society in Barre, Vermont. Organization and preparation of computerized submission manuscript was provided by Lorraine I. Quillon, Specialty Arts & Services, Charlottesville, Virginia.

Editor's Note

Stephen R. Bradley used two spellings of his middle name throughout his life. "Row," apparently the first spelling used, was derived from his mother's maiden name. For unknown reasons, Bradley began to use the spelling "Rowe" sometime after 1775. This book uses "Rowe" but does not change the spelling as it was presented in original documents or publications.

Appendix IV, an index to Bradley's correspondents and their letters, is a comprehensive listing of all persons related to the letters, including ones that are not transcribed in this volume. Biographical information, if known, is also provided.

TABLE OF CONTENTS

Acknowledgments	vii
Editor's Note	viii
Foreword by H. Nicholas Muller III	1
Introduction	5
Abbreviations and Notes on the Transcriptions	9

Background and Biography

Origins of the Family Name (by John C. Bradley)	13
Bradley Family Tree (by Henry K. Willard)	15
Biography	23

Correspondence, 1771 to 1831	47
Appendix I. List of Documents	397
Appendix II. Bradley Flag (U.S.), 1795–1818	407
Appendix III. Memoir and Correspondence of Jeremiah Mason, 1768–1848	409
Appendix IV. Index of Bradley's Correspondents and Their Letters	411
Bibliography	433
General Index	435

Foreword by
H. Nicholas Muller III

After earning undergraduate and M.A. degrees from Yale College during which he published an almanac printed in an edition of 2,000, working for two years as an officer in the Continental service, and studying law under the tutelage of the renowned Tapping Reeve, Stephen Rowe Bradley migrated to Vermont. He first appeared in a public capacity in Vermont in May 1779. He went on to play a prominent and important role on the stage of public affairs in Vermont and the nation for all or parts of five decades until he retired from the United States Senate in 1813. Yet the shadow of time has largely eclipsed Bradley's significance. The painstaking effort to locate, bring together, and transcribe the Bradley correspondence may let more light shine on one of Vermont's most important and distinguished public figures and a leader in the formative years of the United States.

In his monumental 1858 *History of Eastern Vermont, from Its Earliest Settlement to the Close of the Eighteenth Century*,[1*] still regarded as the most useful and comprehensive account of the early years of Vermont east of the Green Mountains, Benjamin H. Hall devotes nine pages to a biographical sketch of Bradley, and the index cites him at some length. Sixty years later Bradley appears frequently in Walter Hill Crockett's five-volume history of Vermont.[2] In 2004 the authors of the outstanding and lengthy one-volume *Freedom and Unity, A History of Vermont* mention Bradley but once.[3] The preceding year, the editors of *The Vermont Encyclopedia* give Bradley about a quarter of a page and, ironically, find an inconsistency of Bradley's Republican politics with his engineering the 1808 presidential nomination of James Madison, who, with Thomas Jefferson, founded the Republican Party.[4]

After arriving in Vermont in 1779, Bradley identified with the faction led by Ethan Allen, his brother Ira Allen, and Thomas Chittenden, who worked to maintain the fragile independence that Vermont had asserted in 1777. He wrote a solid defense of independence in *Vermont's Appeal to the Candid and Impartial World*, a 1780 manifesto in which he argued "Vermont has a natural right of independence," and that it would never surrender "those glorious privileges for which so many have fought, bled, and died." The effort won the approbation of Vermont's leadership and, after the General Assembly had the *Appeal* published, Bradley presented it to the Continental Congress as an agent of Vermont.

In the 1780s Bradley participated actively in state, county, and local public affairs. He practiced law from an office in Westminster, Vermont, where he worked as town clerk and which he represented in the General Assembly for seven one-year terms. He also served as judge of probate for a decade, Windham County judge, clerk to the Superior Court (renamed the Supreme Court in 1782), and for one year as a justice on the Vermont Supreme Court. Though actively

*See Notes on page 3.

involved with Vermont's political leadership, Bradley established the lawyerly demeanor of independence that he maintained throughout his public service. Appointed by the court to represent forty-one settlers who preferred New York to Vermont Authority and whom Ethan Allen had rounded up and carted off to jail, Bradley secured the dismissal of the first six cases. That incited Allen's wrath. Garbed in a resplendent uniform and making his sword conspicuous, he threatened the court exclaiming, "Fifty miles, I have come through the woods with my brave men" to see to the prosecution of "these Yorkers—enemies to our noble state. I see, however, that some of them, by the quirks of this artful lawyer, Bradley, are escaping from punishment they so richly deserve."[5] However angry, the theatrical Allen continued to employ the "artful" Bradley as his personal lawyer, and he later met his young and attractive second wife at Bradley's home where she rented a room.

Bradley's long and distinguished career in national politics began in 1789 when he, again acting independently of the Allen faction, joined the team of commissioners who negotiated with New York and cleared the path to Vermont statehood. He drafted the act that called for a convention to ratify the U.S. Constitution and assumed a leading role in the deliberations that resulted in the ratification and Vermont's becoming the fourteenth state in 1791. In recognition of his efforts and ability, the legislature elected him one of Vermont's first two United States senators. His strong identification with Jefferson's nascent Republican Party cost him reelection in 1794. However, when the Jeffersonians swept to power in 1800, the Vermont legislature returned Bradley to the Senate where he served two more distinguished terms (1801–1813).

In his first term as a U.S. senator, Bradley sponsored the bill that established the flag of the United States. When he began his second term, he became a leader in the small group of men who, with President Jefferson, set policy for the young nation. His colleagues four times elected him Senate President *pro tempore*. He wrote the Twelfth Amendment to the Constitution which required the separate elections of the president and the vice president, thus ending the possibility of repeating the stalemate that followed the election of 1800 when it required a week of bitter wrangling to make Jefferson president. He also became chairman of the Republican caucus in 1804 which agreed on the Jefferson-Clinton ticket. Four years later in 1808, he seized the initiative and called and led the caucus that headed off a Virginia boom for James Monroe and nominated James Madison for president. Although strong party man, Bradley continued to maintain his independence and did not support Jefferson's assault on the judiciary or Madison's call for a declaration of war in 1812.

For an active man at the center of national affairs, Bradley strangely escapes the notice of historians. Dumas Malone's highly regarded six-volume biography of Thomas Jefferson, with a separate volume devoted to each of his terms as president, completely omits Bradley,[6] as does the more recent biography of Jefferson by Willard Sterne Randall, who lives and works in Vermont.[7] Henry Adams's monumental nine-volume *History of the United States During the Administrations of Thomas Jefferson and James Madison* does not include Bradley.[8] Nor does Leonard D. White's standard, *The Jeffersonians, A Study in Administrative History, 1801–1829*.[9] Irving Brandt's six-volume biography of James Madison briefly recognizes Bradley's role in the 1804 and 1808 Republican caucuses, mentions him as "doubtful" on the War of 1812, and confuses him with his son, Congressman William Czar Bradley, in a discussion of Congressional politics during the war, when Bradley had already retired from the Senate.[10] Sean Wilentz's sole mention of Bradley in his *The Rise of American Democracy, Jefferson to Lincoln*, appears in a footnote as "the prime mover in Congress for the slave trade ban,"[11] another achievement lost to historians.

Throughout his lifetime, Bradley did not seek attention. His actions and papers reflect the quiet circumspection typical of an astute legal mind most often working on behalf of others, whether as an attorney or in the public interest. His papers generally remained with his family—unavailable and perhaps unknown to historians. Early Congressional records remain sketchy, and many fell victim to the British burning of the Capitol, White House, and other government buildings in August 1814. This may explain why generations of acclaimed historians have too often neither included Bradley nor recognized his very important contributions to the early history of the United States.

Until the family gave a large cache of material to the University of Vermont in 2000, most Bradley material available to scholars lay unappreciated in the widely scattered collections of his correspondents and other public figures. Locating, often transcribing, and editing the papers of Stephen R. Bradley presented a daunting, expensive, and time-consuming task that Dorr Bradley Carpenter took on and doggedly pursued. In the process, he located previously unknown papers. The publication of this book, which also merits the further subtitle of "Early National and Congressional Leader," will help restore Bradley to the recognition of his important place in the history of Vermont and the United States that his long career in public service earned.

Notes

1. Benjamin H. Hall, *History of Eastern Vermont, From Its Earliest Settlement to the Close of the Eighteenth Century* (New York: D. Appleton & Co., 1858), 593–601.

2. Walter H. Crockett, *Vermont, the Green Mountain State*, 5 vols. (New York: The Century History Co., Inc., 1921–23).

3. Michael Sherman, Gene Sessions, and P. Jeffrey Potash, *Freedom and Unity, A History of Vermont* (Barre, Vermont: Vermont Historical Society, 2004).

4. John J. Duffy, Samuel B. Hand, and Ralph H. Orth, eds. *The Vermont Encyclopedia* (Hanover, New Hampshire, and London: University Press of New England, 2003).

5. Michael A. Bellesiles, *Revolutionary Outlaws* (Charlottesville and London: University Press of Virginia, 1993), 182–3.

6. Dumas Malone, *Jefferson and His Time*, 6 vols. (Boston: Little, Brown, & Co., 1948–81). See volumes 3 and 4, *Jefferson the President, First Term, 1810–1805* and *Jefferson the President, Second Term, 1805–1809*.

7. Willard Sterne Randall, *Thomas Jefferson: A Life* (New York: Harper Perennial, 1993).

8. Henry Adams, *History of the United States During the Administrations of Thomas Jefferson and James Madison* (9 vols., New York, 1889–91).

9. Leonard D. White, *The Jeffersonians, A Study in Administrative History, 1801–1829* (New York: Macmillan, 1951). One treatment, Noble E. Cunningham, Jr., *The Jeffersonian Republicans in Power, Party Operations, 1801–1809* (Chapel Hill: The University of North Carolina Press for the *Institute of Early American History and Culture*, 1963), 112–115, briefly recognizes and describes Bradley's leadership role in the Republican caucuses of 1804 and 1808 that selected their candidates for President and vice president.

10. Irving Brandt, *James Madison* (Indianapolis and New York: Bobbs-Merrill, 1950–1961), Vol. IV, 419 and 424–25, Vol. V, 380, and Vol. VI, 233.

11. Sean Wilentz, *The Rise of American Democracy, Jefferson to Lincoln* (New York and London: W. W. Norton, 2005), 844, fn 7.

H. Nicholas Muller III is the editor of Vermont History *and has published extensively on Ethan and Ira Allen and the early politics of Vermont. He was a professor and dean at the University of Vermont, and served as director of the Wisconsin Historical Society and president of the Frank Lloyd Wright Foundation and Colby-Sawyer College.*

There is a pleasure in literary communication, which none can so fully enjoy, as those who, possessing the means, feel also the mental gratification of dispensing among their fellow creatures, whatever may tend to their amusement, instruction or profit.—John A. Graham

London, 1797 (Stephen R. Bradley's second term Senate clerk)

Introduction

It is exceedingly difficult to write a biography of a person born 250 years ago who kept no diary or journal and served in an army that had virtually no records. Stephen Rowe Bradley's service in Washington as a senator was at a time before the Senate kept good records of its proceedings.

Bradley's early life is an area that is totally unknown. The names of his parents are recorded, but only the number of brothers and sisters is known — not their names. This is not the only gap in our knowledge of Bradley. His army service was in the state militia and not in the Continental Line, resulting in poor records of his service in the central Colonial government veterans' records. The records acknowledge his service in the First Regiment of the Vermont Militia (Bradley's Regiment) as a full colonel, but that is all.[1]* There are numerous books written about General Washington and his correspondence with his officers, but Bradley is not even listed. The *Historical Register of Officers of the Continental Army During the War of Revolution*, by Francis B. Heitman, also makes no mention of Colonel Bradley.[2]

We are very fortunate that the state of Vermont has kept remarkably good records. These are available through the Secretary of State's office at Montpelier.

General Bradley served in the U.S. Senate for more than 16 years. The year after he left this body of lawmakers in 1814, the Senate began to keep a day-to-day record of speeches and vote outcomes. Years later an effort was made to reconstruct the early proceedings and speeches. The result was a series of books called *The Annals of Congress 1789–1814*. These are available to scholars in any government library in the Government Documents Section. Unfortunately, these records are made up from memory, notes, newspaper articles, and the diaries of members of the early Senate. They are both inaccurate and incomplete. In the case of Bradley, they record five speeches in 16 years, in spite of the fact that he was voted President *pro tempore* of this body four times[3] and was a prolific speech maker.

There are literally hundreds of biographical sketches of this man in all sorts of publications. Most of these are fewer than 250 words and similarly phrased. This is understandable because the information came from one book, *History of Eastern Vermont*, 1858, by Benjamin Hall.[4] This publication is found only in the rare book sections of major libraries. The references to General Bradley are found on pages 341–688.

This book is the only one that covers Bradley's life in any significant length. There are other written forms of records besides Hall's book, and these are the basis for this book's account of the life of General Bradley. The sources are Governor and Council Records of the State of Vermont, family correspondence, military and legal records of the Vermont Secretary of State's office in Montpelier, family genealogies, Senate journals, and stories about Bradley written in other books and articles. All of these sources are widely scattered and provide little informa-

*See Notes on page 7.

tion among thousands of words of irrelevant considerations. One purpose of this book is to unite the diverse accounts of Bradley's life.

When General Bradley died in 1830, he was married to Melinda Willard Bradley, his third wife. As a result, the family papers and correspondence passed down through the Willard branch of the family. This was very fortunate as this family not only kept the papers, but also used them in numerous ways.

In 1869, Sarah Bradley Kellogg Willard wrote a book about her grandfather, William C. Bradley (son of Stephen R. Bradley). It was entitled *A Tribute of Affection to the Memory of Honorable William C. Bradley*. Many Bradley letters were used in this small volume, and her narrative provides a better understanding of the family's life in this period. There is one group of letters referred to in this narrative that has never been located. These are the love letters written by William C. Bradley to Sarah Richards during the period 1795 to 1866.

Sarah Willard's son, Henry Kellogg Willard, also wrote a genealogy of his family which covered the Bradley branch, the *Willard-Bradley Memoirs*. It was published in 1924 as a private genealogy of over 270 pages. Many of these letters were reproduced in his book; but, unfortunately, most were in only a fragmentary form. After his book was completed, Henry K. Willard made a gift of the family papers to the Library of Congress and Duke University Library.

The letters sent to the William R. Perkins Library at Duke University included 771 pieces of correspondence. These original documents are available to the public for scrutiny under very controlled conditions. They can be found in chronological order, but neither cataloged, transcribed, nor microfilmed. The letters themselves are virtually unreadable unless one is trained in this area and has a great deal of time as the handwriting is almost indiscernible.

The second large group of Bradley papers was given to the Library of Congress and is found in Series I, II, and III (Bradley Willard Papers). Series II is called the Autograph Collection, and most of these have nothing to do with General Bradley. Series I consists of 450 family and political papers. The last series in this collection is made up of all the "culls" from the other series and are mostly receipts, IOUs, and papers of little or no historical interest. All of these documents are available to the public under close supervision. No advance notice is necessary, but a lengthy procedure is required prior to one's admittance to the archives.

Another large group of letters recently came to light when the Bradley home in Westminster was sold in 2001. The letters, over 600 in number, were given to the University of Vermont. They are available in the documents section of the Bailey/Howe Library. These letters are in excellent condition and are much more easily read than any of the previous collections. They have been put in generally chronological order but not cataloged or transcribed. A total of 200 are transcribed in this book; the remainder are mostly business receipts and letters pertaining to Mark Richards (William C. Bradley's father-in-law). One other interesting note about the Bailey/Howe Library: It has in its collection of rare books a number of volumes from the Bradley family library. The majority of these books were obtained by Stephen Bradley from the court sale of the Crean Brush estate. Schedule C of Stephen Bradley's will contains a complete list of these books and their value.

Radcliffe College has a large quantity of Bradley family correspondence, starting in the year 1813 and continuing through 1954. Only the first 100 documents contain information pertaining to Stephen R. Bradley and his son William.

More than 50 other libraries contributed letters to this book. When they were all examined, some were found to be copies of the original correspondence. Only the library that owns the original is given credit for that document. These libraries are identified on every transcript using the American Library Code.[5]

The transcription work was organized and directed by Jeanne Kerr Cross. She is the former director of the James Madison Papers at the Alderman Library, the University of Virginia. She co-edited 18 volumes of *The Papers of James Madison*. Her assistant in this present endeavor was Ann Decker Cecere, formerly assistant editor of the *John Adams Papers* at the Massachusetts Historical Society.

A photocopy was made of every letter and document from each collection. They were then transcribed and cataloged for this book. On completion of this work, this collection of over 2,500 items was given to the Vermont Historical Society in Barre. This figure represents a total of all known Bradley letters and is very confusing and inaccurate. It is derived by adding the totals of each library's holdings, as *they* report them:

Perkins Library, Duke University	771
Library of Congress	550
Bailey/Howe Library, University of Vermont	600
Fort Ticonderoga Museum	25
Secretary of State Office, Vermont	300
Governor and Council Records	200
Schlesinger Library, Radcliffe College	100
Other libraries	50
Approximate total	2,596

As an example, the Duke University collection has 771 pieces of paper, not all of which are letters. Some letters have as many as four pages and an envelope and are counted as five. Some handwritten speeches have up to 25 pages; however, they translate into three pages of printed text in this book. Unsigned letters and those with no salutations or addressee were eliminated, along with many receipts and IOUs. There were a few letters that simply could not be read. The last group categorized in these collections consist of numerous printed items which were counted in as many as three libraries as an original item. Some items were left out of this book because of space limitations and relevancy. The total transcriptions included in this book are about 550.

Another major source of information on Senator Bradley is a book written by Senator William Plumer of New Hampshire. It is a day-by-day diary of Plumer's service in the Senate from 1803 to 1807. The book is entitled *William Plumer's Memorandum of Proceedings in the United States Senate* and was published in 1923. Bradley plays a significant role in the accounts of this excellent work and is repeatedly quoted on pages 15 to 637. Plumer was of the same political party as Bradley (Republican), and the two voted in generally the same way. In spite of their occasional differences of opinion, the tone of their narrative is one of gentlemanly civility.

General Stephen Rowe Bradley was an important historical figure and deserves recognition as one of the founding fathers of the state of Vermont. This book acknowledges the significance of the life and contributions of this early patriot.

Notes

1. NARA (Washington) card numbers 372, 1732, 7313, and 39135548.
2. Francis B. Heitman, *Historical Register of Officers of the Continental Army During the War of the Revolution, April, 1775, to December, 1783* (Baltimore: Genealogical Pub. Co., 1967).
3. Biographical Directory: Bradley 1889:5.
4. Benjamin H. Hall, *History of Eastern Vermont* (Albany, New York: J. Munsell, 1858).
5. Library of Congress, *Symbols of American Libraries*, 14th ed. (Washington, D.C.: Library of Congress Distribution Service, 1992).

Abbreviations and Notes on the Transcriptions

AD   Autograph document. A handwritten report or other paper that is not a letter.
ADS   Autograph document signed. A document in the hand of and signed by the author.
AL   Autograph letter.
ALS   Autograph letter signed. A letter in the hand of and signed by the author.
AN   Autograph note.
ANS   Autograph note signed.
DS   Document signed. A document or form prepared by another person but signed by the central figure or authority.
Dft   Draft.
LS   Letter (non-autographic) signed by the author.
Tr   Transcript.

Depository Symbols

In the provenance section following each document the first entry indicates the source of the text. If the document was in a private or public depository in the United States, the symbol listed in the Library of Congress's *Symbols of American Libraries* (14th ed.; Washington, 1992) is used. The location symbols for depositories used in this volume are:

AXY   Thomas Jefferson Library, Charlottesville, Virginia
CSmH   Huntington Library, San Marino, California
CtY   Yale University, Sterling Memorial Library, New Haven, Connecticut
DLC   Library of Congress, Washington, D.C.
DNA   National Archives, Washington, D.C.
DSI   Smithsonian Institution, Washington, D.C.
MB   Boston Public Library
MCR-S   Radcliffe College, Schlesinger Library on the History of Women in America, Cambridge, Massachusetts
MHi   Massachusetts Historical Society, Boston
NcD   Duke University, Durham, North Carolina
NFtW   Fort Ticonderoga Association Museum and Library, Ticonderoga, New York
Nh   New Hampshire State Library, Concord
NjP   Princeton University Library, Princeton
ViU   University of Virginia, Charlottesville

Vt	Vermont State Library, Montpelier [or Vt-PR, Vermont Public Records]
VtHi	Vermont Historical Society, Barre
VtU	University of Vermont, Burlington

Bradley Family Name Abbreviations

EBD	Emily Bradley Dorr	**MAB**	Merab Ann Bradley
SWMB	Sarah Williams Merry Bradley	**EPB**	Emily Penelope Bradley
SBK	Sarah Bradley Kellogg	**WBD**	William B. Dorr
JDB	John Dorr Bradley	**JDBII**	John Dorr Bradley II
SRB	Stephen Rowe Bradley	**RMB**	Richard Merry Bradley
RB	Richards Bradley	**SMerryB**	Sarah Merry Bradley
SCB	Susan Crosman Bradley	**WCB**	William Czar Bradley
SR	Sarah Richards Bradley	**WCBII**	William Czar Bradley II
ACB	Arthur Crosman Bradley	**WBD**	William B. Dorr
EBD	Emily Bradley Dorr	**SMinaB**	Susan Mina Crosman Bradley
SMB	Sarah Merry Bradley	**EB**	Emily Bradley (b. 1868)
SAWB	Sarah Ann William Bradley	**MR**	Mark Richards

Short Titles

AofC	Annals of Congress
BFP	Bradley Family Papers
JCC	Journals of the Continental Congress

Editorial Method

Punctuation is presented as written, except:
    Extra flourishes and dashes filling space at end of line have been deleted
    Dash following abbreviation has been changed to period
Run in multi-line closing
Change ye. to the
All paragraphs indented
[ ] indicate added or changed letters or words
< > indicate interpretations of illegible or missing letters or words

Background and Biography

Origins of the Family Name
(by John C. Bradley[*])

The word Bradley is Anglo-Saxon, compounded of *brad*, broad or wide, and *ley or lea*, a field or pasture.

The earliest mention in England of the name Bradley, thus far known, is in 1183 at the feast of St. Cuthbert in Kent when Lord Hugh, Bishop of Durham, caused to be described all the revenues of his whole Bishopric.

This survey of Hugh Pudsey, called Bolton Buke, mentions, in Wolsingham, which contains three hundred acres, Roger de Bradley, who holds forty acres at Bradley, and renders half a marc, besides forest service, to wit: forty days in the fawn season, and forty in the rutting season.

In 1437 there is mention of Bradleys of Bradley. In the will of Ralph Snaith, which was proved March 23, 1472 or '73, he mentions a farm had of Bradley. Again, in 1475, the will of Sir John Pilkington, Knight of Yorkshire, bequeaths to his brother Charles a place named Bradley. The name seems to have been applied to places in England at a comparatively early date; but from what source they sprung is not ascertained. At the present time there are in England a number of townships which bear the name in Cheshire, Lincolnshire, Derbyshire, Southampton, and Staffordshire, which is about the largest, containing three thousand three hundred and seventy-six acres.

There are also Great and Small Bradley parishes in Suffolk, and Lower and Upper, or Bradley Both, in Kildwick, Yorkshire.

John Bradley was Bishop of Shaftesbury in 1539.

In 1578 Alexander Bradley resided in the see of Durham, and about the same year Cuthbertus Bradley was curate of Barnard Castle.

Thomas Bradley, was Doctor of Divinity and chaplain to King Charles the First, afterward prebend in the Cathedral Church of York, and rector of Ackworth in County Ebor.

His son, Savile, was Fellow of Magdelene College in Oxford, and another son, Thomas, a merchant in Virginia. About this time the persecutions in England led many to emigrate to America. This emigration so increased that a tax was levied on all those who left the country; but this, instead of decreasing the number of emigrants led many to slip away by stealth, and thus leave no record of their departure. Among the original lists of emigrants, religious exiles, etc., a number of Bradleys are mentioned as having embarked for America. These lists of course are very imperfect, and there are still many unpublished documents, which, when brought before the public, may help to mend the broken links in many family histories.

---

[*]*John C. Bradley,* Brief Sketches of a Few American Bradleys, with reference to their English Progenitors *(Hoosick Falls, New York: Press of Hoosick Valley Democrat, 1889), 1–6.*

There are several distinct branches of Bradley family in the United States, the founders of which came from England, and were, perhaps, descended from a common ancestor, as the same names are often repeated.

Daniel Bradley, who was born in 1615 in England, and came to this country in the ship "Elizabeth" from London in 1635, founded the "Haverhill" branch.

He married, May 21, 1662, Mary, daughter of John Williams, of Haverhill, where he resided; the Indians killed him, August 13, 1689. He had three children, two of whom, Mary and Hannah, were killed by the Indians on March 15, 1697.

There was also a Peter Bradley, a mariner, who lived in New London in 1654. He married and had children.

Francis Bradley was the founder of the "Fairfield branch." He married Ruth, daughter of John Barlow, by whom he had six children. He died the latter part of 1689.

Then there is the "North Haven branch," which was founded by Isaac Bradley, whose descendants are numerous and widespread.—*History of the Bradlee Family, by Samuel Bradlee Doggett.*

In the early part of the seventeenth century there resided in the market town of Bingley, in the West Riding of Yorkshire, England, a family by the name of Bradley. What his Christian name, or occupation was, has not been determined. We know, however, that he was twice married. By his first wife he had one son named William, and by his second wife one daughter and four sons named, respectively, Ellen, Daniel, Joshua, Nathan and Stephen. William, it is said, was a staunch dissenter and an officer in Cromwell's army. He emigrated to America in 1643 or '44 and joined the New Haven Colony.

Hearing of his father's death a year or two later, he sent for his stepmother and her children, the one daughter and four sons named above. They doubtless accepted the invitation to emigrate to America immediately, for we soon find them all living under William's care, in New Haven, where they continued to reside till the younger members of the family attained to manhood. About this time Daniel was accidentally drowned. This sad event occurred in December 1658. Joshua was married in New Haven, and there one son, named Joshua, was born December 31, 1665. No further trace of this family has been discovered. Possibly they removed; but more probably the family became extinct.

Nathan and Stephen, the two youngest, removed to Guilford, Connecticut, when quite young, and there they continued to reside during the remainder of their lives. They testified in court, in Guilford, as appears by Guilford Records, in 1658, then Nathan was twenty years old, and Stephen sixteen. They probably became citizens of Guilford that year, or, perhaps, the year previous. The mother subsequently married and settled in Guilford, where she died in January, 1683.

"It is recorded that Nathan Bradley with Governor Leete and others bought the township of East Guilford, now Madison, of Uncas, the Indian Sachem. On that occasion they took dinner on a rock near the place where the old gristmill now stands, on the bank of the Hammonasset River, about one-third of a mile from where the Shore Line Railroad crosses the River. Nathan Bradley carved his initials upon the rock, and the place having remained in the family, the rock has been preserved with the initials carefully kept clean and free from moss."

William Bradley was the head of the "New Haven branch" of the Bradley family. He married Alice Pritchard, February 18, 1645, and from this union was born four sons and four daughters. Some of his descendants reached distinction in public life, and many of his widespread posterity are now eminent businessmen.

John C. Bradley — March 1889

BRADLEY FAMILY TREE
(BY HENRY K. WILLARD)

In 1924, Henry K. Willard published a history of his family under the title "Willard-Bradley Memoirs." This information has been passed down through subsequent years. However, it appears that Mr. Willard missed one generation early in the family. Given the resources available at the time of his compilation, this is not difficult to understand.

Mr. Willard indicated that Abraham Bradley married Sarah Bassett. The known child of that union was shown as Moses Bradley. The corrected lineage was presented in a family Bible in possession of Amy Suter Wilson. It states that Abraham Bradley married Ann Thompson, and Daniel Bradley was married to Sarah Bassett. Other on-line documentation supports this addition.

With the exception of this modification, bringing some lines up to modern date, and minor editing, a digest of Mr. Willard's family history is being presented here. However, a more extensive family history is also being prepared for separate publication.

The brothers Bradley, thought to be six or seven in number, arrived from England in about 1650. Previous to this, William Bradley, the eldest, had served with Cromwell's Ironsides. He became the first settler in North Haven, Connecticut. The land belonged to Governor Theophilus Eaton and was part of a large tract west of the Quinnepiae River. His brother Stephen Bradley became a resident of New Haven and took up his profession as a silversmith. It is believed that the brothers Stephen, Daniel, Joshua, and a sister Ellen were half-siblings to William.

William Bradley married Alice Pritchard on February 18, 1645. She was the daughter of Rodger and Frances Pritchard.

William Bradley and Alice Pritchard had the following children:

    I. Joseph Bradley, baptized January 1646
   II. Martin Bradley, b. October 1648
*III. Abraham Bradley, b. October 24, 1650
  IV. Mary Bradley, b. September 30, 1655
   V. Benjamin Bradley, b. April 1657
 VI. Esther Bradley, b. September 29, 1659
VII. Nathaniel Bradley, b. February 26, 1661

Abraham Bradley married Ann Thompson[†] [Mr. Willard had Sarah Bassett], date not known, and they had several children.

---

*Asterisks indicate more complete information to follow.
[†]One on-line source shows her name as Anne and gives the marriage date as December 25, 1673, in New Haven, Connecticut. It also provides the names of her parents as John Thompson and J. Ellen Harrison.

Left: Henry K. Willard. *Middle:* Reuben Atwater (1728–1801). *Right:* Mary Russell Atwater (1726–1807).

Daniel Bradley was one of their sons. He married Sarah Bassett, and they also had several children. Only the name of the second son is recorded. His name was Moses Bradley, and he resided in Cheshire, Connecticut.

Moses Bradley married Mary Row, only daughter of Daniel Row of Mt. Carmel (now Hamden, Connecticut).

Stephen Rowe Bradley, son of Moses and Mary Row Bradley, was born February 20, 1754, in Wallingford, Connecticut. He graduated from Yale with a degree of AB in 1775, and a degree of AM in 1778. He received honorary degrees from Dartmouth and Middlebury Colleges of L.L.D.

He enlisted in the American Service in January 1776 and was appointed captain of the "Cheshire Volunteers." Served as aide-de-camp to General Wooster in the attack on Danbury, April 1777. Appointed a lieutenant in the Vermont militia in August 1780 and raised to the rank of colonel in the Vermont militia in October. In 1784, served under General Ethan Allen as commander of the "Westminster Militia," better known as the "Green Mountain Boys." Promoted to general Vermont militia, Eighth Brigade, January 26, 1791.

He served in the General Assembly of Vermont 1780; as a selectman for the city of Westminster, an office he held for ten years. Appointed judge for Windham County in 1788. Was a member of the State Constitutional Convention in 1798. Became the first United States Senator for the new state of Vermont in 1794 and served three terms. When Kentucky and Vermont were added to the Union, he proposed a new flag with fifteen stars and fifteen stripes (May 1, 1795). This flag was used for twenty-three years and today is known as the "Fort McHenry" flag.

Stephen Rowe Bradley married (1) May 16, 1780, Merab Atwater who was born June 19, 1757, died April 7, 1785. She was the daughter of Reuben and Mary Russell Atwater.

Stephen Rowe Bradley married (2) April 12, 1789, Gratia Thankful Taylor who died January 10, 1802. He married (3) September 18, 1803, Melinda Willard, born August 29, 1784, died April 10, 1837. He died December 9, 1830, and was interred in the Bradley Tomb in Westminster.

Stephen Rowe Bradley and Merab Atwater had the following child:

*I. William Czar Bradley, born March 23, 1782

Stephen Rowe Bradley and Gratia Thankful Taylor Bradley had the following children:

II. Stella Czarina Bradley, born March 8, 1796, died December 13, 1833

The Bradley Tomb in Westminster, Vermont.

III. Stephen Rowe Bradley II, born January 5, 1798, died June 27, 1808
IV. Adeline Gratia Bradley, born April 28, 1799, died June 24, 1852

Stephen Rowe Bradley and Melinda Willard Bradley had the following children:

V. Louise Agnes Bradley, born December 20, 1809, died November 30, 1811
VI. Mary Rowe Bradley, born August 11, 1811, died October 23, 1882

William Czar Bradley born March 23, 1782, the son of Stephen Rowe and Merab Atwater Bradley. He married 1802 Sarah Richards, born March 9, 1783, died August 7, 1866.

She was the daughter of Mark and Ann Ruggles Richards.

William entered Yale College at thirteen years of age and was expelled while a freshman. Graduated from Amherst College with an AB and a law degree. Yale conferred on William an Honorary MA

Melinda Willard Bradley (1784–1837)

Left: William Czar Bradley (1782–1867). *Above:* Sarah Richards Bradley (1783–1866).

Left: Mark Richards. *Right:* Ann Ruggles Richards.

in 1817. In 1851, Yale and The University of Vermont both gave him Honorary degrees of LL.D.

He was elected to the State Legislature 1805. Was a representative to Congress 1812. Appointed an ambassador of the United States under the Treaty of Ghent. Again represented Vermont in the Congress for two terms, 1823 to 1827. At the age of sixty-eight was elected a member of the State Legislature, and at seventy-four (1856) he became President of the Legislature.

He died March 3, 1867, and is buried in the Bradley tomb, Old Cemetery, Westminster, Vermont, with his wife of sixty-six years.

William Czar Bradley and Sarah Richards had the following children:

   I. Emily Penelope Bradley (adopted daughter) born 1799; married Nathaniel Dorr; died 1865, Brattleboro, Vermont
*II. Jonathan Dorr Bradley, born April 17, 1803, died September 8, 1862
  III. Merab Ann Bradley, born February 4, 1806, died March 27, 1845

Jonathan Dorr Bradley, son of William Czar Bradley and Sarah Richards Bradley, graduated from Yale and from Yale Law School. Practiced law first in Bellows Falls, then about 1832 he removed to Brattleboro. He represented Brattleboro in the State Legislature in 1856–57. He served on the Board of Directors of the Vermont and Massachusetts Railroad Company. Jonathan Dorr Bradley married Susan Mina Crosman. She died November 10, 1892.

They had the following children:

   I. William Czar Bradley II, born December 17, 1831, died May 1908
*II. Richards Bradley, born January 25, 1834, died October 2, 1904
  III. Stephen Rowe Bradley III, born March 15, 1836, died August 6, 1910
  IV. Arthur Crosman Bradley, born September 18, 1849, died November 2, 1911

Left: Nathaniel Dorr. **Right:** Emily Penelope Bradley Dorr (1799–1865).

Left: Merab Ann Bradley (1806–1845). *Right:* Jonathan Dorr Bradley (1803–1862).

Richards Bradley engaged in the wholesale mercantile business in New York City, but returned to Brattleboro in 1856. In 1858, he purchased the estate called "Hill Top" which became his home. Later, he bought the West River Farm and the Rice Farm, which he managed at a considerable profit. He was a member of the staff of Governor Horace Fairbank, 1876–78. He married Sarah Ann Williams Merry.

Richards Bradley and Sarah Ann Williams Merry Bradley had the following children:

    I. Robert Merry Bradley, born March 31, 1857, died April 6, 1857
   II. Susan Mina Bradley, born January 13, 1859, died September 1925
*III. Richards Merry Bradley, born February 10, 1861, died December 16, 1918
**IV. Jonathan Dorr Bradley II, born February 9, 1864
***V. Emily Bradley, born June 20, 1868
  VI. Sarah Merry Bradley, born October 20, 1868, married June 17, 1891, Russell Tyson, born December 1, 1867, Shanghai, China. They had no children.
 VII. Walter Williams Bradley, born August 24, 1870, died September 17, 1880

Susan Mina Crosman Bradley (?–1892)

Left: Richards Bradley (1834–1904). *Right:* Sarah Ann Williams Merry Bradley.

*Richards Merry Bradley married Amy Owen Aldis March 24, 1892. She was born April 2, 1865, and died December 16, 1918.

Richards Merry Bradley and Amy Owen Aldis had the following children:

  I. Amy Owen Bradley, born July 3, 1893. She married August 28, 1920, Philip Hales Suter, born October 30, 1888. They had the following children: Amy Aldis Suter, born June 29, 1921; Philip Hales Suter, Jr., born October 8, 1923, and Gurtrude Suter, born 1926.
  II. Helen Aldis Bradley, born February 25, 1895. She married January 1, 1925, Charles Morgan Rotch, born May 19, 1878.
  III. Walter Williams Bradley, born July 17, 1895, died March 18, 1901
  IV. Sarah Merry Bradley, born March 9, 1898. She married Clarence James Gamble, born January 10, 1894. They had the following children: Sarah Louise Gamble, born October 31, 1925; Richards Bradley Gamble, born April 9, 1928; Walter James Gamble, born December 1, 1930; Mary Julia Gamble, May 14, 1934; and Robert David Gamble, born March 9, 1937.
  V. Mary Townsend Bradley, born June 13, 1901. She married Edward Stanley Emery. They had the following children: Edward Stanley Emery, born August 2, 1935; Charlotte Emery, born July 13, 1937; and Richard Bradley Emery, born July 14, 1940.
  VI. Edith Bradley, born January 3, 1903. She never married and had no children.
  VII. Ruth Bradley, born November 29, 1905, died December 18, 1906

**Jonathan Dorr Bradley II graduated Harvard University class of 1886 and Harvard Law class of 1891. He married Francis Elvira Kales September 9, 1896. They removed from Brattleboro to Chicago, Illinois, in 1889. Built an estate at 1414 North Greenday Road, Lake Forest, Illinois, in 1900.

J. D. Bradley was a real estate lawyer. He was co-founder and president of the Building Managers Association of Chicago. He was President of the Chicago Chapter of the Harvard Club and President of the Chicago Chapter of the National Geographic Society. He was a charter member and on the Board of Directors of the Onwenstia Club of Lake Forest, Illinois.

Jonathan Dorr Bradley and Francis Elvira Kales Bradley had the following children:

  I. Alice Pritchard Bradley, born January 13, 1899. She married October 22, 1921, Frederick Taylor Fisher. They had the following children: Bradley Fisher, born July 10, 1923, died June 28, 1995; Walter Lowri Fisher, born April 26, 1925; William Nickols Fisher, born October 18, 1929; Frances Fisher (Brookfield/Wilson), born August 15, 1932; and Alice Snow Fisher (Blood) born September 27, 1936.
 II. Eleanor Bradley, born June 1, 1902. She married June 24, 1925, Benjamin Carpenter, Jr. They had the following children: Benjamin Carpenter III, born November 8, 1926; Dorr Bradley Carpenter, born November 15, 1928; and Helen Carpenter, born 1931, died 1947.

***Emily Bradley, born June 20, 1868. She married June 30, 1887, William Fesenden Wesselheoft, born March 5, 1854. They had the following children:

  I. Margaret Wesselhoeft, born October 25, 1888. She married June 10, 1916, George Hoyt Bigelow, born November 13, 1890.
 II. Susan Wesselhoeft, born July 1, 1891. She married October 25, 1913, Renout Russell, born September 4, 1891.
III. Alice Wesselhoeft, born February 3, 1893. She married July 27, 1913, Leverett Saltonstall, born September 1, 1892.
 IV. Emily Wesselhoeft, born April 14, 1897. She married July 10, 1920, William Andros Barron, Jr., born December 16, 1892.

Biography

Stephen Rowe Bradley was born in the county of Wallingford, Connecticut, in the town of Cheshire, February 20, 1754. His early life is totally lost to history. It is believed that he had four brothers and four sisters, but no record of their names exists.[1]*

The first document that pertains to him is his enrollment in Yale College in the fall of 1771. At Yale he produced an almanac for the year 1775[2]; two thousand copies were printed, and it was published by Ebenezer Watson on November 1, 1774.[3] The almanac consisted of an extensive poem, the twelve months almanac, and an appendix of local herbal remedies. There is no indication as to the authorship of the poem; if it was written by Bradley, it is the only example of his use of this literary form that exists.

Bradley graduated from Yale with a Bachelor of Arts degree on July 25, 1775. Three years later, on September 9, 1778, he received an M.A.[4] His law studies were directed by Tapping Reeves, who afterwards founded the Lichfield Law School. Middlebury College appointed him a fellow of the college on November 1, 1800, a position he held until his death. Both Middlebury and Dartmouth colleges awarded him honorary LLD degrees.

After graduating from Yale, Bradley was commissioned a captain in the Connecticut Militia. His first command was a company of foot soldiers known as the "Cheshire Volunteers."[5] Early in 1776 (on January 4) he was ordered to New York, and his pay order to Congress of June 26, 1776, indicates that he and his company were deployed in that area for about six weeks.[6] Two other pay orders confirm this, dated January 25 and February 25, 1776.

During this service he came to the attention of not only George Washington, but a number of other senior officers in the Continental Line as well. Just before his promotion to major, again in the Connecticut Militia, he was discharged as commander of the Cheshire Volunteers.

Headquarters New York 19th Feby 1776.
   There being no farther Service at present, for Capt. Bradley's Independant Company of Connecticutt Volunteers, they are hereby dismiss'd from any further duty. The General at the same time returns his sincere thanks to the Officers & Men for their Zeal and alacrity in the service of their Country; and their good behavior since they have been embodied.
                                                                    Charles Lee Major General
TO Capn. Stephen R. Bradley

He accepted a position as adjutant and quartermaster[7] for a few months prior to his appointment as aide-de-camp to Maj. Gen. David Wooster.[8] It was during this service that he first came to know Dr. Andrew Graham, a surgeon of eminent reputation whose medical practice dated back to 1759 and the Indian Wars. Both Maj. Bradley and Dr. Graham were serving General Wooster when he fell mortally wounded on April 27, 1777, during the Battle of Danbury. It is interesting to note that there was another officer on the staff in this unit who became a long-time friend of Bradley's: Captain Aaron Burr.

*See Notes on pages 44–45.

Stephen Bradley's part in the third engagement of this battle is well recorded in *Farmers Against the Crown*, by Keith M. Jones (Connecticut Colonel Publishers, Ridgefield, Connecticut: 2003, 60). The British forces under the command of Maj. Gen. William Tyron and Gen. Sir William Erskine attacked the Continental supply depot at Danbury, Connecticut. They were partly successful and captured supplies of rice and tenting. The guns and powder had been removed prior to this action that the British call the "Danbury Raid."

As the Tory and British forces retreated south on their way to New York, they were attacked in three engagements by Patriot forces under the command of Maj. Gen. David Wooster and Brig. Gen. Benedict Arnold. The first attack on the British rear guard had little effect, and Gen. Wooster personally reorganized his command and made a second attempt. It was during this action that Gen. Wooster was mortally wounded. This action has become known as the Battle of Danbury and is considered an American victory. In 1859, Constantino Brumidi painted his scene of the dying Gen. Wooster attended by Dr. Andrew Graham and the general's aide-de-camp, Maj. Stephen Bradley.

The Patriot soldiers, mostly untrained militia, were by then in total disarray and had scattered to seek the protection of the nearby woods. This left Maj. Bradley in command of what remained of the regiment. He soon consolidated and rallied his forces, and without orders marched south with the intent of making a flanking attack on the British who were attacking the main Continental forces under Brig. Gen. Benedict Arnold at the barricade located in the center of Ridgefield, Connecticut.

Bradley arrived too late; the fourth phase of the "Battle of Ridgefield" was over. The British had prevailed in spite of Gen. Arnold's extraordinarily courageous conduct. His actions were so exemplary that Congress voted to strike a new medal of valor in his honor; it was never presented, for obvious reasons.

There are two postcripts to this story:

First, one of the officers under Gen. Benedict Arnold at the barricade was Col. Philip Burr Bradley, a local resident. He commanded the 4th Connecticut Volunteer Regiment; his men were known as "Bradley's Regiment." Col. P.B. Bradley's commission was for three years and ended in early November 1780. Care

Top: Charles Lee. *Above:* Maj. Gen. David Wooster.

must be taken not to confuse this man with Stephen Bradley, who later commanded the 1st Regiment Vermont Volunteers, which was also known as "Bradley's Regiment."

Secondly, a family named Goodrich lived in Ridgefield. Stephen Bradley's third daughter (by his second wife) Adeline Gratia Bradley, married Samuel Goodrich in 1817.

In 1778 through part of 1779 Major Bradley was employed as a commissary officer in New Haven. He also taught at a school in Cheshire in his spare time.

For reasons unknown, he resigned his commission in the Connecticut Militia and journeyed to Vermont. He arrived in Westminster on the 26th of May, 1779.[9] This was a very special day, as the Superior Court of Judge Moses Robinson was in session with an important case. The defendants did not have council: Bradley was prevailed upon to act for the defense. His performance in this case and his

Aaron Burr

"The Death of General Wooster." In 1776 a depot of military equipment and supply was established in Danbury, Connecticut. A raid was made on this depot by the Tory Governor Tyron of New York on April 27, 1777. The successful raiders retreated south and were attacked near Ridgefield by the Continental forces under Major General David Wooster, who was mortally wounded in the conflict. This action has become known as "The Battle of Danbury" and is considered an American victory. In 1859, Constantino Brumidi painted the fresco shown above (S-128N) on plaster. It is located on the north wall of the Senate Appropriation Room of the United States Capitol Building, Washington, D.C. The gentleman in shirt sleeves on the right is Doctor Andrew Graham of Woodbury, Connecticut. The young officer in the middle is a staff officer; his name is Captain Aaron Burr. On the left, at the feet of General Wooster, is his Aide de Camp, Major Stephen R. Bradley of Cheshire, Connecticut.

knowledge of the law at once gained him the esteem of the community. Judge Robinson made him his clerk of the court and later, state's attorney for Cumberland County. The controversy respecting land titles of the New Hampshire Grants had been a problem for some time when Bradley entered this political fray. It was said of Bradley, "Having popular manners and a keen in-sight into society, he became a prominent political leader, and exercised a large influence in laying the foundation of the state of Vermont."[10]

On October 20, 1779, Governor Chittenden made an appointment of five agents to present Vermont's claim to Congress. The five men were Gen. Ethan Allen, Jonas Fay, Paul Sponer, Stephen Bradley, and Moses Robinson. There were numerous communications pertaining to Bradley's appointment. The most important were dated February 1, 1780, and February 5, 1780.[11] The task of writing and presenting the views of Vermont in this vital question of Vermont's rights fell to Bradley.

Bradley, who was only 26 years old at the time, had little knowledge of the intricacies of the subject when he started his investigations into this problem. Within two months this young lawyer became the controlling member of the group and completed a well-written account of the position taken by the state in this controversy. The paper was read before the governor and council at Arlington on December 10, 1779, and was approved and published. "Vermont's Appeal to the Candid and Impartial World"[12] was a major aid in supporting Vermont's claim to a separate and independent state government.

Bradley, accompanied by Moses Robinson and Jonas Fay, made the trip to Philadelphia with the intent of reading the "Appeal" before Congress. They were never granted the opportunity to appear before any committee of Congress.[13] It should be noted that the *Journals of Congress* dispute some of these statements and that Bradley's committee were "duly notified, declined to attend" the Sept. 27 meeting of Congress in 1780. It would appear that Bradley had succeeded when he thought he had failed. All of Bradley's correspondence with Congress had been read into the Journal including his appeal.[14] In early September of 1780, on his second visit to Philadelphia, Bradley became convinced that Congress was determined to decide the question without Vermont's opinion. After discussion between the three emissaries, Bradley composed a remonstrance to Congress that set forth their views and denounced the policy that would divide Vermont between New Hampshire and New York.[15]

Bradley's qualifications in the military had not escaped the attention of the leaders of his adopted state. He was commissioned an officer in the First Regiment of Vermont Militia on August 27, 1780. His rank was raised to full colonel on October 15.[16] At this point he was so disillusioned with his perceived failure in the area of politics that he requested active duty with his regiment.

This particular regiment of mostly Green Mountain Boys was operating in the Hudson River Valley south of Fishkill under very difficult circumstances. The river valley was very important to the British as a means of communication and supply from New York to Canada via Albany. It was an area fought over regularly. The following letter gives one a good idea of just how perilous the situation was:

Moses Robinson

> To the Honorable the General Assembly of the State of Connecticut now Siting at Hartford in said State. The Memorial of the inhabitants of the town of Woodbury in said State Humbly Sheweth that notwithstanding the Provision allready made for supplying the soldiers of this state in general and of this town in particular belonging to the Continental Army with suitable cloathing, we find to our great grief and dissatisfaction that many of our soldiers whom we are more immediately to provide for are not supplied, tho Sutable Provision has been made by your Honours Memoralists, and many others unseasonably Supplied so that they have their summer cloathing in winter and winter cloaths in summer, which in our opinion is not only unprofitable, uncomfortable and unhealthy but Cruel and Destructive to the soldiers. We beg leave further to observe oftentimes it so happens that the cloathing we provide for our sons in the Army remains on hand in this state for six of twelve months before they come or get to our children by Means of which they Suffer beyound Account, which to Prevent, Your Honours Memoralists Pray that they may Send their own cloathing to their own men in the Army taking their receipts in order to account with the State therefore and also Pray that your Honours would take up the matter of the above complaint in such a manner as to find out the true Cause of the above neglect and also grant that your Memoralists may from time to time [one word illegible] Orders from the Pay Table for the above Services in transporting Sd Cloaths on to the Treasurer of this State and your Honours Petitioner as in Duty bound shall ever Pray.
>
> Hartford Jan. 18, 1779
>
> ANDREW GRAHAM in behalf of sd town.

This letter is signed by Dr. Andrew Graham, the same surgeon who served with Bradley when he was aide-de-camp to General Wooster. An advertisement appeared in the *New York Packet* and the *American Advertiser* on Thursday, June 1, 1780, indicating that Dr. Chauncey Graham operated a hospital in this area.[17]

> Whereas, the house built in this place, for a public seat of learning, has been for upwards of 4 years past, & still is occupied as a general hospital for the sick of our army; & not knowing how long it may be used for that purpose, we have opened our public seminary in a house contiguous to it, belonging to Col. Abraham Brinckerhoff; where Reading, Writing and Speaking correctly, the Learned Languages, with every branch of the Mathematicks, and polite Literature, are faithfully taught; and a special regard had to the morals of youth.
>
> CHAUNCEY GRAHAM, Pres.
> Fish-Kill, State of New York
> March 17, 1780

In the Hudson River area, a regiment of Vermont and Connecticut Volunteers found itself at war with the English. Bradley's men fought no major battles, but his troops were decimated by sickness and the lack of proper food and equipment. When the English army under Cornwallis advanced on Hackensack, the Continental General Nathanial Greene ordered the sick and wounded sent to the country.[18] A specific order in the fall of 1780 from Washington's headquarters signed by General Stark was received addressed to "Bradley's Regiment" as it was known.[19] It cautioned Bradley to use care in not disturbing the region with undue foraging. The regiment was to proceed north and prevail upon local medical help for the sick and wounded. Approximately 100 men were left with Dr. Chauncey Graham at Fish-Kill and the remainder were marched to West Point, and then crossed the Hudson River and went into winter quarters at Valley Forge. Bradley's force was so under-manned by this time that it was broken up and its men assigned to other military units. In this case it was to be expected because this unit was made up of men from Connecticut as well as Vermont.

Colonel Bradley did not participate in any military actions for the remainder of the war. The resignation of his commission was accepted on March 2, 1787, and for about four years he did not engage in military activities. This was not the end of his army career, as he was appointed brigadier general of the Eighth Brigade Vermont Volunteers, on January 27, 1791.[20]

His military experience was very important to him and shaped his thinking in many ways in his later life. This was particularly noticeable after he became a U.S. senator prior to the War of 1812.[21] It is also observable in the attitude of his son, Congressman William C. Bradley. Both went to great lengths to try to prevent a second war with England. When Senator Bradley worked with Thomas Jefferson and James Madison, the position of the Republican Party was to avoid war. Bradley never wavered in this idea; both presidents modified their positions because of public pressure. Senator Bradley, who was conceded to be the ablest democratic senator, "earnestly counselled Madison against it [war]."[22] So dissatisfied was Bradley with the country's national policy that on March 4, 1813, at the end of his senatorial term, he withdrew from public life. His attitude toward the war and his failure to keep America out of the 1812 conflict had a strange result. He believed that he had failed as senator in his life's most important objective: peace for his country. On the other hand, he was very proud of his military service; from this time on he would allow no one to address him as "Senator" but was very pleased to be called "General Bradley."

There exists a postscript to this story. An unusual letter written by William Page refers to Bradley's change of attitude as regards to force of arms[23]:

Thomas Jefferson

Charlestown May 1st, 1789

Dear Sir

    Mr. Brooks of Haverhill desired me to sent you the inclosed letter and receive your answer which you will please give to the bearer. You doubtless remember of once calling on me for a Sword, you then was in pursute of honor and Cash, I think to cut and slay the Yonkers, having Accomplished all this and having Not only changed your manner and mode of attack but your weapon also—you will please send me the sword by the bearer, for as all other weapons fail me it is time I take Sword. I am Sir your most Obet Set   W Page

Honble Stephen R. Bradley Esquire

    From 1781 to 1791 Bradley held many elective and appointed offices.[24] These are all duly recorded, but on the other hand there is almost nothing said about how he conducted these offices. Bradley was made a selectman of Westminster in 1782 and served as a clerk of that town from October 6, 1787, to October 9, 1788. He was a probate judge for Windham County from December 1781 to March 1791 and appellate judge of the county court in the place of Samuel Fletcher in February 1783. From October 1788 through October 1789 he was a side judge of the State Supreme Court. He was the representative of the town of Westminster in the State Assembly for the years 1780, 1781, 1784, 1788, 1790, and 1800, and was elected speaker of the session of 1785. He served as a member of the State Constitutional Convention in 1791 and was made a member of the council in September 1798. Prior to the state's being admitted to the Union,

James Madison

Bradley was made a commissioner on October 21, 1790, to establish the line between New York and Vermont.[25]

After the admission of Vermont to the Federal Union, Stephen Bradley and Moses Robinson were chosen to be the first United States senators from that state.[26] On October 31, 1791, Robinson took his seat, and Bradley was seated on November 7, 1791. Lots had been drawn for the purpose of determining to which of three classes each would belong. Bradley drew first and was of the "class of which seats would be vacated at the expiration of four years from March 1791." Robinson drew the longer of the two terms and was seated for six years. Elijah Paine was selected to replace Bradley in 1795. He served only one term and was then replaced by Bradley in March 1801.

At the time Bradley was seated for his second term, the president pro-tempore of the Senate was particularly important. Thomas Jefferson had been elected president in a highly contested election with Aaron Burr; Burr refused to take office as vice president. In the absence of Vice-President Burr, the president pro-tem of the Senate would take his place as president of the Senate.[27] At this time there was no precedent set for replacing this official in the case of his death or absence. As a result, Senator Bradley served in the capacity of president of the Senate for over a year.

Bradley now became the second most powerful man in America, a position that he did not relish. He was never officially vice-president in spite of the fact that he received many marks of personal esteem from Jefferson[28] and was a personal friend. Jefferson presented Bradley with a special gift of a miniature on ivory. It was an oval 2½ inch × 1⅞ inch oil painting of Jefferson's head and shoulders on a blue background. The photograph of a family painting showing Melinda Willard Bradley, clearly depicts this item (page 17). "An original miniature of Thomas Jefferson given by him to Senator S. Bradley of Walpole NH and given to me by his daughter Mrs. Mary R. Tudor Jan 1877 (signed) George E. Hoadly." The miniature remained in the family until it was sold through the Harry L. Sterns Ltd. firm of Chicago.[29] It was boxed in a gilt frame 6¾ inch by 5 inch and lined in cloth.

One of the surviving documents in the published *Annals of Congress* records a speech made by Bradley on February 18, 1802. It was titled "Senate Proceedings Choice of Electors,"[30] and concerned a change in the Constitution of the United States. In reality this was the first draft of what was to become the Twelfth Amendment of the Constitution. It was a new set of rules to elect a president and vice-president so they would not represent differing parties. Problems such as those involving Aaron Burr would be avoided.

Senator Bradley was desirous of securing a successor to Jefferson who would think along their lines, particularly concerning the question of war with England.[31] Bradley also wanted to make sure that George Clinton did not get the nomination. The newspapers and the general population were mostly in favor of war over the question of impressment of American seaman into the British Navy. Bradley did not have the authority to do what he did next, but with the silence of Jefferson (and most likely his concurrence), he took it upon himself to personally nominate James Madison to be the next president. For this purpose he sent out a call for a special caucus:

> Sir: In pursuance of the power vested in me as president of the late convention of republican members of both houses of congress, I deem it expedient, for the purpose of nominating suitable and proper characters for president and vice-president of the United States at the next presidential election, to call a convention of said republican members, to meet at the senate-chamber on Saturday, the 23rd inst., at six o'clock P.M., at which time and place your attendance is requested, to aid the meeting with our influence, information and talents.
>
> S.R. Bradley   Dated at Washington   19th January, 1808

Many members of the House and Senate refused to attend, unwilling to agree to Bradley's "usurpation of power ... [or] to countenance, by their presence, the midnight intrigues of any set of men who may arrogate to themselves the right (which belongs only to the people) of selecting proper persons to fill the important offices of president and vice-president."[32] Those that did attend were ninety-four members from both houses, only one of which was from New York. This was important because Clinton was from New York, and a large number of representatives from that state would have caused Bradley trouble. Madison was nominated (apparently unanimously) and subsequently elected president, with a great deal of the credit due Senator Bradley. It should be noted that Madison modified his initial stand against war before his second run for president to facilitate his re-election.[33] In spite of this, relations between Madison and Bradley remained on friendly terms, and Bradley conducted numerous legal and personal affairs for Madison and his wife.

General Bradley's relationship with Mrs. Madison was very cordial. He saw much of Mrs. Madison, and was quite gallant in his "devoirs" to the lady. There is an amusing correspondence carried on between father and son, concerning certain shoes and slippers which Mrs. Madison wished to procure from a Quaker shoemaker in Lynn.[34] In a letter to his son, who was then in Washington, he wrote, —

> Remember me with the most cordial affection to Mrs. Madison. I am not unmindful of her request to her religious friends in Lynn. I have written to Mr. Breed, informing him of her commission, and of the honor shown them by her "whose shoe-strings they were not worthy to untie." The business shall be accomplished, and the shoes forwarded; and you may assure Mrs. Madison they shall have the simplicity of the Quaker, the elegance of the court, and, in some measure, the quality of the Jewish slippers in the wilderness, that lasted forty years.

Mrs. Madison paid for the shoes, though the Quaker shoemaker charged more for them than the stern general thought was reasonable.

Bradley was without doubt the leading Republican senator during his day, but he was not blindly loyal to Thomas Jefferson and James Madison. He gave no support to Jefferson's disagreement with John Marshall and the federal judiciary.[35] Jefferson would have revised the total system of the federal court, and the structure as we know it today would not exist. In the time before and during Thomas Jefferson's second term, Bradley made several comments pertaining to the president that could be misconstrued as being anti–Jefferson. The fact is that they did not always agree, but remained on very friendly terms over a long period of time. The comments are as follows:

Dolley Madison

> This same Bradley told me (Senator Wm. Plumer), he really hoped Delaware Connecticut and Massachusetts would maintain their federalism. That he was sick and heartily satiated with democracy. That Mr. Jefferson was a visionary man — never qualified for the presidency.[36]
>
> ... The presidents of the United States have taken more pains to acquire popularity than to promote the interest of the United States. This was the case with General Washington — This is the case with Mr. Jefferson. He is now catching at every thing that he thinks will aid his popularity.[37]
>
> ... The president had long discovered his design to avoid on every popular question, all responsibility — That he believes the president did not wish us to repeal the duty on salt — That he recommended it believing it would give him popularity, trusting that the Senate would negative it. That yesterday a member of the House told him he had voted for repeal — That he dare not do otherwise — for if he had, he should have hazarded his re-election.[38]

It must be realized that these statements were made in private conversations with a good friend, Senator

William Plumer. They were not published until 1923.

Bradley was an able and hard working senator with a ready wit and endless store of amusing anecdotes which made him very popular with his colleagues.

There are numerous individuals who played a part in the life of Stephen Rowe Bradley. The majority of these people related to Bradley's life over a long period of time, so the method of their presentation is designed to achieve a maximum degree of continuity.

General Ethan Allen was a much older man than Stephen Bradley, but they remained friends from their first encounter in 1779 until 1789 at his death. The following describes their first meeting in detail. What it does not include is the effect this court case had on forming the lasting friendship between Bradley, Robinson, Allen, and Noah Smith. Bradley arrived in Westminster virtually by accident on the date of this trial. As the defendants had no lawyer, the court (Judge Moses Robinson) requested

William Plumer

that Bradley defend the accused. He had no time to prepare and knew nothing of the situation. It became quite obvious to Judge Robinson and State's Attorney Smith that Bradley had taken control of the task when Bradley presented a motion to quash the indictments against six of the defendants. General Allen was angered by this turn of events, but his wrath was not directed at Bradley. In fact, he was so impressed by Bradley's performance that Bradley became his personal attorney.

Stephen Row Bradley's First Appearance in Westminster[39]

On April 21, 1779, William McWain, a sergeant in the First Regiment, Vermont, took in his possession two cows, one belonging to Clay and the other to Williams, in default of refusing to serve in the Militia of the State. He gave notice that a week later they would be disposed of in Putney at public auction. The Yorkers were determined to resist. On the morning of the 28th, about one hundred of the residents in the neighboring towns, who were friendly to New York, assembled unarmed in Putney and vainly endeavored by calm arguments to stop or postpone the sale. Satisfied that force alone could prevail, they took possession of the cows, restored them to their owners, and returned to their homes.

On May 18, Sergeant McWain entered a complaint against those who had been engaged in the rescue of the cows. Lawful Money Writs were issued signed by Ira Allen for the arrest of forty-four persons charged with "enemical conduct" in opposing the authority of the State. Thirty-six were taken and confined in the jail at Westminster; the prisoners, among whom were Bela and Joseph Willard, were men of influence and ability.

An adjourned session of the Superior Court was held at Westminster on May 26, 1779. Moses Robinson, of Bennington, presided as chief judge. To guard against interruption during the session the people of the town who supported the jurisdiction of Vermont forcibly seized the public stock of gunpowder, amounting to one hundred pounds, which had been provided by the State of New York, and placed twenty-five pounds of it in the hands of their friends. Preliminaries having been arranged, the prisoners, under a strong guard, were marched from the jail-rooms in the lower part of the county hall to the court-room in the second story. Noah Smith, the State's Attorney, exhibited a complaint against the delinquents, in which he stated that they were assembled at Putney on the 28th of April previous, "in a riotous and unlawful manner;" that they, at that time, made an assault upon one William McWain, "a lawful officer in the execution of a lawful command," and rescued out of his hands and possession two cows, which he had taken by legal measures. He charged that such "wicked conduct" was a flagrant violation of the common law of the land, and contrary to the force and effect of a statute law of the State, entitled, "An act to prevent riots, disorders, and contempt of authority within this State, and for punishing the same."

Much time having been occupied in perfecting the arrangements incident to the occasion, and the day being far spent, the court announced a recess until the following morning. On their return to the jail, the prisoners held a consultation in order to decide upon the course which in the present emergency could be pursued with the greatest advantage. Of their number was Micah Townsend, of Brattleboro, a lawyer of ability. By his advice they addressed a petition to the judges of the court, in which they set forth the peculiarity of their situation and the want of impartiality in the proceedings then in progress against them. They averred that on account of the recency of their apprehensions, and the strictness of their confinement, they had been unable to procure any writings or witnesses to substantiate the pleas which they might wish to offer, and, further, that they could not be "justified to their consciences and to the world" should they omit any "prudent and lawful measures to acquit themselves." They also desired the privilege of obtaining counsel from another state to plead their several causes. To obtain these ends, they prayed that the court might be adjourned, for at least one month. To this petition were subscribed the names of twenty-eight of the prisoners. Its only effect was to procure as counsel for the delinquents, Stephen Row Bradley, then of Bennington, the temporary clerk of the court.

When the court resumed business on the morning of the 27th, the State's attorney having become satisfied of his inability to sustain the complaints which he had instituted against three of the prisoners, John Kathan, Jr., and Lieutenant Daniel Kathan, all of Cummerston, entered a *nolle prosequi* in their cases and withdrew the suits. At the same time the defendants' attorney, Mr. Bradley, presented a motion to quash the indictments preferred against Stephen Greenleaf, Jr., of Brattleboro, Joseph Goodhue, of Putney, and Josiah White, on the ground of the nonage of the parties. The motion was granted and the court was about to proceed with the trial of the remaining prisoners when an unexpected interruption took place. Ethan Allen and his men had been engaged at Westminster in assisting the sheriff and guarding the prisoners. He had watched with interest and satisfaction the transactions of the preceding day, and had expressed great pleasure at the manner in which the goddess of justice seemed to be preparing to punish the rebellious Yorkers. He was not present at the commencement of the second

Ira Allen

day's session; however, having heard that some of the prisoners were obtaining their discharge, he resolved to stop such flagitious conduct and teach the court their duty. Accoutred in his military dress, with a large cocked hat on his head profusely ornamented with gold lace and a sword of fabulous dimensions swinging at his side, he entered the courtroom breathless with haste. He pressed through the crowd which filled the room and advanced towards the bench whereon the judges were seated. Bowing to Moses Robinson, who occupied the chief seat and who was his intimate friend, he commenced a furious harangue, aimed particularly at the State's Attorney, Noah Smith.

"I would have the young gentleman to know that with my logic and reasoning, from the eternal fitness of things, I can upset his blackstones, his whitestones, his gravestones, and his brimstones." Here he was interrupted by Moses Robinson, the Chief-Justice, and was gravely informed that it was not allowable for him to appear in a civil court with his sword by his side. Allen replied by a nod, and taking off his chapeau threw it on the table. He then proceeded to unbuckle his sword, and as he laid it aside with a flourish, turned to the judge and in a voice like that of a Stentor, exclaimed,

> For forms of government, let fools contest:
> Whate'er is best administer'd is best.

Having delivered himself in this style, and, observing that the judges were whispering together, he listened for a moment and then cried out: "I said that fools might contest for forms of government — not your Honors! not your Honors!" He then turned to the audience and, having surveyed them for a moment, again addressed the judge as follows:

Fifty miles I have come through the woods with my brave men, to support the civil with the military arm; to quell any disturbances should they arise; and to aid the sheriff and the court in prosecuting these Yorkers — the enemies of our noble State. I see, however, that some of them, by the quirks of this artful lawyer, Bradley, are escaping from the punishment they so richly deserve, and I find, also, that this little Noah Smith is far from understanding his business, since he at one moment moves for a prosecution, and in the next wishes to withdraw it. Let me warn your Honor to be on your guard, lest these delinquents should slip through your fingers, and thus escape the rewards so justly due their crimes.

Then, with great dignity, he replaced his hat and, having buckled on his sword, left the court room with the air of one who seemed to feel the weight of kingdoms on his shoulders.

The defendants were found guilty and fined, the State being the recipient of the proceeds. Ira Allen expressed what may be regarded as the sentiments of the more moderate portion of the partisans of Vermont.

It is not our design to treat the inhabitants of this country with severity, but with as much

Ethan Allen

lenity as the nature of the case will admit. Yet the authority of this State must be supported, for commissions from two different States can no longer subsist together. We mean not to boast our victory over those gentlemen that were in favor of New York in this county, but hope to make them our friends, and have the pleasure of treating them as such. We mean this movement as a defiance to the old government of New York, with whom we have long contended for our properties.

The first legal work Bradley conducted for Ethan Allen concerned the ownership of a rifle.[40] Gen. Allen had a very good relationship with his men, and he liked to feel that they could count on him in any type of trouble. William Stewart was "one of the old Green Mountain Core ... as he is a poor man I desire you will plead his case and charge it to me, my warriors must not be cheated out of their fire arms." Bradley won the case, regaining the gun and sent Allen a bill for two pounds, two shillings for his services.

A second court case involving General Allen concerned a note which had been signed by him and was overdue in payment. The witness lived in Boston and could not possibly attend, and a continuance was needed. Bradley, to obtain the desired order, denied the signature on the note. This procedure was in accordance to accepted tradition. Unfortunately, Allen was in the courtroom and heard his lawyer gravely deny the signature. Allen rebuked Bradley loudly and firmly.[41]

> Mr. Bradley, I did not hire you to come here and lie. That is a true note; I signed it, I'll swear to it, and I'll pay it. I want no shuffling, but I want time. What I employed you for was to get this business put to the next Court, and not to come here and lie and juggle about it.

The judge granted the continuance.

During the next few years, Bradley had become a leading citizen of Westminster and had built a large home in town just north of the courthouse.[42] General Allen was a regular visitor. He always was welcome in spite of their major differences in politics and perspectives. Bradley was in favor of Vermont's becoming an independent state of the Union, and Allen spoke openly of Vermont as a British Province.[43] As a result, Allen lost his commission of general in the Green Mountain Boys, and many of his friends would not speak to him. Bradley's friendship never wavered.

Crean Brush, an Irish lawyer and New York Tory, had accumulated 60,000 acres of Vermont land, all with New York titles.[44] By an order of the Governor dated June 17, 1778, all of it was confiscated and turned over to the court to be sold.[45] Stephen Bradley purchased some of this land, including lot 58 in Westminster, and some books. Shortly after this, Brush committed suicide in Boston. His wife remarried and became Mrs. Patrick Wall. She and her daughter Fanny came to Westminster, Vermont, with the intention of recovering some of the family's lost property. Fanny Buchanan was the young widow of a British Army officer killed in the Revolution. At 24, she was a very beautiful and "dashing woman."[46] As there were only two places in town to reside, the two women took up residency in the home of Stephen Bradley; the local tavern was not acceptable for visiting ladies. Bradley was hired by Mrs. Wall, but no land was recovered.

Over the period of the next few months, Ethan Allen was a regular visitor at the Bradley home, at first as a visitor of Bradley's, and then he became Fanny's suitor. The local tavernkeeper, John Norton, spoke to her on the street in a familiar manner, "Fanny, if you marry Gen. Allen, you will be queen of a new state!" "Yes," she replied, "if I should marry the devil, I would be queen of hell!"[47] The aversion with which she regarded her old suitor disappeared over time.

Left: Mrs. Patrick Wall. *Right:* Fanny Wall Buchanan.

Wedding — Ethan Allen[48]

One morning, while General Bradley and the judges were at breakfast, General Allen, with his sleigh, horses, and driver, appeared at the gate, and on coming into the room was invited to partake. He answered that he had breakfasted at Norton's and would, while they were engaged, step into Mrs. Wall's apartments and see the ladies. Entering without ceremony, he found Mrs. Buchanan in a morning gown, standing on a chair, and arranging some articles on the upper shelves of a china closet.

After recognizing her informal visitor, Mrs. Buchanan raised up a cracked decanter, and calling General Allen's attention to it, accompanied the exhibition with a playful remark. The General laughed at the sally, and after some little chat said to her, "If we are to be married, now is the time, for I am on my way to Arlington."

"Very well," she replied descending from the chair, "But give me time to put on my Joseph."[49]

Meanwhile, the judges and their host, having finished their breakfast, were smoking their long pipes. While thus engaged the couple came in, and General Allen, walking up to his old friend, Chief Justice Moses Robinson, addressed him as follows: —

"Judge Robinson, this young woman and myself have concluded to marry each other, and to have you perform the ceremony."

"When?" said the Judge, somewhat surprised.

"Now," replied Allen. "For myself," he continued. "I have no great opinion of such formality and from what I can discover, she thinks as little of it as I do. But as a decent respect for the opinions of mankind seems to require it, you will proceed."

"General," said the Judge, "this is an important matter, and have you given it a serious consideration?"

"Certainly," replied Allen, "but," glancing at Mrs. Buchanan, "I do not think it requires much consideration."

The ceremony proceeded, until the Judge inquired of Ethan whether he promised to live with Frances "agreeable to the law of God."

"Stop! stop!" cried Allen at this point. Then pausing, and looking out of the window, the pantheist exclaimed, "The law of God as written in the great book of Nature. Yes! Go on."

The Judge continued, and when he had finished, the trunk and guitar case of Mrs. Allen were placed in the sleigh. The parties took their leave and were at once driven off to the General's home.

In May of 1785, General Allen retained Bradley to sell a lot his wife Fanny had inherited in Westminster.[50] Over the next few years Allen wrote a number of letters to Bradley, most of which are still in existence.[51] They are unusual in that they are legible; unfortunately, they were written after Allen was out of politics and concerned farming and family life. The originals of these letters can be seen at the Fort Ticonderoga Museum.

The subject of the New Hampshire Grants involves a very complicated and lengthy political intrigue and is covered here only as it pertains to Stephen Bradley. It also should be noted that when Bradley's Regiment was activated to quell a specific riot, it is unlikely that Colonel Bradley was actually on the scene. Bradley held two offices through most of this time (early 1780s): commanding officer of Vermont's 1st Regiment of Militia and State's Attorney at Westminster. His attitude about force and the use of the military was well known; it was to be used only as a last resort. The courts were his preference and in this idea he was backed firmly by Governor Thomas Chittenden and Judge Moses Robinson.

In a simplified illustration, if Crean Brush had sworn allegiance to Vermont, he would have most likely retained his land. He was not willing to do this, before or after the court took over his land, and the result was disastrous for him. There were hundreds of these cases.

One of the more colorful is the situation surrounding Lt. Col. Benjamin Carpenter.[52] He commanded a regiment of Green Mountain Boys in the southern part of Vermont. He was very effective and used force of arms almost to the point of an art. The story starts when Colonel Timothy Church, a New York Yonker, was captured and turned over to Col. Bradley who sent him under strong guard to Gov. Chittenden at Arlington.[53] On receipt of the prisoner, the governor sent the following reply:[54]

> Dec. 24, 1782 — I received your letter with the prisoner, and approve of your conduct. Have sent to Col. Robinson to call the superior court immediately for his trial, and I hope and trust justice will be done him. I have sent twelve pounds powder agreeable to your request. As to sending or ordering a standing force to Guilford, I had rather hang them (the Yonkers) one by one, until they are all extirpated from the face of the earth. However, I wait for the return of the officers that commanded the posse to send orders to the sheriff to collect the fines and cost, when, if they continue obstinate, a force must accompany the sheriff sufficient to silence them. I am not without hope that the consequence of Church's trial will have some good effect.

This action on the part of the Governor and Bradley resulted in rioting in Brattleborough and other Vermont towns by Tory and others forces aligned with New York. A large force, under the command of Brig. Gen. Fletcher, made up of 200 men consisting of the units of Col. Bradley's and Col. John Sergeant's regiments were already in place to quell the disturbance.[55] A short passage from *History of Eastern Vermont* sums up what happened next.[56]

> The day that witnessed the defeat of the deputy at Brattleborough by means of "guns and Pitchforks," beheld an assemblage at Guilford numbering more than seventy Yonkers, armed "with dangerous and offensive weapons." Their rage on this occasion was directed against Benjamin Carpenter, a staunch Vermonter, who had already held many important positions both on the field of battle and in the administration of government and of whose physical and mental condition combined his epitaph has

preserved a quaint record, which declares that his "Stature was about six feet. Weight 200. Death had no terror." But even these qualifications, sufficient to disarm the last enemy of his power, were not of a nature to protect their possessor from the attacks of an earthly foe. He was taken prisoner by the Yonkers, and carried away "to his great damage." There is no written, printed, or traditional account to show in what this damage consisted, nor is there reason to believe that it was very serious in nature. Whatever it might have been, he survived it many years, and lived to see the final establishment of the state, of whose constitution and government he was a founder.

The Yonkers had the intention to trade Lt. Col. Carpenter for Col. Church. It did not happen and only heightened the resolve of the Vermonters. There was another factor that entered the equation and that was the U.S. Congress. Vermont had requested help from the Congress pertaining to the problem with New York and

Thomas Chittenden

had not received an answer. On January 16, 1783, Col. Bradley and some of his townsmen, along with a number of men from Walpole, "damned the Congress, and drank a toast to their confusion."[57] It was shortly after this that a company of Bradley's Regiment freed Carpenter from confinement.

John Nott (or Noth) was a very pig-headed man, a Tory, and a farmer.[58] He had settled on Vermont land with a New York title, built a home, and cleared the land. At this point he caused no trouble, but he had not complied with Vermont law.[59] The then current policy of Judge Robinson's court was to acquaint settlers such as John Nott with the law. If they swore allegiance to Vermont, they could retain the land and were given a Vermont title. If they did not do this, the land was taken by the court and sold and the individual was banished from the state under threat of death. If the farmer lost his property to the court, he could still regain it if he petitioned the governor. John Nott did not swear allegiance to Vermont, and the court ordered the militia under the command of Bradley to take possession of the land. A very nasty situation resulted, and John Nott was ordered to leave the state. He retaliated against Bradley with accusations of misconduct in his appeal to the governor; these charges were dismissed by the Governor's Council.[60] These petitions are very interesting reading, but nowhere do they contain any attempt by John Nott to swear allegiance to Vermont. The story has a tragic ending that was strangely ironic: Nott died destitute only a few years later, and Stephen Bradley purchased his land from the court.

George Clinton, five-term Governor of New York, was without doubt the most powerful politician ever to oppose the will of Bradley. He ran afoul of Bradley on numerous occasions over a long period of time. It is interesting to note that on each occasion, Bradley prevailed.

Starting during the Revolutionary War and continuing until 1783, Lt. Col. Benjamin Carpenter had prevented almost all of Gov. Clinton's New York friends from taking possession of what they perceived to be New York land in Vermont. Carpenter had been declared an outlaw, and a price put on his head.[61] Gov. Clinton sent two military expeditions into Vermont to capture and hang Carpenter. It would have to have been extremely galling to Clinton when Col. Carpenter was captured by his Tory neighbors and then released by Stephen Bradley without even a trial. This compounded itself when numerous individuals such as Crean Brush and John

Left: George Clinton. *Above:* John Adams.

Nott were stripped of their New York land and banished from the state, along with the hundreds of former New Yorkers who swore allegiance to Vermont to keep their land. By this time Gov. Clinton was most certainly aware of Bradley, as Bradley never lost a court case.

The next they met was in a political situation. Thomas Jefferson's government was without a vice president in 1802, and a group of Gov. Clinton's friends attempted to have him appointed vice president in the absence of Aaron Burr.[62] There were problems involved. There was no precedent for this situation, and a great deal of opposition to a man of Clinton's age serving in this high position. John Adams and Bradley were discussing this problem and Adams was told, "he is too old and we all are witness that his faculties are failing him."[63] George Clinton was not appointed at that time. However, when Thomas Jefferson was elected for his second term, George Clinton became his vice president.[64]

In 1808 Clinton sought the nomination for president, but was unable to obtain his goal because of Bradley. Bradley's Twelfth Amendment to the Constitution[65] had changed the rules, and Bradley's surprise nomination of James Madison had made it impossible. Clinton was again chosen vice president, but died in office before the expiration of his term. There is no indication of any kind that Bradley ever sought the position of president or vice president.[66]

William Eaton was the son of one of Bradley's old friends.[67] As a young man he had served as a sergeant for over five years in the Continental Army. He then entered Dart-

William Eaton

mouth and graduated in 1790. At that time he asked Bradley to obtain a commission for him in the army. The rank awarded was Ensign U.S.A. Within weeks he was promoted to captain and served against the Indians in Ohio and Kentucky in the army of General Anthony Wayne. Fifteen years later he held the rank of major general and commanded all the United States ground forces in Africa during the Tripolian War.[68] During his army service he and General Bradley corresponded on a regular basis. When Bradley was a senator and Eaton was in Africa, the letters took on an official tone.[69] Many of these letters have survived and they tell a story never told before, from a personal perspective, of a war which is virtually forgotten.

The Graham family and the Bradleys held a long-term association starting in 1777 which has continued for over 200 years.[70] Major Bradley served with Dr. Andrew Graham in the service of General Wooster during the battle of Danbury. Col. Bradley and Dr. Chauncey Graham met in the fall of 1780, when Bradley's Regiment left the wounded in Fishkill at Graham's hospital. Years later, after the war, John Andrew Graham, the son of Dr. Andrew Graham and the nephew of Chauncey, immigrated to Vermont and settled in Rutland. He was a young lawyer and rode the Court Circuit which took him regularly through Westminster, Vermont, the home of Stephen Bradley. John Graham prospered, married, and became a prominent lawyer with a great many influential friends. Unfortunately, he had a dark side and was involved in a mining fraud, a church land grab, and a messy divorce. At this time (1795) he ventured to London, England, to avoid his ex-wife and his creditors. While he was there he wrote a book entitled *A Descriptive Sketch of the Present State of Vermont*. In this book he tells of his claim to be a relative of the Duke of Montrose, of life in Vermont, and describes a number of local residents. One of these gushing commentaries is on Stephen Bradley.[71]

> Mr. Bradley is also a lawyer of distinguished abilities, and a good orator; he has held some of the most important offices in the State, and was late a Senator in Congress; few men have more companionable talents, a greater share of social cheerfulness, a more inexhaustible flow of wit, or a larger portion of unaffected urbanity.

After returning to America he settled with his new wife in Washington. As he was unemployed and low on funds, he asked his old friend Senator Bradley for a job as junior clerk in the senate. This was not a good decision by Bradley, as Graham was an outspoken Federalist and Bradley a gentlemanly Republican. Only a short time later the clash of personalities came to head, when Bradley received a letter[72]:

> Philadelphia Feb: 8th; 1803
>
> Sir,
>
> Though a stranger to your person, I am induced to address you upon a subject interesting to humanity.
>
> Mr John Graham deputy Clerk to the senate of the United states, is now under my Care at a lodging house in this city, afflicted with a severe Attack of derangement. Its cause is unknown to me, nor can any inquiries on my part satisfy me what is his business in Philadelphia. His papers shew that he has been well educated, & that his connections are respectable. The Lady with whom he lodges is unwilling — and unable to keep him under present circumstances in her house. I have this day made an unsuccessful Attempt to procure his Admission into Our hospital. His want of funds, or of a security for the payment of his board there, were the

John A. Graham

Objections made to his admission. He speaks often in his more tranquil moments of you — Judge Smith & Mr Clinton with great respect and Affection. I submit his truly distressing case to your consideration. In the mean while, he shall continue to command my best services, Although, from his present want of Attendants and Accommodations suited to his disease, I fear they will be of little use to him. From Sir with great respect you most Obedient Servant

Benjn: Rush

This situation was simply handled by turning the letter over to John Graham's brother in New York who assumed responsibility for his brother's care.

On recovering his senses somewhat, John Graham blamed all of his troubles on Senator Bradley and started writing letters. The first of these were to William Coleman, the founder and editor of the Federalist newspaper the *New York Post*.[73] This was followed by a letter directed to Senator Bradley. The published articles did not seem to have any noticeable effect on Bradley's senatorial position and he was elected president pro-tem at the height of this controversy.

John Graham became a well-known and respected criminal lawyer in New York and practiced without any blemish on his record for the next 34 years.

The subject of the rights of individuals was of great concern to Stephen Bradley. The first indications of his interest was an appointment of a committee by Governor Chittenden on the local Indian problem. They were being displaced and treated in a manner not to Bradley's liking.

IN GENERAL ASSEMBLY, June 7, 1785

On motion made by Mr. Bradley, Resolved that a Committee of five to join a Committee from the Council be appointed to prepare a bill for the quieting Ancient Settlers & make a report. The members choosen Mr. Tichenor, Mr. Chipman, Mr. Knight, Mr. Weld & Mr. Loomis.

Extract from the Journals
Rosl. Hopkins, Clerk[74]

There are few follow ups on these appointments and what resulted is not generally known.

Bradley was dead set against slavery and repeated his sentiments of displeasure many times. These conversations are recorded on numerous occasions.[75]

Left: Benjamin Rush. *Right:* Nathan Burr Graham.

I abhor slavery — I am opposed to it in every shape — He that steals a man & sells him ought to die[76] — I will on every occasion vote against slavery — I am sorry the question is now called up — I have done everything I could to prevent it — but gentlemen, will stir the question, I am prepared & will on all occasions vote against slavery.

Prior to his election to the U.S. Senate, he was of the opinion that free states such as Vermont should have nothing to say about the slavery question. This was based on the theory of state's rights. After his election to the Senate he was forced to vote on this question. Slavery was debated regularly, but the most important, and well recorded instance that involved Bradley was after the acquisition of the Louisiana Territory. Was it to be a free territory or slave territory? The northern Senators, including Bradley, did not have the votes to prevent the spread of slavery in Louisiana, but they did try to curtail it. Senator Israel Smith,[77] the junior senator from Vermont, and Bradley made a proposal to allow slavery in the territory, but to prohibit any further importation of slaves to America after 1808.[78] This proposal, and every other attempt by Bradley and Smith, ended in failure. The following are a group of quotes by Bradley on the subject from William Plumer's *Proceedings in the United State Senate:*

Isaac Tichenor

> I am in favor of extending slavery to that country, because it is a right they claim, & by the treaty we are bound to grant it to them — but I think that in this bill we had better say nothing on that subject.[79]
>
> I am opposed to slavery in the eastern states; but the resolution under consideration admits the principle of slavery, & therefore I shall vote against it.[80]
>
> The prohibiting slaves in that territory from Africa, & admitting them from the States, will encrease, not lessen slavery. Each State can till 1808 import from Africa, & by this law the slave states may send their vicious slaves to Louisiana.[81]
>
> I am against slavery — but this provision is insufficient and I shall vote against it.[82]
>
> This resolution supports slavery, therefore, I shall vote against it, although it is bro't forward by those who wish to destroy slavery.[83]
>
> John Adams: General Bradley some days since gave notice he should ask liberty to bring in a bill to prohibit the importation of Negroes into the United States after January 1808. He yesterday offered his bill but the opposition continued till adjournment.[84]

The rights of individuals in the courts was another of Bradley's interests. When a man who is accused of a crime is insane, he thought the court should proceed no further. Bradley said, "It is a gross absurdity to convict a man of high crimes & misdemeanors who is insane." There are a number of other quotes that are of interest on the subject:

> It has been said by the gentleman from Kentucky (Senator Brackenridge) That a man charged in a

Israel Smith

Walpole, New Hampshire, home of Stephen Rowe Bradley, 1817–1830.

Unitarian Church, Walpole, New Hampshire

court of law with murder, who is insane, may by his friends appear & plead not guilty, & that under that plea insanity has been proved, & if a defence, it has been received as such. The gentleman is mistaken both in his law and fact. In all capital offences the plea cannot be made by council, it must be by the person accused.[85]

An insane man cannot appoint an attorney — he cannot be tried during his insanity. A lunatic may in his lucid intervals plead & be tried, & under the general issue may prove his lunacy — But no man while in a state of insanity was ever required to plead, much less ordered to trial.[86]

Henry K. Willard's history describes succinctly the last few years of Bradley's life, following his retirement from public life.

After returning to Westminster in 1813 Bradley resided there for only a short time. He evidently had some sort of disagreement with the town fathers; it is not known what it was about. The result, however, is known, and he moved across the Connecticut River to Walpole, New Hampshire, where he lived in quiet retirement until his death in 1830. The home he lived in is still in the family (2002), but is not open to the public.

Family Stories

Reuben Atwater, b. October 1728, Wallingford, Connecticut, the son of Pheneas and Mary Ward Atwater; m. (1) April 19, 1752, Sarah Hull; m. (2) January 18, 1755, Mary Russell; b. November 21, 1726, Derby, Connecticut, d. May 6, 1807, Cheshire, Connecticut, where she is buried. He d. August 19, 1801, Blandford, Massachusetts.

Merab Atwater b. June 19, 1757, the daughter of Reuben and Mary Russell Atwater; m. May 16, 1780, Stephen Rowe Bradley; d. April 7, 1785. Buried at the Bradley Tomb, Old Cemetery, Westminster, Vermont. There is an eloquent epitaph dedicated to her memory, it is written in an unidentified hand.

When Merab Atwater Bradley died she left a young son, William Czar Bradley age 3, and he went to live with his grandparents in Connecticut. A letter written by "Billa Czar" (William C. Bradley) age 6 to his father on Oct. 9, 1788, is a unique document.[87] This letter is of interest because it shows a boy who can write and compose poetry at a very tender age and is an indication of his very high intellect. He was prepared for college at Charlestown, N.H., and entered Yale College as a freshman at age 13. At the age of 17 he wrote and delivered the Fourth of July Oration at the celebration of the 25th anniversary of the Declaration of Independence at Westminster, Vermont.

There were a number of major tragedies in the Bradley family, including the early death of Stephen Bradley's first two wives.[88] A son born of his second wife, Gratia Taylor Bradley, drowned in the Deerfield River on June 27, 1808. He was the General's namesake, Stephen Rowe Bradley II, and was a student at Deerfield Academy. The name was used again for Stephen Rowe Bradley III, IV and V. A daughter, Stella Czarina Bradley, also born of Stephen Bradley's second wife, died of consumption at the early age of 37, followed in rapid succession by the deaths from the same cause of her three daughters, Gratia, Sarah, and Stella, all of whom inherited their mother's charm and character. Next to die was her husband, Colonel Josiah Bellows, and lastly her son, Stephen Rowe Bellows. In the period of a few years the entire family became extinct.

The second daughter, Adeline Gratia Bradley, fared much better and married Samuel Griswald Goodrich on April 28, 1799. The marriage lasted 53 years. Samuel Goodrich wrote children's books under the pen name of Peter Parly and was one of the most prolific and prosperous writers of the early 1800's. Prior to his marriage he enjoyed a rather boisterous and wild bachelorhood, so much so, that a friend of Stephen Bradley's warned him he would be an unsatisfactory son-in-law. Of all the books written by Samuel Goodrich only one mentions Bradley, *Recollections of a Lifetime*.[89] This is a very short quote from it:

> Early in the year 1818 I was married to the daughter of SRB, in Westminster, Vermont. Thus established in life, I pursued the business of bookseller and publisher at Hartford for four years.

Bradley thought a great deal of his son-in-law, and over the following years, Samuel Goodrich handled all of the Bradley family financial dealings in the Boston area. This financial responsibility was taken over by Captain Nathanial Dorr, the son-in-law of William C. Bradley. Captain Dorr[90] was a well respected clipper ship captain when he married Emily Penelope Bradley. After his marriage he became a Boston Harbor Pilot and a leading marine merchant on the East Coast. He was member #561 of the Boston Marine Society. Although he married into the family, he became an integral and lasting part, not only for financial dealings, but because of his name. The name "Dorr" has been used at least once in every generation of the Bradley family since this time.

While reading this biography you will have noticed the use of two spellings: Row or Rowe. The name was derived from Mary Row, Stephen's mother. For reasons unknown, Stephen Bradley started to use the spelling of Rowe sometime after 1775.

The family life of the Bradleys in the period 1782 through 1869 is well documented. The old General's granddaughter, Sarah Bradley Willard, wrote *A Tribute of Affection to the Memory of Hon. William C. Bradley*. This book, although printed privately, has survived and one copy is in the Library of Congress. This book is rich with family stories, letters, and the history of the Bradley family.

One amusing story not in this book is the following[91]: One day he (Stephen Bradley) happened to meet one of his poor Westminster neighbors—he asked how he got along with his large family. "Poorly enough," was the reply.

"Well," said Mr. B., "the next time you come over bring a bag and get some corn."

It was not long before the poor man was at Mr. B.'s with his bag—"What do you want in the bag?" said Mr. B.

"I came after the corn you promised me," was the reply. "Corn! I never promised you any corn," said Mr. B.

"Well," said the man, "my neighbors told me before I started that you would not give me any."

"Go to my bin and fill your bag," replied Mr. B., "and when you get home, tell your neighbors they are all a pack of damned liars."

Notes

1. Henry Kellogg Willard, *Willard-Bradley Memoirs* (Privately printed, 1925), 34.
2. Yale University, Sterling Library, owns the only original copy known.
3. See letter (Dec. 4, 1774).
4. Henry K. Willard, 34.
5. See letter (Jan. 24, 1776).
6. See letter (June 26, 1776).
7. Jacob G. Ullery, *Men of Vermont* (Brattleboro, Vermont: Transcript Publishing Co. 1894), 104.
8. *Hemenways Historical Gazetteer* (C.E.H. Page Pub. Co., 1891) Vol. V, 591.
9. Benjamin H. Hall, *History of Eastern Vermont* (Albany, New York: J. Munsell, 1858), 342.
10. *Governor and Council Records* (Montpelier, Vermont: Steam Press of J&J.M. Poland, 1875) Vol. II, 192. See resolution (Oct. 20, 1779).
11. See letters (Oct. 20, 1779; Feb. 1, 1780; Feb. 5, 1780; Aug. 16, 1780; Sept. 12, 1780; Sept. 15, 1780; Sept. 22, 1780; Oct. 2, 1780).
12. *Governor and Council Records*, Vol. II, 19 and 200.
13. See letters (Sept. 15, 1780, and Sept. 22, 1780).
14. *Journals of the Continental Congress, 1774–1789*, compiled by Kenneth E. Harris and Steven D. Tilley. Wed. Sept. 27, 1780, page 868. Also see Benjamin H. Hall, 596.
15. See letter (Sept. 12, 1780).
16. Henry K. Willard, 36.
17. Graham family letters, owned by The Newberry Library, Chicago, Ill.
18. Lewis C. Duncan, *Medical Men in the American Revolution* (War Dept., 1931), 149.
19. See letter (Nov. 12, 1780).
20. *Governor and Council Records*, Vol. III, 228. See letter (March 2, 1787).
21. Francis S. Drake, *Dictonary of American Biography* (Boston: J.B. Osgood & Co., 1872), 575.
22. Benjamin H. Hall, 600.
23. See letter (May 1, 1789).
24. John M. Comstock, ed., *Principal Civil Officers of Vermont, From 1777–1918* (St. Albans, Vermont: St. Albans Messenger Co., 1918), 12–338. See letters (Jan. 15, 1791 and Feb. 26, 1783).
25. *Governor and Council Records*, Vol. III, 460.
26. Benjamin H. Hall, 598.
27. *Annals of Congress Debates and Proceedings* (Washington: Gales and Seaton, 1852), Tues. Dec. 14, 1802, page 11. See letters (Dec. 13, 1802) and Dec. 14, 1802).
28. Benjamin H. Hall, 599.
29. *Thomas Jefferson Library*, Charlottesville, Va. (Bradley Collection).
30. See letter (Feb. 18, 1802).
31. Benjamin H. Hall, 599.
32. Benjamin H. Hall, 599.
33. Benjamin H. Hall, 599.
34. Sara Bradley Willard, *A Tribute of Affection to the Memory of Hon. William C. Bradley* (Boston: Geo. C. Rand & Avery Pub., 1869), 48.

Biography

35. Francis S. Drake, 575. See letters (Feb. 3, 1802 and March 9, 1802).
36. William Plumer, *William Plumer's Memorandum of Proceedings in the United States Senate 1803–1807* (New York, Macmillan Co., 1923), 476.
37. William Plumer, 574.
38. William Plumer, 527.
39. Benjamin H. Hall, 375–379. See letter (June 7, 1779).
40. See letter (June 8, 1779).
41. John Pell, *Ethan Allen* (Boston, Houghton Mifflin Co., 1929), 257.
42. John Pell, 242.
43. John Pell, 222.
44. John Pell, 243.
45. Benjamin H. Hall, 627-8.
46. Benjamin H. Hall, 629.
47. Benjamin H. Hall, 630.
48. Benjamin H. Hall, 630.
49. Joseph: A garment made like a greatcoat, an allusion to Joseph's "coat of many colors."
50. John Pell, 249.
51. See letters (Jan. 19, 1787; Nov. 6, 1787; Nov. 9, 1787; Nov. 12, 1788; etc.).
52. Jacob G. Ullery, 63.
53. Benjamin H. Hall, 478.
54. Benjamin H. Hall, 477.
55. Benjamin H. Hall, 444. See letter (Sept. 13, 1782).
56. Benjamin H. Hall, 505.
57. *Governor and Council Records*, Vol. III, 274.
58. See letter (Oct. 5, 1804).
59. Benjamin H. Hall, 509. See letter (Jan. 10, 1783).
60. See letter (Oct. 10, 1799).
61. Amos B. Carpenter, *Carpenter Memorial Our Family* (Amherst, Massachusetts: Carpenter & Morehouse Press, 1898), 126.
62. John J. Duffy, *Ethan Allen & His Kin* (Hanover & London: University Press of New England, 1998), Vol. II, 755.
63. Claude G. Bowers, *Jefferson in Power* (Cambridge: Riverside Press, 1936), 479.
64. William Plumer, 352.
65. *Annals of Congress*, 190 (Feb. 18, 1802).
66. See letter (Jan. 2, 1805). For a different opinion on this, see paragraph 19 of that entry.
67. *Governor and Council Records*, Vol. II, 202 (footnote).
68. William Plumer, 355.
69. See letters (Feb. 22, 1806; Feb. 24, 1806; March 23, 1806; April 7, 1806; Nov. 17, 1806; etc.).
70. Helen G. Carpenter, *The Reverend John Graham of Woodbury, Connecticut and His Descendants* (Chicago: Monestary Hill Press, 1942), 238.
71. John A. Graham, *A Descriptive Sketch of the Present State of Vermont* (London: Henry Fry Publisher, 1797), 111.
72. See letter (Feb. 8, 1803).
73. See letter (Jan. 2, 1805).
74. *Governor and Council Records*, Vol. III, 67.
75. William Plumer, 126. See letter (Feb. 13, 1813).
76. Exodus, XXI, 16.
77. *Annals of Congress*, page 264 (April 20, 1802).
78. William Plumer, 353. See letter (Feb. 13, 1813).
79. William Plumer, 113.
80. William Plumer, 116.
81. William Plumer, 119.
82. William Plumer, 120.
83. William Plumer, 121.
84. William Plumer, 353.
85. William Plumer, 162.
86. William Plumer, 164.
87. See letters (Oct. 9, 1788 and Dec. 30, 1792).
88. Henry K. Willard, 42.
89. Peter Parly, *Recollections of a Lifetime* (New York: Miller, Orton & Mulligan, 1856), 449.
90. Henry K. Willard, 25.
91. Henry K. Willard, 44.

Correspondence, 1771 to 1831

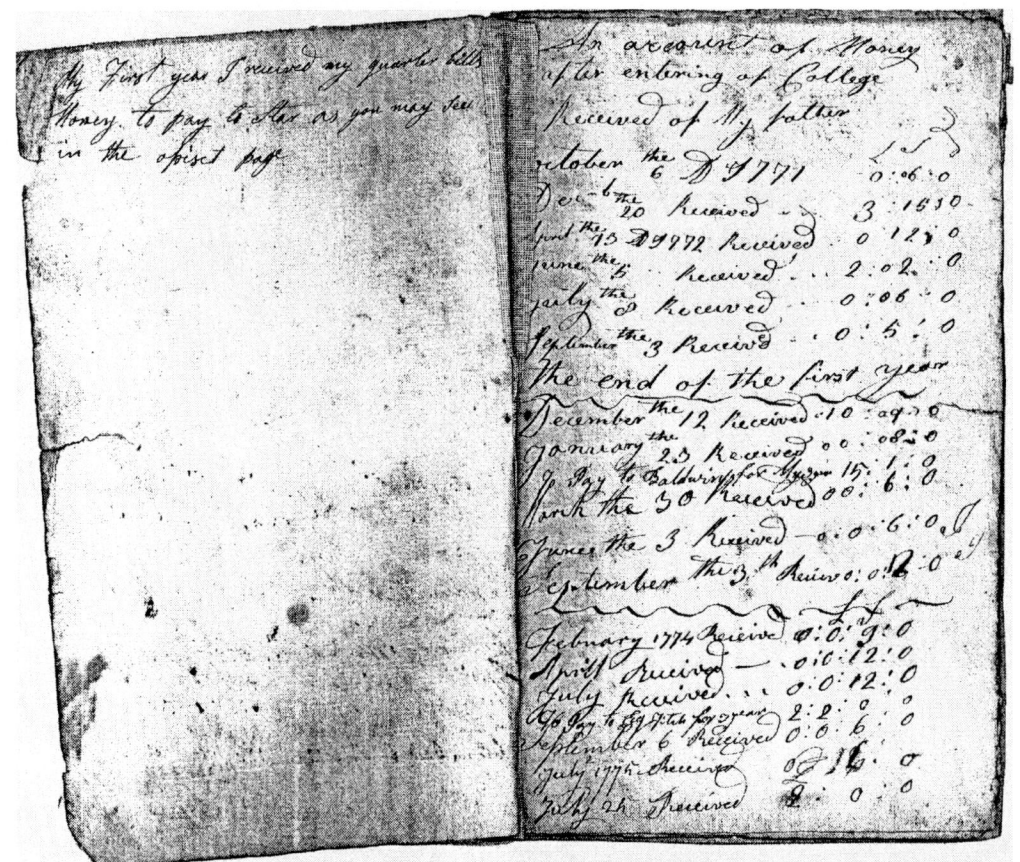

Above and opposite: Stephen Rowe Bradley's notebook of "Colledge Expenses," 1771–1775.

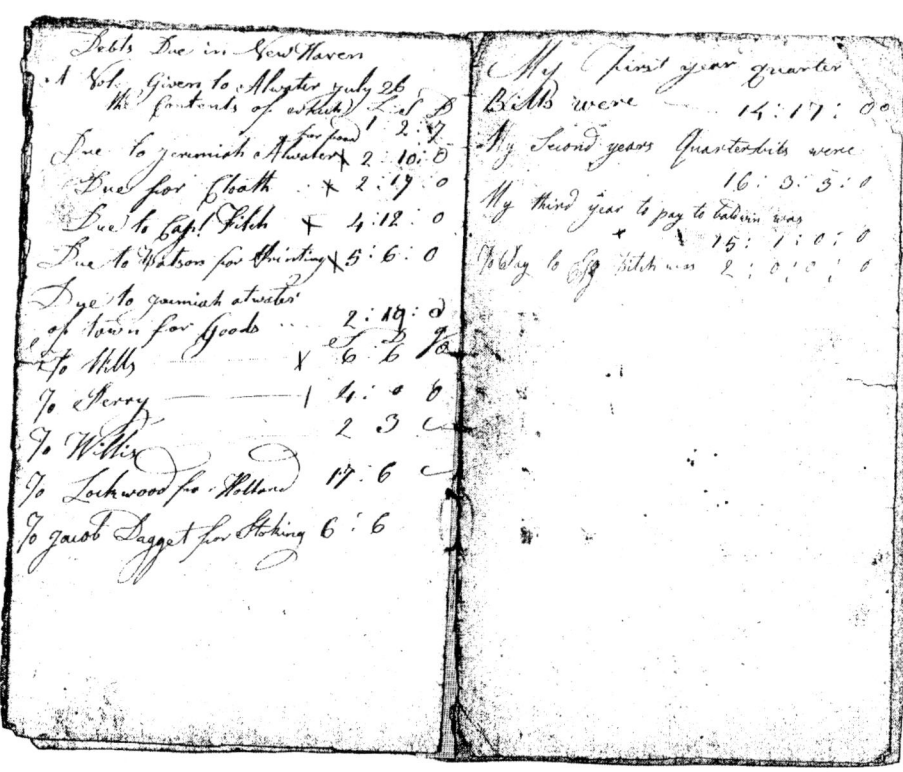

S. R. Bradley's College Expences [1772-5]

An Account of Money Spent at College all the time while there

	£	s	d	
When I went Down first october the 6th 1771 Received	0	6	0	0
December the twentyth then Received	0	9	0	0
April the 13th AD 1772 Received	0	12	0	0
June the 5th Golden Arms Received	0	7	0	0
July the 8 Received	0	6	0	0
September the 3d Received	0	5	0	0
My first years Quarter Bills were	14	17	9	0
December the 12th Received	0	12	0	0
January the 23d AD 1773 Received	0	8	0	0
March the 30th Received	0	6	0	0
June the 9 Received	0	6	0	0
September the 3d Received	0	12	0	0
My Second years Quarter Bills were	16	3	3	0
February 1774 received 9 April received 12 July received 12	1	13	0	0
September 6th Received	0	6	0	0
My third years Bills to Baldwin and Fitch were	17	3	0	0
July 2 1775 Received	0	6	0	0
July the 19th Received	2	0	0	0
To Pay to Jeremiah Atwater	1	11	0	0
To Pay to Esquire Fitch	4	15	0	0
	65	5	0	0

Debts Due in New Haven

	£	s	d
A Note Given to Atwater July 26 the Contents of which	1	2	7
Due to Jeremiah Atwater	2	10	0
Due for Cloath	2	17	0
Due to Capt. Fitch	4	12	0
Due to Watson for Printing	5	6	0
Due to Jeremiah Atwater of Town for Goods	2	19	0
To Mills	6	6	0
To Perry	1	4	0
To Wilcox		2	3
To Lockwood for Holland		17	6
To Jacob Daggat for Stoking		6	6

My first year quarter Bills were 14:17:00
My Second years Quarter bills were 16:3:3:0
My third year to pay to Baldwin was 15:1:0:0
To Pay to Esq Fitch was 2:0:0:0

From Charles Lee

[24 January 1776]

By virtue of authority granted to me, occasionally, by his excellency Gen. Washington, I do constitute and appoint Stephen Rowe Bradley, Esq., to act as captain of the new company of Cheshire Volunteers during the present expedition; and he is to be considered and obeyed as such.

Given, under my hand, at Head Quarters at Stamford, the 24th day of January, 1776.

CHARLES LEE,
Major-General

Printed (*Bradley Family Papers*).

From Charles Lee

Head Quarters New York 19th Feby 1776.

There being no farther Service at present, for Capt Bradley's Independant Company of Connecticutt Volunteers, they are hereby dismiss'd from any further duty. The General at the same time returns his sincere thanks to the Officers & Men for their Zeal and alacrity in the Service of their Country; and their good behaviour since they have been embodied.

Charles Lee[1] Major General

To Capn. Stephen R. Bradley.

LS (MHi).

1. Charles Lee (1731–1782), born in Cheshire, England, first came to America as a British officer serving in the French and Indian War. In 1773 he went to live in Virginia and became a supporter of American independence. His military experience won him a commission as a major general in the Continental army at the start of the American Revolution. Early in 1776 he directed the fortification of New York City. He was captured by the British in December 1776 and gave British general Howe a plan for defeating the Americans, but his treason was not discovered. He was exchanged and joined General Washington at Valley Forge in 1778. Later that year at the battle of Monmouth he prevented an American victory by ordering a retreat of his forces; he was court-martialed and suspended from command for a year; and in 1780 he was finally dismissed from service.

Resolution of Congress

[26 June 1776]

The committee on the treasury, to whom were referred the petition and accounts of Stephen Row Bradley, brought in their report: Whereupon,

Resolved, That there be paid to Stephen Row Bradley the sum of 691¼ dollars, for the service of himself and his company, from the 15 day of January to the 25th of February, during which time they were employed in the service of the continent.

The several matters to this day referred, being postponed,

Adjourned to 9 o'clock to Morrow.

Printed (*JCC*, 5:484).

Receipt from Amos Northrop

<Sawpet?> Rye Jany: 6th: 1777

Receivd: of Majr: General Wooster by the hand of Majr: Stephen R. Bradley Aid de Camp one Hundred twenty four pounds Ball, one Hundred Cartridges Twenty Eight Powder Horns for the use of the New Levies from the State of Connecticutt: Pr.

           Amos Northrop <Condur:?> of Military Stores

ADS (DLC).

From R. Sill

Dear Sir   White Plains Camp 27th July 1778

 Yours by Lt Hitchcok came safe to hand. I improve this first opportunity in returning your favour. In the first place I must inform you the troublesome Disorder of sore Eyes hangs upon me, which will be a sufficient Excuse for bad writing and a short Letter.

 The move of the Army leisure of Business affords me an opportunity of taking my ease in the Country, where I can enjoy all the sweets of female Conversation with the other Luxuries of Rural life, which at some time induces me to determine my situation to be the most disagreable possible. I assure you I never left Connecticut with half the reluctance I parted with N Jersey, a fortunate accident of laming my horse afforded me time in one of their principle Towns to make considerable acquaintance which was extremely agreable. The Young Gentlemen show'd such a fondness of informing themselves as is very uncommon, for two years past they had held meetings somewhat similar to our own *Sinonians* wherein Question respecting Government were disputed with much good sense and Judgment, the Females were beautiful, affable and Clever, think with what reluctance I exchangd these Scenes for my Blankett and a little straw on the ground for my mule Cloth house in which tis impossible to stand straight with my piece of beef & bread — but however the Conquerors of Briton, the defenders of Liberty &c &c are no small matters; I ever am apt to run into companions of this kind, which will rather raise your envy than pity. Stephen tis absolutely determined that (by the leave of providence) I should call to see your *Famosa* <*Perillas*?>, but when it will be is uncertain, have one ready in your Imagination, that the Arrangment need <not in>terfere with the Enjoyment — folly.

 Samme, Preston & myself have a furious fit over a bottle now and then which brings fresh to mind many College scenes. Mr Dwight is Chaplain to this Brigade (which Genl Parsons Commands) we have neither heard him preach nor pray — how he and your friend will agree is uncertain but expect the Jews & Samaritans will have no dealings.

 The particulars of the Action in Jersey you <have it> with the fatigues of a long march in the severest heat ever felt with more exactness than is in my power to relate. The whole Army is now Encampd near the Plains—(*a most grand Army*). We have let our expectations run so fast that at some times we have had the British Troops Prisoners but we are short sighted. Imagination you know is always in the Clouds ever paints the fair tides and is <ever> fallacious. The French Fleet tis said are moved from the hook to Rhode Island.

 From your engagement I suppose tis unnecessary even to desire you to return this your own satisfaction I suppose will be sufficient inducement.

 My Eyes have servd beyond Expectation but cant write another word

 I am Sir Yours &c

                       R Sill

Mr Bradley

 ALS (VtU). Words along the bottom of the recto and the right margin of the verso are obscured.

To the Governor and General Assembly of Vermont

[15 May 1779]

To his Excellency the Govinour and Honourable Assembley of the State of Vermont —

the Petition of Stephen R. Bradley and Miles Powell & Ebenz[er] Fisk and their assosiates humbly Sheweth that their is a Tract of Land in the State of Vermont which has Not been granted to any person and it is adjoining on the West of Poultney to the East bay on the Line within Twenty Miles of the North River also Exstending North to the Latitude of forty five and from thence East to the Lake Champlane and from thence south to the first Menchtioning bounds Containing all the Goar or tract of Land Lying their.

Whereupon Said petitioners would humbly Pray that Said Land may be granted to us being Earnesly Desirous of Pr<om>oting the Settlement of Said State and that Said <la>nd may be granted under such Regulations as your Honour Shall think fit — and your petitioners Shall as in Duty bound ever Pray

Dated May 15 1779

    Stephen R: Bradley
    Miles Powell
    Ebenezer Fisk
    and
    Our assosiates

ADS (Vt: MsVtSP, vol. 21, p. 73). Torn at folds. Docketed on verso, "Petition of Stephn R Bradley & others for Land west of Poulteney / Reced. on file 25th. May 1779."

To the General Assembly of Vermont

[20 May 1779]

To the Honourable General Assembly of the Represent[at]ive of the Freeman of the State of Vermont to be Holden at Winsor in Said State on the first Wednesday of June next —

the Petition of Stephen R Bradley of Wallingford in the State of Connecticut in behalf of himself & Ninety More persons inhabitants of Said State

Humbly Sheweth That Your Honours Petitioner begs Leave to inform Your Honours that He together with Ninety More have Discovered a Certain Gore of Land Lying on the Green Mountains Situate South of a Streight line runing from the North East Corner of Salisbury to the north west Corner of a Certain township Survey'd Under New York by the Name of Middleton Containing all that Gore that Lyet<h> between those towns Surveyd on the East and those Survey'd on the west of Said Gore taking in all Said Gore of Vacant Lands Down as far as the North East Corner of Shrewsbury Runing a Streight line across to the South west Corner of Kensington Supposed to Contain Enough Ground for 3 townships and as Said Land is a Great part of it Mountainous & Broken You[r] petitioner requests it May be Granted on Simp<le> Fees to Your Petitioner and his Associates and You[r] petitioner as in Duty bound will Ever pray

Dated at Shrewsbury the 20th Day of May 1779

    Stephen R Bradley
    Col Roger <Evers?>

ADS (Vt: MsVtSP, vol. 21, p. 74). Docketed on verso, "Petition / Stephen R Bradley / Agent / Recd. on file June 4th. 1779 / fees pd."

To the General Assembly of Vermont

[20 May 1779]

To the Honourable Assembly of the Govr. Council & House of Representatives of the Freeman of the State of Vermont to be Holden at Winsor in Said State on the First Wednesday of June Next —

The petition of the Subscribers of the State of Connecticut Humbly Sheweth

That Your petitioners having knowledge of Vacant Unlocated Grounds in Said State of Vermont Lying in the Northern part of Said State having Survey'd a township Lying north of <Scodayna?> River Bounded on Said River on the Southwest on Fairfield — & North and East on unlocated Grounds which your Honours petitioners Request May be Granded to them by the Name of *Mount Carmel* on Such Considerations as Your Honours in Your Great wisdom Shall Direct and Your petitioners as in Duty Bound will every pray

Dated at Winsor the 20 Day of May 1779

AD (Vt: MsVtSP, vol. 21, p. 73). Signed by SRB and forty-three others. Torn at folds and along the right margin of the verso. Note on the verso reads, Sunderland Octr 10th 1<786> / Rec'd of Ira Allen the Contents [...] / the within Order by being A[...]ed / to Charge the Same on Ba[...]s'd / money having been taken [...] / the Treasury —/ £3.704. 4. 0 / Ira Allen." The note is docketed, "Col. Ira Allen / £3704. 4. 0 / Octr. 10th. 1786 / Continental / No. 2"

Governor and Council Record

[Biographical Notes on Noah Smith, Vol. IV {May 27, 1779}]

... He was admitted to the bar of Vermont at Westminster, May 26 1779, with Stephen R. Bradley — these being the first admissions to the bar of Vermont. Bradley was appointed clerk of the court, and Smith State's Attorney within and for the county of Cumberland, *pro tempore.*

IN COUNCIL, Windsor 3d June 1779

Resolved that Mr. Stephen R. Bradley be & he is hereby appointed to prepare, and bring into this board as soon as may [be] a draft of a Proclamation to be Issued by his Excellency in regard to the diseffected inhabitants of the County of Cumberland.

By order of the Govr. & Council.

JONAS FAY, *Sec'y. P. Tem.*

Printed (Governor and Council Record, vol. 1).

Resolution of the State of Vermont

STATE of VERMONT.

IN COUNCIL, Windsor, 7th June, 1779.

RESOLVED, *That the Captain-General's orders of the 6th of May last, to Colonel Ethan Allen,*[1] *together with an extract of the proceedings of the adjourned Superior Court, held at Westminster, in the south Halfshire of the county of Cumberland, on the 26th day of May last, and his Excellency's proclamation of the 3d instant,*[2] *be published.*

Extract from the minutes,   JONAS FAY, *Secretary pro temp.*

. . . .

State of *Vermont.* } *At an adjourned Superior Court holden at Westminster, in the county of Cumberland, on the 26th of May,* 1779.

PRESENT.

MOSES ROBINSON, Esquire, Chief Judge.

JOHN SHEPHERDSON, Esq;
JOHN FASSET, jun. Esq;   Side Judges of
THOMAS CHANDLER, jun. Esq; and   the same.
JOHN THROOP, Esq;

Noah Smith, State-Attorney within and for said county, exhibited complaint, that

Eleazer Patterson, of Hinsdale, in said county; Elkahan Day, Michael Gilson, Benjamin Whitney, Medad Wright, Bella Willard, Joseph Willard, Beldad Easton, John Norton and John Sessions, each of Westminster, in said county.

Michael Townshend, John Serjeants, Timothy Church, James Blakeslee, Samuel Root and Benjamin Butterfield, each of Brattleborough, in said county; and James Clay, Lucas Willson, James Clay, jun. Ephraim Clay, Daniel Saben, Noah Saben, William Pierce, Noah Cushion, Samuel Wheat, Francis Cummings, James Cummings, Thomas Pierce, Joseph Joy and Thomas Nelson, each of Putney, in said county, did on or about the 28th day of April last, past, at Putney aforesaid, in a riotous and unlawful manner, by force and arms, an assault make upon one William M'Waine, then a lawful officer in the execution of a lawful command, and did also then and th<er>e, viz. with force <and arms, Apprehend and rescue out of the hands and possession of the said M'Waine two cows, which the said M'Waine had taken by lawful command from lawful authority, which wicked conduct was a flagrant violation of the common law of the land, and contrary to the force and effect of a certain statute law of this state, entituled, "An Act to prevent Riots, Disorders and Contempt of Authority within this State, and for punishing the same," as per complaint on file, dated the 26th day of May, 1779.

The delinquents aforesaid being brought into Court, and put to plead to said information: Plead in bar to that part of the said information grounded on the statute in the following words, viz.

"That although by common law they might be holden to answer the information, yet they could not be holden to answer that part thereof brought on the statute, and that because 'twas not in the power of the persons complained of to have known that statute at the time when the crimes were said to have been committed, the said statute not having been promulgated; and this they were ready to verify.

Judgment, &c. &c.

BRADLEY, for delinquents."

The Court overruled the abovesaid plea in bar to be sufficient, and ordered that part of the information brought on the statute to be dismissed.

The delinquents then plead to General <is>sue, Not guilty, and gave in evidence, that they were subjects of the state of N. York, and the facts charged against them on the aforesaid information, were done by virtue of authority granted them by the state of N. York, and thereof put themselves upon the Court for trial.—Judgment, &c. &c.

The Court having heard the evidence, and fully considered the cause, gave judgment, that the delinquents complained of as aforesaid were guilty, and that

Eleazar Patterson, John Serjeants, Elkanah Day and James Clay aforesaid pay a fine, each of Forty pounds lawful money, to the Treasurer of this state.

That Michael Gilson, Lewis Willson and Timothy Church aforesaid pay a fine, each of Twenty-five pounds lawful money, to the Treasurer of this state.

That Micah Townshend, James Blakeslee, James Clay, jun. Benjamin Whitney, Samuel Root, John Norton and John Sessions aforesaid, pay a fine, each of Twenty pounds lawful money, to the Treasurer of this state.

That Ephraim Clay, Medad Wright, Bela Willard, Joseph Willard and Bildad Easton aforesaid pay a fine, each of Ten pounds lawful money, to the Treasurer of this state.

That Daniel Sabin, Noah Sabin, William Pierce, Noah Cushion, Samuel Wheat, Francis Cummings, James Cummings, Joseph Joy, Thomas Pierce and Thomas Willson aforesaid pay a fine, each of Three pounds lawful money, to the Treasurer of this state; and that Benjamin Butterfield aforesaid pay a fine, of Forty shillings lawful money, to the Treasurer of this state. And that the delinquents aforesaid pay cost of prosecution, taxed at £1477:18:0.

A true extract from the original records.

Examined and attested by

STEPHEN R. BRADLEY, *Clerk pro temp.*

. . . .

Printed broadside (DNA: Papers of the Continental Congress, r47, i40, 1:229). Torn at folds.

1. On 2 Apr. 1779 Thomas Chittenden and the Board of War had ordered a militia draft to defend the northern frontier. In Putney, N.Y., militia officers James Clay and Benjamin Willson refused to serve in the Vermont militia. To satisfy the fines against the two men for resisting the draft, Sgt. William McWain seized a cow from each of them to be sold at public vendue on 28 Apr. Col. Eleazar Patterson and one hundred men of Cumberland County's New York militia appeared at the sale and seized the cattle. Under the orders from Governor Chittenden, 6 May 1779, printed in this broadside, Ethan Allen and one hundred armed men arrived in Cumberland County on 24 May and arrested Patterson and forty-four others for riotous and other illegal behavior (*Ethan Allen: Correspondence*, 1:93 n. 2).

2. In the 3 June proclamation printed in this broadside, Governor Chittenden issued a pardon "to all persons residing within this state ... of all public offences, crimes and misdemeanors heretofore committed within the limits of the same ... since the 15th day of January, 1777," which included the rioters arrested by Allen and his men.

From Ethan Allen

Sir   8th June 1779

The bearer Mr. William Stewart[1] one of the old Green Mountain Core having an action at Rutland Superior Court in June instant respecting the title of his Gun which I am very certain he has a Just right to, and as he is a poor man I desire you will plead his case and charge it to me, my Warriors must not be cheated out of their Fire Arms—I am in haste your Friend and very Humble Servant

Ethan Allen

Stephen R. Bradley
    June 1779.
        To   cause at his request for William Stewart
                                  £. S.
                                  2..10..0

AD (Vt)

1. William Stewart (d. 1835) served with Ethan Allen at Montreal and was wounded by a Mohawk's tomahawk. Allen later employed him at his farm in Burlington (John J. Duffy et al., eds., *Ethan Allen and His Kin: Correspondence, 1772–1819* [2 vols.; Hanover, N.H., and London, 1998], 1:94 n. 2).

To the General Assembly of Vermont

Rutland June 10th. 1779.

To the Honbl. General Assembly of Governor Council and Representatives of the State of Vermonte

The petition of us the Subscribers Inhabitents of the United States Humbly sheweth,

That your honors petitioners have discovered a Certain tract of Vacant unlocated Ground which your honors petitioners have Surveyed as follows Viz Begining at a Stake and Stones on <Shunsborough?> one mile East of the falls; from thence running due East by the Needle on Said line five Miles to a pole Marked from thence Runing North ten degrees East two miles and one quarter to Poultney River — Thence on the Same point four Miles to a Pole Marked — from thence Running due west by the Needle five Miles to a tree Marked; from thence Runing South ten degs. west four Miles to the first Mentioned bounds containing about 12,000 acres — which your petitioners Request may be Granted to them as a Township by the Name of Cheshire Upon Simple fees, or if that should Seam unreasonable, that your honors would Grant it upon such Considerations as your honrs in your Great Wisdom shall direct and your petitioners shall in duty bound Ever pray

Barnabas Moss
Stephen R. Bradley

ADS (Vt: MsVtSP, vol. 21, p. 90). Docketed on verso, "Petition of Barns. Moss for the Township of Cheshire / Recd. on file 17th June 1779 / Copy / Attest Joseph Fay Secy."

Certification of Purchase

Septembr 10 1779

To all Concern'd

This may Certafy that I this Day Purchased of Thomas Chandler Esqr Commissioner a Lot of Land in the township of Westminster in Cumberland County Call'd the 58th Lot in the Division of House Lot Said Lot being forfeited to this State by Crean Brush by his Treason[a]ble Conduct[1] for which I gave four Hundred & Twenty five Pounds LM[2] and No more.

Stephen R Bradley

Personally appeared Stephen R Bradley the above Signer and made oath to the truth of the above Certificate

Sept 10th 1779   Pr Me   Reuben Jones Jus Peace

ADS (Vt: MsVtSP, vol. 37, p. 133a). In the hand of SRB, signed by Jones.

1. Crean Brush (1725–1778) was a Dublin-trained lawyer who came to New York in 1762, where he became a member of the New York Provincial Assembly and registrar of New York deeds in Westminster. He married Margaret Schoolcraft, whose daughter by an earlier marriage, Frances Montresor, later became Ethan Allen's second wife. By New York grants, Crean Brush acquired 60,000 acres in the Westminster region near the Connecticut River, and he openly opposed New Hampshire's jurisdiction west of the Connecticut River. In 1775 he was driven out of the New Hampshire Grants for his Loyalist sympathies and escaped to Boston, where he was authorized to seize American property and money. Brush betrayed his British superiors, however, and secretly sailed for Halifax with a boatload of plunder. After being captured at sea, he was returned to Boston and served nineteen months in jail. He escaped to New York by dressing in his wife's clothes, but living in poverty there in May 1778, "with a pistol, besmeared the Room with his Brains." Frances Montresor, when she married Ethan Allen in 1784, was heir to 20,000 acres of Vermont land, the remains of Brush's estate after Allen and the Court of Confiscation seized his Vermont property in 1778 (*Ethan Allen: Correspondence,* 1:17 n. 1).

2. Lawful money.

State Papers of Vermont

Reports of Committees to the General Assembly, vol. IV, p. 10.

Governor Chittenden As Chairman of a Committee of the Whole

State of Vermont }   In General Assembly   Manchester 20th Octr. 1779

At a Committee consisting of the Governor, Council and House of Representatives held at Manchester on the 20th. of October 1779 to take into consideration some matters of importance concerning the State of Vermont.

1st. His Excellency Thomas Chittenden Esquire was unanimously chosen Chairman of said Committee.

2nd. Chose Joseph Fay Esqr. Clerk

3rd. Voted that the policy of the State requires the doors of the House to be shut.

4th. Voted that Genl. Ethan Allen, Stephen R. Bradley, John Throop, Noah Smith, and Nathaniel Chipman Esqrs be requested to attend the Committee.

5th. Voted unanimously that it is the opinion of this Committee that this State ought to support their right of Independence at Congress and to the world in the character of a free and independant State.

6th. Voted to adjourn this Committee to 2 °Clock this afternoon then to meet at this place. Committee met according to adjournment.

7th. Voted that this Committee recommend to the General Assembly of this State to make grants of all or any part of the unappropriated lands within the same (at this present session or in future as their wisdom may direct) that does not interfere with any former grants.

8th. Voted that this Committee be and it is hereby dissolved.

Attest

Joseph Fay   Clerk

Resolutions of the State of Vermont

[20–21 October 1779]

STATE of VERMONT.

In General Assembly, Manchester, October 20th, 1779.

AGREEABLE *to the Order of the Day, his Excellency the Governor, the Council, and House of Representatives, were resolved into a Committee of the Whole, to take into Consideration the Letter of the 25th ult. from his Excellency* JOHN JAY, *Esq; late President of the Congress of the United States of* America, *inclosing certain Acts of Congress, for an equitable Settlement of All Differences subsisting between the States of New-Hampshire, Massachusetts-Bay, and New-York, on one Part, and this State on the other;*[1] *and after some Time spent thereon the Governor resumed the Chair, and the following* RESOLUTIONS *being read several times were agreed to, viz.*

RESOLVED *unanimously,* That, it is the Opinion of this Committee that this State ought to support their Right to Independence, at Congress, and to the World, in the Character of a free, and independent State.

RESOLVED, That this Committee recommend it to the General Assembly, to make Grants of all, or any Part, of the unappropriated Lands within their Jurisdiction, that does not interfere with any former Grants, as their Wisdom may direct.

Extract from the Minutes,

JOSEPH FAY, *Clerk.*

In General Assembly, Manchester,
October 21, 1779.

The Committee of the Whole reported, that they had come to the foregoing Resolutions, which the Clerk was ordered to read; and on a Motion being made, it is Unanimously resolved, by this Assembly, that they agree thereto.

ROSWELL HOPKINS, Clerk.

RESOLVED, That five Persons be chosen, by Ballot, Agents in Behalf of the Freemen of this State, to appear at the Congress of the United States of *America,* on the first Day of February next; and that they, or any three of them, are hereby fully authorised and empowered by the Representatives of the Freemen aforesaid, to vindicate their Right to Independence at that Honourable Board.

And, furthermore, our said Agents, or any three of them, are hereby amply empowered to agree upon, and fully to settle Articles of Union and Confederation in Behalf of this State, with the United States, which shall be valid and binding on us, on our Constituents, and our Successors. And our said Agents are hereby further empowered, to transact all other political Affairs of this State at Congress, as a free and independent State, and report their Proceedings herein to this Assembly as soon as may be.

The Members chosen, Brigadier-General *Ethan Allen,* the Hon. *Jonas Fay,* and *Paul Spooner,* Esquires, *Stephen R. Bradley,* Esq; and the Hon. *Moses Robinson,* Esq.

RESOLVED, That an Agent be chosen to wait on the Honourable the Council, the General Court, of the State of *Massachusetts-Bay,* to negociate the public Business of this State.

Chosen for the above Purpose, by Ballot, Brigadier-General *Ethan Allen.*

Extract from the Journals,

Attest. Roswell Hopkins, Clerk.

Sent up for Concurrence.

IN COUNCIL, MANCHESTER, October 22. 1779.

READ AND CONCURRED.

JOSEPH FAY, Secretary.

Printed broadside (DNA: Papers of the Continental Congress, r47, i40, 1:283); partial copy (ibid., p. 287); partial copy (?, pp. 285–86).

1. The Continental Congress was preparing to debate the issue of the claims of New Hampshire, New York, and Massachusetts over jurisdiction and land titles in the Vermont area, and between each of these three states and the *de facto* independent government created by many of the Vermont settlers (William T. Hutchinson et al., eds., *The Papers of James Madison* [1st ser., vols. 1–10, Chicago, 1962–77, vols. 11–17, Charlottesville, Va. 1977–91], 2:113 n. 2).

Resolution of the State of Vermont

[20–22 October 1779]

State of Vermont. In General Assembly Manchester 20th Oct'r 1779.

Resolved, Unanimously, That five persons be chosen, by ballot, Agents in behalf of the freemen of this State, to appear at the Congress of the United States of America, on the first day of Feb'y next; and that they, or any three of them, are hereby fully authorised and impowered by the representatives of the Freemen aforesaid, to vindicate their right to Independence at that Honorable Board.

And, furthermore, our said agents, or any three of them, are hereby amply impowered to agree, upon, and fully to settle articles of Union and confederation in behalf of this State, with the United States, which shall be valid and binding on us, on our constituents, and our successors. And our said agents are hereby further empowered to transact all other political affairs of this State at Congress as a free & Independent State, and report their proceedings herein to this Assembly as soon as may be.

The members chosen, B. Genl. Ethan Allen, the Hon'ble Jonas Fay & Paul Spooner, Esqrs. Stephen R. Bradley, Esqr. and the hon'ble Moses Robinson, Esqr.

Extract from the Journals.

> Roswell Hopkins, Cl'k.

Sent up for concurrence.

In Council Manchester Oct'r 22, 1779.

Read & concured.

> Joseph Fay, Sec'y.

Printed (*Public Papers of George Clinton*, Albany, N.Y., 1901, 5:225, appendix N).

Petition

Manchester Octor. 22d. 1779

To the Honorable the Genral Assembly of the state of Vermont: mett at manchester: The Humble Petition of Samuel Benton and his asosiates to the Number of Seventy Inhabitants of and frends to this & the united States of america

Humbly sheweth that thare is a Tract of vacant land within this state which hath Never ben Granted Either by the state of new Hamshire or this state Sceituate & Bounded as follows

Begining at a Stake & stones on the south line of Berlin thence Runing west on the line of Berling & moretown Six miles to a stake & stones thence south Eight miles: thence North Six miles thence west Eight miles to the first mentiond bound — Containing thirty thousan Six Hundred & Eighty acres

and as Your Petitioners are desirous of promoting the Setlement of the vacant land in this state & have been Great Sufferers in the Present war have Likewise ben at Expence in Locating sd Tract therfore pray that a Grant of sd Land, Either at the present or at Sum future sessions may be made unto us under such Considerations & Regulations as Your honors in their wisdom may see fitt — & Your Petitioners as in duty bound shall Ever pray —

AD (Vt: MsVtSP, vol. 21, p. 116). Signed by Samuel Benton, SRB, and eighty-three others.

Docketed, "Samll. Benton / Petition for Land Near [blank] / Recd. on file 21t Oct. 1779 / No. <122?>. Another note on the verso reads, "Begining at the Southeast corner of Moriton runing west."

Mss. *Governor and Council*, p. 350.

Vermont's Appeal to the Candid and Impartial World

In Council   Arlington   8th Decr. 1779

Present His Excellency the Governor

Honbl. Joseph Bowker	Timothy Brownson
Moses Robinson	Jeremiah Clark &
Jonas Fay	John Fassett Jur. Esqr.

Resolved that the manuscript entitled "Vermont's apeal to the Candid & Impartial World, Containing a Fair Stating &c." Exhibitted by Stephen R. Bradly [Bradley] be published and promulgated to the States of America.

On the 24th of September, 1779, Congress, by an act, resolved to adjudicate upon the claims of Massachusetts Bay, New Hampshire, and New York, on the 1st of February, 1780. To Mr. Bradley was assigned the task of presenting, for the consideration of Congress, the views held by Vermont on this important question.

With but little knowledge, at the time, of the extent of the subject, the young lawyer commenced his investigations, and in less than two months, had completed a faithful and well-written account of the state of the controversy. This was read before the Council of Vermont, at Arlington, on the 10th of December, 1779, and having been approved of by them, was ordered to be published. It appeared early in the year 1780k, under the title of "Vermont's Appel to the Candid and Impartial World," and aided essentially in supporting the claims of Vermont to a separate and independent government. Benjamin H. HallL: *History of Eastern Vermont*, vol. II, p. 596. *Governor and Council, vol. II, pp. 200–222.*

Resolution of the State of Vermont

December 9th 1779.

Resolved that Jonas Fay, Moses Robinson & Stephen R. Bradley Esqrs. be & they are hereby appointed agents to appear at Congress on the first day of February next.

Printed (Governor and Council Record, vol. 2).

Vermont's Appeal to the Candid and Impartial World

Governor and Council Records, vol. II

APPENDIX D.

VERMONT'S APPEAL to the CANDID and IMPARTIAL WORLD. containing a fair STATING of the CLAIMS of MASSACHUSETTS-BAY, NEW-HAMPSHIRE, and NEW-YORK. the RIGHT the STATE OF VERMONT has to INDEPENDENCE. WITH AN ADDRESS TO THE HONORABLE AMERICAN CONGRESS, and the INHABITANTS OF THE THIRTEEN UNITED STATES. BY STEPHEN R. BRADLEY, A. M.

The LORD hath called me from the Womb, from the Bowels of my Mother hath he made mention of my Name.

And said unto me, Thou art my servant, O V----------t in whom I will be glorified.

And I will feed them that oppress thee with their own Flesh, and they shall be drunken with their own Blood as with sweet wine, and all Flesh shall know that I the LORD am thy Saviour and thy Redeemer, the Mighty One of Jacob.

ISAIAH XLIX.

HARTFORD: Printed by HUDSON & GOODWIN.

STATE OF VERMONT,

In Council, Arlington, 10th Dec. 1779.

THE following Treaties, intitled, Vermont's Appeal to the Candid and Impartial World, containing, &c. being read and carefully perused, is approved of; and Resolved, that the same be published to the World.

By order of the Governor and Council,   JOSEPH FAY, *Sec'ry.*

****

INTRODUCTION.

THE reader, doubtless will wish to see a fair stating of the claims, of *Massachusetts Bay, New-Hampshire,* and *New-York*; before he enters on the important subject of the independence of *Vermont*. On the eighth day of October last past, his Excellency Governor Chittenden, received by express from John Jay Esq; late President of Congress; a copy of an act of Congress of the 24th of September last; informing, that each of said states, claimed the state of *Vermont* against each other, as well as against the inhabitants, as appertaining in the whole or in part to them respectively; together with a resolution of Congress, to judge and determine the cause on the first day of February next. But as the inhabitants of this state, view themselves intitled with the rest of the world, to that liberty which heaven bequeathed to Adam, and equally to all his posterity: we cannot think it worth our while, to shew the absurdities, and clashing inconsistencies, of various grants made by the British crown, from the time of king *James* the first, A.D. 1606, down to the present Æra. We do not expect to stand upon any derived power from an arbitrary king; we cannot conceive human nature fallen so low, as to be dependant on a crowned head for liberty to exist; we expect to stand justified to the world, upon that great principle of reason, that we were created with equal priviledges in the scale of human beings, among which is that essential right of making our own laws, and chusing our own form of government; and that we, nor our fathers, have never given up that right to any kingdom, colony, province, or state, but retain it now among ourselves as sacred as our natural existence.

AND here the reader is desired to observe, that the claims are not for property only, but they claim a right to jurisdiction a power of governing us as a people, and pretend to have derived that right from the British crown: when the crown of *Great-Britain*, never had any right, but the mere consent of the people, and of course that right died when the people assumed government.

'TIS very curious to see how many shapes, *Massachusetts Bay*, *New-Hampshire*, and *New-York*, are able to make his most sacred Majesty appear in; he certainly according to the vulgar notion, much exceeds the devil.

WHILE his adjudications were in their favour he had the immutibility of a God, but when against them, the design of a villain.

THE claims of *Massachusetts Bay* and *New Hampshire*, especially at this period of time are very extraordinary in their nature, and unaccountable upon any other principle, unless they think by puting in so many frightful claims, they scare us to surrender to some one rather than run our chance of being devoured by the whole. It is now upwards of forty years, since *Massachusetts Bay* and *New-Hampshire*, came to a full settlement of boundaries, there had for a long time before, disputes and controversies subsisted, between them: And for settleing the same his Majesty was pleased, by his order in Council, dated the 22d of January 1735, to direct, that Commissioners should be appointed to mark out the dividing line, between the said provinces, and on the 9th day of February 1736, a commission was accordingly issued out; with liberty to either party who should think themselves aggrieved by the determination of the said Commissioners, to appeal therefrom to his Majesty in Council, which said Commissioners did make their report, too tedious to insert here. The cause was appealed to his Majesty in Council, for a final determination, and the following is an authentic copy of what then passed.

"AND whereas appeals from the determination of the said Commissioners, have been laid before his Majesty by the agents for the respective provinces, of the *Massachusetts-Bay*, and *New-Hampshire*, which said appeals have been heard before the Committee of Council for hearing appeals from the plantations, who after having considered the whole matter, and heard all parties concerned therein, did report unto his Majesty as their opinion, that the northern boundary of the said province of the *Massachusetts Bay*, are and be a similar curve line, pursuing the course of *Merrimack* river, at three miles distance on the north side thereof, beginning at the atlantic ocean, and ending at a point due north of a place (in a plan returned by the said commissioners) called *Pantucket* falls; and a strait line drawn from thence due west cross the said river, till it meets with his Majesty's other governments; and that the rest of the commissioners said report, or determination, be affirmed by his Majesty. Which said report of the committee of council, his Majesty hath been pleased with the advice of his privy council to approve, and to declare, adjudge, and order, that the northern boundary of the said province of the *Massachusetts Bay*, are, and be a similar curve line, pursuing the course of *Merrimack* river, at three miles distance on the north side thereof, beginning at the atlantic, and ending at a point due north of a place in the plan returned by the said Commissioners, called *Pantucket* falls, and a strait line, drawn from thence due west cross the said river, till it meets with his Majesty's other governments; and to affirm the rest of the Commissioners report or determination. Whereof the governor or commander in chief of his Majesty's said provinces for the time being, as also his Majesty's respective councils and assemblies thereof, and all others whom it may concern are to take notice."

THIS boundary line as then established by his Majesty in Council, *Massashusetts-Bay* did fully acquiesce in, and hath now for above forty years observed it as sacred, and acted accordingly. We find in the year 1744, *William Shirley*, Esq; then Governor of the province of *Massachusetts-Bay*, complained of *New-Hampshire*, to the Duke of *New-Castle*, one of his Majesty's principal Secretaries of State, for neglecting to take possession of, and to provide for a fort, called *Fort Dummer*; which had been built by the *Massachusetts* government, about twenty years before, but by the above recited line, fell within the limits of *New Hampshire*, in which complaint are these words: "Not thinking ourselves obliged to provide for a fort which no longer belongs to us."

WHICH complaint, being laid before the king and council on the 6th day of Sept. 1744; his Majesty was pleased to order, that as said fort, was within the province of *New-Hampshire*, they must support and maintain the same,; "or His Majesty will find himself under a necessity of restoring that *fort*, with a proper district contiguous thereto, to the province of the *Massachusetts-Bay*, who cannot with justice be required, to maintain a *fort* no longer within their boundaries."

THIS *Fort Dummer* was several miles north of *Massachusetts* line, as then established, and west of *Connecticut* river. All which shews that *Massachusetts Bay* ever since, conceived that line to be their northern boundary, and fully agreed to it. So late as the 3d of October 1767, the commissaries on the part of the *Massachusetts-Bay*, among which was *Thomas Hutchinson* their great historian; dont doubt to treat that line as sacred; they say in their proposals to *New-York*, to establish a boundary line between the two governments in the following words, viz.

"THAT a line being extended due north from the north corner of the colony of *Conecticut*, until it comes to the distance of twelve miles from *Hudson's River*, and another line being extended due west, *upon the north boundary of the Massachusetts province, according to the settlement thereof with New Hampshire,* until such line comes to the like distance &c."

WHICH evidently proves, that there was a fair tryal before the king and council, and a boundary line established between *Massachusetts Bay* and *New-Hampshire*; which has ever since been agreed too, and deemed as sacred on all sides above forty years, and is now the fixed line between the *Massachusetts Bay* and *Vermont*. And for *Massachusetts Bay* to claim over that line a part of this state, by virtue of a right derived from the crown of *Great-Britain*, when by that, they are expressly bounded to that line; is very surprising, after their own tacit consent so long. They and all the world must acknowledge, that had we not bravely defended our rights against the state of *New-York*; but had tamely submitted to that government, *Massachusetts Bay* would not at this time of day have laid in a claim.

We shall trouble the reader no further with the *Massachusetts* claim, being persuaded he must see the principle on which it stands, and how frivolous it is in itself.

The states of *America*, cannot now judge of the propriety and fitness, by which the crown of *Great-Britain* established the various lines on the continent. This undoubtedly should be observed as an invariable rule; that wherever the parties have mutually agreed for a succession of years, and accordingly down to the late revolution, those lines, and adjudications, ought to be held as unalterable and sacred.

The claim of *New-Hampshire*, stands on nearly the same principles as the former, every unprejudiced mind will acknowledge, that after the beforementioned line was established, down to the year 1764, *New-Hampshire* had an exclusive right to all this territory. This appears from the before recited adjudication, and especially in the instance of *Fort Dummer*; as well as from the various Commissions, sent the Governors of *New-Hampshire*, impowering them to sell and dispose of all this territory; in which period of time the inhabitants of *Vermont*, purchased all the territory they are now in actual possession of; excepting some small remnants; of the Governor of *New-Hampshire*, and gave a valuable consideration to the benefit of the crown. After this there arising a dispute respecting boundaries; the government of *New-York*, by very unfair means, obtained an adjudication in the following words *to wit*.

"At the court at *St. James's* the 20th day of July 1764.   Present,

"The Kings most Excellent Majesty.

"Lord Steward.   }   Earl of Hilborough.
"Earl of Sandwich.   }   Mr. Vice Chamberlain.
"Earl of Halifax.   }   Gilbert Elliot Esq.
"Earl of Powls.   }   James Oswald Esq.
"Earl of Harcourt.   }

"Whereas there was this day read at the board a report made by the right Honorable the Lords of the Committee of Council for plantation affairs, dated the 17th of this instant, considering a representation from the Lords Commissioners for trade and plantations, relative to the disputes that have some years subsisted between the provinces of *New-Hampshire* and *New-York*, concerning the boundary line between those provinces: His Majesty taking the same into consideration, was pleased, with the advice of his Privy Council, to approve, of what is therein proposed and doth accordingly hereby order and declare, the western banks of the river *Connecticut*, from where it enters the province of the *Massachusetts Bay*, as far north as the forty-fifth degree of northern latitude, to be the boundary line between the said two provinces of *New-Hampshire* and *New-York*. Whereof the respective Governors, and Commanders in Chief, of his Majesty's said provinces, of *New-Hampshire* and *New York*, for the time being, and all others whom it may concern, are to take notice of his Majesty's pleasure hereby signified and govern themselves accordingly."

Which royal mandate, was most fully agreed too by the province of *New-Hampshire*, and they governed themselves accordingly, down to the late revolution; and cast the people of the Grants, now the inhabitants of *Vermont*, out of their government, and refused any connection with them, published a proclamation, ordering the said people to conduct accordingly, which they have done, and by their own valour, under God, have maintained their liberties; and now *New Hampshire* in their fit of frenzy, are claiming us back again; like a peevish child, flings away its play-thing, and then roars for it.

The governor of *New-Hampshire* wrote to governor *Tryon*, on the 19th day of October 1771 in these words: "That he had invariably recommended implicit obedience to the laws of

New-York, and upon all occasions positively disavowed any connection with those people." By the same reason that *New-Hampshire* disavowed any connection with us when in distress, we now positively disavow any connection with that government, and mean to govern ourselves accordingly. We could mention many public acts of their legislature; one so late as the 8th day of January 1772, viz.

"At a Council held as *Portsmouth* by his Excellency's summons on Thursday the 8th day of January, 1772.

PRESENT

"His Excellency *John Wentworth*, Esq; Governor,
    "and

"Theodore Atkinson,	Daniel Pierce,
"Daniel Warner,	George Jeffery,
"Peter Levius,	Daniel Rogers,
"Jonathan Warner,	Peter Gilman,
"Daniel Rindge,	Thomas W. Waldren,

"The premises being read, it is considered, that by his Majesty's order in Council 20th July 1764, the western banks of *Connecticut* river was then commanded to be the west bounds of this province, and that this government has been and is entirely obedient thereto." Which shews that *New Hampshire* did fully agree to, and acquiesce in that royal mandate. We might further observe that the State of *New Hampshire*, by the writings of their supreme legislature, since the revolution, have implicitly acknowledged the State of *Vermont*,* and given encouragement to our agents, sent there from time to time, that we think it very ungenerous for *New-Hampshire* to claim us now, after they have publickly disavowed any connection with us more than fifteen years; and ordered us to govern ourselves accordingly. That we shall forever dismiss the claim of *Massachusetts-Bay* and *New-Hampshire*, after reminding them, that 'tis very similar to the claim the Pretender has to the Crown of *Great-Britain*. And it is more probable he will govern the British nation, than either of those States will *Vermont*.

We now pass on to the old dispute, *New-York* against *Vermont*. In the first place we absolutely deny, and we believe the candid world will join with us, that *New-York* ever had the least pretended right to this territory, before the adjudication of the King and Council A.D. 1764; though they pretend the Dutch first discovered the continent, and took up all the last west of *Connecticut* river, to *Delaware* bay. No person of sense will ever believe that, for they were ever considered by the English as intruders, and no historian

---

The reader will here observe how implicitly they acknowledged Vermont by the following letter, viz.

"Exeter, July 19, 1777.

"SIR,

"I was favoured with yours of the 15th instant yesterday by express, and laid the same before our General Court who are sitting. We had previous thereto determined to send assistance to your state: They have now determined that a quarter part of the militia of twelve regiments shall be immediately drafted, formed into three battalions, under the command of Brigadier General John Stark, and forthwith sent into your State, to oppose the ravages, and coming forward of the enemy; and orders are now issuing and will all go out in a few hours to the several Colonels for that purpose. Dependence is made that they will be supplied with provisions in your State, and I am to desire your Convention will send some proper person or persons to No. 4, by Thursday next, to meet General Stark there, and advise with him relative to the fort and disposition of our troops, and to give him such information as you may then have, relative to the manoevres of the enemy.

In behalf of the Council and Assembly,
    I am, Sir, your most obedient humble Servant,

MESHECH WEARE, *President*

Ira Allen, Esq; Secretary of the State of Vermont.

that ever wrote, has been able to give any charter of the government of *New York*, or bounds to its territory.*

But is it not very strange indeed if there ever were any grants made to the Dutch of this country, that they never were obtained, and exhibited in the controversy between the Dutch and English, which subsisted for more than twenty years? Equally strange is it also, that all the historians who have written concerning them have given no account of the country which they described, or of any limits or boundaries whatsoever expressed in them. The authorities and vouchers which have been now recited give abundant evidence, that the Dutch claim to New England, or to any part of North America was without any legal foundation: and that their title to any part of the country, was never, at any period, allowed in England. The court of England ever disowned it, and treated them as usurpers. They were not the first discoverers of the country and therefore could not claim it on that footing. They had no grant of it, specifying any particular boundaries, first or last, which any historians have ever been able to certify. A grant for an exclusive trade on Hudson's river in 1614, and a grant to the West-India company in 1621, without any description of the country granted, without the least mention of boundaries, is all that their ablest historians pretend. A grant to the West India company, observe, not to any corporation, or body of men, in New-Netherlands, or in New-England. Nay, this, grant was so far from warranting the Dutch to settle on the lands at New-Netherlands, now New York, and exercise jurisdiction there, distinct from the government of England, that even the States General, who, it is pretended, made the grant, disowned their having ever given orders for any thing of this nature.

FURTHER, it appears that the English, of the united colonies, ever considered the right of the Dutch, as confined entirely to the lands which they had purchased and settled, AND NO MORE. In a word, governor Hutchinson has said, on the best ground, that the suffering the Dutch to extend so far as Greenwich, 20 miles east of Hudsons river, was mere favor and indulgence to these intruders. The New England patents and the derivative grants, had a western extension to the south sea, included the whole province of New York, and made an ample conveyance of all that part of it, which had not been settled prior to them.

THEY have likewise made much noise about a grant to *James Duke of York*, afterward King of *England*, but after all they prove too much, for if that proves any thing, it will give them a right to all the lands west of *Connecticut* river, which will take a great part of *Connecticut* and *Massachusetts-Bay*, and a large tract from the province of *Quebec*. And further it is very evident from what passed by the King and Council 1744, that the territory of *Vermont* was then considered and adjudged to be within the province of *New-Hampshire*, for the adjudication was expressly. "That *Fort Dummer* was within the province of *New-Hampshire*." And *Fort Dummer* was west of *Connecticut* river, and most clearly within the territory of *Vermont*, now claimed by *New York*. Hence we say that the territory of *Vermont*, never did belong to the *Dutch*, and was never considered as appertaining to *New-York* government before the royal mandate passed in 1764; on the other hand they could not claim by any authority but a few miles east of *Hudson's* river.

AND thus stood the case on the 20th day of July 1764: *New-Hampshire* relinquished all their claim to this territory, and *New-York* obtained a royal command affixing it to their government, over which before they could not have the least pretended right.

AND upon this point turns the whole dispute, between *New-York* and *Vermont*, without going one step back from the year 1764; either that royal mandate, is absolutely unavoidable in it's nature, and binds all beings within it's limits equal to the moral law. Or if it is voidable

---

Says Mr. Trumbull an able Historian, in a treatise upon the ancient charters.

undoubtedly *Vermont* is intitled to freedom and independence. For never, no never did a people take more pains to avoid the operation of an oppressive act, than the people of *Vermont* have done. Our greatest enemies cannot say we ever associated with the government of *New-York*, or ever admited their jurisdiction further than compelled by force. But on the contrary, we have ever since 1764, opposed them with all our might and strength even to blood.

THE cause must then stand upon these two points, in the view of every unprejudiced mind, first had *King George* the III on the 20th of July 1764, any right to grant the see of the land, now called the state of *Vermont*, to the government of *New-York?* and secondly had the King of *Great-Britain*, ever a right by his royal mandate to abridge the *Americans* of that great privilege, of making their own laws, and chusing their own form of government?

TO the first we answer, that 'twas always a maxim in the English nation, that "the King is not above law" and that "The law cannot do wrong." Now, as we had before purchased this territory, and given a valuable consideration to the Governor of *New-Hampshire*, who was authorised by the king of *Great-Britain* to sell it, and acted as an agent under him when he gave grants of this very territory. 'Twas the same, and as binding on his Majesty, in the eye of all law and reason, as if the king had sold it himself. If then the king had once sold this territory, and taken a valuable consideration, had he any right the second time to convey it away? and if he could the second time, might he not as well twenty or a hundred, and so on *ad infinitum?* and consequently there could be no security from a king. The voice of reason and common sense tell us, that he could not convey it away but once, and as we had before purchased it, 'twas out of the king's power to convey it to *New-York*, therefore that royal mandate which *New-York* obtained A.D. 1764, was null and void in itself, at conveying any see of the land.

TO the second question we answer as every true American whig ought to do, that 'tis not a king, nor any other beings, under God, that have a right to abridge mankind of their natural liberties without their consent. What right ever had king *George* delegated to him to frame government for us, and to bind us in all cases whatsover? None; he had in the nature of things as good a right on the 20th of July 1764, to have subjected the Angels of God, to the government of New-York, as he had the people of Vermont. For if he could abridge twenty thousand, he could one hundred thousand, and equally three millions of their liberties. And if *Vermont* had not a right to resist that act of oppression, *America* has now no right to resist, but ought to submit to all the usurpations of the British crown.

SO that view that royal command in what light soever, as either granting the see of the land, or the right of jurisdiction, it can be of no validity longer than a *George* stands with an iron rod of tyranny to support it; but is now as dead, as all other of his arbitrary acts, committed heretofore in *America*, against the peace and dignity of human nature. Will any one pretend to say that his royal mandate respecting the Quebec bill is now to be observed as sacred? Certainly not. And yet the Quebec bill much exceeds in point of authority. The truth is, those sovereign acts of oppression and tyranny, went out, and died, when the king in the declaration of independence, was removed to his Britannic regions of despair; and they who now seek to revive them; are as great enemies to the civil liberties of mankind as George III.

HENCE then we are imbolden to say that *Vermont* must live over the claims of all her enemies, *Massachusetts-Bay*, and *New-Hampshire*, by their dereliction, or utter forsaking, have lost all their pretended right; or in the words of the *Mosaic Law* they have given *Vermont* a bill of divorce, and have sent her away, and now she may not in any wise return to them again.

AND let *New-York*, ground their claim upon what principle they please, when reduced to a scale of reason, it must like self-righteousness fail, and leave *New-York* without hope.

THUS we have briefly stated the controversy to the world, we now proceed to treat of the independence of *Vermont*.

****

VERMONT's APPEAL,&c.

WERE it possible for rational men, to entertain so mean an idea of the Great Author of our existence, as to believe he intended a part of the human race, should hold an absolute unbounded power over others, destined by his Sovereign will and pleasure, to wear out a servile life, as vassals and tenants, to cruel lords and masters; in that case *Vermont* might demand of *New-York*, and all others who pretend to that power; some evidence of their having such a dreadful commission from Heaven; for condemned criminals, are not obliged to submit to the awful sentence till the executioner has shewn his warrant.

But reason and common sense, must convince all those who reflect upon the subject one moment, that all the claims made to this State, are founded on principles of the greatest injustice, cruelty and oppression, subversive of the rights of mankind, tending to destroy those great revolution principles upon which the United States are built up, and do in the end point an insult to the divine author of our existence. They need only a candid stating to receive a compleat refutation, for with as great propriety in the fitness of things might *Vermont* claim the territory of *New-York*, and demand their right to independence, as *New York*, can *Vermont's*. In which case we make bold to say, *Vermont* would get no other answer, than *Britain* has frequently got from the mouths of cannon in asking the same question. "Yet knowing to what violent resentment, and incurable animosities, civil discords are apt to exasperate, and inflame the contending parties; we think ourselves required by indispensable obligations to Almighty God, to our fellow countrymen, and to ourselves, immediately to use all the means in our power" not incompatible with out independence, for stoping the effusion of human blood, and to make known to the impartial world the justice of our cause.

BUT before we enter there upon, must beg leave to inform the world, of the unfair means that have been used to deprive *Vermont* of her unalinable and inestimable rights. For the truth of which, we can appeal to many worthy characters, and to the august council of Congress, whether *New-York*, has not in the darkest hours of the present conflict with *Great-Britain*, when our united wisdom and strength, were requisit to oppose the common enemy; made the greatest struggles at Congress, and even by threats, has attempted to obtain a decree exparte; against the State of *Vermont* from no other view but because she thought her own political importance in the scale of *America* was vastly superior to that of *Vermont's*; and that Congress would rather crush *Vermont* than loose the friendship of *New-York*; when not only *New-York*, but every person, that has taken the least pains to inform himself, knows that they never had any other right of jurisdiction over the territory of *Vermont*, but what they obtained by their own wicked craft and *British* tyranny; and that the inhabitants of *Vermont* as a people have never, submitted to the jurisdiction of *New-York*, no not from the very earliest period. For the proof of which we can now appeal, to the marks on the backs, of their then civil Magistrates (if any there be who have not joined the common enemy) who came from time to time, to execute cruel laws, such that the Satarp of an eastern Despot would blush at; made on purpose to ruin the inhabitants of *Vermont*, which will be an eternal disgrace to the records of *New-York* so long as it has a political existence; for particulars of which the reader is refered to *General Allen's "brief narrative of the proceedings of the government of New-York."*

BUT finding Congress possessed of too much wisdom and integrity to carry their vile purposes into execution, they have left no stone unturned, whereby they might ruin *Vermont*. And to gain their point, to the great detriment of the United States, have imbraced, and nourished in the bowels of this State, sworn enemies to the liberties of *America*, and endeavoured to screen them from contributing their might, toward the salvation of their country in times of the greatest danger; and that too, when called upon by officers under commissions from the *American* Congress; for no other reason, but because those persons were avowed enemies to *Vermont*.

THEY have secretly confered commissions on the sculking neutrals, who leaving to others the heat and burden of the day, have used all their diabolical schemes, to dis-hearten and divide the freeborn sons of *Vermont*.

THEY have received private persons, stealing away from this state, into their legislature, under pretence of their being representatives from certain towns, contrary to the very letter; and spirit of their own constitution.

IN a word, they have tryed all means in their power, to extirpate and distroy the State of *Vermont*; altho' we have in all our public writings assured *New York* of our readiness to settle all controversies; respecting lands in dispute, in some equitable way, when the great cause of *America* would permit.

AND now diffident of our own opinion, we leave the candid world to determine, how far *New-York* might have their own influence in view, by strenuously urging, and insisting, that Congress should determine such an important cause, at a period of time, when they think their State from many circumstances, is become the great key of the continent and to affront them must be very detrimental to the confederacy; but let *New-York* remember, that we have a northern as well as they a southern key, and are determined to maintain and support our independence and freedom, or take refuge in that blessed State; *where the small and great are, and the servant is free from his master.*

THE independence of *Vermont*, will be argued under the following heads, viz.

I. The right the State of *Vermont* has to independence.

II. Her interest and advantage in being independant.

III. The necessity she is under of supporting her independence.

IIII. The advantage that has and will accrue to the other States of *America* from the independence of *Vermont*.

UNDER the first of these heads, we can support the right the State of *Vermont* has to independence, upon the same scale of reason, that all kingdoms and States maintain theirs. In a state of nature man knows no ruler, every one (under God) is his own legislator, judge, and avenger, and absolute lord of his property. Had man continued, pure and holy through time, as he came from his Creator at first, there would doubtless have been no need of government; his wants would naturally have created society, but wickedness would never have produced government. Obeying the dictates of a pure conscience, man would have needed no other law-giver; and *jurisdiction* that necessary evil at best would never had it's name. But conscience, nature's great foundation of legislation, being corrupted by the introduction of sin, necessity absolutely required man to be under some further regulation, than the mere impulse of a depraved conscience; which we find soon after the fall, excited the perpetration of most horrid crimes in the children of disobedience; and would fill the world, with the greatest horror and misery unless restrained. From hence government took it's rise, to prevent and punish wickedness, or in other words, negatively, to promote the happiness of society by restraining vice.

FROM whence it most evidently follows, that the very end and design of government, is security of life, liberty, and property, to every member of society; and the form that best answers that end, is of all others the most preferable.

THE human race being in the order of creation all equal, that there is neither high or low, rich or poor, bond or free, for they are all one; until that equality be destroyed by some subsequent circumstance, they are all intitled to equal privileges of society; and have each one a sacred indefesible right, to choose that form of government, that shall best secure, life, liberty, and property.

OR to give a more clear representation of the case, let us suppose a number of persons to move and settle within the polar circle, unconnected with any other part of the world. At their first arrival, they would form into society; and while each one remained strictly honest, and just, they would need no further regulations; their views would be the reciprocal good of each other. But so soon as vice, that pest of society, began to creep in among them, they would then find the necessity, of establishing some form of government, to make each other honest: In framing of which, every person ought to have an equal share, in the legislative, judicial, and vindictive powers; and would have an indisputable right, to adopt such a mode of government, as to them should seem best, and ought to enjoy the benefits thereof, unmolested, equal with any other kingdom, or State under Heaven; and for any foreign power, to exercise jurisdiction, and enforce laws upon that people; would be the essence of tyranny.

WE'LL suppose still further, that as soon as our new emigrants, are formed into a state of society, before they have established any form of government, an eastern monarch, should pass that way with a large host of the dogs of war and sons of tyranny the disgrace of human nature, and discover this little honest feeble band, whereupon he should make a formal declaration "that he had full power and authority, to make laws and statutes, of sufficient validity, to bind this society in all cases whatsoever." And should order and decree that these new settlers in the wilderness, should be abridged of all their natural rights, and be bound to *New-York*, and subjected to the laws ordinances and jurisdiction of the same, upon pain of having his dogs of war let loose to destroy them. And notwithstanding frequent petitions, remonstrances, and asserting their just rights, were nevertheless compelled to remain in this condition, for ten long years; at which period of time, they arrive to that degree of strength, with the assistance of some honest neighbours, that they rise and cut in too that power, *which was of sufficient validity, to bind them in all cases whatsoever*, and thereby get loose from the cords of bondage. We ask in the name of reason; whether the world ought to assist in spliceing that power, to bind them again to *New-York*; or whether they ought not in equity, and the eternal rules of right, immediately to be put in full possession of that inestimable privilege, which they have so long been unjustly deprived of, *that of making their own laws, and choosing their own form of government.*

SIMILAR is the State of *Vermont*; whose inhabitants, at the expence of their fortunes, and hazard of their lives, without the least charge to any Colony, Province, or State, from which they removed, by hard labour and an unconquerable spirit, they have procured settlements, in the wilderness of *Vermont*; have faced death and danger; undergone unspeakable hardships, in perils by savages, in perils by wild beasts of prey, in cold, in nakedness, in hunger, and in want. But above all have they suffered, from the cruelty of *Great-Britain* and her emissaries. Nevertheless, from the first day of their entering into said wilderness, they never adopted, or choose any kind of government, any further than compelled by the murdering sword, nor did they ever form into a State of society, with any other Colony, Province, or State, but kept a well regulated association among themselves, for the protection of life, and property, until the 15th of January 1777, when by the united voice of the people, they declared themselves a free and independant State. For the truth of these things we can appeal to many undeniable facts; so late as March 1774, previous to the battle of *Lexington*, the judges of *New-York*, were led in fetters of iron, within the gates of their own city, for sheding innocent blood at *Westminster* , in murderously attempting to enforce the laws of that province, upon the people of *Vermont*. And as the territory of *Vermont* did not originally appertain to *New-York*, and seeing the inhabitants did never associate with that province; it is manifest they have as good a natural right to independence, to make and execute their own laws, as any body of people on this continent.

AGAIN, the State of *Vermont* has an undoubted right to independence, from the situation and extent of it's territory.

As we have before shewn, the government that best answers the ends of society, is of all others the most preferable, being instituted to promote happiness, and not increase misery: Now whenever government fails in answering the end of it's institution; or in other words creates more evils than it prevents, it becomes a burden, and ought in the course of things to be dismissed; hence it is, that when the reason of parental government ceases, the government of course ceases. And by the same reason that the other *American States* have assumed government; *Vermont* is of age to act for herself. And to suppose the territory of *Vermont*, which is 160 miles in length, and 60 miles in breadth; with near thirty thousand souls, at this time of day, after 3 years independence, under as good regulation, and code of laws as any State on the continent; ought to be affixed to the government of *New-York*; whose morals, manners, and interest's are diametrically opposite; is as absurd, as to suppose the *American States*, ought to be reaffixed to *Great-Britain*. Add further, that if *Vermont* was affixed to the jurisdiction of *New-York*, many individuals must travel 400 miles to the seat of government; which would render it an intolerable burden, and pervert the very ends for which government was instituted.

AGAIN, we might observe, that *Great Britain*, previous to the declaration of independence, had made a distinct government of this territory, and had granted a commission accordingly.

But as matters are now situate, *Vermont* cannot obtain a copy of those writings.

AND that may be one great reason why *New-York*, has wearied Congress to obtain an immediate decisive adjudication, before that evidence can possibly be obtained, least otherwise they should be self condemned upon their own stating.

AGAIN, the State of *Vermont* has merited an indisputable right to independence, in the esteem of every true whig; by her brave and noble conduct, in the gloomy struggle of *America* with *Great Britain*. First in *America* were the Green Mountain Boys, (to their immortal honor be it written) that commenced an offensive war against British tyranny. Under every disadvantage in being a frontier, they nevertheless with their lives in their hands, took *Ticonderoga*, and other important garrisons in the north; so early that *New-York*, as a government, was considered as a dead weight in the continental scale. And like men determined to obtain liberty or death, they pursued the war into *Canada*; there they fought, bled and died, not counting their lives dear, that they might obtain the prize at the race end. Many heroes can *Vermont* boast in the territory of *Canada*, who fell fighting in the glorious cause of American liberty and freedom. Let the brave immortal *Gates*, and deathless *Stark*, tell posterity, that in the year 1777, assisted by the militia of the State of *Vermont*, they humbled the long boasted pride of *Great-Britain* and brought the towering General *Burgoyne*, with his chosen legions, to ask mercy at their feet. In a word, *Vermont*, by her blood and treasure, at the point of the sword, has fairly merited liberty; and by the eternal rule of reason, has a right to independence, from every consideration; she has received it from God, as being created with equal liberties in the scale of human beings; from nature in the formation of her territory; and from her own victorious struggles with *Great-Britain*.

II. THE interest and advantage of the State of *Vermont* in being independant is very certain. This territory has been one continued scene of legislative confusion, and contention, since the royal mandate passed A.D. 1764, till the late revolution, which gave *Vermont* an opportunity to take the staff of government into her own hands. And this contention, being unavoidably founded in the natural opposition of interests, between the State of *New-York*, and that of *Vermont*; that were they to be under one and the same jurisdiction, 'twould render the whole State an eternal theatre of contention, bloodshed and misery. That taking every circumstance into consideration, the greatness and situation of its territory; the strength to which it has already arisen, with the rapid progress of its future settlement; the difference of the morals, and manners of its inhabitants from those of *New-York*; the clashing interests, together with that bitter jealousy, not to say hatred that would forever exist, were they to be affixt to *New-York*, must oblige every impartial man to say that it would be greatly for the interest of *Vermont* to be independent.

III. VERMONT is under a necessity of supporting her independence. Freedom is the gift of the beneficent Creator, to all his subjects: Slavery only appertains to the devil and his followers. All rational beings have a right to expect, that from their natural parents which God bequeathed to them, and left in trust to be handed down unimpaired, to the last child to be born of the human race.

THE State of *Vermont*, we have now clearly shewn, has a natural right to independence; honor, justice and humanity forbid us tamely to surrender that freedom which our innocent posterity have a right to demand and receive from their ancestors. Full well may they hereafter rise up in judgment against us, if, like profane *Easau*, we mortgage away their birth rights, and leave them at the expence of their lives, to obtain freedom. The righteous blood, already spilt in *Westminster* court-house, calls louder than thunder for an everlasting separation from *New-York*.

FURTHER, the State of *Vermont*, is under an absolute necessity of supporting her independence, or incurring, as a people, the greatest guilt in the eye of heaven. They have declared to the world that they are, and of right ought to be, a free independant State; have appointed officers civil and military, who have discharged their various betrustments, punished offenders, ratified and dissolved the most solemn contracts in nature, joined man and wife, have in some instances granted bills of divorce, strictly forbidding the parties ever to cohabit together, have pronounced sentence of death, when twelve men of the vicinage, under the oath of God have declared life was forfeited by the law of the land, and have issued a warrant to take away the same; that should they now give up independence, and thereby confess they had no right to form government; they would acknowledge themselves guilty, of the crying sins of murder, adultery, fornication, robbery, &c. and deserving of that curse pronounced by God on those who part man and wife.

AGAIN, we are under a necessity of supporting our independence, arising from our plighted faith to individuals. Upon the declaration of independence of the State of *Vermont*, many persons of fortune, admiring its constitution, fold all that they had in neighbouring states, moved in and purchased large interests of the government, laid out all their effects, taking the plighted faith of the freemen of the State of *Vermont* for their security; and now to give up our independence, would be destroying all their security, and reducing them by our perfidy, from a state of affluence, to a wretched condition of beggary and want; that could it be possible, every virtuous person would stigmatize the inhabitants of *Vermont* to the latest posterity.

IIII. WE are now to point our the advantage that has and will accrue to the other States of *America* from the independence of *Vermont*.

Omitting a few ******, whom *New-York*, by their bribery, and corruption, have prevented from doing much in the common cause, we venture to assert that no one of the fourteen states now at war with *Great-Britain*, according to their numbers, have done more for the interest of the whole, than *Vermont*. During the first stages of the war, not one State, excepting *Connecticut*, (a free government) excelled the Green Mountain Boys for vigor, spirit and resolution. We will appeal to those Generals who have had the northern command, whether by applying to the Governor and Council of *Vermont*, in times of the most pressing danger, they did not receive much speedier, and as effectual help as by applying to *New-York*. That all the world must confess who have had the least knowledge of the war in the northern district, that the State of *Vermont*, has been of great advantage to *America*, and much more so than if that territory had belonged to any other State.

AGAIN, many advantages must hereafter acrue to the other States of *America*, from the independency of *Vermont*; for we cannot expect those States who are ambitiously grasping at territories to which they have not the least shadow of right, will use the wealth arising therefrom to any better purpose than to oppress their less wealthy and less powerful neighbors. It never will be for the interest of the United States, to have some great, overgrown, unwieldy States. *New-York* is now large enough; and 'tis very probable that if *New-York* should obtain this territory, and the Green Mountain Boys submit to their aristocratical form of government; she would in time, by the same spirit, over run and ruin many of the United States.

VERMONT's APPEAL
To the General Congress of the *United States*

CALLED upon as we are to address your honorable board, on matters of the last importance to the State of *Vermont*; and probably to the thirteen United States, over which you preside. W wish most earnestly to perform this office, with the utmost decency, reverence, and respect; trusting, that should necessity, which knows no law on so uncommon an occasion, oblige us to deviate from that delicate line of honor observed by courts, your candour will impute it to a just attention, due to our own preservation, against those artful and designing States, who abuse your confidence and authority, for the purpose of effecting our destruction; rather than disrespect to your august body.

WE glory in being allied to your goverment, in being connected by the strongest ties of nature, gratitude, and friendship, to those illustrious personages, who by their valour and wisdom, have extricated *America* from ruin, and by securing happiness to others, have erected the most noble and durable monuments to their own fame. We solemnly assure you, that we most ardently wish a permanent union and confederation, might be established between this and the United States, upon so firm a basis, as to transmit its blessings to posterity uninterupted by any future dissentions. Under a full expectation, of reaping equal blessings at the end of the conflict with Great-Britain; the inhabitants of this State have ever stood forth with their lives, and fortunes, to assert and maintain the rights and interests of *America*.

BUT to our unspeakable grief, we find neighbouring States, usurping a more tyrannic power, if it were possible, than ever Great-Britain grasped after, wallowing in luxury, and wanting provinces to drain of wealth, like the debauched Romans, to defray their extravigances, are using the wisdom of serpents, and the intrigue of courtiers, to make the inhabitants of *Vermont*, dupes, and slaves, to their unbounded lust of domination and prey.

AND to our great astonishment, we find some so base, as to be willing their countrymen should be made tributary to such birds of prey; if they might have a small pittance for gathering the tax, even on condition it were demanded at the point of the bayonet.

THE petty tyrants of every country, always wish to have the people dependant on such a power, for under colour of authority from that power, they can carry on their oppressions, vexations, and depredations, and sin without controul.

THAT could any thing add to our grief and surprise; it must be to find your act of the 24th of September last, containing the following Resolutions, *viz.*

"RESOLVED unanimously, That it be, and hereby is most earnestly recommended, to the States of *New-Hampshire, Massachusetts-Bay,* and *New-York,* forthwith to pass laws, expressly authorising Congress, to hear and determine all differences between them, relative to their respective boundaries, in the mode prescribed by the articles of confederation; so that Congress may proceed therein by the first day of February next at furthest.

"And further, That the said States of *New-Hampshire, Massachusetts-Bay,* and *New-York,* do by express laws for the purpose, refer to the decision of Congress, all differences and disputes relative to jurisdiction, which they may respectively have with the district aforesaid; so that Congress may proceed thereon, on the said first day of February next.

"RESOLVED unanimously, That it be, and hereby is recommended to the States of *New-Hampshire, Massachusetts-Bay,* and *New-York,* to authorise Congress, to proceed to hear and determine, all disputes subsisting, between the grantees of the several States aforesaid, with one another, or with either of the said States, respecting title to lands lying in the said district, to be heard and determined by Commissioners or Judges to be appointed in the mode prescribed by the ninth article of the confederation aforesaid,

"And further to provide, that no advantage be taken of the non-performance of the condition of any of the grants of the said lands; but that further reasonable time be allowed for fulfilling such condition.

"RESOLVED unanimously, that Congress will and hereby do pledge their faith, to carry into execution, and support their decisions and determinations in the premises, in favour of whichsoever of the parties the same may be to the end that permanent concord, and harmony may be established between them, and all cause of uneasiness removed.

"RESOLVED unanimously, that Congress will on the said first day of February next, proceed without delay, to hear and examine into the disputes and differences relative to jurisdiction aforesaid, between the said three States respectively, or such of them as shall pass the laws before mentioned on the one part, and the people of the district aforesaid, who claim to be a separate jurisdiction on the other, and after a full and fair hearing, will decide and determine the same according to equity; and that neither of the said States, shall vote on any question relative to the decision thereof; And Congress do hereby pledge their faith, to execute and support their decisions and determinations in the premises,

"And whereas it is essential to the interest of the whole confederacy, that all intestine dissentions, be carefully avoided and domestic peace and good order maintained.

"RESOLVED unanimously, That it is the duty of the people of the district aforesaid, who deny the jurisdiction of all the aforenamed States, to abstain in the mean time, from exercising any power over any of the inhabitants of the said district, who profess themselves to be citizens of, or to owe allegiance to any or either of the said States; but that none of the towns, either on the east or west side of *Connecticut* river, be considered as included within the said district, but such as have heretofore actually joined in denying the jurisdiction of either of said States, and have asumed a separate jurisdiction which they call the state of VERMONT.

"And further, That in the opinion of Congress, the said three States aforenamed, ought in the mean time to suspend executing their laws over any of the inhabitants of the said district; except such of them as shall profess allegiance to, and confess the jurisdiction of the same respectively. And further that Congress will consider, any violence committed against the tenor, true intent, and meaning of this resolution, as a breach of the peace of the confederacy, which they are determined to keep and maintain. And to the end that all such violences and breaches of the public peace may be the better avoided in the said district, it is hereby recommended to all the inhabitants thereof, to cultivate harmony and concord among themselves, to forbear vexing each other at law, or otherwise, and to give as little occasion as possible to the interposition of magistrates.

"Resolved unanimously, That in the opinion of Congress, no unapropriated lands or estates, which are or may be adjudged forfeited or confiscated lying in the said district, ought until the final decision of Congress in the premises to be granted or sold.

"Ordered, that copies of the aforegoing resolution, be sent by express, to the States of *New-York, New-Hampshire,* and *Massachusetts Bay,* and to the people of the district aforesaid; and that they be respectively desired to loose no time in appointing their agent or agents and otherwise preparing for the hearing aforesaid.

"The aforesaid resolutions being read over and a question taken to agree to the whole.

"Resolved unanimously in the affirmative.

"*Extract from the Minutes,*

"CHARLES THOMSON, Sec'ry."

As *Americans*, as freemen, or as men of common sense; we cannot view ourselves holden, in the fight of God or man, to submit to the execution of a plan, which we have reason to believe, was commenced by neighbouring States without policy; and must be prosecuted by means, incompatible, with the fundamental principles of liberty. Which appears, not only big with injustice and impiety; but carries immediate ruin to ourselves and posterity, as soon as they become human beings. We have examined it minutely, we have viewed it in every point of light, in which we were able to place it; and with pain and grief, we sincerely declare we cannot close with the terms of those resolutions, for these reasons.

1. Because, all the liberties and privileges of the State of *Vermont*, by said resolutions, are to be suspended, upon the arbitrament and final determination of Congress; when in our opinion, they are things, too sacred ever to be arbitrated upon: And that we cannot stand acquitted to our own conscience, to the world, or posterity, to give them up, by reason of the adjudication of any man or body of men, but must hold ourselves under the most sacred obligations to posterity, to defend them at every risk.

2. Because, the Congress of the United States has no right to intermeddle with the internal police, and support of civil government in this State, for us, not for Congress, has government been instituted here, and we cannot conceive that any other legislature, has a right to prescribe modes to determine our fate, or abolish our own internal institutions. We most chearfully at the same time, will accede to any propositions made by Congress, for the equitable settlement of all disputes relative to property, when admitted to union with the other States.

3. Because, we conceive this State to exist independant of any of the thirteen United States, and not accountable to them, or their representatives, for liberty, the gift of the beneficent Creator; having existed as an intire corporation, or body politic, before the union or confederation of the other States. The first association, and oldest body politic on the continent, upon the late revolution establishment; and therefore cannot belong to the confederacy.

4. Because, the State of *Vermont* is not represented in Congress, we cannot submit to resolutions passed without our consent, or even knowledge, which put every thing near and dear at stake. We esteem it an essential unalterable principle of liberty, the source and security of all constitutional rights, that no state or people can be bound by the acts of any legislature without being represented. "It is with the deepest concern that we have seen the sacred

security of representation that great bulwark of liberty, silently passed over," and acts, rendering the liberty, and lives of the inhabitants of *Vermont* precarious, passed unanimously. We have carefully weighed the matter, and can see no material difference, in being dragged to *Philadelphia* or *Great-Britain*, and there, untried and unheard, obliged to deliver ourselves up as victims to court pleasure. Let the prejudiced amuse the world, and confound the ignorant with their jargon; freedom and dependence on a power, over which we have no influence nor controul, is slavery, or we are yet ignorant of the word.

5. BECAUSE, there appears a manifest inequality, not to say predetermination by said resolutions in that Congress should request of their own constituents, power to judge and determine in the cause, and never ask the consent of thousands whose all are at stake, which evidently purports one of these two things; either that the rest of the world, are not intitled to equal privileges with their constituents, and that Congress have a right *to make laws to bind them in all cases whatsoever*, without their consent or even knowledge: Or, that Congress already have pre-determined us to belong to the thirteen United States and of course have a deligated right to judge in the cause; either of which, as freemen, it is our indispensible duty by all lawful means to oppose.

6. BECAUSE, said resolutions, are either inconsistent in themselves, or incompatible with the liberties of free States; in that Congress implicitly acknowledge, that as Congress, they have no right to take up the matter by requesting of *New-Hampshire, Massachusetts-Bay,* and *New-York* special laws to authorize them to judge in the cause; and then go on to pledge the faith of Congress, to execute and support their decisions, and determinations, in the premises, if only one State, *to wit, New-York* should pass the law, which amounts to this; that *New York* can give Congress power to pledge the faith of the United States; and even of those States who refuse to submit the cause to Congress.

THESE are our sentiments upon this important subject, and least they should be misconstrued, or misunderstood, we again declare to you, sirs, and to the world, that we are not contending for lucre or filthy gain, we are willing to agree with any equitable proposals, made for the settlement of all differences relative to the see of lands in dispute; and are not anxious of being judges in our own cause. We further most solemnly assure you, that we are, and ever have been willing, to bear our proportion of the burden, and expense of the present war with *Great-Britain*, from it's first commencement; when ever admitted to union with the other States: Esteeming it just, that those who equally participate of the blessing of liberty, should bare equally the burdens of the war in obtaining it. At the same time, we cannot be so lost to all sense, and honor, or do that violence to our feelings, as freemen, and as *Americans*, that after four years war with *Great-Britain*, in which we have expended so much blood and treasure, we should now give up, every thing worth fighting for, *the right of making our own laws and choosing our own form of government*, to the arbitrament, and determination of any man or body of men under heaven.

"Who noble ends, by noble means obtains;
"Or failing smiles, in excile, or in chains.
"*That man is great indeed.*"

POPE.

VERMONT's APPEAL
To the Inhabitants of the United States of
AMERICA.

COUNTRYMEN, FELLOW CITIZENS, & BRETHREN.

UNDER the strongest ties of friendship, as men who have equally suffered together, from the iron rod of tyranny, in the late cruel measures of *Great-Britain*; and have gone hand in hand, and stood by each other, in times when threatened with ruin, tyranny, and death; we beg your most serious attention by our address to this very important subject. And whilst like the Dove in the fable, you bend the branch, to save the poor Bee struggling for life; remember it may be in our power, to sting the fowler so severely, when drawing the net to insnare the Dove, as may hereafter procure your liberation. We can never believe that the present inhabitants of the United States, are so lost to all feelings of humanity, benevolence, and religion, that while they extend their right hands to Heaven, and weary unbounded grace, in praying to be delivered from *British* tyranny and oppression, they should with their left hands, be forming shackles of slavery for their *American* brethren. It gives us pain and grief, to mention the intrigues, and artifices, used by wicked and designing men, to destroy the inestimable liberties, and priviledges of the State of *Vermont*; and that too by those ungrateful ones, who have been preserved from Indian cruelty, by our brave and strenuous exertions during this present war.

We need not inform you, that all those despotic claims of jurisdiction, over this State, made by any powers of the neighbouring States, originate from the same seeds of corruption and tyranny, that raised the war between *Britain* and *America*, to wit the power of taking from us our property without our consent; or in other words, to reduce us to a state of abject tenantcy, binding us down as tenants, and then domineering over us as Lords.

We need not warn you of the dangers that threaten you in our destruction, those who have once feasted on the spoils of their countrymen, and tasted the sweet of living upon the labor and sweat of tenants, like the voracious wolf, will never leave till they have devoured the whole flock of *American* yeomanry. We have seen the liberties of *Poland*, and *Sweeden*, swept away in the course of one year, by treachery and usurpation; the free towns in *Germany*, like dying sparks are quenched one after another in the destructive greatness of their neighbours.

We beg leave to recall your attention, to the present most critical situation of the inhabitants of the State of *Vermont*; many of us were soldiers in the provincial army during the last war, between *France* and *Great Britain*, and suffered inconceivable hardships, in successive campaigns, in striving to support the honor of the *British* nation, and to conquer and defend this territory of land from Indians, Canadians, and French, at which time 'twas we discovered the excellency of the country, and determined, if ever circumstances would permit to settle the same.

At the close of the war, *Canada* being ceded to the British crown, and a general peace prevailing in *North-America*, gave us an opportunity to begin settlements on the Green Mountains, then a wilderness, filled with savages, scorpions and beasts of prey; and notwithstanding all our fatigue in assisting to conquer said territory, that we might not give offence, we applied to the governor of *New-Hampshire*, at that time an agent or factor, to sell extra-provincial or crown lands in *America*, for the king of *Great-Britain*; and purchased all the territory of *Vermont* at a very high price, excepting a small tract in the northern part of this state, and continued making settlements in the wilderness, by an invincible fortitude, surmounted every obstacle. In this situation, in the midst of a howling wilderness, we had very little to do with any other colony, or province, never sending abroad to obtain legislation, but kept a very good regulation among ourselves; acknowledging *New-Hampshire* to be our parent State, because we had purchased our land there, and expected to have it warranted and defended by them, but never associated with them as a people in a state of society; for we never had a single voice in their house of representatives, and consequently were not contained within the jurisdiction of their laws. In this situation the king of *Great Britain*, starting the idea of raising a revenue from the American colonies, and considering the

New-England colonies as too popular to begin with, and entertain any prospect of success, he therefore adds all the territory of land north of *Massachusetts* line, and west of *Connecticut* river, (which we had before purchased) by an arbitrary command, to the jurisdiction of *New-York*; thinking as part of that province was held by tenure, he could carry on his plans with greater ease, by adding greater power to the servants of the crown, decreasing the number of freemen, and consequently increasing the number of slaves: We think the greatest reason will justify this assertion, for no sooner had the governor of *New-York* obtained jurisdiction, but he patented out all the territory we were in possession of, to a few of his nobility and lords, who were favorites of administration, and ordered us to pay the annual rents usual for servile tenants, or quit our possessions immediately; and that "we should not tarry to reap the crops then growing." We replied in the most humble, but positive terms, "That we had purchased our lands of the crown at a dear rate, and had suffered infinite hardships in gaining settlements, and now to give them up, or acknowledge ourselves tenants to any lord was what we would not at the risk of our lives." And from thence sprung the long dispute; we, on our part, refusing to submit to their government, and they striving to dispossess us of our lands and tenements; in the course of which time, we frequently petitioned *New-Hampshire* most earnestly, that they would take us under their protection, and prevent our being devoured by those who sought our ruin; and had as often the misfortune to find them deaf to all our intreaties, and at last had the bitter mortification to see a proclamation, issued by the Governor and Council of *New-Hampshire*, wherein they relinquished all right to the jurisdiction of said territory; put us out from under their protection, and directed us to govern ourselves accordingly. We then found ourselves reduced, to the melancholy necessity of quitting all, and from a state of affluence to commence beggars; to submit as servile tenants to haughty lords, or as freemen, to face death and danger and support our rights; we determined upon the latter, and choose rather to die with honor than live with shame. In this condition, detachments of their militia were frequently sent to dispossess us, whom we opposed even to blood. It ought to be observed, that as soon as *New-Hampshire* refused us any relief, and relinquished their claim, we sent immediately agents after agents to *Great-Britain*, with petitions in their hands, to lay at the foot of the throne, praying for relief, who at first were received very cooly, but after the plan of the stamp-act failed in *America*, the crown listened to our cries, and gave a decree, in part suspending that jurisdictional power in *New-York*, *until his Majesty's further will and pleasure should be known*; afterwards we obtained one or two reports of the Board of Trade in our favour, but remained very much in that situation, until the eve of the present war, when we understood that king *George*, to answer some other tyrannic views, had given Governor *Skeen* a commission to preside as governor over most of this territory, who came once to visit us, but finding the inhabitants no better disposed toward him, than toward *New-York*, soon made his exit and left us to govern ourselves.

"WE shall decline the ungrateful task, of describing the irksome variety of artifices, the acts of oppression, the fruitless terrors, and unavailing severities," that for the course of twelve years were dealt out by the legislature of *New-York*, in their endeavours to execute their unreasonable and cruel measures. And not to wound humanity, leave untold those black acts of outlawry and death, passed against Englishmen, and freemen, and that too by a legislature, wherein they could have no representation, placing them as common marks for the arrow, wherein they not only proffered absolution to any person that should kill them, but even offered rewards, to those who would imbrue their hands in their blood, for no other crime but defending their just rights and privileges. Driven as we were by fatal necessity, while we remained in that condition, to submit either to ruin, slavery and death; or declare ourselves a free and independant State; we determined upon the latter, being assured, that our struggle would be glorious, since in death we could obtain that freedom, which in life we were forbid to enjoy.

We have now existed as a free independant State almost four years, have fought Britains, Canadians, Hessians, Waldeckers, Dutchmen, Indians, Tories and all, and have waded in blood to maintain and support our independence. We beg leave to appeal to your own memories, with what resolution we have fought by your sides, and what wounds we have received fighting in the grand *American* cause; and let your own recollection, tell what *Vermont* has done and suffered in the cause of civil liberty and the rights of mankind, and must we now tamely give up all worth fighting for? No, sirs, while we wear the names of *Americans*, we never will surrender those glorious privileges for which so many have fought blead and died; we appeal to your own fealings as men of like sufferings whether you would submit your freedom and independence, to the arbitrament of any court or referees under heaven? if you would after wasting so much blood and treasure, you are unworthy the name of *Americans*; if you would not, condemn not others in what you allow yourselves. To you we appeal as the dernier resort under God; your approbation, or disapprobation must determine the fate of thousands. It is not the intrigueing courtier, the elequent lawyer, or the learned judge that we fear; we tremble least posterity should read, that the arms of the glorious *Americans*, after working wonders in the cause of liberty, were tarnished and disgraced, and vilely used as instruments to deprive their brethren, of their inestimable rights and privileges.

Our enemies gives us approbrious names, they call us insurgents and rebels, we have stated the matter clearly before you in the course of this *pamphlet*; you see wherein our rebellion consists, and if that can be called rebellion; shew us a period in the history of the present war, in which you have not been equally rebellious; we conjure you by that friendship which has so long subsisted between us, by the blood and sufferings we have exhibited in your cause, by your own honor, and liberties which are at stake; to rise and crush that spirit of oppression, now exercised in making our destruction, be assured that if you suffer us tamely to be devoured by those greedy powers who have laid plans for our ruin, that spirit will not sleep long, before you must fare the same fate; for we conceive the liberties of the whole, to be absolutely connected with every part of an empire, founded on the common rights of mankind. We have coveted no man's estate, we have at all times been ready to submit all differences relative to the see of lands in dispute to impartial judges, and now solemnly declare to all the world that we are contending only for liberty the gift of the Creator to all his subjects, the right of making our own laws, and choosing our own form of government, and will God be pleased to dispose the hearts of our countrymen to save the inhabitants of the State of *Vermont* from tyranny and oppression, to grant them their liberties in peace, and to see the things which belong to their political salvation, before they are hidden from their eyes.

To the Commonalty of *New-Hampshire*, *Massachusetts-Bay*, and *New-York*.

We conclude this address to you, in short, to remind you that your liberties are challenged as well as ours; you are now engaged in a bloody war in defence of the same; remember, the measure you meet out to others, heaven will measure back to you again. Can you stand before the throne of God and seek to be protected and defended in your cause, while you are striving to overthrow and destroy the liberties of the State of *Vermont*, which stands on as large a scale of reason for independence as any other State on the Continent.

Again we request you seriously to consider, whether the object is worth the pursuit before you rush head long like the horse into the battle. Force is seldom imployed with success to change the opinions, or convince the minds of freemen. But admiting that you should conquer us and affix us to any of your governments. Will that enrich you? Certainly not: Will it make us better neighbours? it cannot: Will our destruction secure your liberties? By no means. What then will you obtain finally, for all your trouble and expense, not to say bloodshed. Nothing but a conquered depopulated territory, where every single inhabitant, will be so imbittered against you, that you will be necessitated to keep a standing army perpetually, to keep them in subjection, and support government. And that very army in time, being accustomed to trample upon the liberties of mankind, will, with the assistance of the disaffected, like the worm at the root of *Jonah*'s gourd; eat up and devour the whole of your liberties, and thus the righteous Judge of the universe will give that people that deprive *Vermont* of her rights, slavery to drink for they will be worthy.

THE END.

Printed.

To the President of the Continental Congress

Sir Philadelphia Feby. 1st. 1780

Enclosed your Excellency will receive a Copy of an Act of the legislature of the State of Vermont, appointing and impowering Agents to appear and transact their political affairs at the Congress of the United States, as a free and independent State:[1] herewith likewise will be communicated to you "a vindication of the opposition of the inhabitants of Vermont, to the Government of New York" and "Vermonts appeal to the candid and impartial World" published by order of the Supreme executive Authority thereof, the last of which contains some of the principal reasons upon which the inhabitants of Vermont acted, and their right in asuming Government, with an address to the honorable American Congress in answer to their act, of the 24th day of September last, together with a Book containing a Constitution and Code of Laws as established by the freemen of said State; and have only to add that, we are now in this Town, and are ready with full powers on the part of the State of Vermont to close an equitable Union with the other independent States of America, and to pledge the faith of our Constituen<ts> to pay a just proportion of the expence of the presen<t> War with G. Britain whenever a Constitutional requisition therefor shall be made.

Nevertheless we are not authorised, neith<er> does the State whom we have the honor to represent vi<ew themselves holden to close with the terms of the resolutions of> the 24th of September aforesaid, for the reasons published in the appeal before refered to. But could the honorable Congress pass over those reaso<ns> and determine that, they have an uncontroulable right and power to compel Vermont to abide their determinations in the premises yet they cannot conceive it to be just and equitable that, such an important Cause, in which, not only property, but even liberty for <which> we have been so long contending ought to be tryed, and a find<al> Decision so hastily had therein, on a footing so unequal as it m<ust> inevitably be, on the part of Vermont, if done at this time.

All the evidence that can possibly be exhibited, as the cause is now unfortunately placed, must be exparte, and that evid<ence> which must finally prove the Claim of New York and all others groundless, upon their own Stating, is at present out of our powe<r;> for if we are allowed proper time to prove that, in consequence of our remonstrating and petitioning the Court of G. Britain, that power had made a distinct Government of the tract now comprehending the State of Vermont, and appointed Governor Skeene to preside over the same, previous to America's denyi<ng> its Supremacy, it would silence all our Enemies, and oblig<e> every man, even those interested, to acknowledge that, the State <of> Vermont had an equal right with the other American States, to assume an independent Government.

And until we are allowed sufficient time to collect & publish our evidence, the freemen of Vermont, can never Voluntarily surrender those liberties which God and nature have vested them with, by reason of any partial adjudication, for if the Claims on the one side are founded on Arbitrary adjudicati<ons> of the Crown, of Course a Subsequent adjudication by the same <power, respecting the premises, must render the former adjudication> null and void. If they are built on a right of purchase, they must fail, for *we* possess that in seclusion of all others, being of a prior date, and for a valuable consideration, which no other party can pretend to. If on a right of conquest they fail. If on a right of setlement and occupency, in this likewise, as well as on every principle of the Law of nature and nations, they certainly fail.

We sincerely lament that Neighbouring States from local prejudices, or other Views, should raise internal animosities during the severe contest with G. Britain & thereby give fresh resources to our common Enemy to procrastinate the War, and unnecessarily continue the effusion of Human Blood,

And are Sir your Excellency's most Obedt. humbl. Servants

Jonas Fay
Moses Robinson
Stephen R. Bradley

His Excellency Samuel Huntington Esqr.
President of the Congress.

ALS (DNA: Papers of the Continental Congress, r47, i40, 1:313). Torn at margins; words and parts of words in angle brackets have been supplied from printed copy (*Public Papers of George Clinton, First Governor of New York, 1777–1795 — 1801–1804* [10 vols.; New York and Albany, 1899–1914; facsimile ed., 1973], 5:483–86). Docketed, "Letter from Jonas Fay / Moses Robinson / Stephn. R. Bradley."

1. See Resolutions of the State of Vermont, 20–21 Oct. 1779.

To the President of the Continental Congress

Sir   Philadelphia Feby. 5th. 1780

In pursuance of our appointment from the State of Vermont, we have, in discharge of our betrustment, waited on the Grand Council of the United States of America, have delivered to them a Copy of our Credentials, impowering us to close a Union and Confederation with the other States &c. And are now about to take our leave of this City, to meet the Assembly of the State we represent, which are shortly to convene, to adopt measures for protecting our infant frontiers, and vigorously prosecuting the War against our common Enemy.

We are assured that nothing on our part shall deter us, from spiritedly opposing the Savages of the wilderness, or the power of G. Britain. And have full confidence that neither States, or individuals, that are attached to the American cause, can wish to divert us from our fixed purpose. And shall ever stand ready to acquiesce in any requisition, made by Congress, not incompatible with our own internal police

And are with the highest sentiments of esteem your Excellency's most humbl. Servants

Jonas Fay
Moses Robinson
Stephen R. Bradley

His Excellency Samuel Huntington Esqr.
      President Congress.

ALS (DNA: Papers of the Continental Congress, r47, i40, 1:315). Docketed, "Letter from Jonas Fay / Mos. Robinson / S. R. Bradley / Read Feby 7. 1780."

From Chauncey Goodrich

Dear sir, New Haven April 11th. D 1780

I receivd this instant your favor of the 25th. Ult.[1] and am much obliged to you for your kind attention to me in making me one among a very worthy number of Propri<etors?> in your new town of Montgomery. When it is in my power I shall be happy to receive your commands, and return you the favor.

The State of Vermont seems to be verging to her proper place of importance among her sister states. Her independancy <and> prosperity depend upon her own perseverance and wise <doc>trine, and we doubt not her conduct will continue uniformly the same as it has been. This is all, that is necessary to make it happy and great. I sincerely wish she may be so.

We flatter ourselves that the Arts and Sciences will receive an additional improvement if not their perfection in America. The genius of our Countrymen — and governments are particularly favourable to Literature. Our many wise literary institutions hereafter to be amply endowed, and others to be erected are flattering circumstances. Vermont has now an Opportunity to do much for the encouragement of Learning and I am glad to hear from you that she has made so <great?> a provision for it's future increase and progress. In the regulation of this matter I hope it will be your happiness to avoid an inconvenience we so sensible [sic] feel here, a want of a large and permanent income.

I congratulate you upon your success in Vermont, and think that you, with the rest of the young Gentlemen Attorneys may now in the infancy of its constitution, be of signal advantage in placing it's interior polity of Justice upon a right foundation. It is easier to begin well, than to alter a <well? es>tablished practice. You will be so good as to pardon my [...] time when you consider that We Lawyers love to talk. I [...] to make my Compliments to Mr. Shipman and believe me to be Sir Your humble Servt.

Chauncey Goodrich.

Mr. Bradley.

ALS (CtY). Docketed by SRB, "Chauncey Goodrich." Damaged by blots and removal of seal.
1. Letter not found.

To a Committee in Cumberland County, Vermont

Westminster June 23d 1780.

To a Committee from a Number of Towns in the County of Cumberland, to meet at Brattleborough, June 27th 1780.

Gentlemen,

The Legislature of the State of Vermont, considering the unhappy Differences and Disputes, which have so long continued respecting Government in the County of Cumberland, and being earnestly desirous of having Government established on the broad and sure basis; (the perfect Union and agreement of the People) were pleased at their Session in March last, to appoint, Jonas Fay, Moses Robinson, & Stephen R. Bradley, Esqrs., a Committee with full Power to treat with all and every of those Persons who were disaffected with the Government of Vermont: to inquire into the Cause of their Disaffection, and to make such Overtures from Government, as should if possible, make Satisfaction, and remove all grounds of uneasiness. In pursuance of which appointment, we now notify you, and we trust thro' you, the People whom you represent, that we will wait on them in the following manner. At Westminster Court House on the first Day of August next afternoon, at Putney Meeting House on the 2 Day of August next afternoon, at Brattleborough Meeting House the 3 day of August next afternoon, and at Guilford Meeting House the 4 day of August next afternoon.

And should be happy Gentlemen at either of the Places aforesaid to meet you or a Committee appointed by the People for the above Purpose of amicably removing all Differences and are, Sirs, Your most obedient Humble Servant

                                        Jonas Fay,
                                        Moses Robinson,   Committee.
                                        Stephen R. Bradley,

Printed copy (*Public Papers of Clinton*, 5:889–90).

Governor Chittenden to His Excellency Samuel Huntington, President of Congress

BENNINGTON, *July 25th*, 1780.

    SIR,

Your Excellency's letter of the 10th ult. enclosing several acts of Congress, of the 2d and 9th of the same month, I accidentally received, the 6th inst. have laid them before my Council, and taken their advice thereon, and now beg your Excellency's indulgence, while I treat on a subject of such moment in its nature, and which so nearly concerns the citizens of this state.

However Congress may view these resolutions, they are considered by the people of this state, as being, in their nature, subversive of the natural rights, which they have to liberty and independence, as well as incompatible with the principles on which Congress ground their own right to independence; and have a natural, and direct tendency to endanger the liberties of America, which have, hitherto, been defended at great expence, both of blood and treasure.

Vermont's right to independence has been sufficiently argued, and the good consequences resulting to the United States, from its first assuming government, clearly vindicated, in sundry pamphlets, which have been, officially, laid before Congress. I beg leave to refer your Excellency to "Vermont's appeal," &c. particularly from the thirty second to the forty second page; in which, among other things, is contained a particular answer to the resolutions of the 24th of September, referred to in the resolves of the 2d of June last; and a denial of the authority of Congress over this state, so far as relates to their existence as a fre and independent government.

I find, notwithstanding, by a resolution of the 9th ult. that Congress have assigned the second Tuesday of September next, to judge, absolutely, of the independence of Vermont, as a separate jurisdiction. Can Congress suppose this government are so void of reason, as not to discern that the resolves of the 2d and 9th of June aforesaid, so far as the authority of Congress may be supposed to extend to this state, are leveled directly against their independence?

Vermont, as before mentioned, being a free and independent state, have denied the authority of Congress to judge of their jurisdiction. Over the head of all this, it appears that Congress, by their resolutions of the 9th ult. have determined the essence of the dispute; for, if Vermont does not belong to some one of the United States, Congress could have no such power, without their consent; so that, consequently, determining they have such a power, has determined that Vermont have no right to independence; for, it is utterly incompatible with the rights and prerogatives of an independent state, to be under the control or arbitrament of any other power. Vermont have, therefore, no alternative; they must either submit to the unwarrantable decree of Congress, or continue their appeal to heaven and to arms.

There may, in future, be a trial at Congress, which of the United States shall possess this territory, or how it shall be divided among them: but this does not concern Vermont. And it is altogether probable that there have been proposals for dividing it between the state of New-Hampshire and New-York, the same as the King of Prussia, the Empress of Russia, and the Empress of Hungary divided Poland between those three powers; with this difference only, that the former are not in possession of Vermont.

The cloud that has hovered over Vermont, since the ungenerous claims of New-Hampshire and Massachusetts-Bay, has been seen, and its motions carefully observed by this government; who, expected that Congress would have averted the storm: but, disappointed in this, and unjustly treated as the people, over whom I preside, on the most serious and candid deliberation, conceive themselves to be, in this affair, yet, blessed by heaven, with constancy of mind, and connexions abroad, as an honest, valiant and brave people, are necessitated to declare to your Excellency, to Congress, and to the world, that, as life, liberty and the rights of the people, intrusted them by God, are inseparable, so they do not expect to be justified in the eye of Heaven, or that posterity would call them blessed, if they should, tamely, surrender any part.

Without doubt, Congress have, previous to this, been acquainted that this state has maintained several posts on its frontiers, at its own expence; which are well known to be the only security, to this quarter, of the frontier inhabitants of the states of the Massachusetts-Bay and New-Hampshire; and it is highly probable that Albany, and such parts of the state of New-York, as lie to the northward of that, would, before this time, have been ravaged by the common enemy, had it not been for the indefatigable exertions of this state, and the fears, which the enemy have been, and are still possessed of, that their retreat would be interrupted by the troops from those posts and the militia of this state.

Thus, by guarding the frontiers, has this state secured the friendship of part of the private gentlemen and yeomanry, even of those states, whose representatives, it seems, are seeking its destruction. And, having the general approbation of disinterested states, this people are, undoubtedly, in a condition to maintain government; but should they be deceived in such connexions, yet, as they are not included in the thirteen United States, but conceived themselves to be a separate body, they would still have in their power, other advantages; for they are, if necessitated to it, at liberty to offer, or accept, terms of cessation of hostilities with Great-Britain, without the approbation of any other man or body of men: for, on proviso that neither Congress, nor the Legislatures of those states, which they represent, will support Vermont in her independence, but devote her to the usurped government of any other power, she has not the most distant motive to continue hostilities with Great-Britain, and maintain an important frontier for the benefit of the United States, and for no other reward than the ungrateful one of being enslaved by them. True, Vermont have taken an active part in the war, subsisting between the United States and Great-Britain, under an expectation of securing her liberties; considering the claim of Great-Britain to make laws to bind the colonists, in all cases whatsoever, with out their consent, to be an abridgment of the natural rights of mankind: and it appears that the said resolves of the 2d and 9th of June, are equally arbitrary, and that they furnish equal motives to the citizens of Vermont, to resist the one as the other; for, if the United States have departed from the virtuous principles upon which they first commenced of usurping the rights of Vermont, it is time, high time, for her seriously to consider what she is fighting for, and to what purpose she has been, more than five years last past, spilling the blood of her bravest sons.

This government have dealt with severity, towards the tories, confiscated some of their estates, imprisoned some, banished some, and hanged some, &c and kept the remainder in as good subjection, as any state belonging to the union. And they have, likewise, granted unto worthy whigs, in the neighboring states, some part of their unappropriated lands; the inconsiderable avails of which, have been faithfully appropriated for the defence of the northern frontiers; which, eventually, terminates in the support of the interest, and securing the independence and sovereignty of the United States: and, after having faithfully executed all this, have the mortification to meet with the resentment of Congress, circulated in hand-bills and the New York publick papers, representing their conduct, "in contravening the good intention of Congress, as being highly unwarrantable, and subversive of the peace and welfare of the United States." Those resolves serve only to raise the expiring hopes and expectations, and to revive a languishing flame of a few tories and scismaticks, in this state, who have never been instrumental in promoting the common cause of America.

With regard to the state of the Massachusetts-Bay, they have not, as a legislative body, laid any claim to the territory of Vermont; nor have they enacted laws, judicially authorizing Congress to take cognizance thereof, agreeable to the before mentioned resolves; a majority of their legislative body considering such pretentions to be an infringement on the rights of Vermont; and, therefore, the state of the Massachusetts-Bay cannot be considered as a party in this controversy.

As to the state of New-Hampshire, although they have judicially authorized Congress to make a final adjudication of their late started and very extraordinary claim to the territory of Vermont, yet, by recurring back to the original proceedings between the two states, it appears, the General Court of New-Hampshire had, previous to laying the said claims, settled their boundry line with the state of Vermont, and established Connecticut river as the boundry between the respective governments; and, as far as the approbation of the government of New-Hampshire can go, have, previously, conceded to the independence of Vermont; the particulars of which are too prolix to be given in this letter, but are exhibited, at large, in a pamphlet, entitled "A concise refutation of the claims of New-Hampshire and Massachusetts Bay to the territory of Vermont," and which is herewith transmitted as a bar against the right of New-Hampshire to a trial for any part of Vermont.

The government of New-Hampshire, ever since the royal adjudication of the boundry line between them and the government of New York, in 1764, have cast the inhabitants of the contested territory, out of their protection, and abandoned them to the tyranny of New York: and have very lately, over the head of the settlement aforesaid, laid claim to the said territory, and enacted laws as aforesaid, to enable Congress to judicially determine the merit of said claim. How glaringly illegal, absurd and inconsistent, must their conduct as a legislative body, appear, in this respect. Such irregularity among individuals, arises from the ill government of the human passions; but when that takes place in publick bodies, it is unpardonable, as its influence is more extensive and injurious to society.

Hence it appears, legally speaking, neither the states of New-Hampshire or Massachusetts-Bay, can be, with propriety, considered as parties in the controversy; and, consequently, New-York is left alone, a competitor with Vermont, even admitting Congress are possessed of sufficient authority to determine those disputes, agreeable to their resolutions; which, by this government, is, by no means, admissible.

Notwithstanding the usurpation and injustice of neighboring governments towards Vermont, and the late resolutions of Congress, this government, from a principle of virtue and close attachment to the cause of liberty, as well as a thorough examination of their own policy, are induced, once more, to offer union with the United States of America, of which Congress are the legal representative body. Should that be denied, this state will propose the same to the Legislatures of the United States, separately, and take such other measures as self-preservation may justify.

In behalf of the Council, I am, Sir,

Your Excellency's most obedient, humble servant,

THOMAS CHITTENDEN.

His Excellency SAMUEL HUNTINGTON, *Esq. President of Congress.*

All parties now anxiously awaited the decision of Congress, on the second Tuesday of September: and although Vermont strenuously denied the authority of Congress to adjudicate upon the controversy, yet, two of her agents, the honorable Ira Allen and Stephen R. Bradley, proceeded to Philadelphia, to attend the deliberations.

William Slade, Jr., *Vermont State Papers,* Middlebury, 1823, pp. 118–122.

From Thomas Jefferson

Sir　　　　　　　　　　　　　　　　　　　　　　　　In Council Aug. 14, 1780

Your regiment having now received their pay and equipment for marching are put under General Mecklenburg's direction by order of this day is what they will ____ ____ ____ continental service from this time ____ ____.

I am sir with great ____ Your most obedient humble servant

T. Jefferson

ADS (*Bradley Family Papers*). Addressed to Col. Bradley.

Commission

[16 August 1780]

State of Vermont.　　　　　　　　By the Governor.

Whereas the Supreme Legislature of this State did at their Sessions in october last past, resolve "that five persons be chosen by ballot Agents in behalf of the freemen of this State to appear at the Congress of the United States of America on the first day of February next, and they or any three of them are hereby fully Authorised and impowered by the freemen aforesaid to Vindicate their right to independence at that Honorable Board."

And whereas the said Agents appeared at Congress on the said first day of February officially and transacted the business of their Appointment agreeable to their Instructions, and made report to the Supreme Legislature, of their doings, at their session in March last.

And Whereas by late advice <received> from Congress, it Appears requisite that Commissaries should be appointed for the time being to Attend and Deliver officially to Congress such dispatches as shall be sent from the Authority of this State from time to time, And Also to remonstrate against any Acts of Congress which may infringe the rights and sovereignty of this State.

I have therefore tho't fit by and with Advice of Council to appoint and Commissionate Ira Allen and Stephen R. Bradley Esquires, and they are hereby appointed with full power to transact the business aforesaid. Given under my hand and the Common Seal of this State in the Council Chamber at Bennington this 16th. August 1780.

by his Excellency's Command　　　　　　　　　　　　　　　　　Thos. Chittenden.

J<oseph> Fay Secry.

DS (DNA: Papers of the Continental Congress, r47, i40, 1:357). Docketed, "Commission of Ira Al<len> & Stephen R. Bradley / August 16th 1780 / Read Feby. ____" and "No. II / Read Sept 19. 1780."

Resolution of the State of Vermont

BENNINGTON, 18 August 1780.

Resolved that the agreement relative to a printer, between Stephen R. Bradley Esqr. in behalf of the State of Vermont & Mr. Timothy Green printer at New London, (Conn.,) be & hereby is Ratified on Condition that Mr. Green send his son to print for this State in Leu of Mr. Spooner.

Resolved that Mr. Ezra Stiles be and he is hereby appointed and impowered to repair as soon as may be to New London to inform Mr. Green of the Ratification [of the agreement] made between Stephen R. Bradley Esqr. & Mr. Green aforesaid, & Facilitate as much as possible the moving of the Types and other apparatus for the purpose of Printing agreeable to said agreement.

Resolved that Stephen R. Bradley Esqr. be & he is hereby requested as agent to this State to repair to Philadelphia in Company with Colo. Ira Allen to Transact the Political affairs of this State & Report to this Council.

Printed (Governor and Council Record, vol. 2).

To the President of the Continental Congress

Sir   Philadelphia Sept. 12th. 1780.

We do the Honour to forward your Excellency a duplicate of the appointment of Commissaries from the State of Vermont to wait upon the Honourable Congress of the United States.[1]

Herewith You will receive a Letter from His Excellency the Governor of Vermont, with a pamphlet refered to in Said Letter, which we have positive orders to lay before Congress. And are

Your Excellency's Most obedient Humble Servants

Ira Allen
Stephen R Bradley.

His Excellency Samll. Huntingdon Esqr.
President of Congress.

ALS (DNA: Papers of the Continental Congress, r47, i40, 1:555). Docketed, "No. I / Letter from Ira Allen & Stephen R Bradley / Sept 12. 1780 / Read the same day."
1. Commission, 16 Aug. 1780.

To the President of the Continental Congress

To His Excellency Samll. Huntington Esqr.
President of the Congress of the United
States of America —   Dated Philadelphia
Sir   Sept. 15th. 1780.

We request your Excellency when ever debates come before Congress that may in any wise affect the rights Sovereignty or independance of the State of Vermont — that you take the

Sense of Congress <whe>ther we be <admitted a > personal attendance the better, to enable us to <discharge> the end of our appointment

And are Your Excellency's Most Humble Servants

Ira Allen

Stephen R Bradley

ALS (DNA: Papers of the Continental Congress, r47, i40, 1:557). Words and parts of words in angle brackets have been supplied from printed copy (Governor and Council Records, vol. 2). Cover addressed to "His Excellency Samll. Huntington Esqr. / President of Congress" and marked "*Public Service.*" Docketed, "Letter from Ira Allen / Stephen R Bradley / Sept 15. 1780 / Read the same day."

To the Continental Congress

[22 September 1780]

To the Honourable Congress of the United States of North America —

The Remonstrance —

of Ira Allen and Stephen R. Bradley, Commissioners from the Free and Independant State of *Vermont* — appointed for the time being to attend on Congress — With pleasure they embrace the first opportunity, to testify their thanks for the personal honour done them by Congress, in giving them an attendance, though in a private capacity with their Honourable body — at the Same time lament the necessity which oblige them to Say, they can no longer Sit as idle Spectators, without betraying their trust reposed in them, and doing violence to their feelings — to see partial modes pursued, plans adopted exparte, evidence exhibited which derives all it's authority from the attestation of the party, passages of wrightings selected, giving very false representations of facts, to answer no other end but to prejudice Your Honourable body against the State of *Vermont,* thereby to intrigue and baffle a brave and meritorious people out of their rights and <liberties> — We can easily conceive the Secratary's Office of the State of New York may be converted into an inexhaustible Source to furnish evidence to answer their purpose in the present dispute.

Needless would it be for us to inform Congress, that by the mode of trial now adopted, the State of *Vermont* can have no hearing without denying itself — And to close With those Resolutions,[1] which we conceive our enemies have extorted from Your Honourable body, and on which the trial is now placed — would be in fact taking on ourselves that Humility and Self-abasement as to lose our political life, in order to find it.

We believe the wisdom of Congress sufficient to point out, that pursuing the present mode is deviateing from every principle of the Law of Nature or Nations — For if the dispute is between the States claiming on the one part, and the State of Vermont on the other, whether the latter be a State *de jure?* As independent jurisdictions *de facto* they ought to be considered in the course of the dispute til the powers interposing have determined whether the latter be an independant jurisdiction *de jure?* if not? then of course they ought to annihilate the jurisdiction *de facto* but to annihilate the <state> *de facto* in the first place, is Summarily ending the dispute, — to deny the latter any independant jurisdiction *de facto,* is to deny there is any longer parties in the dispute.

Again we conceive the means connected with the end, and upon no principle whatever can we justify that either party should establish the *modes* or Rules to be pursued in determining disputes <with>out confounding every idea of right and wrong — in the present <case> on the one part might the end as justly have been established as <the way> and means to effect the end.

We are far from being willing those brave and <strenuous> efforts made by the State of *Vermont*, in the contest with Great Britain, should be denied by our grasping adversaries (thirsting after domin<ation> and prey) in the <specious> pretext of rioters, tortiously assumeing government, and we thereby lose all Credit for the hours and money we have expended.

Thus while we are necessitated to remonstrate against the proceeding of Congress on the present mode, we are willing at the same <time> any equitable inquiery should be made, the State of *Vermont* being allowed equal priviledges with the other States in the dispute — And that the State of *Vermont* may Stand justafied to your Honourable body, and to the world, both as to her present and future conduct — we are induced as well from principl<es> of attachment to the grand American Cause as a regard we have for peace and harmony among the States of America now at war with Great Britain, to make the following proposals—

first   That the State of Vermont will as Soon as may be forward to the Secretary of Congress an attested return of all male persons liable to duty, agreeable to a Militia Act heretofore exhibited to Congress, in a Code of Laws intitled "the Laws of Vermont["] — And the State of *Vermont* shall for and during the present war with Great Britain from Year to Year furnish an equal number of troops in the field in propo[r]tion to their numbers as Congress Shall estimate the Quota's of the Several united States in propo[r]tion to their Numbers, which sd troops shall be Clothed, Quartered, and paid by the State of Vermont, and at the close of the war, the dispute shall be Equitably Settled by the mediation of Sovereign powers — And nothing herein Contained Shall be Construed to take away the right, any of the United States claim to have in or over the State of Vermont — Or

Secondly   We are willing to agree upon some one or more of the Legislatures of the disinterested States to interpose as mediators and Settle the dispute — Or

Thirdly   We are willing Congress, being possessed of Sovereignty, Should interpose to prevent the Expression of <human blood>— at the same time we reprobate every idea of Congress's Sitting as a Court of judicatory, to determine the dispute by virtue of authority given them by the Act or Acts of the State or States that make but one party.

It gives us pungent Grief that Such an important Cause, at this critical juncture of affairs, on which our all depends, Should be forced on by any Gentlemen professing themselves Friends to the Cause of *America* with such vehemence and Spirit as appears on the part of the State of New York — And Shall only add that if the matter is thus pursued we Stand ready to appeal to God and the world who must be accountable for the awful Consequences that may insue.

Signed at Philadelphia the 22d Day of September   Ira Allen
in the Year of our Lord 1780   Stephen R Bradley

ALS (DNA: Papers of the Continental Congress, r47, i40, 1:575). Words and parts of words in angle brackets have been supplied from printed copy (Governor and Council Record, vol. 2). Docketed, "The Remonstrance of the Commissioners from the State of Vermont / Read Sept 26. 1780."

1. On 16 September 1780, James Madison, delegate from Virginia to the Continental Congress, had introduced resolutions declaring that according to the evidence presented to Congress, the New Hampshire Grants were within the limits of one or more of the United States; that "every attempt by force to set up a separate and independent jurisdiction within the limits of any one of the United States is a direct violation of the rights of such state, and subversive of the Union"; that "it be earnestly recommended to the people who have assumed an independent jurisdiction over the district aforesaid immediately to desist from the exercise thereof"; and that Congress should appoint commissioners to hear the claims of New Hampshire and New York to the New Hampshire Grants. After debating the Vermont issue on 19, 20, and 27 Sept. and 6 Oct. without reaching agreement, Congress postponed further consideration. It was not taken up again until 20 July 1781 (*Papers of Madison*, 2:87–88 and nn.).

To the President of the Continental Congress

Sir   Philadelphia October 2d—1780

We have the Honour to inform Congress that the time of our appointment to attend on Congress expired yesterday in consequence of which we set out this morning to meet the Genll Assembly of the State which are to convene the 12th instant to adopt measures for prosecuting the war in conjunction with the thirteen United States—& for regulating their own internal police—We are assured the Genll Court of the State of Vermont will make every effort in their power to establish the Sovereignty & independance of America and could wish that principle might be invari[a]bly observed by every man in authority throughout the American States.

The dispute respecting the State of Vermont is of such Great concern it appears to us of the highest importance that Congress should be rightly acquainted with the dispute before they interpose on either Side which at present they cannot while America is in her present Situation—we can further observe that we have many papers more authentic than those that have been exhibited to Congress that will Shew our right to sovereignty over the claims of all our adversaries; which we have not here at present.

For these and for many other reasons, we must request Congress to postpone a further inquiery in the premises til a future day

And have the Honour to be Your Excellencys Most Obedient Humble Servants

                                                 Ira Allen
                                                 Stephen R Bradley

His Excellency Samll Huntington Esqr.
President of Congress

ALS (DNA: Papers of the Continental Congress, r47, i40, 1:579). Cover addressed to "His Excellency Samll Huntington Esqr / President of Congress" and marked "*Public Service.*" Docketed, "Letter from Ira Allen / Stephen R Bradley / Octr. 2. 1780. / Read 6.—."

Resolution of the State of Vermont

[14 October 1780]

Resolved that a Committee of nine[1] to join a Committee from the Council be appointed to take under consideration the 6th article in the Report arranging the business of the Session, and that they prepare a bill for quieting ancient Settlers and make report to this House.

Printed (Governor and Council Record, vol. 2).

1. "This committee consisted of Matthew Lyon of Arlington, Joseph Smith of Clarendon, John Strong of Dorset, [later of Addison,] Nathan Hodges of Lyman, N.H., Ebenezer Drury of Pittsford, Thomas Chandler jr. of Chester, Elkanah Sprague of Hartford, Colburn Preston of Rockingham, Stephen R. Bradley of Westmister, and John Bridgman of Vernon. Ira Allen and Jonas Fay were joined from the Council. Oct. 23, this committee was discharged" (Governor and Council Record, vol. 2).

From George Washington

[Headquarters, Passaic Falls, 12 November 1780]

"Directing Bradley to proceed with the wounded, certain detachments of the Connecticut Line, and such baggage '*as shall be sent from thence*' to Winter Quarters, crossing at King's Ferry and marching to West Point, there to await orders from Maj. Gen. Heath.

"The end of the letter contains one of the rare instances in which Washington cautions in writing against the violation of private property along the line of march."

Printed summary (Edward Ambler Armstrong Collection of Washingtonia, item 173, sold at Gimbel Brothers, 1947).

Resignation of Brigadier General Ethan Allen

[April 1781]

... He moreover resigned the office of Brigadier General, though prudently and patriotically promising "to serve the State according to his abilities," if the Assembly went on nevertheless with the investigation, and, on the testimony of Joseph Fay and Stephen R. Bradley, dismissed Hathaway's remonstrance, allowed Hutchins to withdraw, and by resolution appointed a committee to thank Allen for his good services, and informed him that his resignation was accepted "according to his offer," which has been stated above—that is, an offer of his best services when desired.

Printed (Governor and Council Record, vol. 2).

Resolution of the State of Vermont

[5 April 1781]

Resolved, That a Committee of three be appointed to wait on the Convention and inform them that the Union is agreed on by a major part of the towns in this State agreeable to the Articles of Union as proposed; and that this Assembly will wait to receive the members returned to sit in this Assembly, on the Unions takeing place to-morrow morning nine o'clock to take their seats. The members chosen, Mr. Walbridge, Mr. [Stephen R.] Bradley and Mr. Lyon

Printed (Governor and Council Record, vol. 2).

Resolution of the State of Vermont

FRIDAY April 6th 1781.

Mr. Woodward [Bezaleel,] a Representative from the East side of Connecticut River, informed this House that the Representatives elected in the several towns east of said River were waiting to take their seats agreeable to the Articles of Union and the order of the day—whereupon

Resolved that a Committee of three be appointed to wait on the Representatives returned to sit in this Assembly from the towns east of Connecticut River and introduce them to this house—the members chosen Mr. Bradley, [Stepehn R., who took his seat for Westminster at this session,] Mr. Walbridge and Mr. [Matthew] Lyon.

Printed (Governor and Council Record, vol. 2).

To the Superior Court

[4 August 1781]

To the Honourable Superior Court Now Sitting in Westminster within and for the County of Windham

Comes Stephen R Bradley Attory for and in behalf of the Freemen of the State of Vermont and upon his oath presents that Nathaniel Bennet of Tombleson in Said County Did on or about the first Day of August last past at Athens in Said County utter and publish these false and Defamatory Words of the Civil Authority (to Wit of Seth Oak then a Justice of the

Peace), that he (meaning Said Justice has Given a Damned Judgment against me and he meaning Said Justice has perjured himself and Deserves to be whiped D<amnly?>) thereby having respect to a Sentance Said Justice had past as a Minister and Court of Justice in the Execution of his Office.

All which is against the Peace and Dignity of the Freemen of Vermont and against the form force and Effect of a Certain paragraph of a Statute Law of this State Intitled "An act for the punishment of Defamation["] reference thereto being had

Dated Westminster August 4th 1781

Stephen R Bradley Attoy for State

To the Sheriff of the County of Windham his Deputy or either Constable of the Town Tomblison in sd County, Greeting

In the Name and by the Authority of the Freemen of the State of Vermont you are hereby commanded to arrest the Body of Nathaniel Bennet of sd Tomblison and him have before the Honorable Superior Court now sitting at Westminster in sd County, as soon as may be to answer to the above Information.

Hereof fail not and make due Return according to Law.

William Gould Clerk

Dated at Westminster Sepr. 4th. 1781

ADS (VtU).

From Thomas Chittenden

Sir [27 August 1781]

As your Colo is appoin[t]ed Brigedear Genneral you are Dyrected to have the Rigment under your Command to meet at Som proper Time and place by you to be appointed and When Meet them Lead to the Choice of a Colonal and Such other officers as Shall be Nessrey and make Return to me that he or they may be Commitiond

Given at Arlington this 27th Day of august 1781

Lieut Colo Steven R Bradley   Thos. Chittenden Capt. Gnll.

ALS (NcD: Bradley Family Papers).

Resolution of the State of Vermont

[15 June 1782]

Upon the Application of Benjamin Bennet to this Council by his Attorney Stephen R. Bradley Esqr requesting that the Sentence given by the Hon. Superior Court of this State, at their Session in Tinmouth the last week, against the said Bennet, be mitigated by this Board,

Resolved, that as it is the Desire of this Council when consistent with Constitution, & in Case of Penitency, to mitigate the Rigours of the Law upon Offenders, the said Benjamin Bennet is hereby discharged from Three Months & an half of the Imprisonment ordered by said Sentence, upon Condition that he pay to the Sheriff of the County of Bennington, the Fine ordered by said Court, with Costs of Prosecution, Committment, &c; or procure good and sufficient Security to the Acceptance of the said Sheriff, that the same shall be paid within Three Months after liberation,

And the Sheriff of the said County of Bennington, upon such Payment or Security being made, at the Expiration of Fourteen Days next after the rising of said Court, is hereby directed to liberate & discharge the said Benjamin Bennet from his Confinement in the Goal in Bennington.

By order of the Governor and Council, Tho. Tolman *Dep. Secry.*

Printed (Governor and Council Record, vol. 2).

Boundary Disputes Between Vermont, New Hampshire and New York

Concerning Congressional Terms for a Union

PROCEEDINGS OF THE GENERAL ASSEMBLY OF VERMONT, OCTOBER 1781, ON THE RESOLUTIONS OF CONGRESS OF AUGUST 1781

The deliberations and action of the legislature were mainly in a committee of both Houses, and for that reason the journals do not give an account in detail. Ira Allen stated in his history of Vermont that much difficulty was encountered on account of the conflicting interests growing out of the eastern and western unions; however, a result was reached on the 19th of October, when Jonas Fay of the Council, and Messrs. Ezra Stiles, Stephen R. Bradley, and John Barrett of the House, were appointed a committee to "prepare a Bill" agreeable to the report of the committee of the whole. A "bill," in the language of the record, meant an official statement of the action of the legislature. It was as follows:

State of Vermont, Charlestown, October 16th, 1781

The Governor and Council having joined the general assembly, in a committee of the whole, to take into consideration the report of the honorable Jonas Fay, Ira Allen and Bezaleel Woodward, Esquires, who were appointed by the Legislature of this State, in the month of June last, to repair to the American Congress, with powers to propose to, and receive from, them, terms for an union of this, with the United States, &c.

His Excellency THOMAS CHITTENDEN, *Esquire, in the chair*:

The said agents laid before the committee the following papers, which were read by the secretary in their order, viz.

1st & 2[d]. A copy of their letter to the President of Congress, of the 14th of August last, enclosing a duplicate of their commission.

3[d]. The resolutions of Congress, of the 7th and 8th of August last.

4th. Brigadier General Bellows, and associates, petition to New-Hampshire, 25th of May 1781.

5th. Petition of the selectmen of Swanzy to New-Hampshire, June 9th, 1781.

6th. Honorable Mesheck Weare's letter, to be laid before Congress, dated 20th June, 1781.

7th. Messieurs Duane and Ezra L'Hommedieu's memorial and prayer to Congress, of the 3d day of August, 1781; together with Ira Allen and Stephen R. Bradley Esquire's remonstrance to Congress, dated September 22d, 1780.

8th. Resolve of Congress, dated 17th August 1781.

9th. Written proposals to committee of Congress, dated August 18th, 1781.

10th. Questions proposed to the agents of Vermont by the committee of Congress, August 18th, 1781.

11th. The foregoing questions, with the answers annexed.

12th. Resolutions of Congress of the 20th August, 1781.

The further consideration of the report being referred, adjourned till to-morrow morning, nine o'clock.

Governor and Council, Vol. II, pp. 320–323. Newfane, sometimes called Fane, and Patmos. William Slade, Jr., *Vermont State Papers,* Middlebury, 1823, pp. 160–162.

From Samuel Fletcher

Dated Westminster 13th of Septemr 1782

De[a]r Colol. persuent to A Request from Brigadiar Genl. Ethan Allen, to me Directed to Raise in my Brigade two Hundred Able Effective men Equipt for War to assist the Civil Authority in Carrying into Execution the Laws of this State, You are hereby Requested to Raise in Your Regiment by Draft or Vollontears for the above sd Purpose one Hundred able bodied men Every way Equipt for War with three days Provision and march them so as to Randesvose at Landlord <Armses?> in Brattleborough on Monday Evening next in order to advance to Guilford on Tuesday morning

<pr?>Saml. Fletcher Brdr. Genl.

Colol. Bradley

ALS (NcD: Bradley Family Papers).

From Reuben Atwater

Sir   Cheshire Decemr the 9th 1782

I have determin on your proposal that you have one half of my Sixteenth part of the scoonnor, Ruth with the Loading there of Capt E. Tiley master, and is Now at anker at the warff In Middletown a riggen and tackenin her Loaden for a west indie Voige and when that is completed I shall Let you know the Cost there of. At present we cannot tell but by computtation nere £30 at your resk Both profit & Loss and If this coms to hand you may give me an answer this from your Humble Servant

Reuben Atwater

PS Sir sence the above I paid this opetunety to send you that we are well as usual and after Due respect to you and your family aquat you we shall be glad to here from you as offen as you can send to ous. We ofen here Billizer Menchen'd in oure family. Dont Let him lack too much room in yours. A fine Boy and I wish him to be a grait blessing to you and to the world of mankind but remember both are Liable to be Disapointed, and that many ways I think of Nothing New to Wright to you upon I am Now a going this after noon to add<jond?> Society Meeting To Determine the Balance of Power in matters of an Ecclesiastic Natur and so must subscrib your most Humble servant

R. Atwater

Mamma & Brother remember love to you all.

ALS (VtU). Addressed to SRB at Westminster.

From Thomas Chittenden

Dec. 24 1782

I received your letter with the prisoner,[1] and approve of your conduct. Have sent to Col. Robinson to call the superior court immediately for his trial, and I hope and trust justice will be done him. I have sent twelve pounds powder agreeable to your request. As to sending or ordering a standing force to Guilford, I had rather hang them [the Yorkers] one by one, until they are all extirpated from the face of the earth. However, I wait for the return of the officers that commanded the *posse* (which will soon be) to send orders to the sheriff to collect the fines and cost, when, if they continue to obstinate, a force must accompany the sheriff sufficient to silence them. I am not without hopes that the consequences of Church's trial will have some good effect on his connections.

Printed (Governor and Council Record, vol. 3).
1. Col. Church.

To the Inhabitants of Guilford, Vermont

[10 January 1783]

"I officially acquaint you, as Attorney-General for the freemen of the state of Vermont, that government wishes for your welfare as a people, and notwithstanding the coercive measures that are adopted, are willing to do everything for you consistent with the welfare of government; and I now assure you, upon your desisting from your opposition, and returning peaceably to your families, your persons and properties shall be protected; and in order for that, upon your certifying under your hands on your parol of honor to me, or to the sheriff of this county, or his deputy, or to Major Josiah Boyden of Fulham, that you will not directly nor indirectly do any act or thing prejudicial to the state of Vermont, all prosecutions against any of you shall be no further prosecuted till the rising of the next General Assembly, when I trust you may meet with all desired lenity. I except nevertheless all persons who have teen taken by the officers of government, and such as have been banished. What you do in this respect must be soon, as the matter is now become serious."

Printed extract (Benjamin H. Hall, *History of Eastern Vermont* [2 vols.; Albany, N.Y., 1865] ??:509. Addressed "To the inhabitants of the town of Guilford and its vicinity, who have been opposing the government of Vermont."

From Jonas Fay

[26 February 1783]

In Council Windsor Feby. 21st. 1783

Appointed Stephen Row Bradley Esquire Judge of the County Court of the County of Windham in the room of Samuel Fletcher Esqr. who declines serving—

agreeable to Nomination and return of the Representatives of the Co[u]nty of Windham present &c.

Extract from the Minutes

Jonas Fay Secy. Pro. Tem

Sir

I congratulate you on your appointment to the office of Judge of the County Court for the County of Windham.

I hope it will meet your approbation and that you will fill that place to the acceptance of all concerned among whom is

Your most Obedt. Humbl Servant

Windsor 26th. Feby 1783
Stephen R. Bradley Esqr.

Jonas Fay

ALS (NcD: Bradley Family Papers).

From Russel Atwater

Sir   Cheshire April 21st 1783

The Snow was so much gone when we come down that could not come through Windsor. I left the letter on the road & rote one myself but could not hear any thing from Mr Chapman.

Mr Austin was here, but I was gone from home. I have since been up to see Mr Chapman he says that he cannot make no payment untill Decembr. Next he has it in the Law but does not expect it before then. I have sent the note if you are a mind you can exchange. Capt Hotchkiss has not payed he says that he has got glass likewise that he can prove that you offered other people ⅖ Pr mile & he will not accept of that Note as pay if you desire it I will collect part or all of it as you say he says that he will pay it without Cost. I have sent thirty five Dollars & wish you to ad enough for the expences of the lumber down the river & give it to Mr Cone those boards you had & those Mr Fisk was forgot.

Mr Hall promised to give you a Note for the May of six thousands boards which I want Cone to take.

My best Compliments to Merab & Billy from your Most Obedient Humble Servant

Russel Atwater

Stephen R: Bradley Esqr

ALS (DLC). Addressed to SRB at Westminster.

Jonas Fay's Continental Account

[31 July 1783]

Continental Acct.

1779}

June} 15	To cash paid for expenses to} Phila. on public business 31 ds.}	£360..0..0
Augt. & Septr.	To expences in cash to Phila.} on public business 30 days.}	495..6..0
Jany.} 1780}	To expences in cash to Phila.} for self, M. Robinson, Ira Allen} Esqr. and Stephen R. Bradley} 31 day and cash left with} Allen and Bradley pr. Rect.}	4,500..0..0
	To part of Journey to Phila.} vizt. 17½ days @ £10.0.0}	174..16..0
		£5,530..2..0

Sunderland July 31st. 1783
    Errors Excepted

Jonas Fay
Pay Table office Sunderland   July 31st. 1783

The above account approved and the Treasurer of the State of Vermont is directed to pay to Jonas Fay Esqr. five thousand five hundred & thirty pounds of Continental Currency.

Timo Brownson}
Isaac Tickenor} Committee

DS (Vt: MsVtSP, vol. 8, p. 252–253). Docketed, "Jonas Fay Esqr / £5,530..2..0 / March 10 1784"; "Bennington 10th. March 1784 / Recd the Contents of the Treasurer / Jonas Fay."

From Reuben Atwater

Sir   Cheshire October the 4th 1783

The other day I sent you by Cris sundry articles sum of them I purchisd: & paid the money shall be glad you to send me the Money for them by Russel for I have not receivd any for the Goods set out for you; the first Voyage you have by letter seen an account the Way that they went & as to the 2d Voyage there is but a pershal Divition. Viz to 1/32 is 70 G. rum 84 lb sugar 12½ G. of molasses the Remaindr Lyes for a settlement which is to be compleated soon. The Bill when loded out 1/32 was £17. 8. 2 and your horse was Prised at 16£ so that thare remains due from you £1. 8. 2 for out sets in the Last Voyage. I have sent you part of the affects & the articles bought is 1½ lb tea @ 5/0 8 lb 2oz Loose sugar @ 1/6

    £0. 19. 8

4 wine glasses @ 9d 1 Doz plates 7/0	0. 10. 0
1 Cag wine 30/6 Cask for rum 5/ for sugar 1/ smith bill 1/	1. 17. 6
Paid Jonah bill for axed tree 3s	3. 0

and for further Information Russell will be able to aquint you & shall be Glad to see you as soon as agreeable for you to com and see us. Until that Subscrit you Humble sert

                                                                   Reuben Atwater

ALS (VtU).

The Governor and Council Are Petitioned to Impeach a Justice of the Peace

                                          In General Assembly, October 16th 1783.

A petition signed by a Number of the Inhabitants of Springfield praying that John Barrit Esqr. Justice of the Peace for the County of Windsor may be Impeached before the Governor and Council for Mal Administration in said office being Read,

Resolved that the said Barret be Impeached & that Stephen R. Bradley Esqr. be and he is hereby Authorised, to prosecute the said John Barret Esqr. by Impeaching him before the Governor and Council to final Judgment for Mal Administration.

                Extract from the journals   Rosl. Hopkins, *Clk.*

    True Copy.   Attest,   D. Buck, *Secy. P.T.*

The following impeachment against John Barret Esquire was laid before Council:

The Honorable the General Assembly vrs. John Barret Esquire.

To His Excellency Thomas Chittenden Esqr. Capt. General and Commander in Chief, and Honble Council of the State of Vermont, to be convened at Norwich in the County of Windsor on the first Tuesday of June in the year of our Lord 1785, Comes Stephen R. Bradley Esqr. Attorney to the Honble the General Assembly of the State of Vermont, pursuant to the true intent and meaning of a Resolution passed in General Assembly October 16th 1783, authorising and empowering the said Attorney in behalf of the General Assembly to prosecute John Barret Esqr. of Springfield in the County of Windsor, one of the Justices of the Peace within and for said County of Windsor, before the Governor and Council to final Judgment for Male [Mal] Administration, and in behalf of the General Assembly assigns the following facts which the said John Barret Esqr. in the Male [Mal] Administration of his office as Justice of the Peace has done, vizt. For that Whereas the said John Barret Esqr. on the 20th day of May 1781 at said Springfield did cCorruptly partialy and injuriously render judgment and award Execution against Ozemas Holmes of said Springfield at the suit of Caleb Shaw then late of said Springfield, when the said John Barret Esqr. well knew the said Shaw & Holmes to have settled & to have given orders for the said suit of the said Shaw to be withdrawn, And also for that the said John Barret Esqr. at said Springfield on the 28th day of July 1782 did corruptly and injuriously Issue a Summons against Asahel Powers of said Springfield at the suit of Doctor Frink of Keene, and did afterwards render judgment on a certain accompt contained in a Schadule annexed to the Summons and Taxed a large bill of Costs against said Powers to oppress and injure said Powers, and award Execution thereon, when the Said Powers before the Time of Issuing the said Summons, had before the said John Barret Esqr. confessed Judg^t. on the same account, and the said Barret well knew the Same: And also for that whereas the said John Barret Esqr. did Corruptly oppressively and injuriously on the 20th day of August 1783 at said Springfield, did render Judgment and award Execution against Richard Prouty of Brattleborough in the County of Windham at the suit of John Prouty when the said Barret well knew the said John for three years then last past before rendering said Judgment to have been Dead, And also for that the said John Barret Esqr. thro' the whole course of His Administration as a Justice of the Peace, has excited and encouraged many needless & vexatious Law suits to enhance bills of Costs to the oppression of the People, to the great injury of the Common Weal and against the Peace and dignity of the freemen of the State of Vermont.

Signed at Westminster this 3^d day of May 1785.

STEPHEN R. BRADLEY.

Printed. From the *Vermont Journal*, October 23 1783. From *Governor and Council*, vol. III, p. 301.

Election of Delegates and Agents to Congress

From the *Assembly Journal*:

Oct. 17 1783.—Then proceeded by Ballot to chuse Delegates to represent this State in the Congress of the United States, When the Honble Moses Robinson, Esqr., the Honble Isaac Tichenor Esqr., His Honor Paul Spooner Esqr., The Honble Ira Allen Esqr. and Stephen R. Bradley Esqr. were duly chosen according to Constitution.

Printed (Governor and Council Record, vol. 3).

Vermont Governor and Council Record

[22 October 1783]

On receiving Official Information from Stephen Row Bradley, Esqr. of his Resignation of the Office of Side, or Assistant Judge of the County Court of the County of Windham, Resolved, that the same be accepted.

Printed (Governor and Council Record, vol. 3).

Vermont Governor and Council Record

[22 October 1783]

That General Fletcher, with the Advice of the Officers commanding said Troops, augment or dismiss said troops as Circumstances may require.

That the Troops furnish themselves with arms.

That the Commissary General be directed to furnish the Troops with Ammunition, Provisions, and a necessary allowance of spirituous Liquors.

That one Company of said troops be from Colo. Wait's Regiment, and the other Company from Colo. Bradley's Regiment — and that the Officer commanding said Troops appoint the other Officers.

Which Report being read was accepted and Ordered that a Bill be brought in thereon.

Printed (Governor and Council Record, vol. 3).

Account

Westminster Octr 24 1783

State of Vermont

to Stephen R Bradley Dr

to attending on the General Assembly manageing Causes in behalf of the Freemen Drawing Bills &c three pounds £3:00

Stephen R Bradley.

In Genll Assembly October 24th 1783

Resolved that the above account be accepted and that the Treasurer be Directed to pay the Same by Giving Said Bradley an Order on the Collectors of the threepenny Tax

Rect. from the <Treasr?>

<Lem. Chipman?> Clk. P T

ADS (Vt: MsVtSP, vol. 9, p. 329). Endorsed by SRB on the verso: "Received Westminster October 24th 1783 the Contents of the within order in full of the Treasurer in hard money / Stephen R Bradley." Docketed "Col. S. R. Bradley / £3..0.0. / Ocr. 24th 1783."

Account

[25 October 1783]

Genll Ethan Allen Dr

to Stephen R Bradley

October 25th 1783	To Liquor as per Bill	£1: 4:10
	To fifty Six Meals at 9d/0 per Meal	2: 2: 0
	To Eighteen Lodgings at 3d/0 per Night	4: 6
		£3:11: 4

AD (NFtW). Two copies, both in the hand of SRB.

From Russel Atwater

Dear Sir   Cheshire Novbr 24th 1783

Your affairs go on in the same manner as heretofore the Officers still at work, soon after that I return'd saw Lent Hotchkiss he wanted to buy that rum I sold it to him & desired him to get a reprieve of Mr Hilhouse accordingly he did give it the Officer he repriev'd it but immediately Thatcher Attached it again in Woosters name & detains it; I wrote to Mr Chapman when that I was in Hartford but have heard nothing from him if that you would have me put his note in suit you will write soon and what that you would have done with your

Other affairs, Austins affair is put off I hear; Thatcher is a mind to have papa receipt those two horses & if you Choose it he will; Capt Hotchkiss complains much wants to know if you will not leave it to indifferent men to say how much he shall have for his Journey he makes great talk I can sell your part of the Vessel if you desire it.

Thatcher tells of going to Vermont if that you do not come down you will write in full with regard to all your affairs Mr Hotchkiss gave a receipt as your Returnes for the rum; your Rum and sugar is not sold yet &c.

Your brother brought nothing from Harlow if that he does not settle so as your brother can bring it down you will put in suit immediately for I am in great want it; if you will remember me against next spring it will be a great kindness to me and shall ever think myself indebted to you as I shall be entering in to business then and in want of Cash from your ever Sincere friend and Humble Servant

Russel Atwater

Collo. Stepen R: Bradley

N:B: New Haven County Court adjournd to third tuesday December. I have not heard whether Hartfo<rd> adjournd or not but most likely it did.

ALS (VtU).

Account with the Town of Westminster

[1783]

The Town of Westminster Dr.

to Stephen R Bradley

To Cash paid out in the year 1783 to Lieut Wm. Crook as pr his Receipts for keeping the Widow Richard forty Nine weeks & one third of a week Record at s4/ Lawful Equal to s7/ pr week States Money	£17: 5: 4
April 1781 To preparing a petition to the General Assembly for a Sum to repairing the Meeting House being Specially appointed by the Town	1: 16: 0
To Service Done & money paid out to procure a Set of Stocks in the Town and a ~~Bier for the~~ Dead. The Bier for the Dead not allowed	1: 4: 0
To a Large Book purchased for the use of the Town to record Deeds in	0: 15: 0
To a Small Book for the use of the Town to Record the acts & doings of the Town in	0: 8: 0
To 17 Days auditing public accounts at 3/6 pr Day	2: 19: 6
to two Quire & a half of paper at 1/6 pr Quire Expended in auditing the accounts	<u>0: 3: 9</u>
	£24: 11: 7
To a writ against the Estate of Crean Brush Select Men ordered Stoped	0: 4: 0
to a Complaint & warrant to Carry Luis Johnson out of town	<u>0: 2: 0</u>
	24: 7: 7

Deducted for the Bier 3/0

AD (NcD). Docketing, obscured, reads, "Coln Bradley's acco[...] / Due to him £6: 0: [...]."

Nathan Fisk to the Sheriff of Windham County

[12 January 1784]

To the Sherriff of the County of Windham his Deputy or Either Constable of Westminster and for want thereof Experience Fisk of Westminster Greeting.

Whereas Eleazer Church of Brattleborough was this Day Brou<ght> before me the Subscribing authority for Reasonable Conduct against t<he> State of Vermont and was Sentanced to be Confined in Sum Sufficient Goal in this State without Bail or mainprise til Discharged by Due Course of Law.

These are therefore in the Name and by the Authority of the Fre<e>men of the State of Vermont to Command you that You take th<e> Body of the Said Eleazer Church and him Commit into the keeper <of> the Goal in Westminster in the County of Windham who is hereby Commanded to receive the Body of the Said Eleazer Church within Said prison and him Close keep therein without Bail or mainprise til Discharged by Due Course of Law. Hereof Fail not at your Peril Dated at Westminster this 12th Day of Jany. 1784.

Nathan Fisk Jus. Peace

Fees: 0: 11: 0

LS (DLC). In the hand of SRB; signature and notation on fees by Fisk. Right margin obscured.

To the Printers of the Vermont Journal

GUILFORD, January 24 1784.

No doubt the various reports which have gone abroad respecting the measures taken by government against the riotous body of men in this town who call themselves Yorkers, will leave you anxious of hearing the particulars.

On Saturday morning the 17th inst. I received by express from the Commissary General [Farnsworth,] intelligence, that a body of armed men to the number of about 20, the preceding night, had marched from Guilford to Brattleborough, and about the hour of 12 at night, had surrounded the house of landlord Arms, in said Brattleborough, and fired a number of balls into the house where were a number of travellers and others, and had wounded one or two men, and then by violence bursted into the house, and had taken and carried away Constable Waters, who had put up there that night, supposed with a design to take from him a quantity of money which he had been collecting on taxes; and that said body of men were commanded by one Daniel Ashcroft, and William White, of Guilford, who called themselves officers. I immediately sent the express to the high sheriff, who, very soon, made an official demand of 200 men from the *posse* to assist him in the execution of his office, in consequence of which, I issued orders for that number of men to march from this regiment, and to rendezvous at Brattleborough the next day at 8 o'clock in the morning. On the 18th the *posse* were mustered at Brattleborough, to the amount of 200 and upwards, where General Fletcher joined us on his way from Boston, and Lieut. Governor Spooner, who was on his tour to Bennington, to take his seat on the bench of the supreme court. On Monday the 19th, having received information that the whole body of Yorkers who were determined to oppose the collecting taxes, and in short, all government, were assembled at Guilford; we immediately marched the *posse* there, in order to reduce them to the obedience of the laws; upon our appearing in sight with the troops, that body of men betook themselves to flight without firing a gun. The militia were stationed at Guilford meetinghouse till Wednesday the 21st, two days; in which time about 30 of that party came in, took the oath of allegiance, and delivered up their arms. Having previously been informed, that about 40 of those persons were assembled in arms near the south line of Guilford, upon the borders of the Massachusetts: whereupon I received orders from Gen. Fletcher, to take a detachment of 120 men, and proceed with the high sheriff and disperse them; having marched about three miles, we came in sight of landlord Packer's, who lived within half a mile of the south line, where we perceived a number of men turning out of the house and parading; by that time the *posse* had got within twenty rods of the Yorkers, they gave one fire upon our troops, without ever challenging or saying a word, and then retreated.

Printed (Governor and Council Record, vol. 3).

Petition of Cyrel Carpenter

[21 February 1784]

State of Vermont} to His Excellency the Govr. And the Honble
Council of the State of Vermont

The Petition of Cyrel Carpenter of Guilford in the County of Windham Humbly Sheweth

That your petitioner was Convicted at the Superior Court Holden at Westminster in the County of Windham on the first Tuesday of Febr 1784 of being Concerned in a Dangerous Riot and was Sentanced by Said Court to pay a Fine of £20 and Cost of prosecution.

Your petitioner would inform your Honours that he is a poor Man and Entirely unable at present to pay Said Fine and Cost. Your petitioner has Since taken the oath of Allegiance and means for the Future to Consider himself as a Good and peaceable Subject.

Your petitioner would therefore pray your Honours to remit to him his fine or therein Suspend the Collection of it to Some future Day in which time your petitioner may be able to pay the Same and as in Duty Bound your petitioner will Ever pray.

Dated at Guilford this 21st Day of Febr 1784

Cyrryl Carpenter

DS (Vtu). In the hand of SRB.

Account

[2 March 1784]

State of Vermont Dr.
To Stephen R Bradley

Sept. 16th 1782	To one Hundred and Seventy Nine pounds of Beaf	
No I	at 0/3 per pound as per Receipt	£2: 4: 9
Idem	To Sixty one pounds of Salt Beaf at 0/4d pr pound	1: 0: 4
Decembr 20 1782	To Cash paid Seven Men for Guarding Timothy Church 24 hours at Westminster Court House at 3d pr Man	1: 1: 0
	To Seven Gills of Rum for said Guard	0: 3: 6
	To Capt Leonard Spalding for taking Said Church	0: 6: 0
Decr 22d 1782	To Two Days to Genll Fletchers on State Affairs myself and horse at 7/6 per Day	0:15: 0
	To a pair of Hand Cuffs for said Church Sent over the Mountains	0: 3: 0

	1783		
	Decembr 27th	To Articles of Vicutals [sic] and Drink Delivered Majr. Boyden for troops as per Receipt	1:10: 6
No II			
	1784	To Sundries in Victuals and Drinks Delivered	
	Jany. 10	Majr Boyden in Victuals and Drinks pr Receipt	0: 7: 4
	11	To one Quart of Rum to the Use of the Guards at the Court House at 1/6 and one pound of Candles at 0/8	0: 2: 2
		To a pair of Hand Cuffs for <Shadduck?> at 0/3	0: 3: 0
	Jany 17 1784	To 87 Meals of Victuals at 0/8 per Meal to the Guards while Guarding the Court House	2:18: 0
[Line cut off]			
		two Weeks and to Billiting a Soldier 2 Weeks and five Days	0:16: 9
		To Seven Gallons and three Quarts of Rum	2: 6: 6
		To two Gallons and Rum	<u>0:12: 0</u>
			14: 9. 9

A true Account

Attest Stephen R Bradley

March 2d. 1784

then the above & within aCompt swore to before me

Timo Brownson <HSst.?>

Pay Table Office Bennington March 2 1784

This Cer[t]ifies that the within account being Examined is found Due on Sd. account to Colo. S. R Bradley the Sum of fourteen Pounds Nine Shillings and Nine Pence

£14: 9: 9   Eli <Cogsel?> / Commtee.
                      Timo Brownson

In Council 2d March 1784

The Council having Examined the above acct. Resolved that the Treasurer be & he is hereby directed to pay the Same out of the three penny Tax Granted in Oct last being £14. 9. 9.

Attest Joseph Fay Secy

ADS (Vt: MsVtSP, vol. 9, p. 234). Endorsed by SRB in the margin, "Received Bennington March 3d 1784 the Contents of the within Order in Full of the Treasurer / Stephen R Bradley." Docketed "Stephen R Bradley Account / State of Vermont / £14..9..9. / March 2d. 1784."

Account

[2 March 1784]

Pay Table Office

Bennington March 2d. 1784

The within Account being Examined and approved the Treasurer is hereby Directed to Pay the Same to Colo. Stephen R: Bradley or Bearer it being the Sum of two Pounds Six Shillings & Six Pence

£2: 6: 6.

Timo. Brownson / Committee
Eli <Cogsel?> P. T

[Enclosure]
State of Vermont Dr
to Eliakim Spooner
1784

Feby 3d 1784	To two Baggage Horses 13 Days in Service to *[illegible]*	
	Ammunition provision &c at ⅙ per Day per *[illegible]*	
	in a Slay &c	£1:<14: 6?>
	To the use of a Slay Said time	0: <7?>

The Above Horses were for the Use of Coln Bradley's £2: 6: 6
Regiment

    A true Account

          Attest Eliam. Spooner

County of Windham <?> Westminster Febr. 24th 1784

 There personally appeared Eliakim Spooner Signer of the forgoing account and made Solemn Oath that the above account was just and truly made

         Before Me Seth <Oak Justs peac?>

<small>ADS and enclosure (?). Endorsed by SRB: "Bennington March 3d 1784 / Received the Contents of the above order in full by the Treasurer / Stephen R. Bradley." Docketed, "Eliakim Spooners Account Ver / State of Vermont / March 3d 1784 / Stephen R. Bradley / £2..6..6."</small>

Resolution of the State of Vermont

State of Vermont   In General Assembly March 2d 1784

 Resolved that the Treasurer be and is hereby directed to give an order in favour of Serjeant Sylvanus Fisk upon any of the Collectors of the three penny tax in Windham County for the sum of thirty five pounds Lawful money toward his expences of board, surgeons &c. and charge the same to the said Fisk on account he being wounded in the service of this state — And that said Fisk hereafter exhibited his account to the Comtee. of Pay Table for adjustment and that the Treasurer issue orders upon the hard money tax for what shall be due on a ballance for the expences of his sickness and wound received in the service.

         Extract from the Journals

           Ros. Hopkins Clerk

<small>AD (Vt: MsVtSP, vol. 10, p. 25). Endorsed by SRB on the verso: "Received Bennington March 3d 1784 / Orders on the three penny Tax for the Sum of thirty five pounds of the treasurer in Behalf of Sylvanus Fisk pursuant to the within Resolve / Stephen R Bradley." Docketed, "Silvanus Fisk / £35..0..0 / March 3d. 1784 / Stephen R. Bradley."</small>

State of Vermont Pay Order

              [1 April 1784]

A Return of the Orders Given on the Tresy. by the <Comee?>
of Pay Table in the Months of Janr Febr & March 1784

1784			
Janr		Capt Joseph Safford	£7. 8. 4
	<3d?>	Capt Joseph Safford	1. 10. 0
	2d	Capt Daniel Comstock	£0. 18. 6
	12	James Matthews	2. 7. 4
	16	Isaac Colton	0. 16. 8

	22	John G Lord	3. 5. 8
	27	Col Isaac Clark	19. 14. 6
	28th	Lt. Enos Herman	5. 1
	29	Liut Grant	2. 8.
		Jereh Addams	2. 9
		Majr Gideon Armsby	6. 1
		BenjaWellman	1. 8.
		Stephen Rice	1. 18.
		Capt Leml. Bradley	7. 19.
Febr	3	Capt Joseph Safford	56. 16. 0
	6	Capt Joseph Safford	46. 16. 0
		Capt Hezh Armstrong	17. 18. 8
		Capt Jonah Wickwire	9. 9. 4
	2d	Lt Simeon Herman	3. 5. 4
	11	Capt Enoch Eastman	11. 1. 4
	12	Gideon Adams	1. 4. 0
		Capt Jesse Sawyer	3. 0. 0
		James Fuller	0. 6. 3
		Lamberton Allen	0. 18. 9
	16	John Knickerbacor	216. 0. 0
		Capt Henry Venderhoof	10. 0. 10
		Majr McClung	4. 3. 0
		Joseph Harrow	3. 4. 1½
	18	Sergt Phineas Heath	3. 4. 3
Febr	20th	Lt Andrew Barton	£3. 5. 0
		Phineas Freeman	2. 8. 0
	23	E<nsns?> Alexr Brush & Jacob Safford	64. 1. 6
	24	Roswell Hopkins	4. 1. 3
		Capt Willm Sharp	39. 13. 8
		Capt Wm Sharp	6. 15. 0
		Andrew Sharp	5. 5. 0
		James Cowen	0. 15. 0
		Isaac Tickenor Esqr	46. 10. 0
	26	Capt Daniel Culver	33. 12. 7
		Abm Ives Esqr	6. 0. 0
		Peter Cogsel	11. 10. 0
		Lt. Abner Rowler	5. 17. 11
		David Fasset	1. 7. 0
		Capt Joseph Briggs	20. 3. 11
		Capt Isaac Wheeler	45. 18. 2
		Jesse Cook	2. 18. 11
		Jesse Cook	0. 4. 3
	27	Oliver Waters	16. 10. 0
		David Fassett	0. 18. 0
		David Safford Cont. Money	376. 0. 0
	28	Col. Ebenr. Wallbradge	14. 16. 3
		Joseph Rudd	3. 0. 0
March	2d	Capt Silas Burk	165. 1. 10
		Lt Ebenr Parker	42. 18. 0

		Col. Stephen R Bradley	13. 6. 6
		Col. Stephen R Bradley	30. 4. 0
		Eliakim Spooner	2. 6. 6
		Jonas Galusha Esqr	5. 5. 0
		Martin Follert	1. 3. 4
		Silas Walbridge	1. 3. 4
	3d	Nathan Fay	1. 3. 4
		Reuben & Enoch Sackett	2. 6. 8
		Capt Beriah Green	120. 0. 0
		Genl. Fletcher	9. 12. 0
March	3d	Majr Joseph Fay	£4. 13. 0
	5	Jesse Walker	42. 19. 8
		Col. Stephen R Bradley	131. 10. 0
		Lt Ebenr Harris	9. 10. 7
		Genl. Saml. Fletcher	5. 15. 6
		Nathl Seaver	58. 0. 10¾
		Capt. Ezekl Cobb	23. 5. 5
		Honl Paul Spooner	12. 15. 0
		Majr Saml. Billings	32. 0. 4
	6	Peter Alcott Esqr	62. 12. 6
		Capt Wilm. Ward	23. 4. 8
		Nathl. Chipman Esqr	3. 0. 0
	9	Elias Weld	2. 1. 0
		Joseph Farnsworth	555. 15. 10½
		Francis Davis	202. 10. 4
		Biglow Lawrance	1. 10. 6
		Peter Wright Esqr	1. 6. 0
		Simeon Hatheway	2. 9. 6
		Isaac Tickenor Esqr	7. 8. 0
	10	Elijah Fay	0. 19. 0
		Col. Isaac Clark	2. 10. 0
	13	Majr. Gideon Brownson	201. 10. 0
		Isaac Brownson	2. 10. 0
	23	Daniel Marsh	77. 8. 0

Pay Table Office
Sunderland April 1st 1784

Timo Brownson}
Saml. Bartlet} Committee

ADS (Vt: MsVtSP, vol. 10, p. 5–7?).

Account

[ca. June 1784]

Genl. Ethan Allen Dr

To Stephen R Bradley

1781

To managing a Cause in Equity through a Course of Law wherein he was Pl[anti]ff and Levi Allen Defendant Writings Money paid out and for Fees &c. £10: 0: 0

1782

To Money paid out Fees Writings &c wherein he and Ira Allen Esqr. were Pltts and Levi Allen Defendant in an Action of Covenant Broken Sheriffs Fees &c   £ 6:10: 0

1783

Dr Per Bill at Election time   3:11: 4

1784

To two Writs against Coln Hunt and other writing viz Letter of Atty Deed Bond Deposition &c   2:10: 0
To a Journey to Charles Town   1: 6: 0
Detaining Fees on two Causes against Coln Hunt   3: 0: 0
   £26:17: 4
to two Copies one of will the Other the Inventory of Estate of Crean Brush   0:12: 0

AD (NFtW). See also Account, ca. 9 Aug. 1785, which includes these charges.

Deed of Sale

[23 September 1784]

KNOW all Men by these Presents, That <u>I Ethan Allen of Bennington in the County of Bennington and State of Vermont Esqr.</u>

For and in Consideration of the Sum of <u>thirty five pounds</u>

Lawful Money of said State of <u>Vermont</u>

to <u>me</u> in Hand paid, before the Delivery hereof, by <u>Stephen R Bradley of Westminster in the County of Windham & State aforsaid</u>

The Receipt whereof <u>I</u> do hereby acknowledge, have given, ranted, bargained, sold and released; and by these Presents do give, grant, bargain, sell, aliene, release, convey and confirm to <u>him</u> the said <u>Stephen R Bradley his</u> Heirs and Assigns, <u>for Ever One Certain Lot of Land Situate Lying and Being in the town of Westminster in the County of Windham and State of Vermont being Lot Number third in the first Range of Eighty Acre Lotts as Contained in the Plan of said Town Reference thereto being had</u>

To have and to hold, the said granted Premises, with the Appurtenances thereof, to <u>him</u> the said <u>Stephen R Bradley his</u> Heirs and Assigns, to <u>his</u> and their own proper Use, Benefit and Behoof forever: hereby engaging to warrant and defend the said granted Premises, against all Claims or Demands of any Person or Persons claiming by, from or under <u>Me or any Other person whatsoever.</u>

In Witness whereof <u>I</u> have hereunto set <u>my</u> Hand and Seal, this <u>twenty third</u> Day of <u>September</u> in the Year of our Lord 17<u>84</u>

                                             Ethan Allen

Signed, Sealed and Delivered
   in the Presence of us.
Eli Noble
Joseph Fay

                              Day of   17

THEN the above-named
   personally appearing, acknowledged the above-written Instrument to be
      voluntary Act and Deed, before me,
                                             Justice of Peace.

DS (NFtW). The document is a printed form, completed in the hand of SRB and signed. SRB's additions are indicated here by underlining.

Deed of Sale

[23 September 1784]

To all People to whom these Presents shall come, greeting.
KNOW YE, That <u>I Ethan Allen of Sunderland in the County of Bennington and State of Vermont Esquire</u> For the Consideration of <u>forty pounds Lawfull Money</u> Received to <u>my</u> full Satisfaction, of <u>Stephen R Bradley of Westminster in the County of Windham and State aforsd Esqr.</u> DO give, grant, bargain, sell and confirm unto the said <u>Stephen R Bradley his heirs and Assigns for Ever one Certain Lott of Land Situate Lying and being in Said Westminster being Lot Number four in the Second Range of Hundred Acre Lotts as Laid Down in the plan of Said town reference thereto being had being a Lot Lately owned by Crean Brush Esqr. Deceased</u>
To have and to hold the above granted and bargained Premises, with the Appurtenances thereof, unto <u>him</u> the said <u>Stephen R Bradley his</u> Heirs and Assigns for ever, to <u>his</u> and their own proper Use and Behoof.

AND ALSO, <u>I</u> the said <u>Ethan Allen</u> Do for <u>myself &</u> Heirs, Executors and Administrators, covenant with the said <u>Stephen R Bradley his</u> Heirs and Assigns, That at and until the ensealing these Presents, <u>I was</u> well seized of the Premises, as a good indefeasible Estate, in *Fee simple*; and have good Right to bargain and sell the same, in Manner and form as is above writen; and that the same is free of all Incumbrances whatsoever. AND FURTHERMORE, <u>I</u> the said <u>Ethan Allen</u> do by these Presents bind <u>myself</u> and <u>my</u> Heirs forever, to WARRANT and defend the above granted and bargained Premises to <u>him</u> the said <u>Stephen R Bradley his</u> Heirs and Assigns, against all Claims and Demands whatsoever.

In WITNESS WHEREOF <u>I</u> have hereunto set <u>my</u> Hand and Seal the <u>23d</u> Day of <u>September</u> Anno Domini, 178<u>4</u>

Ethan Allen

Signed, sealed, and delivered,
  in the Presence of
Eli Noble
Joseph F Fay

DS (NFtW). The document is a printed form, completed in the hand of SRB and signed. SRB's additions are indicated here by underlining.

Resolution of the State of Vermont

IN COUNCIL, Rutland Octr. 14th 1784.

Resolved that a Committee of six to join a Committee from the House be appointed to receive, sort and count the votes of the Freemen for Governor, Deputy Governor, Treasurer and twelve Assistants for the year ensuing and order declaration to be made public of the persons chosen.

(Signed)   JONAS FAY, Secy. pro Temp.

The aforesaid resolution being read, whereupon Resolved that Mr. Tichenor, Mr. Tolman, Mr. Lyon, Mr. S. R. Bradley, Mr. Knight, Mr. Brown, Mr. Burton, Mr. J. Bayley, Mr.

Baldwin, Mr. Enos and Mr. Strong be a Committee to join the aforesaid Committee for the purpose aforesaid and that they make report of the persons elected to this House.

Printed (Governor and Council Record, vol. 3).

Resolution of the State of Vermont

STATE OF VERMONT. IN GENL. ASSEMBLY, Octr. 16, 1784.

Resolved, that a Committee of five be appointed to join a Committee from the Council to Take under consideration the 2d article in the Aranget. vizt. That an Act be passed putting the Militia of the State under proper Regulation, & that they prepare a Bill and make Report — The members chosen, Mr. Tichenor, Mr. Clark, Mr. Bradley, Mr. Gates, and Mr. Bayley. In consequence Mr. Fletcher and Mr. Olcott are appointed from the Council to join the said Committee.

A Bill from the House appointing Mr. Whipple, Mr. Mattucks, Mr. Bradley, Mr. Bayley and Mr. Brown, a Committee to join a Committee from the Council, to Take proper Measures for the appointment of a Council of Censors, and make Report, Mr. Porter, and Mr. Emmons are appointed to join said Committee.

JONAS FAY, *Secy. P. T.*

Printed (Governor and Council Record, vol. 3).

Account with Ethan Allen

[1784]

Genll Ethan Allen Dr
        To Stephen R Bradley

1781
To Managing a Cause in Equity through a Course of Law wherein he was Pltf and Levi Allen Defendant wri\<tings\> Money paid out and for Fees &c   £10: 0: 0

1782
To Money paid out Fees Writings &c wherein he and Ira Allen Esqr. were Pltf and Levi Allen Defendant in an Action of Covenant Broken Sheriffs Fees &c   £6: 10: 0

1783
Dr Per Bill at Election time   3: 11: 4

1784
To two writs against Coln Hunt and other writing ~~viz Letter of Atty Deed Bond Deposition~~ &c   2: 10: 0
To a Journey t\<o\> Charles Town   1: 6: 0
Detaining Fees ~~in two Causes against Coln Hunt~~   3: 0: 0
    £26: 17: 4

to two Copies one of will the Other the Inventory of Estate of Crean Brush   0: 12: 0

AD (DLC). In the hand of SRB. Damaged along folds.

From Reuben Atwater

Dear Sir   Cheshire Febr 7th 1785

I am Now to Inform you I receivd you Letter Janr 19th and Glad to here but sorry to here of sickness in your Fammely but hope These Lines will find you in heal[t]h the greatest Blessing in Life, if not may God make all His delings toward you & yours a Blessing which if rightly improvd will be so to all that is Hise[.] We are in yousl state of helth and want to much to See you all but Shall not be able to com this winter. We hop to that If Merab should be able the next spring that you bing her down in the spring. It may be for her helth for want to see you & Merab vary much abought could tell you that I can not writ, hope you wont faile avery oppetunity to writ to us and aquaint us of merabs he[al]th. Love to you and merab & Billa Zr from your frend & well wisher

Reuben Atwater

ADS (VtU).

From Elnathan Beach

Dear Sir   Cheshire March 10th 1785

I yesterday had the happiness of a long interview with my good friend Doctr. Potter, who discoursd much upon the case of Mrs. Bradley, & appeard anctious for her health. Woud have wrote to Mr. Bradley, but was Journeying & lacked opportunity, yet desired I woud inform You, that he had an idea, of there being a universal relaxation, & want of action in the solids, & a great deficiency of the nervous energy in the case of Mrs. Bradley to repair which was a work of time, with carefull attention, & in no measure effected by a momentary visit, which alone he <was> able to make. But so far was he from supposin<g> her case out of the reach of Art; that he was confident she may be restored to her former health, in the perseverance of well directed means to the choice of which he will be happy to lend his assistance, in case she can be brot. within the limits of his daily inspection & that she may be with the utmost safety, he is fully certain, altho her imbecility be so great, as to confine her in bed. If now the Judgement of so great a man needs, or can receive coroboration by my feeble auxiliary; would give it as my oppinion, that the most sure, & agreeable way of recovering the health of our friend, is by indulging her in revisiting her native seat, where the sight & conversation of Parents & friends, tend to dispel the gloom, that so commonly attends, & affects, the heart of the Valetudinarian, if this our plan be agreeable, & it be put in execution, you will be carefull to avoid damps, which are all the evils to be feared, for if fever & other complaints at first insue in consequence of the general concussion they are not to be viewd as ominous, — but the contrary. Time forbids elongation with compts. presented close by subscribing myself Yours with esteem

Elnathan Beach

ADS (VtU). Torn in the center.

From Reuben Atwater

11 Clock P.M. Cheshire the 10th of March AD 1785

Agreed in Counsel this evening that Mr Hull set out tomorrow Morning with his slay & horses with som of the Fammely for to Viset you at westminster on acctent of merabs being so long out of helth that If poseble somthing may be don for her that may prove to be for her Health. Exersise and a continuerd Serres in application is the only Lickly way for her helth soposed now If it be thought best to have her com down to the seeside then No dout it is best before the way of a slay that will soon be don with this <season>, we sopose that she can com to Doc potter now in a slay much better than you can guit the Doctr to Westmstr I have bin to him Doct on purpes to perswade him to go up to you but can not prevail for many reason.

And Due advise if merab continues week but able to ride that she come and see us then shee may be nere to Doct potters I should be glad to Due somthing to procour her helth again if posable if not that shee wait Patiantly on her alotment in world that is all order'd in grate wisdom and can only say it Best to act acording our Best Judgment & then Trust provedence for the avent after Love wish you heven Blessing from your Humble sert

Reuben Atwater

ALS (VtU). Addressed to SRB.

Epitaph for Merab Bradley

[ca. 7 April 1785]

Sacred to
Mrs. Merab Bradley
Consort of Col. Stephen R Bradley
who while living was a delightfull
Friend, a virtuous wife, a most tender
Mother, and pious Christian. Whose
Soul made meet for Glory was
Taken to Immanuel's bosom on the
7th. day of April 1785 in the 28th
year of her Age, And whose Body
now lies in this silent Grave

Oh Death! lament, you've lost your richest prize
No more you'll find so meek so good so wise
If native worth and Piety sincere
And every Christian virtue could endear
If patient suffering more than common pain
A cheerful temper and a mind serene
If these from Deaths relentless stroke could save
Our lovely MCRB had escaped the grave
Yet dead, her fair example is not vain
To life she points and thus she lives again
And gives this best of lessons from the tomb
The good are happy in the world to come

AD (DLC). In an unidentified hand.

Continuation of John Barret Case

The Honorable the General Assembly vrs. John Barret Esquire.

To His Excellency Thomas Chittenden Esq[r.] Capt. Genereal and Commander in chief, and Hon[ble] Council of the State of Vermont, to be convened at Norwich in the County of Windsor on the first Tuesday of June in the year of our Lord 1785, Comes Stephen R. Bradley Esq[r.] Attorney to the Hon[ble] the General Assembly of the State of Vermont, pursuent to the true intent and meaning of a Resolution passed in General Assembly October 16th 1783, authorising and empowering the said Attorney in behalf of the General Assembly to prosecute John Barret Esqr of Springfield in the County of Windsor, one of the Justices of the Peace within and for said County of Windsor, before the Governor and Council to final Judgment for Male Administration, and in behalf of the General Assembly assigns the following facts which the said John Barret Esqr. in the Male Administration of his office as Justice of the Peace has done, viz*t*. For that Whereas the said John Barret Esqr. on the 20th day of May 1781 at said Springfield did Corruptly partially and injuriously render judgment and award Execution against Ozemas Holmes of said Springfield at the suit of Caleb Shaw then late of said Springfield, when the said John Barret Esqr. well knew the said Shaw & Holmes to have settled & to have given orders for the said suit of the said Shaw to be withdrawn, And also for that the said John Barret Esqr. at said Springfield on the 28th day of July 1782 did corruptly and injuriously Issue a Summons against Asahel Powers of said Springfield at the suit of Doctor Frink of Keene, and did afterwards render judgment on a certain accompt contained in a Scadule annexed to the Summons and Taxed a large bill of Costs against said Powers to oppress and injure said Powers, and award Execution thereon, when the Said Powers before the Time of Issuing the said Summons, had before the said JohnBarret Esqr. confessed Judg^t. on the same account, and the said Barret well knew the Same; And also for that whereas the said John Barret Esqr. did Corruptly oppressively and unjuriously on the 20th day of August 1783 at said Springfield, render Judgment and award Execution against Richard Prouty of Brattleborough in the County of Windham at the Suit of John Prouty when the said Barret well knew the said John for three years then last past for rendering said Judgment to have been Dead, And also for that the said John Barret Esqr. thro' the whole course of His Administration as a Justice of the Peace, has excited and encouraged many needless & vexations Law suits to enhance bills of Costs to the oppression of the People, to the great injury of the Common Weal and against the Peace and dignity of the freemen of the State of Vermont.

Signed at Westminster this 3^d day of May 1785.

STEPHEN R. BRADLEY.

Printed. Governor and Council Record, vol. III.

From Russel Atwater

Dear Sir   New Haven May 14th 1785

We Arrived at Cheshire last evening all well and had a verry good journey down Billa is verry well and was verry good on the journey. I saw Mr Bullen after that I left you & he engagd the Continental Money and promisd. to procure it directly from Petersham & give it to you on your paying him therefor at one for two hundred I should be glad of it as soon as you Can send it by safe hands, as for the Cattle the sooner you send them better for you & me as they will fetch a better price and quicker Sale. Pappa has Obligations against the Estate Capt. Atwater to the Amount of £30 — and I Can have them and should be glad to get what you Collect into my hands and, I will settle with the heirs. There was a mistake in the Calculating the money I Sent to you by Pappa to Mr Cone. I wish for the Cattle as soon as is Consistant with you as I shall engage them or thier effects soon.

Your Sincere friend and Humble Servant

Russel Atwater

Collo Stephen R: Bradley

ALS (VtU).

Committee for Quieting Ancient Settlers &c.

In General Assembly, June 7th 1785.

On Motion made by Mr. Bradley, Resolved that a Committee of five to join a Committee from the Council be appointed to prepare a bill for the quieting Ancient Settlers &c. and make Report. The members choosen Mrt. Tichenor, Mr. Chipman, Mr. Knight, Mr. Weld & Mr. Loomis. Extract from the Journals.

Rosl. Hopkins, *Clerk.*

A True Copy. Attest, D. Buck, *Secy. P. T.*

Whereupon Resolved that the Honble Moses Robinson Esqr. & the Honble Ira Allen Esqr. be and they are hereby appointed a Committee to join the Above Committee for the Above purpose.

Adjourned to 2 °Clock p.m.

Account

[ca. 9 August 1785]

Genl. Ethan Allen Dr.

To Stephen R Bradley

		£
June 1779	To Managing a cause at his request for William Steward	2..10.. 0
1781	To managing a cause in equity through a course of Law wherein he was Pl[aintif]f & Levi Allen Def[endant] concerning Land in St. Albens, writing Money paid out for all the suit & for fees	10.. 0.. 0
1783 & 4	To managing a cause before Bennington County Court Money paid out writings Cash paid for service of Writs to Sheriffs &c wherein he & Ira Allen wer[e] Plaintiffs & Levi Allen Defendt. in an action of Covenant broken Fees &c	6..10.. 0
Octr 1783	To boarding at Election time as pr. Bill	3..11.. 4
June 1784	To writing (vizt) two writs & Declerations agt. Colo. Hunt Power of Attorney from Mrs. Wall. Very long Deed, Bond, Deposition of Mrs. Wall &c. &c.	2..10.. 0
June 1784	Journey to Charlestown with Genl. Allen to make Demand &c	1.. 6.. 0
June 1784	Detaining fee in two causes agt. Colo. Hunt	3.. 0.. 0
June 1784	To two Copies one Of Crean Brush's Will the other of the inventory of his landed Estate being long	0..12.. 0
Septr. 18th.	To a Journey to Charlestown to procure Witnesses &c &c	0..18.. 0

Septr. 24th.		
	To a Journey to Bennington & managing two causes agt. Samel. Hunt Esqr. obtaing Judgt. &c &c before County Court	6.. 0.. 0
Septr. 23		
	To cash paid at Bennington to Genl. Allen one half To<?>	2.. 8.. 0
1784		
	March 4th.To cash when at Westminster <34/0?>	1..14.. 0
	Augt. 9th.To a Journey to Charlestown to procure evidence agreeing with West &c	0..12.. 0
		£41..11.. 4

AD (NFtW).

Deed of Sale

[25 August 1785]

To all Men to whom these Presents shall come,   *Greeting.*

𝕶𝖓𝖔𝖜 𝖞𝖊 𝖙𝖍𝖆𝖙 I Ethan Allen of Bennington in the County of Bennington and State of Vermont

For and in consideration of the Sum of Eighty pounds

Lawful Money of the said State of Vermont

to me in Hand paid before the delivery hereof, by Stephen R Bradley of Westminster in the County of Windham and State aforsaid

The Receipt whereof I do hereby acknowledge, have given, granted, bargained, sold and released; and by these Presents do give, grant, bargain, sell, aliene, release, convey and confirm to him the said Stephen R Bradley his

Heirs and Assigns forever, all my Right, Title, Interest, Claim and Demand, of, in, and unto two Certain Lotts of Land Situate Lying & being in said town of Westminster being Lott Number Sixth in the fourth Range of Hundred Acre Lotts as Laid Down in the Plan of Said Town also Lott Number Seven in the Second Range of Hundred Acre Lotts as Laid Down in the Plan of Said Town Reference thereto being Had.

𝕿𝖔 𝖍𝖆𝖛𝖊 𝖆𝖓𝖉 𝖙𝖔 𝖍𝖔𝖑𝖉 𝖙𝖍𝖊 𝖘𝖆𝖎𝖉 𝖌𝖗𝖆𝖓𝖙𝖊𝖉 𝖆𝖓𝖉 𝖇𝖆𝖗𝖌𝖆𝖎𝖓𝖊𝖉 𝕻𝖗𝖊𝖒𝖎𝖘𝖊𝖘 with the Apputenances thereof, to him the said Stephen R Bradley his Heirs and Assigns, to his and their own proper Use, Benefit and Behoof forever: I hereby engaging to warrant and defend the same against the lawful Claims or Demands of any Person or Persons whatsoever.

In witness whereof I have hereunto set my Hand and Seal, this twenty fifth day of August one Thousand seven Hundred and Eighty five.

Signed, Sealed and Delivered,   Ethan Allen
    in the Presence of
Jonathan Robinson
Ben West

THEN *the above named*

personally appearing, acknowledged the above written instrument to be   voluntary Act
and Deed, before me

                                                                Justice of Peace.

DS (NFtW). The document is a printed form, completed in the hand of SRB and signed. SRB's additions are indicated here by underlining. Docketed, "Genll Ethan Allen / Deed to Stephen R Bradley." On the verso is a note dated 1 September 1791: "State of Vermont / Windham <sr?> / Personally appeard Benjamin West Esqr. one of the witnesses to the within deed & made solemn oath that he saw Ethan Allen sign seal & deliver the same & that he the Deponent together with Jonathan Robinson at the same time set their names thereto as written before me / Elijah Paine Judge Supreme Court."

From Ethan Allen

Sir, [Bennington, 7 September 1785]

Mr Haswell is about moving into his new House, and office, and has been so hurried, that I have not been able to procure the Philosophy, he has already printed, so as to send it by this weeks post.[1] I will indeavour to send it you, by the next post. He is now printing the 12th Chapter, treating on the Fundimental Christian Doctrine of imputation, of the Sin of Adam to his posterity, and of the re-imputation of that Cursed Sin, to Jesus Christ, and of his enduring the wrath, and Vindictive displeasure of Almighty God for it. That on the Christian scheme, God was Criminal, Judge, & Executioner, and thus having wrought out an everlasting Righteousness, imputed it to a certain Elect number, of favourites, and doomed the residue of the human race, to Everlasting wo, and perdition, "that he might shew his wrath, and make his power known."[2]

I Fancy Sir, you will be diverted when you read the 12th Chapter, it rips up, and overturns the whole notion of Jockeying, alienating, transferring, or imputing of Sin, or Righteousness, from one person to another, and leaves all mankind accountable, for ther own moral agency. This is fatal to the Ministerial Damnation Salvation, and their merchandize thereof. Mr Salmon, in his Geography,[3] computes the Revenue of the pope, and his Clergy "who are absolutely at his devotion,["] to amount to twenty Millions Sterling pr annum, that he has about two millions, of variously denominated Clergy, "scattered into most countries of the World," who for Christs sake, are trafficking in Original Sin, and in Original Righteousness: probably the Revenue of the Protestent Clergy, may amount nearly half as high, as that of the Romish.

In order to carry on this Priestcraft, the Clergy must invalidate the law of Nature, Reason is represented as Carnal, and depraved, and the natural State, a condition of mankind, to be damnable, to make way for their mysteries, insperations, and pious frauds, and thus most of the Human race, have been miserably Priest-ridden.

To remedy the human species, from this Ghostly Tyranny, (as far as in me lay,) was the Object of my writing, the Oracles of Reason, an Object worthy of Genl. Allen, whatever his success may be. Sir if you will send me, two or three half Johanisses,[4] by the next post, or by any safe conveyance, it would assist me, in publishing my Treatise very much, such a favour would be gratefully acknowledged, by your Friend, and Obedient Humle Sert.

Ethan Allen

Printed copy (*Ethan Allen: Correspondence*, 1:181–82).

1. Anthony Haswell (1756–1816), from Fairfield, Conn., was a printer working with David Russell in Bennington who published Ethan Allen's *Reason the Only Oracle of Man* in 1785 (ibid., 1:168–69 and n. 2, 182 n. 1).
2. Romans 9:22.
3. Thomas Salmon (1679–1767), *A New Geographical and Historical Grammar: Wherein the Geographical Part is Truly Modern; and the Present State of the Several Kingdoms of the World is so Interspersed as to Render the Study of Geography Both Entertaining and Instructive* (10th ed.; London, 1766): "The revenues these Monks draw from the Roman Catholic Countries, do not amount to less than Twenty Millions Sterling *per Annum*" (p. 105) (ibid., 1:182–83 n. 3).
4. A half Johannes was a gold coin worth £3.4.0 in New York currency. One pound York could buy a half pound sterling (ibid., 1:183 n. 4).

From Reuben Atwater

Dear sir   Cheshire Septembr 24th 1785

I am glad of this oppertunity to In form you that we remembr you and that we are all well as I hope these may find you. Bille Cazr is Vary well and happy he is Sary oftn saying that his par is Gon to Hartford with his onkel Reuben but not in the least Troubl'd a bougt that, he sleeps well in his Couch nere our bead side he is much better if not quite well of that sharp youmor & broken out in his blood he is Vary con-tented and we hope that you will Let him stay with us we shall Due as well for him as we know how, whatever that we think best for him; Shall be Vary glad to see you at Connecticut wen you can spare time to Com (or Reubn) to see us.

Please to Wright by all oppertunity that we may here of you well fare and also from Reubn If he is likely to make out well. Dus he attend well to his study.

I sopos you to com or send to Russel this fall then hope to have futhr & better time to say other things. This from your frend & humbl Sert

                                                                                               Reuben Atwater

Mr Stephn R. Bradly
   ALS (VtU).

From C. Harrington

Sir,   Cheshire Decr. 22d. 1785

Mr. Atwater inform's that whereas You expect to be at Cheshire in January next, desired that Mr. Hull and myself would delay coming to Your House untill after that period &c.

Sir I should willingly comply with Your <req>uest was it consistant with my business &c. But <I> have so ordered my Affairs since I agreed to study at Westminster with Yourself, that to delay one Moment after there comes a sufficiency of Snow for Sheying, would be attended with much difficulty on my part.

For I have engaged a sufficient number of Teams to transport from this to Westminster five Hhds Rum & twenty Quintles of Cod fish, & have already paid the greatest part for the transportation of the same, which I must consequently loose incase I should go contra from my said Agreement.

Therefore Sir if nothing interfere's more than what I conceive of at present, I shall the first fair Wind together with Snow — weigh Anchor and set sail for Westminster and proceed by th<e> shortest Route & best Navigation &c.

Sir I hope that You will not suppos<e> that the Care or disposal of the above sd. Articles will in any wise deter or hinder me from paying strict attention to my study while under Your Tuition; for Sir You may depend to the Contrary on forfeiture of the whole of sd. Articles incase of failure. Please to excuse this boldness, And sir You will much Oblige Your humble servant

                                                                                                C. Harrington

Collo. Stephen R. Bradley
   ALS (VtU). Some loss of text at tears and where the seal was removed.

From Ethan Allen

Sir [Bennington, 2 June 1786]

Judgement in favour of Mr. Hudson of Hartford[1] is obtained against me and I expect you will settle the debt with Hudson. The execution is not yet taken out. Mr Smith[2] will delay it a reasonable time for you to settle the matter with Hudson. Since you may better do it with him than drive the Cattle across the mountain, I wholly rely on you to settle the matter in a short time (a few days). I shall advance to the Hostile Ground.[3]

Your Humble Servant

Ethan Allen

Printed copy (*Ethan Allen: Correspondence*, 1:199).
1. Barzilai Hudson of Hartford, Conn., a printer with the house of Hudson and Goodwin, printed SRB's tract, revised by Ira Allen, *Vermont's Appeal to the Candid and Impartial World* in December 1779 and Ethan Allen and Jonas Fay's *Concise Refutation of the Claims of New-Hampshire and Massachusetts-Bay to the Territory of Vermont* in January 1780 (ibid., 1:200 n. 1).
2. Noah Smith, an attorney in Bennington, was, with SRB, one of the first two lawyers admitted to the Vermont bar (ibid., 1:200 n. 2).
3. The Wyoming Valley in Pennsylvania (ibid., 1:200 n. 3).

From Ethan Allen

Sir [21 June 1786]

Several reasons have conspired to procrastinate my returning to Wyoming. My "Only begotten son" has been very sick of the Hooping caugh but past the worst and is recovering fast and secondly Congress have accepted of the session of Connecticut a large territory of lands in their western claim beyond the Sisquehannah purchaise for the use of the united States which virtually terminates the right of soil of the Sisquehannah to belong to the Settlers a favourable Event to me and other adventurers and settlers. Besides Pensylvania have beat up for volunteers since my arrival at Wyoming for the avowed purpose of subjecting us to their government and dispossessing us of the Country, and have failed in the attempt. However I purpose to set out for Wyoming in a few days and wholly confide in your Honour that you will settle the Hartford debt which as I have already wrote you Judgment is obtained against me. Squire Smith has the care of the matter and is desirous to favour me or you as far as he can consistent with his duty as an attorney he tells me however that he expects that you will shortly either settle the debt with Hudson or come and do it with him at Bennington. This I rely on you will do and any trouble you are at in effecting the same I expect to allow you in our settlement pray do not fail me I must go immediately to Sisquehannah.

From your Humle Sert.

Ethan Allen

Printed copy (NHi).

From Ethan Allen

Westminster 25th of July 1786

Sir please to deliver to Mr John Norton[1] Thirty Two pounds Lawful money's worth of neat[2] Cattle, now in the Care of Capt. Ephraim Ranney of this Town and it shall answer to you in the settlement of our accounts and you will Oblige your Humle. Sert.

Ethan Allen

To Colo. Stephen R Bradley
   Westminster

ALS (NFtW). A note in the lower margin reads: "pastered five young Cattle from the 25 of July to the 13 of September." On the verso is SRB to Ephraim Ranney, 12 Sept. 1786. Also on the verso is a docket: "Genll Allen's Receipt—£32:0:0."
1. John Norton owned a tavern in Westminster, which according to one tradition was the site of Ethan Allen's marriage in 1784 to Frances Montresor. Another tradition has the marriage taking place at SRB's house (*Ethan Allen: Correspondence*, 1:218 n. 3).
2. *Neat:* the common domestic bovine.

Ethan Allen to Ira Allen

Sir   Sunderland 18th August 1786

After a tour of three weeks I have returned to this place I caused Colo Bradley to settle the Hudson Execution with Mrs Allen's Estate in his hands Mr Neile has sold his farm to Lawyer Adams who has given him notes on other men to Collect more than three hundred pounds under ten pounds are already sewed or Judgments obtained which come before a single magistrate from which there is no appeal. I am drove almost to death for money. I was at Litchfield when the Superior Court set and saw Lawyer Candfield and Strong Candfield says that Huffman is engaged in a Law suite with a Levingstone and needs his money very much but will stay the Judgment next Septr Court on the receipt of forty pounds and did not know but that would do it for one hundred dollars but not under, I received fifteen dollars of a Mr Lucius Allis of Conway and gave him my receipt for it—to pay to Colo Ebenezer Allen for the taxes on three rights on the Heroes but used the money and sent a letter to Col Allen informing him of it and of the names of the original proprietors of the said rights desiring him at the same time not sell them for the taxes as I would soon pay him the said fifteen dollars, pray look Critically into this matter for Mr Allis gave forty pounds for the three rights and I must make good all dammage to him if they are sold. And as to the three ugly rights, in the Heroes I am obligated to procure for Mr John Kelley of New York do not fail to procure them You will remember I have talked with you on this subject fail me not you must git a good title be the land ever so bad, fail not

The President of Pensylvania has wrote to the Inhabitants of Wyoming to know what quantity of the disputed land they will accept of and comply with the Jurisdiction and Laws of that State and they have sent to me to be there as soon as may be. The Court at Manchester sets the 22nd Instant when my Law suits with Colo Hunt Comes on, soon as they are determined I must go to Wyoming Though I have not a copper of money to save me from the Devil. Wee are rich poor Cursed rascals by G–d alter our measures or we shall be a hiss, a proverb, and a bye word, and derision upon Earth

Your Humle Sert

                                                                                                                    Ethan Allen

Colo Ira Allen
   Colchester
      Onion
         River

Typescript (VtHi). Typescript bears the notation, "Copied by H. W. Denio / From the original in the New York State Library, probably now destroyed."

Ira Allen's Account with the State of Vermont

[10 October 1786]

The state of Vermont

Ira Allen Dr.

1779		
Nov 29	To Continental money Spent in a Journey to Maryland and Attending Congress with J. Fay M. Robinson and S. R. Bradley Esqrs.	922 8
1780		
<M>arch 30	To Cash paid in Albany for one Ream of Good writing paper	94 10
[...] 22	To Cash Expended in a Journey to Newbury &c	216 12
[...]6	To Cash Expended in a Journey to Hartford to buy Powder &c	265 2
[...]6	To Cash paid in Hartford to Nathl Patten for 8 Blank Books 2 Quire of Planning Paper for the use of the State	1227 0
[...]	To Cash paid for 3 Reams of Writing paper for the use of the State	120 0
[...]	To Cash Spent in going to Congress by I. Allen and S. R. Bradley	378 0
[...]2	To Cash Expended in a Journey to Albany	226 12
[...]	To Cash Expended in a Journey to Cambridge	254 0
		£3704 4

Ira Allen

Pay Table Office}
Sunderland Oct 10th 1786} No 146

The Above Account is Approvd and the Treasurer is directed to pay the Contents being Three Thousand Seven Hundred and four Pounds four Shillings Continental Money to Col. Ira Allen

£3704. 4. 0

Timo. Brownson}
Saml. Bartlet}   Committe

ADS (Vt: MsVtSp, vol. 8, p. 217). Torn at left margin.

From Ethan Allen

Sir   Westminster 11th of Octr. 1786

On consulting with Mr Wall[1] it is resolved that we will procure the papers at New York relative to Mr Brush's Estate[2] and not dispose of any more of the Estate till we have the papers. We have furthermore appointed Mr Norton & Micah Townsend Esquire[3] to legally administer on the Estate. We Expect to go on with a suite of Ejectment for the recovery of Westmoreland farm but think it advisable to postpone it till we have Examined the papers.

Your Humle Sert.

Ethan Allen

NB

Part of the lands belonging to Brush's Estate lies in the State of New-York the papers are also there and I cannot attend to the settlement of the Estate. Sisquehanna and my other concerns are plenty for me. I shall rely on your continuing to be our attorney in all matters relative to said Estate we expect to have sundry lawsuites. I am sorry you was not at home as I would have beeen glad to have consulted you on many particulars and determine to be here again next Winter. Mr Norton will consult you in matters of Law.

E A

Col. Bradley

ALS (NFtW).
1. Patrick Wall of Boston married Margaret Schoolcraft Brush, mother of Allen's second wife, Frances Montresor Buchanan, soon after her husband Crean Brush committed suicide in 1778 (*Ethan Allen: Correspondence,* 1:218 n. 1).
2. For Allen's involvement in Crean Brush's estate, see Certification of Purchase, 10 Sept. 1779 (first document), n. 1.
3. Micah Townshend (1749–1832) of Brattleboro, a Princeton graduate and lawyer from White Plains, N.Y., served as Vermont's secretary of state, 1781–88 (ibid., 1:91 n. 2, 218 n. 3).

From Ethan Allen

Sir   Sunderland 19th Jany. 1787

Mr Abel White[1] is now with me says he has meet with misfortune and is going to deliver himself to satisfie the Excecution in my favour and save his bondsman and that if I croud the Excecution he must swear or Damn out of goal but at the same time offers me to deed the same land he bought of me back to me again. When I traded with him he had the character of an honest man and now offers to procure either Mr John Norton Judge Sessions[2] or Capt Gilson[3] all of Westminster to be his bondsman that he has not conveyed the land to any others since I conveyed it to him and I do hereby authorise you to act your best Judgment for me in the premises and do for me as you would for your self were you in my case. Mr. White Intimates that if I will not take land back again he must be obliged to deed it to another Credetor and Cite me to hear him sware out of Goal which he does not want to do.[4] If this is the Case I desire you would git security of some of those gentlemen alread[y] named or of some other good or able man that Mr White has not Conveyed the said land to any person or persons since I deeded it to him and take a deed of the same land in my name. I have received sixteen pounds twelve shillings towards the first note which will likeley pay nearly Your Cost let it answer as it may in Case you Judge it expedient for me to take the land though I had rather have other pay if I could. If you think it best for me to take the land you must describe it a<s> lying in Charlottee in the Count<y of> addison &ce containing the one Eq<u>al half both in quantity and quality of a certain two hundred acres of land whi<ch w>as the first division of the original right of Joseph Ferris No. 21.[5] Sir I desire you would attend the general assembly at Bennington next February for I fear that the Existence of the State will be in danger if wisdom does not preside there.

Your old friend

Ethan Allen

ALS (NFtW). Angle brackets enclose parts of words missing owing to a torn margin and ink blots.
1. Abel White of Rockingham was among the wounded at the Westminster Massacre of 1774 (*Ethan Allen: Correspondence,* 1:224 n. 2).
2. Judge John Sessions was assistant judge of the Windham County court (ibid., 1:224 n. 3).

3. Militia captain Micah Gilson was a resident of Westminster (ibid.).

4. In order to avoid imprisonment for debt, White had offered to pay off his debt to Allen in land rather than the cash that Allen wanted. By threatening to convey his land to an otherwise forgiving creditor, White could compel Allen to testify that White had offered payment in land, thus forcing Allen to accept the land or receive nothing (ibid., 1:224 n. 4).

5. Joseph Ferris lived on Quaker Hill in the Oblong, Duchess County, N.Y., and was an original grantee of land west of the Connecticut River who sold land to the Onion River Land Company, a land speculation venture formed by Ethan Allen with three of his brothers and a cousin (ibid., 1:xxxi, 224 n. 5).

From Thomas Chittenden

Sir   Bennington 2d March 1787 —

Agreeable to your request, I have accepted your resignation of your command of the first Regiment of the Militia of this State; You will therefore call the Regiment to the choice (as the Law directs) of a Colonel to Command the said first Regiment, & such other field officers as may be nec[e]ssary; and make returnes to the secretary of Council that Commissions be given accordingly.

Thos. Chittenden Capt Gnll.

Col. Bradley —

LS (NcD: Bradley Family Papers). Addressed to "Colo. Stephen R. Bradley / Westminster." Docketed by SRB, "From Govr. Chittenden / Excepting Resignation."

From Reuben Atwater

Dear Friend   Monday morning Cheshire May 14th AD 1787

Sir this to be convaid you by my son who is returning to his studies with you in to whos Care I Charfully commit him. Billa Czar your Little son is Now standing by me with expecttation that he shall go with his uncle to see his Par at westminster, and said that he shall come again in 2 or 3 Days for he cannot think of Leaving his Grand mammer, I shall indever to due well by him so long as he remans with us he is a very forward Child and wants vary close attention paid to him now while he is young & voletile not a Judgment to carve for Himself, I hope to see you at Cheshire in June Shall not right on Bis<iness> any thing new at Present but informe you of our well fare that we Injoy hel[t]h have detained Reuben Longer then exspected but hope that it will not damage you he can Inform how we Guit along here with us.

The fammely remember there Love & respects to you & Shall be hope to wait on you when you can come to Connecticut these In hart.

Sir I am with esteem your most obedent and Very Humble Se[r]vent

Reuben Atwater

ALS (VtU). Addressed to SRB at Westminster. There is a small hole in the center of the MS.

Account

Coll. Bradley Account	[3 August 1787]
John Chester Williams vs Edward Smith	£ 0 12. 0
Stephen R Bradly Esqr. vs. Elijah pronty And Thomas Whiple	0.12. 0
Abraham Holland vs Jotham Biglow	0. 8. 4
Roswell Morgan vs David Denison	0.14. 4

Asa Averill vs Mary whiple	0.15. 0
Elkanah Day Esqr vs Moses How And Squire How	0. 8. 8
Stephen R Bradly vs Joseph Eliot And others	0.18. 0
Stephen R Bradly vs Edward & C<?> Carpenter	0.12. 0
Stephen R Bradly Esqr. vs Stephen Chase	0.11. 0
Nathan Stone vs Benjamin Gorton	0. 7. 9
Stephen R Bradly vs Simeon Edwards	0.10. 0
Stephen R Bradly Esqr. vs Simeon Edwards	0.10. 0
Stephen R Bradly Esqr. vs Edward Carpenter	0.11. 0
Thomas Parsot vs Samll. Avery	1. 1. 9
Asa Averil vs Lemuel Ames Execution	0 6. 8
Nathl. Gibson vs John Stearns Execution	0 4 6
<Noahdiah Warner?> vs Edward Smith	0 10. 9
Jonas Fairbanks vs Eleaze Kingsbury	0 12 0
George Eayre vs Gideon Burnham	0 7 8
Benjamin Wait Esqr. vs Benjan. Gorton	0 7 8
Timothy Adams vs. Jesse Hildreth	0 3 4
	11.14. 3
Stephen R Bradly vs David Lamb 12/0	0.12. 0
To attend Court @ Westminster 3 days & half as a Witness the freemen vs. James Walsworth	0.10. 6
To travel to attend Court	0. 5. 0
To Serving a precept on David Woods	1. 0. 0
	14. 2. 9

To 11 dollars for Servin[g] on Coll. Church & others as Constable for the freemen Recd. of Coll. Bradly — 7 Dollars

Received on this Bill One pound fourteen being the Service on Wm. Serjants & others and the Service on David Wood August 3d 1787   Elnathan Allen

Received the Contents of the within Bill Excepting the Service Rosel Morgan vs David Denison of 14/4 the Service Day against the Hows 8/8 Averil vs Ames on Execution 6/8 Gibson vs Stearns 4/6 Fairbanks vs Kingsbury 12/0 Ayer vs Burnum 7/8 Wait vs Gorton of 7/8 which Several Services Excepted Coln Bradley has not Settled the Residue are Settled in full Excepting the Charges as a witness in the Cause against James Walsworth & the Charge against the State for Service against Coln Church & others not Reckoned Elnathan Allen

ALS (NFtW). Docketed, "Col. Bradleys Account" and "Sheriff Allen's Account."

From Ethan Allen

Sir.   Burlington 6th of November 1787

I have lately arrived at my new Farm of 14 hundred acres in one body, in which are three hundred and fifty acres of Choice River Intervale a quantity of swaley and rich upland meadow interspersed with the finest of Wheat land and Pasture land well watered and is by nature equal to any tract of land of the same number of acres that ever I saw. I have about forty acres under improvement. The Country settles fast and I wish that you was well settled in it. Little is said about Philosophy here our "talk is of Bullocks and our glory is in the God,"[1] we mind Earthly things. As to business I never was dissatisfied with your management of my affairs at Westminster but for some reason or other or without any reason Mr. Wall was very urgent to have Mr. Norton to settle Brushes Estate and I hated to have him and Mrs. Wall uneased with me about the matter and as you were from home I acted as I did in the Nomination of Mr. Norton and Esquire Townsend as executors, undoubtedly it was in some respects impolitic in me yet it will give satisfaction to Mr. Wall and his Wife though they have not nor are they at all likely to settle the Estates and consequently the Settlement of it will return to its former channel and with respect to any conjectures respecting your making to yourself any Interest in doing the business it matters not, Wall has blown out in his own scheme and I must confess that was it not for your advice I never should have done any thing about the Estate. Finally it is a business which demands talents to manage it and if there can be any thing made in finishing the Jobb I am willing and expect that you will share liberally with me in it you will see the letter I wrote to Norton and Townsend[2] and then seal it and cause it to be delivered to Norton and consult with Mr Harrington[3] and West[4] my attorneys with you and do any thing and every thing in the premises that may be adjudged best for my interest,

I am Sir with due respect your friend and Humble Servant

Ethan Allen

S. R. Bradley.

AD pp. 423–24).
1. "How can he get wisdom that holdeth the plough, and that glorieth in the goad, that driveth oxen, and is occupied in their labours, and whose talk is of bullocks?" Ecclesiasticus 38:25.
2. Letter not found.
3. William Harrington (1756–1814) served in the Vermont legislature, representing Shelburne, 1789–95, and Burlington, 1798, 1802, 1804, and 1806. He was state's attorney, 1791–96 and 1798–1812, and served on the Governor's Council, 1812–13 (*Ethan Allen: Correspondence*, 1:248 n. 2).
4. Ebenezer West, an Albany attorney and justice of the peace, frequently represented Vermont clients in New York (ibid., 1:250 n. 2).

From Ethan Allen

Burlington 9th of November 1787

I am now consul[t]ing Mr. Harring[ton] relative to my responsibility to the creditors of Brushes Estate he has sundry projections relative to securing me in the premases and though I do not hesitate but the Estate is seven times as much as the debts yet a dead man often times has such accounts brought in against his Estate which Bashfulness would have prevented had he been alive. I shall not Enter into a detail of our speculations on the subject since he can in person better inform you. I desire that among other things you would consult my safety in this matter as well as you can, from your Humble Sert.

Ethan Allen

Col. Bradley

ALS (NFtW).

From Reuben Atwater

Dear Sir   Cheshire April 16 1788

This with the returns of spring & my Son he coms to return to his studies and your Care hoping he may be faithfull to him self and to your buisness, and there by Qualefy him Self for furter Lives he shulds have returnd soner but did not know well to spare him before the spring com on that we could not colect any more money this season but hop at the return of a nother season to have a little more of his assistence in Collecting my money. Bille Czr is well and I shall in dever to School him and take Good Care of him as we can while you are willing to spare him to oure Care I exspect a school mastr this sumer with us and think Bille will Do well abought his book as Reubn can Inform you abought him as well as Other things; and shall be glad to see you when ever you can spare time to pay us a Viset and a quaint each other of all matters that shall be Nedfull, In the sametim subscrib your much Esteemed freind and most Humble sert

Reubn Atwater

Mrs atwater remembers Love to you.
Stephen R Bradly Esqr
ALS (VtU).

From Elnathan Beach

Sir   Cheshire April 16th 1788

If nothing of consequence at this time commands your attention possibly this incoherent prattle of a Friend will not much disrupt.

I hardly expect to amuse much less instruct by any epistulary abilities I am possess'd of but it satisfaction to think this personates the Author & is now enclosed in your friendly Hand.

To enter largely into the discussion of so nice a point as the health & circumstances of your & my Friends is at present needless as Mr. Atwater is competent to that task & will do it at leisure but a recapitulation of the Journey to Vermont a recognition of the pleasing interview with a Friend the Idea of having been one that formd the Jovial circle whose hilarity was encreased by the big mouth bottle and consummated by Arguments demonstrative of Isaac's being Abrahams Son: these are pleasing sensations which he nor any stranger intermeddle with. The revival of those scenes make me almost impatient to revisit the place of there origination: but as that is incompatible at present I smother the Idea lest it kindle into Flame.

Coln. Bradley your multiply'd favour lay me under such Obligation as to require something more than barely an acknowledgement of them: yet as that is all I am able to give by way of compensation please to accept the flimsy reward.

Sr. we flattered ourselves of waiting on you here last winter, but failing of that we still hope to in May or June.

Mrs. Beech fully sensible of your Friendship presents her respects.

Please to remember us to your Friends &c.

I am Dear Sr. with Sentiments of Esteem your Friend & very Humble Servt

Eln. Beech

Coln. Bradley

N B I have sent a very small quanty of different kinds of seed such as I had. I do not deal much in them you will therefore excuse my sending so few.

ALS (VtU).

From Gen. Jonathan Warner

Sir   Hardwick June 17th. 1788

I Conclude you have compleated the Business which Majr: Howe & Myself left with you to Frame out with Mr Wheat of Putney, and have taken Such Security of him as was mentioned you. Mr Wheat Engaged to pay fifty Pounds in the month of June in Pott & Pearlash Deld. at Hardwick, and I was to Load his Teems back with Salt &c, which I have on hand.

Please to press the matter, that he pay the fifty Pounds According to Agreement, as that was the only Inducement for us to wait for <the> Remainder.

<Es>qr Keys is the Bearer of this, who will be a Safe Conveyance for the Securitys you have taken of Mr Wheat in favour of me.

I am Sir with Respect your Friend & Humbl. Servt.

Jona. Warner

ALS (DLC). Addressed to SRB. Damaged by removal of seal.

Contract with Thomas Pearsall

[July 26, 1788]

Know all Men by these presents that we whose names Are under written have agreed between ourselves, that the said under signer Bradley shall sue for and take every legal method to secure to the under signer Pearsall a certain tract of Land in the Township of Reading claimed by said Pearsall of three thousand six hundred & Eightysix Acres, the said suits and prosecutions to be free of all expense to the said Pearsall, and the said Pearsall & his part agrees to convey to the said Bradley One Quarter part of all the land, said Bradley shall save, or recover, or otherwise secure to the said Pearsall.

In whitness whereof the parties have hereunto set their hands & Seals this 26 day of July 1788.
Thomas Pearsall
Stephen R Bradley

Signed Sealed and
deliverd in the
presence of
Elijah Pell
Rudolph Bogert
ADS (VtU).

From Justin Ely

S R Bradley Esqr
Sir   West Springfield 29 Sepr. 1788

Mr Mathews from Claremont in New Hampshire is now with me. He says the Tender Law in New Hampshire is expired as to all Debts, except such as were contracted during the Life of the Tender Law — and also that John West is a man of property with a good Farm and a Stock of Cattle and he thinks can pay the Debt. I beleive General Olcott did not take the Debt of West. I have wrote by Mr Mathews to West that I would take Pot or Pearl Ashes, or Grain, or Salts of Lye of him therefor delivered here and that I had sent to you to take out the Executions thereon — which I wish you to do, if they can be taken out with out a Sine facias or suing the Judgment. I wish the Debt collected as soon as may be and all mine under your Care — Cash will sute me better than any Thing else, but where you cannot get Cash I would take Pot or Pearl Ashes or Salts of Lye delivered here at the going prices here — pay write me a

State of my Affairs and send me what Cash you may have collected for me by Genl Olcott or his Son or some other safe Conveyance and you will oblige

Your hum Sert

Justin Ely

ALS (VtU).

Report on the Petition of Jonathan Hunt

[Petition]

Octr. 20th 1788 —

To the Honorable Legislature of the State of Vermont now Convened

The petition of the Subscriber Humbly sheweth that in consequence of the Grant of a Township in October last, your petitioner has caused the same to be surveyed and Lotted into Severalty, but your petitioner is informed that a Charter is already Issued to Colo. Allen of the same Tract of Land which may cause future Embarrassment & Terminate in the loss of sd. Township, your petitioner has Complied on his part in the payment of about £170 in <solid?> coin, & is now ready to Nearly compleat the payment in case the premises can be rendered free of Incumberence your petitioner, unwilling to be involved in Law Suits, prays your honors to cause enquiry to be made & in case sd. Land has been Chartered in an unconstitutional manner to render it null & void by a Sovereign act, to prevent the preplexity of a suit at Law, or take such other measures as your wisdom shall direct, your Petitioner Would further Suggest to your honors that, in this sd. Township there is a Large Pond which Covers about 1,200, acres Together with Large Swamps unsuitable for Cultivation & is not so Generally Good as was Immagined at the time of perfixing the Granting fees, your petitioner would suggest to Your honors the Propriety of Lessing the fees of sd. Township for the above Reasons, Together with the Extreeme difficulty of Obtaining hard money — & on acct. of the fees being much higher than Lands of the Same Quality & Situation has heretofore been Granted for

Humbly Submitted by —

Jonathan Hunt

[First Report]

The Committee to whom was Refered the within Petition to wait on his Excellency & inquire whether any Charter had Issued Signed by His Excellency under the Seal of this State of the premises therein mentioned beg leave to Report that his Excellency Gave for Answer that he did without advice of Council in October 1786 a Day or two before the Genll Assembly Sat at Rutland in pursuance of a flying Grant that had been made to one <Woodleridge?> which was forfeited make out and Sign in a private manner to Ira Allen Esqr. a Charter which for Aught he knows Covers Some of the premises that he did at that time take a Large bond of sd Allen to indemnify him & the Reason which he principle Gave for Doing it was the fear that the state would wrong[1] sd Allen in his Capacity as a Surveyor General that when the Question was Asked his Excellency whether sd Charter was <Cleared?> or not he answered he did not know — that in the Oppinion of Your Committee his Excellency has violated the Trust reposed in him by the Constitution to keep the public Seal of this State Sacred and has Converted it to private Sinister Views and Submit to the House what Orders Shall be taken and that in the Opinion of your committee said Charter was fradulent and Ought to be Declared Null & void by Act of Legislation.

In Assembly 23d Oct 1788 Stephen R Bradley
Read & accepted [*illegible*] Marvin
    attest Stepn Jacob, Clerk Phinehas Freeman

[Second Report]

The Committee to whom was Refered the Within Petitition [*sic*] to take into Consideration the Granting Fees as heretofore assessed Report that in their oppinion thro' mistake of the Quality of the Land in sd Township the Granting Fees were set too high and that instead of Ten pounds for Every three Hundred & thirty Acres which was heretofore assessed sd Hunt & Associates pay Only Nine pounds for Every three Hundred & thirty Acres.

24th Oct 1788 In Assembly Bradley for Committee

read & accepted

attest Stephen Jacob Clerk

    ADS (Vt: MsVtSP, vol. 18, p. 71). Both reports in the hand of SRB, written on the verso of the petition along with two dockets. The first docket reads: "The petition of / Jna. Hunt / Filed Octr. 23d. 1788. / In Assembly 23rd Ocr. 1788 / Read & refered to Messrs Bradley, Marvin & Freeman to Enquire of his Excellency whether he has issued a Charter under his hand & the Seal of this State, to any other person, of the Lands within mentioned. / Attest S. Jacob, Clerk." The second docket reads: "In Assembly 23rd Octr. 1788 / The report of Committee read accepted & Col. Bradley J. Smith Esqe & Mr. Freeman appointed to Draw a bill agreeable to the recommendation of sd Committee & to take under Consideration the other part of [*illegible*] Hunts Petition & report to this house / Attest Stephen Jacobs, Clerk
    1. Bradley originally wrote "Cheat," then crossed through it and interlined "wrong."

Report on the Petition of Ozias Clark

[Petition]

Manchester Octr. 22d 1788

To the Honorable General Asseml. of the State of Vermont now siting at Manchester in said State

The petition of Ozias Clark of Pawlet in the County of Rutland and State aforesaid Administrator on the Estate of Capt. Elisha Clark late of Orwell in the County of Rutland aforesaid Deceased humbly sheweth that the said Elisha Clark in the month of August in the year 1784 did bargain and sell to Smith Clark of said Orwell one hundred acres of land in said Orwell being a second Division Lot on the Original right of Paul <Macheaus?> that the said Smith Clark in consequence of said Bargain went into possession of said land and hath continued to possess occupy and improve the same ever since That the said Smith Did pay to said Elisha the full sum agreed on for said land agreeable to contract, that the said Elisha was always willing to Execute a Deed of said land but through a hurry of business it was neglected Your petitioner therefore prays your honors to pass an act enabling your petitioner to Execute a Deed of said land to the said Smith Clark as fully and as amply as the said Elisha in his lifetime would have Done and Your Petitioner as in Duty bound shall ever pray

Ozias Clark

[Report]

The Committee to whom was Refered the within petition Report that the prayer of the petition be Granted upon this Express Condition that the judge of Probate in the District where the Land Lies be Ascertained that the Sum was paid which was Contracted to be paid to the Deceased in his life time or in Case the Whole has not been paid that the Judge See to it that the Sum which Remains Due with Interest be made Secure to the Heirs and that the petitioner has Leave to bring in a Bill on these Conditions

Accordingly

Bradley for Committee

ADS (Vt: MsVtSP, vol. 18, p. 76). Report in the hand of SRB, written on the verso of the petition along with a docket: "Ozias Clark admr. on the estate of Elisha Clark / Petition —/ filed Octr. 22d. 1788 / attest Rosl. Hopkins Secy / In Assembly 22nd. Octr. 1788 — Read & refered to Messrs Paine, Bradley & J. Smith / attest Stephen Jacob, Clerk."

From Ethan Allen

Sir   November the 12th 1788

Mr Harrington the bearer of this informs me that Mr Norton and you have bid of at Vendue those lands in Westminster &ce the property of the Heirs of Crean Brush deceased[1] for them it is time you was repaid I conclude the time of redemption is nearly out but I am not concerned about either of you taking advantage of it. I shall be at your House next winter and pay you the money interest &ce you paid at the Vandue for the lands and consult you farther on the subject of that Estate.

Your Hume. Sert.

Ethan Allen

ALS (NFtW). Addressee not indicated.
1. For Crean Brush's estate, see Certification of Purchase, 10 Sept. 1779 (first document), n. 1. Brush's widow, her husband Patrick Wall, and Fanny and Ethan Allen attempted to gain some value from Brush's estate by redeeming at tax vendues and then selling lands Brush had acquired in Westminster by New York grants, but the problem of conflicting New York and New Hampshire titles prevented them from making any great profit (*Ethan Allen: Correspondence*, 1:248 n. 2).

Record of Judgments by SRB as Judge of the Superior Court

[13 November 1788–25 July 1789]

The Within Book contains the Record of Judgments rendered before Stephen R Bradley Esqr while Judge of the Superior Court in 1788 and 1789.

Judgments Rendered by me as Judge of the Superior Court beginning Novr 13th 1788
New Fane ss Windham County Novr. 13 1788

Personally appeared before me John Rickee of   in the County of Rutland and Confessed Judgment on a Note to Jonathan Fuller of Rockingham in the County of Windham for the Sum of forty pounds as pr Note on file.

Execution Issued Novr 13th 1788   Coram Stephen R Bradley Judge

John Rickee   The Defendant personally appeared and Confessed Judgment to said
vs   }   John Rickee on a Note for the Sum of forty pounds as per Note on file.
Jonathan Fuller

Exect. Issued Novr 13th 1788

Fees not paid

paid

Shubal Geere   The Defendant personally appeared & Confessed Judgment to the
vs   }   Plaintiff on a Note for four pounds thirteen Shillings & two pence
Thomas Chandler   Debt & one Shilling Cost as per Note on file Novr 29th 1788.

Execution to bee stayed 1 Month

paid on this Judt by Major Chandler   Received in full

£3: 6: 8   Coram Stephen R Bradley Judge
             the Above Judgment paid & Discharg

Benjamin West Esqr. vs James Richardson	The Defendant personally appeared & Confessed Judgment to the Plaintiff on a Note for twenty four Shillings & three pence Debt & Six Shillings & Nine pence Cost as per Note on File Novr 26 1788.

Mr West Receipted three Bushels I Receipted three bushels for Debt of Wheat Boy worked out Cost

           Coram Stephen R Bradley Judge

Elias Olcott vs Timothy Parker	Note taken back by Nathan Thuston

Peter Wright vs Joseph Underwood	The Defendant personally appeared & Confessed Judgment to the Plaintiff on a Judgment obtained in the Superior court in New Hampshire for four pounds Eighteen & two pence Debt and one pound 10/8 Cost as pr Judt on

File by Copy Decr 22d 1788.

           Coram Stephen R Bradley Judge

Thomas Craige & Heny Pomeroy vs Joshua Wells	The Defendant appeared and Confessed Judgment to the Plaintiff for four pounds Ten & Nine pence Debt & Eleven Shillings & Eight pence Cost on a Note on File Decr 22d 1788.

Execution Issued Decr 22d 1788

           Coram Stephen R Bradley Judge

John Lane vs Joseph Bullen	At a Justices Court Holden at Westminster in the County of Windham on the 4th Day of Febr. 1789. present Stephen R Bradley Just <Davis?>

The Plaintiff appeared by his Atty and the Defendant in person the Plaintiff Demanded four pounds on Back Accounts Due the Court having heard the parties and the Evidence adduced tis Considered by the Court that the Plaintiff recover against the Defend £1: 19: 0 Damage & no Cost to be taxed to Either party.

Isaac Wesson vs Ebenezar Holtontis	At a Justices Court Holden on the 1st of June at Westminster the Pltf appeared but the Defendant tho thrice Called appeared not, whereupon Considered by the Court that the Pltf Recover of the Defend £1: 9:3 Damage and his Cost Taxed at £0: 7: 7.

to be paid in Wheat Rye or Indian Corn

Execution Issued June 30th 1789

Isaac Wesson vs Timothy Parker	At a Justices Court Holden at Westminster on the 1st Day of June 1789 the Plaintiff appear'd and the Defendant tho thrice Called appear'd not whereupon tis Considered by the Court that the Pltf Recover of the Defendant £0: 6: 0 Damage & Cost Taxed at £0: 12: 7.

Wheat

Execution Issued June 1st 1789

Lot Hall Esqr. vs Salmon Dutton and	At a Justices Court Holden at Westminster on the 1st Day of June 1789 the Pltf appeared but the Defendants tho thrice Called appeared not whereupon tis Considered by the Court that the Pltf recover of the

John Coffen   Defendants his Just Damage assessed at £5: 1: 3: and Cost Tax at £0: 15: 6.

Cash

Exct Issued June 1 1789

LH 3/0 paid

Lot Hall Esqr.   At a Justices Court Holden at Westminster on the first Day of June
   vs   } 1789 the Pltf appeared but the Defendant tho thrice Called appeared
Consider Orentt   Not whereupon tis Considered by the Court that the Pltf recover of
                            the Defendant his Just Damage assessed at £0: 18: 0 and his Cost
                            Taxd at £0: 13: 2.

Execution paid in Maple Sugar Delivered at sd Halls

Issued June 1 1789 and Renewed to Octor 24th 1789

L. H 3/0 paid

Joshua Webb Esqr.   At a Justices Court Holden on the 20th Day of May 1789 the parties
   vs   } being present the Cause was adjourned to the 21st Day of May 1789
                            at Nathan Thuston 9 oClock forenoon at which time the Pltf.
                            appear'd but the Defendant tho three times Solemnly Called
                            appeared Not whereupon tis Considered by the Court that the Pltf
                            recover his Just Damages assessed at £2: 2: 4 and his Cost Taxed at
                            £0: 14: 8.

Execution Issued 20th of May 1789

Lot Hall Esqr   At a Justices Court Holden on the 20th Day of May 1789 the Pltf
   vs   } appeared but the Defendant tho thrice Called appeard not where-
                            upon Davis & Levi Locklintis Considered by the Court that the Pltf
                            Recover his Just Damage assessed at £3: 13: 1 and his Cost Taxed at
                            £0: 10: 4.

Execution to be paid in Neat Stock Delivered at the Pltfs in Westminster

Issued 20th May 1789

LH 3/0 paid

Isaac Wesson   At a Justice's Court Holden on the 16th Day of May 1789 before
   vs   } Stephen R Bradley Justice of the Peace the Plaintiff being called
James Bundy   appeared the Defendant tho' thrice Called appeared not whereupon
                            tis Considered by the Court that the Plaintiff Recover his Just
                            Damages against the Defendant assessed at £0: 16: 2 and his Cost
                            Taxed at £0: 7: 1.

Isaac Wesson   At a Justices Court Holden on the 16th Day of May 1789 before
   vs   } Stephen R Bradley Just Peace the Parties being Called appeared &
Daniel <Shepth?>   went to tryal after Due Consideration tis Considered by the Court
                            that the Plaintiff Recover of the Defendt his Damages assessed at
                            £0: 5: 5: 3 & his Cost Taxed at £0: 8: 11.

Execution Issued May 16th 1789

Renewed to the 16th October

Elkanah Day   In an Action on the Case the Parties appeared.
   vs   } The action adjournd to the 16th Day of March Next at 2 o'Clock
Reuben Jones   afternoon at this place.
                            Settled & Discontinued

Elkanah Day vs Nicholas Smith	At a Court Holden the 23d Day of February 1789 the Pltf appeared & the Defendant tho' thrice Called appeared Not whereupon tis Considered by the Court that the Plaintiff Recover of the Defendant £1: 3: 7 Damage & his Cost Taxed at £0: 11: 9 HM. paid & Satisfied in full by said Smith April 6th 1789 P[er] Elkanah Day
Shubal Geer vs Elkanah Day	At a Justices Court Holden on the 9th Day of March 1789 the Plaintiff appeared. Settled & Discontinued
Nathan Fisk vs Jonathan Fuller	At a Justices Court Holden the 20th Day of April 1789 before Stephen R Bradley Justice of the Peace the Pltf being Called appeared the Defendant tho thrice Called appeared not whereupon the Court Consider that the Pltf Recover his Just Damages against the Defendt assessed at £7: 12: 2 and his Cost Taxed at £0: 7: 5.

Exeut Issued 20th April 1789

Jonathan Fuller vs Elkanah Day	At a Justices Court Holden the 27th of April 1789 before Stephen R Bradley Justice of the peace the Plaintiff being Called appeared the Defendt tho' thrice Called appeared not whereupon tis Considered by the Court that the Plaintiff recover his Just Damages assessed at £4: 19: 7 & his Cost Taxed at £0: 9: 7.

Execution Issued 27th of April 1789

Isaac Wesson vs Ebenezar Holton	At a Justices Court Holden the 16 of May 1789 before Stephen R Bradley Justice of the Peace the parties being Called appeared and on Motion of Defndt tis Considered by the Court that the Pltf Writ abate & the Defendant be <assesd> his Cost Taxed at 2/3 which the Pltf paid him in Court.
Edward R Campbell vs Enos Lovell	At a Justices Court Holden at Westminster the 1st Day of June 1789 the Pltf appeared but the Defendant tho thrice Called appear'd not whereupon tis Considered by the Court that the Pltf Recover of the Defendt £2: 1: 7 and his Cost Tax at £0: 9: 4.

Cash

Exct Issued June 1 1789

LH 3/0 paid

Freeman vs <Eliub?> Burk	July 25 adjourned to the 23d Day of Sept at 1 oClock afternoon

AD (VtU).

From Thomas Pearsall

Respected Friend Newyork 10th April 1789

I have received a Letter from Hilkiah Grout of Weathersfield, informing me that his Son is ejected off of Lot No 12 in that Township by the Town, as it was laid out under the New-

Hampshire Grant for a School. As he purchased this Lot of me, he has wrote to have my Opinion of the Matter; I have by this Conveyance referred him to thee for thy Opinion — & shall be glad thou wilt give it to him; & also to defend the Case if adviseable. I expect almost all the Rights in Weathersfield, were purchased by the Petitioners for a Grant under New York, & when this Grant was made by Newyork, I expected that vacated or disannulled the former Grant. If the Town is disposed to settle this Matter by Compromise & are willing to accept a part, perhaps that Mode will be most advisable, I should prefer it, as I would much rather assist a School in that Town than discourage one. If this Case should be determined by Law & go against me, shall I be obliged to pay more than the purchase Money & costs of Suit? Must I also pay for Improvements? Thy Answer when convenient will much oblige thy Friend

Thomas Pearsall

Stephen R Bradley
    ALS (VtU).

From William Page

Dear Sir   Charlestown May 1st. 1789

    Mr. Brooks of Haverhill desired me to send you the inclosed letter and receive your answer, which you will please to give the bearer.

    You doubtless remember of once calling on me for a Sword, you then was in pursute of honor and *Cash*, I think <...> to *cut slay* and *destroy* the Yorkers, <...> having Accomplished all this and having Not only changed your *manner* and *mode* of *Attack* but your *weapon also*— you will please to send me the sword by the bearer, for as all other *weapons* fail me it is time I take *Sword*.

    I am Sir your most Obet Set

W Page

Honble Stephen R Bradley Esquire
    ALS (DLC). Damaged by removal of seal. Cover addressed by Page, "Honble Stephen R Bradley Esquire / Westminster / Vermont." Docketed "From Doct Page," and "William Page." Enclosure not identified.

From Thomas Pearsall

Respected Friend   Newyork 29th June 1789

    I now deliver to thee Miles Johnsons Deed to me for 900 Acres of Land in Windsor, which request may be recorded. I sold him this Land a few years past, please to examine if it is clear of Incumbrance, which I have not the least doubt of.

    I also inclose thee twenty papers being copies of Deeds Quit Claims and Surveys and is a conveyance of 5200 Acres of Land in Ludlow which I purchased of Miles Johnson at 4/ Per Acre is £1040 — york. I wish thee to examine the Titles & get the best information thou canst of the quality & value of the Land as I apprehend, I have given too much for it; if so I will endeavor to get him to release me if possible and will then take Lands in Wallingford: If thou could find out the value of his Forge and quality of Lands in Wallingford I should be glad. I wish thee to make the necessary enquiry respecting the Lands in Ludlow & write me as soon as possible and send the Original and copy to Hartford, by different conveyances & order them forwarded by Post — and also those in Wallingford. I also deliver thee a mortguage from Wm. Ward for about 140 Acres of Land in New Fane, for four hundred & forty five pounds 6/8 Newyork currency dated 17 August. 1784 on which no payment has been made, I request thee to take possession of this Land as soon as thou can and rent it out to a Tenant who will pay. I also deliver thee Luke Knoultons mortgage for about 170 Acres of Land in Newfane for £400 Newyork cy — dated 17 Augst 1784. As there has been no payment made on this I wish to have further Security by mortgage unless he should make a payment in three, or four months. If agreeable to thy judgment, I wish him to purchase the Widows Dower of Daniel Whipples Farm if it can be had at One hundred pounds Newyork currency.

I know not what to write thee concerning the Chaffee Lot in Westminster. Samuel Avery ought to pay rent immediately, or give possession, but I wish to have possession at all events next Spring. I also wish thee to press paymt. of the mortgage from Stone, as I want the money much pot ashes are worth £42 paper money pearl ashes £48 P[er] Ton and is good payment — paper money is about 2 P[er] C[ent] worse than Specie at this time. Inclosed is a List of sundry Debts owing to me in Weathersfield, I wish thee to press them to make me payment in Newyork in pot or pearl ashes or any other Articles that will bring the money — and whatever Sum thou canst get paid in this way I will chearfully Agree to allow thee two & half P[er] Cent.

I am with respect thy Friend

Thomas Pearsall

Stephen R Bradley Esqr
   ALS (VtU).

From Mrs. Ennis Graham

[ca. 22 July 1789]

Mrs. Graham Respectful Compliments to Col: Bradley begs he will deliver the inclosed Bond to Lewis Morriss Esqr Vermont — taking his Receipt for the same.

   AL (DLC). A note in the lower margin reads: "Springfield 22d. July 1789 — Received from the Honble. Colonel Bradley a Bond dated the twenty fifth day of Feby. Anno Domini seventeen hundred & seventy four given by John Church to Ennis Graham and conditioned for the payment of Forty seven pounds, thirteen shillings & ten pence NYork Currency — Witnessed by John Kelly, and Crean Brush. / LR Morris." Docketed, "Coln Morriss' Receipt for a Bond vs John Churches Estate."

Account

[ante 24 October 1789]

The State of Vermont
        To Stephen R Bradley

June 1786   To a Journey to Randolph as a Member of the Committee to fin<ding a p>lace for the College appointed by the House of Representatives Eight Days B<earing?> my own Expences at s10/ pr Day
        £4: 0: 0

Stephen R Bradley

Pay Table Office   Westminster [...] 1789

Examined and passed the Above <acco>unt of four pounds and the Treasurer is hereby Directed to pay sd. four pounds to Stephen R Bradley Esqr. or his order.

Elijah Pa[...] {Comtt. of
Phinehas Fr[...] {Pay Table

£4. 0. 0

Octr. 24 1789 Re[ceive]d in full Stephen R Bradley

ADS (DLC). Text obscured by repairs made along a fold.

Resolution of the State of Vermont

[27 October 1789]

On a Message from the House requesting the Governor and Council to join the House in Grand Committee to consult the propriety of choosing Agents to Congress. The Committee having met, they Resolved to appoint three Agents. The Ballots being taken, the Honble Isaac Tichenor, Esqr. Stephen R. Bradley & Elijah Paine Esqrs. were declared to be duly chosen.

Printed (Governor and Council Record, vol. 3).

From Lewis R. Morris

Sir, Springfield 10th Novr. 1789 —

When we were at Woodstock, I supposed that I had among my papers a copy of an Act of the Legislature of the State of New York appointing Commissioners to treat with the State of Vermont — but upon examination I can only find a Letter from those Commissioners to <Go>vernor Chittenden, which I do myself the honor to enclose — and am with great Respect & Esteem your most obedt. hum servt

LR Morris

ALS (Vt: MsVtSP, vol. 24, p. 31). Angle brackets enclose letters missing owing to a tear. Cover addressed by Morris, "The Honble. Stephen R Bradley Esqre. / Westminster." Docketed, "from Lewis R. Morris / Papers altogether." Enclosure not found.

Lewis Morris

From Charles Marsh

Sir Hartford 23rd. Nov. 1789

The business of this letter, I hope, will be deemed an apology for the interruption. It comes to introduce to your acquaintance Mr Mason, a young Gentleman of distinguished abilities & equally distinguished acquirements— He is desirous of getting into the practice of law in this state & for that purpose expects to go through a regular clerkship therein, in some office where he can have good opportunities for the acquisition of legal knowledge — I have taken the liberty to recommend yours to my friend (from its general reputation) as being one of that description and beg leave to assure you that Mr Mason's character among his acquaintance is such as to induce an universal belief, that he will do honour to the office where he is instructed and honour to the profession of law.

I have the honour to be, Sir, your very humble servant

Charles Mar<sh>

Hon. Stephen R. Bradley Esquire.

ALS (DLC). Docketed by SRB, "Charles Marsh."

Receipt from Brent Willard

[11 December 1789]

Received Decr. 11th 1789 of Stephen R Bradley a Black and white Cow — to winter for her milk and to return to Said Bradley in the Spring when he Calls for her.

Brent Willard

DS (DLC). In the hand of SRB.

From Simeon Baldwin

Sir   New Haven Decr. 26th. 1789

As Mr Mason the bearer of this informs me, he expects to pursue his Studies in your Office, it is with Pleasure I can recommend him to your Confidence & favours as a Gentleman of amiable Manners — a good Scholar — & much esteemed by his Acquaintance. During the time he was in my Office, he was very attentive to the Study of Law — his proficiency it will better become you to judge of than me — As I <nev>er had the Happiness of a personal acquaintance with you — I can claim nothing in his favour on the ground of friendship — yet I doubt not his merit will insure to him your Friendship & Patronage —

I have the Honour to be your most Obedient & very humble Sert.

Simeon Baldwin.

The Hon. Stephen R. Bradley —

ALS (NcD: Bradley Family Papers). Damaged by removal of seal. Cover addressed to "The Hon. Stephen R. Bradly, / Westminster / Vermont / Pr Mr Mason" and docketed by SRB, "From Mr Baldwin."

List of Lands Owned by SRB

[ca. 1790]

The following is a List of the lands owned by General Bradley.

In Granby

15 rights of 320 acres each originally granted to

Medad Dudley	320	Thomas Rice	320
John Stephens	320	Samuel L. Bradle	320
John Thompson	320	Abraham Kimball	320
Daniel Warner esqr	320	James Drake	320
Nathl. Chauncey esqr	320	Joseph Bartholomew	320
Philemon Johnson	320	Jonathan Barker	320
Jacob Parker	320	Timothy Barker	320
Dedimus Parker	320		

also 9 rights originally granted to}

Joshua Ray	320	Hezekiah Hamblet	320
Joshua Couleler	320	John Phillips	320
Jesse Parker	320	Ebenezer Haithorne	320
Samuel Ives	320	Stephen Andrews	
John Willoughby	320		

also 3 rights of which the original Proprietors were}

Samuel Whittlesey	320			
Jonathan Marks	320			
Daniel Hubbard	<u>320</u>			
	8320			

Also   12 rights originally granted to}   Ac[re]s

Abel Hall	320	David Hubbard	320
Andrew Parker	320	Thomas Howell	320
Gamaliel Parker	320	Joseph Atkins	320
Isaac Parker	320	Oliver Dudley	320
John Hall	320	Ebenezer Ball	320
Joshua Ray junr	320	Nathanl Merrill	320

Also   2 rights of which the Original Proprietors were}

Charles Whittlesey	320
Benjamin Hall <2d>	320

Also   from the rights of

Elihu Hall	200
Samuel Mansfield	135
Samuel Baker	320
James Blanchard	231
Elihu Hall	130
&	

undivided land bot. of Col Robt Johnson Sheriff of Orange County}

500

Also   2 rights in Orange County originally granted to

Theophilus Doolittle	320
Chauncey Whittlesey	320

<u>In Brunswick</u> from the rights of

Benjamin Seley	208	James Barns	200
William Barns	208	Read Ferris	200
Stephen Barns	208	Nathl Sherborn	200
George Stillman	208	Elijah Hubble	208
John Bostwick	200	David Calhoon	208
Jonah Camp	208		

2d & 3d division of

Zadock Clark	200

& from the right of

William Kennedy	208
Joseph Calhoon	208
Morgan Noble	208
Seth Kent	208

<u>In Minehead</u>

Of Lands purchased of Robert Johnson Sheriff as will appear by the records of sd. County}

770

also from the right of

John Marsh	331

Heth Garlick	331
Joseph Davis	331
James Calhoon	331

<u>In Averill</u>

The whole of the original rights granted to

Samuel Barlow
James Barlow
Oliver Sanford
Reuben Booth

and of the rights of

Richard Hayson	300
Theodorus Bray	300
John Temple esqr	60
John Downing esqr	49
John Sanford	291

Also the rights the original proprietors of which were

Seth Sanford	360
Stephen Gould	360
Seth Samuel Sanford	360
Ebenezer Green	360
Thomas Reed	360
James Hall	360
James Barlow	360

<u>In Maidstone</u>

of the rights of

Thomas Latten	250
Edmund Leavenworth	220} from the 2d & 3d
Thomas French	220} divisions of sd.
Benja. Booth	220} rights in said
Gideon Wheeler	220} Town
Samuel Averill	100} in sd. 2d.
Seth Crane	140} Division
James Calhoon	40

Thos. Wooster; Jonathan Judson[;] Luke Summers; Henry Custis & Elnathan Lake }
                80 acres each

<u>In Guildhall</u>

from the rights of

Edmund Ward	250
Elihu Hall Junr	100 3d Division
Saml Sharp Bedle	100 Do.
John McClave	200
John Hall 5th	100 acres No 5 <range 13th>
	<½ of> No 7 <range> 3d
John Moss	100 in the 3d division

<u>In Eden</u>

5 rights of which original proprietors were

Samuel Safford	360
Joseph Barber	360
Joseph Hunnewell	360
John Knickerbacor	360
William Mead	360

<u>In Fayston</u>
5 rights of which original proprietors were

Abel Prescott	360
William H Kinsman	360
Thomas Ashley	360
James Fletcher	360
Ebenezer Cobb	360

<u>In Elmore</u>
2 rights of which original proprietors were

Elisha Perkins	360
Erastus Sargeant	360

In Waitsfield
6 rights of which original proprietors were

Stephen Jacob	360
Roger Enos Junr	360
George Dennison	360
Pascal P. Enos	360
Stephen Keyes	360
James Hawley	360

& of the rights of

Roger Enos	210 Lot No 132 excepted
Beriah Green	210 Lot No 119 excepted
<Roodiah> Biscale	210 Lot No 107 excepted
Denming Spears	210 Lot No 210 escepted
Ephraim Smith	210 Lot No 135 escepted
Eli Willard	210 Lot No 122 excepted

In Concord
1 right of which the original propritor was

Simeon Ellis	360

In Walden
The 2 original rights of

Nathan Fawcett	360
Thomas Lindsey	360

In Littleton
1 original right of

Charles Grant	360

<u>In Burke</u>
part of the original right of

Jacob Hinsdale	90

<u>In Pocock</u> (alias Bristol)

a right of
Samuel Willis   270

<u>In Goshen</u>
The 4 original rights of
Orlando Bridgeman   360
Abraham Lansing   360
Abel Stone   360
Ebenezer Pitcher   360
also part of the right of
John Cole   175

<u>In Kingston</u>
5 rights of which the original proprietors were
Justice Mitchell   360
Ebenezer Right   360
Thomas Bliss   360
John Hubbard Junr   360
Asaph Sheldon   360

AD (VtHi). Docketed, " Genl. Bradleys List of Lands."

Vermont Commissioners to New York Commissioners

NEW YORK, No. 151 Water Street, Feby. 9, 1790.

To the Honble. the Commissioners of the State of New York.

Gentlemen:—In pursuance of an act of the State of Vermont, passed the 23d October 1789, which we had the honor to communicate in November last, and in consequence of your letter to us of the 21st December, we have arrived in this city, and are ready to receive any communications from you on the subject of our appointment. With sentiments of esteem we are your obedient and very humble servants.

ISAAC TICHENOR,
STEPHEN R. BRADLEY,
NATHL. CHIPMAN,
ELIJAH PAINE,
STEPHEN JACOB.

Printed (Governor and Council Record, vol. 3).

Moses Robinson to Samuel Mattocks

Sir,   Bennington April 23d 1790

Please to pay Stephen R Bradley Esqr Ten pounds in hard money it being for the Expence he has paid more than he Recevd. in his Journey to New york as Commissioners on the part of this State to Treat with Commissioners appointed by the State of New york Respecting the Boundary line &c—from your Humble Servant

Moses Robinson Govr.

To Saml Mattocks Esquire Treasurer
£10..0.—

ADS (Vt: MsVtSP, vol. 10, p. 336).

From Thomas Pearsall

Respected Friend   New York 31st July 1790

    I received thy Letter of the 8th. Instant by Verplank and note the Contents, but as thou does not acknowledge receipt of the Letter I wrote thee per Col: Morris which I forwarded sometime before the one I wrote ⅌ Judge Knoulton in which Letter I inclosed two of Silas Roy's Notes I think for one hundred dollars each I hope they are not lost. I note that Knoulton had informed thee that I had no objections to allow him three hundred Dollars for the Widow's thirds in the Whipple Farm, in answer thereto I may inform thee that I told him I had no objections to allow what thou thought the Value or something to that purpose as I did not mean to counteract thee in this matter but I know nothing of the Value, and did not mean to fix any price. I expect this contract must be finished with him before the other contracts, as it is necessary I should have a full Title to this Land. I have made particular enquiry about the patentees Deeds of Weathersfield made to General David Wooster mentioned by thee which I heard of at Newhaven in the hands of David Daggett who has brought it here for my inspection, I find it recorded in Weathersfield in the State of Vermont in Lib: 1 Fol 456 by Gershom Clark Town Clark 25 August 1786 I will thank thee to have the Records examined immediately And write me that I may send thee an Authenticated copy if necessary as I am not certain I can get the original Sent to Vermont. I now inclose thee Copy of Miles Johnsons receipt which is now in my hands I expect these Deeds were put into Elijah Robinsons hands to transact I believe I have never received any Notes or any Money or any Notes on these Lands of Miles Johnsons or Elijah Robinson that I can find entered I therefore wish thee to call on E Robinson and get a particular Account of him if thou cantst and collect all the money or produce of him thou canst for Debts owing to me. I settled with M Johnson for £36 Lawful money he received of O Kidder. I dont know nor have not entered £16: 13: 8 received of him on Butters Notes I think it is very probable my affairs in the State of Vermont may not wear a favourable Aspect But I intend to make the best of them I can and Shall be glad of thy assistance and now enclose thee my power of attorney for that purpose, and State of the Notes. I wish thee to collect all the Pot and Pearl A<sh> thou canst of my Debtors and forward to me by way of Hartford to the care of John Morgan. I wish thee to press payment in these articles, and I will give the height of the Market for them I also intend to take Barreled Beef in the Fall if delivered at Hartford in Connecticut at John Morgans but it is best to keep this out of sight at present as it might prevent me from collecting Ashes. As I now give thee full power to collect my Debts in Weathersfield I hope there is not any that will refuse or keep back payment I believe Robinsons demand against me cannot be large I expect it ought to be Small he can have no demands against me unless for the Deeds before mentioned everything prior was settled as will appear I trust. I wish thou would endeavour to collect Some money or Ashes which last I prefer in a moderate Way from Paine of Windsor I am not a little pleased that thou art like to get the Remainder of the Debt due from S Avery secured, I hope he can Spare me a little more as I wish that he should live Comfortably.

    I am with respect thy Friend

                                                                                       Thomas Pearsall

    P: S: I have Still a good Opinion of my Friend Miles Johnson, I believe he means well but is embarrassed. I wish thee to give Hilkiah Grout Assistance in defending the Lands I sold to him, do what is necessary.

Stephen R Bradley

    ALS (VtU).

To the Legislature of Vermont

Castleton Octr 21t. 1790

To the Hon.

The Legislature of the State of Vermont

Your Commissioners appointed to treat with the Commissioners of New-York, on a Boundary Line between the two Governments and the removal of certain Obstacles, which prevent the Admission of Vermont into Union with the United States — Report —

That in January last they commenced to their Negotiation — that after sundry communications & Conferences the Business terminated in a repeal of the Act giving powers to the Commissioners on the part of New-York; And a new Act was passed by the Legislature of New-York then in Session, appointing Commissioners with full & direct powers to treat with us on the Objects of our Appointment. After opening a negotiation with them, We agreed to adjourn to Stockbridge the 6th. of July then ensuing, at which time We convened, but by reason of the Indisposition of two of the Commissioners on the part of New-York, We were necessitated to adjourn to the 27th. of September then ensuing at the City of New-York, when the Negotiation was resumed, and closed on the 7th. Instant by reciving from the Commissioners of the State of New-York, their *Official Act* which We now present to the Legislature for their Consideration.

> Isaac Tichenor
> Stephen R. Bradley
> Nathl Chipman
> Ira Allen
> Elijah Paine
> Israel Smith

ALS (Vt: MsVtSP, vol. 24, p. 33). Docketed, "Report of the Commisrs. appointed to treat with the Commissrs. of N. York / Oct 21t. 1790 / read in Committee —/ In Committee of the Gen Assembly 22d. Octr. 1791 / Read with the Act of Congress." Enclosure not found.

Vermont Governor and Council Record

IN ASSEMBLY, Oct. 22 1790.

The report of the Commissioners appointed to treat with Commissioners from the State of New-York, and the act of the Commissioners on the part of the State of New-York, were read; and,

On motion of Mr. [Stepehen R.] Bradley,

Resolved, That this House go into Committee of the whole for the purpose of discussing the above business.

Mr. Olin in the Chair. — Lewis R. Morris, Clerk.

On motion, the act of the Commissioners on the part of New-York, was read.

Same day, 2 P.M. — The House met pursuant to adjournment, and went into a Committee of the whole, &c.

Mr. Bradley rose, and in a sensible and masterly manner, gave the Committee a full statement of the business — when, on motion of Mr. Marvin, Chief Justice Chipman was requested to give his sentiments on the subject.

His Honor the Chief Justice observed, That colonel Bradley had anticipated everything he could say, and therefore declined trespassing on the patience of the Committee.

Printed (Governor and Council Record, vol. 3).

Resolution of the State of Vermont

[22–25 October 1790]

IN GRAND COMMITTEE, Oct. 22 1790.—On motion of Mr. [Stephen R.] Bradley, Resolved, That this Committee do recommend to the Legislature of this State to pass an Act to call a Convention of the people, to take into consideration the Constitution of the United States, and see whether they will accede to the same.

Oct. 23, Stephen R. Bradley, Samuel Hitchcock, and Lemuel Chipman were appointed by the Assembly to draft a bill to call a Convention; and on the 25th the bill was passed.

Printed (Vermont Governor and Council Record, vol. 3).

Constitutional Convention to Adopt the United States Constitution

AN ACT TO AUTHORIZE THE PEOPLE OF THIS STATE TO MEET IN[1] CONVENTION TO DELIBERATE UPON AND AGREE TO THE CONSTITUTION OF THE UNITED STATES.

OCTOBER 27TH, 1790

Whereas in the opinion of this Legislature the future interest and welfare of this state render it necessary that the Constitution of the United States of America, as agreed to buy the convention at Philadelphia, on the seventeenth day of September, in the year of our Lord, 1787, with the several amendments and alterations as the same has been since established by the United States, should be laid before the people of this state, for their approbation,

It is hereby Enacted by the General Assembly of the State of Vermont, That the first constable in each town shall warn the inhabitants, who by law are entitled to vote for representatives in General Assembly, in the same manner as they warn freemen's meeting, to meet in their respective towns on the first Tuesday of December next, at 10 o'clock forenoon, at the several places fixed by law for holding the annual elections, and when so met, they shall proceed in the same manner as in the election of representatives, to choose some suitable person from each town to serve as a delegate in a state convention, for the purpose of deliberating upon, and agreeing to, the Constitution of the United States, as now established, and the said constable shall certify to the state convention the person sho chosen in manner aforesaid. And,

It is hereby further Enacted by the authority aforesaid, That the persons so elected to serve in state convention as aforesaid, do assemble and meet together on the first Thursday of January[2] next, at Bennington, in the County of Bennington, then and there to deliberate upon the aforesaid Constitution of the United States, and if approved of by them, finally to assent to, and ratify the same, in behalf, and on the part of the people of this state, and make report thereof to the Governor of this state for the time being, to be by him communicated to the President of the United States, and the legislature of this state.

Printed. *Mss. Laws of Vermont,* Vol. 3, pp. 330–331.
1. *State Papers of Vermont,* Laws of Vermont, 1785–1791, pp. 522–523. Also found in *Governor and Council,* Vol. III, pp. 464–465.
2. For the proceedings of the convention for adopting the *Constitution of the United States,* see January 10, 1791, *post.*

Vermont and New York Settle Boundary Dispute for Thirty Thousand Dollars

AN ACT DIRECTING THE PAYMENT OF THIRTY THOUSAND DOLLARS TO THE STATE OF NEW YORK, AND DECLARING WHAT SHALL BE THE BOUNDARY LINE BETWEEN THE STATE OF VER-

MONT AND STATE OF NEW YORK; AND DECLARING
CERTAIN GRANTS THEREIN MENTIONED,
EXTINGUISHED.

OCTOBER 28TH, 1790

It is hereby Enacted and declared by the General Assembly of the State of Vermont, That the state of Vermont shall, on or before the first day of June 1794, pay the State of New York thirty thousand dollars. And the Treasurer of this state, for and in behalf of this state, and for the purposes mentioned in the act of the commissioners aforesaid, shall pay to the State of New York the sum of thirty thousand dollars or on before the first day of June, 1794. And,

It is hereby further Enacted, That the said line described in the said act of the said commissioners, shall, henceforth, be the perpetual boundary line between the state of Vermont and the State of New York; and all grants, charters, or patents of land, lying within the State of Vermont, made by or under the government of the late colony of New York, except such grants, charters or patents as were made in confirmation of grants, charters or patents made by, or under, the government of the late province or colony of New Hampshire, are hereby declared null and void, and incapable of being given in evidence, in any court of law within this state.[1]

Printed, *State Papers of Vermont,* Vol. XIV, Laws of Vermont, pp. 532–534.

1. The report of the Vermont Commission was made to the Legislature sitting at Castleton, October 22, 1790. Stephen R. Bradley "in a sensible and masterly manner," as the record says, gave a full statement in regard to the negotiations, after which Judge Elijah Paine offered a resolution providing that agreeable to the act of the Commissioners, the State of Vermont would pay to the State of New York the sum of $30,000 on or before June 1, 1794. On a yea and nay vote the resolution was adopted on October 25 — 92 yeas, and 12 nays — and Israel Morey, Elijah Paine and Israel Smith were appointed a committee to bring in a bill. This measure carried into effect the agreement already described and was passed October 28, 1790. Walter H. Crockett, *Vermont, The Green Mountain State,* Vol. II, pp. 458–459.

From Benjamin Greene

Sir   Windsor 3 Decr 1790

Mr Chaplin by his misconduct & and the unjust Award of certain Arbitrators in a Case between him & Dr Fletcher finds himself involved in absolute Ruin, and wants your Assistance & Advice. He has mortgaged Lands to me sufficient to secure you or any Gentleman who will assist him & which shall remain as a pledge for their payment. I am Sir your huml Servt

                                                            Benja Greene

Stephn R Brandly Esqr
ALS (VtU).

From Roswell <Clesson?>

Sir   Rockingham December 12th. 1790

I am agoing to attach a Quantaty of Brick as the property of Peter Tozer to Save a Debt that said Tozer owes me & I aispect that Doctr. Alexander Campbell will replevey the Brick — and I Shall want your assestance — and I dont know but that I Shall bring an action against Campbell — & Shall want your assistance. I have Sent you a Note against Joseph Tele of about 20/ for you to Colect & take as a fee but if the Note wont answer I will pay you your Reasonable retaining fee the first time I see you.

                                                   Roswell <Clesson?>

Stephen R Bradley Esqr Westminster
ALS (DLC).

Adoption of the Constitution of the United States

Independent Statehood, Jan. 6 to Mar. 4, 1791
A List of Members of the Convention for Adopting the Constitution of the United States

Bennington, January [6] 1791

THOMAS CHITTENDEN, president.

MOSES ROBINSON, vice president.

Roswell Hopkins, secretary.

[NOTE: Pages 2–11 omitted (Mr. Bradley did not speak in the early deliberations).]

FRIDAY, *January [7.]** Three o'clock P.M.

Mr. Farrand again advanced the motion of discussing the constitution by paragraphs.

Mr. Emmons rose, and observed, that the matters under consideration were so weighty he wished them not to be hurried — he expressed a fear that the people would suffer in their landed property — he said he was for himself doubtful, and believed others were so too, whether, in case land trials should be brought before the federal court, the least attention would be paid to the late treaty with Newyork — doubts, he observed, prevail, whether that state had in reality a right to cede to Vermont the property of individuals.

Mr. Bradley, Mr I. Smith, and others, answered mr. Emmons — they went into a lengthy and well arranged train of arguments on the right of Newyork to proceed in the manner they had done. Mr. Bradley eloquently defined the right of sovereignty in the several states — adverting, in his speech, to the conduct of bvarious sovereignties, both ancient and modern.

Mr. Buck rose, and objected to the motion. He said it appeared to him that if the constitution was taken up paragraph by paragraph, it would in effect foreclose any general observations upon the question which was first to be attended to — that if those who had any objections to make kept to the question before the convention, they would be confined to those which arose from the constitution itself, and could not, without departing from the point, offer any general observations upon the expediency or inexpediency of taking it up at all, supposing it to be ever so good — which appeared to him a question that ought first to be attended to.

Here several members observed, that the motion was calculated to bring on those debates — and that the door was now open for them. They expressed their wishes, that the subject might be treated with the utmost candour, and clearly investigated — that if there were any who had any general objections they would come forward. Mr. Buck rose again, and in a lengthy speech observed, that it appeared to him there were reasons to be offered against the adoption of the constitution at the present time. Supposing the constitution to be ever so good an one, yet, in order to a fair investigation of the question, as to the expediency of adopting it, perhaps it would be necessary to consider the original cause of all government: he urged that it originated from necessity; that, were it possible for a man to enjoy the blessings of society, security of his person, liberty, and property, without the protection of gov-

---

*[Editor's note: This date in the Gazette *was a blunder of the printer, which was followed in each succeeding date. The Convention met on the 6th and dissolved on the 10th of January 1791.*]

ernment, he must be happier in that state than to be under the controul of it; that, in entering into compact and forming government, each individual of the community must necessarily sacrifice such a part of his natural liberty, his interest, and privileges, as to coincide with the common interest of the whole; yet this sacrifice must be in some measure proportionate to the diversity of interest to be found in the several parts of the community — that the sacrifice of the individuals of a smal community must be less than those of a large one, where the interest must be supposed more diverse. He observed, that Vermont, by her local situation, had an uniformity of interest; that there was no mercantile and landed interest found clashing here, and that of othe lord and the tenant was not known; the laws, therefore, were simple and suited to the whole; the affairs of government were managed, as it were, under the eye of the people, and the machine was so small that every one could look and see how the wheels moved, and for this reason it was observable, that the people were all politicians. But if Vermont came into the union, the sacrifice she made must be great — her interest must then bend to the interest of the union — where those clashing interests before mentioned were to be found. He said, the blessings resulting to Vermont from her union with an extensive empire, enumerated by the honorable member from Rutland, though very plausible, would not apply to the bulk of the people: some few favorites of fortune, who from circumstances of birth, and advantage of education, might consider themselves fair candidates for some post in government, might be animated by the magnitude of the object and soar to the height of science; but this number must be but small, while on the other hand, the affairs of government being at such a remove from the eye of the people they could have no knowledge of their transactions, and would naturally degenerate into a state of ignorance. He observed, that all extensive governments had a natural tendency to destroy that equality among the people, which was necessaryto keep one part of mankind from oppressing the other; that there was such a thirst for dominion and power implanted in the human breast, that men were ever ready to make use of the advantages they had to tyrannize over others; that as the stimulous to improvement in knowledge, resulting from our union, would operate on a few only, it would serve but to place them as tyrants over an ignorant multitude.— For the truth of these observations, he referred to the present state of the kingdoms of the world, and observed, that the rich, wise, powerful, and great, bear a tyrannical sway, while they view the bulk of mankind in the same light as we do those domestic animals that are subservient to our use; and as to the salutary effects that our union would have on the morals of the people, we should in all probability experience quite the reverse of what was suggested by the worthy member from Rutland — for it was observable, that luxury, debauchery, and licentiousness, were the attendants on power. The court, he said, was the foundation from whence immorality was diffused among a nation: this was so true, that it had become a common saying, that sincerity and honesty were strangers at court; while real virtue and simple honesty were to be fond in the cottage. It must therefore be a given point, that Vermont (taking into view the bulk of the people) must be much happier unconnected with any other power, than to be in the union — and nothing but necessity could warrant her accession to the federal constitution; therefore, if it was possible for her to support her independence, it was her wisdom to remain independent. He said there were but two things that could ever render it impossible, or prevent it. He agreed, that in case of war between Great britain and America, it would be impossible. But he urged, that there was no prospect or probability of a war again taking place between those powers; he likewise acknowledged that the local situation of Vermont was such, that it was in the power of congress so to embarrass and hedge her up, as to render it impossible for her to exist; but it was easy to determine whether congress would ever exert this power by considering the state Vermont stood in, with respect to the united states; and what probably would be the motives by which congress would be influenced in her conduct — he said it would be that of her interest. He said it was a just observation, that individuals were generally influenced by their interest; but when applied to political bodies the rule was without an exception: we might therefore fix upon it for certain, that the view which congress had of their interest, would be the helm by which they would invariably steer the federal ship; it remained therefore only to shew, that it could not be for the interest of congress ever to lay any embarrassments on us — and this, when we considered our situation in respect to the union, was very apparent, for, upon the present plan of taxation, which in all probability would not be altered as long as peace remains, we paid, and ever should pay, every whit as much towards the support of the federal government, as though we were in the union, it could therefore, never, unless upon the prospect of an immediate war, be for the interest of congress to take measures to compel us in. — But on the contrary, the moment we were received into the union, our senators, representatives, district judge, &c. must make an additional expanse to the federal government — besides, if congress set us upon the same footing with other states, she must assume our expenses of the war; congress must therefore, instead of gaining by our union, be the losers. He observed, that congress had never noticed us, or taken one step that indicated a wish for our union — that all that had been done was in consequence of movements of Newyork, who had, until congress sat in that state, stood our avowed enemy; and that it was easy to see the motive which caused Newyork so suddenly to change her policy. He said, Newyork viewed the seat of the federal government as an object of greater importance than their claim to Vermont, they had therefore sacrificed that, and were now exerting themselves, to the utmost, to bring Vermont into union; that thereby they might add another weight to the northern scale. But by the doings of congress, we found that there were a majority in that body who were pursuing an object which clashed with the view of Newyork, and that the same voices which decided that the seat of government should be carried to the Potomac, would, in all probability, decide, that Vermont should not be received until the permanent seat of federal government should be unalterably fixed. Therefore, as the advantage Vermont would receive from the union, would by no means be adequate to the sacrifice she must make — as she had long existed as an independent state, and might long continue so — and as in all probability she would be rejected by congress, if she made application, there could be no necessity or expedience in acceding to the union, or adopting the constitution.

Mr. Bradley answered Mr. Buck — and went into a full consideration of the reasons offered by the worthy member against the adoption of the constitution at the present time — he observed that most of the arguments would equally apply against our ever adopting the constitution, and many of them against the government in general — he clearly pointed out the state and situation in which Vermont stood, totally incapable of supporting the rights of sovereignty, or protecting her own citizens from invasions — that the evil would be equally ruinous in its consequences if the united states should withdraw their claim of sovereignty, and consider Vermont a sovereign state, as it would should they attempt to annihilate the jurisdiction, and enforce obedience to the laws of the union — if as a sovereign state, they will treat her as such, and withdraw from her all protection — if as belonging to the united states, and for whose conduct they must be responsible to the nations of the world, they will undoubtedly exercise their jurisdiction over her; and in case Vermont refuses to adopt the constitution and become a member of the union, they will either compel her to come in by force, or dismember her among the united states — that in fine the important decision of this convention will determine congress the part they have to act — he said the worthy member from Norwich had stated two instances, in which it would be impossible for Vermont to maintain her independence; one was, in case of war between Great britain and America; the other, when congress should treat her as a sovereign state — or in other words, embarrass and hedge her up — he appealed to the judgment of every member, whether the true interest of the state did not require, in their present situation, an immediate union with her sister states, that they might grow up together in friendship under the same government — rather than wait the uncertainty of those events, which may oblige this government in a servile manner to seek protection from those who will then have it in their power to grant it on such terms as they please — he reprobated, in the most severe terms, every idea that had been thrown out against congress, or the state of Newyork; and said the sacrifice that had been made by the state of Newyork, and several of the united states, might teach that gentleman a lesson, that governments were capable of acting from noble, extensive and disinterested views — he considered the objections raised against being received into the union by congress as having no weight — and said the acquisition of one hundred thousand free persons to their government, and extending empire over the whole, was an object not to be compared with the trifling expense that might accrue by that addition — he considered the many advantages that would be derived form the union — that Vermont would enjoy a full participation of the benefits of every seaport in the united states, a recognition of her sovereignty, protection from foreign invasion, security against intestine convulsions, and the many blessings ensured by a mild and energetic government — he declared he could not think the worthy member serious when he talked of the sacrifice that Vermont must make — and entered minutely into the power given congress by the constitution — and clearly showed that the rights surrendered were of such a nature, though claimed by this state as an independent sovereignty, that they had in but very few instances ever been exercised — he went through the several paragraphs in the constitution — defined the powers of congress — and pointed out in every particular the nature and extent of that power, and the necessity of its being lodged in some general head for the protection of the whole — and concluded with some just remarks upon the excellency of the constitution: that while it gave congress the power necessary to secure and protect the sovereignty of the whole, it ensured to each state the sovereignty necessary to secure and protect the rights of persons and property.

Mr. Bradley was ably supported by mr. Hitchcock, mr I. Smith, and several others.

Adjourned untill to-morrow.

SATURDAY, January [8.] Nine o'clock A.M.

The question with respect to the expediency of an immediate adoption of the constitution still under consideration:

Mr. Buck rose and said, that having the evening before more closely attended to the constitution in question, than his leisure had before permitted, he had obtained conviction that the danger of losing the sovereignty of the separate states, by entering the union, was not so great as he had imagined; the cession of power to congress was not so great as he had conceived it to be, and the rights of the state sovereignties more guarded. He however still retained the sentiment that it was not adviseable for Vermont precipitately to seek for union. Congress has yet never solicited Vermont to adopt the constitution, or even made the most distant overtures to her on the subject: to rush forward therefore, uninvited, and before real property was permanently secured, appeared to him not only unnecessary but improper.

Mr. I. Smith in a consise and masterly manner obviated the seeming difficulties mentioned by mr. Buck and others, and declared himself much in favor of the motion.

Mr. Loomis rose and observed, that he approved of the federal constitution: he thought it well calculated to serve the interest of those states by whom it had been adopted, and had no doubt in his mind but what it would be best for Vermont to adopt it at a proper time; but there were certain matters necessary to be attended to, at least in his view, previous to that step being taken, viz. Congress ought previously to ratify the late treaty with Newyork, and the debt of this state incurred by exertions in the common cause, during the late war, ought to be assumed by the union. The act of Vermont for specifically fulfilling contracts, required, in his opinion, careful attention: for should the constitution now be adopted, it would operate as a repeat of this act, and of course work an injury to the subject: — he believed it to be an indisputable fact, that contracts now existing for grain, cattle, &c. were made twenty-five or perhaps thirty per cent higher on account of said act; the consequence of an immediate adoption therefore, would be an augmentation of the demand of the creditor of near thirty per cent, and a great injury to the debtor.

Mr. Green observed, That the gentlemen who had spoken before him, had so clearly elucidated the subject, particularly in his view, on that side of the question he meant to espouse, that he could scarcely indulge the hope of giving additional light on the topic. It appeared to him that the question was now reduced to this, whether Vermont would become a member of the union, or remain an independent sovereignty. If an independent sovereignty, congress would doubtless treat us as other aliens; and the immediate consequence would be destruction to the energy of our government; it would become the interest of the union to foment discord among us; it must totally destroy social intercourse between us and them, and irradicate the idea of credit. For what man, says he, would venture his property with his neighbor, to any considerable amount, when the debtor, by only crossing a river or lake, may place himself in a sovereign state, free from the power of his creditor.

But were these difficulties removed, the very idea is inadmissible, that congress will consent to have an independent sovereignty within their lines of jurisdiction. Were the united states still under the old confederation, possessed only of a power to advise and recommend, we might perhaps with advantage remain free and independent. But the government is now efficient; and surrounded as we are on three sides by its members, were they to prohibit our traffic with them, what would become of Vermont? where should we carry our produce? perhaps some may say to Canada, but Canada it is well known is a poor market, and soon overstocked. And indeed from the part of the state he represented, it would never answer, even were the markets tolerably good, to export many articles to Canada; he instanced pot and pearl ashes, &c., the consequence of which, said he, need not be pointed out to the enlightened understanding of this house. Congress can compel us to join the union, on their own terms, without having recourse to arms: Let them only prohibit exportation to or importation from Vermont, and we must sink or comply. This must be the case, continued he, or their revenues will be defrauded by reason of illicit traffic, which could easily be carried on with Canada, through Vermont. From every view of the subject therefore, as no gentleman had objected to the constitution itself, but only to the expediency of present adoption, he was clearly of opinion that by entering the union at present, our state government would acquire energy at home and respectability abroad.

Adjourned till two o'clock P.M.

SATURDAY, January [8.] Two o'clock P.M.

The conviction met according to adjournment, and the clerk pursuant to order, read the constitution, making a short pause between the paragraphs, to give suitable opportunity for objections. The constitution having been read, together with the articles of amendment annexed,

Mr. Farrand rose and wished for information, whether the articles of amendment annexed to the constitution, and just read by the clerk, had received the sanction of congress, so far as to become a part of it? if not, he queried, whether there would not be an impropriety in Vermont's adoption the whole.

Dr. Green replied, that the adoption of the constitution, with the amendments, could not be deemed improper, as a precedent of that kind already existed, viz. the mode adopted by Rhodeisland.

Mr. Bradley introduced a motion, seconded by mr. Hitchcock, that convention proceed to choose a committee of five to make a suitable draft of a form of assent to the constitution, and lay it before convention on Monday morning.

Mr. Emmons said, he viewed the matter under consideration, and the determinations of convention, to be of the most serious consequence: he wished therefore to proceed with the utmost deliberation. Our present transaction, says he, may not perhaps be unaptly applied to the act of Adam in eating the forbidden fruit. Were we only acting in town-meeting, or even as legislators, the importance and solemnity of the matter would be vastly less, said he, in my view, since the mistakes of one session may be rectified at another. We are now acting for future generations, and the determinations of this body will most probably affect posterity even to the end of time. He wished therefore, for an adjournment of the convention untill some future day, perhaps the beginning of October next. The people are not yet clear in the idea of the propriety of entering the union at present. It is but a short period since they looked on the constitution as a thing in which they were deeply interested. The difficulties which have lain in the way are now removed by the treaty with Newyork, but people still entertain jealousies respecting the conduct of that state; they do not really perceive the reason of so great a change in their state policy, and feel fearful lest some trap should be found hidden by a fair disguise. I conclude, said he, they would wish for more time, that they might obtain light in this point and gain a more competent knowledge of the constitution. He was the more firmly persuaded of the propriety of this measure from observing what the consequence had been of several states being cautious of entering the union: to this alone he imputed the several existing amendments.

Mr. Chipman said, he could not see the propriety of adjourning the convention by any means; he believed the gentleman who spoke last had declared his real sentiment, with respect to people's wishing to enter the union at present, but he must impute it to his want of general information. In the town mr. Emmons represents, remote from every channel of intelligence, people may entertain groundless jealousies; but the freeman of Vermont at large, continued he, as far as my acquaintance has extended, are in favor of an immediate adoption. The matter, he observed, was not new, it has been, says he, the topic of conversation for years, and a favorable opportunity carefully and dilligently sought for the admission of Vermont into the federal union. By the late negociation with Newyork, obstacles are removed, but with this proviso, that Vermont adopt the federal constitution within two years. The people have a general knowledge of the principles of the federal government; this is all they will ever attain to; it is not to be presumed that they will study it as they do their alphabet: communities attain such knowledge by delegation: the delegates are virtually the people themselves. The freemen have doubtless chosen men to form the present convention, in whom they implicitly confide, or with whose sentiments, and the reasons on which they are founded, they have made themselves acquainted. It is a matter of great consequence, said he, to secure to Vermont the advantage of the late treaty with Newyork, which depends on a speedy adoption of the constitution in question. No reason therefore existing in his mind, for postponing the business, but weighty considerations operating in favor of the measure, he wished mr. Bradley's motion to be attended to.

Mr. Loomis coincided in sentiment with mr. Emmons. He could see no reason for doing business in a hurry — America being now perfectly at peace with all nations, Vermont could not be endangered by taking a few months for consideration. — He wished the people to have opportunity to become better acquainted with the constitution, and obtain satisfaction with respect to the real security of their landed property.

Mr. Bradley rose to enforce the necessity of immediate adoption. He spoke in the most respectful terms of Newyork, and contrasted the trifling relinquishment of claims they had made to Vermont, with the noble sacrifices they made to the union, at the period when they adopted the constitution. At that time, said he, they enjoyed advantages peculiar to themselves, — advantages which enabled them to discharge their public debts with facility, and even to accumulate wealth in their public coffers, by means of their state imposts, &c. But they generously relinquished all to join the general government, and advance the interest of the union. He requested the particular attention of the convention, to a short matter of fact, which his having had the honor to act as a commissioner in the late negociation with Newyork, enabled him to state, and which would perhaps have a tendency to remove jealousies respecting the security of landed property, in any wise affected by the treaty with Newyork.

At the period of the final ratification of that treaty, said he, there were three fair copies thereof engrossed on parchment, one of which was designed for and is now lodged in the secretary's office in Newyork, one in the secretary's office of this state, and the third to be carried forward to the seat of federal government, whenever we applied for admission into the union, to be deposited in the archives of congress, as the foundation for admission of Vermont into the federal union. This, says the honorable gentleman, was the idea entertained by the commissioners of both states, and several members of congress present at the time joined fully in the sentiment, that the stipulations of that treaty would form the basis of our admission into the union.

Mr. Niles made many pertinent observations on the impropriety of defering the adoption till a future day. He wished matters to be treated with the greatest candor. Let every member, says he, state his objections freely, and let every argument be duly attended to—but suffer not division of sentiment to prevail in community if possible to avoid it. It is a certain truth that warm spirits exist among us—these warm spirits may be heated, and being heated may diffuse of their warmth to others, and by so doing may kindle a flame in society the effec tof which may be destructive to its peace.

The motion for appointing a committee to draw up a suitable form of ratification, &c. was put and carried in the affirmative by a great majority.

The convention adjourned untill Monday morning nine o'clock.

MONDAY, January [10] nine o'clock A.M.

Convention met pursuant to adjournment.

The committee reported a form of adoption of the federal constitution, to be entered into by Vermont, which being read produced some debate, in the course of which mr. I. Allen proposed an amendment to the form, which being agreed to by the house, the grand question was put and carried by a unanimous vote.

Appendix I.
Ratification of the U.S. Constitution

ACT AND RESOLUTIONS OF THE CONVENTION, *transmitted to the General Assembly of Vermont, and the President of the United States.*[1]

STATE OF VERMONT —

In Convention of the Delegates of the People of the State of Vermont.

Whereas, by an Act of the Commissioners of the State of New York, done at New York, the Seventh day of October, in the fifteenth year of the Independence of the United States of

America, one thousand seven hundred and ninety, every impediment, as well on the part of the State of New York, as on the part of the State of Vermont, to the admission of the State of Vermont into the Union of the United States of America, is removed; — In full faith and assurance that the same will stand approved and ratified by Congress; —

This Convention, having impartially deliberated upon the Constitution of the United States of America, as now established, submitted to us by an Act of the General Assembly of the State Vermont passed October the twenty seventh one thousand seven hundred and ninety, Do, in virtue of the power and authority to us given, for that purpose, fully and entirely approve of, assent to, and ratify the said Constitution; And declare that, immediately from, and after, this State shall be admitted by the Congress into the Union, and to a full participation of the benefits of the government now enjoyed by the States in the Union, the same shall be binding on us and the people of the State of Vermont forever.

Done at Bennington, in the County of Bennington, the tenth day of January, in the 15th year of the Independence of the United States of America, one thousand seven hundred and ninety one. — In testimony whereof we have hereunto Subscribed our Names —

THOS. CHITTENDEN, *President*,
MOSES ROBINSON, *Vice President*

Tim° Brownson	Martin Powel	John Forgason
John Fasset	Abel Waters	Reuben Thomas
John Strong	James Shafter	Thomas Jewett
Jonathan Hunt	Edward Aiken	Asaph Fletcher
Gideon Olin	Simon Stevens	Elijah Lovell
Stephen R. Bradley	Abel Thompson	John Rich
Janna Churchill	Joshua Wood	John Barron
Eben[r.] Wilson	Nath* Chipman	Amos Brownson
John White	Tho[s.] Hammond	David Hopkinson
Daniel Shearman	Benja. Holcomb	Dan* Kingsbury
Israel Smith	Peter Briggs	Sam* Harrison
Benj. Greene	John M'Neile	Peter Pennock
Andrew Selden	Oliver Gallup	Martin Chittenden
John Marsh	Lem. Chipman	Josiah Pond
Gardiner Chandler	Samuel Miller	W[m] Slade
Timo[y] Todd	Asahel Smith	John Spafford
Calvin Knoulton	Simeon Smith	Peter Sleeman
Timothy Bliss	John Shumway	Jonas Whitney
W. C. Harrington	Silas Hathaway	Nath[el.] Niles
Josiah Edson	Tho[s.] Porter	Alex[r] Harvey
Mich'* Flynn	John Smith	W[m] Chamberlain
Cornelius Lynde	Elisha Barber	Nathan Daniels
John N. Bennet	W[m.] Ward [of Poultney]	Jason Duncan
Jonathan Brewster	Joseph Beeman	Elias Curtis
Jona M'Connell	Heman Durkee	Sam[el] Beach
Benj Henry	E. [Emanuel] Case	Benj[a.] Emmons
Samuel Lathrop	N. [Noah] Lee	Alex Brush
Oliver Pier	Isaac Lyman	Daniel Gilbert
Nathl Stoughton	Daniel Jewet	Ira Allen

*[Editor's note: From the original, now in possession of the Vermont Historical Society.]

Timothy Castle	Daniel Buck	Sam* Gatt [Gates.]
Eleazer Claghorn	Daniel Farrand	Eben[r] Allen
Silas Tupper	Abraham Morrill	Enos Wood
David Palmer	Beriah Loomis	Sam* Hitchcock
W[m] Perry	Asahel Jackson	
Joseph Warner	Jon[a.] Arnold	

STATE OF VERMONT SS *Bennington January* 10th. 1791.

The foregoing ratification was agreed to, and signed by one hundred and five, and dissented to, by four; which is a majority of one hundred and one.

THOS. CHITTENDEN, *President.*

Attest, ROSL. HOPKINS, *Secy of Convention.*

STATE OF VERMONT. *In Convention Bennington Jany.* 10*th.* 1791—

Resolved (the Governor of this State being President) that the Vice President be and hereby is directed to transmit to his Excellency the Governor Duplicates of the act of this Convention ratifying the Constitution of the United States of America to be by him transmitted to the President of the United States and the Legislature of this State.

Attest   ROSL. HOPKINS Secy.

NOTE: On comparing the signatures to this act with the roll of delegates, it is found that the dissenters were Daniel Heald of Chester, Moses Warner of Andover, Benjamin Perkins of Bridgewater, and Enoch Emerson of Bridgewater.[†]

For proceedings of the General Assembly on this subject see *ante,* pp. 218–20, 223–4, 226 note, 227.

Printed (Governor and Council Record, vol. 3).

*[Editor's note: From the original, now in possession of the Vermont Historical Society.]
†[Editor's note: In Errata, page 514, it was indicated that Enoch Emerson was from Rochester.]

Vermont Governor and Council Record

[19 January 1791]

Mr. Bradley, Mr. Hitchcock & Mr. Paine being a Committee from the House to Confer with the Council upon the act sent from Council to the House for appointing Senators, & to inform the Council of the reasons for not passing the Same into a Law of this State, Resolved that Mr. Tichenor, Mr. Arnold and Mr. Walbridge be appointed to Confer with said Committee on the Subject.

On Motion of Mr. Lyon the Committee Resolved to appoint Senators to attend the Congress of the United States. They also Resolved a Sub Committee of Ten to prepare certain articles to lay before this Committee to be recommended to the Legislature, in consequence of the recommendatory restrictions [resolutions in the Assembly journal] of the Late Convention of this State, — Members choosen, His Excellency the Governor, Honble Gideon Olin, Isaac Tichenor, Stephen R. Bradley, Nathl. Niles, Elijah Paine, Samuel Hitchcock, Jonathan Arnold, Israel Smith, and Ira Allen Esquires.

A Message from the House was recd. by Major Robinson requesting the Governor and Council to join in Grand Committee for the purpose of Electing [United States] Senators, whereupon Resolved that the Governor & Council join the House in Grand Committee for the purpose of Electing Senators to represent the Legislature of this State in the Senate of the United States.

Being Met His Excellency the Governor in the Chair, Rosl. Hopkins Esquire Clerk, the Ballots being taken the Honble Moses Robinson Esqr. & Stephen R. Bradley Esqr. was declared to be duly elected.[1] The Committee Dissolved.

On the petition of Stilman Foot, Resolved that Mr. Niles join the Committee of the House to Take the Same under Consideration State facts and Make Report.

Printed (Governor and Council Record, vol. 3).

1. "By letters of Oct. 10 1791, addressed to Gov. Chittenden and Speaker Olin, Senator elect Moses Robinson stated that it had been suggested that the election of U.S. Senators at the previous session was premature, and urged a decision of that question as soon as possible, inasmuch as Congress was to meet in the last of the then present month. Oct. 15, one of these letters was read, when Matthew Lyon moved, and the House resolved, that the election was premature. Probably the ground taken was, that the election on the 19th of January 1791 preceded by six weeks the date fixed by Congress for the admission of the State into the Union. Both houses joined immediately in grand committee, and after a long debate in the morning session and extending into the afternoon, the question was decided in the affirmative, and the 17th was fixed for another election. On the morning of that day, says the *Assembly Journal*, " General Bradley appeared on the floor of the House, and in a handsome and well adapted speech resigned the credentials of his election as a member of the Senate of the United States, into the hands of the Secretary of State." Neither the official records nor the Vermont newspapers give the names of the unsuccessful candidates; and the only clue discovered is a copy, in the *Vermont Journal* of Oct. 18 1791, of a humorous hand-bill which was posted in Windsor on the day preceding the election. It characterized the election as "Federal Racing," and described the racers thus: "Eastern Racers—The Past-Time [Stephen R. Bradley,] Peacock [possibly Elijah Paine,] Pretty Town Horse, Old Roger [Enos,] Narraganset Pacer [Jonathan Arnold,] Connecticut Blue [Nathaniel Niles.] Western Racers—The Old Script [Moses Robinson,] Jersey Sleek [Isaac Tichenor,] Figure, Bold Sweeper [probably Matthew Lyon,] Northern Ranger [probably Hitchcock]" (Governor and Council Record, vol. 5).

Resolution of the State of Vermont

In General Assembly Jany 20th 1791

Resolved that The Treasurer be and hereby is Directed to pay Unto Experience Fisk Administrator on the Estate of Nathan Fisk the Sum of forty one pounds fourteen Shillings in Satisfaction for the Money paid by the said Nathan Fisk for a Lot of Land in Westminster Suposed to have been Confiscated as the Estate of Crean Brush which has since been Recovered by Leonard B<rut?>

Extract from the Journals

£40 13 8

Attest LR Morris Clerk

    Red. in full 20 Jany 1791
        In behalf of Experience Fisk

Stephen R Bradley Atty

ADS (Vt: MsVtSP, vol. 11, p. 11). In the hand of SRB, signed by Morris. Docketed, "1st. / Experience Fisk's Acct £40.13.8."

To the General Assembly of Vermont

[24 January 1791]

The Committee To whom was Refered the within petition beg leave to Report that in the Opinion of your Committee the Surveyor General ought to ascertain what Quantity of Land is Cut off from the Township of Salem by the Charter of Derby & that the proprietors of Salem have refunded to them Such proportion of their Granting fees & Interest as it Shall apear they lose in their Lands by its being thus Cut off.

for Committee

S R Bradley

24th Jany Read and accepted

Attest LR Morris Clerk

[Enclosure]

To the Honourable the General Assembly of the State of Vermont The Petition of Jacob Davis humbly Sheweth — That in September 1787 your petitioner purchased a Township of Land in the Northerly part of this State — paid the charter fees & had the same chartered to him & associates with corporate privileges by the Name of salem containing a Grant of Six miles Square. In consiquence of which your pet[it]ioner has made sale of some considerable part of sd. Lands — And your pet[it]ioner now finds that in consiquence of a Resolution of the Assembly passed October 1787 a charter of the Town of Derby has been since made out & Issued by the Governor granting a considerable part of those same Lands to other persons which charter is antidated & has the appearance of a prior grant to that made to your petitioner which lays a foundation for a long & tedious dispute & renders it incertain which Grant will <h>old sd. Lands — Your petitioner therefore prays your honours to render his title certain by vacating sd. charter which in fact was Subsiquent to that of your petitioner though antidated & has the appearance of a prior one — or otherwise to take a resignation of sd. charter made out to your pet[it]ioner & refund to him in hard money the Sum which he gave for <sd.> Land with six pr. Cent interest thereon — And in duty bound will ever pray —
Bennington 18th. Jany. 1791

Jacob Davis

ALS (Vt: MsVtSP, vol. ?). SRB's report is written on the verso of the petition. Angle brackets enclose parts of words missing owing to tears. Docketed, "Petition of Jacob Davis Esqr. / filed / In Gen Assembly —/ 19th Jany 1791— / Read & referred to Messrs. Bradley, I Allen & Johnson / Attest LRMorris Clerk / Jany. 26th 1791 / Refered to next Session —/ Novr 3d. 1791 / Refered."

Governor and Council Record

[24 January 1791]

The Governor and Council Met in Grand Committee Agreeable to adjournment and proceeded to the Choice of Brigadier Generals to the first and Eighth Brigades of the Militia of this State. The Ballots being Taken, Arad Hunt was declared to be duly choosen for the first Brigade and Stephen R. Bradley Esquire for the Eighth.

Printed (Governor and Council Record, vol. 3).

Jeremiah Wadsworth to the Secretary of State*

Sir   Feb 22 1791

Nathaniel Chipman Esq. is the most proper person in Vermont for District judge. I believe he is without a competitor in the state. Their present Attorney General is Samuel Hitchcock, but I do not believe he would relinquish his State appointment for a federal one as the latter would be less lucrative. Israel Smith Esqr. would be suitable for the office. There are other Lawyers in the State of some eminence — Stephen Jacob Darius Chipman Daniel Farrand Isaac Tichenor. I have placed them as they rank in my opinion. I should have placed at the head of the list Stephen Rowe Bradly Esq. but I have no doubt he will be a Senator. At Allborough I know no person fit for a Naval officer. Stephen Keyes is a Man of education with little property, who I believe would remove from Burlington Bay for the office and could procure Bonds for the faithfull execution of the office. — I am sir Your H Svt.

Jere Wadsworth

*[Editor's note: At this time, Thomas Jefferson was serving as Secretary of State.]

RC (DLC: Washington Papers); at foot of text: "The Secretary of State." Not recorded in SJL.

On the same day Theodore Sedgwick wrote TJ: "I have been informed this morning of the characters recommended by Mr. Wadsworth to fill offices in Vermont. I very fully, from all the information I have received, concur with him in opinion" (RC in DLC: Washington Papers; addressed: "The Honorable Mr. Jefferson"; not recorded in SJL). The next day Sedgwick joined with Fisher Ames in addressing another letter to TJ, perhaps on the same subject (recorded in SJL as received 23 Feb. 1791 but not found).—Wadsworth was correct in thinking that BRADLEY would become a Senator: he took his seat on 4 Nov. 1791 and drew by lot a four-year term (JS, I, 336, 337).

Papers of Thomas Jefferson, Princeton.

The Vermont Company in Gen. Wayne's War Against the Northwestern Indians—1792 to 1795.

Under the act of Congress of March 5, 1791, for the protection of the frontiers, which added three regiments to the army, President Washington assigned the first company of the third of these regiments to Vermont, and appointed as its officers Captain William Eaton, Lieutenant James Underhill, and Ensign Charles Hyde. Eaton, who owed his appointment to Stephen R. Bradley, then resided at Windsor; Underhill is supposed to have been from Dorset; and Hyde from Poultney. The enlistments were for three years, the bounty for each recruit eight dollars, and the monthly pay of privates three dollars. A recruiting office was opened by Ensign Hyde at Bennington about the first of May, and under the spurs of glittering promises of glory, and fervid appeals in prose and verse, the ranks were filled, and the *Vermont Gazette* of Aug. 31 announced the departure of the company for the seat of war as follows:

> This morning the company of recruits raised at the rendezvous in this town, under the command of captain William Eaton, consisting of near 70 of the hardy and brave sons of Vermont, set out on their march for the western country. It has been observed by the muster master and other gentlemen who have seen a number of the other companies of levies, that capt. Eatons company is by far the best that have marched from any rendezvous whatever. They left the ground in good spirits and with that military ambition that becomes a soldier.

Governor and Council. William Eaton Appointed Captain. Vol. I, page 478, Appendix F.

From Samuel Bayard

New york 25th July 1791.

Mr. Bayard request Col. Bradley to Acquaint the Sheriff, who is now become answerable for Col. Stone's Debt, that Mr. Bayard will accept of One half the Principal & Interest of the Debt, provided it is *paid* to *him* on or before the first Day of November Next; and the remaining half on or before the first Day of May following. And that for the performance of this engagement the Sheriff execute to Mr. Bayard such Securities as Col. Bradley shall think necessary to take. The expences to be wholly defrayed by the Sheriff.

Col. Bradley

ALS (NcD: Bradldey Family Papers). Docketed in an unidentified hand, "Samuel Bayard."

Governor and Council Record

[20 October 1791]

Honble. Brigadier General Bradley Resigned his Command of the Eighth Brigade of the Militia of the State of Vermont, which was accordingly accepted.

Printed (Governor and Council Record, vol. 4).

From John Morgan

Stephen R. Bradley Esqr.
Dear Sir					Hartford 7th Novr 1791

Our mutual friends, Thomas Pearsall & John I. Glover as Pearsall & Glover, Pearsall & Pell & Thomas Pearsall & son & John I. Glover have requested me to forward to you by an express their Notes against Josiah Huntington of Wethersfield in this County — with a view to have his property attached to secure their Debts. He has kept up a Store for some time past at Claremont in N Hampshire which has been tended by John Russel, I am not certain whether in his own name or the name of Mr Huntington, the property is however Josiah Huntingtons, I have therefore to request you would without delay attach as much property as you can find of his to secure their Debts. He has a Mortgage of Land, (two pieces, one of 80 & the other I think of about 30 Acres) formerly belonging to a Doctr. Carter of Wethersfield in your State & which before this was to be deeded by absolute Deed. It may be it is still held as a mortgage. You will take such methods as are legal to <get hold> of that, with every other property you can find of his. The bearer of this Jonathan Olcott will wait the issue of the business — by whom you will please to forward me a State of your proceedings have inclosed a Line from the Gentlemen mentiond within in which they point out the different Notes against him I have below given you a List of them which I forward as thought it best to attach with some of them what property I could find here. May be you have a Law by which you can compel his Debtors to account for the sums he has against them, it is expected that every thing legally obtainable will be taken hold off.

Col. Bradley, was in New York at the writing the inclosed & informd those Gentlemen that, two young Gentlemen living with him, would transact the business. To them I address myself as doing Col Bradleys Law business — & in behalf of Messr Pearsall & others mentiond I have once more to request as early a compliance as possible. I suppose there will be no difficulty <in> securing his property in N Hampshire. Should [...]ear that further power Atty or anything of that sort are necessary they can on your Intimation, be forwarded before tryal. I hope you will be able to find some P Ashes at his works. I think his Store is kept about a mile from Wethersfield — on N Hampshire side of the river. I would venture to suggest to you the propriety of going with the Officer who attaches, as Mr Russel may have property of some other person which may be wrongly taken. I have heard he was about to take goods, for Jona Huntington, brother of Josiah, but believe he has not yet, Mr Russel I believe is too honest to secrete his effects, his present patron can now do him no service & his future support will depend on his Honesty. In full confidence of your early Attention to this business I subscribe myself yr. most Obt.

John Morgan

1 Note Thom: Pearsall & Thom: Pearsall Junr. 21 July on Intt. from 6th	90.. 0. 6
1 Ditto Thom: Pearsall & John Glover 21st July Intt. from 1st	216.. 11. 4
	£306. 11. 10

Please to give a Rect. to the bearer.

ALS (VtU). Damaged by removal of seal.

From the Eighth Brigade Artillery Company

Springfield 23d. Novr. 1791.

We the subscribers desirous of forming a company of Artillery to be annexed to the Eight Brigade of the Militia of this State do hereby engage to equip ourselves as the law directs, and as soon as a sufficient number have subscribed we do hereby engage to proceed to the choice of Officers— under such directions as we may receive from the Brigadier General or other our superior Officer— and thereby subject ourselves to the rules and regulations established by Law for the better ordering the Militia of this State.

AD (VtU). Signed by 31 subscribers.

From Stephen <Hull?>

Sir,   Windsor, 10th. May 1792

I Yesterday returned from the District Court at Rutland, where, as usu<al> we had nothing to do. On my return I saw Col. Brush of Bennington, who <said> that our Members at Congress had recd very disagreeable impressions of the Conduct of our Friend Eaton since his appointment—in his not repairing to the place of Rendesvous &c.

As I was convinced from the manner of his Information, that some Enemy had been buisy with his fame—I thot it my Duty as a frien<d> to truth & to Mr Eaton, to inform you that every insinuation to his disadvantage on the subject of his appointment & consequent conduct is without just foundation. He has resided in my family & I have been acquainted with his whole conduct in this business. He recd your Letter informing of his appointment, & on the 5th of April recd one from Secretary Knox of the 17th of March giving him official Information of his appointment to the command of a Compy of Infantry. He the same Day wrote to the Secretary & yourself signifying his acceptance. He then with the advice of his friends made a Journey to Connecticut to take leave of his father—was absent but just ten Days, so as to be sure of being at home when any Dispaches might arrive, he also wrote to Ensign Hyde at Bennington, if any Dispatches should arrive at Benning[ton] that concerned him, to give him immediate Notice. He has ever since been waiting here for some return from the Secretary at War—But has recd nothing either from him or Hyde—nor has any intimation been given from any Quarter what was expected of him 'till Brush yesterday mentioned the matter to me—& said he had long been expected at Bennington. I suppose the dispaches must have been sent by the way of Worcester—and the Post not come from thence but once in 2 weeks. I have been thiss particuler because Brush mentioned many malicious things that were said of Mr Eaton both with regard to his journey to Connecticut, & his not being at Bennington, which he says is the place of Rendesvous. I know he has been anxious to receive orders, & has been very buisy in engaging troops, & would by this time, in my opinion, had he have recd seasonable orders have had a considerable part of his Company engaged—as many of our best young men, not withstanding the smalness of the pay—ar<e> disposed to accompany him.

I hope no person has injured him in your good opinion, I am well convinced you will, from his good conduct in the time of his appointment, never have just reason to regret the exertions you have mad<e> in his favour.

Mr. Bradleys family were well last week. I am, Sir, with sentiments of respect, your very humble Servt.

                                                                      Stephen <Hull?>

Honble Stephen R Bradley Esqr.

ALS (VtU). Damaged by removal of seal; right margins obscured.

To Samuel Minott

Brigade Orders

Sir   Head Quarters Westminster July 17th. 1792

You are hereby required to See that the Several Companies in Your Regiment parade at the Meeting house in Westminster on the first tuesday in October next at ten o'Clock in the morning Compleatly armed and accoutred for review as Law directs. You will direct what Uniform the Officers & Soldiers in your Regiment Shall wear on their Hats &c on the parade and the General recommends that Each Company be furnished with a Baggage wagon to be paraded in the Rear of the Regiment agreeable to Camp Regulation and Strictly forbids all disorderly firing on or about the parade on Said Day on penalty of a Breach of General Orders.

Stephen R Bradley Brigadier Genl

N. B. It is Expected that Your adjutant make a Return of the State of Your Regiment as Law directs.

Coln Samll Minott Esqr.

ALS (NcD).

To Thomas Pearsall

Sir   Westminster August 14th 1792

Since writting to You Yesterday the Bearer Mr Lemuel Cone a Neighbour of mine has applyed to me to recommend him to You to take up Goods upon a few months Credit as he was Coming into New York and has some money to lay out. I have Given him a letter of Credit on Pearsall and Son for Eight Hundred Dollars he has large Connections in this part of the Country who are Connected with him in Business and do procure many Ashes. I have taken Sufficient Security to indemnify me and have no doub[t] they will make the remittances to You in the Time Should they not I will transmit the Money to You on the Earliest notice Should wish if You let him have Goods You would let him have them as reasonable as You Can as he is an honest Man and Very punctual please to take Notes of him for What You Credit him that Should I pay them they might be Signed over.

I am with Esteem thy Friend

Stephen R Bradley

Mr Thomas Pearsall

ALS (DLC).

To the General Assembly of Vermont

August 17th. 1792

To the Honorable the Council & House of Representatives of the State of Vermont to be assembled in October 1792   Humbly shew

Your petitioners that it would be a measure of great publick utility as well as private advantage that communications should be opened throughout the town of Montgomery in the County of Chittenden & State aforesaid, by various publick roads as speedily as conveniently may be. Your Petitioners beg leave to suggest to your Honors that a publick highway should be laid out from the town of Berkshire adjoining, through the aforesaid town of Montgomery to Haysen's road so called, by which an easy & very advantageous communication will be opened from the Coos country to Saint Johns in Canada.

The reasonable prospects of an immediate settlement of the Country to which this petition relates, has induced your petitioners from motives the most liberal & disinterested to present this application. And that the object of it may be accomplished without delay your petitioners pray that a tax for the purpose be granted of One penny <?> upon the acre, which, from the number of streams that water the country, is a sum which your petitioners think no more than adequate.

And your petitioners shall ever pray

>Solomon Fisk Proprietors Committee
>Isaac Fisk two shares.
>P. Edwards, two right
>Stephen R. Bradley Eleven Rights
>Joshua <Clap?>

ALS (Vt: MsVtSP, vol. 18, p. 341). A note on the verso (damaged by tape at folds) reads: "To the Honou<rable the> General Assembly <of Vermont> / Your Comm<ittee> to whome was R<eferre>d the Consideration of the within petition Report / That from <the> Information your <...> Can Collect The Roads th<erein> Mentioned are <abso>lutly Necessary for the advanta<ge> of the public as <well> as the Interest of the Several <Towns> throw which they <...> we are therefore of Opinion that a Tax of one penny be Granted on Each acare of Land in the Township of Montgomrey (publick Rights Excepted) and that <the> petitioners have Lea<ve to b>ring in a bill for that purpose. / <...> Harvey} for Committee." Docketed, "Petition for road thro' Montgomery / Filed Octr. 16th. 1792 / Attest / Lem. Chipman <...> / In Genl. Assembly / Octr. 17th 1792. Read & ref<erred> to Messrs. Harvey, Leaven<worth?,> Hatch, Shelden & Chamblain." Another docket reads: "In Genl. Assembly Octr. 31st 1792. The above Report read <& a>ccept. Attest / R Whitney Clerk."

To Edward R. Campbell

Head Quarters Westminster August 25th. 1792

Capt. Edward R. Campbell Commanding the Light Infantry Company in Westminster is Requested to take Effectual Means for filling up his Company and Leading them to the Choice of Such Officers as may be Necessary for Compleatly Organizing the Same with Officers for that purpose he is Impowered to Inlist Men out of any of the Companies of Militia in Coln Minotts Regiment or any other persons not belonging to the Artilery or Cavelry. Serjant Jabez Brown by leave of his Officers is permitted to Inlist into Capt. Craiges Company & on producing a Certificate to that purpose Capt. Campbell will Discharge him from his Company.

AD (DLC). In SRB's hand.

From Lewis R. Morris

Sir   Chester 1st. Septr. 1792

Enclosed you have Captn. Watkins's Letter to me requesting that he may liberty *[sic]* to resign his Commission — I wish Sir — it may be accepted, as it is the only means of restoring any order in the company. I wish your answer as soon as convenient — that the vacancy may be filled before Muster.

I am Sir with Respect your most ob<edt. Servt.>

LR Mor<ris>

Brigr. Genl. Bradley

ALS (DLC). Cover addressed by Morris to "Brigadier General Bradley / Westminster." Damaged by removal of seal. Enclosure not found.

To Stephen Hayward

Brigade Orders.

Westminster October 18th. 1792

Stephen Hayward Captain of a Company in the first Regiment in the Eighth Brigade is required to warn his Company to meet at some convenient time and place to be by him Appointed and the Company so met to Lead to the choice of an Ensign in the room of Ensign Jonathan Gibson who had the Generals permission to resign, and make return according to law: and return the name of each officer to the General.

Stephen R Bradley Brigadier Genll.

Tomlinson Novr. 8th 1792

In presuance to the within orders I have Called the Company togeather in order to Chuse an Ensign in the Room of Ensign Jonathan Gibson who had the Genll premition to Resign and they made Choice of Joseph Axtill for their Ensign.

Stephen Hayward Capt.

ALS (AXV). Thomas Jefferson Library, Charlottesville, Virginia.

To Jonas Holden

Sir   Westminster, Octor. 18. 1792

You may have, the refusal of the 1100 Acres, of land in Ludlow, adjoining Wallingford gore, bought, of Capt Johnson, untill the 20th March next, at Three shillings, and Eight Pence, ℘ Acre to be paid, One half, in two Years from, next May the other half in four Years from said May, to be on Interest, from, this date

(signed) Stephen R Bradley

Mr Jonas Holden

Tr (VtU). In the hand of Thomas Pearsall. Enclosed in Pearsall's letter of 26 Feb. 1793, below.

Account

[ca. 19 October 1792]

Novr Term 1788	The State of Vermont Dr to Stephen R Bradley. To Manageing a Cause for the State wherein John Norton was Pltt & Eliakim Spooner Defendant in an <...> of Ejectment for Confiscated Land before the County Court to Judgment	£ 1:10: 0
August Term 1790	the State Dr to manageing the Same Cause to Judgment before the Supreme Court	1:10: 0
		3: 0: 0

The above is a true account

Errors Excepted

Stephen R. Bradley

I <cer>tify that Stephen R Bradley was States attorney for windham County when the Above Charge is Dated & did manage for the State the Above Cause as Charged

Luke <Knoulter?>

ADS (Vt). Torn at folds. A note on the verso reads: "Auditors Office / Windsor Oct 19th. 1792 / No. 13 / £3-0-0 / The within <bein>g Examined is allowed the Treasurer is directed to pay the same to Stephen R Bradley or bearer it being Three pounds. / Elisha C<...>"

To Andrew Hull

Brother Hull   Philadelphia Jany. 30th 1793

I have nothing new to write you under God's Heavens it's the Same old Jargon as when you was here business progresses Slowly nothing certain from Europe Since you left here no information as yet from Carollina I have inclosed you the two last papers from which you will learn more in half an hour of politicks than if I were to write Six Days a further assumsion of the States Debts has been carried in the house of Representatives and is now depending in Senate it was determined by the Speaker the members being equally divided I rather think it will not pass the Senate.

I have heard parson Sage is married God's Children love flesh as well as Cash my respects to Mrs Hull and Friends and with pleasure I Subscribe your Friend

Stephen R Bradley

Esqr Hull

ALS (DLC).

From Joseph Fay to Thomas Jefferson

Dear Sir   Bennington 13th. Feby. 1793

I had this day the honor of your letter of the 27th. Ulto. in which you lay me under too much obligation by your friendly apology for not shewing me that attention which you really meant while I was in Phila. Be assured sir, that I was so far from entertaining a thought of any Neglect on your part, that I felt as tho I had committed an *error* in not paying that attention to you which I conceived due your Station. Mr. Bradley informed me of your friendly intention which you express in your letter, and I desired Mr. Robinson to be particular in making my best Compliments to you, and to excuse my not Calling on you again, as business required my immediate return to N. York. I took the Liberty a few days ago of enclosing you the last Canada papers, and shall send you more as they come to hand. Please to accept the best wishes of your Sincere friend and Servant   Joseph Fay

RC (MHi); at foot of text: "Mr Jefferson"; endorsed by TJ as received 1 Mch. 1793 and so recorded in SJL. Fay must have enclosed the Canadian newspapers in a letter to TJ of 10 Feb. 1793, which is recorded in SJL as received 1 Mch. 1793 but has not been found.

From papers of Thomas Jefferson, Princeton University.

From Robert Troop

Sir   New York 26 May 1793

Certain lands have been regularly appraised & set off to me in your State under an execution issued upon a judgment I obtained against Walter Livington. My right under this judgment may be affected by a judgment lately entered against Mr. Duer for Mr Johnson. Mr.

Paine who has charge of My interests in your State will inform you of particulars and I beg leave to refer you to him for this purpose. The object of this letter is to request you to be concerned with Mr Paine as one of my counsel in his endeavours to set aside Johnson's judgment. I shall by the first safe opportunity remit you a fee & at the same communicate my ideas to Mr Paine to be submitted to you. In the mean time I wish that the business may be particularly attended to and that nothi[n]g may be left undone that may tend to my advantage. I shall most chearfully pay you generously for your services. The holding of the lands under my judgment is a serious object to me and every nerve must be strained to defeat the title of my adversaries. The setting of Johnsons judgment aside may save me a very troublesome & expensive controversy respecting Walter Livingston's title in opposition to Duers at the time the different attachments were issued.

I am Sir, Very respectfully, Your humble Servt

Rob Troop

P.S. I have written to Mr West upon the same subject.

Stephen R Bradley Esqr

ALS (NcD: Bradley Family Papers). Cover addressed to "Stephen R Bradley Esqr / Vermont"; docketed by SRB, "Robert Troop / N York."

Bond to Dan Foster

[3 October 1793]

Know all Men by these presents that I Stephen R Bradley of Westminster in the County of Windham and State of Vermont am held & Stand firmly bound unto Dan Foster of Weathersfield in the County of Windsor and State of Vermont in the full & just Sum of one hundred & Eighteen pounds Nine Shillings lawful money to be paid to the said Dan Foster his Certain Attorney Executors administrators or Assigns to the which payment well and truly to be made & done I bind myself my heirs Executors and administrators firmly by these presents Sealed with my Seal Dated this 3d Day of Octbr. A.D. 1793.

The Condition of the Above bond is Such that whereas a dispute in Law has heretofore arisen of and Concerning a Certain Lot of Land Situate lying and being in Said Town of Weathersfield being Lot Number twenty four in the fourth Division and the Same lot of Land on which John Lawrence now lives in said Weathersfield which said Lot Thomas Pearsall purchased by Deed of Genll. Wooster and on the 6th Day of Decr. 1784 Conveyed the Same by Deed to the said John Lawrence for the Consideration of three Certain Notes Given by the said Lawrence to the said Pearsall bearing date the same Day & year last aforsaid for the Sum of Sixty one Dollars Each on Interest & to ensure the payment of the said three Notes the said John Lawrence at the same time by a Morgage Deed conveyed the premises to the said Pearsall Conditioned to be Void on payment of the said three Notes which same lot is Claimed by the Said Dan Foster and Thomas Prentice of Weathersfield aforesaid in right of the first Settled minister and it being mutually agreed between the parties for the ending of all disputes that if the Said Dan Foster & Thomas Prentice pay unto the Said Thomas Pearsall the Sum of fifty Nine pounds four and Six pence being one half the Sum contained in the principle & Interest of the sd three Notes Given by said John Lawrence to the Said Thomas Pearsall with the Costs that have arisen in prosecuting the Same then the Said Thomas Pearsall Should release & Quit Claim to the said Dan Foster all his right & title in the premises and assign to him the Said Morgage with all the appurtenances thereto belonging and the Said Dan Foster & Thomas Prentice in further prosecuting Said agreement have Each of them Executed to the Said Thomas Pearsall two Notes bearing date with this [r]epresents the

Contents of the two Notes Executed by the Said Foster being thirty Seven pounds Seventeen & ten pence half payable in one year the Other moiety in four years the Contents of the two Notes Executed by the Said Thomas Prentice being twenty one pound Six Shillings & Eight pence one Note payable two years after Date the Other three Years after Date Now if the said Thomas Pearsall Shall within a reasonable time after said four Notes Shall have been paid release & forever Quitclaim all his right & title of in or to the before described Lot of Land and also make over and assign to the said Dan Foster his heirs & assigns forever the before mentioned Morgage to the Sole Use Benefit & behoof of the Said Dan Foster — then the above Bond to be Void & of No Effect but in default thereof to be & Remain in full force & Virtue.

The words "One Hundred & Eighteen pounds Nine Shillings" in the fifth Line Wrote on razure before Signing.

Signed Sealed & Delivered in presence of   Stephen R Bradley
    Wst Thomas Prentis
    Joel Stark

ADS (VtU). In the hand of SRB. Docketed by SRB, "Bond to Print."

Receipt

Boston Novr. 6. 1793.

Mr Mark Richards to Samuel Cheney Dr.
To Schooling Nathaniel Dorr from August 6 3 Months   £1: 0: 0
Received the above in full.

Samuel Cheney

ADS (DLC). Nathaniel Dorr later became a clipper ship captain and married Stephen Row Bradley's granddaughter Emily Penelope Bradley.

To William Czar Bradley

[5 December 1793]

I have sent a newspaper of this day, wherein you will see that the French, a great and powerful nation, who have been oppressed by kings, priests, and a certain class of men called nobles, who are frequently worthless, being designed to abuse the rest of mankind, are making repairs in their government, dethroning their king. If they should, it will make an important revolution in the history of this world, from which period will spring the daystar of liberty; and you will hereafter read with rapture the effort made by the French people, which, in its effect, will not only redound to their good but to yours and mine, and nations yet unborn.

Printed (*Bradley Family Papers*).

An Act Making an Alteration in the Flag of the United States

[13 January 1794]

STATUTE I.

CHAPTER I.— An Act making an alteration in the Flag of the United States.[1]

Be it enacted by the Senate and House of Representatives of the United States of America in Congress assembled, That from and after the first day of May, Anno Domini, one thousand seven hundred and ninety-five, the flag of the United States, be fifteen stripes alternate red and white. That the Union be fifteen stars, white in a blue field.

APPROVED, January 13, 1794.

<small>Printed (Act of 13 January 1794, ch. 1, *Stat.* 1).
1. On 23 December 1793, SRB proposed a bill making an alteration in the flag of the United States. The bill was read in the Senate for the first time on 26 December. The following day it was read a second time and amended. On Monday, 30 December, the bill was read a third time and passed (*Annals of Congress*, Senate, 3rd Congress, 1st Session, p. 24).</small>

From Thomas Forrest

To Stephen Bradly Esq.   Philadelphia 20 June 1794.

In hopes this will find you enjoying the Pleasures of the sum<mer?> permit me to address you in a few lines. The Political horizon seems to <be?> so loaded with Matter, that it is utterly impossible to judge wh<at> will happen in the present Campaign in Europe. Pray God it may <not?> last, and that peace may succeed Devastation.

As I hope soon to be a land holder of Windsor. I with great pleasure send you a copy from a late publication of mine,[1] amongst Plan<s> & Views, there is an account of a Chineze aquatic manuvre never used I believe but by them, altho, the advantages are obvious. I mean to try the Chineze scull on the Connecticut when I receive your summons to repo<rt> thither, and shall be much obliged if youl point out the most prope<r> Rout. Being most respectfully, Sir, your most obedient Humble Servant

                                                                 Thos. Forrest

Please to direct at Mr Grammds 2d Street.

<small>ALS (VtU). Margin obscured.
1. *A Voyage from Calcutta to the Mergui Archipelago, Lying on the East Side of the Bay of Bengal;* ..., London, 1792.</small>

Senator Stephen R. Bradley[1] to Governor Chittenden

                                                          Rutland October 10th 1794

Sir

I take the liberty of enclosing a transcript from the Journal of the Senate of the United States of the 7th November 1791 by which you will perceive, the Seat I have the honour to hold in the Senate will be Vacant on the 4th Day of March Next —

I need not mention the importance of it's being early communicated to the Legislature, to enable them seasonably of public affairs in their opinion may require —

I have the honour to be with the Greatest Respect

                         Your Excellency's
                         Most Obedient
                and Very Humble Servant
                                   Stephen R Bradley

His Excellency Thomas Chittenden Esqr
Govr &c &c —

[The original letter in the hand of Stephen R. Bradley, including the wax seal at the folds.]

1. He was a member of the commission that settled the controversy with New York and the one that fixed the boundary between that State and Vermont. He was, next to Chipman, the most powerful man in the Convention of 1791, called to ratify the Federal Constitution and to take action on the admission of Vermont to the Union. Walter H. Crockett, *Vermont, the Green Mountain State*, Vol. V, pp. 61–63.

Mss. Vermont State Papers, Vol. 24, p. 74.

Ephraim Welles to Amos Carpenter

Sir   November the 11 1794

Pleas to Deliver unto Ebenezer Goodhue the Lot of Land that you Live on the first day of may next you will not cut any ash timber nor mapel you are to git your wood make Shuger and Live on Sd place untill the first of may you are not to plow any on Sd place nor Sow any Grain.   Ephraim Welles

P S pleas to Let me have 40 or 50 wait of Shugar in the Spring.

To Amos Carpenter at Westminster

ALS (DLC).

From Augustus Van Horne

Sir   New York Decemr: 26th: 1794

I have received yours of the 24th. instant, and this day Call'd on Mr: Thomas Pearsall and Received from him the One hundred Dollars you transmitted to him for me, for which I thank you — and have placed the Same to your Credit On Accot: of monies you Collected for me in the State of Vermont.

I am Very respectfully Sr: your mo: Obt: Servt:

Aug: V: Horne

Honble: Stephen R Bradley Esqr.

ALS (VtU).

Governor Chittenden Approves and Signs a Town Meeting Warning to Elect a Representative to Congress

[13 January, 1795]

By His Excellency
THOMAS CHITTENDEN, Esquire
Captain-General, and Commander in Chief, in and over the
State of Vermont.

A WARRANT.

To the first Constables of the several Towns in the Counties of Windsor, Windham, and Orange; or, in their Absence, to the Selectmen of said Towns,   Greeting.

WHEREAS it appears by the Returns of the County Clerks of the Eastern District, that no Person has a Majority of all the Votes of the Freemen in Said District, to represent this State in the Congress of the United States — the Statement of Votes being as follows, viz. for

Nathaniel Niles,	673
Daniel Buck,	452
Jonathan Hunt,	235

Stephen Jacob,	233
Lewis R. Morris,	177
Cornelius Lynde,	100
Paul Brigham	71
Lot Hall,	58
Elijah Robinson,	28
Stephen R. Bradley,	17
Samuel Cutler,	16
Reuben Atwater,	13
Daniel Farrand,	12
Royal Tyler,	11
Benjamin Green,	7
Benjamin Henry,	5
James Whitelaw,	3
Oliver Gallup,	3
Asa Burton,	2
Israel Morey,	2
Isaac Green,	2
Benjamin Emmons,	2
Alexander Harvey,	1
William Buckminster,	1
Samuel Knight,	1
William Bigelow,	1
Ephraim Wheelock,	1
John Bridgman,	1
Joseph Lewis,	1
Alden Spooner,	1

You are therefore directed to warn all the Freemen of your respective Towns, to meet at the usual Places of holding Town-Meetings, on the *Second Tuesday of February next,* at two o'Clock P.M. for the Purpose of choosing a Person to represent this State in Congress; and you are further directed, at the opening of the Meeting, to read, or cause to be read, the Statement of the Votes of the Freemen, at their former Meeting, as returned by the Clerks.

Given under my Hand at Williston, *this 13th Day of January,* 1795.

Tho's Chittenden.

Mss. Vermont Historical Society Collections.

To Hezekiah May

Sir,   Philadelphia Jany. 31st. 1795

Yours of the 20 Instant has Come Safe to hand in return I send you last evenings paper in addition to the News therein Contained we have received a priv\<ate\> letter anouncing that Mr Jay has Completed the busines\<s\> of his Mission and that a treaty of Amity Commerce & navigation has been Signed between the United States & G. Britain.

I am in hast[e] Yours

Stephen R Bradley

Mr May

ALS (Private Owner). Docketed, "To Hezh. May." Right margin obscured.

From Stephen Williams

Honored Sir   Springfield 25th. May 1796

    I herewith send you a Note <signe>d by Capt Goodell, Lt. Eaton & Mr Ho<lt?> that it may be collected as soon as possible. Having waited several Years & called in vain repeatedly for the Payment & finding no prospect of obtaining it by other Means I am induced to request you to take the most proper & effectual Means for the speedy collection of what remains due. The endorsement will inform of whatever has been received & the Time of Reception.

    As the Bearer waits I cannot enlarge but depend on your own Discretion &c.

    I remain hond Sir your humbl Servt.

                                                                   Stephen Williams

Honble. S. R. Bradley

    ALS (VtU). Damaged by removal of seal.

From Martha Olcott

                                                         Springfield Sepbr. 6 1796

General Bradley to Martha Olcott Dr

To boarding your son from fourth of July 1792 to 12th October 1793

Septber.	Absent 1 week	
October	Absent 2 weeks	
June	Absent 5 weeks & 1 day	
	Absent 2 weeks & 1 day	
October	Absent 2 weeks & four days	
12	went home returned 12th December	
Dr.	To trimmings for Cloaths	£0..1..10
Febry. 1793	To overhalls & trimmings	..16..8
15th	" Taylor works for your son	..5..
	" 1 doz. of buttons	..1..3
	½ yd. Holland	..1..8
	" 2 yds. <Ricksete?> at Mr. Deanes	..10..8
Cr.		
August 29	By Cash 30 Dolls.	£9.. ..
1792		
May 20 1793	" Cash 23 Dolls.	6..13..
By Mrs. Bradley 6 dollars		£15..18..

Billy went home 12th of October and returned the 12 of December. I have lost the account of his return home. I have made no separate charge of his mending and candles—if you think them of any consequence you may make me some consideration.

                                                                    Martha Olcott

    ADS (NcD). Notation by SRB, "3: 3: 2 / [minus] 1[:] 16: 0 / [equals] 1: 7: 2."

Petition of Abner Miles

Petition of Abner Miles to the General Assembly of Vermont (Summary). *27 September 1796, Putney.* On 12 May 1777 Miles purchased one hundred acres of land in Putney from Isaac Bard, who now resides in West Springfield, Massachusetts, for £133.6.8. After receiving payment in full, Bard entered into a bond with Moses Johnson to give Miles a deed to the land in six months from the date of purchase. Miles then took possession of the one hundred acres and made improvements on it, including building a house and barn and clearing and planting fruit trees during a period of over nineteen years.

When he did not receive a deed, Miles commenced a suit against Bard and Johnson. In the Windham County supreme court held in August 1790 he recovered £75 and costs, but Bard brought an action of ejectment against Miles to recover possession of the land, and in the supreme court term of September 1794, Bard recovered fifty acres, the part of the farm that includes Miles's house, barn, and orchards. Believing the jury in the case made a mistake, Miles asked that a new trial be held in the case, but the court did not allow it. Miles asks the General Assembly to grant him either a new trial or such other relief as they shall deem reasonable.

ADS (Vt: MsVtSP, vol. 19, p. 313a). 3 pp. There are several notes and dockets on the verso of the last page of the petition. The first note reads: "State of Vermont / Windham Ss / To Asael Goodridge an indifferent Person to Serve & return / Greetings / By the authority of the State of Vermont you are hereby Commanded to summon the within named Isaac Bard of West Springfield in the Commonwealth of Massachusetts to appear before the Honorable General Assembly of this State at their next Session to be holden at Rutland on the Second Thursday in October next (by leaving a true and attested Copy of the within Petition and this Citation with Stephen R Bradley Esqr. of Westminster in sd. County of Windham Attorney to the sd. Isaac) and shew Cause if any he has why the Prayer of the within Petition should not be Granted. Given under my hand at Westminster this 29th Day of September 1796 / Lot Hall Judge Sup, Court." The second note reads: "Westminster Octr. 1st. 1796. Then I Served this Precept by delivering a true & attested Copy of the Petition & Citation thereto annexed into to the hands of the above named Stephen R. Bradley Esqr. at his Dwelling house in Westminster. / Attest. / Asael Goodridge." The third note reads: "Personally appeared Asael Goodridge Signor of the above return and made solemn oath to the truth thereof this 10th day of Octr. 1796 / Before / Lot Hall Jus. Peace." The dockets read: "Abner Miles / Petition 1796 / vs Isaac Bard / Filed Octr. 19t. 1796 / Rosl. Hopkins secy."; "In General Assembly. / 22nd Octr. 1796. / Read & referred to Messrs. Chittendon, Joshua Chamberlin & Royce to join, State facts &c. / Wm. R Whitney Clks."; "In Council Oct the 22 Day ad 1796 read & resolved that Messrs White & Williams be appointd to Join sd Committee / Attest <T. Squier?> / Secry."

To Asa Porter

Sir   Westminster December 13th. 1796

Since I saw you I have had a meeting of the Inhabitants settled on the Land of the late William Smith in Chester they were very generally together between thirty and forty — and unanimously rejected your proposition. They say that unless they Can have the land to average about Nine or ten Shillings pr acre they are determined to try it on in the Law — and that they informed you the Same when at Chester. In short I could do nothing with them toward a Compromise that would in the least meet your Expectations. Some of them propose to Let you take their farms if you will pay them for the buildings & improvements as the Same Shall be apprised by Indifferent Men. I give you this earliest information in my power that you may order your Conduct accordingly.

I am Sir with the highest Esteem Your Humbl Servt

                                                                            Stephen R Bradley

Coln Aas Porter

ALS (VtU).

To James Madison

Dear Sir   Westminster February 18th. 1797

Previous to Coln. Monroe's departure for Europe he transmitted to me papers and documents accompanying a Claim to five thousand acres of Land in the Township of Middlesex in this State in right of his wife,[1] this Township was held under a Patent from The late province of New York and was one (among many) of those patents which were extinguished in the late treaty or Settlement between New York & Vermont and for which This Government has paid to New York Thirty thousand Dollars for the benefit of those whose titles were thus affected. New York have of late appointed Commissioners to apportion to each sufferer his Share of the thirty thousand Dollars The Commissioners have met this Winter in Albany I have exhibited Col. Monroe's Claim to them they have as Yet Come to no decision probably they will in the Course of the Summer what Col Monroe's proportion will be remains Yet to be determined—The claims however are so extensive that it is not probable the Sum will be large.

With Sentiments of the highest Esteem I am Sir Your Most Obedt Hble Servt.

                                                       Stephen R. Bradley

Hon. James Madison Jur. Esqr.

ALS (DLC). Docketed by Madison, "Bradley Stephen Feby. 18. 1797."
1. Before leaving for Paris in 1794 to take up his position as U.S. minister to France, James Monroe gave Madison a power of attorney that included authorization to "receive whatever is obtained from Genl. Bradley from the sale of our Vermont property, or otherwise from the sale or upon acct. of it" (*Papers of Madison*, 15:346–47 and n. 2).

From James Monroe

Dear Sir   New York July 12. 1797.

I enclosed you before my departure for Europe a power of Attorney with deeds plats &ca for certain lands in Vermt. with a view that you might endeavor to turn them to the best acct. for Mrs. Monroe to whom they belonged. I trust you recd. them as they were forwarded according to the direction of Govr. Robinson, I flatter myself also you have been able to do something in the business for our advantage. I have requested Colo. Fay to confer with you on this subject, & wish if nothing is done that you and he determine what course is to be taken, if any, & if none in Vermt. that you be so good as deliver them to him that he may use them here as he thinks fit. I am happy in this opportunity of renewing to you the assurances of my sincere esteem & respect, being with best wishes for yr. welfare yrs.

                                                       James Monroe

ALS (DLC). Cover addressed by Monroe to "General Bradley / Vermont / By Colo. Fay." Docketed by SRB, "From Mr Monroe."

To James Monroe

Dear Sir   Westminster in Vermont July 22d 1797

I received your favor of the 12th. Instant by Coln. Fay and have the pleasure to acquaint you that upon a full Examinat<ion> of your Claim, I was induced to believe your best Course to obtain any thing, lay in applying to the Commissioners of New York who had declared your title or Claim to Cease accordingly in the Course of last winter I caused your Claim to be Seasonably Exhibited to the Commissioners at Albany who I understand have adjourned to Some time in September Next when it will be Necessary Still to prosecute the

Claim before them and Exhibit the papers & documents to Suport the title I have transmitted to you by Coln. Fay all the papers the Expence hitherto accrewed in prosecution the busi<ness> is thirty one Dollars and Sixty five Cents I have appo<in>ted that to be paid to my Friend Thomas Pearsall of New York and have Given him a Draugh[t] on you for the Same — and have the pleasure of repeating to you my sincere Esteem and <Regard> and am with Sentiments of the highest Respect Your Most Obedient Humbl Servt

Stephen R Bradley

Hon James Monroe

ALS (VtU). Margin obscured.

From Jonathan Robinson

Dear sir   Bennington August 22d 1797

It was my intention to have been at New Fa<ne?> Court & had an Oppertunity of Chat with you on that *Subj*<ect> to which every thing else gives place, the War of Senti<ment> in America — as well as Europe runs high, and since we have an expectation of a Battle to be fought at Windsor in October next we have a desire to have you take an Important post in the Action for this Purpose Mr Spooners friends have Sent a Man to Westminster with Several Letters from Gentlemen here ardently requesting him to give his Support in the Election to you. The fact is we have been Worsted in our last action in Octr last and are unwilling to risque another withou[t] you. I fear friend Bradley you are not as Ambitious of an Office over Republicans as you ought to be. In my early life as a Legislator I fought und<er> you. I wish once more to hear your Eloquenc<e> Shakeing the Legislature of Vermont. Dont be asleep it is no time for Generals to be Idle. Esqr. Selden the bearer of this has an acquaintance with you and will deliver you our Nominations give him all the Assistance you can and forward to all those you dare the Nominations. You are acquainted with Smith and know him to be a man of talents & of Integrity. You best are acquainted with the Charecters at Westmin<ster> best by some Means or other do you appear as a Member this year or never show your face aga<in.> You have my sincere thanks for your Exertion to Save Esqr Whitney. God be praised that you have Succeeded. The Nomination for Councilors we have sent to the North end of the State in several directions and are very Certain Mony will Succeed. We have put Spooner into the list to lure his Opposition to you, besides he is a man of Real Republican Sentiment is there no way you can heal the difficulty between you. Recommend Esqr Selden to such Charecters in the different Towns in the County as You consider Will be safe.

I am dear sir with sentiments of Esteem your Cordial friend

Jonathan Robinson

Stephen R. Bradley Esqr.
Westminster

ALS (VtU). Margin obscured. Docketed in an unknown hand, "from Jon Robison."

From George Clarke

New York Sunday 10 Spt: 1797

On my Arrival at New York I found myself exceedin<gly> <disap>pointed in not having received your Opinion relative to the <Wallums>chaick Case, more especially as my stay was to be short; & I <purpo>rsely brought up some Papers in order to Consult Coll: Hami<lton>.

In a former Letter I informed you that I had given orders <for> <i>mmediate payment of 40 dollars, which was accordingly done, [...]day called on Mr: Pearsall who informed me he had given you [...] that Amount. I therefore should esteem it as a particular [...] you would transmit me (to the Care of Jacob Le Roy & Sons) the [...] your researches & Opinion founded on the Basis of your Laws & [...] as soon as possible from Sir your most Obt:

Geo: Clarke

<Stephen> R Bradley Esqr

ALS (VtU). Margins obscured.

To George Clarke

Sir   Westminster Sept. 17th 1797

Herewith I transmit you an opinion of the Case Stated respecting Wallumschaick Patent as no documents statement was made of the <dedicate?> of your title under that Grant I give no opinion concerning the Same but have considered it as a Trust Granted that the Chain of title to you was is legal & proper. I have laid the Grant of Benningto<n> under New Hamshire out of the Question for if the Wallumschaick Patent did Convey a title no subsequen<t> Grant could affect that title til it was lost or done away, I enclose you the Statute commonly Called our Quieting Act refered to in the Statement which is the only limitation Act that respect<s> real Estates that has run in our Governmen<t>. I have been obliged to abridge the observation<s> from the many [*illegible*] that turned came up in the Case and Especially the Quotations to Show the aforesaid limitation Act is different from all others, I have only cited Massachusetts New York and Connecticut, Instances might have bee<n> adduced from Every state in the Union and alm<ost> Every well regulated Government under Heaven I Should have sooner transmitted you the papers had it not been for business I have been Called for the [*illegible*] professional been in my power, the shortness of the time I have had to attend to the Subject will be an Excuse for the imperfection<s>.
I have the Honour to be Sir Sir your Most Obedient Hbl Srt

Stephen R Brad<ley>

George Clark Esqr

ALS (VtU). Margin obscured.

Bond to Mathias Gorham

[30 January 1798]

Know all Men by these presents that I Stephen R Bradley of Westminster in the County of Windham and State of Vermont am Held and Stand firmly bound unto Mathias Gorham of Yarmouth in the County of Barnstable and State of Massachusetts in the final Sum of two thousand Dollars to be paid to the Said Mathias Gorham his Certain Attorney Executors administrators or assigns to the which payment will and truly to be made and Done I bind myself my heirs Executors & administrators firmly by these presents Sealed with my Seal Dated this 30th Day of Januay 1798.

The Condition of the above bond is Such that if the above named Mathias Gorham his heirs Executors or administrators shall on or before the 15th Day of May Next pay or Caused to be paid to Stephen R Bradley five Hundred and fifty Dollars and procure to be Executed and delivered to the Said Bradley a Note to be Signed by the Said Gorham, Atherton Hall Esqr and Scotto Clark of Said Westminster for the Sum of four Hundred Dollars payable the first Day of January 1799 with the Interest for the Same from sd 15 Day of May Next and if the Said Bradley upon his performing the Same Shall Deliver to the Said Gorham a Note Signed by Joseph Ide Dated June 21st 1797 for the Sum of Nine Hundred Dollars payable on sd 15th Day of May Next and Shall also Cancel and deliver up a Morgage Deed of Sd Joseph Ide's place bearing Date with said Note then the above bond to be Void and of no Effect but if said Gorham Shall fulfill on his part and Sd Bradley Shall Neglect or refuse to be and remain in full force and Virtue.

N B Gorham wrote on Razure

Signed Sealed & Deliverd

in presence of

Noah Sabin Junr

Joseph Ide

AD (VtU). In the hand of SRB.

Congressional Pugilists

Political Cartoon dated February 15, 1798

Caption reads:

> He in a trice struck Lyon thrice

Political cartoon

Upon his head, enrag'd Sir,
Who seiz'd the tongs to ease his wrongs,
And Griswold thus engag'd, Sir.

Congress Hall,
in Philad[a] Feb. 15. 1798.

Caption under picture of fighting cocks hanging on the wall at top of illustration:

Royal Sport

<small>Reproduced from the Collections of the Library of Congress; handwritten numbers 320920 and LC-USZ62-1551.</small>

From Peter Stuyvesant

Dear Sir   Bowery House N. york the 4th June 1798

Yours of the 16th December 97[1] I have before me, my not answerg: it before is Owing to a letter I reced: from D. Fraser about the Same time in which he informs me that William Holton would be in N. york certainly in May and pay of his Debt but as I have heard nothing farther from them since, I desire you will proceed against them as will compell payment in the Shortest time it can be Done. You desire me to Send you the bonds, I think there may be a great risque to send the bond will it not do if I Send a Coppy under a notoral Seal. *I think you might proceed on the Lease & release* which are recorded at Large in Brattleborough town records for deeds, on page 15 & 16 by Samuel Knight town Clark and Acknowledged before Saml: Knight Justice <of the> peace. William Holton's acknowledged & recorded before & by the Same <per>son or persons on the 13th January 1785[2] on page 17 & 18 — if they are not Come to N. york or comming Soon to Settle the Debt you will please to write me soon what Will be best for me to do & how I must proceed — I am in great haste Dr Sr. yr Very Humbe Sert.

Per: Stuyvesant

Stepn: R Bradley Esqr.
Westminster
   Vermont

<small>ALS (NcD: Bradley Family Papers). Damaged by removal of seal. Cover addressed "To / Stephen R Bradley Esqr: / in / Westminster / Vermont / Via Hartford"; docketed by SRB, "From Peter Stuyvesant." Another copy of this letter (LS [ibid.]; marked "Coppy") includes an undated postscript in Stuyvesant's hand: "Dear Sir / Since I wrote you the above I have not reced: a line from you and I was very much Surprisd when I heard you had been in New york and did not Call at my House, I think it would have been a very good opport<y.> for you to have got the Necessary papers. As I am in great haste I referr you <to> the foregoing of the 4th June Last and request an Answer — I am Dr Sr: your Obedient Humbe Ser<t.> / Per: Stuyvesant."
1. Letter not found.
2. LS reads "1795."</small>

To Samuel Mattocks

Sir   Westminster July 7th 1798

    Nathan Robinson the first Constable of this town moved away from here in the Course of last winter and left with me the Care of Settling the Cent Tax I am engaged to Judge Williams of Rutland who is doing business for the State to pay him One Hundred & fifty Dollars before the first of August the remainder of the money I have ready and will transmit to the treasury if I have an opportunity befo<re that>t time if not I expect to be at Vergennes some time <in> August & will settle it I wish no extent to issue nor no Cost to be made as the tax shall certainly be paid there will be a considirable Drawback on account of the Surveyor Generals returning the town at large.

I am &c Sr. Your Hble Servt.

Stephen R Bradley

Samuel Mattocks Esqr
    Treasurer —

LS? (Vt: MsVtSP, vol. 24, p. 209). Cover addressed to "Samuel Mattocks Esqr. / Vergennes / Vermont" and marked "post" and "Walpole, July 7." Docketed, "S. R. Bradley."

To Samuel Mattocks

Sir   Westminster August 15th. 1798

I have heretofore agreed with Judge Williams to pay to the Treasurer One Hundred & fifty Dollars for the Cent Tax on the Town of Westminster I suppose he has done it I have Sent by Genll Fletcher Ninety Dollars which will Make two Hundred and forty Dollars that with the Deduction and what will be Certified by the Select men amount to The Tax the papers necessary from the Select Men &c I will bring when the Assembly sits and Close the business— til that time I wish the business might lie as the whole Tax is paid that is Due or Can be Collected under the Act.

I am Sir With Great Esteem Your Humble Servant

Stephen R Bradley

To Samll Mattocks Esqr
Treasurer

ALS (Vt: MsVtSP, vol. 24, p. 196). Cover addressed to "the Honble Samuel Mattocks Esqr / Vergennes." Docketed, "Bradley Letter."

To Mr. Richards

Westminster August 18th. 1798

Mr Bradley requests Mr Richards to enclose the within Bill to some of his Friends in or Near Boston and if paid he will take the money here, he will Thank Mr Richards to give directions that if Coln. <Brattle?> utterly refuses to accept or pay the bill to send the same back and not be at the Expence of haveing it protested tho' he thinks there is no doubt it will be paid

He remains with respect

Stephen R Bradley

Mr. Richards

ALS (NcD: Bradley Family Papers). A note in the lower margin in an unidentified hand reads: "Amount of the above bill was Fifty three Dolls Sixty Cents."

To Samuel Mattocks

Westminster May 23d 1799

The Honble. Samll. Mattocks Esqr.
Sir

The Select Men of the Town of Westminster have recieved your Letter of the 6th Instt. on the subject of a balance due on account of a Tax granted for the purpose of averaging the cost of raising 300 Men in 1782 — They are not a little surprized that the old Claim should be revived at this time as the Town actually settled said Tax agreeable to the requ[i]sition of the then Law about fifteen years since with Mr Fisk who was then a Man in good standing and well able to pay and if the Treasurer suffered the money to ly in his hands six or seven years without ever calling for it until Fisk failed they conceive it must be the latches and neglect of the Treasurer by which the money was lost and that they cannot in any legal view of the subject be answerable for the same.

However at their request I have determined to wait upon you on the subject sometime about the 20th of June next and desire that no measures may be pursued or steps taken that in their consequences may be disagreeable either to them or you till that time

And am Sir. With perfect Esteem Your Most Obedient Humble Servant

Stephen R Bradley

PS Please to acquaint me by letter if Judge Williams of Rutland has settled 150 Dolls with you on the Cent Tax which he stipulated to do ten months ago.

LS? (Vt: MsVtSP, vol. 24, p. 245). Cover addressed to "The Honble Samuel Mattocks Esqr / Treasurer of Vermont / Middleburg" and marked "Westminster 24th. May 1799" and "12½ cts." Docketed, "Stephn. R. Bradly Letter."

Permit

[3 July 1799]

Know all Men by these presents That I Aaron Wales Appointed to Superintend the affairs of the Meeting House in the Eastern Parish in the town of Westminster have granted permission to Stephen R Bradley of said town to swing his bell in the Belfray in the Steeple of Said Meeting House free of all expence to Said Parish to remain under the directions of Said Bradley and to be Subject to his Controll til regulations between him and the Parish Shall be agreed on & Settled.

In witness whereof I have hereunto Set my hand this 3d Day of July 1799

Aaron Wales} Superintendant

Samuel Pratt

of the Meeting house

DS (NcD). In the hand of SRB.

Petition of John Noth

Windsor October the 10 1799

To the Honl: Genl: Cort Now Seting at Windsor T'n October the 10. for the year of our Lord 1799 the Humble Petishon of John Noth of Springfield in this State to which I Beg Leve to adress my Self & most Humbly I Pray your Exelence the Govenar & the Honl: Counsil & the Honl: house of Reprezentetives I pray your honrs to hear the grate Destressis that I am forced to Undergow By the most Cruel & unlawful Procedings off Stephen R Bradley Lewis R Morris Jeremiah Mayson Isaac Tower Elisha Brown Thomas Barritt & Silant Cutin did on the 11 day of August in the year 1790 Go to my house in Springfield in my abcenc & my wife was abcent also & in an Unlawful & Rietus manor as Band of Robers Got one of my Children out of my house by force & then Set my house on fire & Birnt it up & a part of my Goods was Birnt with it & By the assistance off these men Bradley hes Robed me off all my Liveing To the Valeu of a Thousand Pounds he hes Tuck my farm from me & Converted it to his own Use without law or Rite or the Coler of Rite without Even giveing me any Notis or worning &

So I am Ruined & intirely ondon for by Being so disstrest that I Could not Provide for my famiIey my wife hes gon & left me & my children are all Scatter'd about & I have No Place on Earth that I Can Call my own to live on & I have lost the Use of my Rite hand in part So that my labour is Very Small to Suport me in Life: & bradley hes By the Asistanc of this Band of Robers kept me off of my farm 9 years the 11 day of August last & Now there is no way on Earth for me to Bring these Vilins to Justis for the Want off a Bondsman which I Cannot Git for the law knows No Bondsman But one that hes got money to pay the Cost if these men Should Chanc to git Clear & I cant be my own Bondsman for I am Stript of Every thing that I Ever had & I am forced to Begg my Bread from dore to dore & Now I Pray in the Name of almity God that your Hors: will Take my hard Case into your wise Consideration & grant me Releaf as your wisdom thinks best Ither that the Cheif Judg of the Cort may Grant me a Speshal Rit in my own Name or Innable me to Bring this Band off Ryetous Robers to Justis as the Law in this State directs for it was Neaver known No whare Elce on Earth that Ryetous Robers Theafs or Murders Should go unponished for the want of a Bondsman or Because that the Pason So Robed could Not git a Rit So that Those Robers mite be apprehended & Brought to Justis for as the law is in this State if Bradley & Morris & all the Rest had Cut all my Children's Throats & a thrown them all into the fire & Bornt them in the house I Could not have Prosecuted no Beter then I can Now. There is Sum will Say that Bradley nor none of the Rest hes Neaver Bin Sited to hear this petichon as to that it was Neaver known that Ryetous theafes was Ever Sited any other way but Only By a Spachal Rit to apprehend them & Bring them to Justis & Now I Pray your Honrs. to Consider that there is no whare Elce for me to go in this State for Releaf But Only to this Assembley whare the law was first arected that No Sute Can be Brought against Criminals without a bonds man & if this is not the Place for me to go then I in the Name of God Pray your Honrs: to direct me. & Now I Pray your Honrs: to Consider how I am Oprest for I Cant have my Petichon Red withou I Can pay twenty shilings Except your Honrs: take pety on me & So Reed it without the fee & twenty Shilings is a Very Grate Sum for me to Pay out of Nothing I Most Humbly Submit my Self to the Good & Lawful Law off the State & Pray for the Wellfair of the Same & in the Name of almity God I Pray your Honrs: to Grant me Releaf in that Way as you in your Wisdom think Best. & I in duty Bound will Ever Pray —

John Noth

One word more I would inform your Honrs: that the Evedence is Sofishant to prove the Ryetous action of these men & So there is No way on Earth that they Can get Cleair of Being Brought to Justice if they are but prosecuted & as this is the head of the law in this State & there can no act be past hear or grant made here that can be Revoked any whare Elce in this State I therefore aply to you for Releafe & if I an Not Relevead & my Intrust Returned Back to me again that Bradley & Morris & Mayson & Tower & Brown & Barritt & Cutin hes Robed me off by Birning my house & Clubing me off of my farm without law or Rite then I must Sofer Unless the State Support me for I am 68 years Old & I am a Cripel for I have Lost the use of my Reite hand in part by Being frose on the Lake & therefore Most Humbley Pray for Releaf as your Honrs think Best. & in duty Bound will Ever Pray

John Noth

ADS (Vt: MsVtSP, vol. 20, p. 335). A note on the verso reads: "John Noth / Petition / Filed Octr. 15t. 1799. / Ro<?> Hopkins Secy / In Genl Assembly / Octr. 16t. 1799. / Read & dismissd / Attest Saml C <Cress?>."

Indenture with Samuel Lincoln and Samuel Lincoln Jr.

[21 October 1799]

 This Indenture made this twenty first day of October in the year of our Lord Seventeen Hundred Ninety and Nine between Stephen R Bradley of Westminster in the County of Windham & State of Vermont of the one part and Samuel Lincoln and Samuel Lincoln junr of Westmoreland in the County of Cheshire and State of New Hampshire of the other part Witnesseth that the party of the first part for and in consideration of the covenants and undertakings of the parties of the second part herein after expressed hath demised granted and to farm let to the said Samuel Lincoln & Samuel Lincoln junr and their Heirs all that certain tract or parcel of land lying and being in said Westminster known by the name of Lot Number three in the second range of Hundred acre Lots in said Westminster with the house and barn standing thereon & all appurtenances thereto belonging to have and to hold the same from the first day of instant October unto the fall and and term of forty three calendar months to wit to the last day of April in the year in the year of our Lord Eighteen Hundred and three and the said Stephen R Bradley doth covenant and agree with the said parties of the second part that he will put one yoke of oxen and ten cows upon the place to be used and improved thereon for and during said Term and fifteen sheep to receive thereof and herein after provided.

 And the said Samuel Lincoln & Samuel Lincoln junr. For themselves and their Heirs Executors and Administrators do covenant with the said Stephen R Bradley his Heirs & assigns that the said Samuel Lincoln junr. Shall move on to the premises & continue to improve and cultivate said farm according to the rules of good Husbandry during said Term that they will make no let strip or waste nor suffer any to be done that they will at the expiration of said term to wit on the last day of April Eighteen Hundred and three deliver up the quiet and peaceable possession of the premises in a good tenantable repair and situation that they will put said cattle and farm in the list as though they were their own and pay all taxes that shall be assessed on the same during said term. And the said Samuel Lincoln and Samuel Lincoln junr de further covenant promise and agree to and with the said Stephen R that they will on or before the first day of January Eighteen Hundred and one pay or cause to be paid to the said Stephen R Bradley for the use and improvement of the said farm and Stock before mentioned the sum of sixty six dollars and sixty seven Cents in port beef better Cheese or grain to be at the price the merchants pay for the same in Cash and shall in like manner pay or cause to be paid to the said Stephen R on or before the first day of January Eighteen Hundred and two the sum of sixty six dollars and sixty seven Cents and shall in like manner pay or cause to be paid to the said Stephen R on or before the first day of January Eighteen Hundred and three the sum of sixty six and sixty seven Cents and the parties of the second part do farther covenant that they will during said term make or cause to be made one Hundred Dollars worth of stone wall to be erected on the out side lines of said farm where the said Stephen R shall direct good double wall to be estimated at ninety one Cents per rod And the said parties of the second part do further covenant with the said Stephen R that at the expiration of the term aforesaid to wit on the last day of April in the year of our Lord eighteen Hundred and three they will deliver to the said Stephen R said Oxen said ten cows and fifteen sheep in good flesh for store Cattle or creatures with Hay enough to carry them through <ere> then spring and if any of the said creatures other than by the immediate act of God should die or perish be disabled or rendered unfit for use the parties of the second part covenant to replace them with others equally as good the calves and the lambs the spring the creatures are delivered back to the said Stephen R to be and belong to the said Stephen R.— And the said parties of the second part do further covenant with the said Stephen R that they will not cut fell destroy or carry away any more trees timber wood or fuel standing or being on the premises than is necessary for fire wood for the place and for the purpose of making repairs and improvement. The said party of the first part is to furnish hay enough on the premises to keep the stock through the ensuing winter and spring and to keep one Cow and a two year old Colt for the parties of the second part.

In witness whereof we have hereunto interchangeably set our hands and seals the day and date first above written.

Signed sealed & delivered in presence of	Samuel Lincoln
Wm Cz Bradley	Samuel Lincoln Jur
<Sam> Holten	Stephen R Bradley
	[1 January 1801]

Jany 1st. 1801 Samll Lincoln Jur paid Sixty Six Dollars & Sixty Seven Cents for the Years rent Ending April 30 1801.

DS (VtU). Notation of 1 Jan. 1801 by SRB.

From J. Eastman

Hon. Stephen R. Bradley Esqr.
Sir,   Fort Jay 4. February 1800.

I was honoured with your very obliging favour of the 26. Jan. and can, in no way, express my gratitude for the exertions you have mad<e> on my behalf, so much so by assuring you, on the hono<ur> of a Soldier, and a gentleman, that no effort on my part shall be wanting, to deserve the confiden<ce> with which you have been pleased to honour me.

I should forever detest myself, should I, by a want of faithfulness, or industry, in the discha<rge> of the duties of the Office, give you cause to blush that you had, by your influence promoted me to that station.

I have the Honour to be, my Much Hond Patron, Your Honour's Most Gratefu<l> and Most Obliged Humble Servt.

J. EASTMAN
Lieut. Artillsts

Hon. Stephen R. Bradley Esqr
Washington City

ALS (VtU). Margin obscured. Notation by SRB, "84: 49 [plus] 6 12, 2 [equals] 90, 61 2."

From Mark Richards

[8 February 1800]

At a Parish Meeting legally warned & held at the Meeting House in the East Parish in Westminster on the 12th day of Decr 1799 (was Voted Ninthly)

9th That John Sessions Esqr & Mark Richards be a Committee to wait on the Honl Stephen R. Bradley Esqr & enquire of him respecting the Bell's belonging to the Parish or not, so as to enable the Parish to take measures to take Care of the Same & to make report.

For John Sessions Esqr & Myself
A Coppy   Mark Richards} Committee

Parish [...]

Westminster 8th Feby 1800

Sir agreeable to the above vote passd by the Parish on the 12th Decr 99 — we the Comittee wait your answer & shall report accordingly & remain respectfully Yr Huml Servants

For John Sessions & myself — Committee

Mark Richards

ALS (NcD). Damaged by removal of seal.

From Elisha Tracy

Honlb. Stephen Roe Bradley Esq

Dear Sir   Norwich (Connecticut) Feby 22nd 18[00?]

The civilities received from you while at [...] & a desire to make some inquiry respecting the state of busi<ness> I left there, perticularly as respects our prospect of adju[...] differences with foreign powers, has induced to trouble [...] my correspondence; that we who are in a minority in [...] no means of communication but with Gentln. from oth[...] a fact so well known to you, that I trust it will be my [...] that an anxiety pretty generally pervades the minds of [...] of the United States is certain, but agricultrial interest s[...] generally to acquiesce in the embargo measure, the meve[...] being more generally *Federal* are more clamorous & of course distrusted. I do trust & hope the measure will be persiste<d> [...] Great Britain is brought to her senses, & a just estimat[...] rights. With France we must take the consiquences her[...] but it would seem that the court of Saint James with F[...] dependances & now Russia & all the North of Europe upon [...] & would not persist in provoking a Warr with us. If we [...] to make a treaty with them that will secure our Just rig[...] is certainly the favourable moment, & I for one feel tha<t> [...] may be placed in the United Wisdom of our Counsel to reason Warr is to be deprecated by all, but a line between that & free & friendly intercours<e> may be drawn that will be preferable to running the Gauntlet with our Commerce between the proclamations of the British King on one side & the Arrets of Saint Cloud on the other & if our affairs remain unsetled with England — will not a non impo<r>tation act be thought of before the session closes. I ask you not for impropper disclosures I know you will Judge for yourself, but if the embargo is to continue as it now stands is there not danger that the country will be drained of spec<ie> it will be difficult to restrain our merchants from sending it away; there is not much patriotism in them. I hear much grumbling & complaining as well might be expected in Connecticut but I do not see much real distress for money when good security can be given for it. I beg you to excuse the liberty I have taken & to believe me to be — with high Consideration of respect & much personal Esteem Dear Sir your humble

Elisha Tracy

ALS (VtU). Margins obscured. Endorsed, "Elisha Tracy."

From Charles Blake

Sir,   Keene N Hampshire March 9th 1800

I had the honor to receive yours of the 20th Ult. Since which have seen Doctor Kingsbary and by him am informed that he should prefer an appointment in the Navy, but will gladly accept an appointment of Surgeons Mate in the United States Army.

The Doctor would prefer being Stationed at Some Post in New England.

I have Sir, the honor to be with the utmost respect & esteem yr. Obdt. Hbl Servt

Charles Blake

Honb. S. R. Bradley
ALS (VtU).

From Peter Gerard Stuyvesant

Dr Sir   New York March 20th 18 — [1800]

Your departure from this City early on the morning of the 22nd of the last month, prevented me the pleasure of an Interview, which I at that time, much desired, particularly on account of the business you had committed to my care; tho, the steps I have since adopted, will, I flatte[r] myself meet with your approbation.

Mr Coleman's return the present week has enabled me to commence the prosecution on the notes. He was very desirous I should wait the result of his application, to you, and Mr Houghton, this however I could not think myself Justified in consenting to, considering the instructions I had received from you, were of so diametrical a nature; Mr Coleman will I presume (from what has passed between him and myself) propose refering the case to three gentlemen of the bar, an objection to that I can suggest, Would be, that a greater delay possible might be occasioned from the reference than to continue it in its present course, and some claim as a set of might be brot in, which may effect your demand, and which he could not avail himself of at the trial, this however I submit to your consideration.

He might also estimate that we cannot recover Judgment against him until Octr or Jan next, but I confidently think that Judgment Will be obtained by July.

Your determination on this subject, I hope you will transmit me immediately, as probable he will urge as a plea to my not persevering in the business, that he has not received your answer, to his proposals.

Mr C has lately been appointed to the office of Clerk of the Circuits a post of great emolument, four circuits are held annually in this City which I suppose will average a thousand dollars each, one will be held next week, & another in the month of June.

Pray sir, inform me if Northfield, the place at which the notes are dated, lies in Vermont or New Hampshire, and w[h]ere Eliot Gilbert, the witness to the notes, resides. By the rules of our Supreme Court it is necessary w[h]ere a Plff resides out of the state he should file security for costs (if Judgment goes against him) a line from you to my father, Mr Pearsall or any one of your friends here will be necessary.

I remain Dr Sir Your Obdt Servt

Peter Gerard Stuyvesant

Stephen R Bradley Esquire

ALS (NcD). Docketed (by SRB), "Mr P G Stuyvesant." Filed under 1818 in the Bradley Papers (NcD). Date determined here by comparison with Stuyvesant's 25 Nov. 1800 letter to SRB.

Resolution of the State of Vermont

State of Vermont, In General Assembly, Oct. 10, 1800.

Resolved, That Mr. Robinson, Mr. S. R. Bradley, Mr. Witherell, Mr. Jacob Smith, Mr. Chipman, Mr. Niles, Mr. Hay, Mr. Beardsley, Mr. E. Sheldon and Mr. Crafts be appointed on the part of the house, jointly with such Committee as may be appointed on the part of the Council, to enquire whether any and what amendment ought to be made to an act entitled "An act regulating Goals and Goalers, and for the relief of persons imprisoned therein." Extract from the Journals.

         Attest SAML. C. CRAFTS, *Clerk pro tem.*

Printed (Governor and Council Record, vol. 4).

Resolution of the State of Vermont

In General Assembly Oct. 24, 1800.

Resolved, That a Committee, consisting of a member from each County, be appointed to join a Committee from Council, to enquire if any and what amendments are necessary to the act, Entitled "An act for the support of the Gospel," and report by bill or otherwise.—Members Chosen—Messs. Butler, Safford, Stanley, Bliss, Spooner, Jas. Fisk, S. R. Bradley, G. Olin, Wood and Smith. Extract from the Journals.

         Attest N. OSGOOD, *Clerk.*

Printed (Governor and Council Record, vol. 4).

From Cephas Smith Jr.

Sir   Rutland Nov. 1. 1800

Herewith is transmitted three Commissions two for taking testimony of Witnesses in the Causes of Norman et ux agt. Spooner—and also of Norman et ux agt. Rand—the other for taking testimony in perpetuam rei memoriam as well between those as all others wherein the proof of the same facts may be necessary.

The Commissioners names are not inserted in either—and I hereby authorize you in my behalf to insert them—it having been suggested to me by Doct Graham that Joseph Wilson Esq is not the Consul of the United States now resident in Ireland.

I would suggest the propriety of sending the Interrogatories agreed upon by the parties with the Commissions.

I am sir with Sentiments of esteem your humble Servt

                         Cephas Smith Jr.

Stephen R Bradley Esqr.

ALS (VtU). Marginal note by Smith, partly obscured by seal, reads, "for want of p[...]ment one of the commissio[...] paper."

Account with Abel Carpenter

[12 November 1800]

Dr Stephen R. Bradley to Abel Carpenter

To Cash collected of Joseph Willard on a note of hand dated the 12th Novr 1800 for $12.37 payable in 60 days with interest	12.49
To Cash collected of Jos. Willard on note v. him of the above date for $20. paybl in 30 days on interest	<u>18.90</u>
	<u>$31.39</u>

Received June 4th 1801 the Sum of thirty one Dollars & thirty Nine Cents in full of the Above bill.

Abel Carpenter

ADS (DLC).

From Peter Gerard Stuyvesant

Dear Sir New York Novr 25th 1800

Your causes against Mr Coleman have been noticed for trial at a circuit court which commences this day, I see no obstructions to our obtaining a verdict during its session, & final Judgment in January; I have reason to believe he is about negociating for a settlement, if so, I should not think it advisable to accept of any proposals short of the payment of the principal & interest by January, my information to you on this subject I have no doubt will be concealed from Mr Coleman

I am Dr Sir Your Most Obdt Servt

Peter Gerard Stuyvesant

Your friend Col Burr has been kind to offer his assistance in the business

ALS (NcD: Bradley Family Papers). Cover addressed to "Genl Stephen R Bradley / West Minster / by way of Hartford"; marked "single" and "17"; postmarked New York, 26 Nov. On the verso of the cover is a note in the hand of SRB: "when there is a possibility that the transaction may be fair the law will not suppose it iniquitous without proof (2 Black 380)." On the verso of the ALS are various doodles, names, and figures, including a list of legal expenses, in the hand of SRB, totaling 38:75, and the names "William C. Hatch," "WCHatch," "SRB. Esq," "Esqr. Attwater," and "Esqr. <Duncan?>."

From Jonathan Dorr

Honble Stephen R Bradley

Sir, Roxbury, th[e] 15 Decemr. 1800

I have taken th<e> liberty to address you for the purpose of gaining some information respecting our present Political situation, plac'd as we are some hundreds of miles from the seat of goverment, we have rumours and storys almost daily to aid some speculation as circumstances now appea<r>.

I should be extremely happy to hear your Oppinion respecting the Embargo law, wethe<r> you think it will be rais'd so far as respec<ts> Neutral Nations before Congress rises or not, believ<e> me Sir your Oppinion will have great weight with me, and likewise if you think the Non Intercou[r]se Act with England, & France, will go into Opperation soon. I am Extremely sorry to add I have just receivd a letter from my brother Joseph in the U States service who you was so good as to patronize has lost his wife, she died th[e] 14 Oct after an Illness of only three days. Mr. M Richar<ds> was with us a few days since, he Observ'd all our Westminster friends were well, If you will be so kind as to write me on Recpt of this I shall take it as a great favor and you will much Oblige, Your Most Obedt humble Servt,

Jona. Dorr

ALS (VtU). Margin obscured

Contract for Thomas Pearsall

Westminster Decr 24th 1800

This Certifies as Atty to Thomas Pearsall I have agreed with Jacob Warner & Asa Warner that upon their Geting the Morgage Deed they this Day Executed to Thomas Pearsall of Certain Lands in Wallingford where John Sutherland & Sons live Recorded in the Town Clerks Office in Walling<ford> and produceing a Certificate From the town Clerk that there is no incumbrance on Said Land Except a Morgage Said Suther<land> Gave Thomas Pearsall and Shall bring said Morgage Deed S[o] recorded and the Certificate together with two notes which they have Executed to Said Pearsall of five Hundred and Sixty three Dollars & fifty three Cents to me in that Case I am to Discharge the Morgage Given by said John Suthe<r>land and John Sutherland Junr the 12th Day of August 1794 of the same premises with a Quantity of other Lands and to Deliver thence said Sutherlands two notes which I now hold in my office payable to said Pearsall for whi[ch] the former Morgage was Given said Notes are to be Canceled before they Go out of my hands.

For Thomas Pearsall
Stephen R Bradley At<ty.>

ADS (VtU). Margin obscured.

From Joseph Fay

Honl. Stephen R. Bradley Esqr.

Dr. sir N. York 2 Jany 1801

The papers you intrusted to my Care for Governor Monroe are yet in my hands. He has requested of me to enquire of you the State of his business respecting the application for Compensation for Lands he lost in Vermont and whether he is entitled to a dividend of what has been recovered from the State of New York, and if any thing, how he is to obtain it. He adds to this his best respects to you, & begs to know if you are Compensated for your Trouble. I will thank you for your information on this Subject by return of post, and am very respectfully your friend, & Servant,

Joseph Fay

P S. no official decision of Election or the late Convention with France.

J. F

ALS (VtU).

From John H. Buell

Dear Genl. Hebron January 5th. 1801

In Consequence of Orders from the Commandents I expect to leave Connecticut to Join my Regt. within a few days, say next monday, I am to Receive furder Orders at Fort Pitt, which leaves it unsertain at what Post I shall be statened at; and the Lenth of time which I may remain with the Regiment or in the Army is eaquelly unsertain. I have strong inducements to remain, and I have strong inducements to return to Private life, the Scale is near on a Paige which way it will turn I am not determined. Should ther be a reduction of the Army I shall sertainly improve it and return. It seems that your side has caried the day and that Mr. Jefferson will be Our President, I do not know what your Opinion of Mr. Burr is, or what it has bin, but as a Military man I ought not to interfar with Po<liticks?> or with the appointment of my first and 2d. Master.

I shall refer you to Mrs. Bue<ll's> Letter for domastick intelligence as it relates to family matters, and shall only observe that my Children are pleased with her and that there is every apperence of there injoying themselves well with her and she with them in my absence.

I shall do myself the honor to write you again from Fort Pitt and will always be happy to Receve a Line from you. Please Sir to present my best respects to your good Lady and Compliments to Mr. Wm. and family.

I have the honor to Remain Sir with great respect and Esteem your Huml servt

John H Buell

N B Sally wishes you to be so kind as to send her word when you have Recev'd, the thousand dollars for her in the Lottery and she will go after it herself.

<Genl> Bradley

ALS (VtU).

From John H. Buell

Dear Sir   Wilkinson Ville on the Ohio May 16th. 1801

After a Jurney of 1700 Miles I landed at this incampment on the 4th. of April two months from the time I left home, my Jurney was rather pleasent then otherwise, both by Land and Water and my health much better then when I Came from Connecticut — and I am now well, enclosed is a Report of the Officer of the Day after the Tornado, but as it was made immediately after the thing hapned it did not imbrace near all the Dammage sustaind, the Scane must have bin dredful beyound description. This <Cantownment> is a 1100 Miles from Pittsburgh and 17 miles above the Mouth of the River, on a high Bank and affords a beutiful prospect of the River but must be considerd a Vary unhealthy place, Colo. Strong Landed here in January last and laid out the Incampment since which we have grounded 40 and 180 now on the Sick List, a serious begining, the land here and 200 Miles above is a perfect Level, we have no Water but what is taken from the River, Our Provision is good and a plenty of it, and we have Vary fine gardins, we have 29 officers and about 600 Troops, we are now ingaged in bilding Our Houses and the Hutts for the Troops, it appears to be designd for a permenent Post, and a military acadimy, but it appears to me that whenever goverment is inform'd of the Situation of the place that we shall be removed, the Commanden in Chief is expected here next month, perhaps our Situation may then be alterd I am sertain it cannot be for the worse, I expect that a part of the Army will be disbanded in the Corse of next winter, if so I intend if possable to quit it.

A short time Since Two gentlemen by the Name of Davis from Kantucka call'd at this Camp on their way to New Orleans with Eleven Negroes for Sale which they had purches'd in Baltemore, Ten miles below this they murderd both of their Masters and hove them overboard and proceeded down the River to Fort Pickering where they was brought too, the Boat being Vary Bloody and no White man on Board they was Suspected by Capt. Sparks the Commanding officer, after keeping them in clost Confinement four days they Confesed the <parties?> are now at this Camp in Irons and will soon be sent forward to Kentucka.

From Pittsburgh to the falls of this River 700 Miles is the finest Cuntry I ever Saw and healthy, you can have no Idea of the Quantity of Produce which goes down this River not a day but more or less Boats pass's one day this Week 25 pass'd before 9 oClock in the morning which careed 5000 Barrals of Flour Bacon Whiskey &c &c.

The day before yesterday the Brig Built at Mariatta and Commanded by Commador Whipple of one hundred tuns pass'd here Laiden with Produce of that Cuntry bound for the

West Indies. On the 6th. Instant I Rec'd Letters from my Sally and also from my four Children, which was the first information I have had from them since I left them. I was never more gratified in my life then by Receiving tho<se> Letters, and also that you and Mrs. Bradly had made a Visit at Our House, immediately on my Return to Connecticut you may expect to have the Visit Returnd.

I am anxious about my family and Lament my absence from them.

At the time I left them I had it in Contemplation to have Resignd at Pittsburgh but finding that there was not any field officers at this Place but Colo. Strong and he at the time Dangerously Sick it would have bin dishonorable to have attempted the thing besides I had some private busness of my Own down th<e> River which made it necessary for m<e> to <assend?> it, which as yet I have not repented, but so soon as I can consisten<t> I shall return and Provably draw my Military Curtain for Life, and become a Citizen. Sally has some little Property in the State of Vermont I do not know the Situation that it is in but I expect that one of our Brothers hav ingage'd to pay the Taxes if they should not be paid by him I will you to do it and I wi<ll> see you honorably paid I wis[h] it to b<e> kept secure for Louisa.

Will you please Sir to wri<te> me immediately on the Recept of this and give me your Opinion respecting politicks so far as respects the Disbanding the Army in particular.

I would write my friend William if I knew whare he was I wish to Receive a Letter from him which shall be Answerd, my best respects to your good Lady and all our family friends and others.

I wrote to my family a few days since which I hope will go safe, Capt. Bissell and Lt. Dell are Present and request me to present there Complements to you.

I am Dear Sir with the greatest Respect your Hum ser't,

John H. Buell

The Honlb. Stephen R Bradley Esqr.

ALS (VtU). Margin obscured. Docketed, "John H. Buell."

Nathaniel Niles to James Madison

Sir   West Fairlee June 9. 1801

... It is doubtful by what political character Mr. Payne will be replaced in the Senate.[1] I am not without hope it will be by a republican, If it should, Genal. Bradley will be the man. But I am much affraid the balance of main st<ren>gth will still turn to the other side....

Printed extract (Robert J. Brugger et al., eds., *Papers of James Madison: Secretary of State Series* [4 vols. to date; Charlottesville, Va., 1984–], 1:283). Nathaniel Niles represented Vermont in Congress from 1791 to 1795 and was a member of the Vermont legislature from 1800 to 1803.

1. Elijah Paine was elected as a Federalist to the U.S. Senate in 1795 and resigned in 1801. SRB filled Paine's vacated seat and served until 1813.

From Jonathan Robinson

Dear sir   Bennington August 7th. 1801

The Republicans on this side of the Mountain feel deeply the Importance of having if Possible a Majority in the Legislature this fall The choice of a Senator may decide the character of the Senate of the United States for this purpose we have Engaged our friend Judge Olin to go to Newfane to converse with you and Such other Charectors as you think will be safe on the Mode & subject of Election of the Chief Magistrates Councilors & Representatives—The Violence of the Federalist<s> is great I am convinced if they carry their Majority we all Sink as a Revenge for the firmness of Mr Jefferson but should we carry a Majority as I pray God we may Certainly our Supreme Court ought to be in some degree at least altered The dignity & safety of the State Require it I wish you to Converse freely and promptly with Mr Olin Respecting the charecter for Chief Magistrate The Republicans this side of the Mountain will at the Assembly agree in any Candidate should we be able to Scatter the Votes of the freemen so that no one is Electe<d.> We wish you to be awake and do all in your power Mr Tyler in his Circuit with Supreme Court can do a good deal if he is hearty in the Cause and you can in your County work a Change of your Members to the Assembly and give us a Strong lift in the list for Councilors but above all dont fail to come as a member to the Assembly I must leave perticulars with Judge Olin exhorting you to perseverance and Sturring your pure Mind by way of Remembrance for the Time is at hand — health & respect

    Yours Cordialy   Jonathan Robinson

I left N York the 1st & came up with the Council of appointment to Albany they are Resolute to Prostrate Federalism & carry republican Candidat<es.>

                                                                                J Robinson

Stephen R. Bradly Esqr
    ALS (NcD: Bradley Family Papers). Docketed by SRB, "Jona Robinson."

From Thomas Sparhawk

Sir   Walpole 24th. Augt. 1801

    I have taken the liberty to leave the bond you gave my brother George K. Sparhawk, in the hands of Genl. Bellows of this Town, and have to request you to be good enough to pay him the amount, as there are weekly opportunities of conveyance hence to Portsmouth. I am with much respect Sir your Obt. Sert.   Thos. Sparhawk

Genl Bradley
    ALS (VtU).

Governor and Council Record

                                                       In General Assembly Oct. 13, 1801.

    A Committee was appointed, consisting of one member from each county, to join such Committee as the Council may appoint, to be denominated the Third land Tax Committee. Members Chosen, Mr. Taylor, Mr. Bradley, Mr. Prentiss, Mr. Marsh, Mr. Wheatley, Mr. Wright, Mr. Vincent, Mr. Law, Mr. Stanley, Mr. Dana and Mr. Sheldon. Extract from the Journals.

                                    Attest   Jas. Elliot, *Clerk*.

    Printed (Governor and Council Record, vol. 4).

To Dr. Nathan Smith

Dear Sir   Westminster October 23d. 1801

    In a confidence of your superior talents and abilitie<s> in your profession I address this to you to request you to Visit Mrs. Bradley at this place as soon as possibly you can, fro<m> alarming symtoms it is feared she is in the first stage of a consumption her complaints have been increase<ing> ever since Last Spring she then took a Very severe cold which Brought on a dry hacking cough which has followed he<r> all Summer and which apparently has been wasting [...] in August and September I carried her to the Sea Side and tryed the Efficacy of the Salt water she returned the latter pa<rt> of September rather worse since which her complaints Evidently increase such as Sweating a Nights cold chills an<d> at times a little fever probably of the hectic kind. Her phisicians are anxious you should Visit her as soon as poss<ible> I hope Sir you will let nothing prevent your coming immedia<tely.> Your demands shall be paid with Gratitude on your arival he<re> and you will permit me once more to entreat you to let noth<ing> prevent your coming unless you Hazard a life thereby more wort<hy> than the one for whom I now interceed.

Assured that you will not deny this reques<t> I have the Honour to be with the highest Esteeme Your Obedient Humbl Servant
Doct Nathan Smith

AL (VtU). Margin obscured.

To Dr. John Wheelock

Doct. Wheelock

Sir, [23 October 1801]

Upon my return home last Evening from the Assembly by the way of the Circuit Court at Rutland I find alarming Symtoms of an approching Consumption in the Case of M<rs.> Bradley who has been a long time out of health I have wrote to Doct Smith this Day Earnestly soliciting him to Visit her as soon as he possibly can but as I have no personal acquaintan<ce> with Doct Smith I have taken the liberty of addressing this to you to request the favor of you to wait on Doct Smith and use your Influence to perswade him to Come immediately as much depends in the Judgment of her phisicians Upon an immediate attention and application to the State and condition of her complaints. I Should not have troubled you on this occasion but knowing your philanthropy and universal benevolence and the Influence you would have with Doctor Smith before any other Character has induced me to make this application to you when the application was made to the Great Phisician he was told that "speak the word and it shall be done" we have such an opinion of Doct Smith in this part of the Country that we Consider him a type of the Great Phisician I hope Sir you will do me this favor which will be ever Gratefully remembered by Sir your affectionate Friend and Very Obliged Servant

SRB

John Wheelock LLD
President of Dartmouth College

ALS (VtU). Margin obscured.

From <Alphonsus> Moore

Dear Sir Peacham Novr 2d 1801

I have lately returnd here from a Tour to the Northward — was consequently deprived of the Pleasure of seeing you at Newbury.

Relative to the Business we conversd upon last June — I did whatever I could do prudentially. In July I travelled through the whole of northern Counties. I found that Mr Smith was put up on the other side of the mountain for Govr & that consequently the Votes for a Repn Govr would be divided if not totally lost. In that Case I thought it best and did my Endeavours to promote what has taken place your appointment of Senator. I am happy that the Choice has given us a decided Majority in the Senate.

Living so far removed from the Seat of Government I must request the Honour & favour of your Correspondence in some moments of your Leisure when at Washington. It is of importance to the present Administration that true information relative to the political Machine should be disseminated, in the remote parts of the Union. At this Distance and at this particular place I can get no Information of Facts except after being mutilated & tomahawk'd in the Aristo Papers. It is necessary to be well arm'd with true statements, in order to oppose the Anti-Reps with Success. In this particular part of County the leading men are averse to the present administration. The upper part of the State are much more pliable and a short period I think will make them what we wish — good Republicans. Any Newspapers or pamphlets of importance that you can inclose will be very gratefully received. I am sorry to request a favour of this kind if it should give you any inconvenience. As I have made a purchase of a Situation in this State probably for Life — it may be in my power to reciprocate favours, now & hereafter.

I am Sir with respect your friend & hle St

Alphs Moore

S R Bradley Esq

ALS (VtU).

From Samuel Avery

Sir,   Athens Novr: 3: 1801

I have Sent my Son Samuel Over to Vermont with powe<r> to Sell my Kingston land, a Right I had of Capn: Burk in Chittend<en> and my Gould ten Acre lot, I wish you to buy them, If you will n<ot> buy them, I would ask your friendship in the matter, and that you would Advise and Assist my Son, Any friendship shown him shall b<e> greatfully acknowledged, My exclusive priviledge in the waterworks<—>I allso wish you to purchase — I shall be over in the winter when my son will again be over in a Slay for some things we left behind — I should have been over myself before this, had it not been for the dispute respecting our title here with Pensylvania, which we are tryin<g> to bring to an amicable Setlement, Commissioners are appointed on both sides to meet and try to adjust the dispute, I expect they will meet N<ext> month — My Son can Inform you of our wellfare.

Wishing every needed Blessing to you and Yours I am Your very Humble Servant
Samuel Avery

ALS (VtU). Margin obscured. Addressed to SRB at Westminster.

To Unidentified

Sir   Westminster Novr. 16th. 1801

I have enclosed the sum of seventy dollars agreeable to your directions for the payment of that bill — in two bank notes 1 of 50 & the other of 20 Dolls — hope they will arrive safe.

I Have not as yet found any of the Bennington papers you mentioned. My files of those papers were mislaid and I fear lost. Should any of them however be met with I shall take measures to transmit them to you.

Be so good as to give me notice of the arrival of this by return of Post.
I am sir Your humble Servant

Stephen R Bradley

L (VHS). Written and signed in an unidentified hand.

From Jabez Penniman

Dear Sir,   Westminster December 7th 1801.

You recollect that it was the advice of Doctr. Smith when last here, that Mrs. Bradly should go into a course of Iron and omitt Callomel and ohium, she pursued it three or four days and found she could not bare it, as it increased the cough very much; was obliged to omit it and return to the use of callomel and ohium as formerly — this relieved her immediately — but the salutary effects were not long felt, before other sympto<ms> equally troublesome and more dangerous were perceived and happily obviated — a diarrea and colliguative sweats came on which produced a general debility, and reduced her very fast for two or three days— every attention was now necessary; I was so fortunate as happily to check them both soon — she now takes a decoction of the Bark six times in twenty four hours two teaspoonfulls each time, which setts easy and well, and gives strenth and increases the appetite as yet — she takes likewise opium Joined with a small quantity of Ipicacuanha night and morning. Mrs. Bradly's spirits and expectations are yet good — but grows more anxious about the cough — she thinks on the whole that she has lost strenth since you left us, I fear she is not deceived — — how long Mrs. Bradly will continue in this situation, is impossible for me or any one to say; but this much I will assure you, that no attention or exertion of mine shall be wanting at any time or season to make her as happy and as comfortable as possible in the nature of things— and am sure that William has and will do all he can to make his Mothers situation as pleasant and easy.

Wiliam, I suppose, writes you weekly, but as he cant know all the peticulars, I have taken the liberty to be minute; well knowing the anxiety you must feel — I likewise wish, that if you learn any thing new, to hear, it immediately on the subject — or if any new publications comes out on this or any other complaint that you would obtain it for me.

This is an important day at Washington's-City — a day in which the wise Sages of our nation are convened in council to deliberate on the common and best possible good for our Country — notwithstanding the care and anxiety we feel at home for our patient — yet in our moments of relaxation we look forward with pleasure and anticipate much good yet to come — Peace in Europe and the American Eagle so happily changed from one complexion of Citizens and so generally by the people given its those who have long and still continue to be their friends— all calmly and loyally done in their sober moments, — is a period rarely to be mett with in modern times— and may the Godess of liberty and prosperity extend her wand over these United States to the great mortification of all disappointed Torys and Federallist so <cosled?>, they cant leave of their strictors on the President and every other man now in place — they are scared shut Isiah Thomas of Worcester is removed from office — and they would complain if Belzebub the prince of Devils was turned out of *his* place as it would mititate very must against *their cause.*

To hear from you occationally the news and what is of importance would be gratefully received and acknoledged.

By all your friends and <add?> new obligations to your friend and very humble Servant

Jabez Penniman

Supervisorship wont be forgot I hope.
Honorable S. R Bradly.

ALS (VtU).

From Gurdon Huntington

Respected Sir, Walpole Decr. 10th. 1801

Having lately ben inform'd that the offic\<e\> of Superintendant of the armory Department at Springfield M—s. is now or soon to be vacant, & having ha\<d\> some information from the serviving officers of that department (through the Channill of a person now in public trust,) respecting my willingness to serv\<e\> the Public in the capasity above mentioned— I ha\<ve\> taken the liberty to inform You that, my services a\<re\> at the controle of the Public; & knowing Sir, Your readiness to serve any Person of Industry & enterpriz\<e\> & Your influence undoubted, do request Your assistance \<in\> procuring this office for me. Your services shall be generously rewarded. The recommendations accompanying this letter will inform You respecting my capasities, the signers of which You are Personally acquainted with, & havi\<ng\> lived neighbours to me upwards of fourteen Years, has induced them to come forward in this friendly way to assist me in obtaining this office of trust. I have been imployed the three Years past in manufacturing arms f\<or\> the U. States, & have had the making of all the swaiges machines for ours & Messrs. Allen & Cos. factory. But I sho\<uld\> not undertake to recommend myself as a person to fill \<the\> office, well knowing that abilities & the trust that a per\<son\> is capible of having commited to him, is the object to \<be\> consulted. If sir, the forgoing Subject should meet approbation, Your exertions in bringing it to effect would lay me under the strongest Obligations to You. With due respect Sir, am Your most Obedient & Humble Servt.

Gurdon Huntington

Honbl. Stepn. R. Bradley.
ALS (VtU). Margins obscured.

From Anthony Lamb

Hackensack New Jersey
Dear sir December 15th 1801

I take the Liberty to introduce to your Acquaintance, my Friend, Colonel Hughes, who was Deputy quarter Master General in the american Army, at the Commencement of the Revolution, he is attending Congress, for the purpose of procuring a Settlement of his Accounts with the public, there being a considerable Balance due to him; he once had them in a train of Settlement, when Genl. Hamilton was Secretary of the Treasury, but owing to his being Sick at the time of the Session of Congress which succeeded his Application to them, he was not able to pursue the Business to effect; as his meritorious Exertions in the Revolution, are universally acknowledged I flatter myself he will obtain from the present Congress, the justice to which an old revolutionary officer is entitled.

I am Dear sir With Sentiments of Respect Your most Obt. servt.

Anthony Lamb

General Bradley
ALS (VtU).

From Joseph Bullen

Honored Sir   Chickesaw Nation Decr. 18. 1801

At the Request of Mr. Colbert, I return you His humble Thanks—for the valuable Book; you sen<t> him — no act — you Could have done of the Same Magnitud<e> Could more Conduce to establish your Reputation in this Part of the Country—as a Gentleman of Piety & Charity—th<e> Book is much read—and those who read it—believe it to expr<ess> the real sentiments of the Giver—& when I see them — say — that General Bradley must be a very Great — Good man[.] Mr James Colbert to whom you sent the Book—asks one expression more of your Friendship—about seven years ag<o> he went to Philadelphia with a number of Chickesaw and Choctaws in Character of Interpreter one John Chisolm was employed by Government to Conduct them safe Home—as usual—money was advanced for the expence at Richmond they were detained waiting for their Presents longe<r> than they expected— Chisolm got out of money—& applied to Colbert—who had money—to Borrow for the United State<s> assuring him it would be replaced at Knoxville—by Col. Henley—Mr. Colbert Considering him (Chisolm) an Officer of Government Lent him 232- Dollars depending o<n> the Faith of the United States for repayment—Chisolm on receiving the Money—gave him his own Note for it—Colber<t> not used to white People's Methods supposed it right— at Knoxville Col. Henley would not replace the Money—& our Friend has never yet been able to get it—& the credi<t> of the States suffers—& an Honest Chickesaw suffers more for want of his Money—Mr. Colbert was a stranger to Chisolm & would not have Trusted him one Dollar on any other Sco<re> but the Credit of the States—we Consider it in a Manner Certa<in> you succeed Mr. Paine in Senate—any way Mr. Colbert wishes your aid in Getting his Money—and will pay a generous Fee for the service—we think it would be best to Petition Congress—the Documents may be found in the war office—but every thing is submitted to your wisdom—the Colbert Family are very influential & noted Frien<ds> to white People.

We are in usual Health & things go as well with us as we Could expect—respecting the sum Due you—on Note & Mortgage—Please to send me the Date & sum—also the Date & sum of endorsement—& whether any—& if any—what Discount you will make to receive the Money—next summer or Fall. Please to Present the Ladies my respectful Complements & in My Name—Congratulate your amiable sister-in Law Mrs Metcalf on her Late Marriage with that truly Brave Officer Major Buel—I can wish them no better than a Long, Happy Life a Numerous & virtuous Issue—a Hopeful Death & Blessed Eternity.

I am, Hond. sir—with great Deference yours

                                                              Joseph Bullen

Honble. Stephen R. Bradley Esqr.

ALS (VtU). Margins obscured.

From Samuel Davis Parmele

Sir   Newyork December 21st. 1801

Although a most total Strainger to you, I am emboldened from a knowledge of the goodness of your heart, to solicit your kind attention for a a few moments. Ever entertaining a Strong propensity for military tactics, and my youthful fancy having indulged many pleasing thoughts on the subject, I feel myself at this period, much inclined to gratify my once juvenile disposition. Possessing a Small knowledge of the theory of military operations, I feel the more confidence in soliciting your patronage.

I have been informed, that there is at present severa<l> vacancies in the Marine Corps which will in all probability be filled this present Session of Congress. If I can not get an appointment in the Marine Corps, I solicit a Commission in the 2d. U. S Regiment of Artillerists and Engineers, which Regiment I am informed, that there are several vacancies at present. Should such be the case, and, you Sir, when you are informed that I am a Son of Captn. Alexander Parmele, deceased, late of Windsor, Vermont (which will in a great degree make you acquainted with my conne<c>tions, character, &c) can feel yourself at liberty to sanction my first request, by an interference in my behalf I shall feel myself bound by every tie which endeers grateful esteem.

I am Sir, With every Sentiment of Respect, Your most obedient and Humble Servant

Samuel Davis Parmele

No. 13, Front Street, Newyork.

N B To make you more acquainted with my Character, I beg leave Respectfully to refer you to the Books of the Secratary of the Navy, where, I presum<e> you will find it entered by Daniel McNeill, Esqr., Commander of the United States Boston Frigate.

I shall continue here in this City till next June, and, Sir, if you will condesend to answer my request, you will confer an obligation which will never be obliterated. You Sir, being a Senator from my native State, I have thought proper to request you to make my intentes known to Goverment — not doubting but you will do every thing in your power to render yourself serviseble to one of your Humble Constituents.

Stephen R. Bradley, Esqr.
Senator of the United States.

ALS (VtU). Margin obscured.

From Elias Bull

Hond: & Dear Sir Rutland Decr. 31st. 1801

Colo Graham has Confidentially Communicated to me his Wish for an Appointment as a Consulate to Som<e> of the European Powers. It would be assuming arogan<ce> in Me to attempt any additional Information on the Subj<ect> as you are So well acquainted with his Person, his natura<l> and acquired abilities, and of which you are a Far mor<e> Competant Judge, and of the Wishes of Colo. Graham he Informs me he has made you Personally acquainted and on your Friendship he Confidentially Relies. Permi<t> me never the Less as a Confidential Friend to accompany his Wish by Submiting to your Honr Superior Considerat<ion> Colo Grahams abilities and Persevering Promptitude, his Friendship for his Country, his Indifateegable Assiduity & Laudable Ambition to Excell, which I doubt not wil<l> meet your approbation and Frendly Patronage.

With Highest Esteam and Consideration yrs.

Elias Bull

The Honl Stephen R: Bradley Esqr

ALS (VtU). Margin obscured.

From Sarah Blackden

New York January the 4th. 1802.

Sir No. 260 Pearl Street

At the period of your late Visit to Colo. Blackden and myself, you was Kind Enough to promise your Support — to the application which he intended to Rend<er> to Congress on the Score of arrears of Compensation du<ring> his Services and Sacrafices as an officer in our Revolutionary War. And we then Mutually indulge<d> the hope that he would have had the Satisfaction to [...] his second Effort Crowned with Success, but Sir I am Reduced to the melancholy task of Informing you tha<t> he became Seriously attack'd by Indisposition short<ly> after your departure, and that he Expired on the Evening of the 22nd. ulto.

Thus left in a state of Widowhood affliction and want. Than by Recommendation of his Honor the Vice President and other Respectable Characters Concluded to offer a Petition in my own name. It was forward under the present date to General Bailey, who was so Kind as to introduce the subject last Session, and I am free to Solicit your friendly Co-operation with that gentleman and others favora<bly> disposed towards me, also your Influence with leading members in each House, as far as the same Can with propriety be Extended in my favor. To the End that I may Receive such Relief and protection, as under an Investigation of all Circumstances, Congress may find it just and proper to afford me.

With great Respect I am Sir Your Distress'd & Mo Hble Servt.

Sarah Blackden

the Honble. Stephen R Bradlee Esqr.
Washington

ALS (VtU). Margin obscured.

Senate Proceedings: Judiciary System

[3 February 1802]

Mr. BRADLEY thereupon rose.— Mr. President, I shall vote for the repeal, because it seems to me that we have got no use for these courts. The business was decreasing when they were appointed, and the old system seems to me to be much better than the new one. The lawyers of Philadelphia like the new one best, but it is for their interest to have a great many courts. Now, Mr. President, I look upon the repeal of this law only as one part of a great system. The system recommended by our worthy President, is a system of more glory than our country ever had. This system is to be completed by lessening all our expenses; by reducing our Military Establishment; by disciplining our militia; by repealing our internal taxes; and then, sir, we shall soon pay our debts, and with a great population of free citizens, we shall make all the tyrants of Europe tremble on their thrones, and in the middle of their armies. None of them will dare to attack this country. This is a glorious system. And then, Mr. President, I do not see how this can be so unconstitutional as the gentleman in the opposition pretend. The words in the Constitution, "to hold during good behaviour," have been interpreted very differently in different States; so I think we cannot apply to the States to fix a right meaning to these words. Well, who then shall we apply to? It seems to me we ought to apply to that country where these words were first used. Now, sir, in that country an act of Parliament can put down any courts or judges, though they do hold their offices during good behaviour. I do not see then, sir, why an act of Congress should not put down courts and judges in this country. The judges will still hold their offices during good behaviour, as much as they do in England.

Besides, Mr. President, I think if we interpret the Constitution as these gentlemen propose, it will amount to a perpetuity for this expensive system; because when a judge dies out, the President is bound to fill up his place; and even if they should all happen to die together, he must appoint sixteen new ones; so I don't see how we are ever to get rid of this system; 'tis an absolute perpetuity, unless God should be moved, as he was by the sins of the old world, to destroy us all by a flood. So, sir, I shall vote for the repeal.

Printed copy (*Annals of Congress,* 7th Cong., 1st sess., 161).

To Stella Bradley

My dear Stella   WASHINGTON. FEBR. 13th. 1802

YOUR Pa, after leaving you that morning he came away proceeded on to this place and after a long and tedious journey has arived here and Remembers you with great love and esteem he feels very anxious for you now you have no Ma—for fear you may be abused and for fear also you will not behave well. Remember Stella to behave well is the only way to fare well and as you will now stand in need of many friends in life so conduct [...] that you may never want them be kind to your grand Ma—friendly to your Brothers and Sisters and pritty to all Your play mates. Remember to take good care as you can of your little brother Stephen as he has no Ma—and a little boy you must be a Ma—to him and above all my dear learn to read and learn to write what a pleasure it would be to your Pa—if you could now write to him and let him know how you are if you are well and if they use you well and how you learn I have sent you a little book to read and Remember your Pa by and when I Return I design to bring you a little watch good bye my charming little girl and forget not your fond parent and dearest friend

Stephen R Bradley

ALS (VtU). Damaged by removal of seal.

Senate Proceedings: Choice of Electors

[18 February 1802]

Mr. BRADLEY communicated sundry resolutions of the Legislature of the State of Vermont; which were read, as follows:

State of Vermont, in General Assembly:

Resolved, That, in the opinion of the Legislature, the following amendments to the Constitution of the United States would conduce to the happiness of the citizens thereof, by the establishment of an uniform mode for the choice of Electors of President and Vice President of the United States and of Representatives to Congress:[1]

1st. That after the third day of March, in the year one thousand eight hundred and one, the choice of Electors of President and Vice President shall be made by the Legislature of each State, dividing the State into a number of districts equal to the number of Electors to be chosen in such State, and by the persons in each of those districts who shall have the qualifications requisite for Electors of the most numerous branch of the Legislature of such State choosing one Elector in the manner which the Legislature thereof shall prescribe; which district, when so divided, shall remain unalterable until a new census of the United States shall be obtained.

2d. That the elections of Representatives to serve after the third day of March, in the year one thousand eight hundred and three, shall be by dividing each State, by the Legislature thereof, into a number of districts, equal to the number of Representatives to which such State shall be entitled, and by the people within each of those districts who shall have the qualifications requisite for Electors of the most numerous branch of the Legislature of such State choosing one Representative in the manner which the Legislature thereof shall prescribe; which district, when so divided, shall remain unalterable until a new census of the United States shall be obtained.

Printed copy (*Annals of Congress,* 7th Cong., 1st sess., 190).

1. The twelfth amendment to the U.S. Constitution, specifying the electoral procedures to be used in presidential elections, was passed by Congress on 9 Dec. 1803 and ratified on 15 June 1804.

From James Elliot

Sir,   Brattleborough March 9th. 1802

We are yet ignorant of the fate of the bill to repeal the judiciary act, in the House of Representatives. I find, however, that the Federalists, in this quarter, are as well convinced as the Republicans, that the repealing bill will pass, and some of them have the candou\<r\> to say that it ought to pass. I am not a little surprised, also, to find that the minor politicians of th\<e\> minority differ from their principals, and almost unanimously acknowledge the constitutional powe\<r\> contended for by the majority in Congress. I sincerely wish, Sir, that Mr. Gouverneur Morris could witness the effect of his eloquence and reasoning among hi\<s\> own party here—Some of them say that he may be honest, but if so, he must be a greater enthusias\<t\> than any democrat—Others suspect his sinceri\<ty\> because they say that he discovers talents inconsistent with the sincere support of doctrines so absu\<rd\> and pernicious as those which he advocates. Ou\<r\> Federalists are very averse to irrepealable laws "unchangeable and eternal Courts," or useless and sinecure judges.

The most curious thing that has transpir\<ed\> in the House of Representatives, is, the threatened *Appeal to the People*. Whatever diversity of opinion may exist, upon the question of expediency, I wish to God the sentiments of the people could be taken upon the constitutional question. The result would be so unflattering to federal pride, that every aristocratic leader would hide his diminished head, before the Majesty of the People. But it is astonishing, my respected Sir, that certain politicians never thought of appealing to the people, untill the people had appealed from them to the Constitution, and to the primary principles of our republican institutions. Not three years since, the *vox populi,* instead of being considered as the *vox Dei,* was treated, by these same men, with insolent derision. The mild and manly expression of the public sentiment, if it contravened their views, was denounced as the tumultuous thunder of fury and of faction. The ink which recorded the triumphant deeds of the enemies of American Freedom, is scarcely dry. The pen of the annalist, employed to perpetuate the memory of scenes disgraceful to our country, is not yet laid aside. And yet Aristocracy dares to appeal to that people which it so lately insulted and persecuted. It dares to set itself up as the guardian of that republican system, which it so lately laboured, with infernal industry, to annihilate. Alas, poor human nature! Is it not dangerous for the enemies of truth to prosecute an appeal, which may produce a still more powerful expression of the public voice? Let them answer the question themselves.

While parties in the Senate were equal, and you, Sir, had not yet taken your seat, it was confidently reported here that you would incline the scale in favour of Aristocracy. Some persons here, whom I need not name to you, asserted that you were pledged, on this particular question, to the friends of the present judiciary system. I repelled the insinuations with spirit—A few republicans were doubtful—I assured them you could never abandon the interests of Repub\<lican\> [...] Our fond expectations were gratified. And I believe, Sir, that every one of your real friends approved your conduct.

I take the liberty, Sir, to inclose to you two Numbers of the National Ægis, edited by Francis Blake Esq. in the management of which I have occasionally some concern — as specimens of the zeal with which we are labouring to support the Administration —

I have the honour to be, Sir, With high respect and esteem, Your obliged and humble Servant

James Elliot.

Honble. Stephen R. Bradley—

ALS (NcD: Bradley Family Papers). Damaged at margins. Cover addressed to "The Honourable Stephen R. Bradley, / Senator in Congress, / Washington" and marked "Brattleboro' V. Mar. 9." and "Free."

From Samuel Parmele

Dear Sir, New York, March 16, 180[...]

During 1801 I did myself the honor to address you on the subject of entering the army of the U.S. In your polite reply which I have by me, yo<u> mention the probability that little encouragement would be afforded at th<at> period, and dissuaded me from [...] intention from that circumstance. Military tactics, have ever been my darling pursuit, and now, while the probability offers that my country will [...] the help of her citizens, I beg leave aga<in> to solicit your *friendship* and *advice*. The [...] object of my petition is to obtain the appointment of Capt. either in the Artillery or Infantry.

So circumstanced, it would be the pride of my life so to act, as to insur<e> the respect of my *superiors*, ever bearing in mind the *exalted character* to whose bounty I have been indebted.

I am, Sir, your Obt. Servant

Samuel Parmele

ALS (VtU). Text obscured by several stains. Margin obscured.

From James Elliot

Respected Sir, Brattleborough March 26. 1802

I take the liberty to address you at this time, by the particular request of Mr. Eli Sargeant, Executor of the will of Colonel John Sargeant, deceased, for whom you instituted an action of debt against the Sheriff grounded upon the following facts— Mr. Sargeant, in his said capacity, at June Term 1800, recovered judgment against Stephen Gorton, an absconding debtor for $77.39 damages and 13.48. costs— and another judgment for about the same sums— sued out Executions June 23d. and delivered it to R. Metcalf, Deputy Sheriff, who within sixty days (21st. August) caused a certain part of a saw mill, the property of Gorton, to be appraised to Sargeant, and gave him possession — but did not cause the executions to be duly returned and recorded untill after the expiration of five months from the date of the judgment —(24th November)— in the mean time Adonijah King, having notice of all these proceedings, sued out a writ of Execution upon a judgment on a subsequent attachment, and on the last day of the five months or the next day after, had the land appraised to himself and obtained possession — Mr. Paine, who was counsel with myself and Mr. Whitney for Mr. Sargeant, at December term last, was of opinion that the action (the declaration being in debt, to which the defendant demurred) was not sustainable — He was inclined to believe that when you instituted the suit, in the hurry of business, you had not paid perfect attention to the subject. Still, however, our great deference for your opinion and practice in a case of this kind, induced us, notwithstanding the decided opinion of Mr. Paine, not to abandon the action. We gave judgment and reviewed.

It would seem, Sir, that this case is not analogous to that of an escape from the Sheriff of a prisoner in Execution, in which instance the debt at once attaches to the Sheriff. It may also admit of a question, whether Sargeant ought not to contest the title with King, before he sues the Sheriff? If there should not be a probability that Congress will rise soon, I will thank you, Sir, in some leisure moment, to review the subject, and drop me a line upon it, as Mr. Sargeant is extremely anxious for your further opinion in the case.

I have the honour to be, Sir, with perfect respect, Your most obedient Servant,

James Elliot.

The Honourable Stephen R. Bradley, Esq.

ALS (VtU). Docketed, "J. Elliot."

From Eliakim Spooner

Sir   Westminster April [1]st. 1802

I understand by the papers that on the fo<urth> of March that glorious day the day on which the Law of Liberty arose and caused the Elustrius Jefferson to be plaist in the Presidential Chair, that you was plaist at the Head of that august asembly of Herows and Sages th<at> met for its Celebration — I thank my God th<at> I have lived to see liberty once more triumphant and can almost say with the sage of old, now let thy servant depart in peace — but this I ca<n> truly say that I sincearly Congratulate you in the Honor conferd. and also our state for the hon<or> they have Recd. threw you on that occation.

As for news I can only say that their has bin a considerable Revolution in <wallpoot?>, a Magoraty of Vots has bean given for Langdon for Governer.

This from your Humble Servant

Eliakim Spooner

General Bradley

ALS (VtU). Margin obscured.

From Gideon Granger

My friend —   Genl Post Office Augt. 6th. 1802.

Yours of the 29th. Ulto.[1] is before me. My Situation was such I could not with propriety refuse to contract with Mr. Brewster, he had made a Journey of 500 miles — was well recommended, and had been for years employed by the department & performd. with fidelity — I do not see why Sykes will not take the contract from Suffield to Brattleboro. I will divide it so that he shall not be responsible for any failure of Brewster. I have in my contract with B. used my full powers and introduced evry necessary Check. 1st. I require that his Surety be approved by Judge Woodward & Mr. Gilbert of Hanover. 2d. I inflict a fine of $15. in evry instance where the mail is found out of the body of the Carriage — 3d. I retain the power of taking the Mail from him when I please after the 3d. failure — All this in Addition to the Common restrictions & penalties & I have solemnly assured him that I was determind rigidly to adhere to the Contracts & enforce all the penalties. If he should fail of giving the surety I can negociate with Sykes otherwise I cannot. While at Suffield I again & again pressed Sykes to go to Hanover & determine on the business — but to no purpose.

Your friend

Gidn Granger

Stephen R Bradly Esq
  Westminster Vt.

Copy? (NcD: Bradley Family Papers).
1. Letter not found.

From Samuel A. Otis

Dear Sir Boston August 23d 1802

Having done myself the honour to write you several times since my arrival here this is to inform you that the President US without my solicitation hath unexpectedly appointed me a Comr. of Bankruptcy under the late law, but the emolument will not amount to one half what I am allowed as Secretary of the Senate. On this & other considerations I shall be induced to decline the appointment; Trusting that the nomination will not operate to deprive me of the office I now hold under the Senate — Acquired by fair election — The duties of which are familiar to me & its stipend necessary to the support of my family. Should an attempt of this kind be made I flatter myself your candour will resist so unfair a measure.

I flattered myself with expectation of seeing you or your son before this time and still hope it. Presuming the arrangement we talked of will be adopted.

Be so good as to write the VPresident on the subject of my appointment, which I fear took place with no friendly views. And any other measures you may think will serve me, will oblige your friend & humble Sert

Sam A. Otis

Post office will come safe to hand

ALS (DLC). Addressee not indicated.

From Thomas Jefferson

Dear Sir Monticello Aug. 27. 1802.

I am afraid some want of sufficient explanation has prevented my recieving recommendations of proper persons as Commissioners of bankruptcy for your state. I had thro' a particular channel desired that the favor might be asked of yourself & judge Smith to recommend; & understood it would be done on your return home. A recent circumstance however makes me doubt whether you had so understood it. I have therefore now to ask the favor of you, as I also do of Judge Smith[1] to name three or four persons, lawyers or merchants, of republican principles, convenient for the exercise of the office at the place where the federal court holds it's session in your state, and whose understandings and integrity qualify them for the office. To avoid the infinite number of nominations which would be necessary to spread these officers over the whole face of every state, most of which would be useless, we instruct the attorney of the district to apply to the Secretary of state whenever any case arises too distant for the general commissioners, & to recommend others for the special case. Accept assurances of my great esteem & respect.

Th: Jefferson

The honble Genl. Bradley
  Vermont.

ALS (ViU); press copy (DLC).

1. In a letter to James Madison of 13 Sept. 1802, Israel Smith wrote that Jefferson's 27 Aug. 1802 letter to him was "the first intimation which I have received that the President wished me to make a recommendation." Smith proposed that six commissioners of bankruptcy be appointed in Vermont—three in the vicinity of Rutland and three near Windsor. He recommended Samuel Prentiss, Darius Chipman, and Richard Skinner and suggested that SRB was more qualified to nominate from the eastern district (*Papers of Madison: Secretary of State Series*, 3:569).

From Samuel Hanson of Samuel

Sir   City of Washington, 10th September, 1802

Understanding that there is some probability of a New appointment of Secretary to your House, at the commencement of the approaching Session, I beg leave, in that event, to present myself as a Candidate for the office. Should my character and pretensions be such as to justify your favouring and advocating my application, your doing so will lay me under a Singular obligation.

With great respect, I am Sir Your most obedt.

S. Hanson of Saml

J. [sic] R. Bradley Esqr.

ALS (NcD: Bradley Family Papers).

To Thomas Jefferson

Sir   Westminster Sept. 13th. 1802

I have the honour of acknowledging the Receipt of Your Letter of the 26th. August Yesterday and can assure you it wa<s the> first intimation that you, *the President of the Uni<ted> States,* expected a Recommendation from me of proper cha<racters?> to be appointed Commissioners of Banktruptcy in this <state.> Had it before come to my knowledge <I would> certainly have embraced the earliest opportunity of Giving You all the assistance in my power— You will permit me to observe th<at> this State has a range of Mountains runing North and so<uth> nearly through the whole length <such?> that most of <the> Inhabitants are Setled on the East and west Sides of the state and but very little commerce or intercourse acrost the mou<ntain and> that the Legislature Hold their Sessions alternately on each side <as do> also the Courts of the United States, I sh<ould consider> it most expedient to appoint four on each <side> of the State that is four in the district in which Judge Smi<th> lives and four in the district in which I live I mentio<n> four that in Case of Death or other Causes that might in<capaci>tate one, there might be a sufficient number in the district— Under a Conviction of its Expediency I will take the Liberty to recommend four Suitable persons living on the eastern Side of the Mountains expectin<g> Judge Smith will recommend proper Characters <on> the western Side and will Name Mark Richar<ds> & Reuben Atwater of Westminster James Elliot of Rutla<nd,> and Oliver Gal<lup> of Hartland[1] the first is a respectable Merchant the three last a<re> Lawyers— they are all M<en> of known probity, Abilities, and firmly attached to Repu<blican> principles. I cannot but rem<ark> before I close this letter that last week the Election took place through out this State <for> members of the Legislature, nothing can equal the diabolical e<fforts> Made by the Feds the lies falshoods and spurious productions they <have> published would disgrace the <fire> of an Infernal— and all we flatter ourselves to no purpose from the returns we have received we are induced to believe the Legislature at their ensueing Session next month will be more republic<an> than they were Last year.

I am Sir With Sentiments of the highest resp<ect> Your Most Obedient Humble Servt.

S R B

Th Jefferson Pr. U S.

<small>Draft (ViU). Heavily corrected, with many deletions and blots; parts of words missing in right margin.

1. These four candidates and the three recommended by Israel Smith were all appointed by Jefferson (*Papers of Madison: Secretary of State Series,* 4:31; Jefferson to SRB, 27 Aug. 1802, n. 1).</small>

To Thomas Jefferson

Sir   Westminster Sept. 13th. 1802

I have the honour to acknowledge the receipt of your letter of the 27th. of August, yesterday, and can assure you it was the first intimation, that you expected from me a recommendation of proper persons, as Commissioners of bankruptcy in this State — had it before come to my knowledge, I certainly should have embraced the earliest oppertunity of giving you all the assistance in my power. You will permit me to observe that this state has a range of Mountains runing north and south through almost the whole length of the same, that most of the Inhabitants are settled on the east and west side of the State, and but very little commerce or intercourse across the mountains that the Legislature hold their sessions alternately on each side as do also the courts of the United States. I should deem it most expedient to appoint four on each side that is four in the district in which Judge *Smith* lives & four in the district in which I live, I mention four that in case of Death, or other causes that might incapacitate one, there might be a sufficient number in the district without having to cross the mountains. Under a conviction of the expediency I will take the Liberty of recommending four living on the eastern Side of the mountains, expecting Judge Smith will recommend proper characters on the western side — and will name *Mark Richards,* and *Reuben Atwater* of Westminster *James Elliot* of Brattleborough and *Oliver Gallop* of Hartland. The first is a Very respectable Merchant the three last mentioned are Lawyers, they are all Men of known probity, abilities, and firmly attached to Republican principles, and would no doubt if appointed discharge the duties with faithfulness, required of *them*.

I cannot but remark before I close this letter that last week the Election took place throughout this State for Members of the Legislature. Nothing can equal the diabolical exertions made by the Feds., the lies, falshoods, and spurious productions, they have published, would disgrace the pen of an Infernal and all we flatter ourselves to no purpose, from the returns received we are Induced to believe the Legislature at their ensuing Session Next Month will be more republican than they were last year.

I am Sir With Sentiments of the highest respect, Your Most Obedt Humble Servt

Stephen R Bradley

The President of the United States

<small>ALS (NjP). Endorsed, "Bradley Stephen R. Westminster. Sep. 13. 1802. / recd. Sep. 23. / commis bankruptcy. Windsor / Recommending / Mark Richards / Reuben Atwater / James Elliot / & Oliver Gallop."</small>

From James Whitelaw

Sir   Ryegate Septr. 27th 1802

Your letter of the 10th by Judge Hall was duely received I have also received the hundred Do<llars> and have placed the same to your credit.

I observe what you mention with respect to the Frost lands and shall charge you for no agency after this date except on the lands I b<ought> for you which I will attend to and either get Deeds or redemption money.

Should you send a new list at any time it shall be punctually attended to.

I am Sir with Esteem your most Huml. Servt.

James Whitelaw

Hon. Stephen R Bradley Esqr.

ALS (VtU). Margin obscured.

From Samuel A. Otis

Dear Sir   Boston 1t Octr 1802

Your son whose conversation & manners have made a pleasing impression, handed me your favr. 27 Sept[1]—I have made an arrangement with him to come into the office as soon as he can finish his business at Decr Court; As no inconvenience will arise from his being absent a few days at the commencement of the session, when the business is not very pressing. As to the terms you recollect the law allows at the rate of 1000 dolls year for the engrossing Clerks. He will have an oppor[tunit]y of looking round him, and will soon find whether it will interfear with his other prospects. He appears to have talents superior to meer clerkship, but may hereby be introduced to something better. At all events persuade him to retain his practice as that is an independency.

Mr. Hanson who hath addressed you, probably a circular letter; is a quondam Cashier of the Georgetown bank, dismissed for appropriating a large sum of the Stockholders money to his own use—At least this was the conversation at Washington the last year.[2] His application seems to have been suggested in part from my appointment to be a commissioner of Bankruptcy—An appointment which I have not accepted nor do I intend unless dismissed the service of the Senate. And whatever they may do at another Session, I flatter myself that no present efforts will me [sic] made to displace me—During the revolution of another year If I can obtain anything like an equivalent in or near Boston, I shall prefer being with my family. My salary as Secretary is short of the support of my family. That of Commissioner of Bankruptcy perhaps too small to bear any comparison. I hope therefore you will be at Washington, by the last of Novemr, or at all events by the day on which the session commences, when probably if at all attempts may be made.

I should have been happy in more of your company while in Town, & when you come again hope for a farther indulgence.

I understand Mr Smith is to be your colleague in future. You will oblige me by saying to him what is proper repeating.

Your assured friend & most humble Servt

Sam: A. Otis

The Honble. Stephen R Bradley

ALS (DLC). Cover addressed by Otis to "The Honble. Stephen R Bradley / Westminster / Vermont." Docketed by SRB, "from Secretary Otis."

1. Letter not found.
2. Samuel Hanson of Samuel had served as cashier of the Bank of Columbia from 1793 until 1801, when he was dismissed. He subsequently solicited employment in the federal government, including the position of chief clerk in the State Department. In 1804 he finally obtained the position of purser at the Washington Navy Yard but was dismissed in 1810 after a court of inquiry had examined his accounts (Robert A. Rutland et al., eds., *The Papers of James Madison: Presidential Series* [3 vols. to date; Charlottesville, Va., 1984–], 2:277 n. 1).

Senate Proceedings: Election of a President Pro Tempore

[13 December 1802]

The VICE PRESIDENT being absent, the Senate proceeded to the choice of a President *pro tempore,* as the Constitution provides, and the ballots being collected and counted, the whole number was found to be 17, of which 9 make a majority.

Mr. Bradley had 7, Mr. Tracy had 7, Mr. Baldwin 1, Mr. Dayton 1, Mr. Logan 1.

There was consequently no choice. Whereupon, the Senate proceeded to the election of a President *pro tempore,* as the Constitution provides, and the ballots being collected and counted, the whole number was found to be 17, of which 9 make a majority.

Mr. Bradley had 8, Mr. Tracy 7, Mr. Dayton 1, Mr. Logan 1.

There was consequently no choice. Whereupon, the Senate proceeded to the election of a President *pro tempore,* as the Constitution provides, and the ballots being counted, the whole number was found to be 17, of which 9 make a majority.

Mr. Bradley had 8, Mr. Tracy 7, Mr. Dayton 1, Mr. Logan 1.

There was consequently no choice. Whereupon, the Senate proceeded to the election of a President *pro tempore,* as the Constitution provides, and the ballots being counted, the whole number of votes was 14, of which 8 make a majority.

Mr. Tracy had 7, Mr. Bradley 5, Mr. Dayton 1, Mr. Logan 1.

There was consequently no choice; and the Senate adjourned.

Printed copy (*Annals of Congress,* 7th Cong., 2d sess., 10).

Senate Proceedings: Election of a President Pro Tempore

[14 December 1802]

The VICE PRESIDENT being absent, the Senate proceeded to the choice of a President *pro tempore,* as the Constitution provides, and the ballots being collected and counted, the whole number was found to be 17, of which 9 make a majority.

Mr. Bradley had 9, Mr. Tracy had 7, Mr. Dayton 1.

Consequently, STEPHEN R. BRADLEY was elected President of the Senate *pro tempore.*

Ordered, That the Secretary wait on the President of the United States, and acquaint him that a quorum of the Senate is assembled, and that, in the absence of the VICE PRESIDENT, they have elected STEPHEN R. BRADLEY President of the Senate *pro tempore.*

Printed copy (*Annals of Congress,* 7th Cong., 2d sess., 10–11).

From Joseph Dorr

Honble Stephen R Bradly Esqr
Sir   Fort Detroit Decbr the 14, 1802

I have here enclosed twenty Dollars it being in part of the Monney for which I am indebted to you I do asure you Sir that it would have giving me much more pleasure to have sent the whole sum for which I am indebted but it is not in my pow<er> at present my unavoidable expences useing all the econimy that I am Master of and I flatter my self th<at> I am as prudant as a Man can be I can not suport my Self upon my pay here I have not yet ben abl<e> to send any to Mrs Dorr but I feel in hopes she do<es> not want it. Sir excuse me for my repeated complaints but looking up to you as a freind whose Influance has power to assist me and whose freindship I have so often received I do it with the <most> asureance and Pardon me Sir if I Intrud Could I but be asured that I were to sail the U. S Schooner Tracy that now sails on the Lakes or a Leiut in the Revenue Cutters I then could ma<ke> a calculation to save some thing for a futer day as my family is small at present. But upon t<he> present apointment I must if at this post be end[...] as much as two hundred Dollars pr Annum as I had when I came here some Months pay due I am not yet envolved and shall endevour not to be so hoping to hear Glad tidings from you as such they will be if any such apointment should take place and under those expectations and past asureances I wait with patiance and I am Sir with due respect your Obligated humble Servant.

Joseph Dorr Ensign 1 Regt Infantry

N. B thair is in the 1 Reft Infantry 20 Leiut & Six Ensigns that rank me and upon a moderate calculation it would be twelve or fourteed years before I could git to a Captcy and then the prime of life with me would be over yours with due respect

Joseph Dorr

Honle Stephen R Bradly Esqr

ALS (VtU). Margin obscured. Endorsed, "Jos. Dorr 1802."

From James Madison

Sir,   Department of State, December 22. 1802.

In pursuance of the "Act to revive and continue in force certain parts of the 'Act for the relief and protection of American seamen,' and to amend the same," I have the Honor to lay before the Senate Abstracts of the Returns made to me by the Collectors of the Customs within the United States, of Registered and of impressed American seamen; to which is added a Report, exhibiting an Abstract of Communications received from Agents of the United States, for the relief and protection of their seamen. With High Respect, I have the Honor to be, sir, Your Obedt Hble. servant,

James Madison

LS and enclosures (DNA: RG 46, Reports and Communications from the Secretary of State, 7A-F1). Addressed to the president of the Senate. Enclosures 10 pp. SRB served as president pro tempore of the Senate during the Seventh and Tenth Congresses (1801–3 and 1807–9).

From Nathaniel Ruggles

My dear Sir   Roxbury near Boston Jany 1st. 1803

My last respects to you, were under date of the 25th. Decr. ulto.[1] in which I expressed my feirst *[sic]* opinion upon the abolition of the Loan Offices—since which I have read the Secretary of the Treasury's observations on that subject, as submitted to the Comee. of Ways & Means—The Secretary is of opinion, that the mode proposed will prevent frauds on Government; but we ought to look (and the Secretary seems to, in part) on the other side of the picture, and pay some attention to the Loaners, who are, certainly entitled to some attention in placing their faith in Government—Transfers are daily taking place and purchases making from those who are obliged or inclined to sell, to those who are inclined to hold, & this grounded on the faith in Government, and, in a great measure, upon the easiness of transferrs. And the less accessable the channels in which these transferrs are made, the less of course must be the price of Stock, and of consequence *less* the Credit of Government—And at such distances as some of the states will be from the place of transfer, the more liable to counterfeeit & Imposition to the Holders. It, in my opinion, would be much less liable, to imposition upon individual holders, where there are discreet persons in each State to oversee the transferrs, who are acquainted with the recent or daily transactions in their own State, and the change of property accruing from deaths &c, and who could detect from their own knowledge, early information, or from circumstances within their observation, spurious powers, knavish transactions &c &c — which knowledge of Men, Circumstances & Transactions, could not be known by the Officers of the Treasury at the distance of Washington — And by this mean great injury might arrise to innocent individuals who have placed their whole reliance on their faith in Government —

The foregoing observations are predicated upon the presumption that Government may find men in each State who are discreet & faithful — & in whom they may safely rest the inspection of this business

I think however they ought to be paid according to their services & responsability — 'Tis not my opinion that they should be paid monies, unearnt. —

The plan proposed, I am fearful will have an Aristrocratic tendency — As it throws the whole business more immediately into the Banks, which from the nature of their institutions, tend to aristocracy —

You, my dear Sir, have oportunity of viewing the whole ground, and I write more freely, as I know you will not attach more weight to my observations than they deserve

I am dear Sir with high respect & Esteem Your hume Servt.

Nathl. Ruggles

P. S I have not heard from Stella since she went to School —

ALS (NcD: Bradley Family Papers). Cover addressed to "Honble. Stephen Roe Bradley / S. U. S / City of Washington / District of Columbia" and stamped "FREE."; postmarked at Boston; docketed by SRB, "Nathel Ruggles."
1. Letter not found.

From Uriel C. Hatch

Dear Sir   Cavendish January 4 1803

Yours by the last Post[1] containing a note against Esqr Briggs I duly received and will collect and pay over the money when I see you — As far as I can learn there is no choice for Representative to Congress in this district — In this Town there were 76 votes for Elliot & 2 scattering — We shall do better at the next trial — I have been informed that in Woodstock Elliot[2] will have nearly 100 more votes than before — should this be true and the Republicans generally attend the freemans meeting I think there can be no doubt of his Election —

I am Sir Your Obedient Servant

Uriel C. Hatch

ALS (NcD: Bradley Family Papers).
1. Letter not found.
2. James Elliott (1775–1839), clerk of the Vermont house of representatives, 1801–1803, was admitted to the bar in 1803 and began practice in Brattleboro, Vermont. He was elected as a Federalist to the Eighth, Ninth, and Tenth Congresses (4 Mar. 1803–3 Mar. 1809). After his retirement from Congress he published a newspaper in Philadelphia.

From Ephraim Kirby

Dear sir   Litchfield January 5th. 1803

The enclosed *jeu d'esprit* may afford you some amusement. It holds an unpleasant mirror before the face of some of our federal friends; however, unpleasant as it is, it may do them good. It is proper that public men should know how their actions are estimated by the people although effusions of this sort are not the most perfect test of public opinion, still they furnish a degree of evidence.

Federalism in Connecticut is evidently in a hectick state. With good nursing it may be made to linger along for some time, but can never recover. Its regular decline is marked by heart-rending groans and violent spasms. As in other cases the malady has produced not only a feverish state of the body, but a restless petulence of temper, which seeks relief in the abuse of others.

I shall be happy to know from you the state of the political pulse at the seat of Government.

Accept the assurance of my esteem & respect

Ephm Kirby

Honbl. Stepn. R. Bradley
ALS (Vtu).

From Amasa <Prire>

Dear Sir   Windsor Janry 13th. 1803

I am induced again to address you, on the subject of placeing the office of Marshal for this district, in other hands. I hope by this time, the business of Congress is so far setled, as that you will have <leisure?> to pay some attention to that subject. General Morris has in his possession, papers which shew, that Mr Willard wholly omitted to give bonds, or qualify under his last appointment, un[t]ill ready four months after his first appointment expired, & that notwithstanding he continually executed the office, tho unauthorized. It is unnecessary for me to descend into the particulars of Mr Willards administration, as you are already convinced of the impropriety of his holding the office any longer. I make no doubt but Major Atwater would do the duties of that office well <c>ould he obtain the appointment of Marshal, & would give general satisfaction, & it would be extremely gratifying to me, should you procure him appointed.

I am with great Respect Your Devoted Humble sert.

Amasa <Prire>

Honble. Mr Bradley
ALS (VtU).

From Benjamin Sumner

Dear Sir   Claremont Janu. 19th. 1803.

I shall make no apoligy for writing to you at this time as I know you are ancious to Strengthen the Un[i]on and Render the general Administration happey — you are well knowing there is not a Republican from the State of New Hampshire, in the Legesleture in Either Senet or House — and I assure you — the Same Plan of Election [...] is Caried on this year that was Last; from oure members of Congress; No communication can be had from the seat of government to this State but to, and from feds. — although Letters are Recd. in town from Mr. — — by maney they are not to be seene by you Know whoo and as the Republican party in this State can have no Communication from its members — I pray you sir to forward to me such Statements from the Several Treasu<ry> Departments as shall Render beyond a Doubt in the mind of Every one the true state of oure finances—as you can Do it with out much Trouble or Cost—it will enable me to Do somthing to aid the Honorable John Langdon in to the Chair of New Hampshire—Which will Compleetly Renovvate this state—oure Numbers Increes and I want to Strengthen their facts by such Publications as you may choose to forward to me We have had Several meetings in order to Know oure Numb<ers> and strength—Doctr. Hastings Will be Run for as Member of the general court of New Hampshire for Charlestown, and have the Influance of the Post officer of that Town; and those that Vote for him I Expect will be for Langdon govr.—Claremont and Cornis as well as Plainfield will set up Republican Candidates it is good for us to begin; the good work; if we should miscarey the first time.

I am Sir With much Esteem; most Respectfully yours

Benja Sumner

ALS (VtU).

From Joseph Bullen

Hond. sir   Chickesaws Janr. 24. 1803

I beg Leave to Call your attention a few Minutes from our great national Concer<ns> to your own affairs & to those of an obscure Individual—the Big Debt I owe you—will amount by the third of next May as I calculate to 577. Doll<s.> or thereabouts—Last spring 400 Ds. which I exp<ected> you would have—unfortunately it went into other Hands—Revd. Mr. Taylor assures me—you shall have it—by the first of May next—it will then be 426 Dollars—my View in advancing Last Year & my Petition now, is that on receiving that sum by Mr. Taylor—you will wait another Year—with Cost—for the Remainder—& for the Contents of the othe<r> Note I gave you in March 1800. the considerat[...] in Favor of granting my Petition are—1st. it will be agreeable to the method in which you have allway<s> Dealt with me—2dly. on Recollection & Looking over your Office & other accounts you'll find your Estate is something better for me—3rdly In one Instance you saved by me more than 500 Dollars of a Debt you was in Danger of Loosing—Lastly the money secured as it is will be as safe in my Hands as in your own Chest & will still be earning something—if it be your Pleasure to grant my Petition—please to write me a few Li<nes> by the Mail—Mr McIntosh Late Post-Master here Died In Louisiana—about the 20th of December—of this the Post-Master General ought to be informed—the Profits of th<e> office here will not pay a man for Doing the Busin<ess> my Living here is Scanty—Government Sometimes send<s> People this way to Do Business—if in Future they have any Commands this way—within the Compass of my weak abilities—they may be assured—if Confided to m<e> they shall be faithfully obeyed—I find you are Chos<en> President of the Senate—tis only a Prelude to your further Advancement—two Grades more will bring you to the highest Dignity your Country [...][1] Mr. Baldwin—with Due Deference I am Honored sir—Yours

Joseph Bullen

P. S. For two Hundred Dollars Per Annum I would Do the Post-office Business here—as little as it Can be done for—& I can do it without Interfering with my Missionary Employ.

J. B.

Perhaps I had better be Content with Poverty than meddle with Business inconsistent with my Professional Character.

Honorable Stephen R. Bradley Esqr.

ALS (VtU). Margin obscured.
1. At least one and one-half lines of text are obscured.

In Senate of the United States

[Jan. 1803]

Mr. Bradley, from the Committee to whom was referred

THE BILL

"To divide the Indiana Territory into two separate Governments, and giving the assent of Congress to the proposition of the Convention of the State of Ohio, contained in the sixth section of the seventh article of the Constitution of that State."

Report the following amendments, (viz.)

1   SECTION 5th, line 3d — strike out the word "*were*" and
2   insert the words "*shall be.*"
3   Section 5th, line 6th — strike out "*were*" and insert "*shall be.*"
4   Strike out the whole of the 7th section.
5   Amend the title by striking out all in the same after the word
6   "*Governments.*"

Printed document. U.S. 7th Congress, 1801–1803.

From Benjamin Rush

Sir,   Philadelphia Feb: 8th: 1803

Though a stranger to your person, I am induced to address you upon a subject interesting to humanity.

Mr John Graham deputy Clerk to the senate of the United states, is now under my Care at a lodging house in this city, afflicted with a severe Attack of derangement. Its cause is unknown to me, nor can any inquiries on my part satisfy me what is his business in Philadelphia. His papers shew that he has been well educated, & that his connections are respectable. The Lady with whom he lodges is unwilling — and unable to keep him under present circumstances in her house. I have this day made an unsuccessful Attempt to procure his Admission into Our hospital. His want of funds, or of a security for the payment of his board there, were the Objections made to his admission. He speaks often in his more tranquil moments of you — Judge Smith & Mr Clinton with great respect and Affection. I submit his truly distressing case to your consideration. In the mean while, he shall continue to command my best services, Although, from his present want of Attendants and Accommodations suited to his disease, I fear they will be of little use to him. From Sir with great respect your most Obedient Servant

Benjn: Rush

ALS (DLC). Cover addressed by Rush to "Stephen R: Bradley Esqr / Member of the Senate of the United States. / City of Washington," postmarked Philadelphia, 8 Feb., and stamped "FREE." Docketed by SRB, "from Doct Rush." Also docketed "Doct Rush / re Graham." Benjamin Rush (1745?–1813) was a well-known Philadelphia physician, author, and politician, who had been a signer of the Declaration of Independence from Pennsylvania.

From Joseph Moffett

Sir,   Danville Feb. 9th. 1803.

Relying on your Honor's ex<ert>ions in promoting the Public Good especially the Interest of Your Constituents, I address your Honor at this time relative to the establishment of a Post road from Portland in Maine by the Notch of the white He[...] in New Hampshire &

Danville in Vermont to St Albans. It will be in length about 200 miles, one hundred of whi<ch> will be a turn Pike viz, from Portland to the Notch. The road from St Albans to the Notch is capable of being ma<de> much better, than the road now established from the northern parts of Vermont to Boston & also much nearer. The earstern parts of New Hamshire & maine are very anxious that a communication be opened with Vermon<t> by this rout & have offered large premiums for its promotio<n.> I am persuaded it will greatly promote the interest of this State, considered either in a commercial or political view, and will have a great tendancy to populate & enlighten the inhabitants of New Hampshire & the northern parts of our own State. We, Hon. Sir have turned our eyes to Your Honor as being best able to promote so desirable an undertaking & carry into effect the wishes of every man of business & consequence from Portland in Maine to St Albans in Vermont. It will also have a great tendancy to promote the revanue of the United States by distributing many letters, which are now returned *dead* to the General Post Office.

We also would propose that a mail be extended from Danville to Derby by which a communication will be opened on the eastern part of Vermont with lower Cannada which you are sensible Sir is mostly settled from the northern parts of Vermont & New Hampshire. Had this rout of the Mail have been established but <a?> twelve month ago I am persuaded we should have b<een> able to carry the election for a republican represent<ative> to Congress. We are sensible, Hon Sir, by your e<x>ertions the above routs may be established we th<us?> rest assured of your attention to the wishes of you<r> constituents.

I am Hon. Sir, your most obedient Serv

Joseph Moffe<tt>

Hon. Stephen R. Bradley
Senator in Congress
ALS (VtU). Damaged by removal of seal. Margin obscured.

From David Robinson

Sir, Westminster March 7th. 1803

Your Son informs me that he thinks Probable that you would wish to purchase the Plaice belonging to my Father when Doct. <Heileman> lived it is now for Sale the price will be Six Hundred & fifty Dollars If you should have an inclination to Purchase it I wish you to give me immediate information, as I have not let it and If Doct. Town hires it he wants to Know it immediately if you should conclude to take it you can let him know it and make such araingments with him as you plese I have had a number of applications from different people for it but my Sister Requested I would not sell it till you had the offer of it. I wish you to write me wheither you should incline to purchase or not which will oblige your Humble sert

David Robinson

Genl. Bradley
ALS (VtU).

From Joseph Goodhue

Honored Sir Westminster Aprill 6th. 1803

I receivd orders by the last evenings mail to repair imediately to Portsmouth came this morning to se you am very sorry you are not at home I feel my self under great obligations to you for the interest you have taken in my welfare and hope to have the pleasure of personaly expresing the same.

I hope sir you will be so kind as to attend to our great meadow sute and I will see that you are paid.

The grain note you hold against me I will sittle the first oppertunity William will inform you how much is already paid.

Sir I am with due respect your humble servant

Joseph Goodhue

ALS (VtU). Addressed to SRB at Westminster.

From Samuel Williams

Sir, Rutland April 12. 1803.

There are some matters in agitation here which may possibly be of some consequence to you. A gentleman with whom you was much acquainted at the city of Washington last winter, seems to be much incensed with you and determined to go to any lengths which may affect your reputation or interest.

He avers that he is in possession of some pieces of your writing last winter; that you dictated to him a letter to be published at New-York, and required him to sign it contrary to his incl[i]nations; that it was sent on, and published unknow[n] to him; that many confidential communications were made to him, respecting certain transactions with a Lawyer formerly of Greenfield, but now of New-York; that a trial respecting them is to be had at New-York the beginning of May; that he is to attend as a witness, and has discovered & agreed upon the plan with Mr Benson and General Hamilton; and has evidence to give which you are not apprehensive of; with many other particulars, too many to be mentioned in writing. And that this plan is to be pursued unless you make such compensation as will be satisfactory.

Perhaps the above is too visionary & trifling to deserve your attention. If this be the case you will excuse a well meant (though foolish) attempt to prevent mischief. As to myself I have no doubt but that the person referred to, is going to New-York to attend as an evidence, that he has concerted the plan with C — — m, Benson & Gen. H — — n and that he will go all lengths to obtain money or consequence, let who may be the sacrifice.

If the above is of no consequence, excuse my too officious intermedling. If it is of any use I believe I can furnish you with several particulars relative to his views and declarations &c not to be committed to paper.

I have wrote the above in the most perfect confidence in your honor and judgment. You will not suffer this paper to be seen by any person, or give any kind of intelligence that you have received a line from me on the Subject. At the same time I am willing to declare that if any serious attempt should be made to injure your reputation or property, I am willing to give you any information I have, or may have upon the subject.

With much esteem and respect, I am, Sir, Your obliged & very humble Servant

Samuel Williams.

Hon. S. R. Bradley

ALS (VtU).

From Henry Dearborn

Sir,   War Department May 4th. 1803

Your favor of the 25th. Ulto.[1] has been duly recd.—The promotion of Mr. Allen cannot take place until after a strict examination of his qualifications and a report made thereon by Col. Williams to this Office—Capt M. Lewis the Secy. of the President of the U.S. (who is a Capt in the Army) has undertaken the tour alluded to in your letter & is now nearly ready to take his departure—

I am respectfully your Hume Servt

H. Dearborn

Hon Stephen R. Bradley

ALS (NcD: Bradley Family Papers). Cover addressed to "Hon. Stephen R. Bradley / Westminster / Vermont"; marked "War Department / H. Dearborn" and stamped "FREE"; postmarked at Washington, 4 May; docketed by SRB, "Secretary of Wars Letter of the 4th of May 1803."

1. Letter not found.

Henry Dearborn

To Thomas Jefferson

The President of the United States

Sir   Westminster May 20th. 1803

I have just learnt that James Elliot has resigned as a Commissioner of Bankruptcy and to my surprise that he has recommended his Brother to succeed him. The recommendation of his Brother is an injudicious one, his brother I understand is a young man reading law as a Clerk in an office and has removed to live in the State but a Very Short time I am convinced his appointment would be viewed unfavourably by the best friends to the Government. I will take the liberty to Recommend *Samuel Knight* Esqr. to be appointed *vice* James Elliot he has been a firm Republican through the whole reign of Terror was Chief Justice of our Supreme Court for Several years and was left out by the Federalists when the Government was in their hands, Since which he has never been replaced he is an able Lawyer and well calculated to Discharge the Duties of that office lives in the Same town with Mr Elliot resigned I wish for the sake of the Government he might obtain.

With the highest respect except the Homage of

Stephen R Bradley

ALS (NjP).

From Joseph Dorr

Honerable Stephen R Bradly Esqr

On board the U.S. Schooner Senator Tracy *bad Name*

Sir   Lying off Fort Erie June the 3 1803

I receve'd yours of the 8 January, on the first of April, attended with the Secretary<'s>

Letter, wherein I have the apointment, to the Command of the above Schooner for which I am indebted to you for, except of my sincere thanks, and respect, it has placed me in a very pleasent Situation, I ca<n> not onely suport my self, but my Wife, and lay up Money, I will endevour to discharge m<y> duty, which is intrusted to me, as far as in my power.

I am with due respect your Obediant Humble Servant

Joseph Dorr

Pleas remember me to my friends I rote William sometime since, I have not yet receivd any in return. I have not time to right to all my Westmin<ster> Friends.

Yours

J Dorr

ALS (VtU). Margin obscured.

From Samuel A. Otis

Dear Sir   Boston June 10th 1803

The enclosed resolution was passed during your presidency, & it appeared to me to be the sense of the Senate that it should retrospect to the commencement of the Session. So it was understood the session prior to the last, and I have paid Mathers, as I did for the last session, accordingly. The Comptroller of the Treasury however excepts to the including the days prior to a quorum, unless the President of the Senate will certify that the Senate intended that the resolution should operate from the 1st day of the Session.

Should you think proper to certify the resolution enclosed, I will on your returning it forward it to the Comptroller. Something like the enclosed may answer the purpose, annexed to my copy.

"United States June [1] 1803

I certify that the intention of the Senate in passing the foregoing resolution was to comprehend all the time between 6th. Decr 1802 and twenty days after the recess of Congress, both days inclusive.

{President of the
Senate of the UStates
pro tempore"

After compliments to your family I subscribe

With respect & regard Your most dbedt humble Sert.

Sam: A. Otis

ALS (DLC). Cover addressed by Otis to "the Honble: Stephen R Bradley / A Senator of the UStates / Westminster / Vermont," postmarked, and marked "3././." Docketed by SRB, "Secretary Otis's Letter of the 10th of June 1803 enclosing a resolution." Enclosed resolution not found.

1. Left blank by Otis.

Circular Letter from James Madison

(CIRCULAR)

SIR, DEPARTMENT OF STATE, WASHINGTON, *July* 18, 1803.

THE Proclamation by the President, of which a copy is inclosed, will inform you, that in pursuance of his authority to convene Congress on extraordinary occasions, he has appointed Monday the 17th day of October next for the meeting of the Senators and Representatives of the United States. This anticipation of the commencement of the ensuing session is rendered necessary by conventions with the French Republic, involving a cession of Louisiana to the United States; which may require the presence of both Houses, and of which conventions the ratifications are to be exchanged within six months computed from the 30th of April last. The shortness of the period therefore, to which the necessary proceedings will be limited, with <the> very great importance of the subject to the interest of the United States, claim from every member the most punctual attendance; and I am charged by the President to urge these considerations on your patriotism, and your sense of duty. Assuring myself that they will have all the effect which he justly expects from them.

I remain, Sir, With the highest respect, Your most obedient Servant,

James Madison

[Enclosure]

BY THE

PRESIDENT OF THE UNITED STATES

OF AMERICA.

A PROCLAMATION.

WHEREAS great and weighty matters, claiming the consideration of the Congress of the United States, form an extraordinary occasion for convening them; I do by these presents appoint Monday the 17th day of October next for their meeting at the City of Washington, hereby requiring the respective Senators and Representatives, then and there to assemble in Congress, in order to receive such communications as may then be made to them, and to consult and determine on such measures, as, in their wisdom may be deemed meet for the welfare of the United States.

In Testimony Whereof, I have caused the Seal of the United States to be hereunto affixed, and signed the same with my hand.

Done at the City of Washington, the sixteenth day of July, in the year of our Lord, L.S. one thousand eight hundred and three; and in the twenty-eighth year of the Independence of the United States.

(Signed)   TH: JEFFERSON.

By the President

(Signed)   JAMES MADISON, *Secretary of State.*

_{Printed circular and enclosure (DLC). Circular signed by Madison. Cover addressed to "The Hone. Stephen R. Bradley Esq / Senator of U.S. / Westminster"; marked "hone. by Majr. Levert. G. Tichenor"; franked by Madison; docketed by Bradley, "James Madison / enclosing the President's proclamation."}

From Abel Spencer

Dear Sir.   Rutland July 18th. *1803*

You will be so good as to pardon the liberty I take in addressing you on a Subject in which neither of us can be grately Interested —& in no way any further than we Respect the Interest of others. Mr. Smith of Rutland who has kept the Post office in that place for About Two yeares last past & I believe with grate Satisfaction to all who have hand anything do with him as Deputy post master in Said office — has this day Informed me that Some few persons in Rutland wish to git him Removd from office and that application had been made to you for assistance in that poticulour by persons living in the nabourhood of Rutland. On what account this Should have happened I Cannot say —for thare is no Complaint he is a man of good Standing in Sociaty and I have never heard an Intimation agt. him in Regarde to his office. He is a Very attentive Industerous man tho a man of bad heath having been much afflicted with the Rumatick Complaint. He has been at grate Expence in Shifting his Local Situation to accomidate the Public. I have oneley to ask in this mans behalf that you will not Sir. Influance agt. him untill you have been fulley Satisfyed he is a man that ought not to hold the office. Why is not this Complaint Publickley known in the nabourhood. Why is not Mr. Smith accquainted with this, if a public Evil Exists why not apply to him he lives a nabour to the Postmaster & would be willing to Interfare if necessary you will Sir. find the Representation if any has been made of the kind as [...]tered by the postmaster & without foundation and arising wholey from a little misunderstanding betwene Smith & a nabour of his—and for no other cause only that Smith wished to Secure a Demand by attachment agt. a person that had for Some time kept a printing office in his house. I have Said to Mr. Smith that Genll. Bradley would never Interfeare in the little Bickerings and Disputs in Rutland while he had a Brother Senetor Residing on the ground—& who would better know the propriety of a Removal from office in that place.

I am Dear Sir. with much Respect your Obedeant Humble Servt.

Abel Spencer

ALS (VtU). Text obscured by seal. Addressed to SRB at Westminster.

From Isaac Tichenor

Sir,   Augt. 1t. 1803

Inclosed you receive Official notice, that Congress will convene on the 17th. of Octr. next.[1]

It is with pleasure I comply with the request of the Secy. of State in transmitting to you this information—

With due Respect & Esteem I am Sir Your Obt. Sert

Isaac Tichenor

Honl. Stephen R Bradley

ALS (NcD: Bradley Family Papers). Cover addressed to"Honle. Stephen R. Bradley / Westminster"; docketed by SRB, "Govr Titchenors Notice Congress."
1. Circular Letter from James Madison, 18 July 1803.

From Nathaniel Ruggles

My dear Sir   Roxbury Octo. 8th. 1803

As Mrs. Seton is about moving to the Westerly part of Boston, near the place of business of her Husband—I brot. Stella out of Town Yesterday, to make a short vissit, untill Mrs. S— should get settled in her new habitation—In conversation with her I touched upon the subject of Stella's remaining under her tuition (I say "touched["]; for I found the subject must be humored a little) She said, "as Mr Seton's business called him a good deal from home, and as she was so much alone, she had concluded to take two or three misses to instruct"—She expressed some doubts; ["]whether the taking Stella from the place at Cambridge, where she was engaged, wou'd not give offence"—I told her, as she engaged the place it was in her power to make a sufficient apology—She said she wou'd let me know in a few days, whether she would or not—I told her that, by your desire, I should attend to the payment of her Bills—I think Sir, from this Parley, the prospect is, that she will take Stella—I also think her a very capable Woman—In a short time I shall be able to inform you of her determination.

On Thursday last (the 6th.) we paid our last Respects to the remains of Mr. Samuel Adams — there was quite a long & respectable procession — *Here* & *There* a solitary *one* of what is called the *Junto* or Hambletonians, & of them, only those, who felt a sort of obligation, ex officio —

I am with Respect & Esteem Your hum Servt.

Nath. Ruggles

N. B your Cask of wine is ready & in good order}

for your order

<small>ALS (NcD: Bradley Family Papers). Cover addressed to "Honble. Stephen R. Bradley Esqr. / City of Washington / District of Columbia" and marked "20"; postmarked at Boston, 9 Oct.; docketed by SRB, "Mr Ruggles" and "Nathel Ruggles."</small>

To the General Assembly of Vermont

Westminster Octr. 18h 1803

To the honorable the General Assembly of the State of Vermont now sitting at Westminster

The petition of Stephen R Bradley of said Westminster

Humbly sheweth —

That your petitioner is the proprietor of a gore of Land lying between Hopkinsville, Victory, and Concord which was formerly granted by Charter to Thomas Pearsall Esqr of the City of NYork and is without any name whereby it may be designated

Wherefore your Petitioner prays that the same may be erected into a Township by the name of "Bradleyvale" and incorporated with such priviledges as the Legislature may please to grant

And your Petitioner shall ever pray

Stephen R Bradley
by Wm. Bradley his son

<small>DS (Vt: MsVtSP, vol. 44, p. 95). In the hand of William C. Bradley?. A note on the verso reads: "Petition of Stephen R. Bradley / Filed Octr. 20. 1803 / Att. D. Winghen Secy / In Gen. Assemy. Oct. 21st. 1803. Read, prayer granted, and leave given to bring in a bill. Att. A Haswell, Clerk."</small>

From Joseph Bullen

Honored Sir   Chickesaws October 20. 1803.

The subject of this Letter — will — I trust — be a sufficient apology for my writing it — to a Person of your Distinguished Character & Dignified Station — When I heard of the acquisition of Louisiana by Treaty it made me very Glad — I have not been much in it But from Correct Information — it is of immense Valu<e> When I heard it was Likely to be exchanged — for those Little — sultry — barren Provinces— the Floridas — it made me concernd. — Besides the Disproportion in Quantity & Quality of Soil — all our Indians Cross Mississippi to Hunt & the Power which Possesses the Western Bank Commands <them?> another Circumstance which may perhaps have escaped your Honor — the Missisippi is about leaving her old Channel taking a new Course 150 Miles above Orleans where She reaches the Gulf of Mexico 90 or 100 miles west of her former Mouth — which will be likely ere long to Leave Orleans & its Environs — a Dry, inland Country — of no Commercial Importance — & then — if Louisiana belongs to a foreign Power where is the Trade of the western waters? — Your Honor may be assured — this is not a Chimerical Idea — Boats have actualy Descended that western

Branch — & unless my Information is incorrect — it will be no Easy matter to prevent it's taking the whole River — Sense of Duty to my Country — has Induce<d> the above Communication, to the Principal Guardian o<f> her Rights — with whom I have the Honor to be acquaint<ed> such is the Probability — of Indian Hostility — & so little th<e> Prospect of Missionary success at present — we think of passing the winter at Natchez — whether I continue Longer in the service or return to Vermont is not fully Determined.

With Great Respect — Your Honor's Humble Servt.

Joseph Bullen

Honorable Stephen R. Bradley Esq.

ALS (VtU). Margin obscured.

Act Incorporating Bradley-vale Township

[31 October 1803]

An Act incorporating the Gore herein after mentioned, into a Township, by the name of Bradley-vale.

It is hereby enacted by the General Assembly of the State of Vermont, That the Tract, or Gore of Land, lying in the County of Caledonia, and bounded by the towns of Victory, Hopkinsville and Concord, and granted to Thomas Pearsall by Charter bearing date the twenty seventh day of January, one thousand seven hundred and ninety one, be, and the same is hereby incorporated into a Township, by the name of Bradley-vale; with all the rights, privileges and immunities enjoyed by other Towns in this State; except so far as may relate to the right of representation.

State of Vermont.

I David Wing Junr. Secretary of the State of Vermont, do hereby Certify, that the foregoing is a true Copy of an Act passed by the Legislature of Vermont, on the 29th. day of October instant.

In testimony whereof I have hereunto set my hand and Seal of Office, at Westminster, the thirty first day of October, Ao. Di. one Thousand eight hundred and three.

D. Wing Junr.

ADS (NcD). Seal affixed.

From Isaac Tichenor

Dear General   Westminster 7h. Novr. 1803

I recd. your favour of the 19th. of the last Month[1] accompanied by the Militia Returns therein mentioned — it would have added to the pleasure I took in the perusal to have seen a statement of the numbers & Equipments of the Militia of this State — It was in the power of the Secy. at War to have done this.

On receiving the Presidents Circular Letter to the Executives of the several States — the Adjutant General made out, in due form, a Return of our Militia & forwarded it to the War-Office — At the same time I enclosed one to the President, containing a Geographical Description of our military Divisions and specifying the names of the Commanding Generals in each — this was forwarded on the 22d. of March last, & might have had a place in the Secy. return. — I feel myself under particular Obligations to you, in placing it in my power, to do away any improper impressions of neglect of Duty on my part or that of the Adjutant General.

Our Legislature have it in view to rise on thursday of this Week — it would be a fortunate circumstance if the Act recommending an alteration in the Constitution of the U. States should arrive before the close of business.

Through the polit[e]ness of two respectable old-Bachelors, who guard your Mansion-House, I had the pleasure of being introduced to Mrs. Bradley — And I now avail myself of this opportunity of assuring you, that all parties united in doing justice to your Judgement, and to her Merits — She is truly a most amiable Woman — But knowing the opinion you have hitherto entertained of the assumption of powers by Legislative Bodies — it is a matter of surprize to some of your friends — that at this critical period of Affairs, you should leave the most valuable of your property exposed — it cannot add to your security to be told that Liberty & Equality is most eminently enjoyed and is the Order of the Day in both Houses — with very great Esteem & Respect I have the honor to be Your Obt. Sert

Isaac Tichenor

Genl. Bradley

ALS (NcD: Bradley Family Papers). Cover addressed to "Honbl. Stephen R. Bradley / in Congress / Senator / City of Washington"; marked "Westminster Nov. 10" and "Free"; docketed by SRB, "Govr Tichenor."
1. Letter not found.

From Alain Spooner

Sir   Windsor, Jan. 9th. 1804.

Your *goodness* and *freedom*, has emboldened me to request some information from you respecting the Amendment of the constitution. It appears by your information and the journals of the Senate and Ho<use> that our Republican members from this State did not agree in the main question — that our Senators and Mr. Oli<n> were in favor, and Mr Elliot, and the federal memb<ers> were opposed. This conduct of Mr. Elliott has given gr<eat> umbrage to his constituents; considering him as [...] young member, and having been requested by a *very* large majority of the Gen Assembly to support such a motion; and having the exampl<e> of the Senators before him, we cannot view his conduct with approbation, unless he proves to us that he is a man of more *wisdom* than our oth<er> members.

I have received a very long Epistle from M<r.> Chamberlin on the subject pointing out (as he sa<ys>) the impropriety of our Legislature's adopting th<e> Amendment. Many things have been writte<n> on the subject, but all from the *opposition*<.> Some have gone so far as to say, our Senators are not in favor of it — others have said, many of the Republican members who voted for it, hav<e> since declared, that were it in their power they would prevent its taking effect. Now, Sir, as you have had all the information possible, in the nature of things, and as I profess be ignorant of those great *national* questions, I wish you, Sir, to give me your opinion on the subject, if you have altered it since giving your yes on the question, for I expect to be soon called on to give my vote on the same subject, and wish to do right.

Mr. Elliot's high complements paid the Federal side of the house, when he was speaking of the repeal of the Bankrupt Law, does not set very well on the stomachs of the Republicans in this part of the district — his fears of their "shaking the government to its centre," might better been thought than spoken.

I thank you, sir, for the favor which you have done with the Secretary of State. I have sent on my Account to him without filling up the sum, which I could not do, being unacquainted with the sum allowed for the services. Were it not that my finances are very low, I should not have troubled you, sir, or him, on the subject. The federal papers around me, have curtailed me of all the business which I used to have <from?> the Lawyers & Courts, and reduces me to the necessity of working hard and living economically, in order to live at all. But my sentiments (until I am convinced to the contrary) I shall retain until my exit.

I remain your very humble Servant

Alain Spooner

Gen Bradley

ALS (VtU). Margin obscured.

From Isaac Tichenor

Dear General
    11 Jany. 1804

Last Evening I recd. your favor, covering a report of the Secy. of the Treasury[1]—unfavourable to the Conduct of the late Coln. Brush—I am astonished at the sum due, in the management of the business intrusted to him—there must be a mistake some where—it cannot arise from any improper application of public monies, made by him—his Enemies will say, that he was a man of that strict integrity, that no consideration could have moved him, to have made an application of public Monies to his private use—a few Days before his Death Mr Dewey & myself urged him to make his Will—he then particularly mentioned the State of his public & private Affairs—& said that he had a Sum over & above what he had recd. from Mrs. Brush that would assist her in bringing up the little ones—that there would be due to him from the U. S in the settlement of his Accounts, nearly $2000—he had often mentioned this to me before

I called on Mrs. Brush this morning & shewed her the report—She tells that the Accounts which were prepared to be forwarded to the Secy. had been detained under the idea, that they should be able to obtain some evidence of monies lodged in some of the Banks—that had not been transmitted, to the Secy. of the Treasury—the Widow has sent to the banks at Albany & Hartford to obtain information of the Amount of Monies lodged by Coln. Brush in those Banks—The Cashier refuses to give this information unless, she obtains the assent of the Secy. of the Treasury—She intreats me to ask the favor of you to obtain this permission, from the Secy. and enclose it to her.

I have examined the Accounts, as made out by young Mr. Brush—the sum due to the Supervisor on the internal Revenue &ca will reduce the Ballance to nearly $3.500

The Adt. Genl. will transmit by this mail to the Secy. at War the Annual Return of our Militia—I hope Genl. Dearborne will not over look this, in his next general Statement

With very great Esteem & Respect—I am Your Obt. Ser

Isaac Tichenor

ALS (NcD: Bradley Family Papers). Cover addressed to "The Honbe. Stephen. R. Bradley / in Senate / Washington"; marked "Ben Jan 13th 1804," "Free," and "Isaac Tichenor"; docketed by SRB, Govr Tichenor" and "about Crean Brush Estate."
    1. Letter not found.

Senate Proceedings: Military Appropriations

January 17, 1804.

Mr. Bradley, *from the committee to whom was referred the "Bill making appropriations for the support of the military establishment of the United States, in the year one thousand eight hundred and four,"*
Reported the following amendments; which were read and ordered to lie for consideration.

1   Sect. 1. line 21st, Strike out the words "*contingencies fifty-*
2   *five*"—and insert in lieu thereof "*contingent expenses of the war*
3   *department seventy-one*"
4   Strike out the 27th and 28th lines in the printed bill—insert
5   the following at the end of the first section:
6   "*For postage on letters on public service to and fron the offices*
7   *of the adjutant, inspector and paymaster of the army, four thou-*
8   *sand five hundred dollars."*

U.S. 8th Congress, 1803–1805. Microform, U.S. Govt. Library.

To William Czar Bradley

Feby 19th 1804

Mr. Bradley presents his respects to Wm. & Sally [...] inform him that Mr Adams was not a member of [...] Convention the ex President was at that time in E<ngland> [...] the Son too young to be noticed in political life[1] [...] to announce to you with regret the Death of that [...] Man Doct Priestly[2]

AN (NcD: Bradley Family Papers). Damaged at right margin.
1. John Adams served as the first U.S. minister to Great Britain, 1785–88, and thus, as SRB indicates, did not participate in the Federal Convention of 1787. His son, John Quincy Adams, graduated from Harvard University in 1787.
2. Joseph Priestley, the English clergyman and scientist who was one of the discoverers of the element oxygen, immigrated to the U.S. in 1794 and died in Northumberland, Pennsylvania, on 6 Feb. 1804.

Senate Proceedings

February 22d, 1804.

Mr. Bradley, from the committee to whom was referred, the *Bill*, to amend the act, "*To lay and collect a direct tax within the United States,*"

Report the bill with the following amendments, (viz.)

1   Sect. 1, line 5th, after the word "*tax,*" insert the following
2   words, "*and where the time limited by law for the redemption of*
3   *such lands, shall not have expired before the passing of this act.*"
4   Sect. 5, line 5d, after the word, *authority,* insert the following
5   words, "*in all cases where the time limited by law for the redemption*
6   *of lands sold, shall not have expired before the passing of this act.*"
7   Sect. 6, strike out all after the word "*that*" in the first line, to
8   the word "*for*" in the second line, and insert in lieu thereof, the
9   following, "*where any lot or tract of land shall have been sold be-*
10   *fore the passing of this act.*"

(2)

11 At the end of the 6th sect. insert the following—"*Provided,*
12 *That hereafter it shall not be lawful for any collector of the said*
13 *tax, to sell more of any lot or tract of land, than will pay the amount*
14 *of such tax, with the legal charges and costs, and all sales of any*
15 *lot or tract of land, which hereafter shall be made for non-payment*
16 *of the direct tax, and for a larger sum than the amount of such*
17 *tax, with the legal charges and costs, shall be void."*

U.S. 8th Congress, 1803–1805. Microform U.S. Govt. Library.

Senate Proceedings

In senate of the United States, Febr: 24th 1804.

Mr. Bradley from the committee appointed on the 9th of Jany. to consider and report whether any and if any what further proceedings ought to be had by the senate in relation to the message and documents communicated by the President of the United States on the 21st: of December last.

Submitted the following

Report

Upon a careful examination of the message and documents communicated by the President on the 21st. of December, your committee no<w> certain, unauthorized acts and doings of individuals contrary to law, and highly prejudicial to the rights and sovereignty of the United States, tending to defeat the measures of the government thereof, and which in their opinion merit, the consideration of the senate.

They find that on the 15th. of Nov. 1802 and before and subsequent to that day divers controversies and disputes had arisen between the governments of the United States and Spain concerning certain seizures and condemnations of the vessels and effects of the citizens of the United States in the ports of Spain, and for which the government of Spain was deemed responsible, and in the prosecution of which for indemnification, the minister of the United States near the court of Spain, had been instructed to press that government by friendly negotiation, to provide for those wrongs.

Your committee find, while said negotiation was pending and the said disputes and controversies in no wise settled or adjusted, that Jared Ingersoll, William Rawle Jos. B. McKean and P. S. DuPonceau of Philadelphia did at said Philadelphia on the same 15th. of Nov. 1802 and Edward Livingston of the city of New York did at said New York on the 3d. day of the same Nov. in violation of the act entitled "An Act

[*is there a page missing here?*]

Resolved if in the opinion of the Attorney General, such papers documents & evidence or such other evidence as may be presumed from any that is particeps criminis shall be deemed sufficient to warrant a prosecution of the aforesaid persons or either of them. That the President of the United States be and hereby is requested to instruct the proper law officer to commence a prosecution at such time and in such manner as he may judge expedient against Jared Ingersoll William Rawle Jos. B. McKean P. S. DuPonceau and Edward Livingston or either of them, on the Act entitled "An Act for the punishment of certain crimes therein specified" And that he be requested to furnish the Attorney on the part of the United States for the purpose of carrying on said prosecution, with such papers documents and evidence from the executive department of the government as he may deem expedient and necessary.

Tr (VtU). Addressed to SRB.

From Charles Blake

Sir,   Keene N Hampshire March 9th 1804

I had the honor to receive yours of the 20th. Ult. Since which have seen Doctor Kingsbury and by him am informed that he should prefer an appointment in the Navy, but will gladly accept an appointment of Surgeons Mate in the United States Army.

The Doctor would prefer being Stationed at Some Post in New England.

I have Sir, the honor to be with the utmost respect & esteem Yr. Obdt. Hbl Servt

Charles Blake

Honb. S. R. Bradley

ALS (VtU).

From Daniel Lammot

Gen Bradley
Sir,   Baltimore 5th April 1804.

Your esteemed favor of the 25 ulto came duly to hand mentioning that an opportunity offered from Alexandria to Rhode Island, which deprived me of the pleasure of seeing you in Baltimore as I still wish to have accomplished, that which we conversed upon in Washington, I must beg the favor of you to inform me whether it woud be proper to have suit entered & the deposition tak<en> of the woman who can prove adultery on Him, bef<ore> my Daughter will be in Vermont. If it be prop<er> in your opinion I think it had better be done immediately lest the woman should leave this place & we find it difficult to ascerta<in> her residence. I will likewise thank you to inform when your Court Sits & when we had better be in Vermont. It will likewise be wel<l]>to transmit me the form of the deposition that is to be taken and the steps that I am to pursue. I hope Sir you will pardon me for thus troubling you when you consider how deeply the happiness of my Family is Interested in the measure that I am now about to take.

I am Sir with sincere esteem yours &c.

Daniel Lammot

ALS (VtU). Margin obscured.

From Joseph Moffett

Hon. Sir,   Danville 20th. April 1804.

A paper entitled the *Northern Gaze<tte>* we expect will soon be in circulation in th<is> part of the country. It will *faithfully* detail the operations of the general & state governments & be conducted on principles of genuine *Republicani<sm.>*

As we recently have experienced your patronage in the procurement of the route through Danville we again earnestly entreat Your Honor to use your influence i<n> our behalf. We have no doubt but the northern Gazette will have an extensive spread, if we can contract for the carriage of the Mail thro' the whole of the new establ<ished> route—and have it for two or three years. We shall feel greatly obliged to you, Sir, if you will write the Postmaster General or any other person whom you shall think prop<er> upon the subject. We shall then think the way opened for communicating our proposa<l.>

I take the liberty, Sir, to recommend Messrs. Ebenezar Strong & Jonathan Ware as persons well qualified to contract for the Mail on the whole of the new route. You, Sir, will do them a kindness by recommending them.

I would suggest to your Honor whether the Public Good would not be promoted by the removal of the Postmaster at Montpelier Mr. Hubbard & the appointment of Samuel Prentice Esquire & also whether the Postmaster at Peacham ought not to be removed & William Scott appointed.

If You, Sir, should think with us by representing it to the head of the department you would greatly aid & assist in establishing the *Northern Gazette.*

I am, Hon. Sir, verry respectfully your humble Servant.

Jos. Moffett

Hon. Stephen R. Bradley Esqr.
 ALS (VtU). Margin obscured.

Deed

[20 April 1804]

 Know all Men by these presents that I Stephen R Bradley of the town of Westminster in the County of Windham and State of Vermont for and in Consideration of the love and natural affection I have for my Son William C. Bradley of the same town and County and fo<r> the further Consideration of fifty Cents Received to my full Satisfaction of the Said William C. Bradley Do Give Grant Bargain Sell alien convey and Confirm to the said William C. Bradley and to his heirs and Assigns forever the following tracts or lots of land Situate lying and being in said town of Westminster and known described and distinguished as lots Number Seventeen and Eighteen in the division of House lots in said town of Westminster as the same were laid down numbered and Surveyed in the division of said township and is the same farm on which I formerly lived and bounds East on the High way North on <Tyler Cone?> west and south on Decon Ranney.

 To have and to hold the above granted and bargained premises with all the appurtenances and priviledges thereto belonging unto him the said William C Bradley his heirs and Assigns to his and their own proper Use benefit and behoof forever And further I the said Stephen R Bradley do Covenant with the Said William C Bradley his heirs and assigns that from and after the ensealing of these presents neither I my heirs executors or administrators shall have any right title Interest property claim or demand of in or to the premises or any part thereof but from having and maintaining the same shall by these presents be forever barred.

 In witness whereof, I have hereunto Set my hand and SEal this twentieth Day of April in the Year of our Lord Eighteen Hundred and four

Signed Sealed and delivered   Stephen R Bradl<ey>
in presents of—
Samuel Phippen
Ira Goodridge
 ADS (DLC). Torn at margin.

From Daniel Lammot

S R Bradley Esqr

Sir, Baltimore 2nd June 1804

Since I wrote you on the 5th April I am without any of your favors for which I cannot account unless yours or my Letter miscarried, if that be the case I will thank you immediately on rect of this to inform me how I am to proceed and in what manner & form the womans deposition is to be taken & when it will be necessary for my daughter to be in Westminster. The Time is now fast approaching when your court will set and I am very desirous of embracing the earliest opportunity to have my Child released from a monster. Since I wrote you as above the woman has sworn before a magistrate of this City that she is with child of Sower. He has also confessed to this woman that he has lately cohabited with other women. Pray Sir will the confession made to this woman and the deposition of the magistrate before whom she swore, be any way serviceable. As I do not suppose that it will be possible for me to hear from you more than once after you receive this, before your Court sits I will thank you to write me every thing that will be necessary to be done before I leave this place & likewise the form of the deposition of the woman & when notice is to be served on Sower. I hope dear Sir you will consider a Fathers feelings and pardon my Importunities & any service that I can render you in this place will afford me peculiar Satisfaction.

I am with sincere esteem Your ob Sert

Daniel Lammot

ALS (VtU). Notations by SRB, "3 10 [+] 1 17 6" and "8 4 [+] 9 8 [=] 14 0."

From James Elliot

Sir, Brattleborough June 18. 1804.

The following is a copy of your letter to me which is the subject of General Morris's application, *so far* as respects a statement of facts. I shall make no disclosure to General M. untill I have farther communicated with you upon the subject—

"The day before Christmas Mr. Ellery went down the Potomack about 32 miles to a place called Port Tobacco to keep Christmas with a gentleman named Numa who lived there and had marri<ed> his cousin—on Saturday being Christmas, Genera<l> Morris went to the place where Mr. Ellery lodged when in this city and enquired where Mr. E. wa<s> gone, and how long he expected to stay—upon being informed he went away—and on Sunday morn<ing> General M. and Mr. Rutledge set out very early in pursuit of him and went down the Potomack a little beyond where Mr. E. was and put up—and on the afternoon of Sunday Gen. M. waited on Mr. E. with a challenge from Mr. R. Mr. E. told him that he had come there to keep Chris<t>mas, that he was above 30 miles from his friends, that he was shortsighted, unable to see a man five yards, and that in short he should neithe<r> receive or accept any challenge till he had returned to Washington and advised with his friends— Gen M. upon that went away, and on Monday morning called at Mr. Numa's before Mr. E. was up and told Mr. Numa he had called upon the same accoun<t> to insist that Mr. E. should accept the challenge— M<r.> N. told Mr. M. he was surprised he should call on that business again as he had a full answer the day before, that it was a breach of every rule of honour <&> politeness, upon which Mr. M. went away apparent<ly> disatisfied—and he and Rutledge set out and came back about halfway to a place called Piscataway, and there tarried at a tavern where the stage stops— And, on Tuesday as Mr. E was returning and stopp<ed> to get breakfast, and had taken a room, being alone, they burst in, Mr. Rutledge with a large club, and str<uck> Mr. E three times on the head, and cut some places <on> his head before Mr. E. could seize him which he then di<d> and took Rutledge down by the hair of his head — R<ut>ledge tried to gouge his eyes out, which Ellery perceiving took hold with his teeth a little below the eye, on the cheek bone and about bit it out, upon which Rutledge cried out for Mr. M. to help him, upon which General Morris fell on — They were parted, and Rutledge and Morris after washing off the blood made all has<te> to this city to avoid the peace officers."

I am, Sir, very respectfully, Your most obedient Servant

James Eliot.

Hon'ble General Bradley —

ALS (NcD: Bradley Family Papers). Damaged at right margin. Cover addressed to "The Honble. Stephen R Bradley, Esq. / Westminster" and marked "Bratte. June 19"; docketed by SRB, "Copy of a letter Sent James Elliott Concerning Ellery Duel."

From A. & Jno. I. Labogh

Sir   N York Sept. 28th. 1804

Before you had concluded to have the tomb in two pieces, we had requested a person to endeavor to procure it in one if possible, which after long delay, we have now got and finished it in the best manner. We thought that it would do more honor to you & give us more credit as it never could be made to suit the Inscription so well in two since part of it is so connected that upon the whole We thought if we could procure it in one by fall you would be better satisfied; it is one of the best of the size we ever saw, it is American Marble the price is for the Tomb $120, Engraving 28$, the box & Carting &c. 5$, total 153 Dollars. We will send it by the first opportunity as you have directed. Wishing you health and the enjoyment of all needful blessings we remain Sir yours

A. & Jno. I. Labogh

Mr. S. R. Bradley E<sqr.>

Received New York Octbr. 30th. 1804 of Stephen R Bradley one Hundred and fifty three Dollars in full of the within bill as stated in the Letter

A. & Jno. P. Labogh

Sloops Price John <Tuanies?> Master to the Care of Justice & Elias Lyman.

ALS (DLC). Receipt and final notation by SRB.

Petition from John Nott

Springfield October the 5 1804

To the Honle: Genrl: Asemblee Now Setin at Rutland in the State of Vermont for the year of our Lord 1804 on the 11 day of October 1804 I John Nott of Springfield in this State most Humbley Begg Leve to Adress my Self to the Govnr: & his counsl: & to the Honle: House of Reprezentetives & I most humble Pray your Honrs: to Reed my Pepticon for I am So Poor that I Cannot Reed it my Self, by the unlawful Proseedings of Stephen R Bradley: in the year 1790: Stephen R bradley Jeremiah Mayson Elisha Brown Thomas Barritt Silant Cutin on the 11 day of August all com to my house when I & my wife was Both absent & got out 4 of my children out of my house: & then threw out a part of my Goods & then he Set my house on fire & Burnt it up & then: he Brought an action of trespass a gainst me of a hundred Pounds damig out of the county in to New fain: & then in the year 1791: ESQr. John Norton of Westminteir Sent Jonathan fuller to Springfield with a Spech<ial> Rit: & then I was Brought Before him: & then he Demanded me to acknoledg Deeds of Lease & Release from me to Creean Brush of Lot No 99 in the fifth Devizon of Spring field: that was Dated: one on the 15 &: the other on the 16 days of june 1773: Under the Grate Seal of New york: which I Deny, for I Neaver had no Regrant: of my land under New york: Nor I neaver Sold no land under the Grate Seal of New york to Crean Brush nor I Neaver Received one peney of money of Crean Brush & for land nor nothing therefore I wont acknoled them Deeds & Because that I Refuzed to acknoledg them Deeds John Norton Gave Judgment a gainst me without Law or Evedence & then I was prest into New fain jail without one peney of money or Estate of any Name or nator whatever: & then after I had Staid there; 13 dayes: & Se nothing: but that I shall Die: with Cold & Hunger: & then I was forced to acknoled them deeds: or Starve to Death: May Please your Honr: Stephen R Bradley hes com to my house & a Band of men with him in the Same way as a theef in the Night; & without the Least Notis or worning: & he hes Sewd me in an action of Trespas: in the Same way: & John Norton: he hes Brought me before him; in the same way: for there is No otheir Name But his own & Jonathan fuller, to his Rit: may Please your Honrs: this is the way in which he Stephen R Bradley; hes Stole my farm in Springfield By the fire Brand & Club in contempt of the Law Both: of God & man: & he hes tuck my farm from me in this way: & no otheir way on Earth: that is: worth Six thousand Dolars: to me: & Sold it to Benjm Bowker & Broadstreet woods: for two hundred Pounds Lawful money: & he hes Rongfuley keept me out of my farm 14 years the 11 day of last August: & Now your Honrs: may See: that he hes taken: all my Interust from me, By force & I am Now a poor begger: from dore to dore: for food & Rayment: for I have Lost the youse of my Rite hand: by Being froze on Lake champlain: 18 years Back: So that I cannot work for my Liveing: & the Riot is Said to be outlawed & the action of trespas & John Nortons Cort & all for the want of a Bondsman & therefore I most Humbley Pray your Honrs. to Restore me to Law So that I Shall be Able to Bring on a Procection & Recover my farm that Stephen R Bradley hes unlawfuley taken from me: may Please your honrs: I cannot call the high sheriff: for want of a Bondsman: I have wornned Benjm. Bowke & Broadstreet woods in 1801 & in 1804 to take there Efecks & go off of my farm in Springfield that is Lot No 44 that is in the fifth Divon., that was Drown to the Right of John Lyman Junr. that I have Bin in the Posescion of: Ever since the year 1764: & the Land hes Never: Bin clamed by no one nor I have not bin hinderd by no wone Untill Stephen R Bradley come & Burnt my house & Now if you Please to Submit it to a Committe or Let me com on to the flore I Shall be able to Bring on the Evedence to Suporte it in Riteing for I cannot call the Evedenc no other way for I have not got one peney of money to call them on with & therefore I P<ray> you [illegible] take my hard case into your wise consediration & Grant me Release By granting me a Spechal act to call the high Shiriff to put me into the Psecion of my farm that Stephen R bradley has So Rongfuley taken from me in this or any other way as you in your Wisdom Think Best & I in Obedince to the good & lawful law of this State Submit my Self & Pray for the wellfaire of the Same & I in Duty Bound Will Ever Pray

John Nott

ADS (Vt?). Docketed: "John Notts Petition / 1804/ Filed Octr 24. 1804. / Att D. <Wing Jun ?> Secy"; "In Genl Assy Oct. 24 1804 Read & refd. to Messrs Js. Fisk, <Potter?> & Rich to join—/ Att. M. Post Clk."; "In Council Octr. 25. 1804 / Read & Resolved that Mr Loomis join the Come. from the House on this Petition / Att. Wm. Page Jur Secy." The committee report, dated Rutland, 29 Oct. 1804, and written on the verso of the last page of the petition, reads: "The Honble. General Assembly now sitting—/ Your Committee to whom was refered the within petition beg Leave to report, That in our opinion the prayer thereof ought, so far, to be granted, as that the petitioner have leave to bring in a bill, giving him the same priviledge of Law, respecting the premises as [if] the statute of limitations had not run against him—/ which is Respectfully submitted / Beriah Loomis—for Committee." Another note reads: "In Genl. Asy. / Oct. 30, 1804. / Report accepted / Att. M. Post Clk / Bill herein passed into a law."

To Nahum Mower

Mr Nahum Mower

Sir Washington Decr. 28th. 1804

I observed in your windsor gazette of the 11th of Decr. 1804 an address "*To the Electors of Representatives of the N Eastern district in Vermont*" recommendind *Hadlock Marcy* as a Very suitable candidate to represent the district in Congress with my name signed Thereto.

I now inform you that I never wrote or signed that address, or directed, or even knew of any such thing being printed; and declare the same to be a false and fraudulent use of my name, and a base imposition on the Publick — and request you to inform the Publick through the medium of your own paper by what authority or by what inducements you presume to publish such a false forged and Counterfeit thing.

Stephen R Bradley

P. S. Please to give publicity to this letter.

ALS (VtU).

John A. Graham's Address to the Public

[2 January 1805]

TO THE PUBLIC.

Friends, Countrymen, and Fellow-Citizens,

HAVING long believed in that celebrated maxim of the illustrious WASHINGTON — "*To err sometimes is nature; to rectify error is always glory*" — the undersigned wrote a letter of apology to WILLIAM COLEMAN,[1] Esq. which appeared in the Evening Post of February 26, 1803, in the words following, to wit:

NEW-YORK, *Feb.* 24, 1803

SIR,

This will advise you of my arrival in this city on Saturday last. Since my arrival, Sir, I have learned certain facts that have confirmed the suspicions which I have for some time past entertained, that you have been very much injured by the letters which appeared some time since in the American Citizen under my signature. I must say that at the time of *lending* my name to the publications, I did believe that the facts therein stated were true, as I had them from a person in whom I then had the greatest confidence, (so far at least as related to this business); but be assured, Mr. Coleman, I wrote from motives of no enmity against you, and I have been led into this error owing to my having, *(as I do now verily believe)* been most *egregiously deceived,* as the facts there stated were *handed to me* by a person who I then had every reasonable right to expect, would not be capable of deceiving me, but whose name I must at present conceal. If, however, this *same person* should not adjust the matter to your satisfaction, (I conceive this is an *affair* of a personal and private nature, in which politics, by the bye, having nothing to do whatever) I shall furnish you with such documents and proofs as will afford you the means of obtaining from him adequate redress for the injuries you have sustained. I have therefore, sir, under the aforesaid circumstances, to request of you to accept of this as my sincere apology, and which, if you please, you are at liberty to publish.

I am, Sir, your's, &c.

J. A. GRAHAM.

William Coleman, Esq.

Two years having nearly elapsed, and *Stephen R. Bradley,* the person to whom I alluded in the aforesaid letter, whose perfidy, treachery, hypocrisy, and lies, occasioned all the fraud and mischief of that correspondence; I feel it a duty I owe to virtue, to honour, and to common honesty; *now* to unveil that dark transaction, and spread the whole of his villainous conduct before the public: And though it is painful to paint *Stephen R. Bradley* in the colours which his vices and infamy have, in this matter, cast upon him, yet when it is intended to caution others from being too credulous, and to guard them from falling into a like error, which I myself have done, I presume it will carry its own apology with it.

The following is an accurate copy of a letter which has been by him received from me. "*The check or post-note and packet,*" therein mentioned, I have deposited at the bar of the Tontine Coffee-House in this city, for the inspection of the public, that they may see *one* of the legitimate children of *General Stephen R. Bradley*. Should the *emetic* have a *salutary* effect on the *General*, so that he may freely *disgorge*—the *Cathartic*, (which is now ready prepared) will not be administered.

J. A. GRAHAM.

TO STEPHEN R. BRADLEY, ESQ.

Senator in the Congress of the United States, from the District of Vermont.

SIR,

"*Aut virtus nomen mane est. Aut decus et precium recte petit experiens vir.*"

"Either Virtue is an empty name, or the man who makes the experiment, deservedly claims the honour and the reward."

You must be sensible of the great zeal and activity I manifested to effect your election at Newbury for your present situation as a Senator in the Grand Council of the General Government.

It may be needful to remind you, that after your election I repaired to Washington at your particular request, and obtained by your procurement a Clerkship in the Secretary of the Senate's Office, which I was afterwards obliged to relinquish, to appease the clamour of those who were offended at my coming forward at your desire, and lending my name to those facts which were published against William Coleman, Esq. which involved me in the odium of the public mind, and subjected me and Mr. Cheetham,[2] the printer of those documents, in all the penalties attached to a malicious libel. Confiding in your veracity, of which I could not at that period have any suspicion, I was emboldened to make that discovery, and to impress the public mind with transactions, which, if true, would have a tendency to destroy the reputation of a man who had done me no personal injury; but from your statement, ought to be held up as a public monument of execration.

You know with what earnestness you involved me in that dark transaction, and the result thereof; and that I had no motive to injure that gentleman's character, save only in the vindication of your reputation before the public, upon the most solemn assurances that the allegations could be supported in a court of justice, should he dare to contest them.

It is true that the prosecutions against me are relinquished, having, as every honest man ought, (so soon as I discovered the treachery into which I had been introduced by your duplicity) made an ample apology to Mr. Coleman for the injury I had done him.

But what is to become of those suits against Mr. Cheetham, who was drawn into the publications by me, as your *agent?* And upon the credibility of your reputation, which would not then admit of the least doubt, from the high elevation you held as Vice-President pro tem. of the Senate of the United States.

It would be worthy your attention to consider that *two* members of your board, and *another high in office,* were privy to those transactions, and knew in what manner I was drawn into a situation so derogatory to my honour, reputation, and feelings.

It will also be worthy your attention to consider that I am in possession of the documents relative to another transaction, equally disgraceful, to wit: The "*Check, or Post Note, and Packet,*" made up and sealed by yourself, in the presence of our *mutual friend,* directed to Mr. Coleman, for the base purpose, as you then declared, to *trick* that gentleman out of three dollars postage, observing, at the same time "that he was poor, and this would help to keep him so." How will this read, when it meets the eyes of your own countrymen, and those of foreigners, that the Vice-President pro tem. of the General Government should tamper with the honour of a gentleman, and make him the instrument of carrying so black a transaction into execution, to answer the purposes of so trifling a consideration?

Had I put your packet into the Post-Office, which at the time you believed was the case, and the money had been paid by Mr. Coleman, the laws of your country would have consigned you, (in the opinion of counsel learned in the law) to the State-Prison; and I, your accomplice, for aiding and abetting your wickedness, been justly consigned to everlasting infamy.

"Quid quesque vitel, nunquam monini
"Satis cantum est in horas."
"What we ought to be aware of, no man is sufficiently cautious at all hours."

For the future honour and safety of my country, I hold up the mirror to your deformity; and hope, most sincerely hope, you may profit by your past errors, lest the vengeance of our country purge you from her confidence, and the Senate of the United States from their counsels, as being unworthy of a seat in that august assembly.

I forbear even to whisper, for my pen refuses its ink when I attempt to express your corrupt sentiments to me conveyed, at the time of your giving your repeated public dinners to the members of Congress, with a view, (as you then remarked) "to bribe their bellies, thereby to become the perpetual Vice-President of the United States"; adding, at the same time, "that you dare not make the attempt to bribe with gold; therefore you would see what wine and good dinners would do; and you doubted not they would have the desired effect."

I felt an honest glow of indignation, when I heard from your own lips with what contempt you held the honour, independence, and virtue of the representatives of a free people; and thought at the time, that such baseness would have disgraced the practices played off by the election-jobbers upon the Pot-Wallopers of a cornish borough in England.

When you compelled me to relinquish my employment at Washington, you craftily foresaw that a developement of your baseness would have impeded your progress to the gratification of your ambition. To shield you from the thunder of public indignation, the counsels which you gave at the time, to avoid inquiry into particulars of the passing traveller to the state of Vermont, mark your mind — conscience trembling alive at the discovery of your baseness.

Be assured, Sir, that I would sooner court the walls of a dungeon, and leave my cause to be tried in the court of reason before the tribunal of public opinion, rather than to let you escape from the discovery of your iniquity.

"*Non ille pro earis amicis, aut patria timidus perire.*"
"Such a man as this is not afraid to perish in defence of his dear friends, or his country."

The relative duties I stand in to the wife of my bosom, and the children of my affection, are impressive; and the calls of friendship, knocking at the door of my heart, are imperiously persuasive.

I should not have written to you, did not your conduct stand unparalleled in the records of a Sir John Fielding's office, or the register of Newgate; & precludes even the glimmering hope of a state pardon.

"*Nil mortalibus arduum est.*"

"There is nothing too arduous for mortals to attempt."

From delicacy to our mutual friend, if one latent spark of virtue remains in your polluted mind, candour will prompt you to an immediate confession of your guilt, to avoid to painful necessity of involving a gentleman, (for whom I entertain the most profound respect) in a transaction that might in the least degree render him the subject of public animadversion.

Under these considerations, I demand of you, your direct, most categorical, & most unequivocal ultimatum, which will govern me in my future proceedings.

Once more, "*Carpe diem quam minimum credula postero.*"

"Seize the present day, not giving the least credit to the succeeding one."

Your humble serv't,

J. A. GRAHAM.

New-York, January 2, 1805.

Printed pamphlet (*No. I. An Address to the Public, Together with a Copy of a Letter to Stephen R. Bradley, Esq., Senator in the Congress of the United States, from the District of Vermont. By John A. Graham, L.L.D., of the City of New-York* (New York, 1805; Shaw and Shoemaker 8549).
1. William Coleman (1766–1829), born in Boston, in 1801 cofounded the strongly pro-Federalist newspaper the New York *Evening Post.*
2. James Cheetham was the editor of the New York *American Citizen,* a Republican newspaper.

Senate Proceedings: Tennessee Lands

[8 January 1805]

Mr. BRADLEY, from the committee to whom was referred the bill, entitled "An act declaring the assent of Congress to an act of the General Assembly of the state of North Carolina," with instructions to enquire what have been the acts of the state of *North Carolina* and *Tennessee*, in relation to the lands claimed by the United States, within the state of Tennessee, made the following

REPORT: —

THAT it had not been in the power of the committee to possess the advantage of the statute laws of the state of Tennessee; that on as strict examination as the committee had been able to make of the laws of North Carolina, they submit the following digest, which in their judgment comprises the most material doings of that state in relation to the subject.

In April, 1782, an act passed "*For the relief of the officers and soldiers in the continental line,*" in which the state engaged to each officer and soldier a certain quantity of land apportioned to the respective grades in the line, and appointed commissioners to examine, and superintend the laying off the land in one or more tracts.

In April, 1783, an act designated the land on which the officers and soldiers might enter and survey, and bounded the same as follows, to wit: "*Beginning* in the Virginia line, where Cumberland river intersects the same, thence south fifty five miles, thence west to the *Tennessee river*, thence down the *Tennessee* to the Virginia line, thence with the said Virginia line *east to the beginning*"; and by the same act allowed the officers and soldiers the term of three years from the first day of October, then next, to secure their land, and prohibited all other persons from making entries thereon, during said term, except certain settlers on Cumberland river, and empowered the secretary of state to issue warrants of survey. And at the same time designated what lands the Cherokee Indians should have and enjoy, and declared all entries, grants, or purchases made of their lands to be utterly void: —

In October, 1784, an act provided that in case the tillable land within the boundaries laid off for the officers and soldiers of the continental line, should be insufficient to satisfy their claims; the deficiency should be made up on any unappropriated lands within the state.

In November, 1785, an act passed the legislature granting a further time of eighteen months for the completing of surveys as well for all persons who had entered lands with any of the entry takers, as for all warrants granted by the secretary of state to the officers and soldiers of the continental line, previous to the passing of said act; and at the same session by a subsequent act, appointed commissioners to liquidate the accounts of the officers and soldiers of the continental line, and directing that the commissioners should sit as a board the first ten days in April, May, and June, then next, and no longer, and that all accounts which should not be exhibited within that time should be forever thereafter of no effect.

In Nov. 1786, an act passed, allowing a further time of two years, from, and after the expiration of the limitation by law then existing, to complete the surveys west of the Apalachian mountain; and twelve months to the officers, and soldiers of the continental line; and the further time of two years for registering military grants.

Thus stood the law in the state of *North Carolina*, when in November, 1789, the legislature passed an act to authorise, empower, and require certain persons therein named, to execute a deed or deeds, on the part and behalf of said state, conveying to the United States of America all right, title, and claims, which the said state of North Carolina then had to the sovereignty and territory of the lands now comprehended within the state of Tennessee, upon certain express conditions, and subject thereto; among which conditions, the following appear only to be material in the present question, to wit:—"That the lands laid off, or directed to be laid off by any act, or acts of the general assembly of this state, for the officers, and soldiers thereof, their heirs and assigns respectively, shall be, and enure to the use, and benefit of the said officers, their heirs, and assigns respectively; and if the bounds of the said lands already prescribed for the officers and soldiers of the continental line of this state, shall not contain a sufficient quantity of lands, fit for cultivation, to make good the several provisions intended by law, that such officer or soldier, or his assignee, who shall fall short of his allotment or proportion, after all the lands, fit for cultivation, within the said bounds are appropriated, be permitted to take his quota, or such part thereof as may be deficient, in any other part of the said territory, intended to be ceded by virtue of this act, not already appropriated. And where entries have been made agreeable to law, and titles under them not perfected by grant or otherwise; then, and in that case, the governor for the time being, shall, and he is hereby required to perfect from time to time, such titles, in such manner as if this act had never been passed: and that all entries made by, or grants made to all, and every person, and persons whatsoever, agreeable to law, and within the limits hereby intended to be ceded to the United States, shall have the same force, and effect, as if such cession had not been made, and that all, and every right of occupancy, and preemptions, and every other right reserved by any act or acts to persons settled on, and occupying lands within the limits of the lands, hereby inte[n]ded to be ceded, as aforesaid, shall continue to be in full force in the same manner as if the cession had not been made, and as conditions upon which the said lands are ceded to the United States: And further, it shall be understood that if any person or persons, shall have by virtue of the act entitled 'An act for opening the land office for the redemption of specie, and other certificates, and discharging the arrears due to the army,' passed in the year 1803, made his or their entry in the office usually called *John Armstrong's* office, and located the same to any spot or piece of ground, on which any other person or persons shall have previously located any entry or entries, that then, and in that case, the person or persons having made such entry or entries, or their assignee or assignees shall have leave, and be at full liberty to remove the location of such entry or entries to any lands on which no entry has been specially located, or any vacant lands included within the limits of the lands hereby intended to be ceded: *Provided*, that nothing herein contained shall extend, or be construed to extend to the making good any entry or entries, or any grant or grants heretofore declared void by any act or acts of the general assembly of this state."

On the 25th day of Feb. 1790, Samuel Johnson, and Benjamin Hawkins, then being senators in Congress from the said state, by virtue of the power, and authority given to them, in, and by said act, by their deed of that date, conveyed to the United States, all right, title, and claim which the said state of North Carolina had to the sovereignty and territory of the lands now called Tennessee, on the conditions mentioned in the said act. At the same session in which the cession act was passed, in 1789, a law passed, giving a further time of three years for surveying all lands entered in the office of John Armstrong, and for all military warrants issued by the secretary of said state, and all preemption rights in the district of *Mero*.

In Dec. 1794, a law passed, declaring all grants for lands entered in the land office, which had not been registered within the time before allowed by law, should be allowed two years after the passing of said act, to register the same. And in the same session made it the duty of all persons, who entered lands in the entry taker's office to pay the purchase money to the treasurer, and take his receipt for the same. And in Nov. 1795, declared all entries for lands where the purchase money had not been paid to the treasurer agreeably to law, null, and void. And all entries then in future to be made for a greater quantity than three hundred acres, where the purchase money should not be paid within six months from the date of such entry; and if a lesser quantity, twelve months from the date of such entry; all such entries void, and of no effect.

In November, 1796, an act was passed providing that the clerks of the county courts where the books of the entry takers were in their possession, should issue warrants of surveys by order of the court, and declaring that the lands then lying in the counties of Wilks, Burk, and Buncombe, which might have been entered with the entry taker of Washington, and Green in the state of Tennessee, should not be surveyed, until it should be proved in the manner therein provided, that the purchase money for the lands claimed had been paid, and by the same law allowed a further time of twelve months from and after the rising of that assembly for the payment of the purchase money to the treasurer of all lands before entered, even where the entries had lapsed and become void under the operation of the then existing laws; and by the same act all entries of lands that had been made since the 15th day of November, 1797 [1787] unless surveyed as therein directed and grants procured thereon on or before the first day of January, 1799, were declared utterly void and of no effect, and providing also, that in all future entries, unless the person claiming the same should complete his title, by taking out a grant for the same within two years from the date of such entry, the same should become utterly null and void, and the land so entered should be deemed vacant land, saving however entries west of Pigeon river, in Buncombe county. Warrants for military lands and warrants for lands entered in John Armstrong's office &c. and by a subsequent law, the same session empowered the secretary of state at any time before the Congress of the United States should open an office for the sale of their lands, within the bounds prescribed, for the officers and soldiers of the late North Carolina line of continental troops, to issue new grants to such officers and soldiers, whose former grant covered lands which had been before granted, and directed the manner of proceeding therein, and provided further for issuing new warrants where the former warrants had been lost, and prohibited the issuing of grants and warrants from the office of John Armstrong, unless it was proved that the purchase money had been paid.

In November, 1797, an act passed for the limitation of land entries, the first section of which is in the following words, "That all lands heretofore entered with any entry taker in this state and which have not been paid for, and all lands which shall be so entered in the course of the present year, and shall not be paid for, shall continue and remain the property of the enterers their heirs or assigns, so far as an entry without the payment of the purchase money to the state, and without obtaining a grant may be held to vest a title in the same: nor shall any such entries become void, nor shall the lands so entered, revert to the state until the last day of December, 1793, at which time and on which day it is hereby expressly enacted and declared, that all entries now made or which shall be made up to the time aforesaid, that is to say, that all entries now made and which shall be made up to the close of the year 1797, and which shall not be paid for, shall become null, void, and of no effect to all intents and purposes, and the lands which may have been so entered and not paid for, shall on the first day of January, 1799, be considered as having reverted to the state, and as being vacant and shall be liable again for any person to enter and secure the same; and in like manner it shall happen yearly and every year, that is to say, it shall be considered that all lands entered in 1798, otherwise on the first day of January, 1800, such entries shall lapse and the lands shall revert to the state and shall be liable to be entered again by any person wishing the same in common with other vacant and unappropriated lands; the lands entered in such preceding year, being in any event to be paid for in the following or succeeding one otherwise, and in case of failure, all such entries shall become and shall be held as being null, void, and of none effect whatsoever. And by the third section of the same act, the operation of all acts or clauses of acts which came within the purview, and meaning therof, are suspended until the first day of January, 1799, and by a subsequent act of the same session suspended the issuing of military warrants or grants by the secretary, and all grants or warrants from the office of John Armstrong for the space of one year from the rising of that assembly, and appointed a board of commissioners to detect frauds and forgeries committed in obtaining military warrants and for bringing to punishment all persons concerned therein, as well officers of the government as all others.

In Nov. 1798, an act passed prohibiting the issuing of duplicate warrants, and giving a further time until the first day of January, 1800, to all enterers of lands since the 15th day of November, 1777, to accomplish their surveys, and perfect their titles, and allowed a further time to all entries of lands made between the 8th day of February, 1795, and the 1st day of January, 1798, until the 1st day of October then next, to pay the purchase money to the state, and declaring all such as were not paid by that time, null, and void, and should be deemed lapsed entries: and by a subsequent act, the same session, constituted the judges of the superior courts of law, and courts of equity, or any three of them, a court of patents, with power to repeal, vacate, and make void all such grants or patents as appeared to be made against law, or obtained by fraud, surprise, or upon untrue suggestions: and the same session repealed the appointment of Colonel Martin Armstrong, surveyor, and discontinued his office at Nashville, and appointed a board of commissioners, to investigate the frauds suggested to have been committed in the secretary's office, in obtaining land warrants for military services, and in obtaining warrants from the office lately kept by John Armstrong, and in obtaining grants or warrants in either of the above cases, and suspended all further issuing of warrants by the secretary, until the assembly should order otherwise.

In Nov. 1799, an act was passed, reciting that whereas many frauds were suggested to have been committed in the secretary's office, the governor for the time being, was therein empowered to issue a commission to the judges, empowering them to hold a special, and unusual court, as therein pointed out for the trial of such persons as shall or may be apprehended for, or on account of their having committed, or been concerned in the commission of frauds in the secretary's office, or in the office of John Armstrong, or Martin Armstrong, in the fraudulent issuing, procuring, receiving, or transferring land warrants, or in the fraudulent issuing, receiving, or procuring grants on such warrants, at any of the said offices: — And by a subsequent act of the same session, directed all military warrants to be cancelled, which had issued to officers, and soldiers, where it appeared from the muster roll, such officer or soldier had served for so short a time as not to be entitled to so large a quantity of land as expressed in the warrant, and new warrants to issue corresponding with the time of service, and prohibited the issuing any grant, or any warrant where the officer's or soldier's name, in whose favor the warrant issued, did not appear on the muster roll, unless specially authorised by the general assembly, or where they had been reported as just by a former board of commissioners.

In Nov. 1800, an act passed to allow all persons who had made entry of lands since the first day of January, 1799 until the day previous to the meeting of the next annual general assembly to pay the purchase money to the state, till which day it should not be deemed a lapsed entry. And by a subsequent act of the session for the purpose of perfecting the titles of the officers, and soldiers of the continental line of that state; in the fourth section it is enacted, "that all claims for lands by the officers, and soldiers of the continental line of this state, during the revolutionary war with Great Britain, and all demands for the same which shall not be applied for, and received either by the person who performed the service, his heirs or assigns, before the first day of December next, shall be forever thereafter barred, and no military land warrant shall issue after the time aforesaid, on any account whatever, any law, usage, or custom to the contrary notwithstanding."

In Nov. 1801, an act passed, extending the time on all *bona fide* entries of lands made previous to the first day of January, 1793, and which had been paid for, until the first day of December, 1802, to have said lands surveyed, and returned into the secretary's office, and declaring all such lands not surveyed, and returned into the secretary's office, by the day aforesaid, to be void, and lapsed lands to the state, and all lands so surveyed, and returned as aforesaid, where the claimant thereof shall not cause the same to be perfected into grants, before the first day of January, 1804, the same is declared null, and void, and lapsed lands to the state, and by a subsequent act of the same session, the fourth section of the act passed in November, 1800, is repealed, and all claims for lands by the officers, and soldiers of the continental line, which shall not be applied for, and received before the first day of January, 1803, are declared to be forever barred, and no military warrants to issue after that time on any warrant whatever.

Thus far the committee have been able to present to the view of the Senate, a very short statement of the acts of the state of North Carolina, to the year 1802, from that period to the present the committee have not been possessed of sufficient documents to make a correct statement on that subject.

They submit the following amendment to the bill declaring the assent of Congress to an act of the General Assembly of the state of North Carolina;

At the end of the bill, insert the following:

"*Provided*, That nothing contained in this act shall be construed, in any manner to affect or impair any right whatever, which accrued to the United States in virtue of an act of the General Assembly of North Carolina, entitled '*An act for the purpose of ceding to the United States of America certain western lands therein described.*'"

Printed copy ([...], 8th Cong., 2d sess., p. x).

To Henry Dearborn

General Dearborn   Washington Jany 15th. 1805

I enclose you a letter from Nathl. Ruggles Esq of Roxbury to be communicated to the President of the U.S. the representation from that State being such will apolog<ize> for my interfereing in the business, and your acquaint<ance> in Massachusetts with Men and characters has induced me to address you on the Subject tho not within your depa<rt>ment. Mr. Ruggles the author of the Letter is a man of irreproachable character and Collegiate education has been a Magestrate in Roxbury for several years and possesses a handsome estate has been an influencial republican character in that town from the begining and contributed much to preserve the town from being overwhelmed in the high tide of Federalism, is brother in Law to Nathl Fellows of Boston and can I presume if the thing should be contemplated by the President, procure any recommendations necessary from the best republican characters in and near Boston Several of whom have already wrote to me. Your laying the same before the President will confer an obligation on him who has the Honour to be your Obedt Servt

                                                        Stephen R Bradley

ALS (VtU). Margin obscured.

To James Madison

Dear Sir   Washington Jany. 25th. 1805

Permit me through your department to recommend to the President of the United States Stanley Griswold[1] of New Hampshire as a fit and proper character for the Office of Secretary of the territory of Michigan. He is a gentleman of education, talents, and integrity, master of several languages and tho' he speaks not the french with ease is able to do business in that language — his political character is truly republican, and I have no doubt he would discharge the duties of that office to the satisfaction of the people of that territory and to the honor of the nation.

I am Sir with great respect Your Most Obedt. Humble Servt.

                                                        Stephen R Bradley

Hon. James Madison
Secretary of State

ALS (DNA: RG 59, Letters of Application and Recommendation, 1801–9, reel 4, fol. 766–67). Directed by JM to "The President." Docketed by Thomas Jefferson, "Griswold Stanley to be Secretary of Michigan."

1. Stanley Griswold (1763–1815) was a Yale graduate who had been a clergyman in Connecticut and editor of a Republican newspaper in New Hampshire. Jefferson appointed him secretary of the Michigan Territory in 1805, and he held that position until 1808 (*Papers of Madison: Presidential Series*, 2:257 n. 1).

James Smith to Those Who Have Sworn to Support the Constitution

"Notandi sunt tibi mores."

                                                        NEW-YORK, JANUARY 28th, 1805.

ON this day was put into my hands an Address to the Public, together with a copy of a letter to *Stephen R. Bradley,* Esq. Senator in the Congress of the United States, from the district of Vermont, by John A. Graham, L. L. D. of the city of New-York. On the first perusal of this extraordinary production, I conjectured that it was an effusion of a mind under the impulse of fanatic irritation bordering on insanity, which had set at defiance all rules of prudence and decorum. I placed it among the list of those essays which mark the malignant temper of the times, arrived to the summit of licentious degeneracy. But upon a second review, and a more attentive examination of its contents, with a reference to characters of the first respectability, the facts appeared to have all the colour of irrefragable evidence to support the allegations presented before the public; and that the motives which induced the author of the publication, so far from being censurable, entitles him to the esteem of all citizens who are concerned for the purity of the manners and principles of men who compose the General Government of our Country.

IF every citizen would follow the laudable example of Colonel Graham, in dragging infamy to the bar of the public mind, the Augeon Stable would in future be purged of that corruption, which, if permitted to exist within the walls of the Grand Councils of the nation, their guardian virtue would command obedience to its laws, and give that energy to its enactments, so essentially necessary to answer all the purposes of national aggrandizement.

I HAVE been for years endeavouring to impress upon the minds of our fellow-citizens in this district, the absolute necessity of cautious cirumspective examination into the principles, character, and capacity, of those who are to fill and perform the functions of legislators. Political capacity joined to political integrity, are the only preservatives of the permanency of that Constitution, devised by the sages of the Revolution, and purchased by the blood of its heroes. Being fully convinced that its duration cannot long survive the period of its formation, unless it is supported by an inviolable attachment to that uncontaminated virtue which is its vital principle, and which must circulate with full vigour through every capillary vessel which pervades every part of its political frame, from its centre to its circumference.

THE despotism of bad laws, the experience of history has ever proved the worst species of tyranny.

"*Satius est petere fonies quam sectari rivilos.*"
"Better seek the fountains than cut off the rivulets."

IF the high fountains of our Government be corrupt, the streams which flow from so foul a source must necessarily partake of their original depravity. Like a mountain torrent collecting its impurity from every additional quarter, gaining accessions of strength, will swell the current, burst the banks, and inundate the fields they were meant to fertilize.

IF men are placed in office, and seated in great dignity in high places, the leaven of their bad example, like an assimilatory process, will soon taint the whole body of our National Councils, and like a corroding cancer will vitiate every nerve and fibre, unless it receives the amputating knife, which shall cut up by the roots its spreading malignancy.

Principius obsta, is a maxim which stands confirmed by the imperious authority of venerable antiquity, and the imposing testimony of ages. Let us correct evil propensities in their first obliquity by the rigid stern virtue of genuine republicanism.

SHOULD they be permitted to invade the sacred altars of liberty, the flames of the revolution which have ascended to immaculate purity, will soon be extinguished, and indignant Heaven, frowning at the impious sacrifices upon its polluted altars, will remove the ark of the covenant from the temple of liberty, to prevent it from being defiled by a sacrilegious priesthood; and leave the people devoted victims to the machinations of false idols, meditating their destruction.

THE eyes of the people are upon the executive; and, solicitous for their safety and the honour of their Government, demand investigation. If Mr. Bradley has been guilty of the charges as stated by Col. Graham, his name ought to be erased from the records, expelled the

Honourable Senate, and driven back with the marks of infamy stamped upon his *forehead,* as unworthy of that elevation to which he has been raised by the unsuspecting credulity of his worthy constituents; and delivered over to be buffeted by the members, upon and over whom he has palmed himself, as unworthy of their favour. I am warranted to declare that the accuser will appear at the bar of the Senate to substantiate the facts alluded to, and prove that he has not wantonly or maliciously given loose to the impulse of the passions, not under the guidance of deliberate reflection.

I SUBMIT to you whether such a measure would not be the most convincing proof of their wisdom, purity, and integrity, which has hitherto marked the features of the present administration; and will prove that no characters, however elevated by the people, shall shield themselves from investigation, or bask in the sunshine of Executive favour any longer than they shall be worthy of the genial beams of the first Magistrate of a free and virtuous people.

JAMES SMITH, M. D.

Printed pamphlet (*To Those Who Have Sworn to Support the Constitution; Maintain Public Justice; Protect Private Right; and Bring to Justice Every Offender Against the Majesty of the Law, the Peace of the People, and their Dignity; These Few Lines Are Addressed* (New York, 1805; Shaw and Shoemaker 9379).

From Isaac Tichenor

Dear Sir,   Bennington [October] 28t. 1805

I have the honor to transmit to your consideration & management, the enclosed Resolutions of our General-Assembly.—Accept the assurance of my esteem & friendship

Isaac Tichenor

Honle. Stephen R. Bradley

[Enclosure]
STATE OF VERMONT

In GENERAL ASSEMBLY, October 17th, 1805.

WHEREAS the Governor, of this State, has laid before this Assembly, a Resolution of the Legislature of the State of Northcarolina, dated December 4th, A. D. 1804, proposing such an amendment of the Federal Constitution, as shall authorize Congress to prevent the importation of slaves into the United States. Therefore,

Resolved, That our Senators in the Congress of the United States be instructed, and our Representatives requested, to take all legal and necessary steps, and to use their utmost exertions, as soon as the same is practicable, to obtain an amendment to the Federal Constitution, so as to authorize, and empower the Congress of the United States to pass a law, whenever they may deem it expedient, to prevent the further importation of Slaves, or People of Color, from any of the West India Islands, from the Coast of Africa, or elsewhere, into the United States, or any part thereof.

Resolved therefore, That the Governor be, and he is hereby requested, to transmit Copies of the foregoing Resolution to our Senators and Representatives in Congress: And also to the Executives of all the different States in the Union, with a request that the same may be laid before their respective Legislatures for their concurrence and adoption.

Sent up for Concurrence.

Attest—   MARTIN POST, Clerk of General Assembly.

In COUNCIL, October 19th, 1805.
Read and Concurred.

Attest— WILLIAM PAGE, jun. *Secretary.*

A true Copy.

Attest— Dava. Wing Junr. *Secretary of State.*

ALS and enclosure (NcD: Bradley Family Papers). Cover addressed to "Stephen. R. Bradley / Senator in Congress / City of Washington"; marked "Bennington" and "Free"; docketed by SRB, "Negroes" and "Instructions from the General Assembly concerning Negroes." Enclosure is printed, except for Wing's signature.

From Henry Dearborn

Sir War Department December 17. 1805

In answer to your note of this Inst.[1] I have the honor, to submit for the information of Committee, on whose behalf your application is made the following summary of Ordnance and Military Stores, belonging to the United States, selected from the General Return of the Superintendent of Military Stores to this Department viz.

Pieces of Brass Ordnance	407
ditto Iron ditto	1 465
ditto new Iron ditto	80
Muskets	121.891
Rifles	3 255
Pistols	1 940
Cannon Balls	200.946
Shells	60 836
Pounds of Grape, exclusive of some fixed & loose ditto	216 179
Musket Cartridges	1.007.171
Crude Nitre lbs. of	1 403 621
Refined ditto "	2 505
Sulphur "	234 617
Lead "	1.303 106
Powder "	525 774
Swords and Cutlasses no. of	9 061

I have the Honor to be very respectfully, Sir, Your H. Servt—

H Dearborn

Honorable
Stephen R. Bradley

ALS (NcD: Bradley Family Papers). Cover addressed to "Honorable / Stephen R. Bradley / US Senator" and marked "War Dep"; docketed by SRB, "Genel Dearborn / Statement of Arms."
1. Letter not found.

Senate Proceedings: Petition of Seth Harding

[27 January 1806]

Mr. Bradley, from the committee, to whom was referred the petition of Seth Harding, submitted the following

REPORT...

THAT the petitioner during the revolutionary war, was a captain in the navy of the United States, and supported the character of an active, brave, and meritorious officer through the whole course of the same, and distinguished himself in several hard fought actions at sea, against superior force, in which he captured several armed vessels of the enemy, took a number of prizes, prisoners, arms, and implements of war, as stated in his petition.

In examining the merits of his claim on his country, it appears to the committee that the following statement, will exhibit his case substantially before the Senate — "That in the latter part of the late war, and in a severe action between the American frigate *Alliance* and a British frigate, the petitioner in the line of duty, received a wound or hurt in the small of his back or loins, the distressing symtoms of which increased with age, and have for several years now last past, totally disabled him for any business, consumed his property, and reduced him to the necessity of depending on the charity of his friends, or the commiseration and justice of his country, for support.

In thus viewing the case, the committee are of opinion, that it comes clearly within the equity of the provision, made by Congress in the ninth section of the act, entitled "*An act for the better government of the navy of the United States,*" passed the 23d day of April, 1800, as follows: — "*And be it enacted*, That all money accruing, or which has already accrued to the United States from the sale of prizes, shall be and remain forever a fund for the payment of pensions and half pay, should the same be hereafter granted, to the officers and seamen who may be entitled to receive the same; and if the said fund shall be insufficient for the purpose, the public faith is hereby pledged to make up the deficiency; but if it should be more than sufficient, the surplus shall be applied to the making of further provision for the comfort of the disabled officers, seamen, and marines, and for such as, though not disabled, may merit by their bravery, or long and faithful services, the gratitude of their country:" — and therefore report, that Seth Harding ought to be placed on the navy pension list, agreeable to the aforesaid act, at the rate of one half the monthly pay of a captain in the navy, to commence from the passing of the aforesaid act; and for that purpose have submitted for consideration a bill, for the relief of Seth Harding, late a captain in the navy of the United States.

Printed copy ([...], 9th Cong., 1st sess., 1–2).

From William Eaton

Honorable
    General Bradley.   Feb. 22d. 1806.

Hamet Bashaw's letter to Commo. Barron, copy by translation herewith inclosed, was dated at Arab's Tower near Alexandria, about the 15th. Feb. last — Compared with the answer it will show the expectations he had reason to form from our Commander in chief —

Inclosed also is a detail of Commodore Prebbles operations on the station of Tripoli, which will show something of the impressions made on the enemy by his arms and the apprehensions thence impressed —

I have made search in the office of the Navy department for my letter, to the Secretary, of June 804 refusing to recieve any compensation for my service as an agent for that department except the successes of the enterprize, in the estimation of my country, should entitle me to it; but find it has been mislaid. The receipt of it, in duplicate, was acknowledged to me by Mr. Gouldsborough, the chief Clerk at Hampton about the 1t. of July following. Of this document I have no recollection of having kept a copy —

I have the honor to be very respectfully, Sir, your most obed: serv:

Wm. Eaton

[Enclosure]

Copy — Translation

Hamet Ex Bashaw of Tripoli
to Comre. S. Barron &c. &c.

Dear & esteemed

I have to inform your Excellency of my perfect health and to express my sincere wishes for yours. I beg you to be assured of the high regard and consideration I have for your Excellency, and I hope that by the assistance of the Divine Being I shall shortly be at Tripoli, my City, to drive from thence my perfidious enemies.

I make known to you the arrival of Mr. Wm. Eaton my General of the Army & that we have agreed upon a plan of operations, which I have no doubt will lead to that success which we both desire. Said Mr. Eaton begged me to come to Syracuse in order to confer with your Excellency, and to form a personal acquaintance with you. I must inform you, my worthy & esteemed Friend, that time does not allow me to cross the sea, and that I am too much occupied with my camp, consisting of Infantry and cavalry, and would not leave them for the acquisition of the world.

With the present I send you my Secretary of State, <remed> Mahumed, as my proper representative to treat in my stead, whom I request you will receive, and trust your ideas will be similar with regard to the great object we have in view.

My Dear Friend — You must know that I am already on my march with my camp, & I earnestly solicit you to send me as speedily as possible, the following succours of which I stand greatly in need — viz. Powder — Field artilery — muskets, money — & a few soldiers. These once arrived we are agreed with Mr. Eaton on the plan explained in his letter: & further, as provisions of all kinds are very scarce in Barbary, I beg you will send some likewise. I hope that in the course of about fifty days we shall form a system of Co-operations at Mensurat. My dear Friend, consider me in all things as your son, and that my kingdom shall be always as your own.

I salute you with cordial regard & remain &c.

Seal of
Hamet Bashaw

[Enclosure]

Facts.

May 1804.   The President said to me *no money would be offered for the peace or ransom: he believed the energetic measures now arranged would supercede the necessity.* I pledged my life & honor to bring the enemy to America if the cooperation with the legitimate Sovereign should be properly supported.

The Secretary of the Navy said to me *that the coercive measures now going into operation were calculated to compel a peace without money — that the co-operation with Hamet Bashaw formed a part of the means — and that necessary field artilery, 1000 stands of arms, with suitable amunition and 40 or 50 thousand dollars would be put on board the squadron at Hampton roads to aid and give effect to this measure.*

Captain Rodgers declared publicly at the offices that *his name should be written in blood on the walls of Tripoli before he would consent to pay a cent for ransom or tribute.* Such were the resolutions formed when I left the seat of Government to embark in the expedition; and subsequent arrangements, as well of the Government as of the chief commanders, evidence a determination to persevere in those resolutions.

Nov. 1804.   The plan of operations the ensuing season was agreed upon by the Commodores Barron & Preble and myself. I was to go in search of Hamet Bashaw to Egypt, and, if possible, to seize the province of Derne on our return; whence we were to pass to Bengazi and to be transported across the gulf of Sydra to Cape Mensurat by the squadron — and thence advance to the rear of Tripoli. We were to be supported by debarkations if necessary. Commodore Preble was to cause a reenforcement of gun boats and ketches to be provided — and a union of operations was to commence against Tripoli as soon as the season would permit. Our plans succeeded. Derne was captured. The enemy's army, sent to the relief of the province, was defeated — and our march was opened to Tripoli without opposition. The reenforcements arrived in good season. The enemy could not recruit troops for the defence of his capital, the people of the country being paralized by dread of the Americans and in a state of general revolt against the usurper — he was totally destitute of funds and provisions & in want of amunition.

May & June 1805.   Mr. Lear had distinct instructions not to pay money for peace or ransom except compelled by adverse circumstances in our military operations — and, previously to the conclusion of the treaty, the Commodore had been instructed to suspend his attack on Tripoli, until the first of July, for the arrival of reenforcements. Thus every thing was well arranged by Government, and every thing in the most promising train on the spot for arresting the enemy in his capital when the negociator appeared off Tripoli and displayed the flag of truce. There was then but one frigate before the place with a brig or schooner. The Essex, which bore the flag, had not before been on the coast: And, what is very extraordinary in similar cases, arrangements had been made at headquarters to abandon the commanding grounds we held in the enemy's dominions and to withdraw the main body of the squadron at a greater distance from the coast before our commissioner of peace left Malta to enter upon the negociation.

It has been asserted to me, & I believe can be proved by Mr. Denison, Commo. Barron's Secretary & Cap. Jas. Barron, that Mr. Lear made it a condition of his meeting the overtures of the enemy, that our forces should be withdrawn from the eastern provinces. This arrangement had no consideration for Hamet Bashaw — yet by a stipulation of treaty he engages all the persuasive influence of the United States to prevail on him to retire from the Dominions of Tripoli, holding out to him, by the same article, and illusive assurance that in such case, his wife and family should be restored to him — and that, *if found deserving*, provisions for his future support would undoubtedly be made by the U States. Mr. Lear's letter of 6. June 1805 authorized me to make these assurances to that unfortunate prince — through whose instrumentality we now enjoy a peace and free commerce in the Mediterranean — and through whose instrumentality we should have enjoyed a triumph at Tripoli and an acquisition to our national glory if our operations had not been arrested in the full tide of success, our original plans of cooperation abandoned.

W. Eaton

ALS and second enclosure (NcD: Bradley Family Papers); first enclosure (CSmH). Second enclosure addressed to SRB at Washington and endorsed by SRB, "Genll Eaton's Statement"

From William Eaton

Honorable General Bradley,
Sir,   Feb. 24th. '6.

Herewith inclosed is a copy, and translation of Baron Sederstrom's letter to Hamet Bashaw — It has been found among my papers withdrawn with others accompanying my statement to Congress in Feb. 1804 —

I have the honor to be very respectfully Sir, Your most Obedient servant

William Eaton

[Enclosure]

Translation —

The Baron Cederstrom, rear Admiral in the navy of his Swedish Majesty —

To Seid Hamet Caramanly, Bashaw of the Government of Derne.

Your Excellency.

Having had the honor of concerting with your Excellency the project of means to restore you to the throne of the kingdom of Tripoli, a government which is of right your due, and to establish on permanent grounds a peace between Sweden and the said Kingdom, I will do myself the honor to state all that I can at present do for your service —

1e. I will use all my power to aid your Excellency's operations against your brother Seid Joseph Caramanly Bashaw, who has usurped the Government of the kingdom of Tripoli

2d. As soon as the American Commodore shall arrive we will agree upon furnishing you such amunition and cash as we can spare —

3d. If contrary to my disposition the American Commodore cannot or will not enter into a convention to this effect; I will nevertheless do for your Excellency every thing which can be expected from me; which will then* depend entirely on the orders of his Swedish Majesty, to whom I have already reported the subject, & whose answer I expect in two months —

4th. In case that the said convention shall not take place with the American Commodore, and that your Excellency should not chuse to wait here the answer of His Majesty, but rather continue your voyage to Derne, I accompany this with a passport for your Excellency and suit, to the end that you may pass unmolested by the ships of war under my orders, with which you may fall in on your passage — I will even escort your Excellency to Derne by a swedish vessel of war, if circumstances permit, that in case your Excellency do not find your person in security there, the swedish frigate may carry your Excellency to the place you desire.

May God Almighty, the Protector of the just and the Avenger of injustice, aid you to recover the power which has been wrested from you by the perfidy of your brother; and Your Excellency may rest assured that I will do every thing in my power to assist you; and that it will be my greatest satisfaction to re-establish the ancient friendship which long subsisted between Sweden & Tripoli —

It is with the most perfect esteem that I have the honor to be Your Excellency's Most humble & most Obedient servant

(signed) Rudolf Cederstrom —

Translation.

Collated by US N. E. Frumerie Charge of Affairs of His Swedish Majesty in the city and kingdom of Tunis; and it is in every thing conformable to the original. In faith of which I sign my hand and affix the customary royal seal for this regency

Given at Tunis the 3d. December 1802

R. S.   (signed)   N E Frumerie.

ALS and enclosure (NcD: Bradley Family Papers).

*The Swede had orders to act in conjunction with the American!

From Capt. Dent

Honle Gen. Bradley,

Sir, Washington Feb. 26. 1806.

I have the honor to acknowledge the receipt of your letter of this day's date, requesting information on three points relative to the transactions in the Mediterranean — and in reply I have the honor to inform you.

1t. That I considered Commodore Barron's health, during the last winter and spring and until after the negociation, such as to disqualify him from transacting any business, his mind being so much impaired as scarcely to recollect any thing that transpired from one day to another. He was constantly confined to his quarters on shore. And by frequent applications to him for instructions he would loose the recollection of what passed in the course of conversation.

2 I have heard Mr. Lear say repeatedly previously to my going to Derne that he believed the expedition conducted by the Bashaw & Gen. Eaton would prove fruitless, and that they and their adherents would be sacrificed before they reached Derne. The capture of Derne of 27. April was communicated by the sloop Hornet previously to a negociation being opened with the reigning Bashaw. I was the bearer of the intelligence of the defeat of the enemy's army before Derne of the 13th. May, and arrived off Tripoli with this information and with dispatches from the Secretary of the navy wishing the Com. to suspend his attack on Tripoli till the first of July as reenforcements would join him about that time, before the terms of the treaty were concluded. Mr. Lear then observed that we did not want the assistance of Hamet Bashaw's army to bring the enemy to terms for the Navy was sufficient to bring him to any terms.

3d. It was generally believed by the officers in the Mediterranean that Mr. Lear had a great ascendancy over the commodore in all his measures relative to the squadron — and from frequent observation of Mr. Lear's intimacy with the commodore during his debilitated state I am of the same opinion.

I have the honor to be with profound respect Sir, your most obdt ser.

DENT

ALS (CSmH). Endorsed, "Cap. Dent's statement to Gen. Bradley, concerning Lear's negociation."

Senate Proceedings: Claim of Charlotte Hazen

[4 March 1806]

Mr. BRADLEY, from the committee to whom was referred the bill, "Supplementary to the act, entitled 'An act regulating the grants of land, appropriated for the refugees, from the British provinces of Canada and Nova Scotia"; submitted the following
REPORT....

IN presenting to the consideration of the Senate the claim of Charlotte Hazen, the committee are induced to submit facts, which in their opinion, militate against the claim as founded either in justice or equity; indeed a case similar to that of general Hazen's can hardly be conceived to come within the reason of the resolution of Congress of the 23d of April, 1803, which made provision for refugees from the British province of Canada. General Hazen being at Philadelphia in the month of January 1776, voluntarily entered into the service of the United States, was appointed to the command of a regiment, and had advanced to him at that time about three thousand dollars in specie. When the American army retreated out of

Canada, he retreated with it as was his duty, and remained in the service of the United States to the end of the war, with the pay and emoluments of a colonel, and afterwards with the half pay of a lieutenant colonel during life. By documents obtained from the register's office, it appears that during the war he was allowed for his disbursements in Canada for commutation and other purposes, about the sum of forty three thousand dollars in specie, and about forty two thousand dollars in bills of credit subject to some depreciation. That since his death, on the 23d of February, 1803, Moses White and the said Charlotte Hazen as executors of the said general Hazen, did receive from the treasury of the United States, 8,040 dollars 89 cents in specie; and further, that Congress at their last session granted to the said Charlotte Hazen the annual sum of two hundred dollars during her natural life, to commence from the 4th day of February, 1803, and which hitherto she has duly received.

The committee express no opinion how far the claim in virtue of said resolution of Congress is barred by the act, entitled "An act for the relief of refugees from the British provinces of Canada and Nova Scotia," passed April 7th 1798, and not revived by any subsequent statute; they however remark, that the claim of Mrs. Hazen was not exhibited to the secretary of war, until the 10th of May, 1804. They also observe that the report of the commissioners is in favor of "*the widow of the late William Hazen,*" and not in favor of Charlotte Hazen, widow of Moses Hazen. They therefore recommend to amend the bill, by striking out in the 7th and 8th lines the following words "*Charlotte Hazen widow of Moses Hazen, sixteen hundred acres.*"

Printed copy ([...], 9th Cong., 1st sess., 1–2).

From Jonathan Badger

Dear Sir   Westminster March 4th. 1806

Yours of the 18th. of January encloseing a communication from Doctor Mitchill was duly received. I cannot refrain from acknowledging how much I feel flattered by your polite attention, and the essential service that an acquaintance and correspondence with a man of Doct Ms. fame in the scientific world will be to me in the pursuit of usefull knowledge, but more immediately in my profession. I regret however that a presure of business prevents at present my furnishing the information he requires concerning the epidemic that prevailed in this town during the sumer months—but the moment my avocations permit me to investigate & arrange the matter I will with pleasure communicate what has fallen under my observation in practice respecting the *Fevers* he mentions.

Mrs. Badger has recovered a tolerable state of health, and probably I shall commence house keeping in the course of Six or eight Weeks. Previous to your departure for Congress I had some conversation with you respecting that house Mr. Abbey occupies. I should be fond of hireing it for a term of four or five years provided I could come into possession of it by the first of May. If that will correspond with your calculations I wish you to be obliging enough to inform me by the first Mail as I wish to be makeing some calculations on the subject.

I am Sir with great consideration & esteem your most Obt.

                                                                                   Jonathan Badger

Genl Bradley
    ALS (VtU).

From William Eaton

Sir,   Alexa. 23d. March 1806.

Thursday evening was put into my hands, under blank cover, from an unknown friend, a copy of the report of the Committee of the Senate on the claim of Hamet Caramalli — The next morning I waited at your[1] to offer you an expression of grateful sentiment for your homage to truth, respect to justice and pride of national honor — You were out — and I left Washington for this place — I brought the report with me: it has been read by sundry of the most respectable of this village with astonishment; but with admiration — It lifts, say they, the veil of mystery from the transactions in the Mediterranean; shows us why we have been disappointed of our expectations; and places the indelible brand of enfamy on the character who dared attempt an imposition on the credulity, the confidence of his country. Colonel Burr says it is the most manly expression of the national sentiment he has seen since the declaration of independence — It is so much sought for here that I dispatch a special courier with this note for no other purpose than to beg you will please to send me half a dozen copies to be distributed —

I have the honor to remain with profound respect, Sir, your most obedient servant

William Eaton

Honorable General Bradley

ALS (NcD: Bradley Family Papers).
1. Eaton apparently omitted a word here.

To Samuel Barron

Commodore Samel Barron

sir   Washington April 5th. 1806

As chairman of the Committee of the Senate of the United States on the application of Hamet Caramalli I enclose You a Copy of Orders said to have been given verbally by you in the Mediterranean, with a request for information from You on the following points

1st Do You recollect to have given those orders or any other at the time and place alluded to, and if different wherein?

2d Were the Orders (if any) given verbally to Capt. Hull at the time and place alluded to reduced by you to writing or by any other person to the best of Your knowledge and belief

You will please to communicate Your answer in writing as soon as may be convenient and Accept Assurances of my high respect

Stephen R Bradley } Chairman

[Enclosure]

"Verbal orders of Commodore Barron to Capt Hull of the United States brig Argus in presence of the Undersigned on board the President"

Sir   September 15th. 1804

The written orders I here hand you to proceed to the port of Alexandria or Smyrna for convaying to Malta any Vessels you may find there are intended to disguise the real object of your expedition which is to proceed with Mr Eaton to Alexandria in search of Hamet Bashaw the rival Brother and legitimate sovereign of the reigning Bashaw of Tripoli, and to convey him and his suite to *Derne* or such other place on the coast as may be determined the most proper for cooperating with the naval force under my command against the Common Enemy or if more agreeable to him to bring him to me before Tripoli. Should Hamet Bashaw not be found at Alexandria you have the discretion to proceed to any other place for him where the safety of your ship can be in your opinion relied upon. The Bashaw may be assured of the support of my squadron at Bengazi or Derne where you are at Liberty to put in if required and if it can be done without too great risk and you may assure him also that I will take the most effectual measures with the forces under my command for cooperating with him against the Usurper his brother and for reestablishing him in the regency of Tripoli. Arrangements to this effect are confided to the discretion with which Mr Eaton is vested by the Government.

Attest   Isaac Hull
           William Eaton

Draft (NcD: Bradley Family Papers).

To William Eaton

Genel Eaton

Sir   Washington April[1] 5th 1806

As Chairman of the Committee of the Senate on the Application of Hamet Caramalli I request of You information on the following points

1st were you present when the Verbal Orders were given to Capt Hull by Commodore Barron Sept 15th. 1805 and were they the same in substance as those published—

2d were those orders reduced to writing at that time by you or Capt. Hull and signed, and in what manner

3 did Commodore Barron know to the best of Your knowledge and belief that those orders were reduced to writing—

You will please to communicate you[r] answer as soon as may be Convenient

And accept assurance of my respect

SRB—

Draft (NcD: Bradley Family Papers).
1. SRB originally wrote "Feb," which is crossed out and "April" interlined in pencil.

From William Eaton

Hon. Gen. Bradley.

Sir,   Washington April 7. 1806

In answer to your enquiries of 5th. inst. I have the honor to state—

1t. I was present when the verbal orders were given to Captain Hull by Commodore Barron Sep. 15. 1805—and know them to be the same in substance as those published—

2d. I noted those orders with a pencil while the Commodore dictated them in his own cabin; they were repeated by the Commodore in a manner to make them understood—immediately on our return on board the Argus same evening those orders were reduced to writing by Captain Hull & myself; by us witnessed and interchanged; and on the 18th. following copies were forwarded to the department of the Navy.

3d. I do not know whether Commodore Barron was informed of those verbal orders having been reduced to writing in the manner above stated; am inclined to think he was not, as his reason for giving them verbally was to evade any accident which might discover our project with the enemy's brother. It is manifest Captain Hull's movements were governed by them—

I have the honor to be, Sir, very respectfully your obed: huml. sert.

W. Eaton

ALS (NcD: Bradley Family Papers). Cover addressed by Eaton to "Hon. Gen. Bradley / Senate / UStates." Mistakenly docketed by SRB, "Letter to Genel Eaton."

THIRTIETH COUNCIL.

OCTOBER 1806 TO OCTOBER 1807.

Isaac Tichenor, Bennington, *Governor*.
Paul Brigham, Norwich, *Lieut. Governor*.

Councillors:

Nathaniel Niles, West Fairlee,
Jonas Galusha, Shaftsbury,
John White, Georgia,
Beriah Loomis, Thetford,
Noah Chittenden, Jericho,
Eliakim Spooner, Westminster,

James Witherell, Fairhaven,
Asaph Fletcher, Cavendish,
Elias Keyes, Stockbridge,
Samuel Shepardson, Guilford,
Ebenezer Wheelock, Whiting,
Josiah Wright, Pownal.

William Page, Jr., *Secretary*.
William Slade, Cornwall, *Sheriff*.

POLITICAL NOTE.

The foregoing list of executive officers and Councillors is the same as for the preceding year, and with the exception of Governor, the persons named were all on the ticket which had previously been agreed upon, said *Spooner's Vermont Journal*, by the Jeffersonians—doubtless meaning in a legislative caucus at the session of 1805. The Jeffersonian ticket also embraced, for the first time, the name of Benjamin Swan as Treasurer. No official or other record of the etire vote for Governor can be found; but *Spooner's Vermont Journal* for Sept. 15 1806 states that in seventy-nine towns Tichenor had 5065 votes, and Israel Smith 4250. The *Assembly Journal* shows that the votes of twenty towns were rejected for informality, which towns gave 544 for Tichenor, 311 for Smith, and 18 scattering. The House was Jeffersonian by a very large majority, as indicated by the election of Stephen R. Bradley as United States Senator, he having received 120 votes against 60 for all other persons, as is stated in *Spooner's Vermont Journal* for Oct. 27 1806.

The election sermon was by the Rev. Thomas A. Merrill.

Governor and Council Records, vol. v.

To Stephen Jacobs

Stephen Jacobs Esqr
Dear Sir   Westminster Octbr 7th. 1806

I have one favor to request of you, the action between Amasa Paine and myself is appealed to the Supreme court of New Hampshire which sits at Keene on the 3d. Tuesday of this month I do not know whether Mills or Hubbard or both are Attornies for Paine as it will be some inconvenient for me to attend that Court and almost imposible to get prepared, I must trouble you with a request to see if the Attorney for Paine will not agree to have the cause put over to may Term at Charlestown if they will I authorize you to enter into such an agreement and if they do or Do not you will very much oblige me by giving me information thereof by the next Mail I shall be obliged to procure your attendance if possible when ever the cause is tried for all trouble I shall compensate you at meeting with pleasure.

Accept Sir assureance of my personal respect and Esteem

Stephen R Bradley

ALS (CtY). Addressed, "Hon Stephen Jacobs Esquire / Windsor / Vermont / the Post Master is requested to hand this to Mr Jacobs / as soon as may be S R Bradley." Notation, "paid 8." Endorsed, "Honble. S. R Bradley E / Octr. 1806."

From William Eaton

Honle. General Bradley —

Sir,   *[cut off at bottom]* Nov. 17th. 1806.

In support of the truths you have reported, concerning transactions of our squadron and commissioner of peace, with Tripoli, may be improved as witnesses —

Doctr. Thos. Babbet, of Brookfield

Doctr.	Cutbush	Philadelphia	Of the Navy,
Doctr. Jno.	Butler	Brimfield	and on the ground —
Doctr.	Cowdry	Vermont	

Dennison, Secretary to Commodore Barron

Captain Isaac Hull, now at Middleton, Con.

Captain Hugh	Campbell — Mediterranean	of the navy
Lieut. Joseph Bainbridge, Boston		and on the
Lieut.	Wederstrandt	ground —

The Communications from Docr. Geo. Davis, late Chargé des affaires of the United States at Tunis, to the Department of State, from April 1t. to Nov. 1805. — and

The ship's journals, or log books, of the squadron —

Evidence may be deduced from these sources, which, I am confident, will establish, beyond controversy, the truth of the facts reported.

I have felt it a duty I equally owe my country, the honor of your committee, and my own integrity to find out resorts from whence correct information may be obtained on this subject, and to report the result.

Except the event of a renewed coalition of the Northern powers of Europe, against France, should give a favorable turn to our pending negociation with Spain, war with this power seems inevitable. Who shall be trusted to fight our battles? If Burr is to be believed, Wilkinson balances between rebellion and desparation — He was never free of debt — and percieves, perhaps, that he is loosing the confidence of those characters in Government which it would be the pride of every honest man to retain — On whatever side the latter may declare, the former will give the United States trouble except suppressed in the outset — The insinuations concerning him, which have come before the public, are founded in facts.

I promised myself the honor of waiting on you at your seat in Vermont the last season; but the deranged situation of my little affairs at home has confined me to domestic arrangements — Shall however, have that gratification soon after the meeting of Congress — Mean time I have the honor to be with high respect, Sir, your mo. ob. serv

William Eaton

ALS (NcD: Bradley Family Papers). Docketed by SRB, "Genel Eaton's Letter."

From Joseph Dorr

Dear Sir   Fort Pickering Chickersaw Bluffs Decr 2. 1806

I am now at this Post Commanding, Mrs Dorr & myself enjoy health, I have ben informd that their is a pertision gone on to Congress from St Louis to augment the Officers pay and reasons stated, should such a pertision come before the house I would thank you for your influence I have made bold in this, for Reasons nowing you to be my friend and I am with Esteem you Obt & Humle Servant

Joseph Dorr

Honle Stephen R Bradly

P: S, pleas remember me to my Westminster friends I have rote often but cannot hear from them.

J Dorr

ALS (VtU).

To William Lyman

General Wm. Lyman

My Dear Sir   Washington December 5th. 1806

Permit me to call your attenti<on> to a Subject of importance to some persons who live in the back part of Massachusetts, and in Vermo<nt> and who claim to be heirs at Law to an Estate lying in Lond<on> in *Frying-pan Alley* and else where and which has descen<ded> to them from the Lord Mayor of London *Wilson* whose Christian name is now unknown supposed however to be Jeremiah or Benjamin and who must have lived on<e> Hundred years Since or more and whose Coat of Arm<s> was three Greyhounds— the present claimants are able to prove their descent in a direct right line from the said Lord Mayor Wilson — their Lineal descent is stated to be thus the Lor<d> Mayor Wilson had two Sons the eldest's christian na<me> is unknown at this time but who it is supposed said died at an adva<nced> age without Issue the Youngest's sons Name was Benjamin the Lord Mayor devised by *will* all his estate that was not entailed to his wife during her natural life and at her decease to his youngest Son Benjamin, who it seems wa<s> displeased at the disposition of the Estate thus made an<d> came to New England and settled at Charlestown near Boston the said Benjamin had two Sons Nathaniel and Jeremiah[.] Nathaniel died without Issue but Jeremi<ah> had Sons the name of his Eldest Son was Jonathan and Jonathan had a So<n> named Luke who now lives at Putney in Vermont indeed all the heirs at Law now Claim under Jeremiah Wilson as their Grand Father and who was Grand Son to the Lord Mayor — this Jeremiah Died March 22d 1743 in the 77th year of his age Jonathan his son was born at Lancaster Sept 2d 1703 and died March 31th. 1789 — The best information relating to the estate at this distance of time and place is as follows— that Benjamin the son of the Lord Mayor after residing some years in New England and having understood that the Estate had descended to him set out for London to take care of his Estate and died on his passage, that when the news of his death came to his brother at london he immediately sent to his brother's Benjns widow then at Charleston requesting her to send over to him all the writings and papers which she had relating to the subject and he would have the Estate confirmed to her and the heirs who were then two Sons Nathaniel and Jeremiah as stated before after which nothing further appears until about the year 1740 when there came a man from England to the said Jeremiah Wilson who then lived in Lancaster & represented that the buildings were decaying and the Estate would Escheat to the crown if it was not taken care of the said Jeremiah being then an old

Man could not and neither of his sons would go to England but the said Jeremiah together with his Eldest son Jonathan gave Jointly a General power of Attorney to the Man who came over to take care of the Estate to lease &c &c since which the heirs have had no return the person who came over about the year 1740 and took the power of Attoney is said to be a Mr Leigh the power was made & executed before the Hon. Joseph Wilder of Lancaster then a Judge since deceased the heirs have this further information by tradition that Either the lord Mayor or his Eldest Son at a very advanced age married a very young woman and died without Issue by her leaving her a young widow that she afterwards married a Mr Leigh by whom she had several Children and it is supposed that the person who received the power of Atty was a son of that woman's by the last marriage—it is said there were several other Estates beside the one lying in Frying Pan Alley that were devised by the Lord Mayor Wilson to his son Benjamin, and that in consequence of the Eldest Son having left no Issue the entailed Estate descended also to the heirs of Benjamin and they who hav<e> been held and possessed under the power of Attorney from Jeremiah & his Son Jonathan will it is thought save it from the Statutes of Limitations—I have enclosed you the Political Observatory under the Deaths you will observe mention "in England the Hon. Mrs Leigh of Stonely by her death an Estate which 60 years since rented at 17,000 £ per Annum devolves upon some unknown heir at Law"—I have been thus minute in detailing to you such information as at present I possess to give you every possible means to investigate the subject, to ascertain whet<her> the power of Attorney was recorded in England and how far the Estate has been held and possessed unde<r> it and what situation the Estate is now in—the Ninth Artic<le> of the Treaty of 1794 will secure it to the heirs if nothing has intervened to deprive them thereof your attention to the Subject will be gratefully acknowledg<ed> and Compensated and the result of your reserches addressed to me at Westminster in the State of Vermo<nt> under Cover to Samuel A Otis of Boston or Thomas Pearsall of New York Merchant will be forwarded with dispach and the Obligation confered recognized with pleasure by your Friend And Obedt Humble Servant

S R Bradley

Draft? (VtU). Numerous cancellations and interlineations. Margin obscured.

Senate Proceedings: Regulating Grants of Land in the Territory of Michigan

February 4, 1807.

Mr. Bradley made the following motion, to amend the bill,
Regulating grants of land in the territory of Michigan.

1   Sec. 2. Line 1, after the word "*or*," Strike out to the word
2   "*and*," in the 14th line, and in lieu thereof insert, "persons in
3   the actual possession, occupancy, and improvement, of any tract
4   or parcel of land, in his, her, or their own right, at the time of
5   the passing of this act, within that part of the territory of Michi-
6   gan, to which the Indian title has been extinguished, and which
7   said tract or parcel of land was settled, occupied, and improved,
8   by him, her, or them, prior to the first day of July, one thou-

9   sand seven hundred and ninety six, or by some other person or
10 persons, under whom he, she, or they, hold or claim the right to
11 the occupancy, or possession thereof; the said tract or parcel of
12 land thus possessed, occupied, and improved, shall be granted,
13 and such occupant or occupants, shall be confirmed in the title
14 to the same, as an estate of inheritance, in fee simple: *Provided*
15 *however,* That no other claims shall be confirmed by virtue of
16 this section, than such as have been entered with the register
17 of the land office of *Detroit*, within the time, and in the manner
18 provided by law, and by the commissioners aforesaid, have been
19 inserted in their report, transmitted as aforesaid; nor shall more
20 than one tract or parcel of land be thus granted to any one per-
21 son, and the same shall not contain more than the quantity
22 claimed, nor more than six hundred and forty acres."

Printed copy ([...], 9th Cong., 1805–1807, Senate, 2d sess., 1–2).

Senate Proceedings: Regulating Grants of Land in the Territory of Michigan

February 9, 1807

Mr. Bradley, from the committee appointed to prepare and bring in a bill, to regulate the summoning of grand jurors, reported the following.

A Bill

To regulate the summoning of grand jurors.

1   **Be it enacted** *by the Senate and House of Representatives*
2   *of the United States of America, in Congress assembled,* That
3   the clerks of the several circuit or district courts of the Unit-
4   ed States, shall not issue process to summon, or cause to be re-
5   turned, a grand jury, to attend any circuit or district court, nor
6   shall the marshal of any district, cause to be returned, a grand
7   jury other than by process as aforesaid, without a special order
8   of the district judge, or at the special request, in writing, of the
9   district attorney, to issue such process, or to cause a grand
10 jury to be returned as aforesaid.
1   Sec. 2. *And be it further enacted,* that whenever any bill of
2   indictment shall be found by a grand jury, attending a district
3   court, for a crime or offence cognizable only in the circuit court,
4   such bill of indictment shall, by order of the district judge,
5   together with such files, papers, and documents as relate thereto,
6   be transmitted to the circuit court, and there proceeded on, in

7	the same manner as if the same had been found by a grand jury
8	attending the said circuit court, and the clerk of the district
9	court shall transmit the same certified under his hand and seal
10	of the court.

[Handwritten notation: "passed Feby 12"]

Microform, U.S. Government Library; U.S. 9th Congress, 1805–1807. Senate.

Senate Proceedings: Regulating the Summoning of Grand Jurors

FEBRUARY 9, 1807.

Mr. Bradley, from the committee to whom was referred, the *Bill* "regulating the grants of land in the territory of Michigan," and the amendment offered thereto,

REPORTED:

Adopt the amendment, with the following

Amendment:

1	In the 8th line of the amendment, between the words "*to*" and
2	"*the*," insert, "and on."
3	In the 11th line of the amendment, after the word, "*thereof*"
4	insert, "and which said occupancy or possession has been con-
5	tinued to the time of the passing of this act."

AMEND THE BILL,

1	SEC. 2, line 14th — strike out "*this donation*," and insert, "the
2	same."
3	Strike out the 3d section.
4	SEC. 4, line 23d — strike out the following: "*which determi-*
5	*nation shall be final.*"
6	Line 48 — after the word "*transcript*," insert, "shall contain a
7	fair statement of the evidence on which each respective claim is
8	founded, and."
9	Line 57 — after the word "*certificates*," insert, "for each of
10	which certificates the register shall receive one dollar."
11	Line 58 — after the word "*treasury*," strike out, "*on which*,"
12	and insert, "and if it shall appear to the satisfaction of the said
13	secretary, that such certificates have been fairly obtained, ac-
14	cording to the true intent and meaning of this act, then and in
15	that case."

Microform, U.S. Government Library, U.S. 9th Congress, 1805–1807, 2d Sess. Senate.

From William Eaton

Honle. General Bradley

Sir, Feb. 13th. 1807

I request to be informed whether there is a prospect of any provisions being made for Hamet Bashaw this session? Justice, humanity, and national honor dictate the measure — If coupling my name with his interests should go to prejudice unfavorably concerning him, I sincerely wish not to be brought into view.

I have received letters from the Bashaw, importuning my agency in his behalf; it has no influence: I am nevertheless desirous of having it in my power to give him some encouragement

I have the honor to be most respectfully Sir, your very Obed.

W. Eaton

ALS (NcD: Bradley Family Papers).

Senate Proceedings: Tennessee Lands

IN SENATE
OF THE UNITED STATES

FEBRUARY 17, 1807.

MR. BRADLEY, from the committee appointed to inquire whether any, and if any, what further proceeding is necessary to carry into effect the provisions of an act, entitled "An act to authorise the state of Tennessee to issue grants and perfect titles to certain lands therein described, and to settle the claims to the vacant and unappropriated lands within the same,"

REPORTED:

THAT in the absence of the honorable Joseph Anderson, one of the Senators from the state of Tennessee, who has not attended Congress during the present session, the committee proceeded to examine the act of the state of Tennessee, entitled "An act to appoint agents to settle the dispute existing between this state and the United States, relative to the vacant and unappropriated lands within this state, and to procure the relinquishment of the claim of the United States, to the same," passed November 14th, 1801, — and find, that in and by said act, the state of Tennessee did authorise their Senators and Representatives, or their successors, or a majority of them, to procure from the United States a relinquishment of their claim to the lands in the state of Tennessee, in such manner, and upon such terms, as to the said agents might seem proper; and being fully satisfied that the powers vested in the Senators and Representatives from the state of Tennessee, signers of the herein after recited instrument, are ample and sufficient to carry into effect, on the part of the state of Tennessee, the provisions of the aforesaid act of Congress, the committee have received from them the following instrument, signed and sealed by them respectively, to wit:

"BE IT REMEMBERED, That we, the undersigned, Senators and Representatives in the Congress of the United States, from the state of Tennessee, do hereby make known, that in pursuance of the power in us vested, by an act of the general assembly of the state of Tennessee, entitled "An act to appoint agents to settle the dispute between this state and the United States, relative to the vacant and unappropriated lands within this state, and to procure the relinquishment of the claim of the United States, to the same," and by a resolution of the Senate and House of Representatives of the state of Tennessee, passed in the year one thousand eight hundred and two, as instructions therein; WE DO, in consideration of the provisions made in the act of Congress entitled "An act to authorise the state of Tennessee to issue grants and perfect titles to certain lands therein described; and to settle the claims to the vacant and unappropriated lands within the same," for and in behalf of the state of Tennessee, agree and declare, that all right, title, and claim, which the state of Tennessee hath to the lands, lying west and south of the following line, to wit: beginning at the place where the eastern or main branch of Elk river shall intersect the southern boundary line of the state of Tennessee; from thence running due north until said line shall intersect the northern or main branch of Duck river; thence down the waters of Duck river, to the military boundary line, as established by the seventh section of the act of North Carolina, entitled "An act for the relief of the officers and soldiers of the continental line, and for other purposes," passed in the year one thousand seven hundred and eighty three; thence with the military boundary line, west to the place where it intersects the Tennessee river; thence down the waters of the Tennessee river, to the place where the same intersects the northern boundary line of the state of Tennessee, shall hereafter forever cease, and the lands aforesaid, lying south and west of the line aforesaid, within the limits of the state of Tennessee, shall be and remain at the sole and entire disposition of the United States, and shall be exempted from every disposition or tax, made by order, or under the authority of the state of Tennessee, while the same shall remain the property of the United States, and for the term of five years after the same shall be sold.

In testimony whereof, we have hereunto signed our names, and affixed our seals.

DONE at the City of Washington, this twenty third day of January, in the year of our Lord one thousand eight hundred and seven.

          DANL. SMITH,   (*Seal.*)
          WM. DICKSON,   (*Seal.*)
          G. W. CAMPBELL,   (*Seal.*)
          JOHN RHEA,   (*Seal.*)

In presence of
    SAMUEL A. OTIS,
Secretary of the Senate of the United States,
    JOHN BECKLEY,
Clerk of the House of Representatives
    of the United States.

Whereupon,

Resolved, That the Senate do approve of the aforesaid instrument, and order the same to be entered at large on the Journal; and the secretary is hereby desired to cause the original instrument to be deposited in the office of the secretary state.

Microform, U.S. Government Library, U.S. 9th Congress, 1805–1807. Senate.

Senate Proceedings:
Bill to Prohibit the Importation of Slaves

FEBRUARY 24, 1807.

Mr. Bradley, from the conferrees from the Senate, on the disagreement between the two houses on the bill, "*to prohibit the importation of slaves into any part or place within the jurisdiction of the United States, from and after the first day of January, in the year of our Lord one thousand eight hundred and eight,*"

Reported,

That having met the conferrees on the part of "the House of Representatives, they have mutually agreed, in conference, to recommend to pass the bill, with the proviso at the end of the 8th section, amended as follows, to wit:

1   "*Provided however, That nothing in this section shall extend*
2   *to prohibit the taking on board or transporting on any river, or*
3   *inland bay of the sea, within the jurisdiction of the United States,*
4   *any negro, mulatto, or person of color, (not imported contrary to*
5   *the provisions of this act,) in any vessel or species of craft what-*
6   *ever.*" And also to amend the eight section, by striking out the
7   word "*fifty,*" and insert in lieu thereof "forty," and in the se-
8   cond line strike out the words "*as a slave or,*" and insert in
9   lieu thereof, "to be."
10   And in section 9, line 1—strike out "*fifty,*" and insert "forty."
11   And also in section 10, line 1—strike out "*fifty,*" and insert,
12   "forty."

Microform, U.S. Government Library, U.S. 9th Congress, 1805–1807. Senate.

Proceedings: Survey of the Coast of North Carolina

February 24, 1807.

Mr. Bradley, from committee to whom was referred the joint resolution to publish the report and chart of the survey of the coast of North Carolina,

MADE THE FOLLOWING

Report.

1   Line 3—strike out the following words "*cause to be publish-*
2   *ed,*" and insert in lieu thereof, "contract with any person or
3   persons to publish."
4   At the end of the bill insert, "upon such terms and condi-
5   tions as will best accord with the public interest, and secure to
6   the United States one thousand copies of the same, subject to
7   the future disposition of Congress."

Microform, U.S. Government Library, U.S. 9th Congress, 1805–1807. Senate.

Senate Proceedings: Fortifying the Ports and Harbors

March 2, 1807

Mr. Bradley, from the committee to whom was referred the bill making further appropriations for fortifying the ports and harbors of the United States, and for building gun boats,

REPORTED THE FOLLOWING
Amendment.

1   Strike out the second section.
2   And amend the title by striking out the following words: "*and*
3   *for building gun boats.*"

Microform, U.S. Government Library, U.S. 9th Congress, 1805–1807. Senate.

From Israel Smith

Dear Sir—   Rutland May the 26th 1807

Mr. Eleazer Wheelock of this place has for many years been a Contractor for carrying the mail from this Town to Highgate and several other Routes—and has been remarkably faithful and diligent in the business, so as to give intire satisfaction to the public, and Individuals who have h<ad> occasion to employ him to transact any business for them. Any favor that you can shew him which may assist him in obtaining the contracts for which he may bid at a reasonable rate will be to confer a great favor on Mr Wheelock and will be very sensibly felt and acknowledged by himself and me—I think his fidelity and attention to the business for a long period of time [Justly?] intitles him to a preferance in the Contracts if any preferance can be shewn.

I am with sentiment of esteem and respect

                                                                                                          Israel Smith

Hon. Stephen R Bradley

    ALS (NcD: Bradley Family Papers).

From Seth Hastings

Honble: Stephen. R. Bradley Esqr.,

Dear Sir   Mendon June 8th: 1807

The Bearer hereof Mr: Jason Chamberlain Junr., is about to make a journey to the Westward, where he will probably be unknown and a Stranger. Permit me to recommend Mr: Chamberlain to your notice and attention as a young Gentleman of education, talents and good character; he is a Candidate for the Ministry; and has lately been preaching in Douglass in this vicinity.

I am Sir with esteem, very respectfully your Friend and humble Servant

                                                                                        Seth Hastings

    LS (VtU).

From Gideon Granger

Sir, General post Office 11 July 1807.

Mr. White post Master by Letter of the 5 June at Putney Vt. states "My situation from the Stage Road is such that it renders it inconvenient for me to serve as Post Master, especially since the new Arrangement in running the Stage, which stops now in Putney but a few minutes & I am distant from the Stage house about fifty Rods. The Driver considers it a hardship to bring the Mail to my Office and I am unwilling to go after it. I would beg leave to recommend Mr. Joseph Metcalf, who is well situated, and, in my Opinion, the most suitable person in this vicinity."

Such is the information recd. from Mr. White. I take the Liberty of Enclosing you a sett of Papers, (Blanks) for a new Appointment of Post Master at Putney Vt:, which you will be pleased to fill with the name of some Person who will in your Opinion discharge the Duties with care and fidelity. With high Respect and Esteem

Yr. Ob: Servt.

Gidn Granger

Honble: Stephen R: Bradley,
Westminster.

ALS (NcD: Bradley Family Papers).

From Simeon Knight

Dear Sir <Natelutoches?> 24th Aug. 1807

My friend Capt. Pike will hand you this letter his character is so conspicuous I deem it unnecessary to offer any encomiums upon it (which I might do with propriety). Should he want assistance any services you may render him will confer an obligation on your friend.

I am of opinion the late aggressions commited by the British upon our commerce and the insults offered our Flag will be the proximate cause of a War between the two Nations. It appears by Newspaper information the minds of the People are too much exasperated to be immediately calmed without revenge for the lives of several of her citizens.

In case of an a[u]gmentation of the Army I request you will give me your assistance in some of the new Regts, if any considerable Rank can be obtained by the transfer. I presume five years Service a close application to duty and a predilection for the profession would give me preference to any citizen in private life.

I have attained the age of twenty seven years—too old to commence a new profession and could I obtain such Rank in the Army as to encourage a laudable ambition I have for some time past determined to spend the remainder of my life in the Service of my Country. Should no transfers take place from the existing Regts, into the New I have enclosed you a power of atty. to offer my Resignation as second Lieut in the first Regt, of Infantry should you find it necessary But request you not to tender it unless considerable advantage may be derived from it.

Accept assurances of my high esteem and respect your friend

S Knight

Honble, Stephen R Bradley

[Enclosure]

<Natelutoches?> 24th August 1807

I hereby empower Stephen R. Bradley my lawful agent and atty to offer my resignation as second Lieut in the first Rgt, of Infantry to take place on the day of

S Knight 2d Lieut

1. Regt, of Infantry

ALS and enclosure (VtU). Endorsed, "Lieut. Simeon Knight." SRB also received from Knight a duplicate of this letter dated 3 September (VtU).

To the General Assembly of Vermont

Westminster Octbr 7th 1807

To the Hon. The General Assembly of the State of Vermont to be holden at Woodstock on the Second Thursday of October in the Year of Our Lord 1807

The Remonstrance & Petition of Stephen R Bradley of Westminster in said State

Humbly Sheweth

That he is the sole owner and proprietor of a tract of land called Bradleyvale that he purchased the Same many years Since of Thomas Pearsall of New York to whom it was granted at the expense of four thousand Dollars and always designed to keep the Same for an inheritance for his Childred [sic] and for that purpose he applyed to and obtained an act of incorporation of the same Tract by the name of *Bradleyvale* that he has constantly paid the taxes assessed on the Same and during the present year has Chearfully paid a tax of twenty dollars on the Same to build a Gaole in the County where the land lies—that altho there is not at present a Single Settler on the land your petitioner nevertheless has for some time been making provision to erect Mills and make large improvments on the Same but to his surprise a few weeks Since he observed in the *Vermont Journal* public notice given by one Theophilus Grant James Lawton and one James Willard that they should apply to Your Honorable body to have this tract of land annexed to Hopkinville a large tract of land owned by one John Atkinson Esqr in New York against which annexation as well as Vexation Your petitioner would most Seriously remonstrate as he considers the object to be nothing less than to steal Your petitioners land from him which now has become an Object as he has advanced including taxes and Interest not Short of Eight thousand Dollars for the same he therefore humbly prays Your honors that he may be Suffered to enjoy his land in rest and quietness any thing contained in the notice or petition of a *Grant Lawton* or *willard* notwithstanding and if the Legislature deem it expedient to take from you[r] petitioner any part or the whole of his land he hopes it may be applied to the benifit of the public and not by any indirect way to the benefit of those speculating land Jobbers who are constantly preying upon the public & individual property. Your petitioner now freely offers the legislature that if they will authorize the Governor to Issue him a Grant exempting Bradleyvale from all land taxes other than those which shall be necessary for making roads through the Same and the Usual State taxes and that the same shall never be annexed or disposed of to any other town without the Consent of the proprietors or a major part of them that he will in consideration thereof pay into the treasury of the State the Sum of three Hundred Dollars and if the Several towns in the State would do the same or in the same proportion the Interest arising from that Sum would he conceives defray the expense of the Civil list of the State forever as there is not four thousand Acres in Bradleyvale he therefore prays your honors to reject the application of *Grant* & Others and to confirm Your petitioner in the free enjoyment of his land And as in duty bound will Ever pray

Stephen R Bradley

ADS (Vt: MsVtSP, vol. 46, p. 180). Notes on the verso read: "Remonstrance of Stephen R Bradley / Filed Octr 13th 1807 / Att Th <Leverold?> Secy / In Gen. Assembly / Oct. 13t. 1807 / Recd & ref'd to the comee. on the petition from Hopkinville / Oct. 22d. 1807 / Resolved, That the prayer of this petitioner in the concluding part of this petn. & remonstrance be granted & that he have leave to bring in a bill accordingly. / Att. M. Post Clk. / *Bill dismissed.*"

From Joseph Goodhue

Dear Sir   Fort Constitution 10th. October 1807

    I take the liberty to address you in behalf of Capt. Walbach, the Commanding officer of this Garrison. Genl. Storer of Portsmouth, who will be the bairer of this, will present A memorial to Congress, in behalf of the Capt., praying for compensation, for servises in the U.S. Army, for which no compensation has ben made. Capt. Walbach is A very worthy Man, and is well deserving the consideration of Our Goverment, as an officer, and a gentleman of the most unshaken integrity & uprigh[t]ness. He has requested me to address You in his favour; knowing the influence You possess at the seat of Goverment, if You shall think His memorial worthy the attention of the Goverment, I have no doubt You will be willing to use Your influence in His favour. It is long since I have had the pleasure of hearing from You, or your Family, but, I should be very happy to hear from Your Self & them. Mrs. Goodhue joins me in Respects & best wishes for A continuance of Your health & usefulness.

    I am Dear Sir very Respectfully Your Obt. Servt.

                                                       Joseph Goodhue

Hon. S. R. Bradley
    ALS (VtU).

From Jonathan Cook

Honoured Sir,   Rutland Vermont 21st. Octr. 1807

    I again trouble you with a renewal of my request, which I made to you at Woodstock last Augt. of procuring for me an appointment in the United States service; providing there should be War—or an increase of the peace Establishment—I think, I can soon raise a Company of Superlative Greenmountain Artillery Boys, provided I had only the authority of our Excellent President: Thos. Jefferson therefor—Be pleased, if within your wish to use your Influence to procure me a Captaincy & have my Subalterns appointed from our Vermont Young Gentlemen in the Millitary School at West Point—<Justins> Post & Satterlee Clark now Cadets are two promising young Gentlemen. The Honble. Royal Tyler, Theophilus Herrinton & Jonas Galusha are our Supreme Judges for the ensuing year. Be pleased to converse with your Brother Senator the Honble. Jona. Robinson on my request & oblige yours

                                                             Jna. Cook

ALS (VtU). Addressed to SRB.

Senate Proceedings: Peace in the Ports and Harbors

IN SENATE
OF THE UNITED STATES.

November 4th, 1807.

The following motion was submitted by MR. BRADLEY, for consideration.

Resolved, That a committee be appointed to inquire whether any, and if any, what further and more effectual provisions are necessary, in addition to the act, entitled "An act for the more effectual preservation of peace in the ports and harbors of the United States, and in the waters under their jurisdiction"; with leave to report by bill or otherwise.

Microform, U.S. Government Library, U.S. 10th Congress, 1807–1809. Senate.

From William C. Harrington

Gen. Bradley

Dear Sir   Burlington Nov. 11th Ad 1807

I have this day received the Presidents message to Congress, which I have carefully perused & examined and think that it speaks the language of a great & good Man.

Many of my brothers (federalists) wish to find fault, but it is such as would strain at a knot & swallow Camel [*illegible*].

Your transmitting the Message to me has conferred a particular obligation, & sir I shall feel highly honored in receiving frequent Communications from You &c.

In case of War, & You should dare run the risk of mentioning my name to the President for a Commission to command a Regiment or an expedition to Canada, I should readily accept of such an appointment, & should do my best to render such service to the Government as should honour Your recommendation. My Acquaintance and comm[i]sions in Lower and Upper Canada is such as put it in my power to render as great service as any man in this State &c &c.

I hope & believe that Mr Jefferson will do every thing consistent with the honor & dignity of our Government to avoid War, but I am afraid that War is inevitable.

Our Legislature is still in session, Governor Smith guides the helm like a good navigator &c.

We have no account as yet of the proceedings of Congress.

I hope that You will not forget me in Your Communications as occasion may require.

I am Sir respectfully Your Obt. Servant

Wm C Harrington

ALS (VtU). Endorsed by SRB, "Wm C. Harrington."

From William Eaton

Sir,   Wednesday Nov. 18th. 1807 —

This morning, at breakfast, Geo. Dyson Esq. informed me that Captain Dent, who brought Doctor Davis to Syracuse to arrange some affairs with Hamet Bashaw, stated to him that *Tobias Lear*, the negociator of our treaty with the ruling Bashaw of Tripoli, had signed a secret article which was in the hands of that Bashaw's prime minister, and which recedes for a given number of years the right stipulated by public treaty of *demanding the family of Hamet Bashaw*—that this secret article had not been communicated by Mr. Lear to the Government—and that the family would not probably be surrendered without new conditions and further pecuniary sacrifices on the part of the United States—I understood Mr. Dyson that this statement had been confirmed to him by Consul Davis.

From the vigilance and punctuality of Doctor Davis it would seem that a discovery so fraudulent in itself and so degrading to the honor of this nation should have been immediately communicated to the Executive and it is presumed he has taken the proper steps to fulfil this obligation —: dispatches are in the Hornet.

From observations of Mr. Lear I had entertained an early suspicion of his duplicity in this instance; but having no document to support the fact, I could only give it the character of a suspicion.

I think it my duty, at this time, to communicate this information — And have the honor to be most respectfully Sir your very Obedient servant

William Eaton

ALS (NcD: Bradley Family Papers). Addressee not indicated.

From Charles Blake

Sir, Northfield November 20th. 1807

Doctor Charles Jarvis who for several years past has had the attendance of the Marine Hosptal of the District of Massachusetts— died a few days since in Boston. Consequently, it at present is destitute of any Medical Person to attend. Doctor Jarvis received for his services I think $1200 Dollars anually which would afford to a Physician who has a small family a tolerable support.

I know of no Gentleman whose influence I think is greater with the Executive than yours— and would therefore solicit it.

I have Sir, served the United States as Physician & Surgeon almost nine years and during that time flatter myself both in the Army & Navy was found faithful and attentive.

Should you Sir think my pretensions good and should be disposed to name me to the Honb Secretary of the Tresury of the U. States, who I think is the Gentleman who will make the appointment — you will render me a favour which I shall ever remember with gratitude.

With the utmost respect I have the honour to be Sir, yr. Obdt. Humble Servt.

Charles Blake

The appointment mentioned I presume will be immediately made — will therefore thank you for your immediate attention.

Hon'ble S. R. Bradley

ALS (VtU). Endorsed by SRB, "Charles Blake."

From Joseph Dorr

Belle Fontain Near St Louis

Honbl Stephen R Bradly Esqr Upper Louisana Novbr 20th 1807

Sir I am enduced to apply to you for a favour from the former Success I have had in my applications hoping that your friendship Still continues and convinced of the service a few words to the Secretary of War would be to me, from you that is I wish to be statined at the a[r]snell at New Po<rt> Kentucky where I shall have but a Small Command it is true, but I shall not be so liable to be Order<d> about as I have ben which I am almost tired of as my funds is scearcely adiquate to my expences — I would not have troubled you at this time but it is rumord here that the few troops will be dispers<ed> in the Spring not known where which caused me to Seliset your Influence, if their is any fighting to do I wish you to dispence of doing any thing <on?> it, I have ritten to Coll Burbeck who I think my freind a word to him from you would be of great use.

I am with Esteem your Most Obt & Humbl Servant

Joseph Dorr Lieut

1st Regt Infantry

P: S Mrs Dorr desires her respects to you, we are both enjoying health.

J Dorr

ALS (VtU). Margin obscured.

From William Plumer

My dear Sir   Epping (N. H.) November 18, 1807

Just before we seperated last March you assured me that I should hear from you this session. To *stir up your pure mind by way of remembrance,* is the object that now induces me to write. Indeed we have nothing here that is new or interesting to you. As to our affairs with Great Britain, we seem involved in doubt & uncertainty; the report of to day contradicts that of the preceding. Have you any official information of the result of our negociation at the Court of London? Will it terminate favorably — will that haughty, imperious nation do us justice; or must we renounce all intercourse with her? And in the language of the Apocalypse, must we *come out and be seperate from her, least we partake of her plagues & of her punishments?*

Judging from present appearances, whether we have peace or war with Great Britain, it seems that our external commerce is doomed to destruction, by all the belligerent powers. We are told that Great Britain acknowledges no neutral power; but will in future consider all vessels as good prize that are bound to or from French ports, or their allies. And that Napolean, & the government of Spain, have adopted the same rule, in reference to all vessels bound to or from the British dominions. It is with a nation as an individual, there is a point beyond which submission is but another name for meanness & cowardice. But if the honor and dignity of the nation can be preserved, I hope we shall avoid the calamity of war. I would leave the merchants, whose God is gain, to regulate their own commerce — that is, either voluntarily embargo their navigation, or take the risque of capture upon themselves. I would not involve my country in war to defend or insure their voyages. The object is not equal to the expence of a war; & a war in our present circumstances, so far from affording protection to our trade, would increase the means of its ruin. And if we had now thirty ships of the line, and that is more than we can conveniently man & support, would they afford us more protection than Denmark received from her navy?

If you have leisure, I should esteem it a favor to hear from you — of men & measures. Do you continue your nocturnal meetings in the Capitol? They were pleasant to me the last winter, & I often think of you & them.

I am now collecting, preparing & arranging materials for the history of the United States. I will thank you to enclose me, under your frank as many of the documents of the present session as you can with convenience. They will be useful to me; & will add to the obligations you have conferred upon Sir your most obedient humble servant.

William Plumer

Hon. Stephen R. Bradley
Senator
Washington

ALS (VtU).

From Israel Smith

The honorable Stephen R Bradley—

Sir—   Rutland Novr. 29—1807—

In obedience to a request from the Legislature I inclose to you, a resolution enter[ed] into by the legislature of this State for the purpose of procuring an Amendment to the Constitution of the United States, so as to enable the President to remove the Judges, on application for that purpose by both Houses of Congress.

I am with the highest Esteem and respect yours

Israel Smith

ALS (NcD: Bradley Family Papers). Enclosure not found.

From Israel Smith

The honorable Stephen R Bradley—

Dear Sir—   Rutland November 29th 1807

A few days since I had the pleasure of receiving a letter from you[1] covering the Presidents Message and other documents accompanying it. I thank you for the favor. It would have given me great satisfaction to have Learnt from that communication that our disputes with the british Cabinet had been peacibly a[d]justed, for no person I believe more sincerely deprecates the evils and calamities of war than myself. What good purpose can it answer? it will most unquestionably destroy the lives of thousands and shorten and render wretched the lives of thousands more—it will waste and ex[h]aust an emensity of property—it will em[p]ty our Treasury—it will divert a great portion of our Citizens from productive Industrey to that which is worse than unproductive and thereby great[l]y Impoverish the nation it will render the community immoral and vitious and if long continued will place the greater part of the people in a State or Condition that will be poor, and wretched, and blind, naked, what good purpose is it to answer, is it to humble our Enimy? in the bloody Conflict of war we stand an equal Chance perhaps of being humbled ourselves—you will ask then? are we to surrender all our rights as an independent Nation I answer no. but maintain them in a manner the most peacible and inoffencive we should never inflict on an Enemy a greater evil as a punishment, than the Injury received least we provoke new agressions and the maxim in Scripture "that it is better to suffer wrong than do wrong["] is extremely apropos we should never Injure the person or property of our Enemy when other measures less destructive and adequate to the redress of the evil complained off [sic] and for this plaine reason we are to inflict no unnecessary evil on ourselves or others—the punishment inflicted on an enemy in all prob[ab]ility will be more effectual in proportion as it shall appear to grow out of the Injury offered the principal Complaint of the british government is that our merchants participate in the colonial Trade of her enemies what would be the consiquence if our merchants should abandon that trade?—so far it would extend to lessen our ability to trade with England—since the right of Trade is the point in controversy between our government and the English let it cease until the british Government entertain different views on the subject for depend on it the measure will not be ineffectual—perhaps to withdraw intercource from all the belligerents (if necessary for our peace) for a short season while this last violent shock of the war is passing over might be thought prudent rather than be compelled to drink deeply of the dregs of this bitter cup. I believe You will think there is a little enthusiastic od[d]ity in this letter it happened to be the train of which came to mind when I sat down to write and I wrote it. I think with you that Wheaton and some others have received the Just reward of their Labors.

Yours Sincerely

Israel Smith.

ALS (NcD: Bradley Family Papers). Cover addressed to "The honorable Stephen R. Bradley / in Senate / City of Washington"; marked "At Rutland Decr. 3d" and "Free."

1. Letter not found.

From Jabez Penniman

Dear Sir: Swanton December 21st 1807

I am desired by some Gentlemen at Burlingto<n> and in this vicinity to acquaint you that the mail in its progress to the northward is unaccountable staid.

Letters from Washington to this place are eighteen days passage—but the delay is principally from th[...]y north—It is a fact that news comes from New-York to Boston from thence to Windser and from the<nce> to Burlington four days sooner then the same <does> from New-York by way of Albany—Rutland—and fro<m> thence to Burlington—why this s<hould> be the case <is> yet to be learnt—Mr. Whee<lock> who is and has been for a long time the mail carier is desirous to increase the rapidity by going twice a week instead of once if he can have some small compensation in addition to what he now has—he says two hundred dollars—but I think he would for something less then that sum—I am willing to say— too much credit cannot be given to Mr. Wheelock as a faithfull honest man.

Permit me to observe that if anything can be done to expedite the mail to this quarter it will be considered by all your friends in this vicinity as a peticular favour and will add a new obligation to th<e> many already confered on—Dear Sir—your obt. Servt.

Jabez Penniman

Honbl. S. R. Bradly Esqr:

Mrs: Penniman desires to be remembered with much respect.

ALS (VtU). Margin obscured. Several small holes in the center of the MS.

To Thomas Jefferson

To the President of the United States Decr 26th. 1807

Permit me Sir to recommend to your notice as a person well qualified to discharge the duties of a judge of the territory of *Michigan* Reuben Atwater of Vermont; he is a man of amiable manners, Strict integrity, of an unblemished moral and political character, was educated to the law, has followed that profession for fifteen years with reputation and esteem, and is considered as an able judge of the law. One motive which induces me at this time to press the recommendation is, that he is first cousin to Governor *Hull* their mothers were sisters, great intimacy always subsisted between the two families, and I have no doubt he would be of esential service in the present state of the territory, he married the daughter of General Lamb, who, (as many of his friends imagine) was treated with great severity under a former administration, this appointment would give great pleasure to the old friends of that *departed hero*. Mr Atwater is well known to the Vice President, who can give further testimonials, and will I presume cordially support the nomination, if any thing further should be necessary I beg leave to refer to the ample recommendations given on a former occasion when Mr Atwater was recommended to the office of Marshal for the district of Vermont — many of which were from his political enemies.

Accept Sir the Assurance of my high respect & Esteem

Stephen R Bradley

ALS (NjP).

From William Eaton

Honorable General Bradley—

Sir,   Brimfield Dec. 27th. 1807.

The impression is strongly fixed in my mind that the volume of state papers, which you had the friendship to lend me, was returned to your lodgings, if not to your room, immediately after my having used it to assist my application for Hamet Caramelli. May it not possibly be found with books of some other gentlemen of your family; or misplaced in your own library? I certainly left nothing in my chamber at Stelles Hotel — and had no occasion for the volume elsewhere. There is indeed a possibility that I may have left it, in passing, somewhere out of place; but cannot recover any such recollection. It will afford me gratification to be informed tha<t> it is found — it cannot be lost.

Has any thing been done for the Bashaw? Will any thing be done. Dare not this nation be just? There remai<ns> a blemish on our claim to this character whilst that man begs!

I have the honor to continu<e> most respectfully, Sir, your very Obed: servt

William Eaton

ALS (NcD: Bradley Family Papers). Parts of words obscured in right margin.

From Lot Hall

Copy

Dear Sir,   Westminster Jany. 17th. 1808

Since writing the inclosed I have submitted them to the inspection of your Son — & he together with my other friends, having exsp[r]essed a favorable opinion with respect to my ultimate Success — in this undertaking it has increased my own confidence considerably. I beg your advice & assistance as far as is consistant. You will read my Petition together with my reasons, as therein exsp[r]esssed for its great length. If you think it best to hav<e> it abridged or altered in any way whatever. In short I submit the whole mode & management to your Superior knowledge in the business. I readily acknowledge my own ignorance in the management of a business of this nature. But if my cla<im> is well founded agreeable to the present principals that govern the national Government, it would be hard that because I am remote from the sea<t> of Government & ignorant of my right should therefore be deprived of it. I hope your friendship for me & your Love of Justice will prevent my being injured in that way. If it be necessary should Send forward a written letter of Attorney to you or any person you shall nominate, if you will draw One & send it forward & point out the mode of authentication it Shall be complied with. My Petition may be entered and Laid on the files in the mean time if you think adviseable. I submit it myself & Petition into your hands and am yours, &c

(Signed) Lot Hall

[Enclosure]

Copy

Hon. Stephen R. Bradley

Dear Sir Westminster Jan. 15th. 1808

Observing with great Satisfaction that the present administration are determined to render Complete & perfect justice to all its citizens for Services performed in the revolutionary War notwithstanding the lapse of tim<e> and recollecting with greatfull emotion the kind and polite attention you were pleased to afford me in my en<d>eavours to obtain compensation for my Services performed the eary Stages of the revolutionary war. Concious that I have a just claim for two & twenty months wages as L<ieut.> of Marines in the Continental Navy, I have presumed to petition Congress, & ask for a participation in that renumative Justice that seem so <currently?> to disinguish their present conduct. You have very probably forgoten all the particular<s> that took place when I was at Philidelphia but fro<m> the interest I have always felt in this business it has always been by me kept fresh in view. You may recollec<t> that we went to the office of the Commissioners for adjust<ing> the claims, between the State of S. Carolina & the united Stat<es> that business was then retarded for some reason that I cannot now recollect. Therefore it was Judged prematu<re> to petition Congress that Mr. Huges & Mr. Butler then thot that I had so good a Claim on the State of S. Carolin<a> that they advised me to go forward & petition them as they said that their State would never take Shelter under any Statute of limitations, altho, Congress were then about doing it or actually had done it. You may likewise remember that in that office I found my name returned by Capt Robert Cochran as Luit of Marines and a prisoner — in short every thing agreeable to truth. I went into the office where the records of the Old Congress of 1778 were kept and there found my Old petition that I then presented to Congress for money to help carry me home but being very impatient to get home and Mr. James Lovell the member from Mass: who presented my petition offering to Lend me money to carry me home I abandoned my petition & it never was acted upon altho refered to the Marine Comee. all these particulars I have thot. best to remind you of as undoubtedly they have Sliped your mind. You will pardon me for thus troubleing you, and also the still further trouble I am afraid I shall be obliged to give you in the prosecution of this business. How this business will proceede? How it ought to be man[a]ged? I am ignorant & earnestly solicit your friendly advise and assistance as far as is consistant whether it is necessary I should have an agent on the spot? Whether it is inconsistant for you to act as my agent? Whether these matters ever undergo a reexamination before you[r] body after passing the house or not I am ignorant. Altho. I have drawn my petition & sent it forward yet I beg to submit the propriety of this whole business to the advise you and my other friends may be kind eno. to give me in this occasion. I was fearfull that by delaying the matter untill I had time to consult you & my other friends respecting this business it might injure my claim. Such is the confidence I have in your friendship & the other Gentleman I may in future address on this Subject that if upon the Statement of facts contained in my memorial I am intitled to relief I believe you will do every thing that is consistant to speed my claim. If I am not God forbid I should in a fool hardy mann<er> be impertenently troubling Congress or yourselves: what other proof can be necessary to support my memorial than the return of Capt Cochran into the Coms. office as to my entering the service of U.S. & my being taken it as to the time of my return from captivity my Old petition presented to Congress in 1778. if this is not satisfactory the records of the Gov. & Council of Virginia will show my exchange from on board the St. Albans, in Jany 1778. I Saw my Old Letter dated on board <ten> aflot, in their files & they voted to give me £50. & a public horse t<o> help me on my way home as far as York Town Pena. wh<ere> Congress then sit: a Copy of these records may easily b<e> procured. My

Petition! I know is lengthened out to a grea<t> length but I thot it best to be particular in Stating m<y> inlistment under Lieut. Paine his fraudulent attempt to pos[...] himself of One half the prizes in lieu of the State of S. Carolin<a> which certainly goes a great way to explain the reason why I never got my wages. You are personally knowing to my endeavours to obtain it in the winter of 1792 & that untill the liquidation of the Claim between the State of S. Caroli<na> & the U. States, I was then considered as having no claim o<n> the U.S. & as soon as that business was thro with: the old administration barred it with a Statute of Limitations. That Claim became a dead born One if any. If you can consist[...] take the agency of this business & will do it what ever is fit & proper on my part shall be done. If not & you will be so good as to nominate One for me & also I shall leave i<t> to your choice which of our members to present with my memorial to lay it before the house for me.

I hope I have not wrote any thing improper on this occasion. You know that I am now advanced in life have a family to support. If I can obtain the same Justice that is daily extended to others, it will be a great relief in my declining age — & believe me Sir: I shall be Wholly governed by your advise and opinion therefore shall anxiously wai<t> for a line with respect. I am yours.

(Signed) Lot. Hall

Tr (VtU). Margins obscured. Addressed, as copied by the transcriber, "Westminster Jany. 19th. / Free / The Hon Stephen R. Bradley Esq / Member of the Senate of the U.S. / Washington / Judge Hall's hand<writing>." Endorsed, as copied by the transcriber, "Lot Hall SRB's hand."

Note by WCB reads: "Westminster Vermont 8 Jan 1841 I William C Bradley of sd Westminster formerly a Member of Congress do hereby certify that in examining the paper<s> of my late father the Hon Stephen R Bradley deceased I this day for the first time discovered among them (the sd papers having been lodged with me as his Executor) the within letter of five pages comprized in two sheets written to him by the late Judge Lot Hall of this town. I was well acquainted with sd Judge having frequently seen him write & corresponded with him and have no doubt of the said letter being in his handwriting & that the words, "Lot Hall" were written thereon by my late father as the filing thereof when he placed it in the bundle from which it was taken by me Wm C Bradley.

"In addition to what I have above stated I would say that I frequently conversed with Judge Hall in relation to his sd claim and altho I do not now recollect the circumstance I have no doubt from my knowledge of him & his character & from the reference which he makes to me in his letter that the first sheet thereof was exhibited to me by him & that feeling at the time the justice of his application I did in the manner he states express my wishes for his success Wm C Bradley."

Notation by WCB on the enclosure reads: "Copy of letter from Judge Hall to SRB original <dld.> T H H. 31 Jan 41."

To Republican Members of Congress

SIR [Washington, 19 January 1808]

IN *pursuance of the power vested in me as president of the late convention of the Republican members of both houses of Congress, I deem it expedient; for the purpose of nominating suitable and proper characters for President and Vice President of the United States for the next Presidential election; to call a convention of the said Republican members, to meet at the Senate chamber of Saturday the 23d instant on 6 o'clock P.M. at which time and place your personal attendance is requested, to aid the meeting with your influence, information and talents.*

Dated at Washington, this 19th *day of January,* A.D. 1808.

S. R. BRADLEY.

Printed broadside (NcD: Bradley Family Papers).

From Edwin Gray

Sir, Washington City Jany 21st. 1808

Your Proclamation dated the 19th instant and addressed to me, has been received, and I take the earliest moment to declare my abhorrence of the usurpation of power declared to be vested in you — the mandatory style — and the object contemplated therein.

I deny that you possess the right of calling upon the Republican members of Congress, or others at this time and place, to attend a Caucus for the Presidential election.

You must permit me to remind you Sir, that it was a far different purpose for which my Constituents reposed their confidence in me. I will not consent either in an individual or representative capacity, to countenance by my presence, the midnight intrigues of any set of men, who may arrogate to themselves the right which belongs alone to the people, of selecting proper persons to fill the important offices of President and Vice President — nor do I suppose that the honest and unsuspecting people of these United States, can, much longer suffer in silence, so direct and palpable an innovation upon an important and sacred right, belong exclusive to them.

I am sir respectfully yr obt Ser

Edwin Gray

Honble. S. R. Bradley
Senator Unites States

ALS (NcD).

Jonathan Williams to Members of the U.S. Military Philosophical Society

SIR, WASHINGTON, January 23 1808.

There being now in this City a considerable number of the Members of the United States Military Philosophical Society, I think it my duty in conformity to the 3d Section of the 4th Chapter of the Constitution, to call an occasional meeting to be held at the first apartment on the right hand in the War Office, on Saturday Evening 30 Inst. for the purpose of stating to the members, who have not hitherto had an opportunity of meeting the Society, the motives which gave rise to the institution, its object, progress, and present state, together with an account of such communications as have been recently made to it.

Besides the reasons assigned, which have impelled me to this measure, it will be a circumstance of pride and pleasure to see so many respectable characters assembled, by whose good councils the Society may be directed to such measures as will in future facilitate the collection and dissemination of Military Science; and I hope I may anticipate the satisfaction each member will enjoy by a fraternal interview with his associates. This early notice is given to prevent previous engagement, and I trust that there will be a full and punctual attendance: The Chair will be taken at 7 o'clock precisely.

I have the honor to be,

Very respectfully,

Your most obedient servant,

Jona Williams[1] PRESIDENT U.S.M.P.S.

Printed broadside (NcD: Bradley Family Papers). Underlining indicates additions in Williams's hand.

1. Jonathan Williams, first superintendent of the U.S. Military Academy, organized the U.S. Military Philosophical Society at West Point in 1802, hoping to make it "the major scientific society in the country." Among the members

From Jabez Penniman

Dear Sir, Swanton Jany. 26th 1808

I have duly received your favours of the 23th and 27th. ult. by last mail, the latter of which was accompanied by Mr. C<uthbert's> Commission, as mids<h>ipman in the Navy; he is not at this place, but is daily expected at which time I shall deliver the Secretarys package to him.

I have been carefull to watch and make enquiries respecting the British Government in Canada and likewise of the opinion and feelings of the people and have only been able to learn that at Quebec they are proceeding in fortifying and making preperation for war but at St. Johns and Montreal no other preperations are making except an increase of men. The Common and Warlike Stores were principally removed to Quebec last fall which place they consider their strong hold or Girbralter. They have this fall sent on t<o> the lines about two miles from the Custom-house a Lieut: with about twenty men who are stationed at that place — but they have offered no disturbance to us.

This last fall every fifth man was ordered by G[...] to be drafted as recruits. Colo. Raighter whose Regiment lies abjoining our line and is composed principally of people from the States— made his draft — and when his men were called for — only five could be mustered of the whole number — having send <like divals> into this state — and the Americans there cannot be forced to fight against this Country — neither is it supposed the French or Canadia[n]s will — but with them much depends on the force sent and their first impression as they will undoubtedly Join the strongest party. In Montreal they were very much alarmed at the embargo and expected war immediately and of course to be conquored. The Irish, Scotch, and old Tories are clamorious against our Government — and say many <delicious> things of Mr. Jefferson — who has to bare all the blame — but as this is in Canada tis of no consequence.

Should war become necessary and an invasion attempted — prudence and policy would dictate that a respectable force be sent to Canada and that Spirit and determination should mark their proceedings — and the moment discover any thing hostile shall <claim> it my duty to give the earliest information. As the embargo does not include sleighs — large quantities of Pork and Grain are going in — and Salt in abundance is coming out.

I am — Dear Sir — with great respect and Esteem your obt Servt.

Jabez Penniman

Honl. S. R. Bradly Esqr.

Mrs. Penniman and family desire to be remember to you.

ALS (VtU). Margin obscured.

From William C. Harrington

Genl. Bradley

Dear Sir Burlington Feby 2nd 1808

I recd, Your favour of the 27th of last Decr., & should have answered sooner if my health had permitted, but I have been quite sick & just begin to get about <home> &c.

I have read the piece extracted from Bell[...] London paper & think it the most manly piece of composition on the subject of our dispute, that I have ever seen &c.

The embargo begins to be sensibly felt in this State, provisions of every kind find no market, business begins to be so stagnated that the people begin to feel alarmed. Many of the peopl<e> of this part of our State, have been obliged to sell their pork at Montreal for less than $5-pr. hundd. in order to meet their Contracts. There are many busybody's in this Country doing their best to render the Embargo unpopular, but the real friends to Government will not believe such doctrine — they think that our Administration are pursuing the best measures. My brethren *of the federalists* call me a democrat, because I think, & do not hesitate in declaring that Mr. Jeffersons Administration, has been as fine as either Washington's or Adam's. No man regreted Mr. Jeffersons election more than myself, which has Occasioned my attention to the course which he has pursued, & by this attention, I have become convinced of the purity of his motives, & the prudence with which he has conducted our publick affairs — & for me to withhold my opinion thus imbibed, would be doing injustice to my feelings &c. &c. &c.

The Government of Lower Canada are organizing the militia pretending to believe that the french Canadians will fight in the defence of the Province, but I may safely say that in case of a War — $5/6$ths of them will Join the Americans &c.

I have two Students in my office who are Young Gentlemen of publick education. One is a son of [...] Clark of Castleton, the other is a son of a Captain Johnson of this town. Mr. Clark has lately recd a Lieut's Commission in the U.S. Army.

And in case of War Mr. Johnson woul<d> willingly accept of an appointment & I assure You that he is a sprightly Young man, & will make a good officer — his Name is Lewis Johnson & I should feel please<d> in having You remember him in Your recommendations &c &c.

I hope that War will be avoid<ed> as it must prove an injury to both parties.

I hope Sir that You will find leisure moments enough to write me often, for there is no one in Congress that I corresspond with but Yourself.

I am respectfully Your Obt. servant

Wm. C. Harrington

ALS (VtU). Margin obscured. Addressed to SRB at Washington. Endorsed by SRB, "Coln. Harrington Burlington."

From Royall Tyler

Sir   Rutland February 10th. 1808

I did myself the honor of writing to you by the last mail upon a confid<en>tial subject. I must trouble you again at the request of Dr Shaw and other of your republican friends in this quarter, with whom you will please to include my honord associates on the Supreme bench.

We are informed through the medium of the Doctor that there is a vacancy in the bench of Judges in the Territory of Michigan and that our friend Judge Witherell is in nomination as a candidate that he has heretofore been nominated to supply a former vacancy — but that a preference was given to another possessd of the superior advantages of a legal education. If this should be the only objection to the judge on the present occasion and you esteem the opinion of the Judiciary of our State as likely to further his advancement you will have the goodness to state to the proper board That he presided with decorum as first Judge in the County of Rutland for several years — that he was approved by the gentlemen of the bar and by suitors and that the Judgments of that County Court during his presidency so far as they come under our view as a Court of appeals—were technically and substantially correct.

We are told that Mr Elliot proposes to resign in which case there will be many—if not hostile—contending candidates in our district. I think the States atty of Windham County will stand prominant and I have some reason to suppose he will eventually prevail—'tho I should not be surprized if the first vote is productive of no choice.

I shall by next mail write to Judge Robinson on the subject of Judge Witherell in the interem you can communicate this to him.

I hope soon to hear from you and more especially upon the subject of my last as the information requested is a matter of solicitude with some worthy people. With great Respect

Royall Tyler

Royall Tyler

ALS (VtU). Addressed to SRB. Endorsed by SRB, "Judge Tyler."

From William Eaton

Honorable General Bradley

Sir,   Boston Feb. 17th. 1808

I learn with a degree of certainty impressing belief that *Tobias Lear has rendered the United States by treaty compact, tributary to the contemptible regency of Tunis*—and this after our formidable display of naval force in his harbor—gasconade at his court—receiving his minister in our country and sending him back laden with testimonials of our *friendship*, and of our humiliation also!

When Lear went to the Barbary court in 1803 he had *secret instructions* to agree on a tribute with the Bey of Tunis: it was offered; and rejected. In 1804 those instructions were reversed: They may, perhaps, since have been revived. But whether he has acted discretionarily or with obedience, he has, in this concession, fixed one more stain on the honor of our nation. Experience has taught me that the Bey of Tunis is manageable: But he has penetration enough to discriminate between corruption and cowardice, and firm integrity; and he has cunning enough to take advantage of circumstances.

Lear's agency at Algiers has been a series of dishonorable concessions and accumulated sacrifices—And if Government will have the impartiality to investigate the causes and objects of the late Algerine *eight day war* they [...] find compromise if not corruption there.

But to return to Tripoli! There th[...]ter of our nation sunk from manly and firm int<eg>rity [...] pusilanimous duplicity and dastardly speculation [...] was no necessary course for this fatal fall [...] bargained it stands erect in *Govern*[...] while Hamet Bashaw, like our honor, per[...] wickedness. Is there justice here! Has the [...] better servants! Or must fr<aud> find [...] the cowardice which has had occasion [...] I say, there is a higher course for [...] because I am incapable of insincerity. There is nothing in this letter which you have not felt; and very little which you have not expressed — and I am firmly impressed with the confidence that the just sense of honor which has characterized your life will insure a concurrence of your opinion with the feelings I use the liberty here to express.

I have the honor to be very respectfully, Sir, your most obedient servant

William Eaton

Gen. Eaton was *five years* pursuing a claim for reimbursements of advances in favor of the government the justice of which had never been disputed and which ought to have been paid out of the treasury on demand. But, after waiting on four sessions of Congress, he obtained an order for adjustment — But no remuneration for the sacrifice of time and expense! Why — Because Alexander Murray is uncle to Albert Gallatin's wife; and Eaton had presented Murray to his Government and country for unofficer and ungentlemanlike conduct in the Mediterranean! And, what was more *uncourtly*, proved his allega<tions> [...]

[...] any man inform me why Captain <Nichols>on has been retained on the Navy establishment; or [...] been stationed eight years at the Navy yard; [...] pay and emoluments equal to $15000 P[er] [...]here he has litterally no services to render [...]ties to perform? Why? Because Nicholson [...]he Wife of Albert Gallatin; and Albert [...] hles money!

[...] Adams why he labored in the Senate to extenuate [...] and [*illegible*].

ALS (NcD). The bottom right corner of the MS is torn and its bottom edge is frayed and stained resulting in the loss of text.

From Elisha Tracy

Honlb. Stephen Roe Bradley Esqr

Dear Sir   Norwich (Connecticut) Feby 22nd. 1808

The civilities received from you while at Washington & a desire to make some inquiry respecting the state of business since I left there, perticularly as respects our prospect of adjusting our differences with foreign powers, has induced to trouble you with my correspondence; that we who are in a minority in Con[necticu]t have no means of communication but with Gentln. from other States is a fact so well known to you, that I trust it will be my apology; that an anxiety pretty generally pervades the minds of the citizens of the United States is certain, but agricultural interest seem verry generally to acquiesce in the embargo measure, the mercantile Interest being more generally *Federal* are more clamorous & of course more to be distrusted. I do trust & hope the measure will be persisted in untill Great Britain is brought to her senses, & a just estimation of our rights. With France we must take the consiquences hereafter but it would seem that the court of Saint James with France & her dependances & now Russia & all the North of Europe upon her, could & would not persist in provoking a Warr with us. If ever we are to make a treaty with them that will secure our Just rights, now is certainly the favourable moment, & I for one feel that a reliance may be placed in the United Wisdom of our Counsels to reasonably improve it. Warr is to be deprecated by all, but a line between that & free & friendly intercourse may be drawn that will be preferable to running the Gauntlet with our Commerce between the proclamations of the British King on one side & the Arrets of Saint Cloud on the other & if our affairs remain unsetled with England — will not a non importation act be thought of before the session closes. I ask you not for impropper disclosures I know you will Judge for yourself, but if the embargo is to continue as it now stands is there not danger that the country will be drained of specie it will be difficult to restrain our merchants from sending it away; there is not much patriotism in them. I hear much grumbling & complaining as well might be expected in Connecticut but I do not see much real distress for money when good security can be given for it. I beg you to excuse the liberty I have taken & to believe me to be with high Consideration of respect & much personal Esteem Dear Sir your humble s<ervt>

Elisha Tracy

ALS (VtU). Endorsed by SRB, "Elisha Tracy."

From Henry Dearborn

Sir   February 24th. 1808

In answer to your letter of the 22d. Instant[1]— I have to observe that by the latest returns, it appears that there are on hand, belonging to the Department of War, One Million and sixty seven thousand pounds of nitre, one hundred and ninety three thousand pounds of sulphur, and four hundred and ninety thousand pounds of gun-powder. In the event of a war nitre and sulphur would undoubtedly come much higher, than it may now be procured for. It is however believed that the former may be procured in the U:S. but not the latter. There have been some late offers of nitre for sale. It may be advisable to appropriate a sum of money for making purchases, altho' our present stock will probably be sufficient for, from two to three active campaigns. I am very respectfully, Sir, Your Ob: Servt —

H. Dearborn

Honorable
    Stephen R. Bradley

[Enclosure]

Munitions

		Cents
Appropriation for Navy Novr 24 1807 vol. 9 page 3 —	Item for ordinance and Military Stores	$310 554,60
ditto for the navy Febr 10 1808 — page 47	Items for Ordinance for Military Stores	50: 000: 0 9: 654 0
Appropriation for Army March 3 1808 page 58	Items for Ordinance for Tents	45:000: 0 20:000: 0
ditto for arming Abilities April 23 1808 page 120	an annual Sum of two Hundred thousand dollars making in April Either by purchase or manufacture <?> not restricted	400:000: 0
ditto for the support of additional <?> from april 25 1808 page 139	for ordinance	60:000: 0

Ditto for the Army March 3 1809 page 289	for ordinance	75:000: 0
for the navy Idem page 292	for ordinance and small arms	150:000
ditto for the navy the present Session	for ordinance and small arms	75:000
ditto for the Army	$1,194:654:60 Cents for ordinance 200.000 —	
<?> 11 1808	<?> for purchasing arms and salt peter	450:000 — 1.844 543 60
March 3 1808 March 3 1809	page 58 for Arsenals Armories &c 218:642 Magazines page 284 for Arsenals Armories &c 219,034 75 Magazines present session for arsenals Armories 283 574 75 magazines—	721.250 50 1 450:
	during the last Congress	2,565 905 10
	for completing fortifications &c 1,750:000	1,750:000 3 865 905 10 1 450 4,315,905.10
April 18 1806 Jany. 10 1807	Arsenals Magazines & Armories &c Arsenals magazines armories &c	218 542 5 218 542 5 721 250 50 1,158,334 60

ALS and enclosure (NcD: Bradley Family Papers). Cover addressed by Dearborn to "Honorable Stephen R. Bradley" and marked "War Dept"; docketed by SRB, "Genel Dearborn / salt peter &c."

1. Letter not found.

From Daniel Buck

General Bradley   27 Feby. 1808—

In the name of Heaven! What can our Executive be about? Spooner[1] in his last paper says "By information from the seat of Government as late as the 5th. inst. we learn that an accommodation with G — B — was so far progressed, to the satisfaction of our government, that the Secretary of the Navy has informed the Chairman of the Committee on Naval affairs, that the 1272 men, voted the other day to man the gun boats, *will not be* wanted."

My God! Is it possible that our Government should think of an accommodation with

England while the War continues between her and France? What then will be our situation? Our commerce must be protected by the British Navy. This leads directly to an alliance offensive and defensive, and of course to a War with all Europe. In less than one year the Court of St. James, following the example of the King of Portugal, must be transferred to Hallifax. We shall then have the house of Hanover on the North, and France and Spain on the South. Deprived of the Mississippi and St. Laurence, and for ever cut off from the *Fisheries* and *Fur Trade*; cramped up between two formidable powers, and controled by a British Navy: we shall be placed like the Dwarf by the Giant; entangled in an eternal War with all the World, except the bulldogs of Britain, whom we must support and feed, for the notable privilege of bearing their insu[l]ts, and the hard knocks of all their enemies.

Forbid it Heaven! Genius of America! Ghost of Washington! Federalists! Nay ye Republicans forbid it! I will not believe a word of it, untill confirmed by hand and Seal, from the highest authority. And then by G—I will rant and rave, curs<e> and swear, Dam Jefferson and all such timid, old maiden, Republican policy; Deny my country, and flee to Boneparte, or to some solitary and sequestred corner of the earth, where the name of America, shall never again wound my ear.

If our Government can become the mediator between France and England, bring about a general peace, and G—B—will make concessions to the extent of our demands! Amen! But for God sake do not patch up a partial peace; that will be ten thousand times worse than the hotest rage of War; and indeed, instead of avoiding protract it. America is now on high ground. The existance of the British government now rests on us. That life, which by her crimes she has ten thousand times forfeited, is now in our hands, and she is completely at our mercy. By availing ourselves of the present state of France and England, we may extend our power, not only from the Atlantic to the Pacific, but from the Gulf of Mexico to the North Pole, and place America on ground, that will enable us to form a balance against all Europe, even if directed by the energies of a Boneparte. Never had men such a glorious opportunity as our present administration, they may immortalize their names, and bring upon their memory the blessings of unborn Millions if they now conduct with firmness and Wisdom. Is it possible that they should over look those important advantages and by pursuing a narrow, contracted, and timid policy, cramp, shackle and hamstring the Nation! For God sake raise a tempest in the Senate against such policy, that will shake the foundations of Nature! call up the Ghosts of departed heroes & patriots! and make the Executive to stand aghast!

You will see a piece of mine Entitled "War and Wisdom Now." I dare pledge my life that three forths of the people in Vermont will accord to them sentiments. I intended to have followed it up by an expostulatory address to Federalists; but if you are going to patch up an hobling peace, I have done! *And the Lord have mercy on your souls!*

I have the Honour to be with very great Respect Your most Obedt. and Humbe. Sert.

D. Buck[2]

Honble Stephen R. Bradley Esqr

ALS (NcD: Bradley Family Papers).

1. Alden Spooner was editor of the weekly *Vermont Journal* in Windsor between 1783 and 1818 (Brigham, *History and Bibliography of American Newspapers*, 2:1099).

2. Daniel Buck (1753–1816) was a member of the Vermont house of representatives in 1793 and 1794 and again in 1806 and 1807. He was elected as a Federalist to the Fourth Congress (1795–1797) and served as attorney general of Vermont in 1802 and 1803.

From Reuben Attwater

Honbl. Stephen R. Bradley Esqr.

Dear Sir Westminster March 3d. 1808

Your letters of the 17th. & 19th. of Feby last I received the 1st. Instant have observed the contents, and consider myself under Obligations to you for your friendship to me which I am fearful I shall not be able to reward you for, but if in my power should be happy to. The appointment to the Office of Secretary, Commissioner & Collector which you have procured a Nomination for me to fill is very handsome and the Salary good and as I have concluded to accept of the appointments shall make every laudable exertion in my power to discharge the duty attached to them provided the Senate should confirm the nomination. I have been confined for a week with an Inflammatory sore throat at the time I recd your letters I had not been out am now better my Brother Russell has been sick two weeks he is now better will leave me soon. I am in hopes you enjoy good health & will return home to your family which must be pleaseing after spending the Winter at Washington attending to the business of our National Goverment. If I should receive the appointment it will not be in my power to leave here for Detroit as soon as it would have been if I had not been confined but will go as soon as I can leave my small Family in a comfortable situation & arrange my other business. Mrs. Attwater's & My Brother send respects.

With sentiments of Esteem and respects your friend

Reuben Attwater

ALS (VtU).

From Jabez Penniman

Dear Sir. Swanton March 15th. 1808

I perceive by the papers that Congress have a bil<l> before them for increasing the standing force of the United States in order to protect the frontiers mor<e> securely. I hope our Government will not be insensable of the exposed situation of the northern part of Vermont and especially on Lake Champlain which opens the most important communication of any on the frontier and which is subject to outrages both by our own Citizens and their subjects—in consequence of not having a small armed force station<ed> at or near the line—not far from the Custom-Hous<e>.

And since the Embargo I fear more diffi<c>ulty then I have heartofore experienced as Yan<k>ee invention will be exerted to evade the Laws and smuggle Merchandize into Canada.

Since the report of an Embargo on sleig<hs> carriegs and rafts, every exertion has been made to transport Pork and Pot-Ashes to Canada and the raftsmen are outragious—and the slow progress of legal proceedings will never stop men of their feelings that have many of the<m> Embarked their all on board of their rafts and say they may as well die one way as the other.

There will be this Spring not less than two hundred men employed on board of rafts and it is not only necessary to make Laws but it is surely [**is there a page missing here?**] ning.

It has been given out in speeches by the owners of rafts that they have contracts to deliver their rafts at Winmill-Point and will likely take [*illegible*] accordingly—but when there means will be taken by people from Canada to carry them by and no force can stop them with a strong south wind.

If Government consider it of consequence to have a Law of this nature — You will at once perceive that it will require something more then mear sound to put it in operation — an armed force is absolutely necessary. Perhaps one Company stationed part in Alburgh and part on the west side of the Lake on the Shore will have all the effect.

I pray you — Sir — will be pleased to State these facts to the Secretary for his consideration. I have been led to make these observation at this time in consequence of a letter which I have received this day from Judge Robinson — which gives me reason to believe all intercourse will shortly be stoped —*by Law* and I hope to be enabled to see it fully executed.

Permit me to flatter myself with the hope of a line from you.

I am — Dear Sir — with great respect your obt. Servt.

Jabez Penniman

Hon S: R: Bradley Esqr.

ALS (VtU). Margin obscured. Note on the back side of the cover reads: "The non Intercourse act will be a serious evil to man<y> in this quarter — as great preperations has been made for Pot-Ashes and Rafting — for which money only is brought back in return."

To Thomas Jefferson

Sir   Washington March 16th. 1808

Immediately upon being acquainted That Mr Atwater would be nominated Secretary of the Territory of *Michigan* &c I wrote him on the subject to know whether he would accept thereof — And have the Honor to inform you that I received Mr Atwater's Answer Yesterday, that he has concluded to accept if appointed, and will be ready to go on, as soon as he shall receive official notice of his appointment — the reason of the nomination being delayed in the Senate is owing to a doubt expressed by some whether the office is vacant it not being noted that the former Secretary is removed.

Accept the Assureance of my high respect & Esteem

S. R. Bradley

The President of the U.S.

ALS (NjP).

From Elisha Tracy

Honlb. Stephen R: Bradley Esqr.

Dear Sir   Norwich (Con[necticu]t) March 16th 1808

Your verry friendly & polite Letter of the 6th Ins<t.> has been received with much pleasure & a continuance of such favours will at future convenient opportunity be highly gratifying to me.

I am now about to take the liberty to request that throug<h> You the Bearer Mr Jesse Brown of this Town may be enab<led> to make application to the President of the United States or such other officer or branch of Government as may be by Law authorised to grant the relief he wishes.

Mr Brown is one of the House of Jesse Brown & Son they have been verry largely concerned in a trade to Martinique & I am fully persuaded have a large amount of propperty remaining there in the hands of their consignees, (& no Vessel there to bring it away) for want of which they have lately stopped payment & involved many of *their friends*; it is understood here that provision has lately been made by act of Congress to enable Citizens of the United States by a propper application to obtain liberty <of> sending abroad a Vessel in Ballast for the purpose of bringing home their propperty to avail themselves of this license, is at this time the bussiness of Mr. Brown at Washington.

A considerable sum is due or owing from them to the United States on Duty Bonds & I am verry apprehensive that unless some relief be obtained from this propperty now abroad, that the surety's will not be able to meet the demands; & on a full view of this case (free from any personal interest or biass) I am fully persuaded it is one of those meant to be provided for by the verry act said to be passed. Your advice & assistance to Mr. Brown will be suitably acknowledged by Dear Sir Your friend & humble servt

Elisha Tracy

ALS (VtU). Margin obscured.

Senate Proceedings: Appointment of a Committee to Report on the Business of the Present Session

IN SENATE
OF
THE UNITED STATES.

MARCH 17th, 1808.

MR. BRADLEY submitted the following motion for consideration:

* * *

Resolved, That a committee be appointed, to join such committee as the House of Representatives may appoint on their part, to consider and report what business is necessary to be done by Congress in the present session, and when it may be expedient to close the same.

Microform, U.S. Government Library.

From Satterlee Clark

Honble. S. R. Bradley Esquire,

Sir, Castleton 24th March 1808

Although I have not the honor of a personal acquaintance with you, yet, from a knowledge of the dignified and Republican character, which you sustain, no apology for this liberty appears necessary.

By the latest accounts from the seat Government, we learn that Congress is about to raise several Regts. of troops for the defen<ce> of our country. Conscious that in making the appointments the President must rely on the recommendations of the most intel<l>igent members of the National legislature, and knowing that his Excellency places great confidence in your honor's opinion, I have presumed to request the exercise of the influence which you have justly acquired, to promote the Son of a Revolutionary Soldier. I have been induced to make this request, by the friendly assurances of your Son, Wm. C. Bradley Esq. to whom I have written upon the subject. I am now a Lieut. of Artillerists in the service of the U. States, and destined to New Orleans. I wish to be transfered to the Command of a Company of

Infantry in one of the Regts. which are to be raised. My acquirements in Military science are known at the War Office, as I have been three years a Cadet. With respect to my other qualifications, please to enquire of Messrs Robinson, Witherell and Chittende<n> who are all acquainted with me. I can boast of no Military achievments which entitle me to patronage, because I never had an opportunity to serve my country in the field.

If Sir, upon enquiry respecting my character, my abilities, and my Republicanism, you can, consistent with your duty to the public, procure me a Captain's Commission, with the privilege of raising a Company of Green Mountain boys, it shall be my constant endeavour to conduct in such a manner as will do honor to my patron and give satisfaction to my country.

I have the honor to be, Sir, with the highest respect Your Obt. Servant

Satterlee Clark

Honble. Stephen R. Bradley Esq.
ALS (VtU). Margin obscured.

From Thomas Munroe

Sir   Post Office Washington City 24th. March 1808

I am honored with your letter of yesterday,[1] and am very sorry to hear of the unaccountable delay and irregularity in the conveyance of your Letters. My register shews that we have regularly mailed on Mondays & fridays (according to my instructions from the General Post Office) a great number of Letters addressed "Vermont Eastern" and my recollection as well as those of the Clerks in the Office enable us to swear, if necessary, that many letters franked by you have been sent therein. This, Sir, is all that I could do; but if there be any other way of sending them from this Office, which will prevent the inconvenience you have such just cause to complain of it will afford me much Satisfaction to execute directions to that effect; and I beg leave, Sir, respectfully to assure you that, altho' something, not entirely unavoidable, appears to have happened to your letters I believe nothing culpable attaches to this Office. I have enquired at the General Post Office whether our making up the "Vermont Eastern" mails oftener than twice a week, or on days, other than Mondays & fridays, will facilitate the conveyance, and was answered in the negative. I can only repeat, Sir, that I very much regret the delays which have taken place, and will cheerfully do any thing in *my* power to prevent them in future.

I Have the honor to be very respecty. Sr, Yr Ob Servt

Thomas Munroe

Honble S. R. Bradley
ALS (DLC).
1. Letter not found.

From Nathan Smith

Respected Sir,   Hanover March 24th 1808.

Your favour[1] in reply to my application in behalf of G. C. Shattuck,[2] has been received.

I return you my sincere thanks for your exertions in his favour; being fully satisfied, that it was impossible for you to serve him in that instance.

I am happy, however, to learn, that Doct. Shattuck has the present year obtained two medals from the committee of Harvard University, thereby proving himself worthy of the exertions and esteem of those, who have interested themselves in his behalf.

I hope you will afford him your countenance, at any future time, if an opportunity to assist him present[s].

I am, Sir, with greatest respect, Yours &c

Nathan Smith

Hon. S. R. Bradley L L.D.

<small>ALS (NcD: Bradley Family Papers).
1. Letter not found.
2. Letter not found.</small>

From Ethan A. Allen

Sir, Fort Constitution March 29. 1808.

As honor, glory and the service of their country are the principal spring which animate the Soldiers bust, I have so far presumed to transgress on your goodness as to trouble you with this, and hope you will excuse me.

As there is some Cavalry to be raised, and in that Corps I think the young Soldier has the best chance to signalize himself, and as I have had an offer very flattering to me to join I shall be much obliged to your honor to give me some advice respecting it.

Capt. Walbach who is my Commanding Officer expects to be transfered to the command of the Cavalry and requests me to accompany him. He promises to procure for me the appointments of first Lieut. and Adjutant of the Regiment; but I am somewhat afraid the Cavalry will in a short be disbanded altho perhaps some part of it may be continued. As a military life suits me best of all others & I should be left to chance were I to be disbanded I know not what to do. In the Cavalry I should be a Capt. as soon as a first Lt. in my present Corps, & if you will be so good as to give me some surity of my being continued you will add another obligation to the many I already owe you and much oblige your very humble Servt.

Ethan A Allen
2 Lt. US. Arty.

Honble. Stephen R Bradley Esqr.

<small>ALS (VtU).</small>

From Theophilus Harris

Sir, Philadelphia April 1st. 1808

Tho' I have but once had the pleasure of being in your company and that several years ago I take the liberty of applying to you for information respecting Nathanl. Chipman and Harry Chipman of the State of Vermont, I believe they live in or near Charlestown in that state. I wish to be inform'd respecting their characters, their responsibility, their pursuits and their property, I do this the more particularly because I have a considerable interest depending, and I take the liberty of applying to you for information, because I conceive I am applying to a gentleman and man of honour upon whose information I may place the most implicit reliance. I should be glad also to be inform'd respecting a Mr. James H. Bingham his place of residence I do not know. As a fellow Citizen and brother Democrat you will I doubt not pardon this liberty, and you will confer an obligation by your early attention to the inquiries if in your power, and it will always give me extreme pleasure to return the obligation in any manner in my power, hoping for the favour of your answer I beg leave to subscribe myself, Sir, your Mot. obedt. Servt.

Theophilus Harris.

Please to direct to Theophilus Harris Philadelphia

ALS (VtU). Addressed to SRB in Washington. Endorsed, "Theophilus Harris Philadelphia."

From Jabez Penniman

Dear Sir,   Swanton Aprill 8th 1808

I recd: yours of the 19th Ult with much pleasure—am extremly gratified to lear<n> that our government has acted the manly and Pacific part and that British intrig<ue> and cunning is once more defeated. From the documents and correspondance I expect the public mind will be satisfied which has been much agitated from the long suspence. I think Mr. Trigg and *Jonny* will be a little chop-fallen after answer to their Manifesto. The Printer at St. Albans will publish the substance of both.

I am informed that the Governmen<t> of Canada are very much e[n]gaged in organizing the militia—raising new troops and companies of Calvary. One company of troops are now stationed within about one mile of the line. Permit me to enquire if our government do not think of making some preparation to defend this northern frontier in case of a prospect of war. From an enquiry I am led to believe that one company could not be furnished with arms and ammunition in these two northern counties—in case of invation we should be in a wretched [*illegible*]. And there is nothing to hinder three hundred men going to Burlington and distroying all before them—unless we attacked them Bonaparte like—with pitchforks and fire brands.

I am with great respect your obt. Servt.

Jabez Penniman

Honbl. S. R. Bradly Esqr.

ALS (VtU). Margin obscured.

From Jabez Penniman

Dear Sir,   Swanton Aprill 10th 1808

A Maj: <S̶a̶k̶s̶?̶> who lives in Canada and belongs to the Militia of that Government has been with me this day to endeavour to con[...]t some measures to prevent vagrant fellow<s> from plundering the inhabitants on each side of the line in case of war; which he believes is determined on. He is an honest Dutchman and has very candidly told me that an express went in from the British Minister to the Govenor with information that no treaty would be made. About the midle of March he has shortly since returned from Montreal—and says that the Govener has lately made a communication to the House of Assemble the contents he did not learn he says they are raising two Regiments of standing troops a number of companies of Cavalry and rapidly organizing the Militia. That they have now about seven thousand standing troops—that ten or twelve thousand more are expected as early as the spring will admit them up the River and that about ten thousand are now at Nova Scotia.

This looks hostile indeed. Will our Government patiently wait till they actually come and drive us from our Country? I told the Majr. <S̶a̶k̶s̶?̶>, that I hoped his Government would not permit the Indians to come out, — his reply was, that they would not, unless, they were heard pushed, in that case they would in the upper Country.

I am — Dear Sir — with much respect your obt. Servt.

Jabez Penniman

Honbl. S. R. Bradley Esqr.

If I have stated any thing which our Government is not apprised of — you will please to make such use of it as you think proper. I have erased the name for fear this might become public and get to Canada and he Suffer.

ALS (VtU). Margin obscured.

From Elisha Tracy

Honlb Stephen R: Bradley Esqr.

Sir   Norwich (Con[necticu]t) April 10th 1808

Your several Inclosures have been duly received & your poli<te> attention is duly appreciated. The correspondence with England se<ems> to have carried Iresistable conviction even to the minds of *honorable Federalist*. I regret that it had not appeared in Massachusets previous to their Election; tho there is no danger as respects its event, but it would have varied the majority. Messrs. *Madison* & *Munroe* have both increased their laurels & added to their diplomatic celeb<rity> Champagny's Letter has also appeared & must confirm even the wavering in favr. of an Embargo—& the promptness with which that Letter has been publickly Communicated ought to convince evry one that no reserve with respect to communications from the French Goverm<ent> has been practised by our Administation. An attempt is making to impress the public mind with the Idea that this Letter had been long si<nce> received but I take it from a Letter I received a day or two ago from o<ne> of my friends at Washington it is verry recently received.

What measures can or ought be adopted on so momentous an occasion no <one> can Judge well of but him who has a full view of the whole ground. Perhaps a non Importation Law might alarm Great Britain. I am not without hopes that a change of ministry has taken place there which event if realised must be verry favourable to our prospects of adjustment. Happy am I in feeling a full confidence in the talents, integrity & Wisdom of our national Councils. At the request of the Marshall of this State I beg leave to remark that the emoluments of his office are totally inadequate to his support & it is thought here that something more than meerly few as an Officer ought to be given him. Our Lawers are nearly all Federal & purposely avoid bringing suits to the United States Courts, so that the bussiness is meerly nothing perhaps some small salary may be thought propper & I believe would meet general aprobation here. With suitable apology for the libertys I have taken I beg you to accept of assurances of the high consideration of respect & Esteem with which I am Dear Sir your friend & humble servt

Elisha Tracy

ALS (VtU). Margin obscured.

From L. Royse

Much Respected Friends   Hartford July 6th 1808

Altho in thus addressing you I feel Myself inadequate to the language of comfort or condolance yet I can Sympathize with & do most sincerely pity your sorrows for the loss of a darling Child on whom you had plac'd your fondest hopes. He is suddenly torn from your arms & all your expectations in him blasted in the bud. Alass! we are ready to say where was the arm that could have rescued him — & why was he not witheld. We ask — but who can answer. Almighty Wisdom had otherwise ordered. His thread of life was measured & his bounds were set. He is taken in innocence from a World of trouble & He who called will have him in his holy keeping — & he has given us his word That of such is the kingdom of Heaven. I hope & pray you may have consolation from this blessed assurance. Stella & Adeline were informed of the malencholly event as tenderly as possible before we gave them your letter — dated from Suffield — as we learnt by the driver what intelligence it contain'd. Their grief was at first violent & extreme — but they have borne it better than I feared they would & tho they sincerely mourn the loss of their dear Brother they are now calm & more resign'd & as much reconcil'd as we could expect. I recd a Letter from you sir on Sunday morn by Mr John's — in which you mention having previously written to Stella. That letter with the Money — & one for Adeline & one from Mr. W. Bradley for Stella & a Box of apples have all come to hand this morning. We have purchased mourning for them & had such made as will answer for the present — say Bonnets frocks Stockings Gloves Vandykes &c — but as they will want more shall get some colour'd for them which tho they will not be as handsome or durable will do for common wear. Stella mention'd a black silk left by her Mamah which from her description our Mantaumaker thinks will make each of them a handsome frock if it could be sent on — & as black silk grows rotten by lying perhaps it will be best for them to have it now. But should you think otherwise hope you will write by next mail & we will not purchase any others until we hear. Stella & Adeline both wish Me to give you thir best affections Stella says she cannot write at present but begs you to be reconciled. They are very well wish you not to send for them by any means — as they had much rather not return until September — unless it would be a comfort to you — if so they would come. They wish to say more — but know not what to say to alleviate your distress. Stella will write as soon as she feels she can write calmly — at present she does not — & I will write for her till she can. Mamah — Uncle George & Mrs. Chenevard wish you all the consolation of Heaven to support you in your affliction. Stella sends a little transcript of some lines which she has found in a Magazine — & thinks they are applicable. She says she will try to write them herself.

 Stella & Adeline desire Me to remember their thanks for the Apples &c. I beg you will accept My best wishes for your health & that you may be comforted & supported in the day of affliction & depend I will omit nothing that may comfort & console the dear Girls intrusted to My care & believe Me to be Respectfully & Gratefully yours

L Royse

Hon. S. R Bradley & Mrs Melinda Bradley

> How transient is each sublunary joy
> How insufficient every human trust
> The skill of man could'nt save the fav'rite boy
> Nor save his mixing with the common dust
>
> Yes Stephens gone! the finest sweetest child
> His father's darling and his mothers boast
> The worlds great wonder — spotless — undefiled
> But oh alas! the precious jewel's lost!
>
> Did I say lost? No I might better say
> He's far far happier than he was before
> He now can dwell where sacred angels stay
> And think of sorrow and of pain no more
>
> Rest blessed shade! thy justly envied urn
> The prospect of thy everlasting peace

> Mig[h]t make the fondest parent cease to mourn
> And bid the stream of sorrow—calmly cease

A gift of consolation

from Stella

ALS (VtU). Addressed to SRB at Westminster. Poetry transcribed by Stella Bradley.

From Sylvester Day

Dear Sir   Detroit July 8: 1808.

Permit me to tender you my warmest acknowledgments for the many favours I have received from your friendship: a friendship probably arising more from a long and uninterrupted intercouse with my Parrients, than from any particular attachment to m<e> who has not had the pleasure of that intimate acquaintance. From whatever cause this friendship arrises I hope sir you never will have cause to regret or suspect it is undeservedly bestowed.

The Letter you had the goodness to give me to the Honble. Secretary of War I lost no time in presenting and to it I attribute my change of station, a change perfectly to my wishes. I am here surrounded by my N. England friends whose society and friendship can not be too highly appreciated by me. At the head of this list stands his Excellency the Governor who has reconciled the contending factions of this Territory to his mild Administration; the Secretary of the Territory whose affability has secured to him that confidence and respect which his merit deserves: Judge Whitherell, et. at.—— Presuming my repeated solicitiations for your aid will be no burthen I will again freely state to you my request and the reasons for making it. Through your influence I wish to obtain the appointment of surgeon in the army. The reasons for making this application so soon after entering into the service I will explain.

1st. It is the opinion of the secretary of War that surgeons mates have no claim to rank or promotion from their long service.

2nd. There are two vacancies of surgeons in the [*illegible*] Establishment to which I belong which mus<t> be filled by some Gentlemen of the Profession.

3. We have two companies now here & two man a<re> expected to be stationed at this post therefore a Surgeon will undoubtedly be Ordered here.

If you will have the goodness to write to secy of War on the subject and use your influence for me I think I shall succeed. Governor Hull will write for me & others but my dependence is on you.

You will please to make the earliest enquiry respec<ting> the business on your arrival at Washington if the resu<lt> be not know before & communicate the same to me.

A Letter from you at any time would be greatf<ully> received. I remain Sir your Devoted humbl<e> Servant

                                                                                 Syl. Day.

ALS (VtU). Margin obscured. Addressed to SRB at Westminster.

From Alden Spooner

Hon S R Bradley
Sir,   Windsor, July 28th. 1808

I hope your irrecoverable loss will not prevent your attending to the business proposed, at Windsor, as soon as possible, consistent with you<r> own convenience. Had I have known the trouble and cost which will <occure?> in the business before I engaged, in it, I should have left the *thing* to its own course. But I did not believe that it took so much more trouble to put a person out of office who *professes* to be a Republican, though a <menace?> in society, than an honest federalist. Had the P. U. S. ordered him to have published his letters in my paper, as he proposed, it would have settled the business; for he has told some of his friends, that if such an order should be sent him, he would resign before he would co<m>ply. Good Republicanism. Your very Humble servt

Alden Spooner

ALS (VtU). Margin obscured. Endorsed by SRB, "Alden Spooner."

From Stella C. Bradley

Hartford July 29th 1808

Painful as my feelings are at present I will summon up [...] my fortitude & address my Afflicted Parents.

It has pleased an all seeing God <to> take from us our dear little brother while we poor miserable m<or>tals are left to bewail a kind & affectionate brother & a [...] companion. The Bishop of this church is expected in t[...] next week & several of the family intend to receive the right of Confirmation & it is was so good an opportunity Mrs. Royse thought you would wish to have us improve it. Please to write me an answer to this before that time. I was very glad to hear that brother William & his wife were coming down with you in September I wish they would fetch little R[...] I set more by him than ever.

Adeline joins with me in love to [...] Parents & wishes me to inform them that she expects M[...]as letter. Mrs Royce desires her respects to you. I have only to add that myself & sister enjoy very good heal<th.>

While I remain as ever your affectionate Daug<hter>

Stella C Bradley

ALS (VtU). Margin obscured.

From L. Royse

Respected sir Hartford Augst 1808

I perhaps ought to apologise for not writing before in answer to the very generous proposal made Me in Your Letter to Stella of the for which I must beg you to accept My sincere acknowledgments & I shall ever retain a high sense of the obligation. But I will candidly state to You sir the existing reasons which for the present must compel Me to decline giving a definite answer.

I find from experience that My health suffers much from close application & the confinement of a school insomuch that I dare not come under an obligation to keep steadily & as the establishment of a regular school would undoubtedly be the wish of those who would so generously exert themselves in My behalf — this of course would be an objection with them — & this has been an inducement for Me to engage in part to undertake some other business as soon as the Embargo is taken off. I would wish it for the present not be mention'd but that of setting up a Millenary & fancy goods store in Pittsfield Mass in March last I went there on this business alone — & concluded that should the Embargo be taken of[f] this fall to go there.

I am sensible an offer like Yours has full claim to an unconditional answer yet I could wish to have it postpon'd for a few weeks—as if I am under the necessity of attending to a school any where I should prefer going to Westminster & should be happy to give a more decided answer in that time. I feel satisfied that Your goodness will allow every apology for this request—and I will write again as soon as I possibly can—on the subject.

Stella & Adeline are very well & desire to be affectionately remember'd. I beg leave to unite the respects of our Family with My own to Mrs. Bradley & Yourself & I am sir—with a sense of Obligations Respectfully Yours

L. Royse

ALS (VtU). Addressed to SRB at Westminster.

From Hamet Caramelle

Honorable General Bradley

Sir,   Dated Syra (supposed) case, Aug 23d. 1808

If I have not rendered all the services to my country which my friends had a right to claim it is because my volitions and my exertions have been checked by speculation and perfidy, the influence of which I could neither control nor resist. Something I am conscious however of having performed. I claim the merit of your peace, bad as it is, with Tripoli. And the time is not far distant when all men, who chuse to see, will see that if you have not at this moment a civil war it is because I did expose a project of treason which would have embraced more traitors than suspicion itself now implicates, if it had not been for my exposure. I can reflect on no instance of my public duties where either considerations of ease, of fortune or of life have interfered with my pledges of honor and loyalty. I thought I had claims on the confidence of my countrymen; at least so far as to be heard when I solicit for a prince of whose credulity they have profited, and who has been ruined by his credulity. Every sigh of Hamet Bashaw sinks deeply on my soul; and he breathes nothing but sighs! Dare we ask God to prosper us while evidence of our neglect to solemn treaty lives in public view of the world? Have Government lost sight of *justice*, of *integrity*, of *honor*! Shall an apostate, detected of fraud, imposition and treachery against the confidence of his country bask in its patronage, while the man whom his duplicity has reduced to wretchedness remonstrates to unfeeling speculation and prays to insensibility? And is it my duty, witness as I am of this injustice <to> countenance the powers who countenance it? No Sir, except I see liberal justice rendered towards Hamet Bashaw, & merited punishment inflicted on the speculator Lear, I shall feel myself justified in exposing some documents to my country concerning Barbary affairs which shall stagger the devotion of the uninformed to existing administration. The man who will connive at fraud shall sit uneasy, even on a throne, where I am a subject. I was willing to believe, and did charitably believe, that contradictory reports from men equally entitled to his confidence suspended the President's opinion concerning facts, until I knew that he had seen Lear's hand and seal to the testimony of his fraud. I am now compelled to think differently concerning the patronage given him. Why seek to conceal his iniquity with secret injunction & closed doors? There must be a hidden reason for this carefulness to hide his compromise of our national honor. Had I been guilty of his perfidy the stamp of infamy would have been deeply branded on my forehead and in the palms of both my hands; and justly! What has Tobias Lear done to entitle him to an exemption from responsibility? If the Executive have sound reasons for shielding him in duplicity amounting to fraud, I have a right to know those reasons. I shall demand them in a manner which will require an answer. I have not yet suffered under the obligation of patronage—+ have not touched a sincecure **P**—nor smelt the perfumes of Constantinople **H**: There can be therefore between the Executive & me no mutual pledges; and of course no violation on my part of plighted faith. Whatever of obligation I feel goes to my *Country*; and the duties resulting from this allegiance shall be discharged without respect to *men*. I apprise you, Sir, of my intentions, as I have the President.

[Page possibly missing here.]

    I am unchangeably & profoundly respectful

                                   (signed)   Hamet Caramelle

                                               Son of Ali, Bashaw of Tripoli

Genl. Eaton   (seal)

    Tr (CSmH).

From Rufus Hatch

Respected Sir,   Pine Ville (S. C.) October 12th 1808

    Some time ago, I wrote to Govr. Brigham of Vt., and requested him, if possible, to obtain for me a Commission of Captain or 1st. Lieutenancy in the Army now raising for the service of the U.S. he has since informed me, that he had, at present no influence with the Secretary of War; but, that he would solicit your patronage, to assist me in obtaining one, I believe likewise that my Brother (Major Hatch) has, either seen or wrote you on the subject. My ruling passion has ever been for a Military life; and nothing, but, my most eager desire to get a Commission in the forces now raising for the service of my Country, could have induced me, unknown as I am, to you, to have troubled you with this. I am fully sensible, that you will thoroughly investigate the Character and abilities of any one, before you patronize him, in obtaining a Commission; should you, however, from information you may obtain from my friends, in Vermont be able consistantly, to speak in my behalf, I shall ever remember it, with the most heartfelt gratitude, and it will ever be my highest ambition to merit you friendship and my Countries' confidence.

    Robert Marion Esqr who will deliver this to you, has been acquainted with me for near two years past, and I would beg leave to refer you to him, for my Conduct during that period.

    I could hope, you would answer this, as early as convenient, as I expect to leave this, for Vermont in about two Months.

    I have the honour to be Dr sir with great respect your Most Obedt.

                                                                               Rufus Hatch.

    ALS (VtU). Addressed to SRB at Washington.

From T. Hutchinson

Sir   Montpelier Novr. 5th. 1808

    We have chosen our electors—our Ticket succeeded by a majority of eleven. They are— Israel Smith, Jonas Galusha, John White, Samuel Shepardson, James Tarbox, and William Cahoon. We have some squabling in our elections. The feds try to run out every Republican. We however have yet been very successful in balloting, except in your County in the cases of Judge Campbell and Judge Chapin. The Governors speech was the tocsin of rebellion. Possibly the answer may prevent its happening. I wish to interest you in behalf of Major Brown of

Windsor who woud be glad of a Captns. commission in the army raising. Larned Lamb of this town was nominated by the President, and now commands a Company stationed at Burlington under Col. Whiting. For reasons well known to and realized, by our friends Jonn. Robinson, James Fisk and Saml Shaw, I presume the Senate will not approve of the appointment of Lamb. Of course that place will be vacant. The two Lieuts. and Ensign under Lamb are so young men — I have no idea that either of them will expect promotion untill their appointments are sanctioned and they wear their commissions awhile. I have no doubt but they will be pleased with the appointment of Brown as their Captn.

I presume you are acquainted with Major Brown. He was a while cryer of the Circuit Court — Is now & for several years has been a Justice of the Peace. He is quite a military man. Not far different from thirty five years of age. His name is Return Bryant Brown. He is a firm Republican, and as such has labored long in the circumscribed Vineyard allotted him. Shou'd Lamb not obtain a Commission or shou'd another vacancy happen — your Influence in his behalf will confer a favor on him and, thro him, on Your Humble Servant

T. Hutchinson

Honl. S R Bradley Esqr.

ALS (VtU). Addressed to SRB at Washington.

Senate Proceedings: Motion to Refer the President's Message Relating to the Barbary Powers to a Select Committee

MR. BRADLEY'S
MOTION.

November 16, 1808.
PRINTED BY ORDER OF THE SENATE.

WASHINGTON CITY.
PRINTED BY R. C. WEIGHTMAN

1808

IN SENATE
OF
THE UNITED STATES.

November 16th, 1808.

Mr. Bradley laid on the table the following motion, for consideration:

Resolved, That so much of the message of the President of the United States, as relates to the Barbary powers, and the unjustifiable proceeding of the Dey of Algiers towards our consul at that regency, with the documents accompanying the same, b referred to a select committee to consider and report thereon.

Microform, U.S. Government Library, U.S. 10th Congress, 1807–1809. Senate.

From Simeon Knight

Sir,   New Orleans 20th Novr: 1808

I received your letter giving me information of your having obtained for me the appointment of District paymaster much later than the letter from the Paymasters officer enclosing the appointment tho: both of the same date.

I immediately complyed with the necessary Bond, and oath of office required — But receiving no instructions for my government with the appointment, nor information of money having been transmited for the payment of the troops in this District; caused some delay in my commencing upon the duties of my office.

I feel myself under many obligations for your services and assistance in my favour, and hope I shall have it in my power to repay them. Accept assurances of my high esteem and the most sincere wish for the happiness of yourself and family.

Your most Obt, Svt,

S. Knight

The Honorable Stephen R Bradley
   ALS (VtU).

From Andrew Hull Jr.

Dear Sir   Cheshire Decemr. 2d 1808

Your favour of the 8th of last month inclosing The Presidents Message, was duly Recd, since which I have recd the documents attending the same, also the report of the Committee for which I am very gratefull, as it is not Only highly gratefying to me but to my Republican Friends — the communications are even spoken well of, by some Federalists. I am well pleased with the measures the Adminenstrat[i]on appear disposed to addopt — as I consider them the only mode that can be Addopted to save our country from ruin and maintain its independence. Mr. Hillhouses Resolutions are spoken of withe a considerabl Degree of contempt even by Federalists. I apprehend he must look out for a New Turnpike road before he can go on to advantag. I have had it in contemplation to come to Washington this winter and think I shall in case I can afford the expence, as there is very little business going on here at present — should there be any material change or a prospect of a change as it respects our Publick affairs I will thank You for any early information that you may think would be beneficial to me. Our Cheshire Friends are in good health.

Yours very Respectfully

Andw. Hull Junr.

Hon. Stephen R. Bradley
   ALS (VtU).

From William Eaton

Honle. General Bradley —

Sir,   Boston Dec. 6th. 1808.

Since my last,[1] yesterday, I have seen the copy of a letter circular from Tobias Lear, dated Algiers Dec. 16. 07, stating an arrangement of a cash commutation for the payment of our arrearage of treaty stipulated naval stores. There is speculation in this transaction. Why did not the *adjustment of this business* take place before the Dey made captures? Lear had been apprized of danger and had proclaimed it. This is the first instance in story of a Barbary chief having made siezures of the kind and *The people on board the vessels having been treated very well and no pillage of any kind having been committed!* When war was made why was not the Consul sent out of the country.

That our commerce was sick and defenceless is sufficient cause of war — but when seriously made, it would transede the ordinary powers of a consul to negociate peace except on plans previously concerted — I infer this from what I know of Barbary customs. Lear has pocketed another sixty thousand dollars. The President knows him to have passed a fraud on his government and country: Why throw his mantle over him! Be assured, Sir, I will unmask the vilany except there is *energy* enough in the Executive to do it. With the sense of indignation I feel for the stain of cowardice Lear has shed on the stars in our flag I mingle resentment for the laurels he barely swindled from me — And, therefore, till he becomes just, I will pursue him. If, after knowing his frauds, the president protects him, duty will dictate exposure of both. No interest can step between me and duty. I know you think & feel as I do on this subject — I therefore declare my resolutions freely — and cheerfully give the declaration of them to your discretion.

With great pleasure I have found an acquaintance in your son here. He has more reading and correct document than any gentleman of the number of my friends and his years; and equal judgement.

I have the honor to be with fair thinking & true respect Sir, your faithful servt:

William Eaton

ALS (NcD: Bradley Family Papers).
1. Letter not found.

From William H. Cabell

Sir,   Richmond December 10t. 1808.

I have lodged with a merchant of this City for the purpose of being forwarded, by the first opportunity to mr. Henry Thompson of Baltimore, a Map of Virginia lately published by the Right Reverend James Madison[1] and others, and which he is requested to keep in his hands subject to your Order. It is directed to the Governor of Vermont, and is presented on behalf of the Legislature of this State to the Legislature of the State of Vermont. I have long endeavored to transmit it, but having heretofore met with no opportunity, permit me to request that you will have the Goodness to point out to mr. Thompson the best mode of Sending it to the Governor of your State.

I am with great respect Sir, your obedt Servant

Wm. H. Cabell[2]

ALS (NcD: Bradley Family Papers). Cover addressed to "The Honorable / Stephen R Bradley / Senator from the State / of Vermont / Washington"; postmarked at Richmond, 21 Dec., and marked "Free"; docketed by SRB, "Gov Cabel Letter."
1. James Madison (1749–1812), president of the College of William and Mary, was consecrated the first Episcopal bishop of Virginia in 1790. He was also a noted surveyor whose *Map of Virginia* was published in 1807. Bishop Madison was a second cousin of James Madison, fourth president of the U.S. (*Papers of James Madison: Presidential Series*, 1:185 n. 2).
2. William Henry Cabell (1772–1853) was governor of Virginia, 1805–8.

From Reuben Attwater

Hon. Stephen R. Bradley Esqr.

Dear Sir.   Detroit December 15th. 1808

I received your letter of the 12th. of November last, encloseing the message of the President to both houses of Congress, which afforded me great pleasure not only to hear from a friend but to hear what situation our public affairs were in, I lament that the belligerent powers are not disposed to do us Justice, the Inhabitants in this Territory feel anxious to know the event. For your friendly information respecting my landed property in Vermont I feel obligated, when I last wrote you on the subject, I informed you that Mr. Richards had the care of it either to sell or Rent as he thought most for my interest. I also wrote you last summer as an apology for not sending you the money I borrowed of you that Mr. Griswold had not paid over any money, it is not in my power at present to procure such Bills as you will receive, but it will be in my power to soon which I will send to Washington with Interest agreeable to your request. I shall always be happy to hear form you. Doc. S. Day who is stationed here as Surgeon's Mate requests me to inform yo<u> that he feels himself very much indebted to you for your friendship in procureing him this post, but further reque<sts> notwiths[t]anding he is reconciled as to his present situat<ion> that if you Sir and his other friends are of opinion th<at> an Army will be raised and continued in service that his name should come before the Senate as Surgeon that you would give him your assistance, but on no consideration would he relinquish his present appointment unless it is certain that an appointment as surgeon would be parmanent if an Army is raised in addition to the present one. If I was to say that Doc Day was very much esteemed here by the most respectable people not only as a Surgeon but a Man it would be saying nothing more than what I have already said.

With sentiments of friendship & Esteem Your obt. servt.

Reuben Attwater.

ALS (VtU). Margin obscured.

From Elisha Tracy

Honlb. Stephen Roe Bradley Esqr

Dear Sir   Norwich (Con[necticu]t) Decr. 15th 1808

Permit me at the request of Capt Charles Bulkley of New London who is desirous of obtaining the Command of a Revenue Cutter, in case any addition be made to their number to say; that he is a revolutionary officer, who during the War served his Country as a Marine Officer with reputation, he is now an active Man, of good standing of fair & respectable Character, of correct political principles & faithfully attached to the administration & its Measures. Permit me also to acknowledge your repeated civilities.

I beg you Dear Sir, to accept the assurances of high respect & Esteem with which I am Dear Sir, your humble servt

Elisha Tracy

ALS (VtU).

From Ab. Bishop

Sir,   New Haven, 19 Dec. 1808.

It has been intimated to me, that there would *probably* be a removal in the Collectns.

office N London should this be the case, there will be three or four Candidates with Claims not very unequal. Permit me to say, *confidentially*, that in case of any appointment to that office, it would be very important to the harmony of republicans, that such appointment should be made, not to the most pressing, but to the best supported pretensions. I do not presume to express any confident expectation of a removel or any opinion as to an appointment, but meerly wish that all, having hopes on that subject, may have equal oppy.

Am, with great respect sr. y mo. obt Serv

Ab Bishop

Hon. S. R. Bradley
    ALS (VtU).

From William Helms

Dr Sir,   Hall of Representatives 23d Decr. 1808

My friend Col. Jonathan Rhea of Trenton, mentions to me, his haveing put into your hands at Hartford in 1806 certain papers to be delivered to your son for investigation &Ca— and requests me to enquire of you what is done with them, he does not mention to what the papers relate, but I presume they are respecting Lands either in Vermont or Maine. If since I spoke to you on the subject anything respecting them has occured to you[r] memory, be so good as to inform me; if you have no resolution thereof, be so good as to write your son, and on receiving his answer let me know.

Your Obet. Servt.

W. Helms[1]

Genl Bradley

    ALS (NcD: Bradley Family Papers).
    1. William Helms (d. 1813), a Revolutionary War veteran, represented New Jersey as a Republican in the Seventh through Eleventh Congresses (1801–11).

From William Law

Respected Sir,   Cheshire Decem'r 27th 1808

I am much obliged to you for the Presidents Message and the Documents with which you favored me.

General Hull was polite enough to hand me the Report of the Committee on the Subject of our relations to foreing Powers. Likewise Mr Giles's Speech. I consider these as very important Communications. I Sincerely wish that Some way and means could be devised so to distribute them so that every Man in the united States could read or here them. We Shall endeavour to make the best use of them we can. Could an acquaintance with facts become general; no doubt great numbers would be convinced of their errors, notwithstanding the exertions of Pickering, Hillhouse &c. The State of Connecticut need the information contained in them as much as any State in the Union.

Such have been the burthens imposed on the Republicans by the goverment of this State; by persecutions against a number, for haveing endeavourd to expose the injustice of Said goverment, that it would now be difficult to raise money enough to defray the expence of printing usefull communications. I would suggest the Idea whether it would be consistent for the goverment to cause in Some way the Communications from the Executive the Debates on the great <Question?> to be printed and Sent into the States and distributed as the Laws are, and in Such a proportion as would probably make the communication general.

I understand Mr Goodrich has been so candid as to Send a number of the Documents to Mr Babcock, those are the onely ones I have heard of in the State except those you Sent.

Permit me to suggest a few Ideas, which arise in my mind I will thank you to take the trouble at least to peruse them. What is ment by the first part of the forth sect. of the forth Article of the Constitution. To a Republican form of Goverment, guaranteed to the State of Connecticut when the Legislature usurps the Power and declare that the old Charter of King Charles Shall be the Constitution of the State; hereby acknowledging the State to be a Colony of England, and in consequence of haveing no restraint are makeing Such Laws as will forever prevent the real expression of the will of the people. Would it not be consistent to amend the Constitution by inserting after the word goverment; And the people of each State Shall by a Convention for that purpose appointed, form and adopt one[.] Laws are made and inforced in this State to curtail the liberty of the Pres. Do States ought to have the right which is <denied?> the general goverment? Could not the Constitution be so amended as to place the States on the Same ground with the general goverment? And in case of any suit brought for any publication against the State or Court thereof, Would it not be Just to alow an appeal to the Courts of the U.S.? Would it be inconsistant with the liberty of the Press to compel a printer to give up the name of the author, by fine or otherwise? Would not such a regulation prevent grate part of the abuse we now Suffer? I am aware that it may be Said to require a State to make a constitution would be an interference on their Soveranety. But the State would adopt Such an one as they Should see fit. Where then would be the injury. Federalists could not get the people of this State to adopt a constitution (even now) that would not be altogether more favorable to Republicanism.

I wrote you last year on the Subject of a grant of land for the College at Burton. I then expected a Petition would have been sent on from the Trustees for that purpose. This was unanimously agreed on by them, and why it was not done I know not. I now hear that Judge Kirtland Says it Shall be done. In that Settlement there is a good propo[r]tion of New England People and nearly all of them Republicans. Grants have ben made I understand to two Colleges in the Southern part of the State of Ohio, and I believe to one of them two Townships. I have never heard whether the line has been established between the U.S. and the Connecticut land Company. I mentioned that there was a gore of land surveyed by the Company from the Portage to the west line, runing to a point at the west line which belongs to the U.S. This was considered at the time of division <a>s not belonging to the Company; money was annexed to those <t>owns to make them good; and if Congress Should give them <u>p, it will be to Individuals most of them very wealthy and bitter enemies to the present administration. I think if Goverment were to give this tract which I believe contains about 9000 acres; and a Township the portage; to the College in Burton it would be an ac<t of> Benevolence to Society, much better than to give it to enne<mies.> If any grant Should be made I wish it might be made to the College in Burton, For Some designing men wish to remove the College.

I expected Burton People would have Sent a Petition for a Post office, in Burton. That Town was Settled in 1798 and one year after the first Settlement on the Reserve, and has now more inhabitants than all the Towns through which the Mail now runs from Warren to Austinburgh, Which is No 11 Range 5th I believe the Mail now runs from Warren to Mesoptamia No 7 R-5th to No 8 R. 5th to Jefferson No 10 R-3d from thence to Austinburgh No 11 R 5th thence to Grand River No 1<1> R 8th thence to Cleveland No 7 R 12th at left 105 mil<es> where as from Warren to Burton is 25 <miles> from Burton to Cleveland is 30 miles. Now if the Mail sha<ll> go from Burton to G- River it would be twenty three miles further than to go direct from Burto<n to> Cleveland. This would carry the mail two days [...]ner from the Seat of goverment to Detroit and back than the present course and if to go direct from Burton to Cleveland it would make a Saving of four days. This was the rout pointed out by Mr Davis last year.

If this rout Should be established Mr Lemuel Panderson would be a very proper man for a Post Master at Burton. He is a Person of Integrity and a decided Republican and is doing every thing he can for the cause. I believe Mr Granger knows him if not his Brother in law Judge Pees could inform him. Your attention to the Subject of this letter, and your answer to any part of it if you Should think it of so much importance as to take that trouble, would oblige your friend and most Humble Servant

William Law

Hon Stephen R Bradley Esq

ALS (VtU). Margin obscured. Text obscured by blots and damaged by removal of seal.

Appointment of Stephen R. Bradley as President *pro tempore* of the Senate

WEDNESDAY, December 28 [1808].

The VICE PRESIDENT being absent by reason of the ill state of his health, the Senate proceeded to the election of a President *pro tempore*, as the Constitution provides: and STEPHEN R. BRADLEY was appointed.

On motion, by MR. GILES.

Ordered. That the Secretary wait on the President of the United States and acquaint him that the Senate have in the absence of the Vice President, elected STEPHEN R. BRADLEY their President *pro tempore.*

History of Congress, *Proceedings*, December 1808. Senate.

From Thomas Tingey

Sir   Navy Yard Washtn: 20 Jany 1809

I have the honor to state, in reply to your note of this morning,[1] That, the frigates United States, Essex and John Adams— are now in as good order, in their hulls, as on the day they were launched— And can be rigged in a few weeks— if so ordered, and suitable appropriations made.

The frigates Congress and Adams, might also proceed to a station in the mouth of any of our bays, or harbours— but I do not consider their hulls in a situation fit to bear the Sea in heavy weather.

The frigates Constellation and New York, I consider as unfit to proceed from this yard, until they shall have had a thorough repair— And the remaining frigate, the President, is now progressing under a thorough repair— and may I presume be ready for sea in May next, with the number of carpenters now employed here.

I have the honor to be very respectfully Sir Yr Obedt Servt

Thos: Tingey[2]

Honbe Stepn R Bradley

ALS (NcD: Bradley Family Papers).
1. Letter not found.
2. Thomas Tingey, a New Jersey native, commanded the U.S. ship *Ganges*, 1798–99. In October 1801 he became superintendent of the Washington Navy Yard (*Papers of James Madison: Secretary of State Series,* 1:296 n. 10).

From Nathaniel Ruggles

Dear Sir   Roxbury Jany 25th. 1809

As it is, without doubt, agreable to you to collect information from the different sections of our Union; I feel guilty, that I have not, before, contributed my mite to that information, from this quarter; But the only apology I can make is, that I have been & am still diffident of hazarding opinions in these tremendous times, especially to a character who hath a prospect of the whole ground, & in comparison of which, my view must be quit[e] limited. I will however give you a short sketch of the recent doings of the Town of Boston, respecting their late Resolves & their Petition to the Legislature. As my extreme anxiety led me to hear the beginning, the same propensity induced me to attend, their progress & hear their Ultimatum. You will have all the particulars in the papers. The debates appeared to be unpassionate & deliberate. Fanuil Hall, which I presume will hold 6000 people, & perhaps more, was as crow[d]ed as ever I have seen it — And as Mr. Austin, there expressed, "the floors seemed to be paved with faces." As near as I could form an estimate, and I had a situation of a pretty good aspect, there were five sixths of the *Voters* in favour of the resolutions & the Petition to *the*[1] Legislature; The majority has been rated higher, & I should be inclined to estimate them more, rather than less. This Embargo System was opposed, as being unprecedented, unavailing, & particularly the last law, unconstitutional & oppressive — I must confess Dear Sir, that I trembled for consequences, when I read Mr. Gallatin's propositions. From what I gathered from the debates yesterday, similar proceedings are expected to take place in all the states in the Northern section; and the exertions of their Legislatures are expected to devise some mode for redress of grievances. I hope these proceedings will not tend to weaken the Union; when, from appearances, from without, the necessity increases every day, of drawing tighter the cords of union. There ought to be mutual conciliations from Northern to Southern & from the Southern to the Northern States; as there were in the outset of our Federal Constitution — And party spirits ought now to yield to the more important considerations for the public good: for times appear to us here, to be drawing to that solemn Crisis, when we must make our election of the least of the two evils, A war with France or a War with England. As I was an Adventurer, in the Grace, Capt. Linsey bound to Leghorn, which was taken & has been condem'd at Paris (first court) under Bonaparte's decrees, & for the pretence of being spoken with by an English armed Ship; and no pretence of her being boarded — I wish you would be so good Sir as to inform me what has been done by our Government respecting the Captures under those last preposterous decrees & orders. I have the condemnation at the first court at Paris, & an appeal entered from that to a higher Court. If you think any use can be made of it to any effect, at Washington, I will have it translated & forward. Mrs. Mark Richards & Mrs. Clapp are in Roxbury — and your son & Lady expected next week. Mrs. Ruggles presents her respects.

I am respectfully Your hum. Servt.

                                                                       Nathl. Ruggles

Mrs. Clapp took your two casks of wine yesterday for Vermont — pretty good sleighing
Honble. Stephen Roe Bradley Esquire —

ALS (NcD: Bradley Family Papers).
1. Ruggles interlined "our" over "*the.*"

From Jonathan Dorr

Honble Stephen R Bradley
Dear sir   Roxbury 29th Jany 1809

Your Esteem'd favor <of> 14th Inst came safely to hand, and believe me sir I should be very remiss, did I not tender you my tha<nks> for your kind attention in forwarding likewise the Pamphlet contg the Orders of Council Decrees &c which I have perused and with great satisfaction.

At this alarming Crisis of our Public affairs w<e> are all looking with much anxiety for some favor<able> change. We had a flameing town meeting in Boston the other day, (Fedralism) pure and unadulterated presided and Resolutions adopted cut and dry'd for the Occasion which you will see in our Public prints undoubtedly before you receive this. A p[...] of Mr. H G Otis's speech went to say that if the Peop<le> of the Northern States were United they might then s<ay> to Mr. Jefferson and Congress we will have Commerce and Mr. Jefferson & the Southerners answer would be y<ou> shall have Commerce. There was last night a seisure made at Commercial Point about four mil<es> from us in Dorchester about $20,000 worth of English goods which were smuggling onshore from a Schooner th<at> are now in the Marshalls hands. Some of our Westmins<ter> friends are now with us Mrs. Richards Observes she lef<t> your family well. I expect Mr. Wm. Bradley and Wife with us next week. Should any news of Imp<or>tance transpire, if not too much trouble will thank you to write me, and believe me sir I shall eve<r> feel grateful therefor[.] Our family are well Mrs. Dorr desires her respects.

With Esteem sir your humble servt

Jona. Dorr

ALS (VtU). Margin obscured.

From Abel Farwell

Hartland 30th. Jan. 1809

Sir you will recollect that I called on you at Westminster last Spring with a letter from Mr. Luce accompanied with other papers requesting your assistance in procur<ing> me a Capts. Commission in the Army of the U. States — and that you assured me that you would lend your aid in the business but Stated to me that it was uncertain whether you could procure one till forepart winter which time has arrived & I have heard nothing from you o<n> the subject which I have concluded was owing to business of more importance & which has occupied the most of your time for the present Session — but finding those grand questions respecting the Embargo & our situation with those Tyrants of the Ocean settled for the present — & finding a resolution introduced for raising arming an[d] equiping fifty thousand volunteers — I have again renewed m<y> requ[e]st with full confidence of success thro your assistance.

With sentiments of the highest esteem I shall subscribe your obdient humble servant

Abel Farwell

Stephen R. Bradley Senator in Congress

ALS (VtU). Damaged by removal of seal. Margin obscured.

From Elisha Tracy

Honlb. Stephen Roe Bradly Esq

Dear Sir   Norwich (Con[necticu]t) Feby 5th 1809

We are looking hard to the South not only to see what you are doing, but in hopes to discover a ray of light, that will be a harbinger of returning prosperous days, we at any rate hope, that there will be that evidence of determi<ned> firmness & a little more activity of measures at Washington so as to put down the Spirit of sedition & opposition in Massachusets organized to such a height I really believe it is intended to effect their State Elections & in hopes by blust[...] to drive the general Goverment from their Measures, I trust further they d<o> not intend to go. In this State we have not any thing to fear at present they will at any rate wait to see the lead that Massachusets will take & even th<en> am persuaded the people here cannot be forsed into any extravagant opposit<ion> it is necessary the friends of the Goverment should conduct with prudence here, that with decisive conduct at Washington will keep this State steady. Our Supreme Court has been sitting in this Town & our Govenor has been here once last Week & once the Week before closeted with the Court & a Member of the Counsel, his bussiness is meant to [be] wrapped in mistery, but I understand it w<as> on the Secy War's Letter directing the designation of militia at the disposal of the Collectors to prevent any attempt by forse to evade the Embargo—& to consult on the expediency of calling our Legislature, agreeble to a request from New Haven &c. Tho they are close on this subject I am persuaded the Legislature will not at present be called, it would not suit the feelings of a great majority of the people, with respect to the other I regret that the marshall had not been designated to call out the militia & he provided a Deputy in each district it is a novel thing here & not suited to our Genius to have the military placed at the collectors dispo<sal> the Embargo may be enforsed here for any length of time the Goverment, have an idea of persisting in it, if they only had two smart Revenue Cutters constantly cruising between the East end of Long Island & Martha's Vineyard & these would also stop Up Rhode Island as well as that outlet from New York through the sound, but without the Goverment doing any thing & with some of their officers opposed to their measures, its enforsement cannot be expected I hope Vessels will not be let out on any pretence & believe from enquiry the country is well supplyed with Salt, once open the Sluice Gate for that article & a torrent of Vessels & produce will pour out, Vessels are continually arriving with that article especially English ones & I think a duty ought immediately be laid on when imported in foreign Bottoms. Our Vessels are too many of them sailing under British licenses & ought to be denatiolized unless they return immediately a high state of preperation will do more to tranquilise the public mind than any thing else. A memorial from Congress stating at large the intention of Goverment with a full view of situation might be usefull. I know there are objections to this & only suggest it.

I am Dear Sir, respectfully & with much personal Esteem your verry humbl servt

Elisha Tracy

I understand but do not Vouch for its truth, that our Collector would have resigned had not his Brothers disuaded him from it; it is however here verry generally expe<cted> he will be displaced at the end of this or beginning of the next administration in either of these events, will you keep your Eye upon it & pay it some attentio<n> on my account: it cannot be that old man at New London, with all his habits can run a race with me; in case vacansy.

Respectfully yours

E: Tracy

ALS (VtU). Margin obscured.

To James Madison

Sir   Washington 7th Febry 1809

Our friend Doctor Kirkpatrick[1] retires from Congress under circumstances which cannot fail to excite an earnest solicitude for his welfare. Past events which test the merit & Ability of this gentleman & which qualify him for office of high trust & responsibility, justify the anxiety we feel, to continue his usefulness to the Public — his delicacy which refuses its assent to any mode of application not independent of him constrains us to adopt a course which leaves to yourself sir the time occasion & office. Very respectfully yr obt Servts

Richd Cutts	Wll B Giles
Wm: H: Crawford	Tho Newton
Jno. Milledge	S. R. Bradley
Wm W Bibb	David Holmes
Jno. W. Eppes	Geo M Troup
W A Burwell	
John Taylor	

ALS (DLC). In the hand of George M. Troup, who enclosed it in a letter to Madison of 4 Mar. 1809 (DLC).

1. William Kirkpatrick, a physician from New York, retired after one term in Congress, 1807–9. He was superintendent of the Onondaga Salt Springs, 1806–8 and 1811–31 (*Papers of Madison: Presidential Series*, 1:15).

From John Matlock

Hon Stephen R Bradly

Sir   Peacham 9 February 1809

I command a regiment here, if the fifty thousand that are proposed to be raised will be offerrerd from the office of the militia would wish to put in with others that have as little modesty as myself for a regiment, but if they are to be commanded by men who have seen Service & have military merit I dare not insert my name among the applicants.

Will you pardon me Sir for asking your influence to obtain this command if it should be thought that the public [*illegible*] would not thereby suffer but if others apply who have "set a Squadron in the field" I shrink from the comparison & am content to remain in indolence at home altho I could wish to assert the rights of the country & the admi[ni]stration against its enemies forregn or domestic.

With the highest respect Sir your obedient Servant

                                                                            John Matlock

ALS (VtU). Text obscured by several blots. Endorsed by SRB, "John Matlocks Letter."

From Elisha Tracy

Honlb. Stephen R; Bradly Esqr

Sir   Norwich (Con[necticu]t) Feby 16th 1809

The Town Meeting here, called by the Federalist to Vote down the measures of Goverment met this day. On opening the meeting I arose & stated that we were ready to discuss the constitutionallity of the Embargo Laws & the expediency of all the measures of the General Goverment. The Federalist were thunder struck & immediately moved the previous question; after an ardent debate & a few cowardly Republicans joining them, they by a small majority Voted to do nothing we were so nearly ballanced, we thought best to let it rest here. As they called the meeting they were beat.

So you see we can support Goverment here & I hope you will not be drove from your measures at Washington, by any noise from the East; never did I before see the Federal[i]st so mortified here they thought they could raise the devil in this Town.

Please to present my best respects to the Gentln. who quarter with you do not be frightnen stand firm. Our standing as a Town will have some w[e]ight in the State.

Your verry respectfull friend

Elisha Tracy

ALS (VtU).

From Royall Tyler

Dear Sir— Brattleboro March 9th. 1809—

I arrived home yesterday from the Western circuit—and now enclose to you Thirty Dollers am sorry that it is not in my power to send the other twenty—I hope this will arrive in time to save you from any blame—which I think must be the case.

Sterne says "We get forward in this world more by recieving favours than doing them["]—I am sure this is the case betwixt you and I. Now if you will advance the other twenty dollars for me—if it should be necessary—or so accomodate the bussiness for a few days—I shall be able to send you the same—if this is not convenient please to advise me by the next mail and I will send it to you immediately—at any rate if you will call on me the next time you come to Brattleboro on the Hale bussiness I shall probably be able to advance the twenty Dollers.

I have a considerable budget of news for you—among the rest I wish to see you respecting our next candidate for Governour. I am very apprehensive that the State of Govr. Smiths health is such that we must run a new candidate[1]—I have been in several conferences upon the subject in which I have not failed to advocate the rights of the eastern section of the State—but these things are better to talk that write upon.

Your Friend—

Royall Tyler

You will consider what I have observed upon Govr. Smith state of health—as a bona dea mystery.[2]

ALS (NcD: Bradley Family Papers). Docketed by SRB, "Royal Tyler Esq / March 9t 1809."
1. Israel Smith was governor of Vermont, 1807–8. In 1808, he was defeated for reelection by Isaac Tichenor, a Federalist. In the 1809 election, the Democratic Republican candidate, Jonas Galusha, defeated Tichenor. Smith died on 2 Dec. 1810.
2. Bona Dea ("the good goddess") was a fertility goddess in the ancient Roman religion. Secret rites in her honor were attended only by women, and the celebrations seem to have had the nature of a mystery cult.

From Thomas and John Shepherd

Hon S. R. Bradley

Dear Sir, No Hampton 17th June 1809

You will please to accept our thanks for calling o<n> the Secretary of the Navy on the subject of Amer<ican> Duck—by the request of our Mr Thomas Shepherd wh<en> in New York a few days since.

We perceive that the subject of an enquiry into th<e> State of the manufacturing establishments of the united States has been agitated in Congress. As the knowled<ge> of all the facts concerning such establishments must <be> usefull to the government, and as we feel a deep interest in the prosperity of manufacturers, having embarked our whole capital therein, we have tho<t> proper to give you the information of what we have done and what we can do (with proper encourag<e>ment) in that line. We have manufactured 100<0> pieces of Duck 37 yds long & 24 inches wide in a year, and could if proper encouragement were given by the Government encrease the number to 2000 pieces a yea<r.>

The last year we manufactured 50,000 yds Cotton Bag[...] 40 Inches wide; this article met with a quick sale in New York owing to the prohibition of the importati<on> of it from abroad by the Non Importation Act. If a duty of 10 Cents a yard was laid in addition to the present duty on the article we could make 200000 yards in a year. We have begun to erect a Woolen and Cotton manufactory upon a large plan, but fear what may be the determination of Congress with regard to protecting American manufactures. We can make 10000 yds of woolen Cloth in a year from one to two dollars value a yard. The extent of our Cotton manufactory we cannot at present precisely state, but we have every convenience for pursuing it to advantage. We should be glad to contract with the Secretary of the Navy for 1000 bolts duck to be delivered in the year 1810. We will send the Secretary 5 or 6 Bolts as a sample some time this summer.

When you return from Washington we should be very happy if yourself and family would call upon us and spend as much time as you shall find agreable.

We have the honor to be very respectfully your Hble Servants

Thomas & John Shepherd

ALS (VtU). Margin obscured.

From Nathan Smith

Sir.   Dartmouth College August 26th 1809

I once more request your assistance for a Friend & Pupil of mine. Mr. Hubbard Sparkawk of Walpole wishes for an appointment in the Marine Hospital to be established in Charlestown Massachusetts I can sincerely recommend Mr. Sparkawk as a man of good genius & pure moral Character well worthy of public Confidence his advantages in Medicine have been good he has been industrious in his studies & has recd. the Degree Of Bachelor in Medicine at this University if you can render him any service in getting the appointment he wishes for You will by doing it confer a very great Obligation on me & highly gratify many respectable people in this Vicinity.

Your Friend & very Hble. Sernt,

Nathan Smith

Honle, Stephen R. Bradley Esqr,

N,B,

I have forwarded letters to Mr Dearborn & Mr. Smith upon the subject not knowing on which the appointment would depend. It appeared important that they should go on immediately as the appointment might be made if they waited your return You will write & give your aid in this business.

Yours with esteem

N Smith

ALS (NcD: Bradley Family Papers). Cover addressed to "Honble, Stephen R. Bradley Esqr, / Westminster / Vt."; docketed by SRB, "from Doct Smith / pro Doct Sparkawk."

From Stella C. Bradley

My Dear Father,   Hartford September 22d 1809

No apology was needfull for not writing us I knew th<at> you have a great deal of business about this time. We lot very much upon seeing You at H....... in a short time I Suppose you are not going on to Congress then. As to Vermont Bank bills they are good for nothing here. I suppose you have r<ecei>ved our letters by Mr. Francis & Mr. May before this I expect they will get there today I am very glad to hear that Huldah <F>aye is coming to Hartford to school. We have heard of the melancholy news of Grandmah Taylers death but we have long expected it. Hartford is very healthy at present & I hope will remain so. I have only to add that Adeline & myself are very well and desire love to all <the> family I am your affectionate Daughter

                                                                      Stella C Bradley

P S The bills which pass current here are Boston New York Connecticutt & Albany.

ALS (VtU). Margin obscured.

From Jonathan Dorr

Honble Stephen R Bradley Esqr

Sir   Roxbury 9th Decemr. 1809

Your Esteem'd favo<r> of 29th Ult covering the Intelligencers came safely to hand for whic<h> I feel myself greatly Oblig'd to you and for you<r> kind attention in forwarding the same; as [...] very gratifying to us here; to know the passing Events at the seat of Goverment in th<e> present Session; There has been a Rumor with us this day or two of an immediate Embar<go> I see nothing in the Intelligencer which looks lik<e> it Altho I must needs say our affairs with Grea<t> Britain wears a very gloomy Aspect.

I have given to Genl Dearborn by hi<s> request a statement of our Manufactory of fa[...] Soaps to forward on to Washington and we ar<e> now prepareing a small Package containing samples of our fine Soaps which we intend forwarding to our Correspondent at Alexandria with a request to forward it to you at Washington. As I wish very much you should see what we are able to Manufacture in this line: Notwithstanding there is now and will be continually Quantitys of these Soaps Imported, unless Goverment will put a stop to it, by increaseing the Dutys or Otherwises. Should there be any important measures about to be adopted by Goverment wherein it Affects our commercial Intrests if not too much trouble you will give me your Early Oppinion I shall take it a favor.

With Esteem Your Obt humble Servt

                                                                      Jona. Dorr

ALS (VtU). Margin obscured. Damaged by removal of seal.

From William C. Harrington

Messrs. S. R. Bradley — Jona. Robinson & Saml Shaw Esquires

Gentlemen   Burlington December 12th 1809

Genl. Bradley was so obliging as to furnish me with many useful documents in course of the last winter session of Congress. I now return to that Gentleman my grateful acknowledgement for the favour — & request that I may be again favoured by receiving from You all such documents as may be proper to promulgate — for since my becoming a member of the republican family, I have found it necessary to have the tools by me, in order to refute the abominable falsehoods that the modern federalists are continually palming upon the people to strengthen their side. I have many fiery trials with my former brethren, many of whom seem determined to deceive the common people, I mean such of the Inhabitants, as have <not> leisure hours enough to read and investigate for themselves. I am convinced that the common people want nothing but correct information, to form right Ideas, relative to the measures of Government, The fact is that modern federalism, is not unlike old fashioned toryism such, as was in vogue at the time of the revolutionary war, if any different, it consists in the adding of some pounded glass, & Verdigrise kneaded together by old granny T. P. with skim milk and water, which when baked by Governor G — must make a heterogeneous mess, too poisonous for republicans &c. &c. &c.

Aristocracy is so prevalent in Burlington that even the Women have more than a supply. We cannot make republicanism grow in this Village, our soil is sandy & better calculated for raising white & black Beans than any thing else. We are curiously situated in this Village. We have 13 merchants all federalists 13 Lawyers all federalists save four 5 Physicians all feds, who together with tanners, Shoe makers, & coblers make aristocracy flourish.

Out of 230 Voters we have but about 60 republicans, but, I may venture to say that republicanism is gaining, & would in my opinion gain fast, if we could establish a republican press. We have 3 federal news papers printed in this district. We have it contemplation to establish a republican press in this town. I can procure sufficient subscribers in the 3 Counties to support such a press on as good a footing as any in this State — & provided it should happen in Your way to send us an editor well calculated for the business, I should esteem it a great favour. We have made several attempts to procure one, which have hitherto failed. The 3 presses now in operation were too proud to even print the proceedings of our last Legislature. I wish You to send to me weekly or oftener the best news paper printed in Washington City, I fancy that the National Intelligencer will be the best, but shall leave that for Your Judgment. I wish one of You Gentlemen would make a contract with the Editor or printer for a sufficient term to contain all the proceedings of Congress the present session which is my object. If it should be necessary to advance any money — I wish one of You to do it, which shall be refunded.

I really wish to have our Government steer clear of war, nevertheless I hope that Congress will take a bold stand. I had rather fight than cringe, & especially to a Government, who depend more on their strength in our Government than their own. I feel as though the patience of our Government must be nearly or quite exhausted.

With regard to our internal concerns — I do really wish that the Jurisdiction of the Circuit should be altered. You must be sensible that there is a continual clashing between our Supreme & Circuit Court in this District. The fee bill in this State now inforced is not regarded in taxing Costs, besides, the fees that we have to pay to the Clerk of the Circuit Court, is something more than both Court & Clerks fees in our County Courts. There is an other great inconvenience — three quarters of the suits lately brot. in the Circuit Court are for Lands in the northern Counties, & generally against poor men, that cannot muster money sufficient to bear their expences to Windsor, & Rutland, & consequently are driven off, of their farms. I think that Colo. Asa Porter has more than 40 actions of ejectment now in the Circuit Court. This Statement is true & the injury is too great to be born. I fancy that Vermont is the only State, that is deprived of having the Circuit Court set at the seat of Government, & I ask in the name of plain common sense for a reason, for the continuing of sd. Court at W. & R. I think none can be shown. I therefore hope that if we must have a Circuit Court in its present shape, that You will have it established at Montpelier.

I shall feel pleased, if You will frequently drop me a line &c. &c.

I am Gentlemen Your Obt. servant

William C. Harrington

ALS (VtU). Damaged by removal of seal.

Senate Proceedings: Direct Tax

[15 December 1809]

Mr. Bradley submitted the following motion for consideration:

Resolved, That the secretary of the treasury be, and hereby is requested to lay before the Senate, a statement of the payments which have been made by the respective states of the direct tax; designating as far as may be, what sums have been paid into the treasury; what sums are unaccounted for by the supervisors; and what sums are in the hands of collectors; and the persons in whose hands such monies are; and what sums are still due from any of the respective states.

Printed (AoC).

From Jonathan Dorr

Honble Stephen R Bradley Esqr

Dear sir   Roxbury 15th Decr. 1809

I had the pleasu<re> of addressing you on the 9th Curt I have this day put onboard the Ship John Andrew Capt Nicko[...] for Alexandria the small Box contg samples of fine Soaps as before written with directions to our Friend at Alexandria to forward the same to you at Washington. If you will have the goodness to receive it to show it and dispose of it as you may think prop<er> you will Oblige Your Friend and humble Servt

Jona. Dorr

N B. Our Soap Bussiness is conducted under the firm of Nathl Scott & Co Roxbury as you will perceive most of the soaps so stamp'd and of a full Statement of the Manufactory we presume was forwarded to Washington by Genl. Dearbor<n>.

ALS (VtU). Margin obscured.

From Tench Coxe

Sir   Philadelphia Decr. 17. 1809

I observe, that a committee has been appointed on the subject of religious incorporations. I am not acquainted with the names of any of the religious societies nor of the petitioners, and therefore have not any intention to take the liberty of saying any thing for or against them. But, believing that it may be useful to bring into the view of legislators such cases and observations as the enclosed, I have ventured to cover to you a couple of copies.

I am, Sir your respectf. h. Servant

Tench Coxe[1]

Genl. Bradley

ALS (Bradley Family Papers). Enclosures not found.

1. Tench Coxe (1755–1824) was an economist and prolific writer who held several public offices, including assistant to the secretary of the treasury during the Washington administration. From 1803 to 1812 he served as purveyor of public supplies.

From Charles Phelps

Genl.   Townshend Decer. 20th 1809

I recd. the Presidents' Message. Am in hopes of asking for some arrangement in the mail route near us soon, at our own charge. Would wish you to communicate such documents as will reflect some little gleam of light in this *benighted corner*. For every communication shall be much obliged; & will farther renumerate as you shall desire.

I have just recd. by the Boston papers the first ebullitions of rancor against Madison. The twistings, & writhing of those dear little British innocents, who have so long lain at the breasts of their fond mother, show that her corruption has pervaded their system; & they must soon expire in convulsions.

Every turn but more & more testifies their miserable depravity Falsehood & deceit make way for perjury & treason. And God has given them up to strong delusions, that they may be damned.

I am, Dr Sir, with sincere esteem Your Most obt St

                                                                            Charles Phelps

Hon. Stephen R. Bradley
ALS (VtU).

Senate Proceedings: Barbary Powers

[26 December 1809]

Mr. Bradley submitted the following motion for consideration:

Resolved, That the President of the United States, be, and hereby is requested to cause to be laid before the Senate, the amount of all the monies disbursed from the treasury of the United States, in their relation or intercourse with the Barbary powers, subsequent to the signing of the treaty of peace with Tripoli in June, 1805, including the monies paid to that regency at the signing thereof. And to cause to be noted (where the same can be ascertained) the agent or consul to whom the respective disbursements were made, the time when, and place where the respective sums were drawn for, or received by said agents or consuls, and the particular purposes to which the same have been applied; and what sums have been retained in the hands of said agents or consuls, for compensation, salary, commissions, or for any other purpose.

Printed ( ).

From Alexander McRae

My dear General,   New-York 1. Jan. 1810.

I arrived at this great City only the night before last, after a most u<n>pleasant journey. Many of the stage-drivers are extremely careless, and the roads are in very bad condition so that it is frequently, in passing ten or twelve miles, more reasonable to anticipate som<e> unfortunate accident, than to expect safety for any one mile, of so short a route; thank God ho<w>ever, I have at length in safety taken my leave <of> the stages for a few weeks. I shall always, my dear sir, recollect with gratitude, the politene<ss> and friendship you showed me, while I was in Washington, and which were farther manifested, <by> the letters with which I was honored the evening <be>fore my departure.

I spent four very agreeable days in Baltimore, at the Hotel to wh<ich> you were so good as to recommend me, and I cou<ld> not keep supposing that the civilities of my Lan<d>lord (Mr. Barney) who is I think a very worthy citizen, were a little encreased by the informatio<n> I gave him, that you had recommended his Hotel to me.

I remained in Philadelphia (under misinformation) several days longer than I had intended, in the hope of seeing Major Butler; but I finally ascertained that he would not return to that City, 'til the next spring, and therefore moved immediately afterwards on to this place. I am now at the City-Hotel to which you recommended me. On my arrival I delivered your letter to Messrs. Fay & Gibson, and while I am greatly indebted to those Gentlemen for their extreme civility and kindness since my arrival here, I can but repeat my acknowledgments for the friendship on your part, which has procured for me such attention. Mr. Gibson is a very genteel young man, and deserves much to be respected; but I have been peculiarly pleased with Mr. Fay, whose education, manners, and deportment, certainly (as far as I am informed) entitle him to wealth, Happiness & distinction. He enquired in a manner most polite & friendly, after yourself, your Lady, & Family.

As soon as may with convenience be practicable I shall commence my intended voyage, which in prospect, becomes every day, more and more irksome and painful to me; my hopes however are, that the privations I must suffer during a tedious absence, will be in some degree mitigated, by an uninterrupted correspondence with some frien<ds> who will remain on this side the water; and with great pleasure I recollect, that your friendship permitted me, to expect the honor of such a correspondence with you. I will upon my part, [...] the happiness of addressing a letter to you, as ofte<n> as it may be in my power to communicate any thing which I shall beleive to be acceptable, o<r> in the least degree interesting to you, as as I sh[...] not cease wherever I may be, to feel that solic<i>tude which belongs to every real American, f<or> the welfare of my Country; I shall be under addi<ti>onal obligations, for the earliest information y<ou> may have it in your power from time to time to give me concerning it's affairs, and of the measures our Country may find it expedient to adop<t> in relation to them. Be pleased to address all your letters to me at this place, and from hence they will be quickly conveyed to me, by an agent whom I shall appoint for that purpose.

It is rumoured here, that th<e> non-intercourse act is to be repealed, and that American Vessels, will be permitted to sail directly, to England or to France. Be pleased to inform me, whether I may confide in this report;—for if I may, I will certainly wait a short time, and take my passage in a vessel of our own Country, rather than sail on Board a Vessel belonging to any foreign Nation. You have, my dear General, my best wishes for your health and happiness.

<Al: McRae>

I have not yet been able to present the other Letters with which you honored me: Before my departure from the City, I will avail myself of the happiness and benefit they will secure to me.

The Honble.
    Gen: Bradley
        Washington

ALS (VtU). Margin obscured. Endorsed by SRB, "Letter from <Alexander McRae.>" Endorsement obscured by an ink stain.

From William Eaton

Sir, Brimfield. Massa. 15th Jan. 1810

You always seemed willing to indulge the familiarity of my communications. I profit of that indulgence — and transmit copies[1] by translations of papers I received yesterday from Syracuse. They have been a year & an half on the passage. The situation of Hamet Bashaw may have since changed. I have no official information on the subject. But report, on credible authority, reinstates him at Derne. The investigation you have moved, if impartially deliberated & fairly examined will inform our country of transactions of our agents in Barbary to which you will not consent to put the national seal.

I am closely beseiged. The Field Martial of Death has driven in my out posts; is drawing lines of circumvalation about my citadel; and, except I can get reenforcements & a fresh supply of provisions I shall be obliged to resign at discretion. Should be glad to change my position; but have not the means of transportation: the Sexton may, perhaps, furnish them. Happen what will to me I shall never cease to be faithfully & respectfully Sir your obed: serv:

William Eaton

The letter addressed to the President came open. I forbear, on second consideration, to translate it but forward it as I received it.

Honbl. Gen. Bradley

ALS (CSmH).
1. Not found.

From John Willard

Dear sir Middlebury Jany 19th 1810

Your letter of the 31st ult[1] has been received, I am under obligation to you for your attention to my concerns particularly in relation to my reappointment, I will avail myself of your obliging offer to transmit any papers or documents so far as to request you if convenient to send me a file of the National Intelligencer during the session & also such documents as you may think proper.

I am highly grateful to find your sentiments coincide with mine on the great concerns of the Nation. If we can consistent with the honor & dignity of the goverment avoid a war I have no doubt that the outrages of the belligerents by compelling us to rely upon our own resources will change our character & habits & thereby produce a permanent good the effects of which will overbalance all the evils we have sustained.

The perplexed state of our foreign relations requires all the wisdom & all the prudence of the National councils. Whatever may be the result I think you may calculate with certainty on the support of the people. Public sentiment as far as I have had opportunity to observe appears to be united in support of goverment. Tho all classes deprecate war with its concomitant evils yet should it become unavoidably necessary I trust the disaffected would be comparatively but few. Indeed it would be difficult to preserve the <enflamer?> of the opposition in the country but for the violent measure of their members of Congress.

Your correspondence with such documents as you may think proper to communicate will ever be gratefully received.

With considerations of respect & esteem I am Dear sir your Obet servt

J. Willard

Hon S. R. Bradley

ALS (NcD: Bradley Family Papers). Cover addressed to "Hon Stephen R Bradley / Member of the Senate / Washington City"; postmarked 20 Jan. at Middlebury, Vt., and stamped "FREE"; docketed by SRB, "Marshal Willard."
1. Letter not found.

From Isaac Clason

Dear Sir   New-York January 24th. 1810

I have not had the honor of seeing you since I was at Washington about Four or Five year ago. I was in hopes of having that pleasure when you pass'd through our City last Fall, but I was disappointed, and I have now to inform you, that I have renew'd my claim to Congress by my affidavit respecting the loss of my Sh[...] Ambition, and nearly the whole of the Cargo; for the pa<r>ticulars of which I refer you to my Petition and Affidavit asseverated by my Clerk, and if you will be so good, as to us<e> your influence in the Senate, for the purpose of giving m<e> relief in so just a cause, I shall ever consider it as a ve<ry> great obligation conferd upon me; I have paid Hundreds of Thousand Dollars to Government, and always with good faith and punctuality; but when I have to conside<r> the hardness of my case, of being Robbed, by the British Government of such an immense amount of property, and afterwards to be call'd upon by our own to pay Fifteen or Twenty Thousand Dollars, over and above a Total loss, I think it too Cruel; if you Sir can mak<e> it convenient to write me on the subject of my Claim and let me know what prospects I have of success, <I> shall ever consider it as a very particular favor <up>on Dear Sir your very respectful, and most obedient Humble Servt.

                                                                 I: Clason

The Honorable Stpn. R Bradley
Senator in Congress
Washington

ALS (VtU). Margin obscured.

To William Eaton

General Eaton

Sir   Washington Febr 2d 1810

Agreeably to what I promised you in my last letter, I now transmit you under three *Covers* the important document—I was obliged to *decompose* it to bring it within the franking powers—you can easily compose it with a needle and thread—you will perceive the Secretary of the treasury has done ample Justice to the call—and I take the liberty to request you would give me <yo>ur *comments* on the account as you must <ha>ve more knowledge of the Customs of tha<t> Country than any other person in America—all <the?> Large presents for festivals Circumcision &c &c &c he bottoms on Customs of the Country I wish you to express your opinion freely as I know you abhor Cowards & Knaves.

I am with Sentiments of Esteem Your Obedt Humbl Servt

AL (CSmH). Damaged by removal of seal.

From Robert Brent

                                                       City of Washington

Sir,   February 9th. 1810.

Agreeably to my promise, I now give you all the information in my power, respecting Lieut. Joseph Dorr, late of the Army.

It appears from the muster rolls of Capt: Clemson's Company, now in my office, that Lt. Dorr died at Bell Fontaine near Saint Louis, on the 8th. of December 1808: It also appears from the accounts of Lt. Whitlock, that Lt. Dorr received his pay in Clemson's Company to the 30th. of June 1808, but that he has not received it for a later period, I cannot state; neither can I find that he received subsistence money of Lt. Whitlock for any part of the year 1808.

There is likewise an unsettled recruiting account of Lt. Dorr's in my office, in which there is a balance of 3.83/100 dollars stated to be due from him to the United States: I will have this account settled as soon as the harrassing business of my office will permit.

I have the honor to be very respectfully Sir Your Mo. Obt.

Robert Brent
p[ay] m[aster] u s army

The Honbl.
S. R. Bradley
in Senate of the U. S.
ALS (VtU).

From Jonathan Dorr

Honble Stephen R Bradley Esqr
Sir   Roxbury 11th Feby 1810

Your favor of 29th Ulto came safely to hand as did the documents enclos'd by which on perusal I find our Commerce more Embarrassed and shackled than hitherto I was aware of— am happy however to learn tis your opinion that Great Britain will send out another Minister or perhaps settle our differences with our minister in London which must be far preferable to a Rupture at this time. We are daily expecting to hear the fate of Mr. Macons Bill which here is thought doubtful of its passing the Senate.

Tis very gratifying to me the small Box of fancy Soaps was so satisfactory as appears by your Letter. We want but a little encouragement from our Goverment such as to stop the importation of those kind of Soaps by duty or otherwise to make the Bussiness beneficial to ourselves and Encouraging to our own Manufactures. We have an Agent Mr. Gilman at Alexandria nearest to Washington where we are now making a shipment of our fine Soaps we likewise keep them in almost every Seaport town in the States and a constant supply is kept for Sale. The prices we sell for by the quantity are for the white Windsor shaving Soap 60 Cts Pr Dozen wg about 2<tt?> which is 30 Cts Pr <tt?> (the English comes at about 90 Cts to one Dollar Pr Dozn or 50 Cts Pr <tt?>) the Coulour'd fancy Soaps and wash Balls from [...] Dollar to One Dollar twenty five cents Pr Doze<n> are larger and the perfume more costly tha<n> use'd for the Windsor Soap of which we m[...] the greatest quantity. I beg of you sir to acc[...] thanks for the kind attention you have [...] to my concerns and for the Papers and D[...] you forwarded me. Mrs. Dorr joins with [...] in sentiments of Esteem & Respect.

Jona. Dorr

ALS (VtU). Margin obscured.

Senate Proceedings: Barbary Powers

[6 March 1810]

Mr. Bradley submitted the following motion for consideration:

Resolved, That a committee be appointed to inquire whether any, and what further provisions are necessary and expedient, in relation to the intercourse between the United States and the Barbary powers, with leave to report by bill or otherwise.

Printed (AoC).

To Jonathan Dorr

Capt Jonathan Dorr
Sir   Washington March 6th 1810

My worthy friend General Sumter member of the Senate from South Carolina has deposited in my hands fifteen dollars to procure the value of that Sum in your Soaps his memmorandum I have enclosed one third of the colored soap he wishes in balls viz Ten Dollars of the white cakes and five in Colored soaps and balls it is his request that you would pack the Same in a box and direct to him to the Care of Messrs. Lee and Haynsworth of Charlestown South Carolina his factors at that place. General Sumter lives say one or two Hundred miles back of Charlestown in the Country he wishes the Soap for Some friends as samples Should they like it he thinks they will become large Customers. You will please to put the box on board some vessel bound directly to Charlestown the freight will be paid by his agents there. I have wrote this day to your friend Mark Richards Esqr and to my Son Wm C. Bradley, which ever of them will be most convenient for you to draw for the fifteen dollars they will be paid on Sight. You will be so good as to put the invoice of the fancy Soaps into a letter and enclose it to me that I may hand it to Genll. Sumter before Congress adjourns.

My Respects to Mrs Dorr and all our friends and accept the repeated assurance of my personal respect & esteem

                                                                            SRB

ALS (DLC).

From Elisha Tracy

Honlb. Stephen Roe Bradley Esqr
My friend   Norwich Con[necticu]t March 22nd 1810

Will you be so good as to send me the bill you have had before Congress regulating the Quatermasters department of the Army of the U: States (I presume you have them printed) — I have constantly been watching the papers to see the progress of your Torpedo bill & Volunteers — it seems to progress slowly & am also looking sharp for a bill providing for fireing umbrellas from a Gun, these sistem I trust will be matured before the session closes.

Great inquiry is made of me respecting Torpedo's — did you see them, was you present at Fultons lecture; is repeated quick. Before the receipt of this — you have probably heard of John Langdons Election in New Hampshire — you see we are not quite down in New England — we shall have a smart struggle in this State for Governor — the federalist's are compleatly divided between Griswold & Treadwell & if the Republicans can be persuaded to practice policy we will shake the Hierarchy of this State & make old square toes at Farmington tremble like Belteshazzah — please to remember me politely to Mr. Montgomery — Colo. Moore & the other Gentln. at your House & to Doctr. Jones — & please to accept for yourself assurances of my respect & Esteem

Elisha Tracy

ALS (DLC).

From Hull & Foot

Sir   New Haven March 24th. 1810

Vessels are daily sailing from here direct for British Ports under heavy Bonds, calculating on th<e> repeal of the Non Intercourse Law to shield them from the Penalty. We did not like the risk, & have detained ou<r> Brig with Stock at a great expense more than 2 Weeks, daily expecting some news from Washington whic<h> might relieve us from this suspense. If the Non Intercourse Law is not to be enforced the Honest Merchan<t> is suffering, while the unprincipled Adventurer is reap<ing> a rich Harvest from the violation of it.

It does not appear probable that the Law will be revived but We do not feel safe in sending to British Ports at present under Bonds.

If Sir you can give us any Information, whether the Law will be repealed, or when it will expire, or whethe<r> the penalties for Violation will be enforced — you will confer a great favor to your Obliged & Sincere Friends & Humble Servants

Hull & Foot

Honl Stephen R Bradley

ALS (VtU). Margin obscured.

From Reuben Attwater

Hon. Stephen R. Bradley
Dear Sir,   Detroit August 1st. 1810

I wrote you last winter requesting you to give me farther time to remunerate you what I am indebted to you if the favor was granted would reward you for it, not hearing from you flatter myself you have complied with my request if so will forward you some money as soon as I am informed from what source I am to receive my Salary in consequence of the Embargo & nonintercourse I have no money in the Collectors Office. You will confer an additional favor on me to inform me what line of conduct I ought to pursue to receive compensation for my services as Commissioner of the land Board.

Please to accept of Mrs. Attwaters best respects and present hers with mine to Mrs. Bradley and your Daughters.

With sentiments of Esteem your friend & Humbl. Servt.

Reuben Attwater

ALS (VtU).

To the General Assembly of Vermont

Dated October 9th 1810

To the Honorable the General Assembly of the State of Vermont to be holden at Montpelier on the Second Thursday of October A.D. 1810

Humbly Sheweth the memorial of Stephen R Bradley of Westminster in Said State

That your memorialist did deliver to the listers of said town of Westminster a true list of all the rateable estate and property of which he was possessed on the 20th of June last amounting to Eight Hundred and fifty Seven dollars in which was included three Hundred dollars being the Six per Cent on five thousand dollars, which was for obligations and monies on hand over and above what he at that time owed — that at the request of the Listers he did in the month of September last deliver to them an inventory of all the obligations and notes he had <on the> 20th of June together with the money he had on hand and at the same time exhibited to them a list of obligations and contingent debts that were against him leaving a ballance of about five thousand Dollars subject to taxation as contained in the Original list exhibited to the listers— Notwithstanding which the Listers of said town of Westminster unduly influenced as your Memorialist verily believes from political and personal considerations did unjustly assess him the amount of forty thousand dollars and did oppressively add the Sum of Six pr Cent on the Same to his list which made the Same to amount to two thousand Nine Hundred and fifty Seven dolls and fifty Cents— When there is not another person's list in said town that amounts to four Hundred dollars.

Your Memorialist would further observe that the last meeting of Said Listers was held on the 2d Day of Instant October when their final division was made since which time Your Memorialist has had no possible means of Obtaining redress as there are but three Selectmen in said town of Westminster one of whom was absent on a long Journey and one of the other two stood in that relation to him as rendered it highly improper to make application to him for redress— and forasmuch as he is without remedy but through the interposition of the Legislature he prays Your honours to pass a law Granting him Such relief as shall seem Just and Equitable in the premises and as in duty bound will ever pray

Stephen R Bradley

ALS (Vt: MsVtSP, vol. 48, p. 52). An undated note on the verso reads: "To the General Assembly now sitting / Your Committee to whom was recommitted the within petition beg leave to report that having had the same again under consideration they find the facts therein stated to be true and that the petitioner ought to be allowed a hearing of his case by some Justice of the Peace of the Town of Westminster together with the Selectmen of sd Town to consider and determine thereon and have reported a bill accordingly —/ Ezra Butler for Comtte." Other notes read: "Petition of Stephen R Bradley / Filed Octr. 13 1810/ Att Th <Leverold?> Secy / In Gen Ass / Octr 13th 1810 / Read & refd to a cmtee of 3 to join from <cme?> / Attes WD Smith Clk / Mesrs Aiken / Brown / Mason / Cmtee Att WD Smith / In Co. Oct. 14th 1810 read & Resold to join a Mr Butler Appointed to Join / R. C. Mallary / In Gen Assy Octr 18th / Report rejected & recommitted to the same cmtee / Att WD Smith Clk."

Certificate of Abatement

[30 October 1810]

This Certificate maketh known to all whom it doth or may concern

That at a meeting of the Subscribers being one of the Justices and two of the Selectmen of the town of Westminster on the application of Stephen R Bradley of Said Westminster and in pursuance of the Statute entitled "An Act concerning the Grand list of the town of Westminster" we proceeded to hear and determine concerning the list of the said Stephen R Bradley for the year one thousand Eight Hundred and ten and on due consideration we do fix the said list at the sum of Nine Hundred Dollars.

And do by these presents Grant to the Said Stephen R Bradley an abatement of two thousand and fifty seven dollars and fifty Cents on his list for the present year.

In witness whereof we have subscribed our names to this Certificate at Westminster this thirtieth day of October in the Year of our lord One thousand Eight Hundred and ten.

Eliakim Spooner}   Justice of the Peace
of the town of Westminster

John Grant}   Select Men of
Ephm. Ranney Junr}   the town of Westminster

ADS (NcD).

From William Plumer

My dear Sir,   Epping (N. H.) Decr 21. 1810

Having been some time employed in compiling the history of the United States, in which I wish to introduce a considerable portion of the biography of eminent citizens—& having recently seen in the journals of the day, notice <of> the death of your late colleague, Israel Smith permit me to request the favor of your transmitting to me, under your frank, some account of his parentage, education, profession, the offices he held, & of his character.

If you have any spare documents, I should be pleased with receiving as many of them, during the session, as you have leisure to enclose, as they contain information that to me is highly useful.

I should be much gratified, in receiving from your pen, information of the proceedings of Congress, & the state of the nation, at this eventful era.

I am with much esteem, Sir your most obedient humble servant.

William Plumer

Hon Stephen R Bradley
Senator Washington.

ALS (VtU). Margin obscured.

From Jonathan Dorr

Honble Stephen R Bradley
Sir   Roxbury 29th Decr. 1810

I have now the pleasure of addressing you at the great City where last spring you was so kind to shew Mrs D & myself so many civilities the great Topic is here will the Charter of the U States Bank be renew'd, or not; is the great question: will thank you if not too much trouble to inform me your oppinion on the subject. Money in Boston was never known more scarce owing they say to the National Banks calling in for a settlement the want of Money extends to rich & Poor there seems to be general distress and a number of failures have within a few days taken place of considerable magnatude had the pleasure to hear the last week all our Westminster Friends were well.

With much Respect Remain Your Friend & humb servt

Jona. Dorr

ALS (VtU).

From Samuel A. Foot

Sir   New Haven January 4, 1811

Your obliging favors,[1] enclosing the documents accompanying the Presidents Message, & 2 News Papers are recieved, You will please to accept my most gratefull acknowlegements for your kind attention, in forwarding the printed documents of Last Session as well as these. I assure you Sir they have been a Source of much useful Instruction as well as entertainment, they exhibit the State of our Foreign Relations in a Small Compass, & have corrected many false Statements in our News Papers which pass among us for Sacred truths.

You will pardon my Anxiety about the renewal of the non Intercourse with Great Britain, we are interested in the event, anxious to know what will be the operation of the Law if revived, on Vessels now out, arriving after the 2d. Feby. & wholly Ignorant & Innocent — will these Cargoes be seized?

The Charter of the United States Bank is a subject interesting to Merchants, by the Papers of this day it appears the Committee of the House are divided. Banks are a Nuisance, this Counterfeiting by Authority I presume has done more mischief than all the Counterfeiters in New-*Gate Prison*. I have ventured to enclose our *Post Master Book* on the Subject, which may be amusing.

Mrs. Hull with Mrs. Foot present their best Respects.

Respectfully Your Obliged & Obedt. Sert

Saml. A. Foot[2]

Hon Stephen R. Bradley

ALS (NcD: Bradley Family Papers). Enclosure not found.
1. Letters not found.
2. Samuel Augustus Foot (1780–1846) graduated from Yale in 1797 and was engaged in the shipping trade. He later served in the Connecticut house of representatives, 1817–18, 1821–23, and 1825–26, the U.S. House of Representatives, 1823–25 and 1833–34, the U.S. Senate, 1827–33, and as governor of Connecticut, 1834–35.

From Unidentified

Dept. of War Accos. office

Sir Jany. 14th. 1811

Since you were at the office the account of the late Lt Dorr has been investigated as far as the documents in the Department would permit and from thence it appears that a Balance of Two hundred & Sixteen Dollars 44/100 is due for Pay & Subsistence but as the Pay Masters accounts have not yet been finally settled, it is to be understood that the above Balance remains open to correction shoud any information be received prior to application being made by the Representatives of Lt Dorr which might go to alter the Same.

Verry respectfully I am Sir Your Mo obd st

[*illegible*]

The Honle. S. R Bradley Esqr

ALS (VtU).

From Jonathan Dorr

Honble Stephen R Bradley

Dear sir   Roxbury 18th Jany 1811

I had yesterday the pleasure to receive your Esteem'd favor of the 8 Inst and thank you for its contents am happy to find tis your Oppinion the U S Bank Charte<r> will be renew'd in some shape or other as I am a witness to what extreme distress the Mercantile part of society will be driven to be Oblig'd to settle up that Institution on the expiration of the present charter it likewise falls very hard on the Manufacturing Intrest and in fact on almost every class of peop<le> should anything favorable to the renewal traspire if it will not be intrudeing too much will than<k> you to inform me as I have many friends haveing Stock and otherways Intrested who are very Anxious to learn the result.

We have this day an Arrival direct fro<m> Bordeaux but as she comes to a Fedral house we are not as yet permited to know the true state of things all that has as yet transpired is she has a full Load of Brandy &c and comes to a good Market. That Bonaparte is amusing himself a little distance from Paris in hunting &c. and one other Account [(]how far true I cant tell) that the French will not consider their Berlin & Milan decrees the revocation of them to take effect untill the English orders in Council are repeal'd.

Had yesterday the pleasure to hear of all our Westminster friends being well Mrs Dorr is well and joins with me in wishing you a happy New Year.

Am with Esteem yours Respectfully

Jona. Dorr

ALS (VtU). Margin obscured.

From Jacob Bayley

Honbl. Sir, Newbury January 22nd 1811

I <perceive?> that the United States are in danger of being involved in a war Either with Grat Brittain or France. I shall be sory if we have been the agressors [*illegible*] recommendation to be ready, I have been acquainted with all the wars Since the year 1744, and have served under Britton and America Sixteen years, and by Experience have found it expedient always to be prepared. I think the 20000 mentioned in the presidents Message will be raised and held in rediness, if so, I would recommend John Bayley a son of mine, who has been a Major of the Brigade under General Davis, I believe to the Satisfaction of the ofcers and Soldiers, Sir, if you will recommend the above John Bayley to the President for the appointment of an officer in the Twenty thousand men to be raised, it would highly Gratifying to me.

I have had a grant as <Colo?> in the French war so called that ended in 1762. of five thousand acres of Land in west Florida, in Genrll. Lymans Grant. Please to enquire and Corespond with Genrll. Chamberlin respecting the above, and oblige your very humble Servant

Jacob Bayley

The honrll. Stephen R. Bradley

ALS (VtU). Two thirds of a line of text is obscured by a fold in the manuscript.

From Andrew Hull Jr.

Dear Sir New Haven Jany. 24th. 1811

I feel anctious at the present mome<nt> not only as it Respects my own Intrest but for the intrest of my Country. I am not abou<t> to express any opinion about the banking Cistem, but cannot refrain from expresing my surprise at the bill reported by Mr Epps and others respecting Nonintercours. If Congress are disposed to upset the present administration I think the step would be effectual. I have always ben disposed strictly to obey the law<s> of my country at the same time think they ought so to be made that they will <Propably?> be Respected. I Sufered under the Embargo & from Nonintercourse Law at least ten thousand dollars Chearfully by adhearing Strictly to the Laws, I owned at the time the embargo was laid the Principal part of Six Vessels which was eventua<l>ly almost Sacrifised. The last brig was Loaded about Six weeks before the nonintercours Expired She Lay in New Haven harbour four weeks with Stock on deck we expecting the Nonintercourse to be taken off we did not like to give bonds double the amount of vessel and Carg and Send her to an English Port as there was no other to which she could go. Rathar than break the Law and Incur the Penalty we Sold Vessel and Cargo fo<r> less than first Cast on a long Credit. The Purchase<r> Gave bonds Sent her to a british Port and Cleare<d> About Four Thousand dollars and have not as <nec?> as many others ben called to any Account. Since which we have built a Large and valuable Brig having Purchased a cargo about the time of the Presiden<t's> Proclamation had her ready for Sea in Decemr. thinking the Nonintercourse would not go into effect we sent her to sea the first of Jany. Int after waiting several weeks for a fair wind. Will Congress now make a Law that shall Strip thousands of Property the avails of that which was so sent out while the thing was uncertain and could not have foreknolege of what would take Place. And not know that they were to forfeit their All, would it not operate somewhat like an expostfacto Law, will the goverment deprive their citizens from bringing their Property to this country or suffer Revenue <officers?> to become as mad Dogs and Plunder the Property honestly obtained, as well as to Prevent the Revenue from being benefited by the duties. I trust congress will at least make some Provison for those who have honestly attemted to obtain it. After a Law is mad[e] and Promulgated if Men will with their Ey[e]s open violate it, I wish they may be Punished with severity. I am with sentiments of high Esteem and Respect Your obt. Servt

Andw Hull Junr.

Hon. Stephen R. Bradley
    ALS (VtU). Margin obscured.

To Royall Tyler

Confidential

Hon. Judge Tyler
Dear Sir   Washington Jany. 27th. 1810 [1811]

    How far the political arrangment in relation to the State of Vermont that I am now to suggest will meet your approbation must depend on your feelings and Judgment should it strike you favourably it will be of importance you pass through the State in Your circuits to feel the public pulse carefully and with much address You will easily suppose that I am tired of my seat in the Senate, and I believe my Colleague is sick of his,[1] it is now above thirty Years since I first held the appointment of Delagate to Congress — independant of the depreciations of domestic and Social happiness I have Suffered in attending on Congress there is one consideration which has great influence to wean me from any further desire to continue therein — those who were my social acquaintance and most intimate friends but a few years ago in the Councils of the nation are now all dead resigned declined or gone so that I have new acquaintances and Friends to make every Session, and at my age of life the recollection of the past is by no means compensated in the enjoyment of the present. I have conversed with Judge Robinson and Mr Shaw on what I am now about to disclose, to wit, that I shall take Govr. G. place[2] — that you shall take the place I now hold — that Judge Robinson Shall take the place You hold and that D. Chase shall be placed on the Supreme court *vice* Judge H. who may probably wish to retire to preach the gospel to the Baptists I flatter myself that it will be agreeable to You to serve a few Years in the Senate and should the vacancy take place at the next session of the Legislature I have no doubt they would give You the appointment not only for the remainder of my term but for the next Six Years Several precedents from other States may be adduced when in exactly a Similar Situation — I Should be very much gratified with a line from you on the Subject and to know your feelings in relation thereto.

I can give you no more information in relation to our public affairs than the documents I sent you communicate with the aid of the news papers I have touched *mr <Law?>* on the Subject of a donation to the College at Burlington he has determined to present the board with books to the amount of $500 — of the most modern and best collection that can be obtained in Europe or America and has given directions accordingly the Other affair which was mentioned between You and me concerning L. L. D I have placed in a favourable train I think I shall succeed at one if not at two and nearly at the same time — of this however I can give you more correct Information hereafter. You will please to make my respects to your brother Judges and all our friends And Accept the Assurances of my most cordial respect & personal Esteem

Stephen R Bradley

ALS (MB). Cover addressed by Bradley to "The Hon. Royal Tyler Esquire / Chief Justice of Vermont / at / Burlington / Vermont / *via Albany*," with "Burlington" crossed through and "Middlebury" added; franked by Bradley.
1. SRB's colleague in the Senate was Jonathan Robinson, a Democratic Republican who served from 1807 to 1815.
2. Jonas Galusha was governor of Vermont from 1809 to 1813 and again from 1815 to 1820.

From William Plumer

Dear Sir,   Epping (NH) January 31. 1811

On my return from Boston I received your obliging letter of the 3d instant,[1] with the enclosed sketch of the life of your late colleague, Mr Smith; & under another cover a sett of important documents — for all of which please to accept my grateful acknowledgments.

I am happy that my attempt to compile a history of our country meets your approbation; & shall feel myself under peculiar obligations to you, if you can command leisure from time to time to transmit me under your frank such other documents as you can spare. If I should not have health and leisure to compleat the work, I shall at least collect & arrange many of the requisite materials — & I hope leave them to some one who will execute it with more ability than I possess; but be assured that nothing but *imperious necessity* will induce me to abandon it.

A vast majority of our Republican friends are anxious to hear that Congress have definitively refused to renew the charter of the bank of the United States. I have long considered that institution as the most powerful engine that has been raised against Republicanism. And I have for sometime indulged the hope that a republican Congress would not revive & organize a body of disciplined troops to attack them and their constitutients [*sic*]. I am really at a loss to find that part of the Constitution that gives Congress *express* authority to establish a *national bank;* & if that authority is not *expressly* given, it seems to me that the tenth amendment *expressly* prohibits your assuming it by *implication.*

We have agreed again to support your *old* friend John Langdon for the gubernatorial chair. It was with great & real reluctance the old gentleman consented; but the difficulty of agreeing on a new candidate made it necessary. We shall, I think, if no unfortunate events in Europe or in Congress should occur materially affecting public opinion, succeed in our March elections.

I shall at all times be happy to hear from you, not of the events which the journals of the day narrate, but of the motives which influence & direct both the majority & minority in the government — & the real objects they seek to attain. You may safely write me fully, freely & confidentially. Your confidence shall never be by me abused.

With sentiments of much respect and esteem I am dear Sir, Your most obedient humble servant

William Plumer

Hon. Stephen R Bradley
    Senator
        Washington

ALS (NcD: Bradley Family Papers).
1. Letter not found.

From Royall Tyler

Dear Sir   Rutland February 3d. 1811

    I acknowledged the receept of your confidential letter[1] which I recieved at Middlebury by two letters[2] dated on the same day at that place in which I inclosed abstracts of the census of this State from the Marshals returns. As the person of all others from whom it would be desirable to keep the contents was then an inmate in my room I could not reply to it — and I have had no hour until the present which I could call my own.

    The site in the proposed arrangment in which you are personally interested you must know for your friends and even apparent opponents know it has long been a favourite object with me that you should possess as conducive to the gratification of the wishes of your Friends and the dignity and wellfare of the State — and should no other impediments present than such as are personal with me and such as depend on my Friendship and personal exertion to remove the object might be considered as assuredly attainable. The arrangement however embraces the interests and opinions of others who I have no opportunity at present of consulting. I regret that the communication was not made to me earlier as on the receept of your letter I had already quitted the northern counties besides meeting the University Corporation in Burlington the members of which & their influence in the State you well know — as it is — I will endeavour to obtain such information and in such mode as shall be prudent on the subject and communicate the result when we meet in the spring.

    Governour G — met me here on Colledge bussiness and I had a favourable opportunity of conversing with him but as you omitted to mention in your letter that it is proposed that he shall take a seat in the senate — although I conclude this is within the Arrangment and as I considered that you had probably some more favourable medium of access to those principally concerned in the plan — I did not intimate the subject to him. I expect however to see him again at Manchester where I shall probably be until the begining of March — and hope to hear from you in the interim — when if you do not think it preferable to apply to him — if this is to be done — through Judge R. or the Doctor — I shall be happy to aid in such mode as shall be thought advisable.

    I have no doubt that if there was a vacancy in the chair — it would be filled from the east side of the Mountains — but I conclude if there is a change it must be effected by amicable understanding of the Republican Interest — and I am pleased to Learn that this is the object of your friends.

    I am informed in a letter from the States Attorney — that Mr Green is appointed post Master at Brattleboro — this I learn by a letter from Dr Russell Fitch of that Town operates a grevious disappointment to him. I regret that this should have happened — more especially as Dr. F. has influence in B — and more particularly in Guilford his native town. I understand that Mr G — is a promising young man of handsome talents — is it not possible the [sic] obtain the Collectors office for him vacant by the resignation of our Friend Dr. Penniman?

and is there not to be another Collector appointed in the North East part of the State according to Mr Galletins recommendation?

The merchants on the seaboard are anticepating the non intercourse and the new road through the Notch of the white mountains and Caledonia County to Canada is crouded with sleighs loaded with Pork & Ashes. An intelligent man told me yesterday that he rode a section of the road last Week and counted 530- sleighs in 30 miles. The expected non intercourse does not as yet excite much sensation among our citizens Although the federalists begin to whisper their apprehensions of the renewal of those scenes of embarrasment and blood shed which accompan[i]ed the Embargo—if however the law is made explicit and put promptly into execution and followed up by correct decisions of the Foederal Courts there can be no danger of the Non intercourse being effected on our Vermont frontier—but if—if——In other words I have no doubt that if the execution of the law was intrested to the executive and judiceary of this State it would be caried into full effect without exciting insurrections or even Murmerings among the peoplle—for we have no ambition to shew our selves wiser than the law or more independant than the government.

In hopes to hear from you speedely I continue your Assured friend

Royall Tyler

Honble Stephen R Bradley
    Washington

    ALS (NcD: Bradley Family Papers). Cover addressed by Tyler to "Honble Stephen R: Bradley Esqr / Senator of the United States / Washington"; marked "Rutland Vt, Feb, 4th." and "Free"; docketed by SRB, "Letter from Judge Tyler."
    1. SRB to Tyler, 27 Jan. [1811].
    2. Letters not found.

From Nathaniel Ruggles

Dear Sir   Roxbury, near Boston Feby 10th. 1811

It is with reluctance, that I intrude upon your reflections on more important national concerns. But being individually interested—You will excuse my stating my case—and asking your opinion thereon. I have property in Calcutta, part of which, say 10000$, I have ordered ship'd in an American Vessel for the United States, this Vessel (altho: the orders were given some time before) did not sail from the United States 'till about the 10th. Jany last. I do not think it can be the policy of Congress to exclude from entry, any property, *Bona fide*, American, or to prevent the Citizens from getting their property home (In case the Non Intercourse goes into effect agst. England). Without doubt, there are Thousands in the Union in like circumstances and that Congress are making some wise provisions for those cases—but as I have seen nothing, relating to such cases in their debates; I am lead to the enquiry, whether there has been or is likely to, be any provisions made in the Laws for such cases—which Dr. Sir at your leisure please to inform me.

I am respectfully Your huml Servt.

Nathl. Ruggles

Honble. Stephen R. Bradley Esqr.
    ALS (VtU).

From Joshua Chamberlain

Sir, Guilford, 12 of Feb. 1811.

I have the honour to acknowledge the receipt of your favour of the 21 ultimo, covering a Note from Mr. Secretary Hamilt<on.> I am much obliged to you, for your politenes<s> and attention, and tender you my sincere thanks.

Since I saw you, I have been appointed to one of the Professorships in our University; and as the situation is both more lucrative and pleasant than a Chaplaincy in the Navy, I wish that Mr. Hamilton would withdraw his nomination if it be already made, and appoint some other person to fill the place destined for me in that department.

With sentiments of the most perfect respect, I am, Sir, yours sincerely

J. Chamberlain

Hon. S. R. Bradley, Esq.
ALS (VtU). Margin obscured.

From Farnsworth & Churchill

Sir Windsor. Feb. 14. 1811

Yours of the 14th. ult. is recd. with pleasure. The offer to supply us with papers is a testimonial of respect for which we feel the hig[h]est honor. We are now taking one from Washingt<on,> three from Baltimore, one from Trenton and several others from the southward. Should you find any thing you may deem important we shall gratefully receive it from your liberal hand. But our news generally comes sooner by way of Boston papers than any other.

We have only time to inform that the people here manifest the strongest desire that the Bank Charter may not be renewed. With the same spirit they would purge the country of British tories would the wish to clip the speculation and influence of her stockholders. With the same spirit they would establish and maintain a government affording happiness to the people, would they wish to maintain a Bank among ourselves only. Our last news from Congress gives us some alarm more than was anticipated, that the Charter will be renewed. But we hope our fears are of short duration.

We have the honor to be Sir your obt. Servants

Farnsworth & Churchill

Hon. S. R. Bradly [*illegible*] S.
ALS (VtU). Margin obscured.

To Albert Gallatin

Sir Washington Febr 15th. 1811

I take the liberty through you of Recommending to the President of the United Sta<tes> Josiah Demming of Vermont as a very proper person to be appointed Collector for the district of Mumph<rey>magog in the State of Vermont, he is a gentlem<an> educated a merchant but from the peculiar situation of the country has done but little business in that way for a year or two past he possesses an amiable moral Character of Strict integrity is enterprizing and endued with great activity of body & mind. Should the President deem it expedient to give hi<m> the appointment I dare to pledge myself you shall find the laws faithfully executed in that quarter as far as it is in the power of any one man to do the same.

Accept Sir the Assurance of my high respect & personal Esteem

            S R B

the Hon.
Albert Gallatin
secretary of the treasury

 ALS (VtU). Margin obscured.

From John T. Peters

Sir   Hebron Feb 15. 1811.

 The partiality of my friends has made me aspiring — and the Collector's Office at *Middletown* is so pleasant a situation that I cannot resist the temptation to solicit.

 If from *our* slight acquaintan<ce> or the information of others you think me capable and worthy of filling the place of *A Wolcott*, will you have goodness to say so, to our "beloved President" and to your other friend "*inter Divas.*"

 A letter from my friend House accompanies this. Other letters have *also* been forwarded in my behalf.

 Should my *friends* be suspected of partiality — Information may be obtained from the Connecticut Delagation should you wish to know further than that.

 I am with great respect your humble Serv't

                           John T. Peters

Hon Mr. Bradley.

 ALS (VtU). Margin obscured.

From Titus Hutchinson

Sir   Woodstock Vert. Feby 28th 181<1>

 I write with a view to interest you in behalf of Franklin Hunter of Windsor son to Judge Hunter. He is no<w> twenty one years of age, became such about two weeks since. He is a firm republican and as such has stemd the torrent in Windsor Street for several years. Has been a clerk in a store, has a good education of the class not Collegiate — and I understand has made military tactics much his study. He now wou'd be glad of a Lieutenants commission in the light artillery if a vacancy shou'd happen or, on failure of that, in the light Infantry. I cannot speak of his military acquisitions as a matter within my own knowledge — yet have no doubt of their sufficiency. But I can say, without any hesitation, that his genius and manly deportment seem well calculated to enable him to act as Lieutt. with Hono<r> to himself and the Government. I think justice requires me to add, that his connection in the mercantile world has been with those from whom he has no reason to expect assistance in beginning the world for himself on account of his firm Republican principles acted out, young as he was, thro the late embargo struggle. Your interest in his behalf, with the Secretary at War, may confer a great favor upon him and his friends, and elevate his candle upon a bushel where it will give light the world around.

 I am with Great Respect Yours

                          Titus Hutchinson

Hon S. R. Bradley Esqr.

 ALS (VtU). Margin obscured.

From Gideon Granger

Dear friend   Genl. Post Office 26 March 1811

I enclose you a petition respecting the Post Office in Chester, Windsor County, Vermont, which I pray you to peruse & forward me your opinion on the premises.

Mr Smith has left the Department of State, with an offer to go to Russia;[1] other changes are frequently talked about but I am the last man likely to know whether they will or will not take place.

Always your friend

G. Granger

The Honble. Stephen Roe Bradley
    Brattleboro
        Vermont.

[Enclosure]
[Inhabitants of Chester, Vermont, to Gideon Granger]

Dear Sir   March 2nd. 1811—

The undersigned inhabitants of Chester in the County of Windsor and State of Vermont, have to trespass upon a small portion of your time and request your attention to a subject which nearly affects our interest and convenience. The affairs of the Post-office in this Town, for a few years past have been conducted in a manner which we deem improper: and we have to request in behalf of ourselves and friends that you will correct the evil—and if the causes are sufficient that you will remove the present Postmaster Thomas Robinson and put in his place Abner Watkins a man who lives in a situation to accomodate the Mail-Carier, and the Inhabitants, and for whose character and abilities we are willing to avouch.

<Waitstill?> Ranney
C. L. Rockwood—
Nathan Whiting

P. S. The Person we wish to have the office is Abner Watkins a mechanic and a friend to the Government.

... and State of Vermont of Lawful age testify and say that I have during the last year had several letters sent me through the medium of the Post-office. The letters arrived in the office in Chester and were then secreted or witheld by the Postmaster Thos. Robinson for several weeks, on account of which, <information of> great importance was kept from me untill it was to late to transact the business—and then not given up untill I actually proved that the letter was in his hands—one person not receiving an answer to his letters directed to me on business of importance, was put to the troble of coming a [...] two hundred and seventy miles on purpo<se to> see me; which Journey and expense might have been prevented; had not my letters been withheld—other persons friends of mine make similar complaints.

James Fox

Chester in the County of Windsor and state of Vermont March 2nd. AD 1811 personally appeared James Fox signer of the above affidavit and made solemn oath that the facts therein stated are true before

James Miller Justice Peace

LS and enclosure (NcD: Bradley Family Papers). Enclosure addressed to Gideon Granger Esquire / Postmaster General / Washington City"; marked "Rockingham Vt. March 15." and "Free." Damaged by removal of seal and fold in paper.

1. On 19 Mar. 1811, President James Madison met with Robert Smith to ask for his resignation as secretary of state

and offer him a diplomatic post in Russia, which Smith subsequently declined. Smith, who had publicly criticized administration policy, was replaced by James Monroe (*Papers of James Madison: Presidential Series*, 3:xxx–xxxi, 226 n. 1)

From Andrew Hull Jr.

Dear Sir   Hartford March 26th. 1811

    I left home yesterday all well we have heard nothing since you left Cheshire—the subject I conversed with you respecting the loan of some money if you can spare the sum you mentioned will accommodate us very much as in building and loading our brig we Contracted from 4 to 5 thousand dollars which w<ill> be due the fore part of April which paym<ent> we calculated to mete withe avails of the Cargo expected at that time we have rec'd Letters from the Captain he expects to be in with a valuable cargo by the middle of nex<t> month and will do well if we could enjoy it but there must be considerable delay—altho there is no doubt with Judge Edwards respecting taking bonds, after the Property <is Seased and libelled?>—and he tells me that he thinks the<re> is no question but the Secretary will remit Sir will you be good enough to write Hull & Foot New Haven by the next Mail what sum you can spare and when and where it can be received and how the business may be transacted— please to make my best respects to your dear Family—Merab your Son Wm. & Fam<ily.>

    I am with the highest Esp[...] & Respect Yours Respectfully

                                                                                    Andw. Hull Junr.

Hon. Stephen R Bradley

    ALS (DLC). Margin obscured.

From Jabez Penniman

Hono. Stephen R. Bradley Esqr.

Dear Sir   Swanton Aprill 24th 1811

    Your very polite and obliging favour of the 17th Inst. was duly received by yesterdays mail—it would have afforded me greate satisfaction to h<ave> staid one day longer in Westminster that I might have had the pleasure of seeing you and as you say to have "compared notes in relation to our political concerns" but so the fates had ordered it.

    Mrs Penniman does herself the honor of presenting you with a volum of the Oracles of Reason it being the only one She has except one retained at the Authors peticular reque<st> but she is very sorry it is not in a <sound?> condition.

    I am at this time at a loss what to say in relation to your proposal for exchanging my house for lands in Bradly vale as I know nothing of the quality of those lands. But I will take twelve hundred dollars for the house and Garden giving a fair time for pay—it being the amount of what you say three hundred acres would bring.

    I will make enquiry and write you further on the subject.

    I am Dear Sir most respectfully your friend and very humble servt.

                                                                                   Jabez Penniman

    ALS (VtU). Margin obscured.

From Jonathan Dorr

Honble Stephen R Bradley Esqr

Sir   Roxbury 17th Augt 181<1>

Your favor of 4th Inst (Post mark 9th) I duley receiv<'d> and Notice'd the contents, was extreme<ly> happy this day to receive your favor of 12th Inst conteracting the advice of the death of our sister Holton as, where, there is life there is hopes, altho her case must be very doubtful from the r[...] presentation you have been pleas'd t<o> give us of her situation.

The sixteen hundred or Two Thousa<nd> Dollars we will take of you on loan for Nin<e> Months or One Year as may best suit yo<u> on the terms you propose, and shal<l> be very happy to see you at Roxbury. We have no News to communicate by Arrivals yesterday & today from Lisbon it appears confirm'd that the British & Portuguese Armys are coming back to their strong holds near Lisbon and their is a strong probability of our haveing to feed them there the Ensuing Winter.

Our family & friends are well Mrs Dorr Joins with me in remembrance to you & your family and Remain Yr Friend & humbl Servt

Jona. Dorr

ALS (VtU). Margin obscured.

From Joseph Wheaton

Very Dear Sir   Washington City Septr. 7. 1811

The office of Sergeant at Arm<s> has become vacant by the death of Mr. Jame<s> Mathers of the Senate. I therefore in concequen<ce> of the great Sacrifices which I Made in the re<vo>lution by entering into the Service of the United Stat<es> in being disenherited by my parents in concequence of that Service, and the repeated known wounds I received during that period — and haveing Shewn to the world that no charge of defaulcatio<n> could be Supported against me by the P[ost] M[aster] Genl. but that he bona fide owes me $1600=34 [*illegible*] as Settled by two arbitrations under a rule of courts I trust I have given proof of fidelity Zeal and devotion to my Government & Country in the course of more than thirty years Servi<ce> not exhibited by every one — and being advanced in life with a growing family and in very needy circumstances — I make an appeal to your Sence of the Justice of my hope, in your consideration, that I may not be deemed wholly unentitled to some notice of the Senate, and therefore I intreat your interest & Support in obtaining for me the appointment of Sergeant at Arms to the Senate of the Untied States, and for which I Shall tender to you my Homage — My Gratitude, & my fidelity.

I have the honor to be faithfully Sir your obedient Servant

Joseph Wheaton

P.S.
Sir

Mrs. Wheaton expresses the highest confidence that you will make Some exertions i<n> my behalf and My children exult in the circumstance of your Lady & Children Sh<ew> Some interest in them — indeed Sir their hearts are animated in the hope you will make some exertion in my behalf — it would be Mortifying indeed to See them disappointed.

J W —

Stephen R. Bradley Esqr.

ALS (VtU). Margin obscured.

From Christopher Ripley

American Consulate, London,
Sir,   Septr. 8th. 1811.

I herewith send a London News Paper, which alludes to a Non-Importation Order, that is about to be issued by this Government, against the United States. The Order did not appear in last Nights Gazette.

It may be in your recollection, that I call'd on you, at your Seat at Westminster in April 1809, and had some conversation with you about obtaining a Commission in the Army of the United States: at that time my place of residence was Northampton Mass.

I am now employed in the American Consular Office here, and be assured that it would give me great pleasure to have the oppertunity of being serviceable to you.

I have the honour to be your Obedt. Servt.

Christr. Ripley

To The Hon: Stephen R. Bradley,}
              Senator of the U. S.
              Westminster.

ALS (VtU).

From Abraham Bradley Jr.

General Post Office
Sir   Sept. 13th. 1811

I have in the absence of the Postmaster General received your letter of the 5th. instant — and we have pursuant to your agreement forwarded a bond and contract to Randol<ph> to be executed by Messrs. Chase & Brackett. I pray you to accept our thanks for the very satisfactory arrangemen<t> that you have made with those gentlemen. When you arrive here we will repay you the expences arising fr<om> the journey. I have the Honour to be your Obedt serv<t>

Abraham Bradley junr

Genl. Stephen R. Bradley
Westminster Vt

ALS (VtU). Margin obscured.

From James Dickinson

4th. Nov. 1811

The Bearer Doctr. Daniel Chief Surgeon of the Army, is a man of Honor, Inte<l>ligence & Independence. He is lately from the Mississippi and can tell you of the Wonderful doings there; He can also tell you of the hard doings here and moreover of the infamous doings of the Dipper. The Secrty. of War by t<he> Agency of Mr. Jones presses me so hard, that I shall be obliged to strip him bare & show him as he is. How will this be received by our Chief — Wil<l> he stand between his Servants & act & divide with even handed Justice — I hope so & think so, but give me your opinion in a single line by return mail — and may God bless & <preserve?> You.

Truly yours

Ja: Dickinson

Honble Genl. Bradley
 ALS (VtU). Margin obscured.

From Royall Tyler

Dear Sir.   Brattleboro Novr. 12. 1811—
Confidential

    Early in the Legeslative session at Montpellier I observed that interest was making for the next senatorial election accompanied with the uniform assertion that you would decline a reappointment. No person on the ground not even Mr Richards knew your determination on the subject: By the return of Mr R— to West Minster I wrote to the States Attorney in hopes from his answer to be able to state positively and Authoretively that you intended to serve the State another term but recieving no satisfactory reply and observing that attempts were making to engage the leading Members to pledge themselves to the several candidates; your friends consulted together and it was concluded that I should be put on the list of candidates—concluding that if in the event you should incline to accept another appointment —*my friends would be your friends*— and we should have them in some measure embodied and at the least prevent their irretrevebly engaging in an opposite interest.

    If the Election had happened this year I do not know what would have been the result but I conclude that the shew of patronage in my favour was not despicable because after I was mentioned the Zeal to obtain assurances of support for the other candidates suddenly cooled and it was generally observed by their warmest supporters that it would be most advisable to put of[f] the consideration of the subject until another session. I hope however that you will incline to serve another septenary or what would be more desirable that you will have some executive appointment in which you may serve your country as ably and with more ease to yourself. A confidential knowledge of your Ultimate decision as to the senatorship when made — will be beneficial — especially as I expect to see many friends this Winter.

    I was at Westminster yesterday your family & connections are all well — William was preparing to set off for his sister.

    If you should see Mr Law please to remember me in the Most friendly Terms to him. The last evening I read his "Instinctive Impulses" to my family and we concluded our Vespers with the Modern Griselda from the Port Folio.

    If in the calling out of the melitia under the Presidents recommendation an appointment of surgeon should be made in our quarter you will permit me to recommend to your Notice Dr Russell Fitch of this town.

    I hope to be favoured with some communications from you during the sessions and whilst you are engaged in securing our National interests at Washington I expect to be as sedulously carefull of our interests at home.

    Your friend & Servt —

                                                                  Royall Tyler

Honble. Genl Bradley —

    ALS (NcD: Bradley Family Papers). Cover addressed by Tyler to "Honble. Stephen R: Bradley / Senator of the United States / Washington." Docketed by SRB, "from Judge Tyler / Answered."

From Andrew Hull Jr.

Dear Sir   New Haven Novr. 15th. 181<1>

    We were very much mortified in not seeing you when at New Haven Mrs. Hull Betsey and myself were in town at Mr. Foots at the time waiting for a good time to go to New York went on board on saturday You had left N York before we arived Hull & Foot were Particularly anctiou<s> to have conversed with you on the subject of our Bonds gave for the Brig Mars and her cargo of Molasses from Trinidad last spring—we gave Bond<s> for the duties seperate which are Paid the other Bonds have ben sued or rathe<r> a suit comenced or a liebel and the suit continued and cost accruing—it was not in our Power to give any information to the Captain of the Law of the 2d of March last she arived here and Reported from Trinidad where she took in the Cargo—Now if we are to be subjected to the Payme<nt> of the Bonds when there was no Fraud and after Paying the duties it would be a hard Case and more Especially to the Firm of Hull and Foot as they have done every thing in their Power to escape difficulty and not attempting to evade the Laws of the General Goverment and after sacrifising a Considerable Part of the Value of Five Brigs employed in the West indie trad<e> Previous to the embargo we never sent to sea a Cent during the embargo and Former Nonintercours Law—after they ended we built a Brig and sent her to Sea being confident at that time that the Orders in Council would be Revoked in case the French decrees were which was the prevailing Opinion here at that time—I trust that the Majority of Congress will be carefull not to strip their Cit[iz]ens of their *All* when there hath ben no Fraud Intended and the Revenue benefited—we are at a loss what method to Pursue whether to Petition Congress or not—will be very much Oblig<ed> to You for your Opinion—and advice so far as Consistant.

    Yours very Respectfully

                                             Andw Hull Junr.

Hon. Stephen R. Bradley

    ALS (VtU). Margin obscured. Docketed by WCB(?), "Gen Hull of Cheshire."

From Elihu Luce

Dear Sir   Hartland Novr. 24th day AD 1811

    Your favour, the Presidents Message was duly received by yesterdays Mail. I also receved by Newspaper information the communicat<ion> made by the President to Congress of the settlement of the Chesepeake Affair. I fear Sir that this settlement happening at so late a moment is only to <deny?> Congress and will finaly prove another Erskine adjustment which will not be recognized by the British Goverm<ent.> I also receivd the correspondance between Mr. Munroe and Mr Foster respecting our dificulties with Greate Briton. And if I understand Mr. Foster their is no credit to be given to any Official document comeing from the Emperor of the French and that the President of the U. S. is a dupe if he believes any thing of the kind therefore nothing is to credited by our Goverment comeing from France untill it is sanctioned by Grate Briton—&c. This is Fedreal creed also. I hope Sir and I believe that Congress will not be deceived by any more British influence and Federal flattery or threatenings and that the good people of this northern Contry will find energetic measures adopted by Congress to support our National rights against murder plunder and impressment. Should Congress be out managed by Foster and the Fedrealist I hope the wrath of God will be kindled and that Congress will without discrimination be anihilated. I am yours respectfully

Elihu Luce

Hon. Stephen R. Bradley Esquire
ALS (VtU). Margin obscured.

From James Elliot

Sir, [29 November 1811, Putney, Vermont] *[date cut off in copying]*

I thank you for the favour of the President's Message, and will thank you for a newspaper occasionally. I do not wish to trouble you often in that way, but a spare paper once in a while will be agreeable to me in my solitude.

Whatever may have been my opinion as to measures heretofore, I am convinced that a crisis has now arrived, which renders it the duty of all friends of their country to support the National Government. I am determined to support it in future with steadiness, and to the best of my ability. And I am inclined to think that the impression under which I am myself acting, is gaining ground in this quarter, in consequence of the President's Message.

Should an army be raised, I would offer myself a candidate for such a situation in it as I could accept without degrading myself, after having been so long in a high publick situation. I think this ought not to be a lower rank than the command of a regiment—but if it should be your opinion, Sir, and that of the Secretary of War, who knows me well, that I ought not to advance pretensions to such a rank, I would advance none at all. You know, Sir, that I have had some military experience, and my studies have been in a great measure military from my infancy—but I shall rejoice if there shall be found a sufficient number of other military characters, better qualified than myself for the service.

I will acknowledge to you, however, Sir, in confidence, that, in the state of poverty in which I find myself, after a series of misfortunes, and particularly the very large extraordinary expences to which I have been subjected for several years back, in consequence of Mrs. Elliot's ill health, a publick employment, either military or civil, in which I could support myself with due economy, would relieve me from many disagreeable circumstances with which I am at present surrounded.

I am, Sir, with sentiments of high respect, Your most obedient Servant,

James Elliot.

The Honble Stephen R. Bradley, Esq.
ALS (NcD: Bradley Family Papers).

From Jonathan Badger

Hon. Stephen R. Bradley
sir Friday 2 OC[lock] P.M. November 30th. 1811. Westminster

I am under the painfull necesity of stateing to you the unfo<r>tunate situation of your little daughter Louisa. I was called to her last Week on Thursday. She had a high fever, and from her symtoms I suspected Pneumonic inflamations. Shou<ld> have bled her, but was detered by her being so fleshy. I gave a Cathartic of Calomel after the operation of which the fever entirely disappeared.

Mrs. Bradley early on Friday-morning discovered a swelling of the Neck which upon examination I found to be an enlargem<ent> of the Parotid Gland much resembleing Cynanche Parotidna or *Mumps*. This however disappeared by Sunday. Monday nig<ht> she was attacked with pukeing of purulent-matter which has contin<ued> since as often as once in an hour or two, but from whence its source I am totally ignorant. She has refused all kinds of food and drink since she was indisposed excepting a little small Beer.

Doct. Sparhawk has visited her since Tuesday. Dr. Johnson once. Yesterday Dr. Hastings of Charlestown was called. He is of opinion that the chance is against her. I think so myself. Doct. Sparhawk however entertains a different opinion.

Yours respectfully

Jonathan Badger

ALS (VtU). Margin obscured. Louise Agnes Bradley died Nov. 30, 1811.

From Samuel A. Foot

Sir   New Haven Decr. 6th. 1811

Your several favors[1] recieved since your arrival at Washington I have to acknowlege with Gratitude & more particularly yours of 20th. Novr. in answer to our request of your advice & opinion respecting the most proper mode of procedure in the case of the Brig Mars & Cargo.

The prevailing opinion here seemed to be to petition the Secy. of the Treasury or Congress immediately. We had thought differently, & concluded to request your advice so far as was consistent with your situation & are fully convinced of the propriety & policy of the mode recommended by you in that very friendly Letter.

At the request of Mr. Hull I now enclose you an Advertisement respecting a New Bank granted at the last Session of the Legislature & to be established in New Haven. Mr. Hull intended to have written you respecting it, but informed me to day he had forgotten to mention it, & from some conversation with you last spring thought probable you might choose to become a stockholder, if you choose to become a Subscriber you may command our services in the business, which will be cheerfully rendered, with the highest respect I am Sir, very Respectfully your Obedt. & obliged Servt

S. A. Foot

Hon. Stephen R. Bradley

P. S. We were much disappointed that your [...] not make us the expected Visit. I for[...] Letter to him as directed.

Yours &c [...]

ALS (NcD: Bradley Family Papers. Docketed by SRB, "Letter from Mr Foot." Postscript damaged.
1. Letters not found.

From Killian Killian Van Rensselaer

Dear General   Albany Dec 18th. 1811

My private and your political friend Mr Isarah Townsend will do himself the honor to hand you this letter, a Gentleman of fair character and honorable standing in this City and who leaves this with a view of opposing Mr Fultons bill now before the Senate, on the principal that legislative aid or interference may injure the rights of certain Citizens here as well as in other States inasmuch as Mr Fulton has instituted suits in Law and equity against a Company here who have erected two Steam Boats—his right under his Patent is therefore to be tried, and the Courts are Presumed to be competent to decide. This being a private bill I have taken the liberty to call your attention to it and to request you to give the subject all that consideration its importance merits. I have, my good Sir no interest in it (saving that as one of the Sovreigns) but I have at the request of the Gentlemen of the Company here taken the liberty of addressing you on this subject as an old friend, to have the affair properly probed and considered before it is acted on. Any services you can render my friend Mr Townsend consistently in your situation will be gratefully acknowledged by your old friend, Who is with great regard & Esteem Your very humble servt.

K. K. Van Rensselaer

Genl. Bradley

ALS (DLC). Endorsed by SRB, "Letter / K K Van Rensalier."

From Samuel Williams

Sir,   Rutland, Vermont, Dec. 26. 18<11?>

From the intelligence announced in t<he> public papers we understand that it is <in> contemplation to increase the Army of the United States, and to appoint a board o<f> Commissioners to aid and support the collectors of the customs in carrying into execution the laws of the United States in the district of Vermont. Should either be the case allow me to mention to you the name of my Son, major Leonard Willia<ms> as a person that wishes again to be employed in the service of his country. For thirteen years he was an officer in t<he> army of the United States, and was employ<ed> by Mr Dearborn in several offices of trust and confidence, I believe to the full satisfaction of his employers. He is now a Dep<u>ty Collector of the customs and is <much?> engaged in carrying the laws into effect. He flatters himself that his past services a<nd> experience might lead him to hope for a<n> office of Major in the army, or some appointment among the commissioners of t<he> customs, if such a board should be appointed. Referring his hopes and wishes to your discretion and direction,

I am, Sir, With much esteem & respect, Your most humble Serva<nt>

Samuel Williams.

Hon. S. R. Bradley.

ALS (VtU). Margin obscured.

From Ebenezer Breed

Stephen R Bradley Esqr
Much Esteemed Friend   Nahant Lynn 30 dec'r 1811

I have taken the liberty to make and send thee a few pair Gentlemens Slippers, two pa<ir> of them are marked for thyself which I ask thee to accept — two pair are directed to Doctr. S L Mitchell to whom I have written, and ask the favour of thee to hand them to him, one pair are for Thos. Law Esqr which thee will have the goodness to hand to him, and with a view to exhibit to the President of the U States a specimen of the manufacture of the Town of Lynn long known as a famous place for shoemaking, I have sent him two pair Slippers for himself and three pair for his Wife, the former I made myself and the latter I got made in Lynn, I mentioned to several of our leading Shoemakers, my intention of sending a Sampl<e> of our work to thee and the President and others, for the examination of the leading Characters of the nation and they much approved of it, and as thou art well acquainted with us, and what a high opinion and regard the people of Lynn have for the President it is wished that thee will present them in such a manner as thee shall think propper, so that it is understood as a small, or simple testimony of the sincere regard and approbation of a people, who tho' they move in an *humbler* sphere of life, they are industrious, enterprizing and *firm supporters* of the present administeration. Thy slippers and one pair of those for the President, (the light colour'd ones) are made of American Skins, Sheep, I chose this in order to shew to what perfection the manufacture of that article has arived, but a few years ago the pelt would bring only 6 to 10 Cents, now they are worth from 40 to 50, and when dressed as these are of which the slippers are made, will sell for $2.25 — which is equal to the former price of a sheep, — meat wool and all. Mrs. Madison's shoes are made of American Calf Skin dressed in imitation of English kid, it <is> handsome and durable, and we think an excellent Substitute for kid. If they are not as neat as English shoes we hope they will be thought to be tolerably good. Should they meet the Presidents and his Ladie's approbation it will be highly gratifiing, and give me great sattisfaction.

The first bussiness I commenced in Philada was in the Shoe line, and then made my home some time with my kind friend Stephen Collins, he was a respectable merchant, was always my friend, and put me into bussiness, at whose house I have often seen Dolly Paine, now Mrs. M—. She then had shoes of me, I mention this merely to observe, that should these shoes suit I now send it will be doubly pleasing to me. And may further remark, that had I have kept to that bussiness instead of going to Europe after goods I might perhaps have avoided many disappointments, and mortifications which I have since experience'd.

Since we had the pleasure of thy company here last Summer, I have had the sattisfaction to meet at this place Several of my old Southern friends three of them were formerly my intimate friends in Philada: They were very kind and attentive to me, and one of them has helped me since very considerably in a pecuniary way. Knowing thy friendly and benevolent disposition toward me I mention it as an article of agreeable information.

The bundle of Slippers are put in a box with a consignment I have made to Samuel Wheeler of Alexandria, and have requested him to send it up to Washington to thee, in the mean time should thee have an opportunity thee will please to make enquirey of him to know when the vessel arives at Alexandria. She has or will sail very soon from Boston. I have sent him 100 pair of these Gentlemens Slippers for sale, and perhaps some of them may reach some of the stores in Washington, thee will do me a kindness to mention them to thy friends if thee thinks that any one shall wish to purchase any for their own use. Col Law told me when he was here that he thought a lot of such Slippers would sell readily in Washington, perhaps he will inform some of his friends about it.

31st: decer:

I hope my asking the favour of thy attention to these small affairs will not be deem'd an intrusion. I feel a diffidence in thus writing to an eminent Statesman upon trivial matters, especially at this momentous crisis when thy mind must be deeply engaged upon the important concerns of the Nation, yet I have no doubt, that in the exalted station in which thou art place'd as one of the Fathers of the People, thee still posseses a benevolent disposition to assist and accommodate any one of thy friends, or fellow Citizens, however low his condition in life may be. Indeed, Genl: Bradley is now so well known and esteemed in Lynn that many feel acquainted with him, and tho' he is not the Senator of our State such has been his friendly attention to them that the people of Lynn are proud to call him their *Friend*.

If thee should feel at liberty and find a leisure moment to write I shall be highly gratified to receive a line from thee. Perhaps thee can enclose a Nat. Int. I shall be glad to peruse those which may have some of the interesting speeches in them.

A cousin of mine Micajah Collins of Lynn a Quaker Preacher I am informed had a meeting at Washington and invited the Members of Congress to attend it, I should like to know if he was approved of by his hearers there. We esteem him here.

The Hotel on this place is still unsold. I am fearfull we never shall have Genl. Bradley for a Neibour. We remain pretty much as when thee was here. Both of our families unite in love to thee. We hope to have the pleasure of thy company the next season.

Was it one day later, I would offer thee, the acknowledgements of the season, — must however anticipate the day, and beg thee to accept the friend<ly> wishes and sincere regard and esteem of Thy friend

Ebenr: Breed

P S. I may just remark, that the light coloured Slippers are the natural colour of the skin. It is only simply tanned in Shoemack liquor, and then finished off as it now appears. We call it Russett leather. It has become very fashionable for mens Slippers and for Ladies shoes also. The red Slippers, are call'd Lazey Slippers, because they can be Slip'd on without stooping. Perhaps thee may *occasionally need* such.

ALS (VtU). Margin obscured.

From Henry Davis

Hon. Sir,   Middlebury College Jan. 12. 1812.

I have received from you a copy of the Documents communicated by the President to the congress of the U. S. and several letters enclosed, from Professor Hubbard. For these favors, Sir, be pleased to accept my sincere thanks. I avail myself of your politeness to forward a couple of small pamphlets to the Rev. James Laurie of the City Washington. With this gentleman I have no acquaintance. They are sent by the request of Prof. H. I hope, Sir, that you will excuse this freedom.

I am, Sir, with sentiments of high respect, your obliged and very humb. servt.

Henry Davis

Hon. S. R. Bradley. L. L. D.

ALS (VtU).

From Jonathan Dorr

Honble Stephen R Bradley Esqr

Dear sir   Roxbury 12th Jany 1812

I embrace the earlyst opportunity in answering your Esteem'd favor of the 4 Inst, and Notice the large Military force about to be rais'd, in addition to filling up the present Establishment: tis most probable we shall have som<e> of the recruiting Bussiness, before our Contract expir<es> which is on the last of May next.

Respectg Beef Cattle, which are now in the Stalls, tis my Opinion if you have keeping they will bring more the next month or in March than at present, the best Cattle sold the last week at 6$ Pr hund & very tolerable Beef at 5 to 5<½> Dollars, & tis not uncommon that good Cattle in Feby or March should fetch 6 to 7$, & in some Cases 7½; but this will depend greatly on the number of Cattle put into the Stalls this season, I am led to believe there are many. In this case then, your Cattle will turn as well the last of this Month or begining of next, or to wait longer; & particularl<y> if your keepg should grow short.

I am Extremely Oblig'd to you for the Intrest you have been pleas'd to take for me for the Navy Agency at Boston; The present Agent Mr. Johonnot remains about the same as when I last had the pleasure to address you; his complaint <i>s in the Bladder & consider'd very dangerous has had <a> very severe operation perform'd not long since, is <n>ot able to sit up and is very much emaciated; he may live these some Months, I think tis impossible <h>e can survive longer. Should there be a Vacancy I <s>hall embrace the first Opportunity to inform <a>s I am more & more persuaded I should like [...] Agency if it could be Obtain'd without troubleing you too much, if a Vacancy should take place.

I can if it should be Necessary I think <a>t any time get the recommendations of Genl Dearborn our Neighbour & Mr. Henry Payson of Baltimore who <r>ecommended the present Agent & other Gentlemen if Necessary.

I a few days ago Wrote you & took the Liberty of requestg your assistance in procureing Leiut[enan]cy in the Military Service for a Cousin of <m>ine Mr Joseph Plymton who is a fine young man and of very steady Industrious Habits.

Mrs Dorr & our family are well, as we have now good Sleighing we are daily expectg William & his wife to pay us a Visit; as we understook th<ey> were coming by a friend who left Westminster <a> few days since & left all friends well.

Yours very Respectfully

Jona. Dorr

ALS (VtU). Margin obscured.

From Elisha Tracy

Honbl. Stephen Roe Bradley Esqr

Dear Sir   Norwich Con[necticu]t Jany 12th 1812

When I had last the pleasure of seeing my friend at Washington — he thought that while the Horses were fat & the Beef & Poultry plenty & good — it was not best for us to go to War for Commerce how stands my friend now; has he a different view of the subject. I notice an attempt to permit merchants to import Goods from G: Britain so far as they have funds already there for that purpose, permit me to remark to you, that the mercantile part of our community (one of which I am) are not much to be trusted. Remember the game they played with permissions under the Embargo Law.

Precisely so will they practise impositions if this indulgence be granted. Those who may have $5,000 in Great Britain will swear the $50,000 & import a hundred. I have no personal Interest, I have withdrawn from all commercial concerns some years ago but the measure will bear hard on those who do not pretend to funds abroad or who are too consciencious to swear that they have. I know of one House who claim to have 60 or 70,000 dollars in England & who are offered half a million of dollars in Goods from one House in London; indeed under an Idea the orders in Counsel would be removed — I have myself been solicited to remove to New York for the purpose of being concerned in this verry importation in case the orders are removed. A measure of this kind will demoralize Society, it will indirectly bid a bounty on perjury & if the Goverment are really in want of goods suitable for the Indians they had better import them, by means of Agents. War; strict inforsement of restrictions; or abandonment of the whole My Dear Sir are the one possible measures safe to pursue.

Will you be so good as to favour me with a line, with what you feel authorised to Communicate.

Verry respectfull Your obt Servt

Elisha Tracy

ALS (VtU).

From Reuben Attwater

Hon. Stephen R. Bradley
Dear Sir,   Detroit Jany. 14th. 1812.

Yours of the 24th of December last I receiv'd am much indebted to you for your friendly attention in calling upon the President respecting my reappointment. The inhabitants in this part of the Territory was alarmed after hearing of Battle fought on the Wabash by Gov. Harrison & the Prophet, now are quiet but under apprehension we shall have trouble in the Spring, the Indians are at present apparently friendly but troublesome, claim it as a right to be feed by us in consequence of our critical situation I have been more liberal than usual with them, our neighbors his Majesty's subjects from their conduct endeavour to convince us they are friendly, which I doubt when I frequently hear of Indians being sent by the Indian Agent Elliot from Malden to the Prophet with instructions to tell him since the Battle to say nothing, as I conlude to deceive us or not let us know that the British has assisted them; previous to the Battle the Indians visited Malden recd. powder, Ball Guns and presents you Sir, can judge for what purpose, I will not trust the *rascals*. As to our Military force it is trifling our troops in the Garrison does not consist of more than fifty effective Men, our Militia small in number and in confusion, I am making attemps to have organized and equip'd and in readiness but at best miserable, too many profess'd Americans, that at heart are his Royal highness friends of course they will not fight for us. I am of the opinion that this Territory is of consequence to the U. States being one of the frontiers, but Territories are little thought of. When I first came here I did not think we had sufficient force and if so then what now, if War with England, also Indians it will be a long time before any troops from the States could be sent here to Assist. I shall make every exertion in my power to prepare for what ever event may take place, but my means are small and you are sensible that I never had any pretensions of being considered as a Military character. I shall always be happy to hear from you. Please to accept of Mrs. Attwaters best respects and when you write Mrs. Bradley present hers with mine to her and friends in Vermont.

Accept the assurance of my Esteem

                                                                    Reuben Attwater

ALS (VtU).

Senate Proceedings: Claim of Charlotte Hazen

In Senate of the United States.

January 21st, 1812.

Mr. Bradley, from the committee appointed to consider the subject, reported the following bill, which was read and passed to the second reading.

A Bill

Supplementary to the act, entitled "An act regulating the grants of Land appropriated for the Refugees from the British provinces of Canada and Nova Scotia."

1   BE it enacted by the Senate and House of Representatives
2   *of the United States of America in Congress assembled,* That
3   Charlotte Hazen, widow of Moses Hazen, one of the refugees
4   from the British province of Canada, claiming land under the

5	act, entitled "An act for the relief of the refugees from the
6	British provinces of Canada and Nova Scotia," shall be entitled
7	to the quantity of one thousand acres, in pursuance of the re-
8	port of the commissioners made to Congress on the twenty-first
9	of April, one thousand eight hundred and six, which said
10	tract of one thousand acres shall be located in the manner and
11	within the boundaries of the tract designated by the act to which
12	this act is a supplement, and a patent shall likewise be granted
13	for the same, in the manner directed by the last mentioned act.

Microform, U.S. Government Library, U.S. 12th Congress, 1811–1813. Senate. Numbered XVIII.

From Asbury Dickens

American Consulate, London,

Sir,   January 31. 1812.

Mr. Ripley has favoured me with the perusal of the Letter which you did him the honour to address to him on the 18th. ultimo.[1] It affords me high gratification to learn that the favourable opinion which he has formed of me, should have so far communicated itself to you, as that you should, in any degree, have interested yourself in the success of my application for the Consular office at this City. Whatever may be the result of that application, the recollection of the proofs of friendship which the occasion has called forth will always be dear to me: and it affords me grounds of but little less satisfaction in having gained for me the countenance of a man so eminent and so estimable as yourself.

In the hope that you may still be disposed to serve me I take the liberty to refer you to my kinsman and friend Willis Alston Representative in Congress for the State of North Carolina,[2] whom as a steadfast fellow labourer in the sacred cause of our Country, you know, and who has kindly taken charge of my interests near the Government. He will acquaint you with my situation and my views, and with the grounds on which I have claimed the regard of the President. If you should still confide in my integrity, you will, perhaps, act with him for my good.

I congratulate you upon the proud attitude which our Country has assumed. We must go still further before we shall obtain of Great Britain, all that our interest, our honour, our very existance as a nation, call upon us to demand: for, her conduct proves even at this moment, that she injures and insults us, and, as far as she dares, despises us.

I am sir, with great re[s]pect, Your obedient humble servant

                                                                  Asbury Dickins.

General Bradley,
    Senator in Congress for the State of Vermont/

ALS (NcD: Bradley Family Papers). Docketed by SRB, "Mr Deygins / Consul London."
1. Letter not found.
2. Willis Alston (1769–1837), a Republican, represented North Carolina in Congress, 1799–1815 and 1825–31.

From Christopher Ripley

American Consulate, London,
Jany. 31st. 1812

Sir,

I have but just time to acknowledge that I have had the honour of receiving your letter of the 18th. Ultimo. to request you to accept my sincere thanks for the attention you have given to my representations in favour of Mr. Dickins, to assure you that I will make it an object to keep you well informed respecting events that take place here, and to say that I hope to have an oppertunity of sending another letter and some News Papers to you by the Ship which will take this.

I am, Sir, with great respect, Your Obedt. Servt.

Christr. Ripley

To The Hon: Stephen R. Bradley,}
    Senator in Congress,
    Washington.

ALS (VtU).

From Christopher Ripley

American Consulate, London,
Feby. 3rd. 1812.

Sir,

I have the honour to acknowledge the receipt of your letter of the 18th. of Decr. last, and to assure you that I feel myself very much obliged for the attention which you have given to my representations in favour of A. Dickins Esqr. Having said a great deal in my letter of the 29th. of Septr. last, in favour of that Gentleman, I now beg leave to refer you to some of his works which I think will prove that I did not say too much, viz. his letter to The Hon: James Monroe, Secretary of State, dated about the 1st. of Octr. last, and a letter from the Consul here to J. W. Croker, Esqr., Secretary of the Admiralty, London, dated the 10th. Ultimo (a copy of which goes to the Secretary of State at Washington by the Ship Orbit) which was written by Mr. Dickins and approved of, signed, and forwarded, by the Consul. The Consul deserves a certain share of credit for that letter, it was determined in a conversation between himself and Mr. Dickins that the state of his correspondence with the Admiralty required something of the kind, and Mr. Dickins was requested to draw up a letter, which he did. I think that that letter, has had a favourable effect, on the cases of the American Seamen that have been decided on at the Admiralty, since it was received there. I presume that you can see both of these documents at the Secretary of States office in Washington. The Hon: Willis Alston, Member of Congress from the State of North Carolina, is the friend and relative of Mr. Dickins, and has been exerting his influence in favour of Mr. D— and I cannot but hope that the opposition which comes from N. Carolina will prove to be efforts made in his favour. I have communicated the contents of your letter to Mr. Dickins, and to him only, he feels greatly obliged to you and has taken the liberty of expressing his grattitude in a letter to you. He cannot imagine what objections can be made to him from N. Carolina, and most ardently wishes for an oppertunity to remove them, being concious that he can do it, as soon as they are known to him: and I have to request that you will take the trouble to communicate them to me. In my letter of the 29th. of Septr. last, I stated that Mr. Dickins would probably send to the Government testimonials of his Character and ability, from many of the first Mercantile Houses in this City. Mr. Thomas Mullett, senior partner in the House of Thos. Mullett,

J. J. Evans & Co. did write to the Secretary of State (to whom he is personally well-known) strongly in Mr. D—favour: testimonials were likewise obtained from most of the other Houses that I mentioned in my letter, and from some others, but, considera<ble> delay having taken place, Mr. Dickins was of opinion th<at> the appointment would be made before they could arrive, and omitted sending them forward: they will now go to his frien<d> Alston by the Ship Orbit, who will probably communicate them to the Secretary of State. I wrote a few lines to you on the 31st. Ultimo, also on the 1st. Inst. by the Ship Rober<t> Burns and sent a file of the Times fm. the 15th. to the 25th. ultimo inclusive, and the Morning Post & Morning Chronicle of the 1st Inst. I now send a file of the Times from the 27th. Ultimo to this day, inclusive, and Cobbetts Register and the Courier of the 1st. inst. In the Register you will see a Letter on American affairs and I may safely say that Mr. Dickins's influence induced Mr. Cobbett to take up that subject.

I cannot now say much on Political subjects. The preparations for War in America, produce considera<ble> effect here, and it is my opinion, that the determined spirit manifested by Congress, will be more likely to produce a settlement of the points in dispute, than farther forbearance, and profers of friendship, on the part of America.

I am Sir, with great respect, Your Obedt. Servt.

Christr. Ripley.

To The Hon. S. R. Bradley,}
    Senator in Congress,
    Washington.

ALS (VtU). Margin obscured.

From Reuben Attwater

Hon. Stephen R. Bradley,
Dear Sir,   Detroit Febry. 4th. 1812

Your letter of the 4th. of December last I recd. the 1st. instant, also one at the same time in which was enclosed my commission as Secry. of this Tery. for your friendly attention I am greatly indebted, it gives me pleasure to hear that the President of the U. States was pleased to nominate me and Senate approve unanimously; I shall make every exertion in my power that my conduct shall be as unexceptionable as it has heretofore been since I have held said Office. Many gentlemen in this part of the Territory feel disposed to join the Army, I am in hopes Sir, you will excuse me for so often troubleing you to intercede for Gentlemen who wish for Commissions; you undoubtedly recollect Harris H. Hickman Esq. Atty. at Law who married one of Gov. Hull's daughter's he is now Atty. Gen. of the Tery. and of good talents he is anxious for a Commission as Captain in the new Corps. Mr. John Anderson now Marshal of the Tery. and late Lieut. in the U. S. Army resigned with a determination to join the army if we had war but in time of peace considered it too inactive a life he is also a good friend to his Country and will do honor to a Capt. Commission but will not accept of any subordinate one; if by consulting Judge Robinson and other Gentlemen who know's his character you should be of opinion that the Gentlemen abovenamed are deserving of the appointments which they wish for, as I am, you will not only confer a favor on them but if appointed will add two Officers to our Army who will fight manly to defend their Country. I among the many friendly acts received from you shall be grateful. In haste as the mail waiting Sir, I am with sentiments of esteem Your friend

Reuben Attwater

Please to accept of Mrs. Attwaters best Respects.

ALS (VtU). Docketing, by SRB, obscured, "Letter / [...]."

Senate Proceedings: Affadavits and Bail in the Courts
In Senate of the United States

February 7th, 1812.

Mr. Bradley, from the committee to whom was referred, the bill "providing for the more convenient taking of affidavits and bail, in civil causes depending in the courts of the United States," reported the same with the following:

Amendment:

1 At the end of the bill, insert the following section.
2 "*And be it further enacted*, That, in any cause before a court
3 of the United States, it shall be lawful for such court, in its dis-
4 cretion, to admit, in evidence any deposition taken *in propetuem*
5 *rei memoriam*, which would be so admissible in a court of the
6 state wherein such cause is pending according to the laws
7 thereof."

Microform, U.S. Government Library, U.S. 12th Congress, 1811–1813. Senate.

From Christopher Ripley

American Consulate, London,
Feby. 20th. 1812.

Sir,

I have sent two letters, and several News Papers, on board the Ship Orbit at Liverpool for you; which Ship is detained, in consequence of a hope entertained by the Agents, that she will soon be permitted to land a Cargo of English Manufd. Goods in the U. S. I now send the Morning Chronicl<e> of this day. In my letter by the Orbit, I state<d> to you, that the Counsel would send to the Secretary of State by that Ship, a Copy of his letter to John W. Croker Esqr., Secreta<ry> of the Admiralty, London, respecting the Impressmen<t> of American Seamen & dated the 10th. Ultimo. It does not however go by her, but by the Ship Friends, Capt. Hipkins, from this Port to Norfolk: I thin<k> that it is a letter, that is creditable to its author, and, that it is expedient to have the *real* auth[or] known, to those who are to determine, who shall be Consul at London. It was determined in a conversation between the Consul and Mr. Dickins, that the state of his correspondence with the Admiralty required particular attention; most of the points of the letter were noticed, Mr. Dickins was requested to compose a letter that he thought would have the best effect, and he produced the one alluded to. As he is a candidate for the Consular Office, I think that justice requires that he should have all the credit arising from his own works.

I am, Sir, With great respect, Your Obedt. Servt.

Christr. Ripley.

To the Hon: General Bradley,
&c. &c. &c.

ALS (VtU). Margin obscured.

Senate Proceedings: President's Authorization to Ascertain and Designate Certain Boundaries

In Senate of the United States.

MARCH 4th, 1812.

Mr. Bradley, from the committee to whom the subject was referred, reported the following bill, which was read and passed to a second reading

---

A Bill

To authorize the President of the United States to ascertain and designate certain Boundaries.

1   BE it enacted by the Senate and House of Representatives
2   of the United States of America in Congress assembled, That
3   the surveyor-general, under the direction of the President of
4   the United States, be, and he is hereby authorised and required,
5   (as soon as the consent of the Indians can be obtained) to cause
6   to be surveyed, marked and designated, so much of the western
7   and northern boundaries of the state of Ohio, which have not
8   already been ascertained, as divides said state from the terri-
9   tories of Indiana and Michigan, agreeably to the boundaries as
10   established by the act, entitled "An act to enable the people
11   of the eastern division of the territory north west of the river
12   Ohio to form a constitution and state government, and for the
13   admission of such state into the Union on an equal footing
14   with the original states, and for other purposes," passed April
15   thirtieth, one thousand eight hundred and two; and to cause to
16   be made a plat or plan of so much of the boundary line as runs
17   from the southerly extreme of Lake Michigan to Lake Erie,
18   particularly noting the place where the said line intersects the
19   margin of said lake, and to return the same whem [sic] made to
20   Congress.

1   Sec. 2. *And be it further enacted*, That the President of the
2   United States be, and hereby is authorised, whenever he shall
3   deem it expedient, to cause to be ascertained by astronomical
4   observation the point or place where the waters of Connecticut
5   river intersect the northernmost part of the forty-fifth degree of
6   north latitude; and to cause to be erected on the west bank of
7   the aforesaid river, and at the point or place aforesaid, a durable
8   monument which shall hereafter render the same fixed and cer-
9   tain.

Microform, U.S. Government Library, U.S. 12th Congress, 1811–1813. Senate.

From Mark Richards

Stephen R Bradley Esqr.

Dear Sir   Westminster Vt. 15th March 1812

    Your favour of [...] 4th Inst is recd in compliance of your request I have made som<e> examination relative to your Cattle &c &c. You have before this been informed of the loss of one of the fat Oxen. On friday the 6th Mrs Bradley sent to Mr May & myself to advise about the Ox which had been ailing a few days we concluded he would soon get well & advised not to kill him as the Beef would not do to sell when thus disorderd but contra to our expectations the ox di[e]d Saturday night. I find your fat Cattle are not as forward as might be expected. Grant now feeds about a peck of meal daily each. I learn he has fed lighter till lately I think a saving would be made by disposing of them soon in short had they went withe those lately drove from here it could have been done at less expence. E Spencer Nutting & E Burk Joined & drove theirs—was in marke<t> last Monday they got from 6 to $7 P[er] Ct. & they were quick sale. Your man has about 10 Bushel of meal ground up I find about 20 B of Corn in the Granary I advised to geting that out imediately (as the rats are wasting it fast) & get it chiefly ground now while Sleighing lasts the Corn in the <Phipan?> Barn remains untouched as you left it. Corn is now worth 3/[...] rye 4/6 wheat 8/. It will rise more if the winter holds on long as severe as at present snow is still 3 feet deep on a level & many places 30. Hay is growing very scarce many purchacers. Esqr Spooner Mr May Mr Nutting & many Farmers as well as others are buyers the present price of Hay is $10. The Towns ajoining are shorter than we are you have about one Ton yet left at the Robins place about 4½ tons in the North Barn 1/2 do in horse barn 1 ton in <phipan?> barn a few Corn Stalks Straw &c scatterd round which ought to have been given out earlier you have <9?> Calves 21 Lambs have lost a number. I will see your man occasionaly & see if the hay can be made to hold out. I rather think it will. Mrs B tells me she can have a load of Lincoln if needed. Your out door Cattle look pretty well & can be turned of as soon as the Snow gets down. I have been very much confind at home this Winter have a large Stock of Cattle & no help. I have had 4 hired men since you went away but found them [...] much worse than none that I dismissd them & done alone chiefly [...] respecting our public affairs I have (with you) feard the N E States would be revolutionized we are overwhelmed with Washington B. <Sanctin?> meeting Weekly & oftener, but I find very little danger is to be feard from them N Hamshire Election evinces that there is no gain to the Federal party that State is undoubtedly safe Walpole carrid all Republican. Doctr Johnson represents that Town. Drew had 17 over Vose as Senator the Candidates for Govr. tied. This Town has suceded in carrying the Repubn ticket for Town Officers by from 21 to 33 majority at a very full meeti<ng.> Massachusetts will go well by the best information I can g<et.> I must however think Congress must from policy pursue War measures nothing short of War will sattisfy the people under existing circumstances (if we have the information necesary to make a decision<).> The present crisis in an important one we anxiously wa<i>t the result of Congressional procedings in full confidence they will terminate in the best measu<re> for maintaining our National honour & hapiness. Please write me again & if I can render you any service here I cheerfully will do it. I recd of William the 28th day of Jany $336- to account to you therefor I had occasion for some sooner than I could obtain it of the County Treasurer. Please remember me to <Frnds?> Shaw Fisk & Strong. I remain with esteem Your Huml Servt

                                                                                                    Mark Richards

ALS (VtU). Margin obscured. Damaged by removal of seal.

To Eliakim and Capt. Alfred Spooner

Gentlemen   Washington March 16th. 1812

By this presents I authorize and direct you to pay to William C. Bradley any sum or Sums of money due owing or payable to me from you or Either of you to redeem the farm on the hill north of Barnabas Wood's and for which you hold my bond dated Last spring to convey on payment of a certain Sum of money and any receipt by him the sd William C. Given Shall have the same force and effect as if Given by me provided the Sum shall be paid within the term of time limitted by the bond aforsaid.

In witness whereof I have hereunto Subscribed my name the day & date above.

Stephen R Bradley

To Eliakim Spooner Esqr
& Capt Alfred Spooner

ALS (VtU). Cover addressed, "Messrs Eliakim Spooner Esqr / & Alfred Spooner." Notation by WCB, "Specie only can be received by direction Wm C. Bradley."

From Royall Tyler

Dear Sir—   Brattleboro March 16. 1812.

Your favor of the 5th of December last[1] reachd me on the Western Circuit—considering the subject matter better adapted to colloquial than epestolary discussion I made no particular reply to it I will however observe that I have noticed its object on proper Occasions—& to suitable persons.

I was gratified by your assurance that you would not be unmindfull of Dr Russell Fitch and have mentioned it to him as coming from you without my application.

Mr Jones Blake son of John W Blake Esqr has waited upon me and requested that I would name him to you as a candidate for a subalterns Commission in the old regular Army or in case that cannot be obtained to the same grade in the additional army. This young gentleman I believe you know. He is at present Member of the Junior Class in Williamstown Colledge—wants a few months of being adult—is a very personable figure and of peculiar suavity of manners his father has written to the Secretary of War on the subject but his principal reliance is on your influence *[missing line?]* it is if you can be prevailed upon to patronize the Young man which I hope you will do.

The snow was never so deep and *so solid* in Windham County at this day in March since the settlement of the Country. It is now three feet deep in my wood lot and the sun has made no impression upon it for six days past I do beseech you who inhabit a more genial clime to take pity on us and send us some cheering intelligence to dissipate this wintry gloom. It seems to me that another speech like yours on the Volunteer Bill—which is very popular in Vermont—if it did not melt the snow would at least warm our blood to withstand the severity of the season.

I have not heard a word from our friends at Westminster since my return from the circuit.

Please to write me on the receipt of this—and inform me what probability of success for Mr Blake—and if you can with propriety intimate what is to be the Grand Result of your present session.

I am with respect—Your friend &c.

Royall Tyler

Genl Bradley—

ALS (NcD: Bradley Family Papers). Cover addressed by Tyler to "Honble. Stephen R: Bradley / Senator in Congress of the United States / from the State of Vermont / City of Washington"; docketed by SRB, "Judge Tyler."
1. Letter not found.

From Zimri E. Allen

Hon. S. R. Bradley   Conn. Litchfield 21st. March 1812.

Allow me to intrude for a few moments upon your attention.

In 1809. if rightly I remember, I was reccommended by Gentlemen in Vermont, for a Cadet in the U. S. Army. My letters were then answered, in the negative —;in consequence of the School at West Point being full. My name however, was placed on the list of Applicants. These l<et>ters were accompanied by one from my Cousin Herman Allen — with whom, I believe, you are personally acquainted. Since 1809. I have been in the study of Law & am now in the Law School at this place. I however belong to Vermont.

My ardour for military glory has not subsided — my heart still glows with Patriotic zeal. Considering therefore, the situation & circumstances of our Country & also that appointments are now making for the "new Army" I have taken the liberty to request you (if consistent) to make intercessions for a Lieutenancy — in my behalf. If success attends this application & recruiting is the present duty, I think Burlington, Middlbury or Windsor — or indeed Woodstock in Vermont would be excellent places to raise men & should like to be stationed in one of them, particularly the former. I have written the Honbles. Robinson & Shaw on this subject.

In giving yourself the trouble of attending to this business, you will confer a lasting obligation on Sir — your obt. Humble Servt.

                                                                  Zimri E Allen

Hon. S. R. Bradley.
ALS (VtU). Margin obscured.

From Jeremiah Mason

Dear Sir   Portsmouth 27. March 1812

Mr. Nathaniel A. Haven Jur. a young gentleman in whose welfare I take much interest being about to sail for England & intending to visit France before his return has requested me to procure for him letters of recommendation to Mr. Barlow our minister at Paris. On considering how I could obtain for him such letters as would be serviceable I could recollect no person that I could apply to, who probably had more power than yourself to assist my young friend.

Mr. Haven is the son of a very respectable and wealthy merchant of this place who was one of the representatives of this State in the last Congress. I think it probable his character may be in some degree known to you. The son (for whom I request your recommendation) graduated a few years ago at Cambridge College where he was much distinguished as a scholar. Since which he has studied law the usual term under my direction and was lately admitted an attorney & Counsellor of Our Superior Court. He possesses good natural talents which have been well cultivated. He is of good character correct morals & manners. I am confident he will do no discredit to his friends or Country wherever he shall be known The object of his visit to Europe is to acquire knowledge & improvement. If you grant the favour

I request you will confer a benefit on a person worthy of it & much oblige one who is with much esteem & respect yr friend & Obt. Sert.

Jeremiah Mason

Honble. S. R. Bradley Esqr.

ALS (DLC). Cover addressed, "Honle. Stephen R. Bradley / Senator in Congress / Washington." Stamped, "PORTSMOUTH, N. H. / MARCH 30<in> and "FREE." Endorsed by SRB, "Letter / Jeremiah Mason."

From Amos Stoddard

Sir, Fort Columbus 28th. March 1812.

I am greatly obliged to you for your favor of the 22d. instant,[1] and likewise for the information it contains.

If it be found proper to postpone the appointment in question to some future period, I beg leave to request that, when that period arrives, you would be so good as to bear in mind the views I have expressed; and I take this occasion to make the request, as I know not to what part of the union, *or even Canada,* my military duties may call me.

If, on your return home, you would be so good as to inform me of your arrival in New-York, I should be happy to wait on you, and to conduct you over the little dominion under my command.

I am, Sir, with sentiments of high respect, Your very hume. Servt.

Amos Stoddard, maj

Commy

Hone. Mr. Bradley.

ALS (NcD: Bradley Family Papers).
1. Letter not found.

In Senate of the United States.

APRIL 4th, 1812.

Mr. Bradley, from the committee to whom was referred the bill making provision for certain persons claiming lands under the several acts for the relief of the refugees from the British provinces of Canada and Nova Scotia, reported the following:

Amendments:

1 In the printed bill, line 9— After the words "Moses Hazen,"
2 strike out "sixteen hundred acres."
3 At the end of the tenth line insert, "*the heirs of:*
4 Line 11— Before the words "Israel Ruland," insert "*the heirs*
5 *of.*"
6 Line 12 — Strike out "Anthony Buck," and insert, "*the heir*
7 *of Anthony Burk* [sic]."
8 Line 20 — Strike out after the word "Antill," the following.
9 "the heirs of,"— insert in lieu thereof, the word "*and* ."

Microform, U.S. Government Library, U.S. 12th Congress, 1811–1813. Senate.

To Joel Barlow

Dear Sir Washington April 7th. 1812

Mr. Nathaniel A. Haven Jun., son of Doctor Haven late member of Congress from Portsmouth in New-Hampshire is on a tour to europe for the purpose of acquiring General Information and improving his moral and intellectual endowments he intends to visit France.

I take the liberty to recommend him to your *favourable* notice and patronage, he is a young gentleman of Talents, Education, and Merit, you will not find him undeserving of attention — every obligation conferred on Mr Haven will add one more to the many which will always be acknowledged with pleasure by Your old Friend and Very Humble Servant

Stephen R Bradley

His Excellency Joel Barlow
 ALS (VtU).

From Martin Chittenden

D. Sir Washington April 11h 1812

You will accept of my thank<s> for Your politeness, on the Subject of appointments. I have not in view at present any persons, whom I am willing to recommend, that I am Sure will accept. I shall <le>ave this for Vermont tomorrow.

If the appointments can be delayed without any injury to the public untill I return to Vermont — I can probably Select those who will do honor to themselves & their Country.

I am with high esteem & consideration Your Hbl Svt

Martin Chittenden

Genl S. R. Bradley
 ALS (NcD: Bradley Family Papers). Damaged by removal of seal.

From Richard Rush

Treasury department
Comptrollers office.

sir. April the 23d. 1812

I have had the honor to receive your note of the 20th of this month[1] enclosing the deposition of Jabez Jones in the case of Agustus Levaque, a canadian refugee.

The effect of this deposition, I cannot, at this moment, determine. All that I can promise is, that it shall be placed upon the files, and due attention be paid to it.

I have the honor to be with great respect your faithful, & obt. servt.

Richard Rush

Hon: S. R. Bradley.
 ALS (NcD: Bradley Family Papers).
 1. Letter not found.

From David Austin

Hon: S. Row Bradley}
Senator in Congress.

Respected Sir, Norwich (Con) May 5th. A.D. 1812

In your favor of March 6th. 1809: you say—"Watchman what of the night?"—Your observations before the Senate, on the subject of a recess, on or about 25th. Ulto. have reached me this day. Your name recalls former interviews observations &c.—Were I now to answer your question "What of the night?"—Perhaps to save appearanc<es> I might answer you, in the light of public opinion. The Judicious now look at Congress, as men look at a Coal-Pith, smothered with turff—,but now & then a little fire twinkling thro' the crevices. The people, as you state in your observations, "are not irrational"—They wait, & look, & remark. I need not tell you all they say: but some, humbly presume to say: "if you go to war, it is a war of your own making"—you must shoulder the burthen & carry it for yourselves: for they feel neither the calls of interest, or of policy, or of Conscience, urging them to go with you!—*No not a step*. This is the Voice of New England in its popular heath. In fact, notwithstanding all the speeches, remarks of Editors, & public documents, they do *profess to be ignorant* of the matter for which war is threatned.

"Is the war *for Commerce?*"—"We are now allowed more, even by the British, than *our own Government will let us take!*"—"Is the war *for territory?*"—["]We want no body's land Continents or Islands!"—"Is it to get our impressed Seamen home?"—"More will be prisoners by three months war than have been seized in as many years!"—"Is the war to *please Buoneparte?*"—"His <paw?> is already in our scalp as oft as we fall within reach of his talons!" Is the war to make the present administration *popular?*" "Nothing will damn them so soon!"—And thus the accompt now stands. Some laugh, & say it is, but a war of words and the Government do not mean war!—They are only holding a burning match at the nose of John Bull to make him sneeze up a few things. None pretend ye are sold to England or to France: but many marvel that ye send, & send so many messengers to France to have their breech kicked, & then to come home with their finger in their mouth!

The people are not fools. They see that England & France are fighting a deadly battle; &, that either of them should now & then jostle our neutral boat a little is not to them surprizing. Let it be that those powers are to our trade *equally injurious*: still, better voyages are made when the Ships steal thro' the tempest to a strong market, than when the ports are so far free that *all float* in safety, & glut the market!—All the merchants require is, that you would not legislate for them at all. The Insurance Offices they deem better ballances of profit & of safety than all the cuts ye can make, or the power ye can use in their behalf.—As to going to war, in their behalf, *they ask no such thing*.

If you ask, what else can we do?—I answer, *fire Pop-gun No. 3!*—What is that?—Jefferson's Proclaa. *removing the Bristish fleet* because they killed Pierce &c was *Pop-gun No. 1.*—This Shot was felt: the people said Amen! & the Ports were clear: not a hen Roost could their boats approach, but their fingers were hammered by the populace!—*No. 2.*—This was Madison's praclama. respecting the Berlin & Milan decrees!—This was a *flash in the pan*. The Shot was felt *no where!*—The British did not *take it in*. The French danced a little: Buoneparte laughed at the success of the <snare?>; & our own people were partly cajoled, partly robbed & maltreated, & the kingdom filled with smoke!—Now, *what next? Fire Pop-gun No. 3!*—What is that?—Let Mr. Madison charge his piece with the obstructions, requisitions, sequestrations confiscations & burnings of the French: let him *ram down his cartridge well*: then put in a *single ball*, levelled as distinctly at the Intercourse with France, as Jefferson levelled at the

Bitish fleet, trade, intercourse, & whatever he pleases. Such a discharge will take effect in several ways! — 1. It will deliver Mr. Madison from the partial mistake of his last fire. 2. It will set him forth as a Leader of the people on high ground! — it will put trust, energy & public opinion on his side! — The Voice of the *whole nation* would be "Amen to Madison & administration *thus far*!" — 3. — This would set the Belligerents both at distance, & give us *commanding stations on our own shores*. This is all we want for ourselves! — Our high prizes are all in our rear: & all we want is the lawful & peaceful enjoyment of what the God of Heaven & our own prowess & industry have carved out for us! — Higher prizes than Independance: Constitution: Peace: industry & prosperity & the blessing of God on them we can never obtain! — Fight, talk bluster, & even succeed, & then make peace, & ye cannot get better ground than *ye now possess*. Ye can now make *better terms* for yourselves, under *the discharge of No. 3*. than either of the Belligerents would allow you; should either of them attain to a perfect domination of the Seas. — In fact the people demand nothing but themselves in Liberty: their property in safety: & a Government upright: free'd from the snares & lies of *foreign depredators*!

Take station on Capitol Hill: & survey the Ocean under the sound of the third Gun! — Your Coast is in safety, this yr. own Guarda Costas! — The Country is under yr. feet, & for its safety all the people are ready to fight to the last drop! — Cut off then this Section of Creation: & [*illegible*] its Guardians under the banners of the *Prince of Peace*. — This would give to the powers that are, lofty stations in the estimation of the people of every class.

If it be asked "what *shall we do for commerce*?["] Answer, *Nothing at all*! — we are completely independent in this point — our domestic manufactures are so far on, that *we want nothing from any one*! as to foreign communication we want none, farther than *they want us*. The *bread-basket* is all that we can carry abroad to profit: & as the *nations are hungry* they will *cry out*. This cry of necesity will open their ports, and we may *bring home the price*. The trade in bread-stuffs hath given more solid profits than all other voyages of late: & there is little else that we can spare to profit.

When ye have set all the powers *at distance*: ye may easily regulate the mode of intercourse by their example towards you: or leave the enterprize of Commerce to its own hazards: & let the insurance offices regulate the warfare. — This will lift you out of the mire & slough of Commercial restrictions: wh. at present is the *only gulph* in wh. ye wallow.

As to hatred to England as such; or love to France, or the contrary there is no such thing among the people. There is no spring for war with either! — The people are content as they are: the merchants would be so: if *left to themselves*.

As *to Canada*: the people take the same interest in the project they would take in fighting a Bank of snow or of Ice: from wh. they promise thems. no advantage, in case of highest sucess.

After all, may Heaven direct you: continue its protection over our beloved Country: & grant to us the blessings we enjoy & to our seed forever. As I receive yr. remarks before the Senate, thro' the Courier, I hand my hints, thr'o the same medium.

With asurances of esteem

D. Austin

P. S. I did think to send you this line thr'o the Courier: but if it be of any use to you; conn it over a little with Mr. Madison, & if any benefit can come from it well: but rest assured it contains the genuine ideas of all parties this way.

ALS (NcD). Cover addressed, "Norwich / May 6th} Free / Hon: Stephen R. Bradley / Senator, Congress, / Washington-City." Endorsed by SRB, "David Austins Letter."

From Joshua Chamberlain

University of Vermont,
11 of May, 1812.

Dear Sir,

The Rector of William and Mary College has advertised in the Intelligencer, that they are in want of a Professor of Rhetoric and Belle Lettres, Moral Philosophy and Politics. That situation would be much more lucrative and eligible than my present station, and it would require a course of studies, with which I should be pleased. I presume the Senators from Virginia are members of the board of Visitors, and if you could speak to one of them on the subject, with perfect convenience you would confer a great favour.

I am as much pleased with this place, as I could reasonably expect. There were but twenty students, when I came, and by my exertions, I have increased their number to sixty five. But tuition is low and our funds are not sufficiently productive to allow so ample a compensation to the Professors as their stations require. If our funds had been well managed, and there was a fair prospect of an ample and permanent support for the Professors, I should have no wish to leave the place. But at present, I see no such prospects, and feel under no obligations to remain here, if I can procure a better situation.

You will be good enough to accept the homage which every virtuous citizen ought to pay to a wise and Independent Ruler, and of my gratitude for your particular favours to me, and believe me to be, with sentiments of the highest respect, your sincere friend, and much obliged

J. Chamberlain

Gen. Bradley
ALS (VtU).

From Christopher Ripley

American Consulate, London,
May 11th. 1812.

Sir,

Being anxious that Our Government should not be mistaken respecting the real author of such Documents as are creditable to this Office, I beg leave to call your attention to a Letter to John W. Croker Esqr Secretary to the Admiralty London dated April 16th. 1812.

This Letter proceeded from the zeal of Asbury Dickins Esqr. for the Interests of the United States: he was the Author and Writer: Mr. Beasley, the Acting Consul, read it, signed it, read the answer, and directed that copies of both should be transmitted to the Secretary of State at Washington: which, I presume you can see.

You will notice by the answer, that a considerable effect was produced by the Letter: one point was gained: The Lords of the Admiralty consented to investigate the cases of Men on Foreign Stations.

I have before called your attention to an important Letter to the same Gentleman dated Jany. 10th. 1812 which was also written by Mr. Dickins: indeed, he devotes himself daily to the service of the United States, with more zeal than could be expected, when it is considered, that his exertions have a tendency to raise a Rival in the estimation of those, whose confidence he is anxious to obtain for himself. If he was placed in a situation, where he could have all the credit of his own actions, he would be animated with an ambition that would be very useful to his Country.

I am, Sir, With the greatest respect, Your Obedt. Servt.

Christr. Ripley

To The Hon: Stephen R. Bradley,
&c. &c. &c Washington.
ALS (VtU).

From Philip Reed

Dear Sir   Washington City 19th May 1812

The President[i]al Caucus assembled the last evening, in the Senate Chamber, and nominated J. Madison as President and Colo. Langdon, as V. President, the former had, I understand, 82 & the latter gentleman about 66 Votes. Mr. Gerrey 15 or 16. I give you this as I recieved it without pretending to be accountable for its accuracy, tho believe it to be nearly so, if not quite: your return is hoped & looked for. Yours

Phil Reed

Genl. Bradley
ALS (NcD: Bradley Family Papers).

From Philip Reed

Dear Sir   Washington City 24th May 1812

The news papers will have informed you before this reaches Vermont of the arrival at New York of the Ship *Hornet*. The messengers, with the dispatches reached this place on Friday last. Altho' the contents have not yet been communicated it seems to be understood that they do not contain any thing of a very decisive character. I suppose Bonaparte may have made another declaration of his *imperial &* <*loyal*?> "*love* of the americans." Several of your friends would be Very glad to see you here. I am with much respect Dr. sir your Most Obdt

Phil Reed

Hone. S. R. Bradley
ALS (NcD: Bradley Family Papers).

From Gideon Tomlinson

Sir,   Fairfield (Con) June 3d 1812

Such is the mental indisposition of the Collector of the District of Fairfield that his Friends as it is understood have thought it unsafe for him to have the custody of the *public papers* and they have accordingly removed those papers of importance which are attached to the office from his House where they have heretofore been kept.

The unhappy malady of Mr. Smedley having incapacitated him in the opinion of his Friends, for the discharge of his official duties, it is presumed that the office which he has hitherto holden will be vacated. In such an event it will be a ma<tter of> some moment to the Community that it be filled by a *fit* person. The Friends of the Administration in this District, I believe universally, consider Walter Bradley Esquire, a man known to you and a tried Republican, to be such a man and would desire his appointment should there be a vacancy which is deemed inevitable. This Gentleman has, by letter, informed Mr. Gallatin, of his wish to recieve the Appointment and has referred him to Mr. Bishop & other leading republicans in this State for information.

Mr. Bradley's acquaintance with you has induced him to believe that you would not be averse to his appointment and, I have therefore as his Friend and at his desire, ventured to suggest to you his wish to be appointed to the Office of Collector of this District should it be vacated, and to request for him your aid in an application the success of which is interesting to him & his Friends.

Being uncertain whether his letter to Mr. Gallatin has been recieved, Mr. Bradley desires you to take the trouble to ascertain that fact & to make such mention of him to the President & Mr. Gallatin, as you may think your Knowledge of him will justify.

With sentiments of high consideration I am, Sir, very respectfully Your obdnt. Servt.

Gideon Tomlinson

Hon. S: R. Bradley Esqr.
Senator in Congress

ALS (NcD: Bradley Family Papers). Cover addressed by Tomlinson to "Hon. Stephen R. Bradley Esqr. / Senator in Congress / Washington" and marked "Fairfield 3 June" and "Free"; docketed by SRB, "Letter / Gideon Tomlinson / Fairfield." Damaged by removal of seal.

From Nathaniel Ruggles

Dear Sir   Roxbury June 30th. 1812

Your esteemed letter of June 24th.[1] with an inclosure to your daughter came to hand in due course. With respect to my property lying in England, to import which I perferr'd a petition early in this Session — I know not how the present State of the two nations will affect it; but if there should be any way of importing with safety, I should be glad of that privilege — my petition in that respect, states the facts. Respecting my property in the South-Carolina, my Petition to Congress & my letter to Mr. Gallatin state the facts on that head. The South Carolina (destined for Philadelphia) arrived at Charleston S. C in distress, was there seized by the Officers of the Customs, Bonds were there given for the issue, by the friends of the Agent in the Vessel, for Vessel & Cargo, under heavy Commissions, and the property freighted to Philadelphia & consigned to Mr. Gerand. I wrote to my Correspondents in Charleston to Bond my property seperately, but he did not receive my advices, untill after the whole was Bonded by the Agent. I also sent to Charleston all documents & proofs respecting my property. But the last letters from my Correspondent mention, no use had been made of them, owing to there being no district judge at that place. I have expected, under the new state of things, that some general arrangement would be made, wherein an unoffending individual might find redress without spending half the property in obtaining his right, if there was not a general release. It is impossible for me to suggest the mode to you. I conceive the power at present, lies with the Secretary of the Treasury, if any. I wish to release those Bondsmen at Charleston, so far as respects my property, from their Bonds; untill then my property in that Vessel will remain entangled. Or if it is the intention of Government either to enforce Bonds of that description or to let them remain as dead letters, I should wish to have those Bonds exchanged for Bonds I would furnish here for the issue. The property bot. for me with my Bills of 20000 sicca Rupees, after deducting charges in Calcutta, consists of B. S. C.

# 279 @ 290	12 Bales of	Jalapore Sannas	
291	1 "	Jugdia Baftas	
307 @ 322	16 "	John Cathy Goyah Mamoody	
323 " 342	<u>20</u> "	do.	do
making	49 Bales amountg. to, cost		17215 Sicca Rupes

I remain with high respect & e[s]teem Your hume Servt.

Nathl. Ruggles

Honble. S. R. Bradley, Esqr.

ALS (NcD: Bradley Family Papers).
1. Letter not found.

From Asbury Dickens

Dear sir,   London, August 15. 1812.

I had the honour to address you on the 31 Jany. at which time, and on many subsequent occasions, I transmitted to you those of the London publications which I thought might interest you. Some of the many casualties to which the intercourse between the two countries must have been exposed during the unsettled and unfriendly state of their relations, have I fear, interrupted the communication either on your side or mine. But at any event, I cannot suffer the present sure opportunity to pass without conveying to you the expression of my best thanks for your exertions to promote my welfare: and of assuring you that it will be at all times my study to deserve the support of such men as have interested themselves for my success.

This will be handed to you by Mr Ripley. To him I am indebted for the honour of your acquaintance. But my obligations are not to end here. Being about to return to America, he has kindly offered to make those representations on my behalf to the Government, which my absence renders so necessary. He has been for upwards of two years, a near observer of the conduct of all who have been in this Office. To his testimony I beg to refer you for a just view of my character. I trust he will convince you that your support has not been ill bestowed. I would fain hope more. I would hope that you will still aid my cause; that you will, in concert with him and my other friends, make one more exertion to obtain from the Government such an employment as may be commensurate with my zeal and my ability to promote the public welfare.

I congratulate you, as my countryman, upon the elevated station which America has assumed in the rank of Nations.

Accept the assurance of my high respect, and believe me to be Dear Sir, Your much obliged and most obedt servt.

Asbury Dickins.

ALS (NcD: Bradley Family Papers).

From Daniel C. Sanders

University of Vermont

Sir,   Burlington 22d Sept. 1812.

By the Rev. Professor Chamberlain, we had the high satisfaction of receiving in books a very valuable donation from you for our Library. For this instance of your liberality and much esteemed patronage to the State College, the Corporation have requested me to return you very sincere thanks and tender you their best respects. Permit me likewise to subjoin the expression of my own gratitude, and fervant wishes that you may long continue an ornament in the Counsels of your country.

I am, Sir, with the highest respect, Your most obedient and humble Ser't,

Daniel C. Sanders, Prest.

The Hon. S. R. Bradley, L. L. D.

ALS (NcD: Bradley Family Papers).

From Samuel Smith

Dr. Sir/   Balte. 8. Octr. 1812

Our Elections are over, and the State is Compleatly federal, the feds have Such a majority in the House, as gives them a major Vote on a joint Ballot, they therefore will Elect the Govr. & Council, the Senator to the U. S. and all the Justices of Peace &c &c. On the Electoral Election for Prest. this State will given Clinton 5. Votes at least out of 11, and those who know best Say, that he will have Seven Votes. Does your Election fix the Vote of Vermont for Madison? Your Answer will Oblige —

Your Obedt. servt.

S. Smith

Pennsylvania is Staggering, a helping hand from Duane[1] would give Clinton their Vote. No. Carolina will Certainly Vote for Clinton, their legislature is federal.

ALS (NcD: Bradley Family Papers). Cover addressed by Smith to "The Honble Stephen R. Bradley / Westminster / Vermont" and postmarked Baltimore; docketed by SRB, "Genel Sam Smith."
1. William Duane was editor of the Philadelphia *Aurora General Advertiser*.

From Simeon Knight

Dear Sir   New Orleans 14th. Novr: 1812

When I had the pleasure of seeing you in Washington the evening before your departure for Vermont I was in hopes you would have returned before I left the place. But having closed my business as paymaster it became necessary I should return to my duties again and on the 3d of May I left the City for this country via Pittsburgh; not meeting with a passage by water down the Ohio I purchased a pair of horses and came by land through the States of Ohio, Kentucky, and Tennessee and the Chickasaw & Chocktaw Nations of Indians and on the 13th. of July I arrived at Natchez. I met with no extreordinary occurrence on my journey and a detail of particulars would be uninteresting, this is the third time I have been in New Orleans since my return and once to the Pass of Christian on Lake Ponchatrain.

The War in this part of the country has not as yet caused any blood shed nor has it equaled the Sabine or Burr Wars in 1806 & 7. Fears of insurrections among the Negros have occasionally alarmed the people, and a few poor black fellows have been hanged. I believe on suspicion of revolt.

The Petition which you was so good as to present for me at the last session of Congress I hope you will again call up and any attention you may bestow to the same will confer a lasting obligation on your friend.

With great respect & esteem I am Sir Your obt. Svt.

Simeon Knight

The Honble
Stephen R. Bradley
City of Washington

ALS (VtU). Endorsed by SRB, "Simeon Knight."

From Samuel Harrison

Dear Sir   Chittenden Vt. Novr. 28th. 1812

Although I never attempted to Address you in an Epistolary way, yet I cannot refrain, at this time to call to your mind the very flattering Reccomendation, and Introduction, You was pleased to bestow on me, to a num<ber> of your Colleagues, in the Senate Chamber, in the Capitol at Washington in March 1806.

I Corresponded with your cotemporary Senator, since Governo<r>—now, deceased, Israel Smith, who used, by Letter, to communic<ate> to me, an account of the Bussiness, which transpired, at the Seat of Government. Since his Absence from Washington, I have not had any regular Correspondence, excepting a few Letters, fr<om> Collo. Lyon, General Chittenden, and Judge Fisk.

It would gratify me very much to hear from You, while you remain at the Seat of Government.

I lament that the Legislature of Vermont have, this Year, been so amazingly incompetent, to the Duties assigned them; Their Unconstituti<on>al assumption of rights, never delegated by the People, has excluded yo<u> from a continuance in the Senate of the U. S. But I hope, Dear Sir, You will not blame Vermont; When the example is set at the City of Washington: — For, we must be assured, — if *Caucuses and Publ<ic> Nominations, are persisted in, Our Liberties will soon be Eradicated. Public Nominations engender Faction;— And Faction will always destroy the Principles of Republicanism. And it will be succeeded, by Monarchy, and Despotism.*

Had no Faction been engendered, by Public Nominations in our own on<ce?> happy Country; we should not have been involved in the Present War with Great Britain — Nor should we need to fear French influence in our Councils.

I hope, the People will discover their *Error*, and their *Danger*, before it is too late.

I hope, his Excellency the President of the U. S. will not push matters, so far, with Great Britain: but that a *permanent Peace* may be speedily made. NEUTRALITY *ought to be our Motto*.

I have written, a number of Letters, to Mr. Madison, upon the Subject of War. I began to write on the 11th of May, and wrote again on the 11th of Ju[...] and continued writing, at intervals until the 24th. And endeavored to convince him, that it was *improper to Go to War*; I offered 13 Reasons, and was about to proceed to some other; when the news of the Declaration of War came to Vermont; I desisted, until September. Then the tidings arrived, of the Capture of General Hull; I wrote again to his Excellency; and likewise to the Post-Master General, Gideon Granger Esquire, Again, to his Excellency, on the 30th of October, and again today. In some of which Letters, *I offered, my Services to Negociate with the Court of Great-Britain, without any other renumeration, excepting outfits, and expences; If I did not succeed. If I did succeed, then I would be paid, equal to other Plenipotentiaries.*

I am certain that I can (had I the Powers of an Ambassador) *procure an honorable adjustment, of the existing difficulties*: For I am well acquainted in *London*; I have been there, and in many other *Towns*, and *Cities*, in that *Kingdom*: I have acquaintance with many *respectable Characters, in that Nation, who have influence; and, are well wishers to a reciprocity of Interests, between Great-Britain, and the United States.*

But my Letters, and Offers, are treated with Neglect; And I am constrained to *Appeal to You, and to Heaven*; for the Purity of my Intentions.

I love America — I love our Constitution — I hate to see that *Bulwark of Freedom violated. It has received three heavy Shocks of late.* — I am a Friend to Peace. — A Friend to Neutrality — A Friend to Agricultur<e,> Commerce, and Manufactures; But I hate War; and its Concomitant Misseries; Loans; Direct Taxes; — Legalized Rapine; — Blood; Slaughter; and Destruction.

I beg you to use your Influence, while you remain in the Senate, of the United States, to have all return to the *True Principles of the Constitution* — Bear testimony against every deviation *from that Palladium of our Country's Rights.*

Bear testimony against every species of *Legalised Iniquity; every hostile attack, on the Temple of Freedom.*

Never support measures, where the *Injury to our Nation will be Greater, than the Benefit; Where a few Individuals will fatten on the ruin of their Neighbou<rs.>*

The Money that has been thrown away, May I not say foolishly, since the Declaration of War, last June, would have made a Road; as good as a Turnpike, from the Northern part of Vermont, to the City of Washington; And what have we *Gained*, but *Disgrace*, and Disappointment?

And all *Future Warfare* will have a like *termina<l.>*

Was the Money laid out, in Ameliorating the distresses of Mankind, that has been expended, by the present European Competitors, for *Terrene*, and *Maritime Dominion;—Misery would be banished from the Families of Man.*

What has been expended in Spain, and Portugal, for the last three Years, would have *Built a Bridge of Boats across the Atlantic;—* And what has been foolishly squandered, this Season to Subjugate, and to defend Russia, would have *Irrigated* the whole United States of America; that every Man might have had a Boat at his Door, and Access, and recess, by inland Navigation, from Champlain to St. Mary's.

I hope the Time is not far distant, When Wars shall cease, and Man resum<e> his Native Dignity.

If you condescend to write to me, Please to Direct to Samuel Harrison Esquire Pittsford <in?> Vermont. Altho' my residence is in Chittenden there is not any Post Office in the Town and if directed to Chittenden it may stop at some Post Office more remote than Pittsford.

I beseech You to accept of my Salutations, and Respects—and rest assured of <my> best wishes for your Welfare, and that of our Country.

I reamin your Obt. Servt.

Saml. Harrison

<Ste>phen R. Bradley Esqr.
<Sen.> of the United States. A.

<small>ALS (VtU). Margin obscured. Damaged by removal of seal, two small holes, and a corner cut from the manuscript. Cover addressed, "His Excellency James Madison Esquire / President of the U.S.A. / city of Washington." Franked, "Pittsford Decr. 1st. Free."</small>

From Jonathan Morgan

Honbl. Stephen R Bradley Esqr
Dear Sir   Hartford 7. Decr. 1812

The man who plants a tree or Shrubb, is said to feel a stronger Interest in its growth—than any other person—merely because it was his own work. Since my appointment to the business & office of navy Agent I have had almost nothing to do. I sometime have thought it arose from some sly proceeding to counteract the appointment—then that nothing was wanted in the Agency here. In my Letters to Secretary Hamilton—& Mr Turner I went so far as to say that if an agent at N London to be permanently establishd there was wanted, I would remove there.

I expect that post will be considered as a un eligible one for a Navy yard. If so as no agent is in the State so near as this is now appointed—I could wish to have the business—or even for such accidental as may fall in there, if a naval arsenal is not permanently establishd.

I know I can supply the navy with *better* salted provisions than they can obtain elsewhere — and you know that Masts, sparrs — & Timber from the river can be had in plenty & safely transported to N London or N York without risque. This I mentiond in my Letter to Commodore Tingey. No Navy agent is in office East of N Haven — or Derby & I am not very vain when I say my business as Ship Owner & builder of such a number would warrant me to say that I am not ignorant of the business or that I am certainly as well acquainted as any other man. I wish my friend you would think of these observations & if I can have any thing to do in this hitherto nominal business — to be at least worth the confidence of tryal. I write to you from the feeling of the moment — & confidentially in the hopes that you will still afford me your patronage in which you will be joind by M Goodrich. I was disappointed in not seeing you on your way — a more intelligent communication would then have made to you, than in this hurried Letter. Accept my best respects & believe me your friend & Humbl. Servt.

Jno: Morgan

You will have heard of the capture of the Macedonian by Co Decatur — but we have now a report that Comr Rogers is off with the B[...] Acasto — it is yet but report — tho likely [...] true.

ALS (VtU). Damaged by removal of the seal.

From E. S. Swenmore

My Dear Sir   Boston Dec 14 1812

Your Letter of the 3d inst affords me much gratification. I can not say *pleasure* for our Country is certainly in a very deploreable situation and nothing but the good sense of the people can extricate us. I [*illegible*] ever one important consideration — Napoleon (I hope) is so up to his Chin in difficulties he never can wade through. I shall carefully observe your injunction and shall not publish or expose your Letter or mention anything as coming from you — but the observations themselves are too important not to be mentioned as coming from a person whose opinions are to be respected. The southern people appear to be mad — "as mad as a March Hare." They little dream of the destruction that awaits them should peace not take place. I know not how the information comes or from what source but the belief seems to be unqualified — that the British intend an operation upon them of a most serious nature. Is it possible those Southern Slave holders — particularly of S. C. and Georgia are insensible to the worse than "Gunpowder plot" they contain within themselves. I shudder to think of the horrors should a match be put to the [a line missing] Slaves can so easily be made his Executioners is beyond my comprehension. The Slave holders may talk of their Militia as much as they please — but I am very much afraid should the war continue they will want other aid beside their Militia to keep their own Cattle in subjection. I think we may well apply the adage quem Dius vult perdise &c.

On every account the folly of the people of the South is inexplicable. What have they to gain by this war? Irishman like to gain a loss? Why do they trouble their heads about impressment? If it operated injuriously any where it would be among the Eastern States — and our Merchants and Sailors make no Complaints except those employed by the administration to disseminate their false stories and absurd doctrines. But you have (in my opinion) given the true cause of the war — it is the war of France — and if the people will support it — will continue with the career of Buonaparte. But the people will not support it. If Congress can obtain forced loans they may go on for a while — and possibly the *lucre of gain* may draw out something from the monied men — but it *will not* be extensive. There have been some Subscribers to the loan here — but it was upon the supposition that peace would take place which was the prevailing opini<on> for some time past, but now having vanished like the bowless fabric of a vision! There are no more patriots—patriotism vanished with the dream and those who have loaned their mon<ey> now wish they had been asleep and Gallatin to the Devil. Congress dare not lay taxes and the people would not pay if they did. I know not what course the sovereign people will take but I am somewhat of the opini<on> that should Congress rise and no peace and no Act passed for the meeting of the new Congress there will be a Convention of some of the States. Many are wan[...] for calling it immediately—but I hope this will not be done. Our accounts from Vermont are much in favor of a change of sentiments as to Madison and Friends. I believe if the elections had not come on so soon the result would have been different as to President.

But the administration may rest assured that Vermont will join the Eastern States in whatever they may conceive for their safety. They begin to feel the effects of the war and speak [may be a line missing] in price of imported articles—and depressio<n> of their own—and scarcity of money—are too serious inconveniences not to be regarded by a *Green mountain boy*.

But I am writing to one who knows more about Vermont than I do. However—I have conversed with some who have lately been in Vermont and have also heard the observations of those who have conversed with others from there. But all New Englanders are the same—and when they suffer privations will naturally enquire the cause. I have a little Girl that lies dangerously ill of a scald—we fear she will not live. I can say no more at this time.

But am sincerely yours

E S Swenmore

ALS (VtU). Margin obscured. Addressee unknown.

From Jonathan Dorr

Honble Stephen R Bradley Esqr
Dear sir   Roxbury 18th Decr. 1812

A most distressing Accident hapening to my family must Apologise for my not addressing you before on the Subject of the Carriage, On Saturday last Mr<s> Dorr & myself Rode up to Needham about 10 Miles to look a little afte<r> some Estates the late property of Mr. R Smith & before night we were met on the road on our Return by a person on the road who came on purpose to inform that our youngest Child about 4 Months old was very much burnt by the Cradles geting on fire, we got home as soon a<s> Possible but alass our dear babe liv'd but about an hour after. The Girl who had it in charge says she put some diapers on the fender to dry and then put them in the Cradle which was probably on fire & Occasion'd the Shocking Accident [*illegible*] leaving the Child asleep. It is doubly distressing to loose a Child or friend in this way it is almost too much for Mrs Dorr & myself to bear but we must be content to say the Lords will be done.

I have made Enquiry & find the Carriage I spoke to you about I can now purchase for you with tackling compleat for $700–which has been use'd but little is considerd to be as good as New, & cost $1350–. We have no News to day except the return of the British privateer Liverpool Packet on our Coast near Cape Cod last night she captured 4 or 5 Coasters from the Southard with Corn Flour &c which makes a great stir among our Merchants in the Southern trade.

In my last I wrote you something respectg a Contract I wish'd to make for Navy Provisions I find I can make it here with the Navy Agent.

From Daniel C. Sanders

Sir   Burlington, 18th Dec. 1812.

The President's Message and two other communications of accompanying documents have been received.[1] Your kind attention merits the expression of my sincere acknowledgements.

Our College continues in its former state. During the year past, it has received additions to the number of students. But, like other American Colleges, it languishes for the want of competent funds. The pressure of the times will affect us.

A most alarming mortality rages among General Dearborn's Army in Plattsburgh and Burlington. The most fatal disorder is the *"Peripneumonia notha,"* accompanied with severe colds, meazles and dysentary. The most perfect health prevails among the citizens.

I am, Sir, with great respect, Your mo. obt. servant,

Daniel C. Sanders.

Gen. S. R. Bradley.

ALS (NcD: Bradley Family Papers). Cover addressed by Sanders to "The Hon. Stephen R. Bradley Esq. / Senator in Congress, / Washington."; postmarked 21 Dec. at Burlington, Vt.; docketed by SRB, "Daniel C Sanders."
1. Letter not found.

Senate Proceedings: Mississippi Territory

In Senate of the United States.

JANUARY 11th, 1813.

Mr. Bradley, from the committee to whom was re-committed the bill from the House of Representatives, entitled "An act to enable the people of the Mississippi territory to form a constitution and state government, and for the admission of such territory into the Union, on an equal footing with the original states," reported, *in part*, the following bill:

A Bill

To carry into effect, the report made to Congress in February, one thousand eight hundred and three, by James Madison, then Secretary of State, Albert Gallatin, Secretary of the Treasury, and Levi Lincoln, Attorney General of the United States, commissioners appointed in pursuance of the act, entitled, "An act for an amicable settlement of limits with the state of Georgia, and authorising the establishment of a government in the Mississippi territory, in obedience to the provisions of the act, supplemental to the last mentioned act."

1   BE it enacted by the Senate and House of Representatives
2   *of the United States of America in Congress assembled*, That
3   until the first day of January, one thousand eight hundred and
4   fourteen, shall be and is hereby allowed to any person or per-
5   sons claiming public lands in the Mississippi territory, south of

the state of Tennessee, and west of the state of Georgia, under the act, or pretended act, of the state of Georgia, entitled "An act, supplementary to an act, entitled 'An act for appropriating a part of the unlocated territory of this state, for the payment of the late state troops, and for other purposes therein mentioned, declaring the right of this state to the unappropriated territory thereof, for the protection and support of the frontiers of this state, and for other purposes," passed January seventh, one thousand seven hundred and ninety-five, and the evidence of whose claim has been exhibited to the Secretary of State, and recorded in books in his office, conformably to the act of Congress, passed the third day of March, one thousand eight hundred and three, entitled, "An act regulating the grants of land and providing for the disposal of the lands of the United States south of the state of Tennessee," to lodge in the office of the Secretary of State, a sufficient legal release of all such claim to the United States, to take effect on provision being made by Congress for the indemnification of such claimants, conformably to the provisions of this act.

Sec. 2. *And be it further enacted*, That every conveyance or other written evidence of any claim to the said lands, derived from any person or persons whatsoever, since the same was exhibited to and recorded in the office of the Secretary of State, as aforesaid, shall, before the first day of December next, be exhibited by the claimant to the Secretary of State, and recorded as is provided in the aforesaid act; and every deed, conveyance, or other written evidence of any claim as aforesaid, which shall not be exhibited and recorded as aforesaid, before the first of December next, shall be null and void, and incapable of being pleaded or given in evidence in any court whatsoever.

Sec. 3. *And be it further enacted*, That if on or before the first day of January next, such sufficient releases as aforesaid, shall be lodged in the said office of the Secretary of State, as in the opinion of the President of the United States, shall release to the United States, and discharge all claims to the said lands which have been exhibited to the Secretary of State, and recorded as aforesaid, or which may be exhibited and recorded agreeably to the provisions of this act, the faith of the United States is hereby pledged to provide for the indemnification of such claimants. *Provided always*, That such indemnification shall be upon the principles, conformable to, and in strict execution of the terms proposed as the basis of a compromise in the report made to Con-

13 gress on the twenty-ninth of November, one thousand eight hun-
14 dred and four, by James Madison, then Secretary of State, Al-
15 bert Galatin, Secretary of the Treasury, and Levi Lincoln, At-
16 torney-General of the United States, commissioners appointed
17 as aforesaid. *And provided also*, That no claim shall be allowed,
18 or any indemnification made therefor, to any person or persons
19 who have voluntarily surrendered the evidence of their claims to
20 the said lands under the act of Georgia, of the thirteenth of Feb-
21 ruary, one thousand seven hundred and ninety-six, or any sub-
22 sequent act, and which at the time of the surrender would have
23 vested the title in such claimant, had the title from Georgia been
24 valid, or who have received the money deposited as the conside-
25 ration of the purchase of said land thus surrendered; but all
26 such lands shall be deemed and taken to the vested in the Unit-
27 ed States, exonerated and discharged from all such claims with-
28 out any further surrender or release whatever.

1 Sec. 4. *And be it further enacted*, That the Secretary of State,
2 the Secretary of the Treasury, and the Attorney General, for
3 the time being, be, and they are hereby appointed commission-
4 ers, any two of whom shall have full power and authority to
5 carry into effect the provisions of this act, and to apportion the
6 land among the several claimants in proportion to the quantity
7 of land contained within their respective claims; and also to
8 decide, in conformity to the principles of law and equity, on all
9 conflicting claims to said lands, and moreover shall have full
10 power and authority to do and perform all acts and things re-
11 quisite and necessary to carry into full effect the report of the
12 commissioners aforesaid, agreeably to the propositions of com-
13 promise and settlement therein contained.

1 Sec. 5. *And be it further enacted*, That from and after such
2 sufficient releases from the claimants to the United States, shall
3 be lodged in the office of the Secretary of State, as is herein before
4 provided in this act; all such sum or sums of money remaining
5 in the possession of the state of Georgia, which may have been
6 deposited as the consideration of the purchase of the aforesaid
7 lands, together with such interest, if any there be, as may have
8 accrued thereon, shall be set over and paid by the said commis-
9 sioners to the state of Georia, in part payment of the one mil-
10 lion two hundred and fifty thousand dollars, stipulated by the
11 articles of agreement and cessation between the United States and
12 the state of Georgia.

1 Sec. 6. *And be it further enacted*, That if any person or per-

2 sons in pursuance of the act of the state of Georgia of the thir-
3 teenth of February, one thousand seven hundred and ninety-six,
4 or of any subsequent act, shall have taken, received, or with-
5 drawn from the state of Georgia, or from the treasury thereof,
6 any sum or sums of money, which had been paid or deposited
7 as the consideration of the purchase of any of the aforesaid
8 lands, and the person, or persons, at the time of taking, receiving,
9 or withdrawing said sum or sums of money as aforesaid, were
10 not the *bona fide* claimants of the land for which said money
11 had been paid, or deposited as the consideration of the purchase
12 thereof, or if such person, or persons, had not at the time the
13 legal title vested in them, supposing the title from Georgia to
14 have been valid, every such person, or persons, who shall have
15 taken, received, or withdrawn the money as aforesaid, shall be
16 deemed and adjudged to have had, and received the same, to an
17 for the use of the United States, and shall be, and are hereby
18 declared to be holden and liable to refund and pay to the United
19 States, all such sum or sums of money so had and received as
20 aforesaid, with interest, at six per cent. per annum, from the
21 time he, she, or they, so received the same, which said sum or
22 sums of money may be recovered in an action of debt or trespass
23 on the case, at the suit of the United States, in any court having
24 competent jurisdiction of the same; and the aforesaid commis-
25 sioners be, and are hereby further authorised and directed to ex-
26 amine into, and investigate all cases coming within the purview
27 of this section, and to claim such sum or sums, to be paid to
28 the United States, as to them shall appear just and reasonable,
29 and to direct suits to be commenced for the recovery thereof,
30 against any person, or persons, who on due notice of such claim
31 shall neglect or refuse to pay the same.

Microform, U.S. Government Library, U.S. 12th Congress, 1811–1813. Senate.

From Roberts Vaux

Philada. Arch Street 2 Mo. 13. 1813.

The Pennsylvania Society for promoting the Abolition of Slavery &ca, deeply affected in learning that some American Citizens continue to violate the laws of their Country, and disregard the high obligations of Justice, Benevolence, & Honour, by conducting the African Slave Trade under the protection of foreign flags, is induced to memorialize the President, & Congress of the United States, on this important subject.

The distinguished part which thou has acted in the Councils of the Nation, in order to prevent the unrighteous commerce in Human flesh, is recollected with gratitude, & pleasure, by the Society, as it must be, by every friend, of the oppressed Africans.

It is therefore that the freedom is assumed to transmit the Memorial intended for the Senate of the United States, to thy care, accompanied by a request, that thou wilt be pleased to present it, to that Body.

The Committee entrusted with the superintendence of this application, (and of which I am chairman), will cheerfully furnish any information within its power to communicate, that may be deemed necessary to the advancement of the precious cause, for the promotion of which, the Society is ardently concerned.

Be pleased to accept assurances of my respect &c.

Roberts Vaux

Stephen R Bradley Esqr.
   of the Senate of the
      United States.
         Washington City.

ALS (NcD: Bradley Family Papers). Enclosed memorial not found.

In Senate of the United States.

FEBRUARY 15th, 1813.

Agreeably to notice given, Mr. Bradley asked and obtained leave to bring in the following bill, which was read and passed to a second reading.

A Bill

To encourage more effectually the destruction of the armed vessels of the enemy entering the ports and harbors of the United States.

1   BE it enacted by the Senate and House of Representatives
2   *of the United States of America in Congress assembled,* That
3   if any British armed vessel shall be found within the harbors
4   and waters under the jurisdiction of the United States, during
5   the present war with Great Britain (other than vessels coming
6   as cartels or flags of truce) it may and shall be lawful for any
7   person or persons, in any manner whatsoever, whilst such arm-
8   ed vessel shall so remain within the jurisdiction of the United
9   States, to burn, sink, or destroy, every such armed vessel; and
10 for that purpose to use torpedoes, submarine instruments, or any
11 other destructive machine whatever; and a bounty of one half
12 the value of the armed vessel so burnt, sunk, or destroyed, and
13 also one half the value of her guns, cargo, tackle, and apparel,
14 shall be paid out of the Treasury of the United States to such
15 person or persons who shall effect the same, otherwise than by
16 the armed or commissioned vessels of the United States.

Microform, U.S. Government Library, U.S. 12th Congress, 1811–1813. Senate. XXIII.

To Joseph Willard

Westminster July 5th 1813

Mr Joseph Willard
Dept Sheriff

Sir

On Mr Eli Robinsons settling with you for what trouble you have been at on his Execution you may return the Execution to me and take up your Receipt as he informs me the Execution has not been levied.

Stephen R Bradley

ANS (NcD: Bradley Family Papers).

From Charles Storer

sir,   Bellows Falls. Sept. 25th. 1813

According to your directions, after I, as Agent to the Canal Corporation, had made a payment to Samuel Bellows & indorsed the same on the Note which he held against the Corporation, I handed the same Note over to an Officer as Mr. Bellows' property and he attached it on the suit of John Atkinson & James Casey the trading Company at Bellows' Falls by virtue of the Writ assued [sic] from your son's Office. Mr: Bellows did not like the proceeding, and demanded the Note of me. The Officer, however, still holds it, and I presume has made due return thereof. Since this transaction Mr: Bellows has made application to Judge Knight, from whose office has issued the inclosed; which was handed to me this week.

How far the insertion of the name of Jesus Christ may operate in our Court I do not know; but by Bellows' mode of proceeding I am led to fear he may throw the costs of suit upon me, as I must confess judgement on the Note due from the Corporation, for the overplus of the demand of the Trading Company. The business, however, is with you & William to whom I submit it. A line of advice how I am to proceed will much oblige, sir, Yrs. respectfully,

Chas. Storer,
for B. F. Co:

ALS (NcD: Bradley Family Papers). Enclosure not found.

From Jonathan Dorr

Honble Stephen R Bradley
Dear sir   Roxbury 16th Octr 1813

I this day recd y<r> favor by mail & will attend to yr request respectg Mrs Madisons Shoe<s> should they appear. I will likewis<e> send you by the first Oport<u>nity the small Keg of Jamai<can> Spirit & nevertheless small it shall be very good as we have a little as fine as I ever saw.

At the Prospects of Peace through the mediation of Russia our Spirits are low, You Observe Good Spirits are with you scarce, they are likewise so with us and high.

Very respectfully Your Friend & Obt Servt

Jona. Dorr

ALS (VtU). Margin obscured.

From Robert Wright

My Dear sir   Washington Feb 2. 1814—

I am happy to recognize in Your son—a Chip of the old Block. He will be a strong Member. I should put great pleasure in possessing—Your Supper and The Hogs—and Adams Fall. I had some poetry for You, but I have lost it, it was so much in demand. I send You an Annapolis paper—where You will see Alexander Hanson one of the Editors of the "Federal Republican"[1] advertised. That paper is said to be edited by Hanson—Grosvenor of New York[2]—and John H Thomas. *I* call it "The Cyrberean Barker"—a Treble Headed Monster, guarding the British pandimonium, as Cerberus did Hell[3]—that they are three Cowards, and as Tecumseh says have "procter'd," their Tail. Will You have the goodness to give us a poem on pickering[4]—Hanson and Grovnor's Trip to Annapolis to the <Cossack?> dinner. After the Gove[r]nor & Council & these great Guests had dined, at night, they sallied out from the Tavern to parade the—streets—they were attacked by some Boys and Negros, several knocked down and one had his Ear sprung from his Head and were driven back—they rallied but were driven back again,—pickering's Toast—"Britains [*illegible*] I <slew?>.["] Pray my friend let us know you are alive, as it is among my prayers that You may live a long and happy Life. I am yr. servt and Friend

                                                                                            Robert Wright[5]

The papers will shew You how I touch the Traytors, to the quick. It is high Time some honest Judge had said to them his ultimatum—"The Lord have mercy on Your soul."

ALS (NcD: Bradley Family Papers). Cover addressed by Wright to "The Honble. Stephen R: Bradley / Westminster / Vermont / East" and franked; docketed by SRB, "Govr. Wright's Letters."

1. Alexander Contee Harrison (1786–1819), a strident critic of President Madison and the War of 1812, established and edited the *Federal Republican*, an extreme Federalist newspaper, in Baltimore from 1808 to 1812. In 1812 he moved the paper to Georgetown, D.C., after being seriously injured by a mob angered by his articles denouncing the administration. Hanson represented Maryland in the U. S. House of Representatives, 1813–16, and in the U.S. Senate, 1816–19.

2. Thomas Peabody Grosvenor (1778–1817), a Federalist, represented New York in the U.S. House of Representatives, 1813–17.

3. In Greek mythology, Cerebus is the three-headed watchdog who guards the entrance to Hades, permitting new spirits to enter the realm of the dead but allowing none of them to leave.

4. Timothy Pickering (1745–1829), after serving as secretary of war in 1795, and secretary of state, 1795–1800, represented Massachusetts as a Federalist in the U.S. Senate, 1803–11, and in the U.S. House of Representatives, 1813–17.

5. Robert Wright (1752–1826), a Republican, represented Maryland in the U.S. Senate, 1801–6, and in the U.S. House of Representatives, 1810–17 and 1821–23. From 1806 to 1809 he was governor of Maryland.

Indenture with James Holden

                                                                                            [15 May 1815]

This Indenture made this 15th Day of May 1815 between Stephen R Bradley of Westminster in the County of Windha<m> and State of Vermont of the one part and James Holden of Walpole in the State of New Hampshire of the other part Witnesseth that the said Stephen R in consideration of the rent Undertaking and covenants of the said James herein after mentioned hath devised and Let to the said James the following rooms in the Phippen house so called in Westminster to wit the northeast room on the Ground floor and the two back chambers to wit the northwest chamber and the middle chamber in th<e> back part of the house.

To have and to hold the same from the 14th day of the present month for and during and to the full end and term of one year he the said James yielding and paying therefor monthly and at the end of Every month two dollars and the said James doth further covenant that he will pay said rent as above specified that he will keep the rooms in Good repair that if any of the Glass should get Broken he will immediately repair the same that he will commit no Strip or waste and at the Expiration will deliver the quiet and peaceable possession of the premises to the said Stephen R in good tenantable repair as they are now in.

In witness whereof the parties have hereunto set their hands and Seals the day & year above written.

James Holden
Stephen R Bradley

Signed Sealed and delivered in presence of
<Rawsom Lawrens?>
Hezh. Abbey

ADS (VtU). In the hand of SRB. Margin obscured.

Contract with James Holden

[26 May 1815]

This Certifies that I have this day sold and delivered to Stephen R Bradley a black & white Cow now in his said Bradley's keeping which said Cow said Bradley is to keep in his possession and has engaged to let me milk said Cow two months from this date in said Bradley's yard night and morning and if before the Expiration of two months I pay said Bradley for the keeping of said Cow thirty Cents pr week and the rent that shall be then due for the rooms I have hired in said Bradley's house and also pay him Ten dollars which he has this day let me have and the Interest on the Same — Said Cow began to pasture the Nineteenth Day of April Instant — and upon my complying with the Above Conditions said Bradley is to sell and convey said Cow back to me but if I fail to perform the above conditions said Cow is to be said Bradley's free of all Incumbrances whatsoever forever.

Dated this 26th day of May A.D. 1815.

Test   James Holden

Received Novr 16 1815 of Stephen R Bradley five Dollars which in addition to the Ten Dollars he lent me in May last as Contained in the within writing is in full Satisfaction for the within Cow and makes the Sale thereof absolute without any claim or Right of Redemption on my part.

Hezh. Abbey   James Holden

DS (VtU). In the hand of SRB. Notation by SRB, "James Holden's obligation <per?> Cow."

To the General Assembly of Vermont

Westminster Oct. 7th 1815

To the Honorable the General Assembly of the State of Vermont next to be holden at Montpelier on the second Thursday of October instant

The petition of Caleb Clapp of Westminster in the County of Windham Humbly Sheweth that your petitioner is the proprietor of a manufactory for the purpose of manufacturing woolen and cotton cloths in the Town of Westminster in the County of Windham and that the same has been in operation for some years but that he experiences great inconveniencies in conducting the business for the want of those advantages which have been bestowed by the legislature upon most of the other manufactories in the State.

Wherefore he prays that he and his Successors may be constituted a Corporation by the name of the Westminster Manufacturing Company with such privileges and immunities as to your honorable body shall seem meet and proper — and as in duty bound will ever pray

Caleb Clapp

We the Undersigners do hereby Certify that in our opinion it would be expedient and proper that the prayer of the above petition Should be Granted

Stephen R. Bradley
Aaron Wales
Jonathan Badger
Joseph Willard Jr.
Isaac Parker
Isaac Holton
Henry Crawford

DS (Vt: MsVtSP, vol. 51, p. 69). A note in the lower margin, dated 25 Oct. 1815, reads: "To the Genl Assembly now sitting the Committee to whom was refered the above petition Report that in their opinion the prayer thereof ought to be granted & the petitioner have leave to bring in a bill Accordingly / M Richards Jr Committee." Notes on the verso read: "Petition of Caleb Clapp / Filed in Gen. Assy. / Oct. 14. 1815 / Att. W. Slade Junr. / Secy. of State / In Genl. Ass / Octr 14 1815 / Read & refd to the cmtee of manufactures / Att Wm D Smith Clk / In Council Oct. 16th 1815 / Resold to Concur in the Above referenced / RC Mallary / Secy / Octr 23d 1815 / Rept accpt / Att WDS Clerk / read / manufactures."

To William A. Griswold

Wm. A. Griswold Esqr

Sir   Westminster Decr. 14th. 1815

Some time in Octbr 1801 Samll Wetherbee Esqr of Concord gave me a note of $190 payable at a future day — which note some years afterwards I put into Wm C. Bradley's office for collection, and I understood that said Wetherbee had also put into said Bradley's office a note to collect against Smith & <Sias?> of Danville which when Collected was to be applied toward the payment of my demand against said Wetherbee. On the 25th of May 1807 Wm C. Bradley paid me Sixteen dollars and Ninety five Cents and one the 21st of October 1812 paid me a further sum of one Hundred and twenty Eight dollars and twenty Six Cents on my demand against said Wetherbee I then understood it was all the demand against Smith & <Sias?> Collected — those two sums amounting to $145:21 I then acknowledged and Still acknowledge to have received on my demand against said Wetherbee.

I am surprised to find said Wetherbee should make any question in relation to that Sum as he has been in my neighbourhood and done business within a few rods of my house since the receipt thereof and might have received the most ample satisfaction on that score had he not declined calling at my office.

I am Sir Respectfully Your Obedt Servt

S R B

ALS (VtU).

Indenture with John H. Wier

[27 October 1817]

This Indenture made this twenty Seventh day of Octob<er> A.D. 1817 between Stephen R Bradley of Westminster in the County of Windham and State of Vermont of the first part and John H. Wier of Westmoreland in the County of Cheshir<e> and State of New Hampshire of the Second part Witnesseth — that the party of the first part for and in consideration of the rents Covenants and undertakings of the party of the Second part doth devise lease and to farm let to the sa<id> John H. a certain tract or piece of land lying in Walpole in said County of Cheshire being a piece of the farm common<ly> called the Wier farm and is that small piece of land whi<ch> lyeth under the hill adjoining the land and Garden of the sai<d> John on the easterly side of the highway and enclosed with the fence that seperates it from the great pasture with <the?> orchard standing thereon supposed to contain about three Acres be the same more or less.

To have and to occupy & possess the same fro<m> the first day of April now last past for and during an<d> to the full end and term of twelve Calendar months and fully to be Complete and ended yielding and paying therefor at the end of said term fifteen dollars — and the said John H. doth hereby convenant that he will at the end of said term pay unto the said Stephen R. the above said rent of fifteen dollars that he will commit no strip o<r> waste and will at the expiration of said term delive<r> up to the said Stephen R. the Quiet and peacable possession of the premises in as good tenantable repair as he receiv<ed> them.

In Witness whereof the parties have hereun<to> set their hands and Seals the day and date above

Stephen R Bradley
John H. Wier

Signed Sealed and delivered in presence of
N. B. the word "*twelve*" in the 3d line of the Habendum wrote on razure before signing
Josiah Bellows 3d.
Nathl. F Stone

   ADS (VtU). In the hand of SRB. Margin obscured.

To William C. Bradley

My Dear Son   Boston Novr. 9th 1817

Hearing various reports of your Illness and some representing it in the worst point of light so much alarmed your friends here and especially *Sally* that I was induced to take my carriage and bring her and Mrs Dorr to this place with a determination that unless we obtained more favourable news to get aboard of a packet and come to you but learning from a Mr Glover & Capt. Rogers that you was on the mending has induced us to defer the voige til we hear further Sally & Mrs Dorr is now out at Roxbury with Capt Dorr who has been very sick indeed his life has been for Several weeks despaired of I found him however mending last evening when I arived at Roxbury and the prospect now is he will get well tho' he is very low Mrs Clapp his Sister from Westminster has been with him for Several weeks and I dare say has been a fine *nurse* his Sickness has been long — Your friends are all very well at Westminster Mr Richards sets out for Congress on Monday the 17th. Sally & Mrs Dorr would send much love if they knew of the oppertunity but they are at Roxbury & the Packet will wait but half an hour Judge Chipman will Sail in the Packet he has not yet come down and I have not Seen him he is however expected on board every minute — I am inclined to think I Shall return home and leave Sally & Mrs Dorr here to congratulate you on your arival — be mindful not to leave your Quarter<s> at *Lubeck* til you find yourself abundantly able to bear the voige You will be received here and at Westminster by your friends "as *life from the dead*["] — if any thing should turn up more unfavourable injoin it upon Mr Johnson and <Gaas?> to write the earliest information, *our anxiety is Gre<at.>*

I am my Dear Son with the most anxious concerns for Your health & recovery Your affectionate father

Stephen R Bradley

ALS (VtU). Margin obscured.

From William C. Bradley

My dear fatherBoston Nov 19th. 1817

I arrived here this morning in a rather feeble state but improving. I shall start as soon as I have finished this letter for Roxbury to find Sally whom I long to see though I am sure the first interview will be painful.

Your letter my dear father gave me both pain & pleasure — pain to think of the anxiety of which I have been the occasion & pleasure to hear again from my friends.

I shall return to Westminster as soon as I feel strong enough to ride so far — meanwhile I beg you to believe how sensible of & grateful for your solicitude I am & also to give my love to my Mother sisters & children.

Yr truly affectionate Son

Wm C Bradley

Hon S. R. Bradley
ALS (MCR-S).

To Abraham Bradley Jr.

Abraham Bradley Jnr
Assistant P[ost] M[aster] General

Dear SirWestminster Decr 19th 1817

I have just learnt with no small Surprise that measures are taking to remove the distributing Post office from Walpole to Bellows Falls I feel confident that if correct information is obtained at the general Post office no such arrangment will ever take place Walpole is a place five times as large as Bellows Falls & a place where ten times more business is done, there are roads leading from Walpole in every direction and the place is surrounded on every side with a fine cultivated Country not so with Bellows Falls which is locked in by mountains the distributing office at Walpole accomodates all the adjacent towns in Vermont and as most of the trade of the Country is to Boston the place seems well calculated to accomodate this part of the Country on both Sides of the river if removed to B. Falls it would Subject Walpole Westminster and many other towns to the inconvenience of having there letters carried Six or Eight miles or more Directly from them and to lye Some days till the return mail whereas at present the letters go regularly to the Post offices in the Several towns above Walpole when distributed at that place, the Merchants at Walpole are many of them concerned in business very extensively some importers and a large Fur trade with the Indians that I flatter myself the community at large will not be subjected to such disadvantages, to gratify a few restless and angry persons for I understand the scheme has been set on foot by Brewster to be revenged for some personal quarrel he has had with Individuals at Walpole.

I am with Great respect Your Obedt Servt

S R B

Dft? (VtU).

From Abraham Bradley Jr.

General Post Office
Decemr. 26. 1817

Dear sir

I am favoured with your letter of the 19th which I h<ave> shown to the postmaster general. No communication on the sub<ject> of removing the distributing office from Walpole to Bellows falls h<as> been received here. Such a removal would seem to be preposterou<s> for the reasons which you have mentioned, & will not be done without previously consulting you.

I am with great respect your obedt servt

Abm Bradley j<r.>

General Stephen R Bradley
Westminster Vt

ALS (VtU). Margin obscured.

To Mark Richards

Dear Sir   Westminster Feb 20th. 1818

Some time since I inclosed in a letter to your care sundry documents in relation to the claims of Franci<s> Snow and the widow Badger for doctoring & nursing sick So<l>diers they are anxious to learn whether you have received the<m> and what prospect there is of their receiving any remunirat<ion.>

I received your letter of the 4th. instant and observe with so<me> surprise that Genll. St Clair should have the face to make any furth<er> claims on Congress I have no doubt he has been fourfold <re>munirated for any money he advanced if ever he advanced any from his private funds, since many of the papers and documents which related to the transactions of 76 &c have been destroyed and lost he has exhibited claims founded on old rec<eipts> which he obtained from subordinate officers which every Genll & field officer might do who belonged to the army at that time in the deranged state of publick affairs—*Maese & Coldwell* if I mistake not their names acted as pay Master Generals at that time and transmitted to officers commanding seperate departments and to those commanding regiments by Post or otherwise large su<ms> of money which those officers delivered to their subordinate officers taking their receipts when Genll St Clair was appoint<d> General and left his regiment he had a Considerable sum of th[...] money which he delivered over to Major Butler who was then the Commanding officer of the regiment and took his receipt which has been made the Ground of his claim it is very strang<e> that General St Clair should never have set up any of these Claims in the various settlements he made at the treasury nor with the Commissioner who Settld army accounts nor while he was president of old Congress until the papers of that day were mostly destroyed and Major Butler and the other officers dece'd—but you may as wel<l> satisfy the Grave as some of those old officers who were never of muc<h> worth to the public or themselves but to spend money and boast of their heroic deeds which nobody ever heard of but from themselves if a man who has had the advantage of Genll St Clair was a General through the revolutionary war with a commutation of half pay for life was afterwards a Genl for some years in the Indian War where he obtained a mighty defeat was at the same time Governor of the teritory of Ohio and superintendant of Indian affairs and drew pay for all those seperate offices at the same time amounting to above Six thousand dollars a year I say if a man with those advantages will spend all let him beg & be d—n before I would advance him one Cent from the public or private purs<e.>

Nothing new has occured in our little village things remain in Statu quo it has been very cold during this month and a Great plenty of Snow has fallen. Your friends are all very well and your domestic concerns under the Guidance of the Doctor I believe are conducted well.

Accept Sir the Assurance of my personal respect & Esteem

Stephen R Bradley

Hon. M Richards

ALS (VtU). Margin obscured. Endorsed by Richards, "Honl Stephen R. Bradley / letter 20th Feby 1818 / *rcd 1st March.*"

Indenture with Abel Wellington

[9 April 1818]

This Indenture made this 9th. day of April A.D. 1818 between Stephen R Bradley of Westminster in the county of Windham and Stat<e> of Vermont of the one part and Abel Wellington of said Westminster of other part Witnesseth that the said Stephen R for and in consideration the rents covenants & undertakings of the said Abel by him to be done and performed Doth hereby devise lease and to farm to the said Ab<el> let the following farm or tract of land lying and being in said Wes<t>minster and bounded and described as follows to wit being lot number three in the first division of Hundred Acres and is the farm on which the said Abel now lives.

To have and to hold use occupy & possess the same from the first day of April Instant for and during and to the full end and term of one year thence next ensuing and fully to be completed & ended And the said Abel doth hereby on his part covenant & agree with the said Stephen R that he will on or before the first day of Febru<a>ry next as rent for said farm deliver to the said Stephen R at his no<w> dwelling house in said Westminster twenty five bushels of wheat twenty five bushels of Rye twenty bushels of Corn and thirty bus<h>el of Oats and thirty bushels of potatoes and forty weight of flax the Grain & flax to be good and marchantable And the said Abel doth further Covenant that he will give said farm into the list & pay all taxes assessed thereon during said term that he will not cut fell destroy or carry away any timber trees or wood standing lying or being on said Farm other than what is necessary for fuel for his own fires and for repairs on said farm that he will commit no strip or waste that he will carry on the farm according to the rules of good husbandry and will at the expiration of said term deliver the quiet and peacable possession of said Farm to the said Stephen R in as good tenantable repair as it is now in.

In witness whereof the parties have hereunto interchangably set their hands and Seals the day & year first above written.

Abel Wellington
Stephen R Bradley

Signed Sealed & Delivered
In presence of
<Eunce?> Abbey
Julia Abbey

ADS (VtU). In the hand of SRB. Margin obscured.

To William C. Bradley

Dear Sir   Walpole Decr 24th 1818

I enclose to your care a small final settlement note of $58:89 it has been on interest since the first day of January 1783. The statute of limitatio<ns> had barr'd the payment til the late act of Congress whi<ch> I understand has opened once more the door if you w<ill> be so good as to apply to the Treasury department an<d> get the amount in a draft on some bank in Bosto<n> or any other way that the same may be realized you will very much oblige

                                                                             Your affectionate parent
                                                                                   Stephen R Bradley

Wm C Bradley Esqr

P. S. It had been mislaid for a long time & was found the other day.

ALS (VtU). Margin obscured.

To William Czar Bradley

My Dear Sir   Walpole Jany. 1st. 1819

I had calculated to see you before you left home but the solemnities of Christmas, and the call of Friends deprived me of the pleasure I now enclose you a small Final Settlement note of $58:89 it has been on interest since the first day of Jany. 1783 the statute of limitation had barr'd the payment til the late act of Congress which I understand has opened once more the door. If you will be so good as to apply at the treasury department and get the amount in a draft on some bank in Boston or any other way that the same may be realized you will very much oblige

                                         Your affectionate parent & Friend
                                                       Stephen R Bradley

ALS (NcD).

From Samuel G. Goodrich

Dear Sir   Hartford Feby 27. 1819

I should have written you several days before this in reply to your last, if I had had any thing of particular consequence to write. It was our intention to have written by Mr. Hatch, but he went a day sooner than we expected. The chairs I have not yet been able to send as no opportunity has offered. The order on the Bank mentioned in your letter I recd. & (as I think) you will find a memorandum accordingly on a blank page of my letter of Decr. I expect to go to N. York on the 16th. March. If you should not come to Hartford before that time & will authorize Trumbull to give me the note of C[andee] & G[oodrich] I will get it discounted, & save you any trouble on the subject. I mention this, because the money will be of more value to me to take to N. York than under other circumstances; & it is I suppose entirely according to your arrangement.

We are all quite well. Adelines health is perfectly good — our little babe grows every day in weight & graces. If you come to see us this Spring we shall without doubt make you acknowledge that in some respects at least we can equal the productions of Vermont or New Hampshire.

We have no news here — about a fortnight Since, however, a very strange occurence took place here which, altho' it made a great noise, has not yet perhaps reached you. W. H. Imlay had furnished a large capital to F. W. Hotchkiss & B. C. Burdett (the latter Caroline Barbers man) to trade in dye stuffs. The partnership was to expire next month, and as Imlay did not wish to renew it, negotiations for a settlement commenced. In the course of this business however considerable irritation on both sides took place, & finally Hotchkiss & Burdett told Imlay that they should hold the property in their possession untill they procured terms such as they wanted. As they owed Imlay about 50,000 dollars for capital—& as about 30 or 40 thousand dollars of the company property was in *notes* Imlay became very much alarmed. This was increased by their withholding a statement of the companys accounts, & as Imlay says by some other circumstances. He therefore resolved to put a period to the establishment. On saturday evening about seven o'clock (the 13th inst.) He took Trumbull & Smith a sheriff & three negroes down to the store of Hotchkiss & Burdett declared the partnership dissolved according to a provision in the contract—& ordered the officer to attatch all the goods of the firm. He then went with Smith & Trumbull into the counting room of H. & B. & endeavoured to persuade them to give up the books & papers. They however took the notes & money into their possession & declared they would not give them up. Upon this Imlay went out—presently the three negroes rushed into the room—seized Burdett & Hotckiss threw them down upon the floor—& Imlay with a knife cut off the skirts of their coats—& thus obtained Burdetts pocket book which contained the notes—money &c. Hotckiss accidentally saved his pocket Book—tho' he lost the tail of his coat. Several persons in the neighborhood hearing the cry of Murder! forced open the door, but did not arrive till Imlay had accomplished his purpose. Trumbull & Smith were present—& were very much blamed for not interfering. They say however, that the whole affair was so sudden & unexpected they could not do it. They <were?> joined with Imlay in two actions for, tresspass—one for Burdett—laying damages at 30,000 dollars & another for Hotckiss—damages at 25,000. Imlays bank stock—house furniture—goods in store—house &c—were all attatched on monday following the fracas. By subsequent agreement however the matters are to be settled by arbitration.

Thus I have made a long story—perhaps a dull one. Adeline & I returned from Berlin on wednesday where we had been to the wedding of Maryanne—who was married to A. B. Smith—son of Judge Smith of <Rox>bury.

Yrs respy
S. G. Goodrich

ALS (NcD). Bottom margin obscured. Cover addressed, "Hon Stephen R. Bradley / Walpole / N. Hampshire." Endorsed by SRB, "Samll G Goodrich / Letter of/ Febr 27 1819."

To John J. Astor

Sir   Walpole March 8th. 1819

    I take the liberty to recommend to your patronage the bearer Edwin May a young gentleman of good habits and respectable Connections has been well educated in the mercantile line amply competant for store or book keeping or any branch of Clerkship, as business is dull in the Country he is wishing to get into some business in the City and knowing how extensive your Concerns are and the pleasure you take in bringing forward young gentlemen and encouraging them in business, I have ventured to recommend him to you—any favour you may show him will be conferring an Obligation on a meritorious young Man & Much oblige your Humble Servant

S R Bradley

John J Astor Esquire

ALS (DLC).

From Samuel G. Goodrich

Dr. Sir, Hartford April 23. 1819

I this day send by the Stage 3 shad which I hope will reach you safely. We are quite well now — except little Mary who has it is thought the whooping-cough tho' I doubt it myself. A very Severe influenza has prevailed here which confined me to the house three weeks.

It is a good while since we have heard from you except verbally. There is nothing new here.

Yrs. respectfully

Saml. G. Goodrich

Hon. S. R. Bradley

P. S. Hartford April 27. The above was written too late for the mail. Since that date I have recd. your letter. I expect very soon an opportunity to send your chairs if you wish. They are in my store chamber well packed in straw. Shall I send them by a boat if a chance offers? Please write me about this. I send 4 shad by the stage. I cannot but hope that they will arrive fresh as they are unusually fine this season.

In haste yrs

S. G. G.

As it is now shad season & as the election is next week we hope you will be here. Stella has some idea of meeting Josiah here. Will you not bring her down with you?

ALS (NcD).

Indenture with John H. Wier

[12 May 1819]

This Indenture made this twelfth day of May in the yea<r> of Our Lord one thousand Eight Hundred and Nineteen betwe<en> Stephen R Bradley of Walpole in the County of Cheshire and Stat<e> of New Hampshire of the one part and John H Wier of Westmorela<nd> in the Same County of Cheshire of the other part Witnesseth that t<he> said Bradley for and in consideration of the rents covenants a<nd> undertakings of the Said Wier by him to be done and perform<ed> doth hereby demise lease and to farm let to the Said John H Wier a Certain tract or piece of land lying in Walpole aforsaid bei<ng> a piece of the farm commonly called the Wier farm and is tha<t> small piece of land which lyeth under the hill and adjoining t<he> land and garden of the Said Wier's on the easterly side of the hig<h>way and enclosed within the fence that seperates it from the great pasture with the Orchard standing thereon supposed to contain three Acres be the Same more or less.

To have and to hold occupy and possess the same from t<he> first day of April now last past for and during and to the fu<ll> end and term of one year thence next ensuing and fully to be co<m>pleted and ended yielding and paying therefor at the end <of> said term fifteen dollars— And the said John H. Wier doth her<eby> covenant that he will at the end of said term pay unto the <said> Stephen R Bradley the Said rent of fifteen dollars and that he wi<ll> commit no Strip or waste but will carry on said piece of land and improve the same according to the rules of Good Husbandry and will at the expiration of said term deliver up to the said Bradley the quiet and peacable possession of the premises in as good tenantable repair as he received the same.

In witness whereof the parties have hereunto set the<ir> hands and Seals the day and date above

Stephen R Bradley
John H Wires

Signed Sealed and delivered
in presence of
C<h>arlton Wires

ADS (VtU). In the hand of SRB. Margin obscured.

From Samuel G. Goodrich

Dear Sir   Hartford Sep. 30. 1819

Your letter came to hand yesterday. I have this morning purchased for you the Stove as you requested, but have not determined as to the trimming. On the back of your letter I found written "get a copper kettle." I was afraid I might not understand this right. I therefore send you a description of the furniture attatched to the stove—for the purpose of your choosing such as you like. The description is as follows—

1 Thomsons Cooking Stove—with 3 <gr>iddles—2 Round pans—2 rings—1 pair of andirons—1 Sheet iron plate—1 large tin boiler—2 smaller do—1 Tin Tea Kettle—1 Coffee do—1 Tin Steamer—price $49 cash.

The above is similar to William's in all respects except the stove, being cast this season is improved by adding a door to the fire place on the side of the stove.

Another description is as follows—The same stove as above—& the same griddles—pans, rings—andirons—& sheet iron plate—also 1 Iron pan, Square—1 large Copper boiler—2 smaller do—1 Copper Tea Kettle—1 Tin Coffee Kettle—2 tin Steamers—65 Dollars cash. The latter kind is probably cheapest. Mr. Richards bought one like it in New York & paid $65 cash for it there. Mr. May bought one a few days since here & paid $66.

If you will give me your instructions which of them you prefer I will have them sent by the first boat.

You can if you please select from the above descriptions any pieces you please—but in this case a set of furniture is broken & the pieces of the articles selected, disproportionatly enhanced.

We have been disappointed at not Seeing you—but now flatter ourselves you will be here in Nov. I had occasion to send some books to William (which I purchased for him) a few days since. I put in a new book for you—entitled a history of South America—by—Bonnycastle. I hardly know what its character is—but from the <topick,> I should think it interesting. The bin in which it was sent was directed to Hall & Green—Bellows falls.

We are all pretty well—<& expect> tomorrow or next day to Stella Wm. & his wife. Adeline is very curious to know who has had the courage to take off Paulina.

We desire to be remember to all—& I am in haste yrs.resp

                                                                 S. G. Goodrich

Hon S. R. Bradley

P. S. Wms. Stove was bought for 47 or 48 dollars, but this was owing to its being purchased out of season.

ALS (NcD). Damaged by removal of seal.

To William H. Crawford

Sir   Walpole Octbr 12th. 1819

The bearer hereof Mr David Stone of the house of Stone & Bellows will have the honour to call on you for the purpose of making a contract with Government for furnishing a quantity of provisions at[1]

Any perticular attention you may show him will confer an additional obligation on your old friend. The house of Stone & Bellows have had very extensive concerns and done much business in the western country they think it would much facilitate the closing their concerns in that country and to their advantage if they could receive and dispose of the produce and provisions raised there. Mr Stone is a Gentleman with whom I have been long acquainted is a man of honour of the strictest probity and integrity and you may be assured that any contract he may make with the government for furnishing provisions at the place aforesaid will be faithfully and punctually fulfiled.

    I am with the greatest respect your Most obedient and Most Humble Servant

                                                                      Stephen R Bradley

The Hon. William H Crawford
    Secretary of War

ALS (VtU).
1. Remainder of line left blank by SRB.

From Samuel G. Goodrich

Dr. Sir   Hartford Nov. 8. 1819

Agreeably to your request I have examined the house you purchased, & can see no particular defect about it. It smokes badly but by the use of stoves this objection will be done away. The cellar is rather wet & the occupant informs me that it communicates considerable dampness to the house, Would it not remedy this to lay a plank floor. There is no water in the cellar & I believe it is sufficiently drained—& the dampness seems only to spring from the nature of the soil. The well is an excellent one, & retains abundance of water in the dryest seasons. The arrangement of the rooms is good—except that the street door opens into the largest & best room—the only one indeed which is susceptible of being made a parlour. The manner in which the house is finished <is> plain but well enough. The present state of repair is in some respects bad. The paint of the rooms is dirty—& the paper ditto. The fences too as you probably noticed in front of the house are a little out of order.

But on the whole the house is good—& in good condition. I think 100 Dollars in repairs including a floor to the cellar—would make it quite satisfactory. About all these matters we should be glad to have your opinion & direction.

It is our plan provided it corresponds with yours to pull up stakes in a few weeks, & the sooner we are able to do this the better will it enable us to make arrangments for the winter. But we shall cheerfully make our plans conform to yours. We will thank you to inform us be an early mail what you wish us to calculate upon.

We had had no news since you left us. J. Morgan I find was really disappointed that you would not buy his house. Perhaps you have heard that Northampton has subscribed $50,000 for Williamstown college provided it isremoved there. We are all well & desire to be remembered to all friends.

                                                                      Yrs respy.
                                                                      S. G. Goodrich

ALS (NcD). Damaged by removal of seal.

From Samuel Dinsmoor

Sir,   Keene, Augt. 26. 1820.

    I have the honor to inform you that the "United Fraternity" at Dartmouth College have elected you an honorary member of the fraternity; and have requested me to invite you to unite with them, and to lend your influence and aid to promote the interest and respectability of the society.

    I am Sir, respectfully Yr. Obt. Servt.

                                                 Saml Dinsmoor

Hon. Stephen R. Bradley
    ALS (NcD).

From Samuel G. Goodrich

Dr Sir   Hartford Feb. 17. 1822

    During the last week Adeline has gained strength & appetite — and her cough has in some small degree abated. These circumstances have given strength to the hopes which I have entertained from the beginning of her illnes. Dr. Sheldon, of Litchfield, a physician of great reputation in hectic cases has been here four days, and devotes himself entirely to Adeline. His practice consists very much in devising <modes?> of excercise suited to extreme debility — in choosing & regulating drinks & food, in furnishing ammounts & adapting medicines carefully to the changing state of the patient. He has done wonders in other cases, & from the favorable results of his practice thus far, I anticipate a great deal of good. I have before given you some particulars of A's situation — a relation of her state now, will enable you judge of her improvement. She sits up from 3 to 4 hours a day — and is exercised in a swing once or twice. She coughs but little — not more than two or three times in 24 hours — but occasionally for several minutes & with some severity. She has had no turn of coughing however for the last 24 hours. She raises no blood, nor has she — but she constantly expectorates a kind of phlegmy matter amounting often to a pint or more a day. There is however no purulent matter with it, and the quantity has lessened for some days. She is extremely emaciated & is scarcely able to bear her weight. She sleeps quietly — has no pain in the breast — no fever — & no night sweats. The physicians say that she has the best pulse for a person so much diseased, they have ever known. They consider the difficulties of her case to lie in her debility & emaciation, her want of appetite & her profuse expectoration.

    I have not hear from you for many days & I hope soon to hear that you are all well. Adeline tells me to give her best love to you all.

    Yrs. respy.

                                                 S. G. Goodrich

Honl. S. R. Bradley
    ALS (NcD).

From Samuel G. Goodrich

Dr. Sir   Hartford Mar. 5. 1822

    I have not written you for the last fortnight, partly because I could communicate to you no important change in Adelines condition & partly because I have had an affection of the eyes which rendered it difficult for me to write.

As I have been particular to state A's symptoms heretofore, I need only say that they remain much the same — tho' she has gained strength & appetite in some slight degree. She sits up about 6 or 7 hours each day — & rides about the room in a chamber carriage from one hour to one & a half. She can walk about the room — tho she does not much.

My eyes allow me to write no more — but you may rely upon early information of important matters in A's case.

Yrs affy

S. G Goodrich

ALS (NcD).

From Samuel Whittelsey

Dear Sir,   Hartford June 24th. 1822

It has become my painful duty, by the request of Mr Goodrich, to announce to you the Death of your beloved daughter Adeline. She expired this morning, about 6 O clock. Although all hopes of her recovery have, doubtless, long since been relinquished, and the event of her exit anticipated; yet I doubt not you will sensibly feel the stroke that has severed from your embraces a child so dearly & so justly beloved.

We have watched, with no small degree of solicitude, the progress of her disease, and have seen her gradually declining towards the grave; yet we cannot but feel that the event of her death has come somewhat suddenly upon us.

During the whole period of her sickness, Mrs Goodrich has manifested uncommon patience. Not a murmur or a sigh has been heard to escape from her lips. To her native cheerfulness and amenity of temper, have been superadded the graces of evangelical resignation to the divine will and cordial faith in an Almighty Redeemer. These christian virtues have most evidently produced a peace & tranquility of mind, which the world, with all its splendors, could neither give nor take away. Her reason was unclouded till the last moments of her life; her confidence in her saviour remained unshaken; her hopes of heaven seemed to brighten as she approached the closing scene; and she has left, to all her bereaved friends, her fullest testimony to the reality and power of evangelical religion, and the sweet consolation derived from the conviction that she has gone to dwell with Christ in Heaven, & to share the bliss which is prepared for the disciples of Jesus in the mansions of glory.

The solemnities of her funeral are to be [...]d on Wednesday next.

Miss Willard requests me to say to y<ou> that, if your ill health should prevent your coming to Hartford, at the period you have proposed, she will thank you to write, as she wishes to return home as soon as may be convenient after paying her last kind offices to her deceased friend. With respects to Mrs Bradley in which Mrs Whittelsey unites, I am Sir Yours

Saml Whittelsey

ALS (NcD). Damaged by removal of seal.

From Samuel G. Goodrich

Dr. Sir   Hartford 21st. Augt. 1822

It is several weeks since I have either written to my northern friends, or heard directly from them. The truth is that partly withheld by a disinclination to disturb them with my affairs, & still more relying upon your promise to come down at Watermelon time, I have let the time pass away, trusting that the knowledge of my situation communicated by Mr. Whittlesey would furnish sufficient excuses if any should be needed.

I now intend to go to Walpole in Sepr. unless you should bring Mary down before. In the mean time will you do me the favor to let me know your intentions as to coming. I have heard that Margaret is ill—will you please say how she is.

I hope Mary is a good girl—& rewards the good care that I know is taken of her, by her behaviour. I am afraid if she has not forgotten me entirely, she has at least forgotten, by this time, our strict Lord Hill discipline.

Please remember me to Mrs. B. & all friends

respy.

S. G. Goodrich

ALS (NcD).

From Tapping Reeve

Dear Sir   Litchfield Nov 16th 1822

It has given me great pleasure to become acquainted with your Son and has carried me back to former days when you were here studying Law with me. Many public scenes have occupied each of us since that time. You have accumulated great wealth—whilst I have only obtained a competency—the difference is, in some measure owing probably, to a talent which nature has given to *you*—and not to me in understanding how to acquire property under the same means—but until the two last years I had a comfortable living from my Law school which has now passed out of my hands and left me in circumstances comparatively poor—and has driven me to the necessity of collecting all my scattered dues—and in looking over my old account I found that the very small sum which was due to me for your instruction had never been cancelled—and have no doubt but it has wholy escaped your recollection—I determined tho with great reluctance to request that you will have the goodness to excuse me at this late period in calling on you for such an old claim—but do feel Sir that when my situation is taken into view you will allow it—though it is but fifteen or at the most but twenty dollars yet this sum as small as it is with the interest will help me much—the circumstances which called you away and the public affairs which has since devolved upon you has calculated to drive all such small affairs from your memory—but I had a confident feeling that when it was made known to you—that with cheerfulness you would attend to it—and that you would receive it as was intended by me as a friend to a friend—and believe me your friend & Huble Servt

Tapping Reeve

ALS (NcD).

From Joshua Bates

Sir,   Middlebury College Jany. 16. 1823.

By the particular desire of all the members of the Corporation in this vicinity, you are hereby requested to attend a Special meeting of "the President & Fellows of Middlebury College"; to be holden at my house, on Tuesday the 4th. of March next, at 6, o'clock, P.M.

The particular object of the meeting is to inquire into the state of the Institution, in relation to the Professor of Mathe[.] & Natural Philosophy. The business is of a peculiarly interesting nature; & requires the serious deliberation of a full Board. It is hoped, therefore, that nothing will prevent your attendance.

With sentiments of respect &c.

Joshua Bates.

Hon. S. R. Bradley. L. L. D
   ALS (NcD).

From Samuel Smith

Dr. Sir,   Washington 5 Feby. 1823

I have in the Course of conversation said, that in the senate Mr J. Q. Adams, on the subject of impressment of seamen by the British—had taken the ground, "that Great Britain had a right to the services of her seamen, and were justified in taking them wherever they were found. That we employed their seamen, and that when they searched our ships for them, they would sometimes be mistaken, and take american sailors which on proper proof being adduced would be released." In other words justified their taking their seamen out of our ships—such are my impressions and I ask as a favour that you would say whether I am right or wrong that I may unsay if I have done him injustice.

The Presidential Election may have reached you in your retirement. I think the tug will be between Adams and Crawford Mr. Calhoun will probably retire, and Mr Clay Can only get Kentucky and the States on the other side of the Ohio, and Louisiana 44 Votes, General Jackson has a mission which he will probably accept so that he is out of the way—Mr. Adams will I think get all N. England altho: some doubt it. 42 Votes. He may get six Votes in Maryland, and it is thought that Mr. Calhoun will transfer So. Carolina to him 11 Vote and that he has a good Chance for Alabama 5 Votes in all 64 Votes—more I think he will not get.

Mr. Crawford will get Jersey, Delaware—5 in maryland, all Virga. N. Carolina and Georgia and Tenesee. It is *ascertained* that two <thirds?> of the present legislature of N. York are in his favour and that he has a good Chance for mississippi & some little Chance for Pennsylvania, if Calhoun should retire. At present that State it is said are in his Calhoun's[1] favour, and his friends flatter themselves, that he can transfer it to Adams.

I wish you only to answer the first part of this letter—if you answer the residue, let it be in a seperate sheet.

Your Old friend

S. Smith

Stephen R. Bradley, Esqr.
   ALS (NcD).
   1. The preceding name was interlined by Smith.

To Samuel Smith

Dear Sir   Walpole N. H. Febr 14th. 1823

I received your letter of the 5th Instant with much pleasure as it convinced me that you were Still engaged in the great concerns of the nation and shall cheerfully comply with your friendly request you say in your letter "That in the course of conversation you have Said that in the Senate Mr J Q. Adams on the Subject of impressment of Seamen by the British—had taken the ground that Great Brittain had a right to the Services of her Seamen and was

Justified in taking them wherever they were found that we employed their Seamen and that when they searched our Ships for them they would sometimes be mistaken and take American Sailors which on proper proof being adduced would be released — in other words Justified their taking their Seamen out of our Ships — Such are my impressions and I ask as a favour that you would Say whether I am right or wrong that I may unsay if I have done him injustice."

I think your impressions are wrong I never understood Mr Adams to have taken the Ground in the Senate that Great Brittain was Justified in taking her Seamen where ever they were found or that he even Justified or approved of the British taking Seamen out of our Ships. I have heard Mr. Pickering advance doctrine near the whole length of your Statement — and I imagine that led you into the mistake as they were from the same State but you know they never agreed cordially in political Sentiments. What confirms me in my opinion respecting Mr Adams I recollect that in conversation with him at different times he manifested a Strong disapprobation of the conduct of Great Brittain in that respect and expressed a regret that Some measure could not be devised by negotiation that would induce Great Brittain to relinquish that Claim that it would inevitably lead to a war between the two nations as the United States would never submit to it. And once observed to me that he believed the United States were destined as the only nation at some future period to curb the domineering insolence of the British Navy. I have long Since retired from the jaring Eliments of the political world & enjoy my retirement with pleasure and delight.

Accept Sir the assurance of my personal respect & Esteem

S R B

Hon Genl Smith
   Dft? (NcD).

From Samuel Smith

Dr. sir,   Washington 25 feby. 1823

I have received your letter and have mentioned its Contents to the very few Gentlemen, to whom I had ventured to state my recollection. I remember well that Colonel Pickering had made the observations to which I answered, and published my Speech. I remember many other things. I write now to set you right, for I Conjecture, that you suppose I meant to make a publick Charge against Mr. Adams. I meant precisely what I said and have performed what I wrote I meant to do.

It is bad Electioneering to make Charges. I never did. I have always gained my Elections (and I never lost One) by disproving Charges against myself — and those whose Cause I had espoused. I am Dr sir your

S. Smith

ALS (NcD).

From Samuel G. Goodrich

Dr. Sir   Hartford Dec 14. 1824

Mary will take the stage tomorrow morning for Brattleboro', under the care of Mr. S. Whittlesey. I have no prospect of being able to leave for 5 or 6 weeks & as the severe weather is approaching I think it most prudent not to wait. She will be left under the care of Mrs Green as you direct.

In hast yrs respy

S. G. Goodrich

ALS (NcD). Cover addressed, "Hon S. R. Bradley / Walpole / N. H." Stamped, "Hartford Ct. / Dec. 14." Notation, " Sir, / Mary Goodrich is now with us / this momt come half past one morig / Thursday 16th — Yrs & A. Green." Endorsed by SRB, "Samll G. Goodrich's / Letter of Decr 14 1824 / respecting Mary's coming / up."

From Samuel G. Goodrich

Dr. Sir Hartford Feb 26. 1825

I am sorry to trouble you so often, but I want exceedingly to know how Mary is, how she is getting along at school, how your own health is &c &c. It is a very great while since I have heard any thing from you. Please say to Mary that I have bought a little *globe* for her, which I shall send the first opportunity.

I left Washington ten days ago. You get all the news *& more too* in the papers. The election was a very sober business, & disappointed a great many who had flocked to Washington to see a sight. I believe the result must be consonant to your wishes, & I think is acquiesed in as the best choice, by the men of sense & respectability generally in the country, at least north of the Potomac. Please give my best love to Mary & good wishes to friends.

Yrs respy

S. G. Goodrich

Honl. S. R. Bradley

ALS (NcD).

To William Czar and Sarah Richards Bradley

June 8th 1825

Mr & Mrs Bradley request the Pleasure of William & Sally and the rest of the family to dinner to Morrow the 9th. Instant at 1 oClock afternoon.

Please to answer by to Morrow morning Mail.

ALS (NcD).

From Samuel G. Goodrich

Dear Sir, Hartford Augt 19. 1825

I recd. with pleasure your letter informing me that Mary was well & contented at Keene. I had heard that she was there, & was gratified that it was with your aprobation. We have had no rain here for 4 weeks, of any consequence. The earth is parched up & the garden almost wholly ruined. We get a plenty of watermelons, however, & the peaches begin to be good. You have probably heard that the report of the engineers is altogether favorable, & that the completion of the intended improvemts in the <ruin?>, is calculated on here as certain. The Boston banks have been running our banks for specie since April. The result has been that in 5 expeditions of this sort, they have drawn from our banks $189,000 & our banks have retaliated, & drawn in the same period, from them $665,000! It is very deathly here & on the whole, very dull times. The New Haven Canal is actually begun & progressing rapidly.

Please give my regards to all friends.

Yrs respy.

S. G. Goodrich

ALS (NcD). Reverse addressed by SRB, "Miss Mary R. Bradley / Keene / Miss Fisk's school."

From Samuel G. Goodrich

Dear Sir,   Hartford Nov 30. 1825

Mary arrived with her Uncle William last night. She has grown very much & is in fine health. I think she has improved & promises to fulfil all you anticipate with regard to her.

Permit me Sir to mention to you at this time a subject which may be interesting, in some degree, to you & your family. It is my expectation to be united in marriage to Miss Mary Boott of Boston in a few weeks. It would have been my wish, at an earlier moment to have addressed you on this subject, had circumstances permitted it. It would now be to me most gratifying to be assured of your approbation of the step I contemplate making. I could earnestly wish more — that this new connection may not in any degree seperate me from friends in whom my feelings must ever be deeply interested — & with whom I am still connected as well by the dear memory of one that is dead — as the bright resemblance of her, that is living.

It is my intention to go to housekeeping in the course of the winter. May I not expect that my house shall still be a home to any of my northern friends when they come to Hartford. My wish as to Mary, for the present, would be that she should spend a part of the winter with me — as to the future, I shall hope for your opinions & advice respecting her.

    Yrs affy

                                                                           S. G Goodrich

ALS (NcD).

To Jonathan Dorr Bradley

J Dorr Bradley Esqr

Dear Sir   Walpole March 11th 1826

I enclose you herewith the morgage and notes against Joseph Goodridge you will see I have cost the notes and Interest there [*illegible*] <to> April the 19th. 1826 supposing to be about the time of your Courts Sitting and find they will amount on that day to $331:51. You may agree with him if you please about the time he Shall be allowed by the Court for returning the premises I Should wish to obtain Judgment this Court if convenient but if not it must take its <fate?> by continuing it will bring more Cost on Goodridge which I am afraid he is little able to pay. Davis has settled that the writ against him need not be returned he engaged Solemnly to pay Constable Willard his fees for serving the writ which if he does not I will pay you for the same.

    Accept the assurance of my love and Esteem

                                                                       Stephen R Bradley

ALS (MCR-S). Text obscured by several ink blots and tears.

To Mr. Tuttle

Dear Sir   Walpole Augt 11: 1827

I have received your favour of the 3d Instant and very much regret the death of Genll Hull no doubt he would have saved you harmless had he lived. I always found him a man of strict honour & integretity as the event has happned I am willing to give you two or three years to pay the debt and as it is uncertain what day I shall be in Cheshire or how long I shall stay their I expect to go by the way of Boston & Providence and return by New Haven. To prevent any failure I would propose that you execute a note to me signed by your self and some friend payable in 2 or 3 years as will be most Convenient for you and date it Sept 20 1827 Interest to be paid annually at the Hartford Bank or at Hitchcock's store in Cheshire and leave it with William Hitchcock in Cheshire and when I come to Cheshire I will exchange with Hitchcock and leave with him the note of $900 dollars you indorsed to be delivered to you the note on the 20th of Sept will be   principle $900

                                                                 Interest   <u>39:38</u>

Note dated Decr 4 1826   939:38

    Accept the Assurance of my respect & Esteem

                                                                                       S R Bradley

    Copy of the letter Sent to Mr Tuttle
Dft (NcD).

Last Will and Testament of Stephen Rowe Bradley

[15 September 1828]

    I, Stephen R. Bradley of Walpole in New Hampshire being of health & of a sound mind and memory & knowing that I must shortly bid adieu to all earthly possessions do make, ordain & constitute this to be my last will and testament in manner & form following — that is to say — in the first place I commit my body to the dust to be decently interred by my executors hereinafter named and my spirit to my Heavenly Father in an humble hope as he has been pleased to give me a further existence in an immortal state of life and glory —

    In respect to my worldly interest I will & direct the following disposition to be made thereof and that the same be divided & disposed of as follows (viz) I give & bequeath to my wife Melinda the use & improvements rents & profits of the house & farm on which I now live in Walpole including all the lands & buildings more particularly described in a deed[1] from David Stone to me bearing date the 23d day of January A.D. 1817 and also about one hundred rods of land I purchased of Abel Bellows lying between my house & the Meeting house & also all my household furniture of every name & nature including both my clocks to have, use, occupy & possess the same during the term of her natural life subject to the reversion hereinafter provided — *Item* I give to my wife Melinda one Horse & Chaise & Chaise harness, two cows, one yoke of oxen, all my implements of husbandry, all my pork, beef & grain that I may die possessed of — Also all my hogsheads, barrels, tierces & kegs & whatsoever is contained therein together with all my hogs to be to her sole use, benefit and behoof forever — *Item* I give & bequeath to my wife Melinda one thousand dollars to be paid her as soon as convenient after my decease by my executors hereinafter named, the foregoing bequest with what is hereinafter provided for my Melinda in lieu of all dower. *Item* I give & bequeath to my wife Melinda during the period she shall remain my widow & unmarried & no longer full right power & authority & interest to enter on that tract or parcel of land lying in said Walpole adjoining the land reserved for the use of the meeting house & which I purchased of Josiah Bellows, by a quit claim deed & there from time to time & at all times during said period to cut, fell, take & carry away so much wood & timber only as shall be wanting & necessary for fuel to consume in the fires in the house & repairs of the place which is herein before bequeathed to her during her natural life — *Item* I give & bequeath to my son William C. Bradley all that tract or parcel of land lying & being in Westminster being all the land I own or possess on lots number one & number two in the first division of 100 acre lots in said town which is now leased to my son-in-law Josiah Bellows, 3rd. Also my gold headed cane and all my library & manuscripts (excepting my Bibles & other books & pamphlets which I reserve for the use of the family) to have & to hold the same to him, his heirs & assigns forever. *Item* I give & bequeath to my daughter Stella C. Bellows that certain tract or parcel of land lying in said Walpole commonly called & known as the Dana & Bellows farm & is bounded southerly on the highway, easterly & northerly in part on Deacon Stearns and westerly on Thomas Bellows Esq. and also my gold watch to have & to hold the same to her & her heirs & assigns forever—*Item* I give & bequeath to my daughter Mary R. Tudor my Wier farm so called lying in the southwest corner of Walpole containing about three hundred acres & bounded west on the Connecticut River, South on Westmoreland line, East in part on John H. Wier's land & north in part on Lyman's land to have & to hold the same to her & her heirs & assigns forever. *Item* I give & bequeath to my two children William C. Bradley & Stella C. Bellows the reversion of the house & farm on which I now live together with about one hundred rods of land I purchased of Abel Bellows & which is herein before bequeathed to my said wife Melinda during her natural life, they, the said William & Stella to have & to hold the same after my said wife's decease as tenants in common to them, their heirs & assigns forever share & share alike. *Item* I give & bequeath to my two daughters Stella C. Bellows & Mary R. Tudor & to my granddaughter Mary E. Goodrich all my household furniture of what name or nature soever herein before bequeathed to my wife Melinda during her natural life to have & to hold the same after my said wife's decease to them, their heirs & assigns in three equal parts, share & share alike. *Item* I give & bequeath to my grandson Stephen R. Bellows otherwise called Stephen R. Bradley Bellows all that tract or parcel of land lying in said Walpole adjoining the land reserved for the use of a meeting house & which I purchased of Josiah Bellows by a quit claim deed recorded in the records of deeds for the county of Cheshire to have & to hold the same to him, his heirs and assigns forever, subject to the right and authority herein before given to my wife Melinda to take wood and timber as therein provided. *Item* I give & bequeath to my granddaughter Mary E. Goodrich twenty-seven shares in the Hartford Bank to have & to hold the same to her & her heirs with all the profits accruing therefrom subject to the following conditions that the dividends on the said twenty-seven shares shall remain a fund for the support & education of the said Mary Elizabeth until she arrives at the age of eighteen years under the immediate care and trust of my executors herein after named who are hereby empowered to receive & employ the same to the uses & purposes aforesaid and in case my said granddaughter Mary E. shall live & attain the age of eighteen years or shall have issue born of her body before that time then & in that case the twenty-seven shares to be vested in her & to be to her sole use, benefit & disposal forever but in case my said granddaughter should die before she attains the age of eighteen years & before issue born of her body then the said twenty-seven shares to vest in and be equally divided between my three children, William C. Bradley, Stella C. Bellows & Mary R. Tudor to them, their heirs & assigns forever. *Item* I give & bequeath to my granddaughter Mary E. Goodrich four lots of land in Bradley vale in Vermont marked and numbered on the plan as lots number eight, twelve, twenty & twenty-four to have & to hold the same to her & her heirs & assigns forever. *Item* I give & bequeath to my daughter Mary R. Tudor a certain lot of land lying in the town of Hartford containing about five acres & bounds north & west on highways, south on land of Leonard Bacon & east on land of John Babcock & which lot I purchased of Leonard Bacon to have & to hold the same to her & her heirs & assigns forever subject to the following conditions that if the said Mary R. Tudor should die without issue born of her body then & in that case the said lot of land together with the Wier farm so called herein before bequeathed to the said Mary R. Tudor shall revert to and be vested in & be equally divided between my two children William C. Bradley & Stella C. Bellows to them, their heirs and assigns forever. *And* all my just debts & funeral expenses being first paid &

discharged I give & bequeath to my wife Melinda & to my three children, to wit, to my son William C. Bradley & to my two daughters Stella C. Bellows & Mary R. Tudor all my goods & chattels & personal estate, debts, dues & demands of what name or nature soever not herein otherwise disposed of to be divided in four equal parts share & share alike & I do moreover declare & ordain that all mortgages & ground leases shall be deemed and taken to be personal estate altho the conditions should not be fulfilled & the land should revert & be vested in my heirs & shall be equally divided in four equal parts as herein provided for personal estate. *Item* I give & bequeath to my three children William C. Bradley, Stella C. Bellows & Mary R. Tudor all my real estate lands and tenements, wheresoever situate lying or being & not herein before disposed of to have & to hold the same to them, their heirs & assigns forever as tenants in common, share & share alike.—*And* I do further ordain that none of my children shall be charged or held responsible for anything heretofore advanced to them this provision however not to extend to promissory notes for which they are to stand charged & responsible.—*And* I do more over by these presents ordain constitute & appoint my wife Melinda & my son William C. Bradley & my son-in-law Josiah Bellows, 3rd, executrix & executors of this my last will & testament & do authorise them or any two of them to deed & convey by quit claim all such tracts or farms or lands as I may have given bonds or covenants to deed as soon as the conditions shall have been fulfilled & to discharge all mortgages when the conditions shall have been fulfilled & all monies & rents accruing from such contracts or covenants to be considered as goods & chattels in the hands of the executors respectively other than those rents & profits herein before bequeathed—*And* in case one or more of my executors herein named should decline, resign, die or remove to distant parts or by any other contingent event become incapacitated to act whereby two or even one of three named executors shall remain in that case the remaining or surviving executrix, executors, or executor shall have all the power & authority to execute this testament & transact all matters & things relative thereto herein before given to the three or any two of them. *And*, whereas, the land in Westminster herein before bequeathed to William C. Bradley is under a lease to Josiah Bellows the 3rd I will and ordain that the said William C. Bradley shall have the rents and profits of the Dana & Bellows farm in Walpole herein before devised to Stella C. Bellows unless they can otherwise agree during the continuance of the said Bellows' lease after which they respectively to enjoy & possess the herein before bequeathed premises free of all incumbrances—*And* my pew in the old meeting house & my two slips in the new meeting house on the hill I give & bequeath to my wife Melinda & to my daughter Stella C. Bellows & to their heirs & assigns forever, share & share alike.

And I do further give & bequeath the following shares in the Hartford Bank one share to each person respectively, to wit, to my sister the widow Mary Wales one share and to my daughter-in-law Sarah Bradley one share & to Stella C. Bellows one share to Mary R. Tudor one share & to my seven grandchildren Emily Bradley, Jonathan Dorr Bradley, Merab Ann Bradley, Stella Louise Bellows, Sarah Adeline Bellows, Rebecca Gratia Bellows & Stephen R. Bellows one share each to have & to hold the same to them, their heirs & assigns forever.

Signed, Sealed published & declared by the said
Stephen R. Bradley to be his last will and testament
revoking all former wills by him heretofore made in   STEPHEN R. BRADLEY
presence of us the Subscribing witnesses who   LS
subscribed our names in the presence of the Testator
& of each other this fifteenth day of September in the
year of our Lord one thousand eight hundred and
twenty-eight.

SAMUEL GRANT
ABEL BELLOWS
GEORGE B. REDINGTON

I Stephen R. Bradley of Walpole in the State of New Hampshire of sound and composed mind & memory do make and ordain this to be a codicil or supplement to my last will & testament in manner & form following, that is to say, I give & bequeath to my Grandson Henry Bradley Tudor son of Henry S. Tudor and Mary R. Tudor all that tract or parcel of land lying & being in the town of Walpole in the county of Cheshire and State of New Hampshire & bounding east on the highway southerly on land of William Buffum, westerly on Connecticut River, northerly on land of N. Holland and the widow Livingstone and supposed to contain about forty acres, being the same land I purchased of David Stone, as by his deed reference thereto being had to have & to hold the same to him, his heirs & assigns forever subject to the following conditions — that if my said Grandson should die without issue before he arrives at the age of twenty-one years then & in that case the premises with the appurtenances thereof shall be & remain vested in my three children William C. Bradley, Stella C. Bellows & Mary R. Tudor to them, their heirs & assigns forever share & share alike. And whereas the said David Stone holds a bond giving him a right to redeem said land by paying One Thousand Dollars in one or two years from the date thereof, now if the said David Stone shall redeem said land by paying the One Thousand Dollars in one or two years from the date of said bond it is my will and I do hereby ordain that the One Thousand Dollars so paid for the redemption of said bond shall by my executors named in my last will, be vested in stock as securities held in trust for the use & benefit of my said grandson Henry Bradley Tudor until he arrives at the age of twenty-one years & then to be at his or his heirs sole disposal — but if before that period my said grandson Henry Bradley Tudor should die without issue then & in that case the said money stock or securities to be equally divided between my three children William C. Bradley, Stella C. Bellows & Mary R. Tudor, their heirs & assigns share & share alike to have & enjoy the same forever. And I do moreover constitute & appoint executors named in my last will as executrix & executors of this codicil or supplement to my last will & testament giving them & each of them the same authority & power as to the execution of this codicil or supplement as is given them in my last will & testament.

Signed Sealed published & declared by the said Stephen R. Bradley to be a Codicil or supplement to his last will and testament in presence of us the Subscribers, witnesses who subscribed our names hereunto in presence of the testator and of each other this twenty-ninth day of January in the year of the Lord one thousand eight hundred & thirty.

STEPHEN R. BRADLEY
LS

CATHARINE WIER
MARTHA FROST
DANIEL A. JENNISON

Printed (Willard-Bradley Memoirs, by Henry K. Willard, 1924).
1. "In the abstract of title (Vol. 74, page 154 of the Cheshire Country Registry of Deeds), David Stone conveyed the original place containing 30 acres with the buildings thereon to Stephen R. Bradley by Warranty deed dated January 23, 1817, for the consideration of $6000. General Bradley willed this property by reversion to his two children, William Czar and Stella Czarina.
Henry Kellogg Willard, the great-great-grandson of Stephen Rowe Bradley, purchased the original house, barn, and about four acres of land of Miss Fanny P. Mason, August 26, 1913, for $10,000, to be kept in the family *in perpetuo*."

To Abel Perrin

Mr Abel Perrin

Sir   Walpole March 25th 1829

After you was at my house on my applying to Mr Howland to undertake the job for less than I offered you he informed me he had just before undertaken a job to build the factory at Jeppony that was burnt down last fall and that with the Mason house would take him all the Season so that he could not engage to have the house finish til next Season the other joiners here are all engage in job I have therefore concluded to come to your terms and do and will engage to give you two Hundred and Eighty dollars one Hundred in Cash and one Hundred and Eighty to be endorsed on your Lease. I have left it with Dorr to draw the writings to ascertain what you are to do in the job so as to have no dispute.

I am respectfully

Stephen R Bradley

ALS (MCR-S).

From Samuel G. Goodrich

Dear Sir,   Boston May 13: 1829

Mary, who goes under the care of Mr. Buffum, will bring you this, with a set of Clappertons 2d. Journey, and a very amusing work on Spain, written by Capt. Perry, a brother of the Comodore. It will give me pleasure, if you find them worth the perusal.

You will find Mary to have made Considerable advances in grammar, french, & history, with some improvement in readings, writing &c. Perhaps you may not think her progress has been great, but it is sufficient to show that she will easily obtain all the school knowledge with facility. The more experience I get, the more I incline to your opinion that the *forcing system* is not the best, & I think the age is making a great movement toward a change in the treatment of children very much in accordance with your views, which, I confess I once thought not quite orthodox.

I hope to be able to visit Walpole in the course of the summer, but I am not certain that I can do so.

I suppose it will not be best for Mary to go to school while she is in Walpole, & therefore she does not take her books. I had thought it best for her to return to her school here in about a month. Perhaps Stella Bellows will come back with her, as I believe her parents have some idea of sending her here.

Please give my respects to Mrs Bradly.

Ver Respectfully,

S. G. Goodrich

P. S. I have sent some pamphlets & papers which please to give to Bro. Wm. & Josiah when you have done with them.

ALS (NcD).

From Richard H. Bayard

Wilmington Delaware
Sep. 26th. 1830.

Dear Sir.

On the 23d of Aug. I addressed to you a letter in relation to the depositions of my Father the late James A Bayard and of General Smith made in the case of Gillespie & Smith in which you were one of the commissioners to take testimony.

It was addressed to you at Westminster, Vermont and may therefore never have reached you, as I have since learned that your residence is in Walpole New Hampshire.

It was written in consequence of the transmission of copies of the above depositions, by you through the medium of your son, to my Brother Mr James A. Bayard. The object of the letter was to ascertain whether you were in possession of the original depositions or if not, whether you could tell what became of them, and Secondly whether the Copies sent by you were made by yourself from the originals, or had been by you compared with them.

It appears from the copies in question that the deposition of my Father was made before you and George Logan on the 3d april 1806 and certified accordingly. That of General Smith was made on the 15th april 1806 before George Logan and David Stone and certified by them. Upon referring to the Journals of the Senate I find that on Wednesday the 9th april you asked and obtained leave of absence after the following monday (the 14th.) for the remainder of the Session.

You probably therefore left town on that day which accounts for you not having been present on the commission when General Smith made his deposition, which was on the following day the 15th.

It is also highly probable that the proceedings under the commission never afterwards came into your hands but were transmitted by one or the other of your colleagues to the attornies in the cause.

It becomes therefore a matter of importance, in order to prevent all ground for cavilling to know by whom the copies were made, or whether they have the Sanction of your authority as authentick. I have no doubt of the fact myself that they are authentick copies, since that of my Father's deposition corresponds with the rough copy preserved among his papers. Something more however than the private opinion would be required for publication and it is for that reason that I am anxious to have their authenticity established by your authority.

I have the honor to be very respectfully your obdt servt.

Richard H Bayard

The Honle. Stephen R Bradley

ALS (NcD).

To Richard H. Bayard

Dear Sir   Walpole October 1st. 1830

A short time since my Son handed me a letter from Mr James A Bayard requesting to know if I was in possession of the depositions of your Hond Father and General Smith taken in the case of Gillespie vs Smith in which I was a Commissioner. On Examination of my old Congressional papers I found the papers which I directed my Son to transmit to Mr Bayard in the same state I found them filed not having seen them for twenty years that I recollect as they must have been filed and laid away about the period in which they were taken which renders it extreemly difficult to certify[1] recollect with precision transactions of so long standing but according to the best of my recollection the Originals were delivered to Coln Burr and may probably be obtained by writing to him in N Y if they are not lost I did not copy the depositions myself I believe that was done by a person or persons in Coln Burrs service I have some faint recollection of Comparing with Coln Burr the original with the Copies and can now say I verily believe and have no Doubt that the Copies transmitted to James A Bayard are true genuine and authentic Copies of the original depositions and I am rather inclined to think Genll Smith signed as a duplicate the copy transmitted but that may be ascertained by Comparison of his hand. I am persuaded I did not leave the city till the business was Completed. The envelop Covering the Copies Sent James A Bayard with the interogotories and Commission appear to be original from the imperfection of memory and the infirmities of old age and the long time that has elapsed the subject not having been in my mind for about twenty years prevents my giving you a more perticular account as I was in the Senate with Mr Bassett your Grand Father and Mr Carroll now Living when your Mother was a Miss at the boarding School. Accept Sir the Assurance of my respect and Esteem

S R B

Dft (NcD). Notation by SRB, "Copy of / letter to / R H Bayard / 1 oct 1830."
1. The preceding word was interlined by SRB.

Inventory of the Estate of Stephen Rowe Bradley

[15 March 1831]

State of New-Hampshire

CHESHIRE, SS.

The Judge of the Probate of Wills, &c. for said County.

To   Nathaniel Holland, Ephraim Holland, and Stephen Stearns all of Walpole in said County

GREETING

YOU are hereby authorized to take an Inventory of the Estate of Stephen R. Bradley late of said Walpole deceased,

to be shewn unto you by

Melinda Bradley, William C. Bradley and Josiah Bellows 3d.

Who are Executors of the will of said deceased, and to make a just and impartial Appraisement thereof, upon oath, according to the best of your judgement, and when you have completed your Inventory, you are to return the same, together with this warrant, to the said Executors to be by them personally returned into the Registry of the Court of Probate for said County, at or before the fifteenth day of June next.

Given under my hand and the seal of the Court of Probate. Dated at Keene said county this 15th day of March Anno Domini 18 31

Samuel Dinsmoor Judge of Probate.

Schedule A

Inventory of Household furniture and of Houses & lands belonging to the estate of Stephen R Bradley late of Walpole deceased the use whereof is devised and bequeathed to his widow during her natural life.

the Carlton house & land	200	00
the farm south of the road	1500	00
the Mansion house & out buildings	2300	00

Furniture in the sitting room		
1 side board	10	00
1 sofa	6	00
5 chairs	2	50
1 rocking do		75
1 pembroke table	2	75
1 looking glass	7	00
1 carpet	9	00
1 rug	3	00
1 set andirons, fender shovel & tongs	12	00
1 hearth brush		16
1 clock	10	00
1 pair plated candlesticks	3	00
1 do. glass lamps		50
1 do. plated snuffers & tray	3	00
in closet in same room		
37 large blue plates	3	00
33 small do.	1	50
12 soup plates		62
10 bowls	1	50
7 pitchers	2	00
18 large silver spoons	37	00
<1>2 tea spoons	6	00
2 dessert spoons	3	50
2 pr. sugar tongs	6	00
1 silver ladle	8	00
1 cream spoon	1	25
1 pr salt spoons		75
1 pr mustard do.		33
1 silver quart tankard	20	00
1 silver sugar bowl, creamer & tumbler	16	00
1 fish knife	1	33
2 fruit baskets	19	00
Amount carried up	$4197	44
Amount brought up	4197	44
1 set castors	5	00
7 china cups & 13 saucers	1	00
2 small mugs		30
4 sugar bowls	1	25
19 plain glass tumblers	2	50
12 plain wines & 4 egg glasses	2	00
2 glass plates		75
1 goblet		30
4 small decanters, 1 glass mustard		50
2 pair salts		33
1 liquor case & bottles	2	00
phials & medicines	1	00
5 cut glass decanters	2	50

5 plain do.	1	50
2 quart tumblers		50
1 doz large knives & forks & carver	2	00
1 doz small do		50
3 large waiters	1	50
4 small waiters		50
Bed Rooms adjoining		
2 bedsteads & 2 beds	30	00
1 pair card tables	3	33
1 light stand		25
1 wash stand		25
3 chairs	1	50
1 small looking glass	1	00
1 old desk	5	00
2 carpets	7	00
Front Entry		
1 carpet	10	00
1 stair carpet	6	00
1 side board	10	00
1 pair dining tables & 2 ends	10	50
1 breakfast table	1	75
3 chairs	1	50
1 spy glass	2	00
Amount carried over	$4313	45
Amount brought over	$4313	45
West Room		
1 carpet & 1 rug	40	00
1 sofa	10	00
1 pair card tables	10	00
1 doz chairs	15	00
1 pair knife cases & 1 tea chest	2	50
2 prs. shovels & tongs, 1 do. andirons & 1 fender	12	00
1 looking glass	12	00
1 easy chair	35	00
1 pair glass lamps	2	50
Dining Room		
1 cooking stove	12	00
2 old tables	1	50
1 clock	25	00
6 chairs	1	00
1 small looking glass		50
China Closet		
3 glass stands	3	00
27 plain jelly glasses	2	75
12 china soup plates	1	00
17 china plates	1	25
1 china tea set 42 pieces	6	00

13 china platters	4	50
5 china tureens	6	00
3 deep dishes & 1 celery dish	2	00
10 cut wine glasses	1	25
6 cut punch glasses		50
3 salts		33
11 champagne glasses	1	75
1 brittania coffee pot	1	50
3 china dishes		75
3 deep dishes delf	1	00
East Chamber		
1 bed & bedstead	18	00
1 bureau	7	00
1 wash stand & 2 bowls	3	00
1 looking glass & 1 small do	4	00
1 carpet & rug	10	00
6 chairs	3	00
1 card table	2	00
	4573	03
Amount brought up	4573	03
1 light stand		50
4 half window curtains	1	50
Upper Entry		
2 chairs	1	00
Back East Chamber		
1 bed & bedstead	6	00
7 chairs	2	33
1 carpet	3	00
1 looking glass		75
1 table	1	25
West Chamber		
1 bed & bedstead with curtains	25	00
1 pair card tables	10	00
1 carpet & rug	13	00
1 looking glass	5	00
1 wash stand bowl & pitcher	2	75
7 chairs, 1 easy do & 1 small rocker	7	50
1 bureau & dressing glass	14	00
1 light stand		75
1 glass lamp		25
4 window curtains	8	00
3 pictures	2	00
1 snuffers & tray	1	50
brushes & bellows		75
West back chamber		
2 bedsteads & beds 1 set curtains & 3 window do.	28	00
1 card table	2	75

1 light stand		50
5 chairs	1	87 ½
1 case drawers	4	00
1 carpet	3	00
1 looking glass	1	00
5 pictures	1	25
1 stove	1	50
1 wash stand bowl & pitcher	1	00
tongs, shovel & snuffers		50

Bed coverings

7 bed quilts	8	00
3 copper plate spreads	5	25
1 white counterpane	<u>4 00</u>	
	4742	48 ½
Amount brought up	4742	48 ½
19 blankets	19	00
3 comfortables	4	50

Bed & other linen

15 pairs linen sheets @ 150	22	50
17 pairs pillow cases @ 38 ⅓ Cts	5	67
6 fine linen sheets @ 3.00	18	00
8 fine " pillow cases @ 66 ⅔ cts	5	33
14 diaper table cloths	11	00
23 fine towels	10	00
27 coarse towels	4	50
4 old table cloths	1	50
3 green cloth table covers	9	00
1 plaid table cover	1	00

Kitchen & Cellar furniture

1 stove	5	00
4 chairs & 1 chest		50
4 iron candlesticks, 3 brass do. 1 bread tray}		
2 tea pots & 9 custard cups	7	00
1 tea kettle	2	00
1 bell metal mortar	1	50
1 copper dipper		16 ½
pewter platters	2	50
tin ware pails, coffee pots &c	12	00
Iron ware viz, 1 boiler, 3 pots, 2 iron kettles}		
2 basins, 1 spider, 2 bake kettles, 1 tea kettle		
2 grid irons, shovel & tongs, toast iron		
waffle iron & dogs	17	00
2 tables, 3 chairs & wash stand	3	00
3 brass kettles	4	00
2 tubs & 1 coal hod	3	50
6 doz junk bottles	2	25
1 coffee roaster	2	50
churn, meal chest & wooden ware	3	00

4 demi johns	3	00
6 gallon bottles	2	00
1 stone jug & 2 galls & 1 small bottle		37
3 jars & 2 bottles	1	00
1 tunnell		50
1 steel yard	<u>1</u>	<u>00</u>
Amount carried up	$4928	26 ½
Amount brought up	4928	26 ½

Miscellaneous furniture

4 crickets	1	00
1 bed & bedstead	1	00
bedstead wheel & 2 chairs	1	50
1 desk		50
1 trunk	5	00
13 quires writing paper	2	16
1 old secretary	2	50
1 pair fire buckets	3	00
1 bathing tub	2	50
1 short rifle	4	00
4 bottles wine	3	
1 Britta. flaggon	2	50
6 " Tumblers	1	
1 Bed pan	2	50
2 Hatchetts	2	
1 Warming pan		<u>50</u>
Dolrs	4962	92

Recd. the articles contained in this schedule A
Melinda Bradley

Schedule B

Inventory of Cooper's ware & the contents thereof, Implements of husbandry, Grain, Chaise and harness and animals belonging to the estate of Stephen R Bradley late of Walpole deceased and which were by him bequeathed to his widow in perpetuity.

Hooped ware & Contents

[*illegible*]	2	50
[*illegible*]	3	
[*illegible*]	[*illegible*]	
[*illegible*]	[*illegible*]	
[*illegible*]	10	<00>
[*illegible*]	10	00
[*illegible*]	50	00
[*illegible*]	9	00
[*illegible*] 50 Galls.	20	00
[*illegible*]	9	00
10 old casks	1	00
½ tierce of salt	3	50
1 doz casks	1	50

27 dry casks	5	00
8 old casks	1	00
Implements of husbandry		
1 sled		25
1 hand cart	1	25
50 lbs of chains @ 8 Cts pr. lb	4	–
2 axes	2	00
1 Iron bar	1	50
1 grindstone	1	00
5 yokes & 4 rings	3	00
1 beetle & 2 wedges	1	00
2 hoes	1	00
2 ploughs	6	00
2 harrows	5	50
4 old wheels	3	00
~~1 saddle~~	~~2~~	~~00~~
3 whiffle trees	1	50
1 winnowing mill	3	00
1 hand sled		25
1 cradle		75
1 brush scythe		75
2 scythes & swaiths	1	00
	173	75
Amount Brot. up	$173	75
1 rake		25
5 pitchforks	1	00
half bushel & peck measures		65
[*illegible*]	3	00
1 ran		40
4 scythe swaiths		67
2 shovels		50
1 straw cutter	1	50
1 horse sled	2	00
3 cider mill screws	3	00
1 cart	6	00
2 cart wheels	14	00
Grain & vegetables		
85 bushs. corn @ 62 ½ cts	53	12 ½
75 do. Oats @ 30 cts	22	50
38 do. rye @ 66 ⅔ cts	25	33 1/<3>
100 do. potatoes	15	00
4 tons hay @ 8$	32	00
Animals		
1 horse		70 00
1 yoke oxen	65	00
2 cows & 1 calf	40	00
2 hogs	24	00

Other Articles

1 chaise & harness	80	00
half a pew in old meeting house	35	
half of 2 slips in the new one	40	
Dolrs	708	67

Recd. the articles contained in this schedule B.

Melinda Bradley

Schedule C.

Inventory of the library and of the furniture attached thereto belonging to the Estate of Stephen R Bradley late of Walpole deceased & by him specifically bequeathed to William C Bradley.

Christian Register	1	00
King James' works	1	00
Chambers' Cyclopedia 2 v	3	00
Harris' voyages 2 v	3	00
Motherby's Dictionary	2	00
Journals & Documents of Congress 32 v. fol	8	00
Laws of Barbadoes	1	00
Laws of New York	1	50
Williams' Hist of Northern Goverments		75
Hoare's travels	2	00
Montague's <gag?> for papists		25
Charlevoix's Paraguay	1	00
Stannton's Embassy	1	00
Forrest's voyages	1	00
Life of Sr. Wm Jones		75
Mackenzie's Voyages	1	00
Berriman on 1 Timo[.]		50
Gallup on Epidemics	1	50
Pennant's tour in Wales		50
Ferguson's Astronomy		25
Duncan's Cicero	1	50
Wollaston's Religion of Nature		25
Marquis of Halifax's works		25
Chauncey on the Benevolence of the Deity		25
Wynnes Gospels		50
Toland's Amyntor		50
Chas. Lee's Memoirs		50
Warburton's divine legation		50
Volney's ruins	1	00
Memoirs of Ripperda		25
Athenagoras' apology		25
Blackwell's letters—Mythology		50
Shaw's latin grammar		25
Military discipline		25
Schre<uder's> lexicon	1	50
Gillies Greece 3 vs.	2	00

Amount carried up	$41	25
Amount brot. up	$41	25
Hume's England 6 vs	5	00
Mosheim's Eccl. History 6 vs.	3	00
Gibbon's Rome 6 vs.	6	00
Gough's Hist of the Quaker 3 vs	2	00
Hickeringall's works 2vs		50
Sime's Mil. Guide 2 vs.		50
Blair's lectures 2 vs	1	00
Ward's Oratory 2 vs.	1	00
Littlebury's Herodotus 2 vs	1	00
Burgh's pol. disquisitions 2 vs	1	00
Millot's Elements of Mod Hist. 3 v	1	50
Wynne's Hist of America 2 vs	1	50
Winchester's lectures 3 v	1	50
Tooke's Catherine 2 vs	2	00
Sydney on Govt. 3 vs	3	00
Atkinson's navigation		25
Ward's mathematics		20
Magazine of 1745		12 ½
Glass' works		20
Love's surveying		20
Sinclair's address		12 ½
Clarke on the Attributes		50
Allen's theology		25
Fessenden's science of sanctity		50
Turner on the skin		17
Pamphlets in 1 vol		20
Zimmerman on Pride		12 ½
Paine's political tracts		20
Cheyne on health		20
Graham's letters		25
D'orleans' history		20
Bastwick's <coating?>		20
Lewis' dispensatory		25
Grey's Hebrew Grammar		20
Writings of Apostles Gr & Eng		<u>20</u>
Amount carried over	$76	29
Amount brought over	76	29
Instructions for Infantry		25
Scott's Napolean 3 vs.	1	50
Milton's Treatise 2 vs	1	00
Columbus' 1st. voyage		50
Denham & Clapperton 2 vs	2	00
Thiebault's Frederic 2 vs.	1	00
Dela Lolme on Eng. const.		50
Capt. Keppel's travels		50
Lord Keppel's trial		50

Journals, laws & docts of Cong: 74 vs. octavo	35	00
Journals of confederation Congs. 13 do.	9	75
Statutes of Vermont		25
Do of New Hampshire		25
Gilbert on Evidence		10
Slade's state papers		50
Bacon's abridgement 5 vs.	2	50
1st. vol Tyler's reports		50
Kirby's reports		20
Trials per pais 2 vo.		25
Burn's Justice 4 vo.		50
English Stamp laws		10
Rammohun Roy's writings	1	00
Unitarian Miscellany 6 vs	1	50
Madden's travels 2 vs		50
Priestly's Hist of Corruptions 2 vs.	1	00
Original draught of primitive church		20
Bolingbroke's works political 4 vs.	1	50
Smith's wealth of nations 3 vs.	1	00
Plutarch's morals 5 vs.	1	50
Knox's essays 2 vs.		50
Hobbes' tracts 4 vs.		50
Memoirs of Grub street 2 vs.		25
Military tract		10
Jefferson's manual		12 ½
Fletcher of Saltoun's works		10
Addison's freeholder		10
Francis' Horace 4 vs		50
Bossuet's universal history 2 vs.		25
Moores travels		25
Algerine Captive		10
Amount carried up	$144.	91 ½
Amount brought up	144	<91 ½>
Maxims of Father Paul		[illegible]
Bulwark of truth		[illegible]
Locke on civil government		12[illegible]
the Barrister		10[illegible]
Young's prose works		1[illegible]
Gentleman Instructed 2 vs		2[illegible]
Gordon's Cato's letters		10
Chipman's principles of govrmt.		10
Treatise on husbandry		10
Constitutions		12 ½
Phipps' military discipline		10
Greek grammar		6
Hull's defence		10
Madison's rights of neutrals		10
Wolstonecraft's do. of woman		10

Browne's religio medici		25
O'Meara's Napoleon 2 vs.		25
Varlo's husbandry 2 vs.		20
British liberties 2 setts		50
Cranch's customs		20
Montesquieu's reflections		10
Home on bleaching		10
Greek testament		10
Tooke's pantheon		10
Hudibras		10
Swift's works 18 vols	4	50
Blackstone's commentaries 4 vs	1	50
Law of arrests		10
Hawkins' abridgement		10
Law Magazine		10
Lots of pamphlets	1	00
1 writing table		50
1 small desk of manuscripts		25
1 case drawer of papers	2	00
1 paper presser		12 ½
1 pair paper shears		20
1 gold headed cane	3	00
	161	85

Recd. the articles contained in this schedule (C) Wm C Bradley

Schedule E

Inventory of Lands, moveable chattels, notes mortgages & securities belonging to the Estate of Stephen R Bradley late of Walpole deceased and which are not specifically devised or bequeathed by his last Will to any one individual.

Moveable chattels

1 Blue cloth cloak	2	00
1 old blue do		50
1 blue surtout	5	00
1 blk coat	7	00
1 do do	6	00
1 old blk do	1	50
1 pr. pantaloons	3	00
1 pr do.	2	00
1 pr do	3	00
1 pr old do.	1	00
1 vest	2	00
1 do		50
1 Doeskin vest of drawers	3	00
1 pr. boots, 1 do shoes, 1 do slippers, 1 do Indn. rubs.	3	00
1 flannel nightgown	2	00
1 hat cap & pr mittens	1	50
5 thin vests & 2 pr. thin pantaloons	4	50
6 shirts	9	00

3 pr stockings	1	00
4 handkerchiefs	1	50
1 large bore rifle	2	00
1 fowling piece	4	00
1 surveyor's compass & 2 chain	3	00
1 fishing rod		25
1 wolf skin robe	6	00
3 racoon skins do.	15	00
1 cross cut saw	3	50
4 planes	1	00
1 saw		25
4 chisels & 1 spike drawer		50
2 shaves	1	00
1 carriage with its harness	225	00
1 lot of old harnesses	10	00
2 saddles	4	00
1 wolf trap		50
lead pipe	6	00
Amount carried up	$341	00
Amount brought up	$341	00
1 lot of old iron	3	00
4 augurs	1	00
1 double sleigh	5	00
1 old sleigh	1	00
2 waggon	6	00
1 waggon harness	6	00
1 red cow	17	00
1 Bull	10	00
2 three yr old steers	34	00
2 two yr old steers	20	00
1 two yr old heifer	12	00
2 three yr old steers	32	00
1 white face cow	14	00
2 four yr old steers	38	00
1 cow	16	00
2 staggs	48	00
2 calves	10	00
1 heifer	13	00
1 pr. steers	35	00
1 steer	15	00
1 cow	17	00
1 cow	17	00
Oxen at Starkweather's 1 pr	65	00
Amount carried over	776	00
Amount brot over	776	00

Lands

a small piece of land back of the Carleton house about ¾ acre   100

Notes, Mortgages & securities

Geo: Carlisle's note of 1000. & annual interest thereon to 9. Dec. 1830 $260.35	1260	35
Seprelet Wilbur's note & mortgage 12 Dec. 1829 $600 intr to 9 Dec 1830 $35.70	635	70
M Gorham, A Hall & E Ranney jrs 3 notes of 23 Mar 1830 for $450. int to 9 Decr. 1830 $19.28	469	28
W C Bradley's note of 14 May 1827 for $200 int to 9 Dec 1830 $42.84	242	84
A. Wilson E Hodgkins & J Briggs' note of 2. Mar 1829 $225 intr to 9 Dec. 1830 $10.38	235	38
R Leppenerell & D Bemis' note balance of prin & intr. due 9 Decr. 1830	118	90
D Martin, D Johnson & I Smith's note of 13 Mar 1830 $125.00 int to 9 Decr " $5.57	130.57	
R Watkins' note of 29 Oct 1830 $150.00 int to 9 Dec. 1830 $1	151	00
J. Clark's note of 21 June 1830 $105 int to 9 Dec. " $2.93	107	93
J Flanders' two notes of 14 Sep 1829 of $25 each $50 int to 9 Dec " $3.71	53	71
L Starkweather's & Chas Watkins' rent from 1 Apl. to 9 Dec 1830 at rate of $100 pr ann	56	00
Jos Russell & Ezra Hall's rent bal. on 9 Dec. 1830	143	62
Levi Lyman's rent from 1 Mar to 9 Dec 1830 at rate of $90 pr. ann	69	80
Josiah Bellows 3d rent from 1 Jan to 9 Dec 1830 at $50 pr ann	47	23
Roland Carleton's rent 9 Dec 1830	17	33
Lemuel Starkweather's debt for use of cattle	10	00
Zoheth Holton's note of 28 Oct 1830 $18.37 int 12 Cts	18	49
John H Wier's note 18 June 1830 for $9.00 in force ind & int to 9 Dec	9	25
John H Wier's rent from 1 Apr. to 9 Decr 1830 at $9. pr ann	<u>6</u>	<u>20</u>
Dols	4659	64

We the undersigned to whom the above articles contained in this schedule E are devised or bequeathed do hereby acknowledge that we have recieved our respective shares thereof and that the Executors are no longer holden to us for the same.

Melinda Bradley
Wm C Bradley
H S Tudor
Mary R Tudor

State of New Hampshire

To the honorable the Judge of Probate of Wills in and for the County of Cheshire

We The undersigned having been appointed in and by your honor's [*illegible*] hereunto annexed a committee to take an Inventory of the estate of Stephen R Bradley late of Walpole deceased to be shewn them by the Executors of said deceased and to make a just and impartial appraisement thereof having taken upon them that service and having been duly sworn according to law have inventoried and appraised the same at the respective prices entered against each article in the several schedules hereunto annexed amounting as follows viz

The items in schedule A to the sum of	$4962.92
The items in schedule B to the sum of	708.67
The items in schedule C to the sum of	161.85

The items in schedule D to the sum of   16500
The items in schedule E to the sum of   4659.<64>
and amounting in the whole to the sum of   Dolls   26993.08

 All which is by us certified and returned
  Nathl. Holland}
  Ephm. Holland   Committee
  Stephen Stearns

            Trustees
  Wm C Bradley}
  J. Bellows 3d

To Stella Louisa Bellows one share in the Hartford Bank   100   00
To Sarah Adeline Bellows one share in the Hartford Bank   100   00
To Rebecca Gratia Bellows one share in the Hartford Bank   100   00

 Recd. the forgoing three shares for my children above named
    J Bellows 3d

  to Stephen R B Bellows

The hill farm, so called, near the upper meetinghouse in Walpole subject to
the widow's right to take wood therefrom 42 acres   840   00
one share in the Hartford Bank   100   00

 Recd possession of the above for S R B Bellows
    J Bellows 3d

  to Henry B. Tudor

The stone farm, so called, in Walpole, subject to the right of redemption
thereof by David Stone 411 acres $1000   —

 Recd the foregoing legacy for my son H B Tudor
    H S Tudor

DS. The first page of the document is a printed form. Additions to the form are indicated here by underlining. NOTE: Schedule D is missing. Careless photocopying has obscured text on Schedules B and C.

Appendix I.
List of Documents
(Chronological)

Space and content limitations of this volume dictated the exclusion of certain items that were neither Bradley's own correspondence nor the more important letters of others. Items excluded are indicated by an asterisk and can be found at the depository listed.

NcD	College Expenses [1771–1775]	Printed	Resolution of the State of Vermont, 8 December 1779
Printed	Astronomical Diary; or, Almanack for ... 1775 *[1775]	Printed	Resolution of the State of Vermont, 9 December 1779
NcD	Account with Ebenezer Watson, *4 December 1774	Printed	Resolution of the State of Vermont, 10 December 1779
Printed	From Charles Lee, 24 January 1776	Printed	Vermont's Appeal to the Candid and Impartial World [10 December 1779]
MHi	From Charles Lee, 19 February 1776	DNA	To the President of the Continental Congress, 1 February 1780
Printed	Resolution of Congress, 26 June 1776		
DLC	Receipt from Amos Northrop, 6 January 1777	DNA	To the President of the Continental Congress, 5 February 1780
DLC	Orders to Col. Benjamin Carpenter, *9 September 1777	Printed	Ira Allen to Cesar Rodney, *8 February 1780
VtU	From R. Sill, 27 July 1778	NcD	Account with the State of Vermont *[February 1780]
Vt	To the Governor and General Assembly of Vermont, 15 May 1779	VtU	From Russel Atwater, *3 April 1780
Vt	To the General Assembly of Vermont, 20 May 1779	VtU	From Elihu Gridley, *4 April 1780
Vt	To the General Assembly of Vermont, 20 May 1779	CtY	From Chauncey Goodrich, 11 April 1780
Printed	Record of the Vermont Superior Court, *26 May 1779	VtU	From John Fisk, *26 May 1780
		Printed	To a Committee in Cumberland County, Vermont, 23 June 1780
Printed	Governor and Council Record, SRB admitted to bar [27 May 1779]	Printed	Gov. Thomas Chittenden to the President of Congress, 25 July 1780
Printed	Governor and Council Record *[3 June 1779]	Printed	From Thomas Jefferson, 14 August 1780
DLC	Account with Ethan Allen *[4 June 1779]	DNA	Commission, 16 August 1780
		Printed	Resolution of the State of Vermont, 18 August 1780
DNA	Resolution of the State of Vermont, 7 June 1779	Vt	Receipt from Thomas Chittenden, *1 September 1780
Vt	From Ethan Allen, 8 June 1779		
Vt	To the General Assembly of Vermont, 10 June 1779	DNA	To the President of the Continental Congress, 12 September 1780
Vt	Certification of Purchase, 10 September 1779	DNA	To the President of the Continental Congress, 15 September 1780
VtU	From Ezra Stiles, *16 September 1779	DNA	To the Continental Congress, 22 September 1780
Printed	Resolutions of the State of Vermont, 20 October 1779	DNA	To the President of the Continental Congress, 2 October 1780
DNA	Resolutions of the State of Vermont, 20–21 October 1779	Printed	Resolution of the State of Vermont [14 October 1780]
Printed	Resolution of the State of Vermont, 20–22 October 1779	Printed	From George Washington, 12 November 1780
Vt	Petition, 22 October 1779		

397

VtU	From Reuben Atwater, *12 December 1780		NFtW	Deed of Sale, 23 September 1784
VtU	From Titus Hutchinson, *28 February 1781		Printed	Biographical Notes—Thomas Tolman *[October 1784]
Printed	Resignation of Gen. Ethan Allen [April 1781]		VtU	Indenture of David Stone, *6 October 1784
Printed	Resolution of the State of Vermont [5 April 1781]		Printed	Resolution of the State of Vermont [14 October 1784]
Printed	Resolutions of the State of Vermont, 6 April 1781		Printed	Resolution of the State of Vermont [16 October 1784]
NcD	From Thomas Wooster, *15 July 1781		DLC	Account with Ethan Allen [1784]
VtU	From Reuben Atwater, *August 1781		VtU	From Reuben Atwater, 7 February 1785
VtU	To the Superior Court, 4 August 1781		VtU	From Reuben Atwater, *15 February 1785
NcD	From Thomas Chittenden [27 August 1781]		VtU	From Elnathan Beach, 10 March 1785
			VtU	From Reuben Atwater, 10 March 1785
Printed	Statement of Action of the Legislature of Vermont, *16 October 1781		DLC	Epitaph for Merab Bradley [ca. 7 April 1785]
Not found	From Thomas Chittenden *[22 May 1782]		VtU	From Levi Shephard, *30 April 1785
			Printed	To the Governor and Council of Vermont, 3 May 1785
Printed	Resolution of the State of Vermont [15 June 1782]		VtU	From Russel Atwater, 14 May 1785
NcD	From Samuel Fletcher, 13 September 1782			From Samuel Dana, *14 May 1785
DLC	From Oliver Lewis, *28 October 1782		VtU	From Elijah Grant, *25 May 1785
VtU	From Reuben Atwater, 9 December 1782		VtU	From Samuel Hitchcock, *30 May 1785
NcD	Thomas Chandler's Power of Attorney *[16 December 1782]		Printed	Resolution of the State of Vermont, 7 June 1785
Printed	From Thomas Chittenden, 24 December 1782		Printed	Governor and Council Record *[13 June 1785]
Printed	To the Inhabitants of Guilford, Vermont [10 January 1783]		VtU	From Elijah Grant, *4 July 1785
			NFtW	Account [ca. 9 August 1785]
VtU	From Daniel Lyman, *5 February 1783		NFtW	Deed of Sale, 25 August 1785
NcD	From Jonas Fay [26 February 1783]		Printed	From Ethan Allen, 7 September 1785 (Vt)
DLC	From Russel Atwater, 21 April 1783		VtU	From Reuben Atwater, 24 September 1785
VtU	Bond of Thomas Adams, *17 May 1783			
Vt	Jonas Fay's Continental Account, 31 July 1783		VtU	From Thomas Pearsall, *12 October 1785
			Printed	Governor and Council Record *[19 October 1785]
VtU	From Russel Atwater, *23 September 1783		Printed	Governor and Council Record *[19 October 1785]
VtU	From Reuben Atwater, 4 October 1783		VtU	From Russel Atwater, *20 October 1785
Printed	Resolution of the State of Vermont *[15 October 1783]		VtU	From C. Harrington, 22 December 1785
Printed	Resolution of the State of Vermont, 16 October 1783		DLC	From Reuben Atwater, *26 December 1785
Printed	Election of Delegates and Agents to Congress, 17 October 1783		DLC	From Reuben Atwater, *9 January 1786
			VtU	From Reuben Atwater, *1 June 1786
Printed	Resolution of the State of Vermont [22 October 1783]		Printed	From Ethan Allen, 2 June 1786 (Vt)
			VtU	From Reuben Atwater, *5 June 1786
Printed	Vermont Governor and Council Record, 22 October 1783		VtU	From William Biglow, *5 June 1786
			VtU	From Noah Smith, *5 June 1786
Vt	Account, 24 October 1783		VtU	From Unknown, *13 June 1786
NFtW	Account, 25 October 1783		Printed	From Ethan Allen, 21 June 1786 (NHi)
VtU	From Russel Atwater, 24 November 1783		NFtW	From Ethan Allen, 25 July 1786
NcD	Account with the Town of Westminster [1783]		VtHi	Ethan Allen to Ira Allen, 18 August 1786
			NFtW	To Ephraim Ranney, *12 September 1786
DLC	Nathan Fisk to the Sheriff of Windham County, 12 January 1784		Vt	Ira Allen's Account with the State of Vermont [10 October 1786]
Printed	To the Printers of the Vermont Journal, 24 January 1784		NFtW	From Ethan Allen, 11 October 1786
			VtU	From Barzillai Hudson, *1 January 1787
VtU	Petition of Cyrel Carpenter, 21 February 1784		NFtW	From Ethan Allen, 19 January 1787
			NcD	From Thomas Chittenden, 2 March 1787
Vt	Account, 2 March 1784		VtU	From Joshua L. Woodbridge, *23 April 1787
Vt	Account, 2 March 1784			
Vt	Resolution of the State of Vermont, 2 March 1784		VtU	From Reuben Atwater, 14 May 1787
			VtU	From Reuben Atwater, *21 July 1787
DLC	From Elihu Lyman, *8 March 1784		NFtW	Account, 3 August 1787
Vt	State of Vermont Pay Order [1 April 1784]		Vt	From Ethan Allen, 6 November 1787
VtU	From Reuben Atwater, *5 April 1784		NFtW	From Ethan Allen, *6 November 1787
NFtW	Account [ca. June 1784]		NFtW	From Ethan Allen, 9 November 1787
NcD	From David Willard, *24 July 1784		DLC	From Thomas Pearsall, *28 November 1787

List of Documents

VtU	From Thomas Seymour, *13 December 1787		Thousand Dollars to the State of New York, and Declaring what Shall be the Boundary Line Between the State of Vermont and State of New York; and Declaring Certain Grants Therein Mentioned, Extinguished, 28 October 1790
DLC	From William Wickham, *24 January 1788		
DLC	From Lewis R. Morris, *31 January 1788		
VtU	From Reuben Atwater, 16 April 1788		
VtU	From Elnathan Beach, 16 April 1788		
DLC	From Gen. Jonathan Warner, 17 June 1788	VtU	From Benjamin Greene, 3 December 1790
VtU	Contract with Thomas Pearsall, 26 July 1788	DLC	From Roswell <Clesson?>, 12 December 1790
DLC	From Thomas Pearsall, *27 July 1788	Printed	Convention for Adopting the Constitution of the United States, 6–10 January 1791
DLC	From E. Tudor, *8 September 1788		
VtU	From Justin Ely, 29 September 1788	Printed	Adoption of the Constitution of the United States, *10 January 1791 (see 19 January 1791, paragraph 2)
Vt	Report on the Petition of Jonathan Hunt, 20 October 1788		
Vt	Report on the Petition of Ozias Clark, 22 October 1788	Vt	Report on the Petition of Samuel Williams and William Barr, *12 January 1791
NFtW	From Ethan Allen, 12 November 1788		
VtU	Record of Judgments by SRB as Judge of the Superior Court [13 November 1788–25 July 1789]	Vt	To Samuel Mattocks, *14 January 1791
		Printed	Vermont Governor and Council Record [19 January 1791]
VtU	From Thomas Pearsall, 10 April 1789	Vt	Resolution of the State of Vermont, 20 January 1791
DLC	From William Page, 1 May 1789		
VtU	From Thomas Pearsall, 29 June 1789	Vt	To the General Assembly of Vermont, 24 January 1791
VtU	From Thomas Pearsall, *1 July 1789		
DLC	From Samuel Kilbourn, A*15 July 1789	Printed	Governor and Council Record [24 January 1791]
DLC	From Mrs. Ennis Graham [ca. 22 July 1789]	DLC	From Lemuel Chipman, *25 January 1791
VtU	From Thomas Pearsall, *4 September 1789	Printed	Jeremiah Wadsworth to Thomas Jefferson, 22 February 1791
VtU	From Thomas Pearsall, *9 October 1789	Printed	William Eaton appointed captain [5 March 1791]
DLC	Account [ante 24 October 1789]		
Printed	Resolution of the State of Vermont [27 October 1789]	DLC	From Ephraim Kirby, *15 May 1791
		VtU	From Eleazer Miller, *22 July 1791
Vt	Account, *October 1789	NcD	From Samuel Bayard, 25 July 1791
NcD	From James Bowdoin, *5 November 1789	Printed	Governor and Council Record [20 October 1791]
Vt	From Lewis R. Morris, 10 November 1789		
DLC	From Charles Marsh, 23 November 1789	DLC	From Thomas Pearsall & Son, John I. Glover, and Pearsall & Pell, *1 November 1791
DLC	Receipt from Brent Willard, 11 December 1789		
NcD	From Simeon Baldwin, 26 December 1789	VtU	From John Morgan, 7 November 1791
VtHi	List of Lands Owned by SRB [ca. 1790]	VtU	From the Eighth Brigade Artillery Company, 23 November 1791
NcD	From Isaac Tichenor, *15 January 1790		
Printed	Vermont Commissioners to New York Commissioners, 9 February 1790	VtU	First Light Infantry Company to Elihu Mather, *5 May 1792
Vt	Moses Robinson to Samuel Mattocks, 23 April 1790	VtU	First Light Infantry Company to Lewis R. Morris, *5 May 1792
NcD	Receipt, Experience Fisk to Lot Hall, *9 June 1790	VtU	From Stephen <Hull?>, 10 May 1792
		DLC	From Hezekiah Ivers, *24 May 1792
VtU	From Thomas Pearsall, 31 July 1790	DLC	From Ephraim Kirby, *1 June 1792
DLC	From Elihu Lyman, *13 August 1790	NcD	To Samuel Minott, 17 July 1792
VtU	From John Coburn, *26 August 1790	NcD	From Timothy Edwards, *9 August 1792
Vt	To the Legislature of Vermont, 21 October 1790	DLC	To Thomas Pearsall, 14 August 1792
		Vt	To the General Assembly of Vermont, 17 August 1792
Printed	Vermont Governor and Council Record, 22 October 1790	DLC	From Hezekiah Ivers, *20 August 1792
Printed	Resolution of the State of Vermont [22–25 October 1790]	DLC	To Edward R. Campbell, 25 August 1792
		DLC	From Lewis R. Morris, 1 September 1792
Vt	To the General Assembly of Vermont, *25 October 1790	VtU	From Thomas Pearsall, *4 September 1792
		AXV	To Stephen Hayward, 18 October 1792
Printed	Vermont Governor and Council Record *[26 October 1790]	VtU	To Jonas Holden, 18 October 1792
		Vt	Account [ca. 19 October 1792]
Printed	An Act to Authorize the People of this State [Vermont] to Meet in Convention to Deliberate Upon and Agree to the Constitution of the United States, 27 October 1790	NcD	To William Czar Bradley, *30 December 1792
		VtU	From Jonas Holden, *3 January 1793
		DLC	To Andrew Hull, 30 January 1793
Printed	An Act Directing the Payment of Thirty	Printed	Joseph Fay to Thomas Jefferson, 13 February 1793

VtU	From Thomas Pearsall, *26 February 1793
VtU	From Thomas Pearsall, *27 April 1793
NcD	From Robert Troop, 26 May 1793
VtU	From Jonathan Morgan, *10 August 1793
VtU	Bond to Dan Foster, 3 October 1793
Vt	Petition of John Nott, *12 October 1793
Vt	Addendum to the Petition of John Nott, *17 October 1793
DLC	Receipt, 6 November 1793
Printed	To William Czar Bradley [5 December 1793]
Printed	An Act Making an Alteration in the Flag of the United States, 13 January 1794
VtU	From Thomas Forrest, 20 June 1794
Vt	To Thomas Chittenden, 10 October 1794
Printed	Vermont Governor and Council Record *[10 October 1794]
DLC	Ephraim Welles to Amos Carpenter, 11 November 1794
VtU	Ephraim Welles to Amos Carpenter, *16 November 1794
VtU	From Thomas Pearsall, *1 December 1794
VtU	From Thomas Pearsall, *8 December 1794
VtU	From Thomas Pearsall, *25 December 1794
VtU	From Augustus Van Horne, 26 December 1794
Printed	Warrant, 13 January 1795
Private Owner	To Hezekiah May, 31 January 1795
NcD	Receipt from Martha Olcod, *1 February 1795
VtU	From Thomas Pearsall, *7 March 1795
VtU	From Hezekiah Ivers, *25 April 1795
VtU	John Beckley to Unknown, *26 April 1795
VtU	From Richard Wood, *29 May 1795
VtU	From James Arden, *30 July 1795
VtU	From John Kelly, *30 July 1795
NcD	Receipt, *17 September 1795
DLC	From Francis Arden, *25 January 1796
VtU	From Daniel Dunbar, *4 February 1796
VtU	From Reuben Atwater, *8 March 1796
NcD	From Royall Tyler, *23 March 1796
VtU	From John W. Blake, *26 March 1796
VtU	From <WAH?>, *29 March 1796
VtU	From John W. Blake, *31 March 1796
DLC	From Jacob Briant, *16 May 1796
DLC	From Reuben Atwater, *23 May 1796
VtU	From Stephen Williams, 25 May 1796
VtU	From Ebenezer Clark, *25 June 1796
VtU	From Mark Richards, *5 July 1796
VtU	From Ebenezer Clark, *13 August 1796
VtU	From Jonathan Nye, *18 August 1796
VtU	Receipt from Charles Chandler, *6 September 1796
NcD	From Martha Olcott, 6 September 1796
Vt	Petition of Abner Miles to the General Assembly of Vermont, 27 September 1796 (Summary)
DLC	From Ebenezer Clark, *31 October 1796
DLC	From Asa Porter, *3 November 1796
VtU	From John Crain, *13 November 1796
VtU	From Asa Porter, *3 December 1796
VtU	From Eleazer May, *12 December 1796
VtU	To Asa Porter, 13 December 1796
VtU	From Elnathan Beach, *2 January 1797
VtU	From Thomas Pearsall, *4 January 1797
VtU	From Thomas Pearsall, *31 January 1797
VtU	From James Arden, *14 February 1797
DLC	To James Madison, 18 February 1797
VtU	From Thomas Pearsall & Son and John I. Glover, *20 February 1797
VtU	From Thomas Pearsall & Son, *28 February 1797
VtU	From James Arden, *6 March 1797
DLC	From Elijah Paine, *23 March 1797
NcD	Joseph Bullen to Micah Read, *4 April 1797
VtU	From James Sullivan, *11 April 1797
VtU	From James Arden, *14 April 1797
NcD	From William Coleman, *24 June 1797
NcD	From William Coleman, *25 June 1797
NcD	From William Coleman, *6 July [1797]
NcD	From William Coleman, *12 July 1797
DLC	From James Monroe, 12 July 1797
DLC	Ann Richards to Mark Richards, *12 July 1797
VtU	To James Monroe, 22 July 1797
VtU	From Jonathan Robinson, 22 August 1797
VtU	From George Clarke, 10 September 1797
VtU	To George Clarke, 17 September 1797
NcD	From Peter Stuyvesant, *5 November 1797
Printed	Governor and Council Record *[7 November 1797]
DLC	Receipt to Caleb Johnson, *13–29 December 1797
VtU	From James Arden, *21 December 1797
VtU	Bond to Mathias Gorham, 30 January 1798
VtU	From James Arden, *14 February 1798
DLC	Senate cartoon, 15 February 1798
VtU	From Thomas Pearsall, *2 June 1798
NcD	From Peter Stuyvesant, 4 June 1798
DLC	From Caleb Clapp, *1 July 1798
Vt	To Samuel Mattocks, 7 July 1798
Vt	To Samuel Mattocks, 15 August 1798
NcD	To Mr. Richards, 18 August 1798
VtU	From Thomas Pearsall & Son, *18 August 1798
VtU	From Roswell Olcott, *22 September 1798
VtU	From Samuel Delaplaine, *26 October 1798
VtU	From Caleb Clapp, *8 January 1799
VtU	L. Hall to Mark Richards, *13 February 1799
VtU	From John W. Blake, *12 April 179[9?]
Vt	To Samuel Mattocks, 23 May 1799
VtU	From James Arden, *18 June 1799
NcD	Permit, 3 July 1799
DLC	Elijah Paine to [Richards & May?], *3 August 1799
VtU	From R. Hopkins, *28 August 1799
DLC	Elijah Paine to [Richards & May?], *7 September 1799
Vt	Petition of John Noth, 10 October 1799
DLC	Sylvester Sage to Mark Richards, *20 October 1799
VtU	Indenture with Samuel Lincoln and Samuel Lincoln Jr., 21 October 1799
VtU	From James Arden, *1 January 1800
NcD	Pierpont Edwards to an Unidentified Correspondent, *20 January 1800
VtU	From J. Eastman, 4 February 1800
NcD	From Mark Richards, 8 February 1800
VtU	From Elisha Tracy, 22 February 18[00?]
VtU	From Thomas Pearsall, *23 February 1800
VtU	From Charles Blake, 9 March 1800
NcD	From Peter Gerard Stuyvesant, 20 March 18[00]

VtU	From Thomas Pearsall, *21 March 1800		VtU	From Anthony Lamb, 15 December 1801
VtU	From Asher Benjamin, *26 March 1800		VtU	From Joseph Bullen, 18 December 1801
VtU	From James Arden, *15 May 1800		NcD	From Peter Gerard Stuyvesant, *18 December 1801
VtU	From Thomas Pearsall, *20 May 1800		VtU	From Samuel Davis Parmele, 21 December 1801
VtU	From Zenas Cowles, *2 June 1800			
VtU	From Jedidiah Stark, *19 June 1800		VtU	From Elias Bull, 31 December 1801
VtU	From David Goodall, *20 June 1800		VtU	From Sarah Blackden, 4 January 1802
VtU	Mark Richards to Archibald Hopkins, *28 June 1800		VtU	John H. Buell to Gen. Wilkinson, *12 January 1802
VtU	From James Arden, *8 July 1800		NcD	From R. Enos, *20 January 1802
VtU	From S. & Z. Cowles, *22 July 1800		Printed	Senate Proceedings: Judiciary System [3 February 1802]
VtU	From Thomas Pearsall, *25 July 1800			
NcD	Receipt to Joseph Olds, *6 August 1800		VtU	To Stella Bradley, 13 February 1802
VtU	From David Stone, *25 August 1800		Printed	Senate Proceedings: Choice of Electors [18 February 1802]
VtU	From Thomas Pearsall, *16 September 1[800]			
			NcD	From James Elliot, 9 March 1802
VtU	From Josiah Goodhue, *30 September 1800		VtU	From Samuel Parmele, 16 March 180[...]
			VtU	From James Elliot, 26 March 1802
Printed	Resolution of the State of Vermont, 10 October 1800		VtU	From Azarias Williams, *27 March 1802
Printed	Governor and Council Record, *10 October 1800		VtU	From Thomas Pearsall, *1 April 1802
			VtU	From Eliakim Spooner, [1] April 1802
Printed	Resolution of the State of Vermont, 24 October 1800		NcD	From Gideon Granger, *8 April 1802
			VtU	From James Elliot, *20 April 1802
VtU	From Cephas Smith Jr., 1 November 1800		VtU	From Thomas Pearsall, *31 May 1802
VtU	From Robert Bowne, *4 November 1800		VtU	From William and Jonathan Walker, *1 July 1802
DLC	From Rebecca Bayard, *10 November 1800			
			NcD	Receipt from Rigs and Center to John H. Buell, *2 July 1802
DLC	Account with Abel Carpenter, 12 November 1800			
			VtU	Gen. James Wilkinson to John H. Buell, *13 July 1802
VtU	From Oliver Gallup, *15 November 1800			
VtU	From Thomas Pearsall, *17 November 18[00?]		NcD	From Gideon Granger, *17 July 1802
			NcD	From Gideon Granger, 6 August 1802
NcD	From Peter Gerard Stuyvesant, 25 November 1800		VtU	From Thomas Pearsall, *12 August 1802
			DLC	From Samuel A. Otis, 23 August 1802
VtU	From Titus Hutchinson, *2 December 1800		ViU	From Thomas Jefferson, 27 August 1802
			VtU	From J. Sargeant, *31 August 1802
VtU	From Jonathan Dorr, 15 December 1800		NcD	From Samuel Hanson of Samuel, 10 September 1802
VtU	Contract for Thomas Pearsall, 24 December 1800			
			ViU	To Thomas Jefferson, 13 September 1802 (draft)
VtU	From Joseph Fay, 2 January 1801			
VtU	From John H. Buell, 5 January 1801		NjP	To Thomas Jefferson, 13 September 1802
VtU	Joseph Dorr to Mark Richards, *24 March 1801		NcD	From Nathaniel Ruggles, *21 September 1802
NcD	From Royall Tyler, *27 March 1801		VtU	From James Whitelaw, 27 September 1802
VtU	From John H. Buell, 16 May 1801		DLC	From Samuel A. Otis, 1 October 1802
NcD	From Peter Gerard Stuyvesant, *26 May 1801		VtU	James Madison to Mark Richards, *18 October 1802
Printed	Nathaniel Niles to James Madison, 9 June 1801		VtU	From John W. Blake, *22 November 1802
			Printed	Senate Proceedings *[6 December 1802–4 February 1814]. This is mostly a list of attendance
VtU	From B<...>, *31 July 1801			
NcD	From Jonathan Robinson, 7 August 1801			
VtU	From Thomas Sparhawk, 24 August 1801		Printed	Senate Proceedings: Election of a President Pro Tempore [13 December 1802]
DLC	From Elijah Paine, *24 September 1801			
Printed	Governor and Council Record, 13 October 1801		Printed	Senate Proceedings: Election of a President Pro Tempore [14 December 1802]
NcD	From Peter Gerard Stuyvesant, *20 October [1801]		VtU	From Joseph Dorr, 14 December 1802
			DNA	From James Madison, 22 December 1802
VtU	To Dr. Nathan Smith, 23 October 1801		NcD	From Nathaniel Ruggles, 1 January 1803
VtU	To Dr. John Wheelock, 23 October 1801		NcD	From Uriel C. Hatch, 4 January 1803
VtU	From <Alphonsus> Moore, 2 November 1801		VtU	From Ephraim Kirby, 5 January 1803
VtU	From Samuel Avery, 3 November 1801		VtU	From Amasa <Prire>, 13 January 1803
VtU	Bond from Edward Houghton, *10 November 1801		VtU	From Benjamin Sumner, 19 January 1803
			VtU	From Joseph Bullen, 24 January 1803
VHS	To Unidentified, 16 November 1801		Printed	Senate Proceedings: Division of the Indiana Territory [January 1803]
VtU	From Jabez Penniman, 7 December 1801			
VtU	From Gurdon Huntington, 10 December 1801		DLC	From Benjamin Rush, 8 February 1803
			VtU	From Joseph Moffe<tt>, 9 February 1803

VtU	Oliver Gallup to James Madison, *12 February 1803		to Support the Constitution, 28 January 1805
VtU	From David Robinson, 7 March 1803	DLC	Reuben Atwater: Writ, Josiah Deming & Co. vs. John Wyman, *31 January 1805
VtU	From Joseph Goodhue, 6 April 1803		Reuben Atwater: Writ, Josiah Deming & Co. vs. Silas Powers, *1 April 1805
VtU	From R. E. Newcomb, *11 April 1803		
VtU	From Samuel Williams, 12 April 1803	VtU	From Thomas Pearsall, *2 April 1805
VtU	From George Blake, *19 April 1803	NcD	Reuben Atwater: Writ, Mark Richards & Co. vs. William Clapp, *31 May 1805
NcD	From Henry Dearborn, 4 May 1803		
NjP	To Thomas Jefferson, 20 May 1803		E. Spooner, Charge of Assault and Battery vs. Aron Wales [post *1 August 1805]
VtU	From Joseph Dorr, 3 June 1803		
VtU	From Thomas Pearsall, *6 June 1803		
DLC	From Samuel A. Otis, 10 June 1803	NcD	From Isaac Tichenor, 28 [October] 1805
VtU	From James Arden, *21 June 1803	DLC	Asa Washburn: Writ, Mark Richards vs. Justus Lane, *5 November 1805
Printed	Presidential Proclamation, *16 July 1803		
DLC	Circular Letter from James Madison, 18 July 1803	NcD	From Henry Dearborn, 17 December 1805
VtU	From Abel Spencer, 18 July 1803	Printed	Senate Proceedings: Petition of Seth Harding, 27 January 1806
NcD	From Isaac Tichenor, 1 August 1803		
NcD	Invoice of Sundries bought for Sally Richards, *3 September 1803	NcD, CSmH	From William Eaton, 22 February 1806
		NcD	From William Eaton, 24 February 1806
NcD	From Nathaniel Ruggles, *30 September 1803	VtU	D. Buck to James Madison, *24 February 1806
NcD	From Nathaniel Ruggles, 8 October 1803	CsmH	From Capt. Dent, 26 February 1806
Vt	To the General Assembly of Vermont, 18 October 1803	Printed	Senate Proceedings: Claim of Charlotte Hazen, 4 March 1806
VtU	From Joseph Bullen, 20 October 1803	VtU	From Jonathan Badger, 4 March 1806
NcD	Act Incorporating Bradley-vale Township, 31 October 1803	NcD	From William Eaton, 23 March 1806
		NcD	To Samuel Barron, 5 April 1806
NcD	From Isaac Tichenor, 7 November 1803	NcD	To William Eaton, 5 April 1806
DLC	Reuben Attwater, Oath of Office as Commissioner of Bankruptcy, *9 November 1803	NcD	From William Eaton, 7 April 1806
		VtU	From Daniel Boardman, *28 May 1806
DLC	Mark Richards, Oath of Office as Commissioner of Bankruptcy, *9 November 1803	VtU	From Joseph Goodhue, *17 July 1806
		VtU	From David Fay, *24 September 1806
		Printed	List of Vermont Executive Officers and Councillors [ca. October 1806]
VtU	From James Arden, *14 December 1803		
VtU	From Alain Spooner, 9 January 1804	CtY	To Stephen Jacobs, 7 October 1806
NcD	From Isaac Tichenor, 11 January 1804	NcD	From William Eaton, 17 November 1806
Printed	Senate Proceedings: Military Appropriations, 17 January 1804	VtU	From Joseph Dorr, 2 December 1806
		VtU	To William Lyman, 5 December 1806
VtU	From Oliver Gallup, *30 January 1804	Printed	Senate Proceedings: Petition of Seth Harding *[24–31 December 1806]
NcD	To William Czar Bradley, 19 February 1804		
		VtU	Mark Richards, Sheriffs Sales, *23 January 1807
Printed	Senate Proceedings, 22 February 1804		
VtU	Senate Proceedings, 24 February 1804	Printed	Senate Proceedings: Regulating Grants of Land in the Territory of Michigan, 4 February 1807
VtU	From Charles Blake, 9 March 1804		
VtU	From A. Labogh, *14 March 1804		
VtU	From Daniel Lammot, 5 April 1804	Printed	Senate Proceedings: Regulating Grants of Land in the Territory of Michigan, 9 February 1807
VtU	From Jos. Moffett, 20 April 1804		
DLC	Deed [20 April 1804]		
VtU	From Daniel Lammot, 2 June 1804	Printed	Senate Proceedings: Regulating the Summoning of Grand Jurors, 9 February 1807
VtU	From Thomas Pearsall, *8 June 1804		
NcD	From James Elliot, 18 June 1804		
VtU	From James Arden, *10 July 1804	NcD	From William Eaton, 13 February 1807
VtU	From J. Maréchaux, *10 July 1804	Printed	Senate Proceedings: Tennessee Lands, 17 February 1807
DLC	From A. & Jno. I. Labogh, 28 Sept. 1804		
Vt	Petition from John Nott, 5 October 1804	Printed	Senate Proceedings: Bill to Prohibit the Importation of Slaves, 24 February 1807
VtU	From Hadlock Marcy, *19 November 1804		
VtU	From Peter Alcott and Others, *8 December 1804		
		Printed	Senate Proceedings: Survey of the Coast of North Carolina, 24 February 1807
VtU	From James Arden, *13 December 1804		
VtU	To Nahum Mower, 28 December 1804	Printed	Senate Proceedings: Fortifying the Ports and Harbors, 2 March 1807
Printed	John A. Graham's Address to the Public, 2 January 1805		
		NcD	From Israel Smith, 26 May 1807
Printed	Senate Proceedings: Tennessee Lands, 8 January 1805	NcD	James Anderson to Robert Smith, *31 May 1807
VtU	To Henry Dearborn, 15 January 1805	VtU	From Seth Hastings, 8 June 1807
DNA	To James Madison, 25 January 1805	NcD	From Gideon Granger, 11 July 1807
Printed	James Smith to Those Who Have Sworn	VtU	From Simeon Knight, 24 August 1807

List of Documents

VtU	From Simeon Knight, *3 September 1807
DLC	From Elijah Paine, *24 September 1807
VtU	From T. Worthington, *5 October 1807
Vt	To the General Assembly of Vermont, 7 October 1807
VtU	From Joseph Goodhue, 10 October 1807
VtU	From Jonathan Cook, 21 October 1807
VtU	Mark Richards, Appointment as Sheriff, *2 November 1807
Printed	Senate Proceedings: Peace in the Ports and Harbors of the United States, 4 November 1807
VtU	From William C. Harrington, 11 November 1807
NcD	From William Eaton, 18 November 1807
VtU	From Charles Blake, 20 November 1807
VtU	From Joseph Dorr, 20 November 1807
VtU	From William Plumer, 18 November 1807
NcD	From Israel Smith, 29 November 1807
VtU	From Samuel Hinckley, *10 December 1807
VtU	From Jabez Penniman, 21 December 1807
NjP	To Thomas Jefferson, 26 December 1807
NcD	From William Eaton, 27 December 1807
VtU	From Jabez Penniman, *16 January 1808
VtU	From Lot Hall, 17 January 1808
NcD	To Republican Members of Congress, 19 January 1808
NcD	From Edwin Gray, 21 January 1808
NcD	Jonathan Williams to Members of the U.S. Military Philosophical Society, 23 January 1808
VtU	From Jabez Penniman, 26 January 1808
VtU	From William C. Harrington, 2 February 1808
VtU	From Royall Tyler, 10 February 1808
NcD	From William Eaton, 17 February 1808
VtU	From Elisha Tracy, 22 February 1808
NcD	From Henry Dearborn, 24 February 1808
NcD	From Daniel Buck, 27 February 1808
VtU	From Reuben Attwater, 3 March 1808
VtU	From Samuel Hinckley, *11 March 1808
VtU	From Jabez Penniman, 15 March 1808
NjP	To Thomas Jefferson, 16 March 1808
VtU	From Elisha Tracy, 16 March 1808
Printed	Senate Proceedings: Appointment of a Committee to Report on the Business of the Present Session, 17 March 1808
NcD	From Joseph Wilcox, *17 March 1808
VtU	From Satterlee Clark, 24 March 1808
DLC	From Thomas Munroe, 24 March 1808
NcD	From Nathan Smith, 24 March 1808
VtU	From Ethan A. Allen, 29 March 1808
VtU	From Reuben Attwater, *31 March 1808
VtU	From Thomas Leverett, *31 March 1808
VtU	From Theophilus Harris, 1 April 1808
VtU	From Jabez Penniman, 8 April 1808
VtU	From Jabez Penniman, 10 April 1808
VtU	From Elisha Tracy, 10 April 1808
VtU	From Elijah Backus, *14 April 1808
VtU	From L. Royse, 6 July 1808
VtU	From Sylvester Day, 8 July 1808
VtU	From Alden Spooner, 28 July 1808
VtU	From Stella C. Bradley, 29 July 1808
VtU	From L. Royce, August 1808
CSmH	From Hamet Caramelle, 23 August 1808
VtU	From Rufus Hatch, 12 October 1808
VtU	From T. Hutchinson, 5 November 1808
VtU	From James Dickinson, *8 November 1808
Printed	Senate Proceedings: Motion to refer the President's Message relating to the Barbary Powers to a Select Committee, 16 November 1808
VtU	From Simeon Knight, 10 November 1808
VtU	From James Strong, *24 November 1808
VtU	From Reuben Attwater, *2 December 1808
VtU	From Andrew Hull Jr., 2 December 1808
NcD	From William Eaton, 6 December 1808
NcD	From William H. Cabell, 10 December 1808
NcD	From Joseph Wilcox, *10 December 1808
VtU	From Reuben Attwater, 15 December 1808
VtU	From Elisha Tracy, 15 December 1808
VtU	From Ab. Bishop, 19 December 1808
NcD	From William Helms, 23 December 1808
VtU	From William Law, 27 December 1808
Printed	Senate Proceedings: SRB Elected President pro tempore of the Senate, 28 December 1808
VtU	Caleb Clapp to Mark Richards *[28 December 1808]
VtU	From John B. Colvin, *31 December 1808
NcD	From Thomas Tingey, 20 January 1809
NcD	From Nathaniel Ruggles, 25 January 1809
VtU	From Jonathan Dorr, 29 January 1809
VtU	From Abel Farwell, 30 January 1809
VtU	From Elisha Tracy, 5 February 1809
DLC	To James Madison, 7 February 1809
VtU	From John Matlock, 9 February 1809
VtU	From Timothy E. Danielson, *15 February 1809
VtU	From Elisha Tracy, 16 February 1809
VtU	D. Buck to James Madison, *24 February 1809
NcD	From Royall Tyler, 9 March 1809
VtU	From Anthony Lamb, *20 March 1809
VtU	From Thomas and John Shepherd, 17 June 1809
VtU	From Daniel Boardman, *24 June 1809
NcD	From Gaius Lyman, *15 July 1809
NcD	From Nathan Smith, 26 August 1809
VtU	From Daniel Boardman, *20 September 1809
VtU	From Stella C. Bradley, 22 September 1809
VtU	From Jonathan Dorr, 9 December 1809
VtU	From William C. Harrington, 12 December 1809
Printed	Senate Proceedings: Direct Tax, 15 December 1809
VtU	From Jonathan Dorr, 15 December 1809
NcD	From Tench Coxe, 17 December 1809
VtU	From Charles Phelps, 20 December 1809
Printed	Senate Proceedings: Barbary Powers, 26 December 1809
VtU	From Daniel Boardman, *30 December 18[09]
VtU	From Alexander McRae, 1 January 1810
VtU	From Dr. Samuel A. Peters, *8 January 1810
CSmH	From William Eaton, 15 January 1810
NcD	From John Willard, 19 January 1810
VtU	From Isaac Clason, 24 January 1810
VtU	From Turhand Kirtland, *30 January 1810
CSmH	To William Eaton, 2 February 1810
VtU	From Isaac Clason, *2 February 1810
VtU	From Joshua Chamberlain, *3 February 1810
VtU	From O. Farnsworth, *5 February 1810
VtU	From Robert Brent, 9 February 1810

VtU	From Jonathan Dorr, 11 February 1810
Printed	Senate Proceedings: Barbary Powers, 6 March 1810
DLC	To Jonathan Dorr, 6 March 1810
VtU	From Reuben Attwater, *8 March 1810
DLC	From Elisha Tracy, 22 March 1810
VtU	From Hull & Foot, 24 March 1810
VtU	From Nathaniel Richards, *28 March 1810
VtU	From T. Turner, *2 April 1810
VtU	From William Jess<enden?>, *23 April 1<810>
NcD	Deposition of Samuel Gale, *28 April 1810
VtU	From Reuben Attwater, 1 August 1810
VtU	Declaration of A. Green, *8 October 1810
Vt	To the General Assembly of Vermont, 9 October 1810
NcD	Certificate of Abatement, 30 October 1810
VtU	From J. B. Thomas, *18 November 1810
VtU	From Reuben Attwater, *28 November 1810
VtU	From John Griffin, *21 December 1810
VtU	From William Plumer, 21 December 1810
VtU	From Jonathan Dorr, 29 December 1810
NcD	From Samuel A. Foot, 4 January 1811
VtU	From Unidentified, 14 January 1811
VtU	From Jonathan Dorr, 18 January 1811
VtU	From Jacob Bayley, 22 January 1811
VtU	From Andrew Hull Jr., 24 January 1811
MB	To Royall Tyler, 27 January [1811]
NcD	From William Plumer, 31 January 1811
NcD	From Royall Tyler, 3 February 1811
VtU	From Nathaniel Ruggles, 10 February 1811
VtU	From Joshua Chamberlain, 12 February 1811
VtU	From Farnsworth & Churchill, 14 February 1811
VtU	To Albert Gallatin, 15 February 1811
VtU	From John T. Peters, 15 February 1811
VtU	From Titus Hutchinson, 28 February 181<1>
VtU	From James Dickinson, *1 March 1811
VtU	From George Bull, *18 March 1811
NcD	From Gideon Granger, 26 March 1811
DLC	From Andrew Hull Jr., 26 March 1811
VtU	From Samuel Buel, *15 April 1811
VtU	From Jabez Penniman, 24 April 1811
VtU	From Jonathan Dorr, 17 August 1811
NcD	From Dudley Chase, *2 September 1811
VtU	From Joseph Wheaton, 7 September 1811
VtU	From Christopher Ripley, 8 September 1811
VtU	From Abraham Bradley Jr., 13 September 1811
VtU	From John C. Brush, *24 September 1811
VtU	From Reuben Attwater, *2 November 1811
VtU	From James Dickinson, 4 November 1811
NcD	From Royall Tyler, 12 November 1811
VtU	From Andrew Hull Jr., 15 November 1811
VtU	From Elihu Luce, 24 November 1811
NcD	From James Elliot, 29 November 1811
VtU	From Jonathan Badger, 30 November 1811
NcD	From Samuel A. Foot, 6 December 1811
DLC	From Killian Killian Van Rensselaer, 18 December 1811
VtU	From Alpha Kingzley, *22 December 1811
VtU	From Samuel Williams, 26 December 18<11?>
VtU	From William Fay, *29 December 1811
VtU	From Elijah Knight, *29 December 1811
VtU	From Ebenezer Breed, 30 December 1811
VtU	From Jonathan Dorr, *4 January 1812
VtU	From Charlotte Hazen, *11 January 1812
VtU	From Henry Davis, 12 January 1812
VtU	From Jonathan Dorr, 12 January 1812
VtU	From Elisha Tracy, 12 January 1812
VtU	From Reuben Attwater, 14 January 1812
Printed	Senate Proceedings: Bill to Incorporate Moses Austin and Others into the Louisiana Lead Company, *17 January 1812
Printed	Senate Proceedings: Claim of Charlotte Hazen, 21 January 1812
NcD	From Asbury Dickens, 31 January 1812
VtU	From Christopher Ripley, 31 January 1812
VtU	From Mark Richards, *3 February 1812
VtU	From Christopher Ripley, 3 February 1812
VtU	From Reuben Attwater, 4 February 1812
Printed	Senate Proceedings: An Act for the More Convenient Taking of Affidavits and Bail, ... in the Courts of the United States," 7 February 1812
VtU	From Christopher Ripley, 20 February 1812
Printed	Senate Proceedings: "A Bill to Authorise the President ... to Ascertain and Designate Certain Boundaries," 4 March 1812
VtU	From Mark Richards, 15 March 1812
VtU	To Eliakim and Capt. Alfred Spooner, 16 March 1812
NcD	From Royall Tyler, 16 March 1812
Printed	Senate Proceedings: Bill to Incorporate Moses Austin and Others into the Louisiana Lead Company, *18 March 1812
VtU	From Zimri E. Allen, 21 March 1812
DLC	From Jeremiah Mason, 27 March 1812
NcD	From Amos Stoddard, 28 March 1812
Printed	Senate Proceedings: "An Act Concerning the Levy Court of the County of Washington, in the District of Columbia," *1 April 1812
Printed	Senate Proceedings: "Bill Making Provision for Certain Persons Claiming Lands Under the Several Acts for the Relief of the Refugees from the British Provinces," 4 April 1812
VtU	To Joel Barlow, 7 April 1812
NcD	From Martin Chittenden, 11 April 1812
NcD	From Richard Rush, 23 April 1812
NcD	From David Austin, 5 May 1812
VtU	From Joshua Chamberlain, 11 May 1812
VtU	From Christopher Ripley, 11 May 1812
NcD	From Philip Reed, 19 May 1812
NcD	From Philip Reed, 24 May 1812
NcD	From Charles Cutts, *28 May 1812
NcD	From Gideon Tomlinson, 3 June 1812
NcD	From Nathaniel Ruggles, 30 June 1812
DLC	From Samuel A. Otis, *[7?] July 1812
	Statement of the Fifth Company of Green Mountain Farmers, *6 August 1812
NcD	From Asbury Dickens, 15 August 1812
NcD	From Daniel C. Sanders, 22 September 1812
NcD	From Samuel Smith, 8 October 1812
VtU	From Simeon Knight, 14 November 1812
VtU	From Samuel Harrison, 28 November 1812

List of Documents

VtU	From Jonathan Morgan, 7 December 1812
VtU	From E. S. Swenmore, 14 December 1812
VtU	From Jonathan Dorr, 18 December 1812
NcD	From Daniel C. Sanders, 18 December 1812
Printed	Senate Proceedings: "An Act to Enable the ... Mississippi Territory to Form a Constitution and State Government...," 11 January 1813
NcD	From Roberts Vaux, 13 February 1813
Printed	Senate Proceedings: "A Bill to Encourage ... the Destruction of the Armed Vessels of the Enemy...," 15 February 1813
DLC	From Jonathan Bradley, *25 March 1813
VHS	Timothy Phelps to the Grand Jury of Windham County, *12 May 1813
DLC	From Charles Storer, *14 June 1813
NcD	To Joseph Willard, 5 July 1813
NcD	From Charles Storer, 25 September 1813
VtU	From Jonathan Dorr, 16 October 1813
NcD	From T. Turner, *7 January 1814
NcD	From Robert Wright, 2 February 1814
NcD	From Joseph Trumbull, *15 June 1814
VtU	Indenture with James Holden, 15 May 1815
VtU	Contract with James Holden, 26 May 1815
Vt	To the General Assembly of Vermont, 7 October 1815
VtU	To William A. Griswold, 14 December 1815
NcD	Receipt from Jabez Perry, *26 November 1816
NcD	From Samuel G. Goodrich, *15 May 1817
NcD	From Samuel G. Goodrich, *23 June 1817
VtU	Indenture with John H. Weir, 27 October 1817
VtU	To William Czar Bradley, 9 November 1817
MCR-S	From William Czar Bradley, 19 November 1817
VtU	To Abraham Bradley Jr, 19 December 1817
VtU	From Abraham Bradley Jr., 26 December 1817
VtU	From Candee & Goodrich, *22 January 1818
VtU	To Mark Richards, 20 February 1818
NcD	From Samuel G. Goodrich, *7 March 1818
VtU	Indenture with Abel Wellington, 9 April 1818
NcD	From Samuel G. Goodrich, *14 April 1818
NcD	From Samuel G. Goodrich, *21 May 1818
NcD	Receipt from Samuel G. Goodrich, *11 June [1818]
NcD	From Samuel G. Goodrich, *22 June 1818
NcD	From Samuel G. Goodrich, *17 July 1818
NcD	From Samuel G. Goodrich, *11 September 1818
NcD	From Samuel G. Goodrich, *7 October 1818
VtU	From Candee & Goodrich, *8 October 1818
NcD	From Samuel G. Goodrich, *24 October 1818
NcD	From Joseph Trumbull, *7 November 1818
NcD	From Joseph Trumbull, *16 November 1818
NcD	From Samuel G. Goodrich, *4 December 1818
VtU	To William Czar Bradley, 24 December 1818
NcD	To William Czar Bradley, 1 January 1819
NcD	From Samuel G. Goodrich, 27 February 1819
DLC	To John J. Astor, 8 March 1819
	Recommendation for Edwin May, *8 March 1819
NcD	From Joseph Trumbull, *21 April 1819
NcD	From Samuel G. Goodrich, 23 April 1819
VtU	Indenture with John H. Wier, 12 May 1819
NcD	From Samuel G. Goodrich, *18 May 1819
NcD	From Samuel G. Goodrich, *29 May 1819
NcD	From Samuel G. Goodrich, 30 September 1819
VtU	To William H. Crawford, 12 October 1819
NcD	From Samuel G. Goodrich, 8 November 1819
NcD	From Samuel G. Goodrich, *12 December 1819
	Deed from Asa Hurd, *11 February 1820
NcD	From Samuel G. Goodrich, *29 April 1820
NcD	From Samuel Dinsmoor, 26 August 1820
NcD	From Samuel G. Goodrich, *17 September 1820
NcD	From Samuel G. Goodrich, *17 January 1821
NcD	From Samuel G. Goodrich, *27 January 1821
NcD	From Horace Everett, *22 April 1821
NcD	From Samuel G. Goodrich, *24 April 1821
NcD	From Horace Everett, *28 September 1821
NcD	From Samuel G. Goodrich, *18 December 1821
NcD	From Samuel G. Goodrich, 17 February 1822
NcD	From Samuel G. Goodrich, 5 March 1822
NcD	From Samuel G. Goodrich, *7 April 1822
NcD	From Samuel G. Goodrich, *21 April 1822
NcD	From Horace Everett, *24 June 1822
NcD	From Samuel Whittelsey, 24 June 1822
NcD	From Samuel G. Goodrich, 21 August 1822
NcD	From Tapping Reeve, 16 November 1822
NcD	To Unidentified, *9 December 1822
NcD	From Horace Everett, *28 December 1822
NcD	From Horace Everett, *9 January 1823
NcD	From Joshua Bates, 16 January 1823
NcD	From Samuel Smith, 5 February 1823
NcD	To Samuel Smith, 14 February 1823
NcD	From Samuel Smith, 25 February 1823
NcD	From Samuel G. Goodrich, *4 August 1823
NcD	From Samuel G. Goodrich, *5 December 1824
NcD	From Samuel G. Goodrich, 14 December 1824
NcD	From Samuel G. Goodrich, 26 February 1825
NcD	From Samuel G. Goodrich, *7 May 1825
NcD	To William Czar and Sarah Richards Bradley, 8 June 1825
NcD	To the American Unitarian Association, *15 August 1825
NcD	From Samuel G. Goodrich, 19 August 1825
NcD	From Henry Ware Jr., *22 August 1825
NcD	From Samuel G. Goodrich, 30 November 1825
MCR-S	To Jonathan Dorr Bradley, *23 January 1826
NcD	From B. Tyler, *24 January 1826

MCR-S	To Jonathan Dorr Bradley, 11 March 1826	NcD	From Richard H. Bayard, 26 September 1830
NcD	From Samuel G. Goodrich, *23 June 1827		
NcD	To Mr. Tuttle, 11 August 1827	NcD	To Richard H. Bayard, 1 October 1830
NcD	From B. Tyler, *16 February 1828		Inventory of the Estate of Stephen Rowe Bradley [post 15 March 1831]
Printed	Last Will and Testament of Stephen Rowe Bradley, 15 September 1828	Printed	Last Will and Testament of Melinda Willard Bradley, *12 August 1836
MCR-S	To Abel Perrin, 25 March 1829		
NcD	From Samuel G. Goodrich, *7 May 1829	NcD	From Peter Gerard Stuyvesant, *28 March [no date]
NcD	From Samuel G. Goodrich, 13 May 1829		
NcD	From Samuel G. Goodrich, *27 April 1830		

APPENDIX II.
BRADLEY FLAG (U.S.), 1795–1818

From the "History of Congress," Thursday, December 26, 1793, there is the following notation: "Agreeably to notice given on the 23d instant, Mr. Bradley obtained leave to bring in a bill making an alteration in the flag of the United States; and the bill was read the first time, and ordered to a second reading." At this time Senator Bradley's speech, "Kentucky and Vermont have been added to the Union, and they consider themselves of as much importance as the thirteen original Colonies and desire to be represented on the flag. I therefore move that the flag be fifteen stars and fifteen stripes."

On Friday, December 27, "The Senate proceeded to the second reading of the bill making an alteration in the flag of the United States and, having amended the same, the bill was ordered to a third reading."

The final vote took place, Monday, December 30, 1793, "The bill making an alteration in the Flag of the United States, was read the third time, and passed." The Bradley flag was the official flag of the United States for 23 years.

ACTS OF THE THIRD CONGRESS
of the
UNITED STATES,

Passed at the first session, which was begun and held at the City of Philadelphia, in the State of Pennsylvania, on Monday, the second day of December, 1793, and ended on the ninth day of June, 1794.

George Washington, President; John Adams, Vice President of the United States, and President of the Senate; Ralph Izard, President of the Senate pro tempore; Frederick Augustus Muhlenberg, Speaker of the House of Representatives.

STATUTE I.

Chapter 1.—*An Act making an alteration in the Flag of the United States.*

Be it enacted by the Senate and House of Representatives of the United States of America in Congress assembled, That from and after the first day of May, Anno Domini, one thousand seven hundred and ninety-five, the flag of the United States, be fifteen stripes alternate red and white. That the Union be fifteen stars, white in a blue field. (*a*)

Approved, January 13, 1794.

At the time of the first reading of the "Bradley Flag Bill" the Senate was shown an oil painting of the proposed flag. This painting was then hung in the family homes in Westminster and Walpole for the next one hundred years. It was then presented to The Daughters of the American Revolution in a formal ceremony. A copy of the hand bill at this presentation is still in existence, but the location of the painting is not known.

In 1814, during the War of 1812, Francis Scott Key wrote a poem about this flag, "The Star Spangled Banner." This story about the flag became so familiar to Americans that it took on a new name and is now generally known as the "Fort McHenry Flag."

It should be noted that the two flags differed slightly. The Bradley version had two stars in the first row (adjacent to the pole) and the Fort McHenry flag had three stars in the first row. Both flags are correct as the Senate did not specify the arrangement of the stars in the constellation.

APPENDIX III.
MEMOIR AND CORRESPONDENCE OF JEREMIAH MASON, 1768–1848

* * *

As a young man Jeremiah Mason joined the law firm of Stephen R. Bradley as a student. The following is an extract from *Memoir and Correspondence of Jeremiah Mason*. It was published in 1873, by Cambridge Riverside Press. He went on to become a very prominent lawyer in Boston and a U.S. senator from the state of New Hampshire.

* * *

I entered myself as a student in the office of Stephen Rowe Bradley, at Westminster; returned home; visited New Haven, and took up my connections there and went back to Westminster the first part of the ensuing winter. I found General Bradley (that was his usual designation) an extraordinary character. He inherited from nature an ardent and sanguine temperament, with vigorous, natural powers of mind, and strong passions. He was graduated at Yale College in 1775, but his attainments from study were slender. His studies were irregular, as his capricious humors and inclinations directed; without much refinement of any kind, he had an unconquerable love for broad humor and practical jokes, which he freely indulged on all occasions. He was an admirable story-teller, and was never more delighted than when he had an opportunity to set the rabble of a courthouse or bar-room on a roar by one of his overwhelming droll stories. With all this apparent lightness and indulgence in drolleries, he was persevering and efficient in action, rather deriving aid than suffering impediment from them. Many years after the time of which I am speaking, I heard the celebrated Mr. Giles of Virginia, in the Senate of the United States, when expressing his regret for the failure of a certain measure that had been attempted, attribute the failure entirely to General Bradley who had then been a member of that body, saying that of all the men he ever knew, General Bradley possessed the most extraordinary powers in a deliberative assembly to defeat any measure he assailed. Among his other queer fancies he built a pulpit in his office, which was ample, adjoined his house, and opened directly into a parlor, and also into a long piazza, so that a large audience might be accommodated. He occasionally notified meetings and had preaching in his pulpit. On one occasion he gave out that Mr. Murray, the celebrated Universalist, was to preach in his pulpit. This gathered a crowded assembly, when instead of Mr. Murray, an ordinary travelling Universalist preacher whom he picked up, entered the pulpit. He was fluent, and delivered a flaming discourse on his favorite doctrine. Mr. Sage, the minister of the parish, an ardent young Calvinistic Divine of the Orthodox sect, who had attended to protect the purity of the faith, on the close of the discourse immediately challenged the Universalist to a combat of polemic discussion. The Universalist promptly accepted the challenge; General Bradley immediately arranged the combatants at two tables, and assumed a seat for himself as moderator to rule the debate and keep order. Sage assumed the part of assailant and the Universalist that of defender, and the battle began. For two long hours the moderator sat with imperturbably gravity, ruling the questions of order devised by the combatants, and sometimes suggesting questions himself. This furnished him with an ample fund of amusement for a long time.

He was extravagantly fond of narrating the fooleries he had practiced. He often told with great zest a hoax he had practiced as a poor man, by imparting to him, under solemn injunctions of secrecy, a recipe for making the fish called bass out of bass-wood. He had a vast stock of stories of such like feats. His manners were popular and such light conduct did not seem much to injure his respectability in the rude state of society then prevailing in that region.

He professed to attach much importance to the Orthodox religious faith; and with a strong love for money, he suffered but little convenience from rigid principle of any kind. A short time before I entered his office, and married his second wife, an amiable woman of lady-like accomplishments, who exerted a very honorable influence over him. I lived in the family, where all things were pleasant, and occasionally enlivened by agreeable company. There was little or no good society in the place, nor was it much better at Walpole, the village on the opposite bank of the river.

There was then living in Westminster a lawyer of the name of Lot Hall (afterwards a judge of the Supreme Court of Vermont), a man of ordinary natural talents, little learning, and much industry. With him Bradley had long been at feud. As is usual with village feuds, where there can be but few objects to excite the feelings and passions, the mutual enmity had become so violent as to prevent all social intercourse. Justices of the peace had a large civil jurisdiction which was final when under a certain amount of damages. Before these Justices' Courts a great deal of petty litigation was carried on. At these courts Messrs. Bradley and Hall often met, and held discussions not well calculated to soften or sweeten their tempers. Soon after I entered his office, Mr. Bradley, being obliged to be absent at the time of one of these courts, requested me to attend in his stead. I rather reluctantly consented, fearing that I should not be equal to the occasion; but Mr. Bradley encouraged me by professing to hold his adversary in great contempt. I attended, and there argued my first cause, and won it; with which both my client and I were well satisfied. Mr. Bradley was much gratified that I had beat Hall, as he termed it. He said his engagements were such as rendered it inconvenient for him to attend to these petty causes, and offered to give me the whole charge and management of all the business before the Justices' Courts, with all the fees in litigated cases, and one half the income (being the taxed costs) in the cases not litigated. The offer was grossly improper for him to make and for me to accept: my time ought to have been exclusively devoted to study. But I needed money, which I knew my father furnished rather reluctantly, felt pleased with the offer, which flattered my vanity, and immediately acceded to it and launched out into a sea of pettifogging. I continued in Mr. Bradley's office nearly a year and a half, during which I did a very considerable business under this agreement. I commenced a multitude of suits for the collection of small debts, and often appeared as counsel in the petty litigation in the Justices' Courts in Westminster and the adjoining towns. I certainly knew very little law, but that was the less necessary as most of my opponents knew not much more, and the judges I addressed none at all. Being tolerably fluent I got along pretty well. Whenever it was my fortune to meet Mr. Hall, I was careful to treat him with marked courtesy, to show that with his business I had not adopted Mr. Bradley's quarrel. I often studied my little causes with sufficient diligence, and this premature attempt to argue causes helped me to gain confidence in myself; which was highly beneficial to me, for I was exceedingly diffident.

Appendix IV.
Index of Bradley's Correspondents and Their Letters

Entries contain a brief description or biography of Bradley's correspondent if available. Dates are given for letters relating to that person or entry. Asterisks indicate that a letter is not included in this volume; it can be found at the depository listed in Appendix I. Other information can be found via the General Index.

Abbey, <Eunce?>. 4/9/1818
Abbey, Hezh. 5/15/1815; 5/26/1815
Abbey, Julia. 4/9/1818
Abbey, Mr. 3/4/1806
Abbot, James, Esqr. Receiver of money in Michigan Territory. 12/2/1808*
Adams, Gideon. [4/1/1784]
Adams, Jereh. [4/1/1784]
Adams, John (1735–1826). Served as first vice president and second president of the United States. Member of the Continental Congress 1774–1777; signed the Declaration of Independence and proposed George Washington, of Virginia, for general of the American Army; elected in 1788 as the first vice president of the United States with George Washington as president; reelected in 1792 and served from April 21, 1789, to March 3, 1797; elected president of the United States and served from March 4, 1797, to March 3, 1801. 2/19/1804; 2/2/1808
Adams, John Quincy (1767–1848). A senator and representative from Massachusetts and sixth president of the United States. Elected as a Federalist to the United States Senate and served from March 4, 1803, until June 8, 1808, when he resigned; secretary of state in the cabinet of President James Monroe 1817–1825; in 1825, none of the presidential candidates secured a majority of electoral votes, so the election of the president of the United States fell, according to the Constitution of the United States, upon the House of Representatives, and Adams, who stood second to Andrew Jackson in the electoral vote, was chosen and served from March 4, 1825, to March 3, 1829; elected as a Republican to the U.S. House of Representatives for the 22nd and to the eight succeeding Congresses, becoming a Whig in 1834. 2/19/1804; 1/16/1823; 2/14/1823; 2/25/1823
Adams, Peregran, Jr. Of Marlboro. 5/16/1796*
Adams, Samuel (1722–1803). Member of the Continental Congress from 1774 to 1781; a signer of the Declaration of Independence; member of the Massachusetts constitutional convention in 1779; president of the state senate in 1781; member of the state constitutional convention in 1788; lieutenant governor 1789–1794; governor 1794–1797.
Adams, Thomas. Bond from 5/17/1783*
Alcott, Peter. [4/1/1784]
Alcott, Peter. Of Norwich. 12/28/1804
Aldrich, Benone. Money owed C. Johnson 12/13/1797*
Alexander, Mr. Delivered letters to SRB from J. Bowdoin 11/5/1789*
Allen, Ethan (1739–1789). Commanding officer of the Vermont "Green Mountain Boys." On May 10, 1775, he captured Fort Ticonderoga from its British garrison. Was involved in the "New Hampshire Grants" controversy. He wrote "Reason, the only Oracle of Man" (1784). 6/4/1779; 10/20/1779; 10/22/1779; 9/7/1785; 4/6/1786; 6/2/1786; 6/21/1786; 7/25/1786; 10/11/1786; 1/1/1787*; 11/6/1787; 11/9/1787
Allen, Ethan A. 3/29/1808
Allen, Heman. ID — 7/13/1815; 3/21/1812
Allen, Ira (1751–1814). Younger brother of Ethan. Served eight terms in the Vermont General Assembly; held the rank of major general with the Vermont Militia; was deeply involved in the "Olive Branch" litigation with the British courts. 6/4/1779*; 2/??/1780; 5/26/1780*; 8/18/1780; 10/14/1780; [7/31/1783]; 10/17/1783; [10/10/1786]; 1/19/1791
Allen, Levi. 6/4/1779*; [ca. June 1784]
Allen, Mr. SRB recommends promotion 5/4/1803
Allen, Zimri E. Of Litchfield, Conn. 3/21/1812
Alston, Willis. ID. North Carolina congressman. 1/31/1812; 2/3/1812
American Unitarian Association. 8/15/1825*
Anderson, John. Marshal of the Michigan (?) Territory. 2/4/1812
Anderson, Joseph. U.S. senator from Tennessee. 2/17/1807; 12/22/1811*
Andrews, Stephen. SRB purchased land from [ca. 1790]
Appleton, S & N. 5/24/1808
Arden, Francis. 1/25/1796*
Arden, James. N.Y. merchant. 7/30/1795*; 2/14/1797*; 3/6/1797*; 4/14/1797*; 12/21/1797*; 2/14/1798*;

411

6/18/1799*; 1/1/1800*; 5/15/1800*; 7/8/1800*; 6/21/1803*; 12/14/1803*; 6/8/1804*; 7/10/1804*; 12/13/1804*
Armsby, Maj. Gideon. [4/1/1784]
Armstrong, Capt. Hezikiah. [4/1/1784]
Armstrong, John. ID — 3/17/1814
Armstrong, John. Re: Tennessee lands 1/8/1805
Armstrong, Col. Martin. Surveyor. 1/8/1805
Arnold, Mr. Member of Vt. General Assembly. 1/19/1791
Ashcroft, Daniel. Of Guilford. 1/24/1784
Ashley, Thomas. SRB purchased land from [ca. 1790]
Ashley, William. Debt owed SRB 12/10/1807*; 3/11/1808*
Astor, John J. 3/8/1819
Atherton, Abel W. Friend of J. Ruggles. 4/4/1808
Atherton, Mr. 7/2/1813
Atkins, Joseph. SRB purchased land from [ca. 1790]
Atkinson, John. 6/2/1798*; 9/25/1813
Atkinson, Mr. 1/29/1809
Atkinson, Mr. Developer of Hopkinville. 3/27/1802*
Atkinsons, Messrs. 3/29/1807
Attwaiters?, Mr. Of Westminster. 11/14/1801
Attwater, Esq. 11/25/1800; 6/9/1807
Atwater, Ambrose. Brother of Reuben. 6/5/1786*
Atwater, Capt. (deceased) 5/14/1785
Atwater, John. 10/20/1785*
Atwater, Major. 1/13/1803
Atwater, Mary Russell. Mother of Mrs. SRB. 1/9/1786*; 4/16/1788; 3/8/1796*
Atwater, Mr. (Reuben or Russel?) 12/22/1785; 4/12/1799*; 11/4/1800*
Atwater, Reuben (1728–1801). Married Mary Russel January 28, 1755. The daughter of Mary and Reuben Atwater, Merab Atwater, became the first wife of Stephen Rowe Bradley May 16, 1780. 9/1/1780*; 12/12/1780*; 8/??/1781*; 12/9/1782; 10/4/1783; 4/5/1784*; 2/7/1785; 2/15/1785*; 3/10/1785; 5/14/1785; 9/24/1785; 12/26/1785*; 1/9/1786*; 6/1/1786*; 6/5/1786*; 5/14/1787; 7/21/1787*; 4/16/1788; 3/8/1796*; 5/23/1796*; Recommended to be Commissioner of Bankruptcy 9/13/1802
Atwater (Attwater), Reuben, Jr. Brother of Mrs. SRB. 2/15/1785; 9/24/1785; 10/20/1785*; 12/26/1785*; 1/9/1786*; 6/1/1786*; 5/14/1787; 4/16/1788; 4/16/1788; 1/2/1797*; 12/26/1807; 3/3/1808; 3/16/1808; 3/31/1808*; 12/2/1808*;12/15/1808; 3/8/1810*; 8/1/1810; 11/28/1810*; 11/2/1811*; 1/14/1812; 2/4/1812
Atwater, Russel. Brother of Mrs. SRB. 4/3/1780*; 9/1/1780*; 10/28/1782*; 4/21/1783; 9/23/1783*; 10/4/1783; 11/24/1783; 4/5/1784*; 5/14/1785; 9/24/1785; 10/20/1785*; 5/23/1796*; 1/2/1797*; 3/3/1808
Atwater, Sarah Lamb. Mrs. Reuben Jr. 12/26/1807; 3/3/1808; 3/8/1810*; 8/1/1810; 11/28/1810*; 11/2/1811*; 1/14/1812; 2/4/1812
Atwater? (WCB's Aunt "Betsa") 12/26/1785*
Audrian, Peter. Of Detroit. 11/28/1810*
Austin, David. Of Norwich, Conn. 5/5/1812
Austin, Mr. Member of Vermont General Assembly. 1/12/1791*; 1/25/1809
Austin, Mr. 4/21/1783; 9/23/1783*; 11/24/1783
Averill, Samuel. SRB purchased land from [ca. 1790]
Avery, Fanny. Friend of J. Ruggles and J.E. Trask. 8/5/1800; 1/24/1801*; 11/14/1801
Avery, Mr. Debt owed David Stone 8/25/1800*
Avery, Samuel. 9/6/1796*; 11/3/1801; Debt owed Pearsall 9/16/1800*
Avery, Samuel. 5/17/1783*; 10/12/1785*; 11/28/1787*; 6/29/1789; 7/31/1790; 4/27/1793*
Avery, Samuel, Jr. Has power to sell father's land in Kingston 11/3/1801

Axtill, Joseph. Ensign Vt. Militia. 10/18/1792
B<...>. Re: Ingraham vs. Geyer 7/31/1801*
Babbet, Thomas. Of Brookfield. Re: Tripoli 11/17/1806
Babcock, John. 9/15/1828
Babcock, Mr. Of Conn. 12/27/1808
Backus, Elijah. Of Kaskaskia, Indiana Territory. 4/14/1808*
Bacon, Leonard. 9/15/1828
Badger, Dr. Jonathan. Of Westminster. 3/4/1806; 11/30/1811; 2/20/1818
Badger, Mrs. Jonathan. 3/4/1806
Badger, Widow. 2/20/1818
Bailey, Theodorus. U.S. senator from N.Y. 1/4/1802
Bainbridge, Joseph. Navy Lt. 11/17/1806
Baker, Lt. Friend of J. Ruggles. 8/5/1800
Baker, Samuel. SRB purchased land from [ca. 1790]
Baldwin, Abraham (1754–1807). A Republican delegate, representative, and senator from Georgia; served as chaplain in the Second Connecticut Brigade, Revolutionary Army, from 1777 until 1783; author of the charter of the University of Georgia and its president 1786–1801; member of the Continental Congress in 1785, 1787, and 1788; member of the United States Constitutional Convention in 1787; elected to the 1st and to the four succeeding Congresses (March 4, 1789–March 3, 1799); elected to the United States Senate in 1799; reelected in 1805 and served from March 4, 1799, until his death on April 4, 1807; served as president pro tempore of the senate during the 7th Congress. 12/13&14/1802
Baldwin, Mr. 1/24/1803
Baldwin, Simeon. New Haven attorney. 12/26/1789
Bale, William T. 6/14/1813*
Ball, Ebenezer. SRB purchased land from [ca. 1790]
Bangs, Mr. 6/19/1800*
Barber, Caroline. Of Hartford. 2/27/1819
Barber, Joseph. SRB purchased land from [ca. 1790]
Barber, Oliver. Partner in John Holbrook & Co. 2/20/1797*
Barber, Oliver & George W., & Co. 12/8/1794*; 2/20/1797*
Bard, Isaac. Landowner in Putney, Vt., later residing in West Springfield, Mass. 9/27/1796
Bareines, Maj. Wait. 6/13/1786*
Baring, Mr. Lusher. 6/13/1786*
Barker, Jonathan. SRB purchased land from [ca. 1790]
Barker, Timothy. SRB purchased land from [ca. 1790]
Barlow, James. SRB purchased land from [ca. 1790]
Barlow, Joel. U.S. minister to France. 3/27/1812; 4/7/1812
Barlow, Samuel. SRB purchased land from [ca. 1790]
Barnes, Stephen. SRB purchased land from [ca. 1790]
Barney, Mr. Baltimore hotelkeeper 1/1/1810
Barns, James. SRB purchased land from [ca. 1790]
Barns, William. SRB purchased land from [ca. 1790]
Barr, William. Selectman of Rutland, Vt. 1/12/1791*
Barret, John. Justice of the Peace for Windsor County. 6/13/1785*
Barrett, Henry. 3/27/1816
Barrett, Thomas. Accused by John Noth of burning house. 10/12/1793*; 10/5/1804
Barron, Dr. A.? Friend of Joseph Ruggles, Jr. 8/5/1800
Barron, Abel. Of Hartford. Interested in purchasing land in Hartland 11/15/1800*
Barron, Capt. Jas. 2/22/1806
Barron, Samuel. U.S. Navy commodore. 2/22/1806; 2/24/1806*; 2/26/1806; 4/5/1806 [2]; 4/7/1806; 11/17/1806
Bartholomew, Joseph. SRB purchased land from [ca. 1790]

Bartlett, Samuel. [10/10/1786]
Barton, Lt. Andrew. [4/1/1784]
Basset, Mr. U.S. representative. 12/21/1810
Bassett, Mr. Former U. S. senator; grandfather of Richard H. Bayard. 10/1/1830
Bates, Joshua. Of Middlebury College. 1/16/1823
Baxter, Horace. Re: post office in Rockingham 12/29/1811*
Bayard, James A. 9/26/1830
Bayard, James. A., Jr. 9/26/1830; 10/1/1830
Bayard, Rebecca. Sister of Samuel. 11/10/1800*
Bayard, Richard H. Of Wilmington, Del.; son of James A. Bayard. 9/26/1830; 10/1/1830
Bayard, Samuel. 7/25/1791; 11/4/1800*
Bayley, Jacob. Of Newbury. 1/22/1811
Bayley, John. Son of Jacob. 1/22/1811
Beach, Abigail Atwater. Mrs. Elnathan; sister of Mrs. SRB. 4/16/1788; 1/2/1797*
Beach, Barney. Brother of Elnathan. 1/2/1797*
Beach, Elnathan. Of Cheshire; brother-in-law of SRB. 3/10/1785; 4/16/1788; 1/2/1797*
Beach, James E. Brother of Elnathan. 1/2/1797*
Beach, John. Brother of Elnathan. 1/2/1797*
Beach, Col. Miles. Of Hartford. 5/15/1791*; 6/1/1792*
Beach, Miss. Friend of SRB's daughter. 9/21/1802*
Beach, Misses. Daughters of Abigail Atwater and Elnathan Beach. 1/2/1797*
Beardsley, Mr. Member of Vt. General Assembly. 10/10/1800
Beasley, Mr. Acting U.S. consul in London. 5/11/1812
Beckley, John. Clerk of the House of Reps. of the U.S. 2/17/1807
Bedle, Samuel Sharp. SRB purchased land from [ca. 1790]
Begelow, Mr. 5/30/1785*
Bellows, Abel. Of Walpole, N. H.. 9/15/1828
Bellows, Ezra. 7/1/1810
Bellows, Gen. Of Walpole. 8/24/1801
Bellows, Josiah. 11/15/1810; 2/25/1816; 9/15/1828
Bellows, Josiah 3rd. SRB's son-in-law. 9/15/1828; 3/15/1831
Bellows, Mr. 4/14/1818*
Bellows, Mr. 10/24/1818*
Bellows, Mrs. 10/7/1818*
Bellows, Rebecca Gratia. SRB's granddaughter. 9/15/1828; 3/15/1831
Bellows, Samuel. 9/25/1813
Bellows, Sarah Adeline. SRB's granddaughter. 9/15/1828; 3/15/1831
Bellows, Stella C. Bradley. Mrs. Josiah Bellows 3rd. 9/15/1828
Bellows, Stella Louise. SRB's granddaughter. 9/15/1828; 5/13/1829; 4/27/1830*; 3/15/1831
Bellows, Stephen R. Bradley. SRB's grandson. 9/15/1828; 3/15/1831
Bellows, Thomas. 9/15/1828
Bemis, D. Note owed SRB 3/15/1831
Benjamin, Asher. Builder. 3/26/1800*
Bennet, Nathanial. Of Tombleson. 8/4/1781
Benson, Mr. 4/12/1803
Bigelow, Mr. Debt to N. Ruggles. 12/25/1803; 3/6/1813
Bigelow, Mr. Weathersfield (?) tavern owner. 7/15/1789*
Bigelow, Reuben. Town clerk of Peru, Vt. 7/17/1818*
Biglow, Lawrance. [4/1/1784]
Biglow, William. Of Guilford. 6/5/1786*
Billings, Maj. Samuel. [4/1/1784]
Bingham, James H. 4/1/1808
Binney & Ludlow. Of Boston. 11/9/1816

Biscale, <Roodiah?> SRB purchased land from [ca. 1790]
Bishop, Ab. Of New Haven. 12/19/1808
Bishop, Mr. Conn. Republican. 6/3/1812
Bissell, Capt. At Wilkinson Ville 5/16/1801
Bissell, Mr. 9/8/1788*
Blackden, Col. Death of 1/4/1802
Blackden, Sarah. Of N.Y. 1/4/1802
Blake, Dr. Charles. 11/20/1807; 7/28/1814
Blake, Charles. Of Keene, N.H. 3/9/1800; 3/9/1804
Blake, Francis. Editor of National Ægis. 3/9/1802
Blake, G. 7/28/1814
Blake, George. Of Boston. 4/19/1803*
Blake, John. In suit against Ralston 6/9/1809
Blake, John W. Of Brattleboro. 3/26/1796*; 3/31/1796*; 4/12/1799*; 11/22/1802*
Blake, John W. In suit against Coleman 5/26/1801*; Tyler recommends son 3/16/1812
Blake, John W. Attorney for Robert Bowne. 11/4/1800*
Blake, Jones. Tyler recommends 3/16/1812
Blanchard, James. SRB purchased land from [ca. 1790]
Blasdell, Dewey. 9/2/1811*
Bledsoe, Jesse (1776–1836). Senator from Kentucky; member, Kentucky state house of representatives 1812; elected as a Republican to the United States Senate and served from March 4, 1813, until his resignation on December 24, 1814; member, state senate 1817–1820. 1/7/1814*
Bleeker, Mr. U.S. congressman from Albany. 1/11/1812*
Bliss, Frederick. Vt. council election [ca. 10/10/1811]
Bliss, Mr. Member of Vt. General Assembly. 10/10/1800
Bliss, Thomas. SRB purchased land from [ca. 1790]; Re: land deeded to Lemuel Cone 12/30/1809*
Bloggit, Mehitteble? 10/12/1793*
Boardman, Daniel. Of N.Y. 5/28/1806*; 6/24/1809*; 9/20/1809*; 12/30/1809*
Bogert, Rudolph. 7/26/1788; Clerk? for Thomas Pearsall 8/18/1798*
Bonaparte, Napoleon. 1/18/1811; 5/5/1812; 12/14/1812
Bond, Mr. 2/25/1816
Bonds. 5/17/1783*; 10/3/1793; 11/10/1801*
Bonnycastle, Richard Henry. 9/30/1819
Booth, Benjamin. SRB purchased land from [ca. 1790]
Booth, Reuben. SRB purchased land from [ca. 1790]
Boott, Mary. Of Boston. To marry S. G. Goodrich 11/30/1825
Bostwick, John. SRB purchased land from [ca. 1790]
Bowdoin, James (1726–1790). Governor of Massachusetts, 1785–87. 11/5/1789*
Bowker, Benjamin. Bought John Nott's land 10/5/1804
Bowker, Daniel. Capt. 11/5/1789*
Bowker, Mr. Of Chester? Thompson to evict 8/31/1802*
Bowne, Robert. Of N.Y. 11/4/1800*
Boyden, Major Josiah. Of Fulham. 1/10/1783
Boynton, Beman. 9/6/1796*
Boynton, John. 9/6/1796*
Brackett, Capt. Charles. Carries letter from Dudley Chase 9/2/1811*
Bradle, Samuel L. SRB purchased land from [ca. 1790]
Bradley, Abraham, Jr. Of the General Post Office. 9/13/1811; 12/19/1817; 12/26/1817
Bradley, Emily. Daughter of WCB. 5/28/1816; 12/15/1816; 9/15/1828
Bradley, Jonathan Dorr (1803–1862). Graduate of Yale College; practiced law in Bellows Falls and Brattleboro; married Susan Crossman in 1829. 1/23/1826*; 3/11/1826; 9/15/1828; 3/25/1829
Bradley?, Josiah. 3/7/1818*; 4/23/1819; 5/13/1829

Bradley, Capt. Lemuel. [4/1/1784]
Bradley, Louisa. Daughter of SRB. 11/30/1811
Bradley, Louisa & Josiah. 3/9/1813
Bradley, Mary Rowe (1811–1882). Second daughter of Stephen and Melinda Bradley.
Bradley, Melinda Willard (1784–1837). Third wife of Stephen Rowe Bradley. 7/17/1806*; 8/x/1808; 1/1/1810; 3/8/1810*; 8/1/1810; 3/18/1811*; 11/2/1811*; 11/30/1811; 1/14/1812; 3/15/1812; 6/22/1818*; 10/7/1818*; 6/24/1822; 8/21/1822; 5/7/1825*; 6/8/1825; 9/15/1828; 5/13/1829; 3/15/1831
Bradley, Merab. 3/26/1811
Bradley, Merab Ann. Daughter of WCB. 8/25/1814; 3/22/1815; 5/28/1816; 12/15/1816; 9/15/1828
Bradley, Merab Atwater. Mrs. SRB. 4/21/1783; 4/5/1784*; 2/7/1785; 2/15/1785*; 3/10/1785; 3/10/1785
Bradley, Mr. 2/15/1785*
(Bradley?), Paulina. 9/30/1819
Bradley, Sarah Richards (1783–1866). Daughter of Senator Mark Richards and Ann Ruggles Dorr Richards; married William Czar Bradley 1802. 1/20/1802*; 12/25/1803; 3/9/1803; 7/29/1808; 1/29/1809; 1/12/1812; 5/28/1816; 11/9/1817; 11/19/1817; 9/30/1819; 6/8/1825; 9/15/1828
Bradley, Mrs. S.R. (Sally?). 11/7/1803; 2/19/1804
Bradley, Mrs. S.R. (Gratia Thankful Taylor). Second wife of SRB. 3/8/1796*; 9/6/1796*; 1/2/1797*; 4/12/1799*; 1/5/1801; 5/16/1801; 10/23/1801; 12/7/1801; 2/13/1802; 7/17/1806*
Bradley, Stella. Daughter of SRB. 2/13/1802; 9/21/1802*; 1/1/1803; 10/8/1803; 12/25/1803; 6/10/1804; 7/6/1808; 7/29/1808; 8/x8/1808; 9/22/1809; 3/18/1811*; 3/9/1813; 4/23/1819; 9/30/1819
Bradley, Stephen Rowe, I. Son of SRB and his second wife. 2/13/1802; Death of 7/6/1808
Bradley, Thadeus. 9/1/1780*
Bradley, Walter. Recommended for Conn. collector 6/3/1812
Bradley, William Czar. 12/9/1782; 4/21/1783; 2/7/1785; 5/14/1785; 9/24/1785; 10/20/1785*; 12/26/1785*; 6/1/1786*; 5/14/1787; 7/21/1787*; 4/16/1788; 12/5/1793; 12/13/1797*; 1/5/1801; 5/16/1801; 11/10/1801*; 12/7/1801; 3/7/1803; 4/6/1803; 6/3/1803; 1/17/1808; 3/24/1808; 3/31/1808*; 7/6/1808; 7/29/1808; 1/29/1809; 9/20/1809*; 12/30/1809*; 3/6/1810; 3/26/1811; 1/12/1812; 3/15/1812; 3/16/1812; 3/25/1813*; 6/14/1813*; 12/14/1815; 11/9/1817; 11/19/1817; 3/7/1818*; 10/7/1818*; 12/24/1818; 1/1/1819; 5/29/1819*; 9/30/1819; 4/7/1822*; 12/5/1824*; 6/8/1825; 11/30/1825; 9/15/1828; 5/13/1829; 3/15/1831; bill for boarding of 9/6/1796*
Brattle?, Col. Bill to SRB 8/18/1798*
Brattle, Major. Of Boston? Suit against Cole 4/11/1797*
Brattle, Mr. 4/20/1802*
Bray, Theodorus. SRB purchased land from [ca. 1790]
Breed, Ebenezer. Lynn, Mass., shoemaker. 12/30/1811
Brent, Robert. U.S. Army paymaster. 2/9/1810
Brewster, Jacob W. Of Lebanon, N.H. 7/17/1802*; 8/6/1802
Brewster, Mr. 12/19/1817
Briant, Jacob. Of Marlborough. 5/16/1796*
Bridgman, John. Of Vernon. 10/14/1780
Bridgeman, Orlando. SRB purchased land from [ca. 1790]
Briggs, Esq. SRB's note against 1/4/1803
Briggs, J. Note owed SRB 3/15/1831
Briggs, Capt. Joseph. [4/1/1784]
Brigham, Paul. Lt. Gov. of Vt. 12/8/1804*; 10/12/1808; [ca. 10/10/1811]
BroudAngel?, John. Legal case 3/23/1796*

Brown, Ebenezer. Of Norwich. 12/28/1804
Brown, Elisha. Accused by John Noth of burning house 10/12/1793*; 10/5/1804
Brown, Jabez. Sgt. of Vt. militia. 8/25/1792
Brown, Jesse. Norwich, Conn., merchant. 3/16/1808
Brown, Major Return Bryant. Of Windsor. 11/5/1808
Brownson, Maj. Gideon. [4/1/1784]
Brownson, Isaac. [4/1/1784]
Brownson, Timothy. [7/31/1783]; [10/10/1786]
Brush, Alexander. [4/1/1784]
Brush, Col. Of Bennington. 5/10/1792
Brush, Crean. 6/4/1779*; [1783]; [ca. June 1784]; 8/13/1790*; 10/12/1793*; 10/17/93; 10/5/1804; 1/11/1804
Brush, John C. Of Washington. 9/24/1811*
Buchanan, Fanny. Widow of a British Army officer and daughter of Mrs. Patrick Wall; married Ethan Allen.
Buck, Daniel. ID 2/27/1808
Buckingham, Jed P. Vt. Council election [ca. 10/10/1811]
Bucknam, Col. 10/31/1796*
Buel, Samuel. Of Burlington. 4/15/1811*
Buell, John H. 1/5/1801; 5/16/1801; 12/18/1801*
Buell, Louisa. Daughter of John H.? 5/16/1801
Buell, Maj. In Natchez with Gen. Wilkinson 11/14/1801
Buell, Sally. Mrs. John H. 1/5/1801; 5/16/1801; 12/18/1801*
Buell vs. Van Ness. 7/13/1815
Buffum, William. 9/15/1828; 5/13/1829
Bulkley, Capt. Charles. Of New London. 12/15/1808
Bull, Elias. Of Rutland. 12/31/1801
Bull, Lydia. Of Hartford; mother of Lydia Royse. 7/6/1808
Bull, George. Of Hartford; uncle of Lydia Royse. 7/6/1808; 3/18/1811*
Bull, George. Of Hartford; brother? of Lydia Royse. 3/18/1811*
Bull, Hezekiah. Of Hartford; brother of George Jr.? 3/18/1811*
Bulle, Ezra. Vt. Council election [ca. 10/10/1811]
Bullen, Joseph. [11/13/1788–7/25/1789] ; 12/18/1801*; 1/24/1803; 10/20/1803; Debt owed Micah Read 4/4/1797*
Bullen, Mr. 5/14/1785
Bundy, James. [11/13/1788–7/25/1789]
Burbank, Daniel. Of Enfield. 12/26/1785*; 6/1/1786*; 6/5/1786*
Burbank, Seth. 6/1/1786*; 6/5/1786*
Burbeck, Coll. 11/20/1807
Burdett, Mr. B. C. Of Hartford. 2/27/1819
Burk, Capt. Of Chittenden 11/3/1801
Burk, Mr. E. Of Westminster. 3/15/1812
Burk, <Eliub?> [11/13/1788–7/25/1789]
Burkett, Christopher. Bill on T. Peacock 8/18/1798*
Burows, Mr. Works on SRB's house on Lord Hill in Hartford 6/11/1818*
Burr, Aaron (1756–1836). Revolutionary War Lt. Col.; served as vice president under Thomas Jefferson 1801–1804; killed Alexander Hamilton in a duel at Weehawken; was involved with Gen. James Wilkenson in a massive land grab in Louisiana. 1/5/1801; 1/4/1802
Burr, Aaron? 11/25/1800; 1/24/1801; 3/23/1806; 11/17/1806
Burr, Col. 10/1/1830
Burr, Mr. Cashier of the Hartford Bank. 11/16/1818*
Burrows, William. 6/5/1786*
Burton, Elisha. Of Norwich. 12/28/1804
Butler, Ezra. Member of Vt. General Assembly. 10/24/1800; 1/30/1804*

Butler, John. Of Brimfield. Re: Tripoli 11/17/1806
Butler, Major. Of Philadelphia. 1/1/1810
Butler, Major. 2/20/1818
Butler, Mr. 1/17/1808
Butler, Mrs. Of Roxbury, MA. SRB's daughter visits 9/21/1802*; 12/25/1803
Butters, Mr. 7/31/1790
Buzziel, Abel B. Money owed C. Johnson 12/13/1797*
C— —m, Mr. 4/12/1803
Cabell, William H. ID 12/10/1808*
Cabot, Marston. 11/15/1800*
Cahoon, William. Vt. presidential elector. 11/5/1808
Calhoon, David. SRB purchased land from [ca. 1790]
Calhoon, James. SRB purchased land from [ca. 1790]
Calhoon, Joseph. SRB purchased land from [ca. 1790]
Calhoun, John C. 1/16/1823
Cambridge, Dr. 4/1/1814
Cameron, John. Vt. Council election [ca. 10/10/1811]
Cameron, Mr. 4/24/1805; 5/28/1805; 1/24/1811; 8/24/1813
Camp, Jonah. SRB purchased land from [ca. 1790]
Campbel, James. 12/9/1822*
Campbell, Dr. Alexander. 12/12/1790
Campbell, Dr. 6/19/1800*
Campbell, Edward R. Capt. of Vt. Militia. [11/13/1788–7/25/1789]; 8/25/1792
Campbell, Edward R. 2d. Re: post office in Rockingham 12/29/1811*
Campbell, George Washington. U.S. representative from Tennessee. 2/17/1807; 12/22/1811*
Campbell, Hugh. Navy capt. Re: Tripoli 11/17/1806
Campbell, Judge. 11/5/1808
Candee, Mr. 11/7/1818*; 12/4/1818*; 4/21/1819*
Candee & Goodrich. Of Hartford. 1/22/1818*; 5/21/1818*; 9/11/1818*; 10/8/1818*; 10/24/1818*; 11/16/1818*; 12/4/1818*; 2/27/1819
Caramanli, Hamet (Ahmed). Brother of pasha of Tripoli. 2/22/1806; 2/26/1806; 3/23/1806; 4/5/1806 [2]; 2/13/1807; 12/27/1807; 2/17/1808; 8/23/1808; 1/15/1810
Caramanli, Joseph. Pasha of Tripoli. 2/24/1806*; 2/26/1806
Carleton, Roland. Rent owed SRB 3/15/1831
Carlisle, David. 3/27/1801*
Carlisle, David, Jr. Money owed C. Johnson 12/13/1797*
Carlisle, George. Note owed SRB 3/15/1831
Carnargie?, Andrew. Legal case 3/23/1796*
Carpenter, Abel. Account with SRB 11/12/1800
Carpenter, Amos. Of Westminster. Letter from Ephraim Welles 11/11/1794
Carpenter, Lt. Col. Benjamin (1725–1804). Served in Revolutionary War; Lt. Gov. of Vermont under Thomas Chittendon; was a major figure in "New Hampshire Grants" troubles with New York and the "Yonkers"; from Guilford, Vt.
Carpenter, Cyrel. Petition of 2/21/1784
Carpenter, David. 7/17/1818*
Carpenter, Mr. 9/4/1792*
Carroll, Mr. Former U.S. senator. 10/1/1830
Carter, Dr. Of Weathersfield, Vt. 11/7/1791; 8/10/1793*
Casey, James. 9/25/1813
Cederström, Baron. Swedish admiral. 2/24/1806*
Chamberlain, Rev. Prof. Joshua. 2/3/1810*; 2/12/1811; 5/11/1812; 9/22/1812
Chamberlain, Jason, Jr. 6/8/1807
Chamberlain, John C. 12/28/1822*
Chamberlin, Joshua. Member of Vt. General Assembly. 9/27/1796

Chamberlin, William. U.S. congressman from Vt.; candidate for Vermont lieutenant governor. 1/9/1804; [ca. 10/10/1811]
Champagny, Jean-Baptiste Nompère de. French minister for foreign affairs. 4/10/1808
Champion, Genl. 4/21/1819*
Chandler, Charles. Receipt from 9/6/1796*
Chandler, John W. Vt. Council election [ca. 10/10/1811]
Chandler, Mr. 8/26/1790*
Chandler, Mr. 8/3/1811
Chandler, Samuel. 9/6/1796*; 8/29/1813
Chandler, Thomas. [11/13/1788–7/25/1789]
Chandler, Thomas, Jr. Of Chester. 10/14/1780
Chapin, Judge. 11/5/1808
Chaplin, Mr. 12/3/1790
Chapman, Mr. 4/21/1783; 9/23/1783*; 11/24/1783
Chase, Dudley (1771–1846). Member, Vermont House of Representatives 1805–1812; delegate to the state constitutional conventions in 1814 and 1822; elected as a Jeffersonian Democrat to the United States Senate and served from March 4, 1813, to November 3, 1817; chief justice of the supreme court of Vermont 1817–1821; member, state house of representatives 1823–1824; elected as a Republican to the United States Senate and served from March 4, 1825, to March 3, 1831. 1/27/[1811]; 9/2/1811*; 3/17/1814; 4/1/1814
Chase & Brackett. To execute bond 9/13/1811
Chauncey, Nathaniel. SRB purchased land from [ca. 1790]
Chaw, Mr. 5/30/1785*
Chenevard, Martha Bull. Of Hartford; sister of Lydia Royse. 7/6/1808; 3/18/1811*
Cheney, Samuel. Of Boston; teacher of Nathaniel Dorr. 11/6/1793
Chipman, Daniel. Vt. Council election [ca. 10/10/1811]
Chipman, Harry. Brother of Nathaniel. 4/1/1808
Chipman, Lemuel. Member of Vt. General Assembly. 10/22/1790; 1/25/1791*
Chipman, Mr. Member of Vt. General Assembly. 10/10/1800
Chipman, Nathaniel (1752–1843). Federalist senator from Vermont; served as a lieutenant in the Revolutionary War; served in the U.S. Senate from October 17, 1797, until March 3, 1803; state house of representatives 1806–1811; chief justice of Vermont 1813–1815. 1/20/1802*; [4/1/1784]; 1/15/1790*; 2/9/1790; 10/22/1790; 4/1/1808; 11/9/1817
Chipman, Samuel. Justice of the Peace. 10/8/1810*
Chisolm, John. Indian interpreter. 12/18/1801*
Chittenden, Martin. Candidate for Vt. governor 1813–1815. [ca. 10/10/1811]; 4/11/1812
Chittenden, Mr. Character reference for Satterlee Clark 3/24/1808
Chittendon, Mr. Member of Vt. General Assembly. 9/27/1796
Chittenden, Noah. Vt. Council election [ca. 10/10/1811]
Chittenden, Thomas (1730–1797). Revolutionary War officer?; governor of Vt., 1778–79, 1790–97. 9/1/1780*; 8/27/1781; 12/24/1782; 3/2/1787; 1/10/1791*; 1/19/1791; 11/28/1812
Church, Col. 12/24/1782; 4/23/1787*
Church, Eleazer. 1/12/1784
Church, Joshua? 7/24/1784*
Church, Samuel. 4/23/1787*
Church, Col. Timothy. Colonel New York militia; key figure in the "New Hampshire Grants" controversy.
Clap, Capt. Caleb. Friend of SRB. 3/26/1796*; 7/6/1797*; 7/12/1797*; 7/1/1798*; 1/8/1799*

Clap, Mr. President of Yale? 1/8/1810*
Clap (Clapp), Mr. and Mrs. Friends of Bradleys. 6/19/1799; 8/5/1800; 12/25/1803; 1/29/1809; 11/12/1816
Clapp, Mrs. Of Westminster; sister of Capt. Dorr of Roxbury. 11/9/1817
(Clapp?), Nancy. 7/1/1798*
Clapperton, Hugh. 5/13/1829
Clark, Ebenezer. Of Lunenberg. 6/25/1796*; 8/13/1796*; 10/31/1796*
Clark, Capt. Elisha. (deceased) 10/22/1788
Clark, Gershom. Town clerk of Weathersfield. 7/31/1790
Clark, Col. Isaac. [4/1/1784]
Clark, J. Note owed SRB 3/15/1831
Clark, Lieut. Student of Wm. C. Harrington. 2/2/1808
Clark, Mr. Of Castleton. 2/2/1808
Clark, Ozias. Vermont petitioner. 10/22/1788
Clark, Satterlee. West Point cadet. 10/21/1807; 3/24/1808
Clark, Scotto. Signee on note 1/30/1798
Clark, Smith. 10/22/1788
Clark, Zadock. SRB purchased land from [ca. 1790]
Clark vs. Ware 8/13/1796*
Clarke, George. Of New York. 9/10/1797; 9/17/1797
Clason, Isaac. Of New York. 1/24/1810; 2/2/1810*
Clay, Henry. 1/16/1823
Clemson, Capt. Commanding officer of Lt. Joseph Dorr. 2/9/1810
Clephan, Mr. Debtor of A. Williams 3/27/1802*
<Clesson?>, Roswell. Of Rockingham. 12/12/1790
Clinton, George. (1739–1812). Served as a brigadier general in the continental army. Was governor of New York state for 18 successive years. Vice president of the U.S. in 1804 under Thomas Jefferson, he again served as vice president with James Madison and died in office May 20, 1812. 10/8/1812
Cobb, Ebenezer. SRB purchased land from [ca. 1790]
Cobb, Capt. Ezekiel. [4/1/1784]
Cobb, Mr. 12/13/1787*
Cobbett, Mr. Of Cobbett's Register 2/3/1812
Coburn, John. 8/26/1790*
Coburn vs. Chandler 8/26/1790*
Cochran, Capt. Robert. 1/17/1808
Coffeen, John. Representative from Cavendish, was governor of Vermont 1828–1831. [11/13/1788–7/25/1789]
Cogsel, Peter. [4/1/1784]
Colbert, James. Of Chickesaw Nation. 12/18/1801*
Coldwell, Mr. Former pay master general. 2/20/1818
Cole, Henry. In suit against Brattle 4/11/1797*
Cole, John. SRB purchased land from [ca. 1790]
Coleman, William (1766–1829). Journalist, born in Boston, Mass.; co-founded the *New York Evening Post*, a pro-Federalist newspaper, with Alexander Hamilton. 6/24/1797*, 6/25/1797*; 7/6/1797*, 7/12/1797*; 3/20/1800; 11/25/1800; 5/26/1801*; 10/20/1801*; 12/18/1801*; 11/10/1801*
Collins, Micajah. Quaker preacher in Lynn, Mass. 12/30/1811
Collins, Stephen. Philadelphia merchant. 12/30/1811
Colton, Isaac. [4/1/1784]
Colvin, John B. 12/31/1808*
Comstock, Capt. Daniel. [4/1/1784]
Cone, Lemuel. Of Westminster. 8/14/1792; 12/1/1794*; 6/24/1809*; 9/20/1809*; 12/30/1809*; account with Pearsall 6/6/1803*
Cone, Mr. 5/14/1785
Cone, Mr. Debt owed T. Pearsall 2/23/1800*; 3/21/1800*; 4/1/1802*; 5/31/1802*

Cone, Samuel. 12/25/1794*
Cook, Jesse. [4/1/1784]
Cook, Jonathan. Of Rutland. 10/21/1807
Couleler, Joshua. SRB purchased land from [ca. 1790]
Cowdry, Dr. Of Vt. Re: Tripoli 11/17/1806
Cowen, James. [4/1/1784]
Cowles, S. Brother of Zenas. 7/22/1800*
Cowles, Zenas. Of Westminster. 6/2/1800*; 7/22/1800*
Coxe, Tench. ID 12/17/1809
Crafts, Royal. Of Durkee & Crafts. 7/30/1813; 8/10/1814; 1/19/1816
Crafts, Samuel C. Member of Vt. General Assembly. 10/10/1800; Vt. Council election [ca. 10/10/1811]
Craige, Capt. Vt. militia. 8/25/1792
Craige, Thomas. [11/13/1788–7/25/1789]
Crain, John. Of Williamstown. 11/13/1796*
Crane, Seth. SRB purchased land from [ca. 1790]
Crawford, William H. Secretary of War. 10/12/1819; 1/16/1823
Crawford, William Harris. 4/6/1816
Cris? 10/4/1783
<Crocker>, J. Works on SRB' house on Lord Hill in Hartford 6/11/1818*
Croker, John W. Secretary of the Admiralty (British). 2/3/1812; 2/20/1812; 5/11/1812
Crone, Mr. 4/21/1783
Crook, Lt. William. Of Westminster. [1783]
Crozier, Samuel. Engages SRB 3/23/1796*
Culver, Capt. Daniel. [4/1/1784]
Curtis, Tebina. 4/27/1793*
Curtis & Hubbard. Re: J. Frost's lands 1/30/1804*
Custis, Henry. SRB purchased land from [ca. 1790]
Cutbush, Dr. Re: Tripoli 11/17/1806
Cuthbert, Mr. Navy midshipman. 1/26/1808
Cutin [Cretin?], Silant. Accused by John Nott of burning house. 10/12/1793*; 10/17/1793*; 10/5/1804
Cutler, Doctor. 1/1/1787*
Cutter, James. Re: post office in Rockingham 12/29/1811*
Cutting, Lt. Col. 9/16/1814
Cutts, Charles. Writes to SRB 5/28/1812*
Daggett, David. 7/31/1790
Daggett, Mr. 11/16/1814
Dallas, Alexander J. 4/12/1816
Dana, Col. 5/17/1813
Dana, Daniel. Vt. Council election [ca. 10/10/1811]
Dana, Mr. Member of Vt. General Assembly. 10/13/1801
Dana, Samuel. Of Amherst. 5/14/1785*
Daniel, Dr. Chief surgeon of the Army. 11/4/1811
Danielson, Timothy E. Of Marietta. 2/15/1809*
Davis, Francis. [4/1/1784]
Davis, Gen. 1/22/1811
Davis, George. Chargé d'affaires at Tunis. 11/17/1806; 11/18/1807
Davis, Henry. 1/12/1812
Davis, Joseph. SRB purchased land from [ca. 1790]
Davis, Joshua. Writes to WCB 5/24/1808
Davis, Mr. Re: mail delivery to Burton, Ohio(?) 12/27/1808
Davis, Mr. Writ against 1/23/1826*; 3/11/1826
Davis, Mr. and Mr. Of Kentucky; murdered slave traders. 5/16/1801
Davis, Thomas I. Judge of the Supreme Court of the Indiana Territory. 4/14/1808*
Day, Elkanah. [11/13/1788–7/25/1789]
Day, Maj. 6/13/1786*
Day, Dr. Sylvester. 7/8/1808; 12/15/1808
Dayton, Jonathan. Federalist delegate, representative, and senator from New Jersey; during the Revolution-

ary War served in the Continental Army 1776–1783, attaining the rank of captain; delegate to the Federal Constitutional Convention in 1787 and signed the Constitution; delegate to the Continental Congress 1787–1788; elected to the 2nd and to the three succeeding Congresses (March 4, 1791–March 3, 1799); Speaker of the House of Representatives (4th and 5th Congresses); elected as a Federalist to the United States Senate and served from March 4, 1799, to March 3, 1805; was arrested in 1807 on a charge of conspiring with Aaron Burr in treasonable projects but was released and never brought to trial; the city of Dayton, Ohio, was named for him. 12/13&14/1802

Deane, Mr. Of Springfield? 9/6/1796*

Dearborn, Henry (1751–1829). Representative from Massachusetts; during the Revolutionary War was a captain in Stark's Regiment; elected brigadier general of militia in 1787 and made major general in 1789; elected from a Maine district of Massachusetts to the 3rd Congress and reelected as a Republican to the 4th Congress (March 4, 1793–March 3, 1797); appointed Secretary of War by President Jefferson and served from March 4, 1801, to March 7, 1809. 5/4/1803; 11/7/1803; 1/11/1804; 1/15/1805; 12/17/1805; 2/24/1808; 12/9/1809; 12/15/1809; 12/26/1811?; 1/12/1812; 12/18/1812

Decatur, Capt. Stephen. 12/7/1812

Delaplaine, Joshua. Father of Samuel; deceased. 10/26/1798*

Delaplaine, Samuel. Of New York. 10/26/1798*; Account with SRB 3/21/1800*

Dell, Lt. At Wilkinson Ville 5/16/1801

Demming, Josiah. Of Vt. SRB recommends for collector of Mumphreymagog District in Vt. 2/15/1811

Dening, Mr. 9/15/1813

Denneson, Gelbert. Vt. Council election [ca. 10/10/1811]

Denning, Mr. 7/13/1815

Dennison, George. SRB purchased land from [ca. 1790]

Dennison, Mr. Commodore Barron's secretary. 2/22/1806; 11/17/1806

Dent, Capt. Re: Tripoli 2/26/1806

Dewey, Mr. With I. Tichenor and Crean Brush 1/11/1804

Dexter, Mr. WCB to study law with 6/19/1799

Dickens, Asbury (1760–1861). Secretary of Senate? 1/31/1812; 2/3/1812; 2/20/1812; 5/11/1812; 8/15/1812

Dickerman, John, Jr. In suit against James & Thomas Lamb 3/26/1796*; 3/31/1796*

Dickinson, James. 3/1/1811*; 11/4/1811

Dickinson, James. 11/8/1808*

Dickson, William. U.S. representative from Tennessee. 2/17/1807

Dinsmoor, Samuel. Of Keene, N.H.; judge of probate. 8/26/1820; 3/15/1831

Doolittle, Theophilus. SRB purchased land from [ca. 1790]

Dorr, Capt. Of Roxbury; brother of Mrs. Clapp from Westminster. 11/9/1817

Dorr, Jonathan. Of Roxbury. 12/15/1800; 1/29/1809; 12/9/1809; 12/15/1809; 2/11/1810; 3/6/1810; 12/29/1810; 1/18/1811; 8/17/1811; 1/4/1812*; 1/12/1812; 12/18/1812; 10/16/1813

Dorr, Mrs. Jonathan. 1/29/1809; 2/11/1810; 3/6/1810; 12/29/1810; 1/18/1811; 8/17/1811; 1/12/1812; 12/18/1812

Dorr, Jonathan and Nathaniel. Friends of J. Ruggles. 8/5/1800; 10/5/1800

Dorr, Joseph. Brother of Jonathan; in U.S. Army. 12/15/1800; 12/14/1802; 6/3/1803; 12/2/1806; 11/20/1807; 1/14/1811; Death of 2/9/1810

Dorr, Mrs. Joseph. Death of 12/15/1800; 12/2/1806; 11/20/1807

Dorr, Miss. Friend of J. Ruggles. 10/5/1800

Dorr, Mr. 9/28/1819 (WCB)

Dorr, Mrs. Friend of Mrs. WCB. 5/28/1816; 11/12/1816; 11/9/1817

Dorr, Nathaniel. Merchant sea captain; married Emily Penelope Bradley (adopted daughter of SRB). Bill for schooling of 11/6/1793

Downing, John. SRB purchased land from [ca. 1790]

Drake, James. SRB purchased land from [ca. 1790]

Drew, Thomas C. Vt. senator. 3/15/1812

Drury, Ebenezer. Of Pittsford. 10/14/1780

Drury, Esqr. Of Swanton. 1/16/1808*

Drury, Luther. Of Swanton. 1/16/1808*

Duane, William. 10/8/1812

Dudley, Medad. SRB purchased land from [ca. 1790]

Dudley, Oliver. SRB purchased land from [ca. 1790]

Duer, Mr. Judgment against re: Vt. lands 5/26/1793

Duer, Col. William. Estate of, in Chester, Vt. 7/30/1795*

Dunbar, Daniel. 2/4/1796*

Duncan?, Esqr. 11/25/1800

Dunham, Thomas. Of Westmoreland. 12/4/1818*

DuPonceau, P. S. Of Philadelphia. 2/24/1804

Durkee, Isaiah? 8/10/1814; 1/19/1816; 2/2/1816; 3/25/1816; 3/27/1816

Dutton, J., Jr. 7/2/1813

Dutton, Salmon. [11/13/1788–7/25/1789]

Dutton, Salmon? 4/2/1813; 5/1/1813

Duvall, Mr. U.S. comptroller. 4/2/1810*

Dwight, Chaplain. 7/27/1778

Dwight, Dr. Of Conn. 1/8/1810*

Dwight, Mr. Action vs. SRB 9/28/1821*; 6/24/1822

Dwite, Mr. Of Northampton. 8/28/1815

Eastman, Capt. Enoch. [4/1/1784]

Eastman, J. Artillery lieutenant. 2/4/1800

Eastman, Jonathan E. 5/7/1816

Easton, Mr. 12/13/1787*

Eaton, Lt. Legal case 5/25/1796

Eaton, William (1764–1811). Of Windsor; graduate of Dartmouth College in 1790; infantry commander; appointed consul of Tunis in February 1799; took command of U.S. and native forces in Africa in 1805 and captured the city of Derna (Tripolitan War); held the rank of Maj. Gen. U.S. Army. 5/10/1792; 2/22/1806; 2/24/1806*; 3/23/1806; 4/5/1806; 4/7/1806; 11/17/1806; 2/13/1807; 11/18/1807; 12/27/1807; 2/17/1808; 12/6/1808; 2/15/1809*; 1/15/1810; 2/2/1810*; re: Tripoli 2/26/1806; 4/5/1806

Edwards, Judge. 3/28/1810*

Edwards, Pierpont. 1/20/1800*; 9/24/1806*

Edwards, Timothy (1738–1813). Aaron Burr's guardian and uncle and the oldest son of Jonathon Edwards; judge of probate in Berkshire County, member of the Continental Congress. 8/9/1792*

Edwards, William. Of Northampton; son of Timothy Edwards. 8/9/1792*

Eliot, Mr. 8/10/1814

Ellery, Mr. Duel with Rutledge 6/18/1804

Elliot, James. Of Brattleborough. 3/26/1802; 4/20/1802*; recommended to be commissioner of bankruptcy 9/13/1802; resigned as commissioner of bankruptcy 5/20/1803

Elliot, James. Same as James Elliott (1775–1839); Federalist congressman from Vt., 1803–1813? 3/9/1802; ID —1/4/1803; 1/9/1804; 6/18/1804; 11/29/1811

Elliot, Mr. Possible candidate for Congress from Vt. 12/2/1800*
Elliot, Mr. 2/10/1808
Elliot, Mr. British Indian agent. 1/14/1812
Elliott, James. Clerk of Vt. General Assembly. 10/13/1801
Ellis, Mr. 8/22/1808
Ellis, Simeon. SRB purchased land from [ca. 1790]
Ellsworth, John. Vt. Council election [ca. 10/10/1811]
Ellsworth, Mr. Son of the judge. 9/17/1820*
Ely, Abishae. Account with Pearsall 6/6/1803*; 4/2/1805*
Ely, Joel. Account with Pearsall 6/6/1803*; 4/2/1805*
Ely, Justin. 9/29/1788
Ely, Mr. SRB to defend on behalf of Pearsall 3/21/1800*
Enos, Mr. Re: J. Frost's lands 1/30/1804*
Enos, Mr. 7/13/1815
Enos, Pascal. SRB purchased land from [ca. 1790]
Enos, Paschal P. 3/25/1816; 3/26/1816
Enos, R. 1/20/1802*
Enos, Roger. SRB purchased land from [ca. 1790]
Enos, Roger, Jr. SRB purchased land from [ca. 1790]
Epps, Mr. 1/24/1811
Everett, Mr. 6/14/1813*
Everett, Horace. Of Windsor. 4/22/1821*; 9/28/1821*; 6/24/1822*; 12/28/1822*; 1/9/1823*
Farnsworth, Commissary General. 1/24/1784
Farnsworth, Joseph. [4/1/1784]
Farnsworth, O. Of Windsor. 2/5/1810*
Farnsworth & Churchill. Of Windsor. 2/14/1811
Farrand, Mr. 10/17/1814
Farwell, Abel. Of Hartland. 1/30/1809
Fasset, David. Prominent Vermont family (Bennington). [4/1/1784]
Fawcett, Nathan. SRB purchased land from [ca. 1790]
Fay, Col. Carries letters to and from J. Monroe 7/22/1797
Fay, David. Of Bennington. 9/24/1806*
Fay, Dr. 2/??/1780
Fay, Elijah. [4/1/1784]
Fay, Jonas. Secretary pro tem; Vt. Governor's Council. 2/26/1783; 6/3/1779*; 10/20–22/1779; 12/9/1779; 10/14/1780; [10/10/1786]; Account of [7/31/1783]
Fay, Joseph. 1/2/1801
Fay, Maj. Joseph. [4/1/1784]
Fay, Mr. Of New York. 1/1/1810
Fay, Nathan. [4/1/1784]
Fay, William. 12/29/1811*; 4/2/1813; 5/1/1813
Faye, Huldah. Will attend school in Hartford 9/22/1809
Fellows, Nathaniel. Of Boston; brother-in-law of Nathaniel Ruggles. 1/15/1805
Felt, James. Re: post office in Rockingham 12/29/1811*
Ferris, Reed. 5/30/1785*; SRB purchased land from [ca. 1790]
Ferris, Zebulon. 5/30/1785*
Fesdenton, Joseph. 7/8/1800*
Fessenden, John. 8/10/1814; 1/19/1816
Fessendon, Joseph. 12/10/1811; 7/30/1813; 10/4/1813; 8/10/1814; 1/19/1816; 2/2/1816; 3/25/1816; 3/27/1816
Fessendon, Mr. 6/14/1813*
Field, Mrs. Regarding land in Chester. 12/3/1796*
Fisk, Capt. 4/3/1780*
Fisk, James. Member of Vt. General Assembly. 10/10/1800; 1/30/1804*; 11/5/1808
Fisk, John. Of Stockbridge. 5/26/1780*
Fisk, Js. Member of Vt. General Assembly. 10/5/1804
Fisk, Judge. 11/28/1812
Fisk, Miss. Of Keene, N.H. Mary Goodrich attends school of 8/19/1825

Fisk, Mr. 3/15/1812
Fisk, Mr. Father of John. 5/26/1780*
Fisk, Mr. 4/21/1783
Fisk, Mr. 9/8/1788*
Fisk, Nathan. Justice of the peace. Letter to Sheriff of Windham County 1/12/1784
Fisk, Nathan. [11/13/1788–7/25/1789]
Fisk, Nathan, Jr. 5/17/1783*
Fisk, Solomon. Brother of John. 5/26/1780*
Fitch, Major. 9/16/1800*
Fitch, Russell. Dr. of Brattleboro. 2/3/1811; 11/12/1811; 3/16/1812
Fitch, William. Money owed C. Johnson 12/13/1797*
Flanders, J. Note owed SRB 3/15/1831
Fletcher, James. SRB purchased land from [ca. 1790]
Fletcher, Mr. 12/3/1790
Fletcher, Sam. Vt. Council election [ca. 10/10/1811]
Fletcher, Samuel. Vt. brigadier general. 9/13/1782; 2/26/1783; 10/22/1783; 1/24/1784; [4/1/1784]; 8/6/1800*
Fletcher, Dr. Thomas. Of Burlington Bay. 8/18/1796*
Fletcher & Horton. Re: land in Chester 2/14/1797*
Follert, Martin. [4/1/1784]
Foot, Samuel A. ID 1/4/1811; 11/15/1811; 12/6/1811
Foot, Stilman. Member of Vt. General Assembly. 1/19/1791
Forrest, Robert. Re: father's estate 1/4/1797*
Forrest, Thomas. Author of *Voyage from Calcutta*. 6/20/1794
Fosdick & Procter. Of Boston; in suit against Jonathan Smith. 3/21/1796*; 3/31/1796*
Foster, Dan. Of Weathersfield, Vt. Bond from SRB 10/3/1793
Foster, Mr. 11/24/1811
Fox, James. 3/26/1811
Fr[...], Phinehas. Member Vt. Committee of Pay Table. [ante 10/24/1789]
Francis, Mr. WCB's clerk. 8/3/1811
Francis, Mr. Carries letters from Stella Bradley to SRB 9/22/1809
Francis (Frasier?), Mr. Of Royalton. 1/19/1816
Frasier (Fraser?), Daniel. Bond to Stuyvesant 11/5/1797*; 6/4/1798
Freeman, Mr. [11/13/1788–7/25/1789]
Freeman, Philip. Landowner in Rockingham, Vt. 11/5/1789*
Freeman, Phineas. [4/1/1784]
Freeman, Phinehas. Member of Vermont General Assembly. 10/20/1788
French, Thomas. SRB purchased land from [ca. 1790]
Frost, John. Formerly of N.Y. 7/1/1802*; 9/27/1802; 1/30/1804*; 5/28/1806*; 9/20/1809*; 12/30/1809*
Frost, Martha. 9/15/1828
Frumerie, N. E. Swedish charge d'affaires at Tripoli. 2/24/1806*
Fuller, James. [4/1/1784]
Fuller, Jonathan. [11/13/1788–7/25/1789]
Fuller, Jonathan. Delivered writ to John Nott 10/5/1804
Fulton, Robert. 12/18/1811
<Gaas?>, Mr. 11/9/1817
Gales, Joseph, Jr. 1/15/1814
Gallatin, Albert (1761–1849). Senator-elect and a representative from Pennsylvania; born in Geneva, Switzerland; immigrated to the United States in 1780; served in the Revolutionary Army; member, Virginia House of Representatives 1790–1792; elected to the United States Senate and took the oath of office on December 2, 1793, but a petition filed with

the Senate on the same date alleged that Gallatin failed to satisfy the Constitutional citizenship requirement; in early 1794, the senate determined that Gallatin did not meet the citizenship requirement and declared his election void; elected to the 4th, 5th, and 6th Congresses (March 4, 1795–March 3, 1801); served as secretary of the treasury from 1801 to 1814. 1/11/1804; 2/17/1808; 2/3/1811; 6/3/1812; 6/30/1812; 7/2/1813; 3/8/1810*; 2/15/1811; 1/11/1812*; 12/14/1812

Gallup, Mr. 1/29/1809

Gallup, Oliver. Of Hartland. 11/15/1800*; 1/30/1804*; John Frost's estate 5/28/1806*, 9/20/1809*; recommended to be commissioner of bankruptcy 9/13/1802

Galusha, Jonas. Vt. Supreme Court justice; gov. of Vermont 1815–1819; married a Chittenden daughter. [4/1/1784]; 10/21/1807; 11/5/1808; 3/9/1809; 1/27[1811]; 2/3/1811; [ca. 10/10/1811]

Garlick, Heth. SRB purchased land from [ca. 1790]

Garrand, Mr. ? Of Philadelphia. 6/30/1812

Geere, Shubal. [11/13/1788–7/25/1789]

Gerry, Elbridge. U.S. senator from Maine. 5/19/1812.

Geyer, Mr., and sons, F. & T. Geyer. Friends of Bradleys. 6/19/1799

Gibbs, Rufus. Lister for the town of Westminster. 10/8/1810*

Gibson, Jonathan. Ensign Vt. Militia. 10/18/1792

Gibson, Mr. Of New York. 1/1/1810

Gibson, William. Signee on note 4/4/1797*

Gilbert, Eliot. Of Northfield, N.H. or Vt.; witness to notes in suit vs. Coleman 3/20/1800

Gilbert, Jesse. Of New Haven, Conn. 1/3/1793*; 2/26/1793*

Gilbert, Mr. Of Hanover, N.H. 8/6/1802

Gilbert & Allen. 1/17/1821*

Giles, William Branch. 5/28/1812*; 12/27/1808

Gilman, Mr. Of Alexandria, Virginia. 2/11/1810

Glover, John I. 11/1/1791*; 11/7/1791; 9/4/1792*; 2/26/1793*; 2/20/1797*

Glover, Mr. 11/9/1817

Glover, Mr. Of N.Y. 10/8/1818*

Glynn, James. 8/6/1800*

Glynn, Joseph. 8/6/1800*

Goldsborough, Charles W. (1779–1843). Chief clerk in the Navy Dept. 2/22/1806

Goodale, Rev. David. Legal case 3/23/1796*

Goodall, David. Suit vs. Jedidiah Stark 6/19/1800*; 6/20/1800*

Goodell, Capt. Legal case 5/25/1796

Goodhue, Ebenezer. 11/11/1794

Goodhue, James. 1/19/1816

Goodhue, Joseph. 4/6/1803; 7/17/1806*; 10/10/1807

Goodhue, Mrs. Joseph. 7/17/1806*; 10/10/1806

Goodhue, Josiah. Of Putney. 9/16/1800*

Goodhue, Nathaniel. Brother of Joseph. 7/17/1806*

Goodman, Richard. Of Hartford. 11/7/1818*; 11/16/1818*

Goodrich, Adeline Bradley. Mrs. Samuel Griswold; daughter of SRB. 7/6/1808; 7/29/1808; 8/x/1808; 9/22/1809; 3/7/1818*; 7/17/1818*; 12/4/1818*; 2/27/1819; 5/18/1819*; 5/29/1819*; 9/30/1819; 12/12/1819*; 4/29/1820*; 9/17/1820*; 1/27/1821*; 12/18/1821*; 2/17/1822; 3/5/1822; 4/7/1822*; 4/21/1822*; death of 6/24/1822

Goodrich, Chauncey. (1759–1815) Federalist representative and senator from Connecticut; member, state house of representatives 1793–1794; elected as a Federalist to the 4th, 5th, and 6th Congresses (March 4, 1795–March 3, 1801); elected as a Federalist to the United States Senate to fill a vacancy; reelected and served from October 25, 1807, until May 1813, when he resigned to become lieutenant governor. 4/11/1780; 12/27/1808

Goodrich, E. Brother of Samuel. 5/15/1817*

Goodrich, Elizur, Jr. Of Candee & Goodrich. 11/7/1818*; 11/16/1818*; 12/4/1818*; 4/21/1819*

Goodrich, Mary Boott. 2d wife of Samuel G. Goodrich. 6/23/1827*

Goodrich, Mary E. Daughter of Samuel G. and Adeline Bradley Goodrich. 12/4/1818*; 2/27/1819; 4/23/1819; 12/12/1819*; 4/7/1822*; 4/21/1822*; 8/21/1822; 8/4/1823*; 12/5/1824*; 12/14/1824; 2/26/1825; 5/7/1825*; 8/19/1825; 11/30/1825; 6/23/1827*; 9/15/1828; 5/7/1829*; 5/13/1829; 4/27/1830*

Goodrich, Samuel Griswold (1793–1860). Author of children's books, better known under the pseudonym of "Peter Parly"; married Adeline Gratia Bradley; member of the Massachusetts House of Representatives and the State Senate. 5/15/1817*; 6/23/1817*; 3/7/1818*; 4/14/1818*; 5/21/1818*; 6/11/1818*; 6/22/1818*; 7/17/1818*; 9/11/1818*; 10/7/1818*; 10/24/1818*; 11/16/1818*;12/4/1818*; 2/27/1819; 4/23/1819; 5/18/1819*; 5/29/1819*; 9/30/1819; 11/8/1819; 12/12/1819*; 4/29/1820*; 9/17/1820*; 1/17/1821*; 1/27/1821*; 4/24/1821*; 12/18/1821*; 2/17/1822; 3/5/1822; 4/7/1822*; 4/21/1822*; 6/24/1822; 8/21/1822; 8/4/1823*; 12/5/1824*; 12/14/1824; 2/26/1825; 5/7/1825*; 8/19/1825; 11/30/1825; 6/23/1827*; 5/7/1829*; 5/13/1829; 4/27/1830*

Goodridge, Asael. Summons server. 9/27/1796

Goodridge, Joseph. Writ against 1/23/1826*; Mortgage against 3/11/1826

Goodwrich, Major. 5/26/1780*

Googins, Edmond. 8/11/1809

Gore, Christopher. Gov. of Mass. 12/12/1809

Gorham, M. Note owed SRB 3/15/1831

Gorham, Mathia. Bond to 1/30/1798

Gorton, Stephen. Sargeant vs. Gorton 3/26/1802

Gould, Stephen. SRB purchased land from [ca. 1790]

Gould, William. Clerk of the Superior Court? 8/4/1781

Graham, Dr. Andrew (1729–1785). Resided in Woodbury-Southbury, Conn. and attended Yale College; served as a regimental surgeon at the Battle of White Plains, and again in the Battle of Danbury; he is the father of John Andrew Graham and Nathan Burr Graham. 1/18/1779

Graham, Dr. Chauncy (1727–1784). Graduate of Yale College in 1747. An ordained pastor of the independent Christ Church of Rumbout Precinct. In 1759 the Rev. Chauncy Graham joined an expedition to Canada as chaplain and surgeon under the command of Lord Maj. Gen. Jeffery Amherst. During the Revolutionary War he operated a school and hospital at Fish-Kill, N.Y. He was the father of thirteen children, on of these was John Andrew Graham. 6/1/1780

Graham, Col. Seeks appointment in U.S. consulate in Europe 12/31/1801

Graham, Dr. 11/1/1800

Graham, Lt. Col. John Andrew (1764–1811). He married (1) Jan. 24, 1788, Rachel Hodges and (2) Margaret Lorimer, May 26, 1796. Was involved in mining and land enterprises of a doubtful nature. He was the third lawyer admitted to the Vermont Bar. While in England he became embroiled in the international case involving the ship "Olive Branch." On returning to America he became a clerk of the U.S. Senate for Sen. Stephen R. Bradley. He lived out the remainder of his life in New York City as a criminal lawyer.

Grammds, Mr. Of Philadelphia. 11/6/1793
Granger, Col. 2/5/1783*
Granger, Gideon. U.S. administrator; Postmaster General, 1801–1814; father of Francis Granger (1767–1822). 4/8/1802*; 7/17/1802*; 8/6/1802; 7/11/1807; 3/31/1808*; 12/27/1808; 3/26/1811; [ca. 10/10/1811]; 12/29/1811*; 11/28/1812; 3/18/1814; 3/25/1814
Grant, Charles. SRB purchased land from [ca. 1790]
Grant, Elijah. 5/25/1785*; 7/4/1785*
Grant, John. Westminster selectman. 10/30/1810
Grant, Lieut. [4/1/1784]
Grant, Samuel. 9/15/1828
Gray, Edwin. U.S. rep. from Virginia. 1/21/1808
Green, Mr. A. Of Westminster. 10/8/1810*
Green, Mr. A. Of Brattleboro. 12/14/1824; to look after Mary Goodrich 6/23/1827*
Green, Mrs. A. Of Brattleboro. To look after Mary Goodrich 12/14/1824
Green, Beriah. SRB purchased land from [ca. 1790]
Green, Capt. Beriah. [4/1/1784]
Green, Ebenezer. SRB purchased land from [ca. 1790]
Green, Isaac. Of Windsor. 4/12/1816
Green, Mr. Apptd. postmaster at Brattleboro 2/3/1811
Green, Mr. Of Brattleborough. 5/7/1816
Green, Mr. Carries letter to WCB 4/12/1813
Green, Timothy. Printer at New London, Conn. 8/18/1780
Greene, Benjamin. 12/3/1790
Greenleaf, Ensign. 8/24/1813
Greenleaf, Mr. Draft on by <WAH?>. 3/29/1796*
Gridley, Elihu. 4/3/1780*; 4/4/1780*
Gridley, Nathaniel. 9/1/1780*
Griffin, Ebenezer. Legal case 3/23/1796*
Griffin, John. Of Detroit. 12/21/1810*
Griswold, R. 4/14/1808*
Griswold, Mr. Money owed Reuben Atwater Jr. 12/15/1808
Griswold, Mr. 1/8/1810*
Griswold, Mr. Of Illinois. 12/21/1810
Griswold, William A. 12/14/1815
Grosvenor, Thomas Peabody. ID — 2/2/1814
Grout, Hilkiah. Of Weathersfield. 4/10/1789; 10/9/1789*; 7/31/1790
Guilford, Joshua. 8/28/1815
Guilkey, Mr. 4/3/1780*
H — —, W. A. Of Charlestown. 3/29/1796*
H — — g, S — — l. Of Northampton; enemy of William Coleman. 6/25/1797*
Haithorne, Ebenezer. SRB purchased land from [ca. 1790]
Hale, J. R. WCB handles estate 5/24/1808
Hale, Mr. 6/14/1813*
Hale, Mrs. 5/25/1785*
Hall, A. Note owed SRB 3/15/1831
Hall, Abel. SRB purchased land from [ca. 1790]
Hall, Atherton, Esqr. Signee on note 1/30/1798
Hall, Benjamin. 12/9/1822*
Hall, Benjamin, 2d. SRB purchased land from [ca. 1790]
Hall, David. 6/2/1800*
Hall, Elihu. SRB purchased land from [ca. 1790]
Hall, Elihu, Jr. SRB purchased land from [ca. 1790]
Hall, Esq. Potential witness for Coburn vs. Chandler 8/26/1790*
Hall, Ezra. Rent owed SRB 3/15/1831
Hall, Isaac. 1/25/1791*
Hall, James. SRB purchased land from [ca. 1790]
Hall, John. SRB purchased land from [ca. 1790]
Hall, John, 5th. [ca. 1790]

Hall, Judge. 9/27/1802
Hall, Lot, Esqr. Judge of Windham County, Vt., supreme court. [11/13/1788–7/25/1789]; 9/27/1796; 1/17/1808
Hall, Mr. 4/21/1783
Hall, Mr. 12/29/1811*
Hall, William. 4/2/1813; 5/1/1813
Hall & Green. Of Bellows Falls, Vt. 9/30/1819
Hamblet, Hezekiah. SRB purchased land from [ca. 1790]
Hamilton, Alexander. 12/15/1801; 4/12/1803; 2/12/1811; 12/7/1812
Hamilton, Col. 9/10/1797
Hamilton, Mr. 6/13/1786*
Hanson, Alexander Contee. ID — 2/2/1814
Hanson, Samuel. Of Hanson. 9/10/1802; 10/1/1802
Harding, Seth. Petition to U.S. Senate 1/27/1806
Harlbeet, John, Jr. Re: land deeded to Lemuel Cone 12/30/1809*
Harrington, C. 12/22/1785
Harrington, Joseph. Letter to WCB 9/28/1819
Harrington, William C. 11/11/1807; 2/2/1808; 12/12/1809
Harris, Lt. Ebenezer. [4/1/1784]
Harris, Mr. Dispute with Caleb Clapp 7/1/1798*
Harris, Theophilus. Of Philadelphia. 4/1/1808
Harrison, Samuel. Of Chittenden, Vt. 11/28/1812
Harrison, William Henry. Gov. Indiana Terr. 1/14/1812
Harrow, Joseph. [4/1/1784]
Harwington, Capt. 1/9/1786*
Hastings, Dr. Candidate for N.H. General Court for Charlestown. 1/19/1803; 11/30/1811
Hastings, Seth. Of Mendon. 6/8/1807
Hatch, Lucius. Brother of Uriel. 2/27/1814
Hatch, Major. Brother of Rufus. 10/12/1808
Hatch, Mr. 2/27/1819
Hatch, Narcissa and Hariet. Daughters of Uriel? 10/28/1813
Hatch, Reuben. Vt. Council election [ca. 10/10/1811]
Hatch, Rufus. 10/12/1808
Hatch, Uriel C. 11/10/1801*; 1/4/1803; 6/5/1807; 6/3/1808; 11/15/1810; 2/27/1811; 5/17/1813; 7/2/1813; 9/15/1813; 10/28/1813; 11/22/1813; 10/4/1814; 10/17/1814
Hatch, William C. 11/25/1800
Hatheway, Simeon. [4/1/1784]
Haven, Dr. Father of Nathaniel; former member of Congress. 4/7/1812
Haven, Nathaniel A., Jr. Of Portsmouth, N.H. 3/27/1812; 4/7/1812
Hawkins, Benjamin. U.S. senator from North Carolina. 1/8/1805
Hawley, James. SRB purchased land from [ca. 1790]
Hay, Mr. Member of Vt. General Assembly. 10/10/1800
Hayden, William. Works on SRB' house on Lord Hill in Hartford 6/11/1818*
Hayson, Richard. SRB purchased land from [ca. 1790]
Hayward, Stephen. Capt. Vt. Militia. 10/18/1792
Hazen, Charlotte. Widow of Moses Hazen. Petition to U.S. Senate 3/4/1806; 1/11/1812*
Hazen, Gen. Moses. 3/4/1806
Hazen, William. 3/4/1806
Heath, Sgt. Phineas. [4/1/1784]
<Heileman>, Dr. Of Westminster? 3/7/1803
Heilemens?, Mr. Friend of SRB. 11/14/1802
Helms, William. ID 12/23/1808
Henley, Col. 12/18/1801*
Herman, Lt. Enos. [4/1/1784]
Herman, Lt. Simeon. [4/1/1784]
Herrington, Theophilus. Vt. Supreme Court justice. 10/21/1807

Hickman, Harris H. Attorney general of the Michigan (?) Territory. 2/4/1812
Hilhouse, Mr. 11/24/1783
Hill, Benjamin. 8/11/1809
Hill, Timothy. 6/14/1813*
Hillhouse, James. U.S. senator from Conn. 12/2/1808*; 12/27/1808
Hinckley, Samuel. Of Northampton. 12/10/1807*; 3/11/1808*
Hinkby, Mr. Attorney in Northampton. 4/11/1803*
Hinsdale, Jacob. SRB purchased land from [ca. 1790]
Hinsdale, Capt. James. Transports SRB's trunk from N.Y. to Vt. 5/31/1802*
Hipkins, Capt. Of the *Friends*. 2/20/1812
Hitchcock, Judge. Of Vergennes. Bondsman to Colo. Keyes 8/28/1799*
Hitchcock, Lt. 7/27/1778
Hitchcock, Samuel. Of Manchester; married Ethan Allen's daughter; Member of Vt. General Assembly. 5/30/1785*; 10/22/1790; 1/19/1791
Hitchcock, Valentine. 6/5/1786*
Hitchcock, William. Of Cheshire, Conn. 6/23/1827*
Hodges, Nathan. Of Lyman, N.H. 10/14/1780
Hodgkins, E. Note owed SRB 3/15/1831
Holbrook, John. Partner in John Holbrook & Co. 2/20/1797*; 2/28/1797*
Holbrook, John & Co. Of Brattleboro. 12/8/1794*; 12/25/1794*; Money owed Pearsall & Son and Glover 2/20/1797*; 2/28/1797*
Holbrook, Mr. 2/2/1816
Holland, Ephraim. Of Walpole, N.H. 3/15/1831
Holland, Mr. 1/15/1814
Holland, N. 9/15/1828
Holland, Nathaniel. Of Walpole, N.H. 3/15/1831
Ho<lt?>, Mr. Legal case 5/25/1796
Hopkins, R. Of Vergennes. 8/28/1799*
Hopkins, Roswell. Secretary of Vermont General Assembly. 10/20–22/1779; [4/1/1784], 10/22/1788, 1/10/1791*; 1/12/1791*, 1/19/1791; 9/27/1796
Hopkinson, Joshua. Regarding Clark vs. Ware 8/13/1796*
Holden, James. Indenture with SRB 5/15/1815; Contract with SRB 5/26/1815
Holden, Jonas. 10/18/1792; 1/3/1793*; 2/26/1793*
Holden, Sowtell? 8/22/1808
Holton, Ebenezar. [11/13/1788–7/25/1789]
Holton, Mr. 6/3/1808
Holton, Ms. Jonathan Dorr refers to as "our sister Holton" 8/17/1811
Holton, William. Bond to Stuyvesant 11/5/1797*; 6/4/1798
Holton, Zoheth. Note owed SRB 3/15/1831
Hosford, Aaron. Partner in John Holbrook & Co. 2/20/1797*
Hotchkiss, Capt. 4/21/1783; 11/24/1783
Hotchkiss, Mr. F. W. Of Hartford. 2/27/1819
Hotchkiss, Lent. 11/24/1783
Hotchkiss, Mr. 4/5/1784*
Houghton, Edward. Of Guilford, Vt.; in suit with SRB vs Coleman. 3/20/1800; 5/26/1801*; 10/20/1801*; 12/18/1801*; Bond to SRB 11/10/1801*
How, Simon. Of Guildhall? 8/13/1796*
Howe, Major. 6/17/1788*
Howe, Samuel, Jr. Purchases land from Pearsall 3/21/1800*
Howell, Thomas. SRB purchased land from [ca. 1790]
Howland, Mr. 3/25/1829
Hubbard, Daniel. SRB purchased land from [ca. 1790]
Hubbard, David. SRB purchased land from [ca. 1790]

Hubbard, Elijah. 9/1/1780*
Hubbard, John, Jr. SRB purchased land from [ca. 1790]
Hubbard, Jonathan H. Of Windsor. 4/12/1816; 9/20/1809*; 12/30/1809*; 12/28/1822*; 1/9/1823*
Hubbard, Mr. Postmaster at Montpelier. 4/20/1804
Hubbard, Mr. Attorney for Amasa Paine. 10/7/1806
Hubbard, Mr. 9/28/1821*
Hubbard, Prof. Of Middlebury College? 1/12/1812
Hubble, Elijah. SRB purchased land from [ca. 1790]
Hudson, Barzillai. 1/1/1787*
Hudson & Goodwin (firm?) 6/5/1786*
Huges, Mr. 1/17/1808
Hughes, Col. Former deputy quarter master of U.S. Army. 12/15/1801
Hull, Andrew. SRB's brother-in-law. 1/30/1793
Hull, Andrew, Jr. 12/2/1808*; 1/24/1811; 3/26/1811; 11/15/1811
Hull, Mrs. Andrew, Jr. 11/15/1811
Hull, Betsey. 11/15/1811
Hull, Dr. 1/25/1791*
Hull, Elizabeth Mary Ann Atwater (Mrs. Andrew). 1/30/1793
Hull, Gen. Delivers papers to Wm. Law for SRB 12/27/1808
Hull, Gov. Cousin of Reuben Atwater, Jr. 12/26/1807; 2/4/1812
Hull, Capt. Isaac. At Tripoli. 4/5/1806 [2]; 4/7/1806; 11/17/1806
Hull, Mr. In New Haven. 12/6/1811
Hull, Mr. 3/10/1785; 10/20/1785*; 12/22/1785
Hull, Mrs. 1/4/1811
Hull, Samuel. Of Cheshire, Conn. 10/6/1784*
<Hull?>, Stephen. Of Windsor. 5/10/1792
Hull, Gen. William. Capture of 11/28/1812; 8/11/1827
Hull & Foot. Of New Haven. 3/24/1810
Hunnewell, Joseph. SRB purchased land from [ca. 1790]
Hunt, Arad. Brig. Gen. First Brigade Vt. Militia. 1/24/1791
Hunt, Col. [ca. June 1784]
Hunt, Jonathan. Vermont petition 10/20/1788
Hunt, Mr. Debt to N. Ruggles 12/25/1803; 10/7/1811
Hunt, Samuel. 6/4/1779*
Hunter, Franklin. Of Windsor, Vt. 2/28/1811
Hunter, William. Vt. Council election [ca. 10/10/1811]
Hunter, Judge William. Of Windsor, Vt. 2/28/1811
Huntington, Gurdon. Of Walpole. 12/10/1801
Huntington, Jonathan. Brother of Josiah. 11/7/1791
Huntington, Jonathan. 1/4/1797*; 1/31/1797*; account with Pearsall 6/6/1803*
Huntington, Josiah. Of Rochy Hill near Weathersfield, Conn. 11/1/1791*; 11/7/1791; 8/10/1793*
Hutchinson, Alexander. 8/29/1813
Hutchinson, J. S. 6/3/1808
Hutchinson, T. 11/5/1808
Hutchinson, Titus. Of Woodstock, Vt. 12/2/1800*; 2/28/1811
Hyde, Ensign Charles. Of Bennington. 5/10/1792
Ide, Joseph. Money owed C. Johnson 12/13/1797*; Signee on note 1/30/1798
Imlay, W. H. Of Hartford 2/27/1819
Ingersoll, Jared. Of Philadelphia. 2/24/1804
Ingraham vs. Geyer. 7/31/1801*
Ivers, Hannah. 2/14/1797*
Ivers, Hezekiah. Of N.Y. 5/24/1792*; 8/20/1792*; 4/25/1795*; 2/14/1797*; Death of 1/25/1796*
Ivers, Mary. Sister of James Arden. 6/18/1799*; 1/1/1800*; 5/15/1800*; 6/21/1803*; 12/13/1804*
Ivers, Mrs. Lands in Chester 3/6/1797*; 4/14/1797*

Ivers, Thomas. 8/20/1792*; 2/14/1797*; 3/6/1797*; 4/14/1797*
Ives, Abraham, Esqr. [4/1/1784]
Ives, Mr. 12/13/1787*
Ives, Samuel. SRB purchased land from [ca. 1790]
Jackson, Andrew. 2/18/1815; 1/16/1823
Jackson, Deputy Sheriff. 12/13/1787*
Jacob, Mr. Of Hartland or Windsor? 12/3/1796*
Jacob, Stephen. Clerk of Vermont General Assembly; Vt. commissioner. 10/20/1788; 2/9/1790
Jacob, Stephen. SRB purchased land from [ca. 1790]
Jacobs, Esqr. 10/12/1793*
Jacobs, Stephen. Of Windsor, Vt. 10/7/1806; 3/31/1808*
Jarvis, Dr. Charles. Physician and surgeon to the Marine Hospital in Charlestown, Mass. 11/20/1807
Jay, John. 12/25/1794
Jefferson, Thomas (1743–1826). Served as governor of Virginia from 1779 to 1781; Minister to France from 1784 to 1789; secretary of state under George Washington; third president of the United States of America. 8/14/1780; 1/5/1801; 1/24/1801; 4/1/1802*; 9/13/1802; 5/20/1803; 12/26/1807; 10/21/1807; 11/11/1807; 1/26/1808; 2/2/1808; 3/16/1808; 1/29/1809; 5/5/1812
Jennison, Daniel A. 9/15/1828
Jessenden(?), William. Of Brattleborough. 4/23/1810*
Johns, Mr. Delivers letter from SRB to L. Royse 7/6/1808
Johnson, Caleb. Receipt to, for debt collection 12/13/1797*
Johnson, Capt. Of Burlington. 2/2/1808
Johnson, D. Note owed SRB 3/15/1831
Johnson, Dr. Attends SRB's daughter Louisa 11/30/1811
Johnson, Dr. Of Walpole. 3/15/1812
Johnson, John. French Negro in Rutland, Vt. 1/12/1791*
Johnson, Lewis. Student of Wm. C. Harrington. 2/2/1808
Johnson, Luis. [1783]
Johnson, Miles. 7/27/1788*; 6/29/1789; 7/1/1789*; 9/4/1789*; 10/9/1789*; 7/31/1790; 7/2/1791; 10/18/1792; 10/26/1798*; 9/16/1800*
Johnson, Mr. Vt. land claim 5/26/1793
Johnson, Mr. 11/9/1817
Johnson, Moses. Bondsman? 9/27/1796; 7/24/1784*
Johnson, Philemon. SRB purchased land from [ca. 1790]
Johnson, Col. Robert. Sheriff of Orange County. SRB purchased land from [ca. 1790]
Johnston, Samuel. U.S. senator from North Carolina. 1/8/1805
Johonnot, Mr. Naval agent at Boston. 1/12/1812
Jonah? 10/4/1783
Jones, Dr. Of Washington. 3/22/1810
Jones, Jabez. 4/23/1812
Jones, John Rice. Of Illinois. 11/18/1810*
Jones, Judge. Of Illinois, later Mississippi. 12/21/1810
Jones, Mr. Re: J. Frost's lands 1/30/1804*
Jones, Mr. Of Washington? 11/4/1811
Jones, Reuben. [11/13/1788–7/25/1789]
Judson, Jonathan. SRB purchased land from [ca. 1790]
Kelly, John. Of N.Y. 7/30/1795*; 5/15/1800*
Kennedy, William. SRB purchased land from [ca. 1790]
Kent, Seth. SRB purchased land from [ca. 1790]
Keyes, Col. 8/28/1799*
Keyes, Elias. Deeded land to Lemuel Cone 12/30/1809*
Keys, Esqr. 6/17/1788*
Keys, Stephen. SRB purchased land from [ca. 1790]
Kidder, O. 7/31/1790
Kilbourn, Samuel. Of Hartford. 7/15/1789*

Kimball, Abraham. SRB purchased land from [ca. 1790]
King, Adonijah. 3/26/1802
King, Rufus (1755–1827). Politician, diplomat; represented Massachusetts at the Continental Congress (1784–87) and the Constitutional Convention (1787); became a U.S. senator representing New York (Fed.; 1789–96); served as ambassador to Great Britain (1796–1803); returned to the Senate (Fed., N.Y.; 1813–25) and was the last Federalist to run for the presidency (1816); retiring from the Senate, he went back to Great Britain in 1825 as the U.S. ambassador, but illness forced him to come home (1826) where he soon died. 1/20/1802*
Kingsbary, Dr. Seeking appointment as surgeon's mate 3/9/1800; 3/9/1804
Kingsbery, Major J. 11/13/1796*
Kingzley, Alpha. Of Tennessee. 12/22/1811*
Kinsman, William H. SRB purchased land from [ca. 1790]
Kirby, Ephraim. 5/15/1791*; 6/1/1792*; 1/5/1803
Kirtland, Turhand. 1/30/1810*
Knickerbacor, John. [4/1/1784]; SRB purchased land from [ca. 1790]
Knight, Capt. 9/16/1814
Knight, Mr. 5/29/1795*
Knight, Elijah. Of Rockingham. 4/4/1797*; 12/29/1811*
Knight, Judge (Elijah?). In Rockingham, Vt. 5/26/1807; 9/25/1813; 9/16/1814
Knight, Samuel. Brattleboro town clerk & justice of the peace. 9/17/1795*; 6/4/1798; 5/20/1803
Knight, Simeon. 8/24/1807; 11/20/1808; 11/14/1812
Knights, Judge. Attorney for Major Brattle 4/11/1797*
Knoulton, Judge. 7/31/1790; 6/7/1805
Knoulton, Luke. Mortgage in Newfane. 6/29/1789
Knoulton, Luke, & Co. 6/7/1805
Knowlton, Ekekiel. 5/25/1805
Knox, Henry. Secretary of war. 5/10/1792
Kreps?, J. 8/24/1813
Labogh, A. Re: tomb for 2d Mrs. SRB. 3/14/1804*; 9/28/1804
Labogh. Jno. Re: tomb for 2d Mrs. SRB. 9/28/1804
Lake, Elnathan. SRB purchased land from [ca. 1790]
Lamb, Anthony. Of Hackensack. 12/15/1801
Lamb, Anthony. Candiate for office of military agent for N.Y. 3/20/1809*
Lamb, Gen. Anthony. 12/26/1807
Lamb, James. Of Boston. In suit against J. Dickerman and <Samuel?> Smith. 3/26/1796*; 3/31/1796*
Lamb, Larned. Of Montpelier. Nominated for Captain's commission 11/5/1808
Lamb, Thomas. Of Boston; in suit against J. Dickerman and <Samuel?> Smith. 3/26/1796*; 3/31/1796*
Lamberton, Allen. [4/1/1784]
Lammot, Daniel. Of Baltimore. 4/5/1804; 6/2/1804
Lane, John. [11/13/1788–7/25/1789]
Langdon, Chauncey. Vt. Council election [ca. 10/10/1811]
Langdon, John? 5/19/1812
Langdon, John. N.H. governor. 1/19/1803; 3/22/1810
Lansing, Abraham. SRB purchased land from [ca. 1790]
Larrabee, Benjamin. Money owed C. Johnson 12/13/1797*
Latten, Thomas. SRB purchased land from [ca. 1790]
Laurie, Rev. James. Of Washington. 1/12/1812
Law, Mr. Member of Vt. General Assembly. 10/13/1801
Law, Mr. 4/12/1813
Law, Thomas? Of Washington. 11/12/1811; 11/9/1816

Law, Thomas. Of Washington. 12/30/1811
Law, William. 11/16/1814
Law, William. Of Cheshire. 12/27/1808
Lawrence, John. Of Weathersfield. 10/9/1789*; 10/3/1793
<Lawrens, Rawsom?> 5/15/1815
Lear, Tobias. 2/22/1806; 2/26/1806; 11/18/1807; 2/17/1808; 8/23/1808; 12/6/1808
Leavenworth, Edmund. SRB purchased land from [ca. 1790]
Leavenworth, William. Writes to WCB 5/7/1816
Lee, Capt. Claim against 3/7/1818*
Lee, Maj. Gen. Charles (1731–1782). Born in England, first came to America as a British officer serving in the French and Indian War. Joined Washington's army in 1775 as a major general. He left the Continental Army under a cloud and was dismissed in 1780. 1/24/1776; 2/19/1776
Lee, Mrs. Mother of Mary Boott Goodrich. 6/23/1827*
Lee, Seth. 9/1/1780*
Lee & Haynsworth, Messrs. Of Charlestown, S.C. 3/6/1810
Leib, Michael. ID — 3/17/1814; 3/25/1814; 4/1/1814
Leigh, Mr. Re: the estate of Lord Mayor Wilson of London 12/5/1806
Leigh, Mrs. Widow of the Lord Mayor Wilson of London 12/5/1806
Leppenerell, R. Note owed SRB 3/15/1831
Le Roy, Jacob, & Sons. 9/10/1797
Levaque, Agustus. Canadian refugee. 4/23/1812
Leverett, Mr. 4/22/1821*
Leverett, Thomas. Of Windsor. 3/31/1808*; 4/12/1816
Lewis, Meriwether (1774–1809). U.S. explorer with William Clark. 5/4/1803
Lewis, Oliver. 10/28/1782*
Limeg, Mr. (alias Church). 4/23/1787*
Lindsey, Thomas. SRB purchased land from [ca. 1790]
Linsle, Joseph, Jr. Of N.Y. Atty. for J. Frost 1/30/1804*
Livingston, Edward. Of N.Y. 2/24/1804
Livingston, Robert R. (1746–1813). Lawyer, diplomat; member of Continental Congress (1775–76, 1779–81, 1784–85); secretary of the Department of Foreign Affairs (1781–83); ambassador to France (1801–04); chancellor of New York (1777–1801). 5/26/1801*
Livingston, Walter. Vt. land claim 5/26/1793
Livingstone, Widow. 9/15/1828
Locklin, Davis. [11/13/1788–7/25/1789]
Locklin, Jonathan. 9/17/1795*
Locklin, Levi. [11/13/1788–7/25/1789]
Logan, George. (1753–1821). Republican senator from Pennsylvania; member, state house of representatives 1785–1789, 1795–1796, and 1799; appointed and subsequently elected as a Republican to the United States Senate to fill a vacancy and served from July 13, 1801, to March 3, 1807; published several agricultural pamphlets. 12/13&14/1802; 9/26/1830
Loomis, Beriah. Member of Vt. General Assembly. 10/5/1804; [ca. 10/10/1811]
Loomis, Mr. 12/13/1787*
Lord, John G. [4/1/1784]
Lovejoy, Mr. 5/14/1785
Lovell, Enos. [11/13/1788–7/25/1789]
Lovell, James. 1/17/1808
Low, (Nicholas?). Agent for A. Thompson's land in Chester 12/21/1797*
Luce, Elihu. Of Hartland. 11/24/1811
Luce, Mr. 1/30/1809
Luis, Gabriel. Letter to WCB 1/16/1803
Lull, Mr. Friend of SRB. 2/10/1802; 11/14/1802

Ly — — n, Wm. Enemy of William Coleman 6/25/1797*
Lyman, Daniel. Of New Haven. 2/5/1783*
Lyman, Elias. Of Hartford. 4/1/1802*; 7/15/1809*
Lyman, Elias. Tomb of 2d Mrs. SRB shipped to 9/28/1804
Lyman, Elihu. Of Northampton. 8/13/1790*
Lyman, Elihu. Of New Haven. 3/8/1784*
Lyman, Gaius. WCB orders shad from 8/4/1814; 7/15/1809*
Lyman, John, Jr. Land claim in Springfield 10/5/1804
Lyman, Justice. Tomb of Mrs. SRB shipped to 9/28/1804
Lyman, Justin. Of Hartford. 4/1/1802*; 7/15/1809*
Lyman, Levi. Rent owed SRB 3/15/1831
Lyman, Mr. Of Northfield; deputy sheriff 6/25/1797*
Lyman, Gen. Phineas. French & Indian War 1/20/1802*; 1/22/1811
Lyman, William. 12/5/1806
Lyon, Asa. Vt. Council election [ca. 10/10/1811]
Lyon, Matthew. Of Arlington. 10/14/1780; 4/5/1781; 4/6/1781; 1/19/1791; 11/28/1812
Macdonough, Commodore Thomas. 9/16/1814
Macheaus?, Paul. Vermont landowner. 10/20/1788
Macon, Mr. U.S. senator? 2/11/1810
Madison, Dolly Paine. 12/30/1811; 10/16/1813
Madison, James (1751–1836). Fourth president of the United States; served in Continental Congress during the Revolution; became secretary of state upon Jefferson's accession to the presidency in 1801; best known for his success in the Tripolian War and the purchase of Louisiana. 4/10/1808; 2/7/1809; 12/20/1809; 1/8/1810*; 12/30/1811; 5/5/1812; 5/19/1812; 10/8/1812; 11/28/1812
Madison, Rev. James. ID 12/10/1808*
Maese, Mr. Former pay master general. 2/20/1818
Mahumed, <Remed>. Secy. of state of Hamet Bashaw. 2/22/1806
Mallory, Mr. 1/25/1791*
Mansfield, Samuel. SRB purchased land from [ca. 1790]
Mantson? Mr. 6/13/1786*
Marcy, Hadlock. Of Westminster. 11/19/1804*; 12/28/1804
Maréchaux, J. Stella Bradley's French instructor. 7/10/1804*
Marion, Esqr., Robert. Delivers letter from Rufus Hatch 10/12/1808
Marks, Jonathan. SRB purchased land from [ca. 1790]
Marsh, Daniel. [4/1/1784]
Marsh, John. SRB purchased land from [ca. 1790]
Marsh, Mr. Member of Vt. General Assembly. 10/13/1801
Marsh, Mr. 4/22/1821*
Marshall, John (1755–1835). Chief justice of the U.S. Supreme Court. He was secretary of state from June 6, 1800, to March 4, 1801, under John Adams. His appointment to the Supreme Court was dated January 31, 1801.
Martin, D. Note owed SRB 3/15/1831
Marvin, Mr. Member of Vermont General Assembly. 10/20/1788; 10/22/1790
Mason, Jeremiah (1768–1848). Studied law in Westminster, Vermont, under Stephen R. Bradley; became a U.S. senator. 12/26/1789; 3/27/1812; Accused by John Noth of burning house 10/12/1793*, 10/5/1804
Mathers, James. Late sergeant at arms of the U.S. Senate. 9/7/1811
Mathews, Mr. Of Claremont, N.H. 9/29/1788

Matlock, John. Of Peacham. 2/9/1809
Matthews, James. [4/1/1784]
May, Edwin. 3/8/1819*
May, Eleazer. Father of SRB's clerk. 12/12/1796*
May, Hezekiah. 1/31/1795
May, Mr. Carries letter to WCB. 5/7/1799; 1/24/1801; 2/10/1802
May, Mr. Carries letters from Stella Bradley to SRB. 9/22/1809
May, Mr. Of Westminster. 2/3/1812; 3/15/1812; 9/30/1819
Mayes, Mr. Clerk of SRB. 6/25/1796*; 12/12/1796*
Maynard, Mr. 12/29/1811*
McAllister, Robert. Account with Pearsall 6/6/1803*; 4/2/1805*
McClave, John. SRB purchased land from [ca. 1790]
McClung, Maj. [4/1/1784]
McIntosh, Mr. Former postmaster of Chickesaw Nation/Mississippi. 1/24/1803
McKean, Jos. B. Of Philadelphia. 2/24/1804
McNeill Esqr, Daniel. Commander of U.S. Boston frigate. 12/21/1801
McRae, Alexander. 1/1/1810
Mead, William. SRB purchased land from [ca. 1790]
Mecklenburg, Gen. 8/14/1780
Meigs, Return J., Jr. ID — 3/17/1814; 3/25/1814; 4/1/1814
Merrick, Samuel? 8/11/1809
Merrill, Nathaniel. SRB purchased land from [ca. 1790]
Metcalf, R. Deputy sheriff. Sargeant vs. Gorton 3/26/1802
Miles, Abner. Of Putney, Vt. Petitions Vt. General Assembly 9/27/1796
Miller, Eleazer. Of N.Y. 7/2/1791
Miller, Joe. Vt. Council election [ca. 10/10/1811]
Mills, Mr. Attorney for Amasa Paine 10/7/1806
Minchin? & Welch. Write to WCB 5/24/1808
Minott, Samuel. Colonel of Vt. militia. 7/17/1792; 8/25/1792
Minturn & Champlen. Of New York. Attaches property of Oliver & George W. Barber & Co. 2/20/1797*
Mitchal, Isaac. 5/14/1785
Mitchel, Justus. Re: land deeded to Lemuel Cone 12/30/1809*
Mitchell, Justice. SRB purchased land from [ca. 1790]
Mitchell, Dr. S. L. Of Washington. 12/30/1811
Mitchill, Dr. 3/4/1806
Moffett, Joseph. Of Danville. 2/9/1803; 4/20/1804
Montgomery, Mr. Housemate of SRB in Washington. 3/22/1810
Montgomery, Richard. ID WCB-7/4/1799
Monroe, James. 7/12/1797*; 7/22/1797; 1/2/1801; 4/10/1808; 11/24/1811; 2/3/1812; 4/6/1816
Moore, <Alphonsus>. Of Peacham. 11/2/1801
Moore, Col. 3/26/1796*
Moore, Col. Housemate of SRB in Washington. 3/22/1810
Morgan, Capt. 1/17/1814
Morgan, Mr. J. Of Hartford. 1/22/1818*; 5/21/1818*; 9/11/1818*; 10/7/1818*; 10/8/1818*; 10/24/1818*; 11/16/1818*; 11/8/1819; 9/17/1820*
Morgan, Johnathan. Hartford merchant. 7/31/1790; 5/15/1791*; 11/1/1791*; 11/7/1791; 8/10/1793*; 3/18/1811*; 12/7/1812; 3/25/1813*
Morris, Chief Justice. 1/24/1788*
Morris, Col. 7/31/1790
Morris, Gen. 9/22/1798*
Morris, Gen. 1/13/1803
Morris, Gen. (Lewis Richard?) Duel between Ellery and Rutledge 6/18/1804

Morris, Gouverneur (1752–1816). Delegate and senator from New York; member, New York provincial congress 1775–1777; lieutenant colonel in the State militia in 1776; member of the Continental Congress in 1778 and 1779; signer of the Articles of Confederation in 1778; Pennsylvania delegate to the convention that framed the Constitution of the United States in 1787; minister plenipotentiary to France 1792–1794; elected in 1800 as a Federalist to the United States Senate to fill a vacancy and served from April 3, 1800, to March 3, 1803; chairman of the Erie Canal Commission 1810–1813. 3/9/1802
Morris, Lewis Richard (1760–1825). Representative from Vermont; member of the state house of representatives 1795–1797 and 1803–1808; elected as a Federalist to the 5th, 6th, and 7th Congresses (March 4, 1797–March 3, 1803). 10/22/1790; 1/12/1791*; 10/12/1793*; 7/30/1795*; 1/30/1804*
Moseley, Judge. Of Rutland. 12/13/1787*
Moss, John. 6/5/1786*; SRB purchased land from [ca. 1790]
Mower, Nahum. 12/28/1804
Mullett, Thomas. Senior partner of Thos. Mullett, J. J. Evans & Co. (British). 2/3/1812
Murray, Alexander. 2/17/1808
Negus, Mr. Of Charlestown? 4/30/1785*
Ness, Miss. Re: Stella Bradley 6/10/1804
Newcomb, Richard E. Partner of William Coleman. 6/24/1797*; 6/25/1797*; 7/6/1797*; 7/12/1797*; 4/11/1803*; 8/28/1815?
Nicko[...], Capt. Of ship *John Andrew*. 12/15/1809
Nicholson, Capt. 2/17/1808
Niles, Nathaniel. Member of Vt. General Assembly. 1/19/1791; 10/10/1800; 1/30/1804*
Noble, Morgan. SRB purchased land from [ca. 1790]
Norman, John. Of Ireland. 11/17/1800*
Norman, Mr. Bills Jacob and Asa Warner 4/2/1805*
Norman, Mr. and Mrs. In suits vs. Spooner and Rand 11/1/1800
Norman, Thomas. SRB sends bills drawn by to Pearsall 11/17/1800*
Norton, John. Justice of the peace and tavern owner in Westminster, Vermont. 10/12/1793*; 10/17/1793*; 10/5/1804
Norton, Mr. 4/3/1780*
Nott [Noth?], John. Petitioner against SRB. 10/12/1793*; 10/5/1804
Numa, Mr. 6/18/1804
Nutting, Mr. Of Westminster. 3/15/1812
Nye, Jonathan. Of New Braintree. 8/18/1796*
Oak, Seth. Justice of the peace. 8/4/1781
Olcott, Gen. 9/29/1788
Olcott, Elias. [11/13/1788–7/25/1789]
Olcott, Jonathan. 11/7/1791
Olcott, Martha. Of Springfield. Bill from, for boarding WCB 9/6/1796*
Olcott, Mills. Brother of Roswell. 9/22/1798*
Olcott, Roswell. Of Norwich. 9/22/1798*
Olds, Benjamin. 8/6/1800*
Olds, Benjamin, Jr. 8/6/1800*
Olds, Col. 8/6/1800*
Olds, Joseph. Of Marlborough. 8/6/1800*
Olin, Gideon. Member of Vt. General Assembly; U.S. congressman from Vt. 10/22/1790; 1/19/1791; 10/24/1800; 1/9/1804
Olin, Henry? Member of Vt. General Assembly. 1/30/1804*
Olin, Judge. 8/7/1801
Olmsted, Joseph. 7/17/1818*

Index of Bradley's Correspondents and Their Letters

Onion, Ichabod. Money owed C. Johnson 12/13/1797*
Orentt, Consider. [11/13/1788–7/25/1789]
Osgood, N. Clerk of Vt. General Assembly. 10/24/1800
Otis, Harrison Gray? 5/28/1812*
Otis, Harrison Gray. 1/29/1809
Otis, Samuel A. Of Boston; Secy. of the Senate of the U.S. 12/5/1806; 2/17/1807
Pa[...], Elijah. Member Vt. Committee of Pay Table. [ante 10/24/1789]
Packer, Mr. Of Guilford? 1/24/1784
Page, Col. Surveyor of Rockingham, Vt. 5/26/1807
Page, Mr. Owed money by John Atkinson 6/2/1798*
Page, William, Jr. Secretary of Vt. Council. 10/5/1804; 10/28/1805; 4/2/1813?
Paine, Amasa. 11/4/1800*; 10/7/1806
Paine, Elijah. Member of the Vermont General Assembly and a U.S. senator from Vermont. 10/22/1788; [10/27/1789]; 2/9/1790; 1/19/1791; 12/18/1801*; 9/24/1807*
Paine, Lieut. 1/17/1808
Paine, Mr. Representing Robert Troop 5/26/1793
Paine, Mr. Of Windsor. Debtor of Pearsall 7/31/1790; 4/27/1793*
Paine, Mr. Counsel for Col. John Sargeant 3/26/1802
Palmer, Aaron H. Works? at the White House 1/8/1810*
Palmer, Mr. Clerk of Vt. Gen. Ass. canvassing committee. [ca. 10/10/1811]
Panderson, Lemuel. Recommended to be postmaster of Burton, Ohio(?) 12/27/1808
Parker, Andrew. SRB purchased land from [ca. 1790]
Parker, Daniel. Clerk of War Dept. 1/7/1814*
Parker, Dedimus. SRB purchased land from [ca. 1790]
Parker, Lt. Ebenezer. [4/1/1784]
Parker, Gamaliel. SRB purchased land from [ca. 1790]
Parker, Isaac. SRB purchased land from [ca. 1790]
Parker, Jacob. SRB purchased land from [ca. 1790]
Parker, Jesse. SRB purchased land from [ca. 1790]
Parker, Mr. Agent or attorney of Lemuel Cone. 12/30/1809*
Parker, Timothy. [11/13/1788–7/25/1789]
Parmele, Capt. Alexander. Father of Samuel D. 12/21/1801
Parmele, Samuel Davis. Of N.Y. 12/21/1801; 3/16/18[02?]
Parsons, Gen. 7/27/1778
Partridge, Joseph. Money owed C. Johnson 12/13/1797*
Patrick, Joseph. Of Kingston. 12/30/1809*
Patten, Nathaniel. [10/10/1786]
Pattison, Judge. Death of 9/24/1806*
Payson, Henry. Of Baltimore. 1/12/1812
Peacock, Thomas. Money owed C. Burkett 8/18/1798*
Pearce, Mr. Employer? of Joseph Ruggles, Jr. 6/19/1799
Pearsall, Thomas. 10/12/1785*; 11/28/1787*; 7/26/1788; 7/27/1788*; 4/10/1789; 6/29/1789; 7/1/1789*; 9/4/1789*; 10/9/1789*; 7/31/1790; 11/1/1791*; 11/7/1791; 8/14/1792; 9/4/1792*; 2/26/1793*; 4/27/1793*; 10/3/1793; 12/1/1794*; 12/8/1794*; 12/25/1794*; 3/7/1795*; 1/4/1797*; 1/31/1797*; 7/22/1797; 9/10/1797; 6/2/1798*; 10/26/1798*; 2/23/1800*; 3/20/1800; 3/21/1800*; 5/15/1800*; 7/25/1800*; 9/16/1800*; 11/17/1800*; 12/24/1800; 4/1/1802*; 5/31/1802*; 8/12/1802*; 6/6/1803*; 6/8/1804*; 4/2/1805*; 12/5/1806
Pearsall, Thomas C. Son of Thomas. 11/1/1791*
Pearsall, Thomas & Son. 2/20/1797*; 2/28/1797*; 8/18/1798*; 7/1/1802*
Pees, Judge. Brother-in-law of Gideon Granger. 12/27/1808
Pell, Elijah. Of Persall & Pell. 7/26/1788; 11/1/1791*
Penniman?, Dr. 2/3/1811

Penniman, Jabez. 12/7/1801; 12/21/1807; 1/16/1808*; 1/26/1808; 3/15/1808; 4/10/1808; 4/24/1811
Penniman, Mrs. Jabez. 12/21/1807; 1/26/1808; 4/24/1811
Penniman, John. 6/2/1800*
Pennine?, Dr. Of Westminster. 11/14/1801
Perham, Lemuel. 5/14/1785
Perkins, Elisha. SRB purchased land from [ca. 1790]
Perrin, Abel. 3/25/1829
Perry, Capt. 5/13/1829
Peters, John T. Of Hebron. 2/15/1811
Peters, Dr. Samuel A. Of New York. 1/8/1810*
Platt, Mrs. Client of WCB. 11/21/1812
Phelps, Charles. Of Townshend. 12/20/1809
Phelps, Miss. Student of Mrs. Seton. 12/15/1816
Phelps, Mr. Action of ejectment vs. 8/9/1792*
Phelps, Samuel. Bondsman for Jesse Ware. 6/25/1796*
Phillips, John. SRB purchased land from [ca. 1790]
Phippany, Mr. 5/25/1785*; 7/4/1785*
Pickering, Timothy. ID — 2/2/1814; 12/27/1808; 12/1/1809; 2/14/1823; 2/25/1823
Pike, Capt. Delivers letter from Simeon Knight 8/24/1807
Pitcher, Ebenezer. SRB purchased land from [ca. 1790]
Plumer, William. Member of the U.S. Senate from New Hampshire 1803–1807. 11/18/1807 [2]; 12/21/1810; 1/31/1811
Plympton, Joseph. 1/4/1812*; 1/12/1812
Pomeroy, Hen[r]y. [11/13/1788–7/25/1789]
Pomeroy, Mr. 10/20/1785*
Porter, Asa. Of Haverhill. 11/3/1796*; 12/3/1796*; 12/13/1796
Porter, Mr. 7/28/1814
Post, <Justins>. West Point cadet. 10/21/1807
Post, Martin. Clerk of Vt. General Assembly. 10/5/1804; 10/28/1805
Potter, Dr. Of Cheshire? 3/10/1785; 3/10/1785
Potter?, Mr. Member of Vt. General Assembly. 10/5/1804
Potter, Capt. Reuben. Of Brattleborough. Claim to Brattle lands 4/20/1802*
Power, Col. Hunt. 6/4/1779*
Pratt, Capt. 8/25/1800*
Pratt, Samuel. Witness on permit 7/3/1799
Preble, Edward. U.S. Navy commodore. 2/22/1806
Prentice, Samuel. Recommended for postmaster of Montpelier 4/20/1804
Prentice, Thomas. Of Weathersfield, Vt. 10/3/1793
Prentiss, John. 8/22/1825*
Prentiss, Mr. Member of Vt. General Assembly. 10/13/1801
Prescott, Abel. SRB purchased land from [ca. 1790]
Presstis, Samuel. Of Lunenberg. 8/13/1796*
Preston, Colburn. Of Rockingham. 10/14/1780
Preston, Samuel? 7/27/1778
Pride, Mr. Westminster friend of WCB. 6/19/1799
Priestley, Joseph 1733–1804. English chemist and clergyman; wrote "The History and Present State of Electricity" 1767, "Essay on the First Principles of Government" 1768, 4-volume "A General History of the Catholic Church" 1790–1802; discovered element oxygen as "dephlogisticated air" independently of Karl Scheele 1774; immigrated to U.S. 1794. 2/19/1804
<Prire>, Amasa. Of Windsor. 1/13/1803
The Prophet. Fought battle on the Wabash. 1/14/1812
Purkins, William. 4/3/1780*
Putnam, G. Works on SRB' house on Lord Hill in Hartford 6/11/1818*
Putnam, Seth. 5/17/1783*

Quinton, Joseph. 12/13/1797*
R., Sally. Friend of WCB. 6/19/1799; 11/14/1801?; 2/10/1802
Raighter, Col. 1/26/1808
Ralston, Alexander, Jr. Writes to WCB 6/9/1809
Rand, Mr. Sued by Mr. and Mrs. Norman 11/1/1800
Randol, Elisha, & Iszeble his wife. Of Springfield, Vt. 10/12/1793*
Ranney, Benjamin. Lister for the town of Westminster. 10/8/1810*
Ranney, Ephraim, Jr. Westminster selectman. 10/30/1810; 3/15/1831
Ranney, Waitstill? 2/14/1798*; 6/18/1799*; 1/1/1800*; 5/15/1800*; 6/21/1803*; 12/14/1803*; 3/26/1811
Ranney & Williams. Offer to buy Ivers land in Chester 3/6/1797*
Ransom, Amos. Proprietor of Hartford Coffee House. 3/18/1811*
Ranstead, Mr. 8/4/1814
Rawle, William. Of Philadelphia. 2/24/1804
Ray, Joshua. SRB purchased land from [ca. 1790]
Ray, Joshua, Jr. SRB purchased land from [ca. 1790]
Read, Micah. Of Westmoreland. Collection of note for 4/4/1797*
Red(d)ington, George B. 6/23/1827*; 9/15/1828; 4/27/1830
Reed, Philip. 5/19/1812; 5/24/1812
Reed, Thomas. SRB purchased land from [ca. 1790]
Reeve, Tapping. Founder of the Litchfield Law School. 10/12/1793*; 11/16/1822
Reynolds, Peter. Land owner in Peru, Vt. 7/17/1818*
Reynolds, Samuel. Land owner in Peru, Vt. 7/17/1818*
Rhea, John. U.S. representative from Tennessee. 2/17/1807
Rhea, Jonathan. Of Trenton. 12/23/1808; 6/9/1809
Rice, Col. 7/28/1814
Rice, Stephen. [4/1/1784]
Rice, Thomas. SRB purchased land from [ca. 1790]
Rich, Charles. Member of Vt. General Assembly; Vt. congressman. 10/5/1804; 2/18/1815
Richard, Widow. Of Westminster. [1783]
Richards, Alexander. Money owed Pearsall 7/25/1800*
Richards, Mark. 7/5/1796*; 1/8/1799*; 2/8/1800; 12/15/1800; 9/13/1802; 12/15/1808; 3/6/1810; 2/3/1812*; 3/15/1812; 11/9/1817; 2/20/1818; 9/30/1819; Pays bill for schooling of Nathanial Dorr 11/6/1793
Richards, Mark? Sheriff?. Of Westminster. 11/14/1801; 9/30/1803*; 12/25/1803; [ca. 10/10/1811]; 11/12/1811; Carries letters for WCB and SRB 6/19/1799; 2/10/1802; 10/28/1813
Richards, Mrs. Mark. 1/29/1809; 1/29/1809
Richards, Mr. SRB sends bill to 8/18/1798*
Richards, Mr. Possible candidate for Congress from Vt. 12/2/1800*
Richards, Moses. 12/9/1822*
Richards, Nathaniel. Of New London. 3/28/1810*
Richards & May. Money owed Pearsall 7/25/1800*
Richardson, James. [11/13/1788–7/25/1789]
Rickee, John. [11/13/1788–7/25/1789]
Right, Ebenezer. SRB purchased land from [ca. 1790]
Riley, Capt. 9/23/1783*
Ripley, Christopher. 9/8/1811; 1/31/1812; 2/3/1812; 2/20/1812; 5/11/1812
Ripley, Eleazar Wheelock [name from list]. 12/15/1800; 1/31/1812; 8/15/1812
Ripley, Mr. SRB purchases land from in Hartford? 4/24/1821*; 8/4/1823*
Roberts, John, Jr. Of Putney. 11/15/1815
Roberts, Judge. Of Guilford. 8/24/1813

Roberts, Thomas. Works on SRB' house on Lord Hill in Hartford 6/11/1818*
Robinson, Col. 2/??/1780; 12/24/1782
Robinson, David. Of Westminster. 3/7/1803
Robinson, Eli. 7/5/1813
Robinson, Elijah. 7/27/1788*; 7/1/1789*; 7/31/1790
Robinson, Jonathan (1756–1819). Senator from Vermont; member, state house of representatives 1789–1802; chief justice of the supreme court of Vermont 1801–1807; elected in 1807 as a Republican to the United States Senate to fill a vacancy; reelected in 1809 and served from October 10, 1807, to March 3, 1815; member, State house of representatives in 1818. 8/22/1797; 8/7/1801; 10/21/1807; 11/5/1808; 12/12/1809; 1/27[1811]; 2/3/1811; 11/16/1814?
Robinson, Judge. 2/10/1808; 3/15/1808; 3/24/1808; 3/31/1808*
Robinson, Major. Member of Vt. Assembly. 1/19/1791
Robinson, Mr. Member of Vt. General Assembly. 10/10/1800
Robinson, Moses. Judge of the Superior court, Westminster, Vt.; served one term as a U.S. senator; he and Stephen Bradley were the first two senators from Vermont. 10/20–22/1779; 12/9/1779; [7/31/1783]; 10/17/1783; [10/10/1786]; 1/10/1791*; 1/19/1791; [ca. 10/10/1811]
Robinson, Thomas. Postmaster, Chester, Vt. 3/26/1811; 8/3/1811; 3/18/1814
Rockwood, Cepha L. 3/26/1811; 12/7/1816; letter to WCB 2/24/1814
Rodgers, Capt. 2/22/1806
Rodgers, Capt. John(?). 12/7/1812
Rogers, Capt. 11/9/1817
Rogers, D. Works on SRB' house on Lord Hill in Hartford 6/11/1818*
Rosebrook, William. Of Guildhall? 8/13/1796*
Rowe, Joseph. Account with Pearsall 6/6/1803*; 4/2/1805*
Rowler, Lt. Abner. [4/1/1784]
Roy, Silas. 7/31/1790
Royce, Mr. Member of Vt. General Assembly. 9/27/1796
Royce (Rice?), Samuel. Of Landaff, N.H. 10/6/1784*
Royse, Lydia Bull. Of Hartford; teacher of Stella and Adeline Bradley. 7/6/1808; 7/29/1808; 8/x/1808; 3/18/1811*
Rudd, Joseph. [4/1/1784]
Ruggles, Joseph, Jr. Friend of WCB. 5/7/1799; 6/19/1799; 8/5/1800; 10/5/1800; 1/24/1801; 4/4/1808; 7/28/1814
Ruggles, Martha. Daughter of Nathaniel. 11/12/1816
Ruggles, Nathaniel. Of Roxbury, MA. 9/21/1802*; 1/1/1803; 9/30/1803*; 10/8/1803; 12/25/1803; 1/15/1805; 1/29/1809; 2/10/1811; 10/7/1811; 6/30/1812; 11/20/1812; 8/24/1814; 11/12/1816
Rush, Benjamin (1745–1813). Graduate of the College of New Jersey (now Princeton); M.D. Univ. of Edinburgh 1768; professor of chemistry at the College of Philadelphia; member of the Continental Congress 1776–1777; signer of the Declaration of Independence. 2/8/1803
Rush, Richard. 4/23/1812
Russel, John. Of Claremont, N.H. 11/7/1791; 8/10/1793*
Russell, Ben. 7/28/1814
Russell, Joseph. Rent owed SRB 3/15/1831
Rutledge, Mr. Duel with Ellery 6/18/1804
Ryan?, Elijah. 8/28/1814
Sabin, Judge. 7/4/1785*
Sabin, Noah, Jr. Signee on bond 1/30/1798

Sackett, Enoch. [4/1/1784]
Sackett, Reuben. [4/1/1784]
Safford, David. [4/1/1784]
Safford, Jacob. [4/1/1784]
Safford, Capt. Joseph. [4/1/1784]
Safford, Mr. Member of Vt. General Assembly. 10/10/1800
Safford, Samuel. SRB purchased land from [ca. 1790]
Sage, Parson. 1/30/1793
St. Cair, Gen. Arthur. 2/20/1818
Salter, Richard, Jr. Crockery merchant to marry Miss A. H. 6/19/1799; 8/5/1800
Sanders, Daniel C. Controversial Unitarian Universalist minister 1815–1829; conservative Unitarians objected to his liberal views; after his withdrawal as minister in 1829, he was a frequent orator at public events and held various elected offices (from the Rev. Richard A. Kellaway, First Parish Unitarian Universalist Church, Medfield, Massachusetts, "A Sermon Celebrating 350 Years," 11 Feb. 2001, http://www.firstparishmedfield.org/350thanniversary.html). 12/18/1812; 9/22/1812
Sanderson, Capt. 3/26/1796*; 3/31/1796*
Sanford, John. SRB purchased land from [ca. 1790]
Sanford, Oliver. SRB purchased land from [ca. 1790]
Sanford, Seth. SRB purchased land from [ca. 1790]
Sanford, Seth Samuel. SRB purchased land from [ca. 1790]
Sargeant, Benjamin. Putney merchant. 7/15/1816
Sargeant, Eli. Executor of will of Col. John Sargeant. 3/26/1802
Sargeant, Erastus. SRB purchased land from [ca. 1790]
Sargeant, Ezra. Of Chester? 8/31/1802*
Sargeant, J. Of Chester. 8/31/1802*
Sargeant, Col. John. Sargeant v. Gorton 3/26/1802
Sargeant, Rev. Samuel. 3/18/1814
Sargent, Mr. 6/9/1807; 1/22/1809
Sargeant vs. Gorton 3/26/1802
Saunderson, Mr. 3/29/1807
Sawyer, Capt. Jesse. [4/1/1784]
Scott, Nathaniel, & Co. Name of Jona. Dorr's soap business. 12/15/1809
Scott, William. Recommended for postmaster at Peacham 4/20/1804
Seamans, A. Writes to WCB 4/2/1813; 5/1/1813
Seamans, Mr. 12/29/1811*
Seaver, Nathaniel. [4/1/1784]
<Sebroot>, Mrs. John. Land abuts that of P Stiversant in Hartland 11/15/1800*
Sedgwick, Mrs. 7/28/1814
Selden, Esqr. Carries letter from J. Robinson 8/22/1797
Seley, Benjamin. SRB purchased land from [ca. 1790]
Sessions, Esqr., John. Of Westminster. 2/8/1800
Seton, Mrs. Instructor of Stella Bradley and WCB's daughter Merab. 9/30/1803*; 10/8/1803; 8/25/1814; 3/22/1815; 5/28/1816; 12/15/1816
Seymour, Horatio. Vt. Council election [ca. 10/10/1811]
Seymour, Thomas. 12/13/1787*
Sharp, Andrew. [4/1/1784]
Sharp, Capt. William. [4/1/1784]
Shattuck, G. C. (Dr.) 3/24/1808
Shaw, Dr. 2/10/1808
Shaw, John. Letter to WCB 6/7/1805
Shaw, Mr. [1/27/1811]
Shaw, Robert Gould. 4/24/1805; 5/28/1805; 1/24/1811; 8/24/1813
Shaw, Samuel. U.S. rep. from Vt. 11/5/1808; 12/12/1809; 3/15/1812
Shelden, Asaph. SRB purchased land from [ca. 1790]

Sheldon, Dr. Of Litchfield. 2/17/1822
Sheldon, Mr. Member of Vt. General Assembly. 10/10/1800; 10/13/1801
Shepardson, Samuel. Vt. presidential elector. 11/5/1808
Sheperd, Thomas and John. Cotton manufacturers in Northampton. 6/17/1809
Shephard, Levi. Of Northampton. 4/30/1785*
Shepth?, Daniel. [11/13/1788–7/25/1789]
Sherborn, Nathaniel. SRB purchased land from [ca. 1790]
Sherer, John. Signee on note 4/4/1797*
Shipman, Mr. 4/11/1780
Sikes (Sykes), Col. 7/17/1802*; 8/6/1802
Sill, R. 7/27/1778
Simcoe, John Graves. Gov. of Upper Canada. 1/19/1803
Skinner, John. 6/24/1822; 12/28/1822*
Slade, Mr. [ca. 10/10/1811]
Small, Salisbury & Co. 5/24/1808
Smedley, Mr. Conn. Collector. 6/3/1812
Smith, Mr. A. B. Son of Judge Smith of Roxbury. Marriage of 2/27/1819
Smith, Asakel? 7/2/1813
Smith, Benjamin. Writes to WCB 8/29/1813
Smith, Cephas, Jr. Of Rutland. 11/1/1800
Smith, Charles. Studied law with WCB. 4/25/1811; 5/20/1812
Smith, Daniel. U.S. senator from Tennessee. 2/17/1807
Smith, Miss E. Friend of J. Ruggles. 8/5/1800; 10/5/1800
Smith, Ephraim. [ca. 1790]
Smith, Gen. 9/26/1830; 10/1/1830
Smith, I. Note owed SRB 3/15/1831
Smith, Isaiah. 8/6/1800*
Smith, Israel (1759–1810). Republican representative and a senator from Vermont; member, state house of representatives 1785, 1788–1791; delegate to the state constitutional convention in 1791; upon the admission of Vermont as a state into the Union was elected to the 2nd Congress; reelected to the 3rd and 4th Congresses and served from October 17, 1791, to March 3, 1797; member, state house of representatives 1797; chief justice of the state supreme court 1797–1798; elected to the 7th Congress (March 4, 1801–March 3, 1803); elected as a Republican to the United States Senate and served from March 4, 1803, until his resignation on October 1, 1807, having been elected governor; governor of Vermont 1807–1808. 1/19/1791; 1/20/1802*; 5/26/1807; 11/11/1807; 11/29/1807[2]; 11/5/1808; 3/9/1809; 12/21/1810; 9/13/1802; 11/28/1812
Smith, J. Member of Vermont General Assembly. 10/20/1788, 10/22/1788
Smith, Jacob. Member of Vt. General Assembly. 10/10/1800
Smith, James. 7/2/1813
Smith, John. Land abuts P. Stiversant's land in Hartland. 11/15/1800*
Smith, Jonathan. Of Brattleboro; in suit against Fosdick and Procter. 3/26/1796*; 3/31/1796*
Smith, Joseph. Of Clarendon. 10/14/1780
Smith, Judge. Of Roxbury. 2/27/1819
Smith, <Lory?>. Works on SRB' house on Lord Hill in Hartford 6/11/1818*
Smith, Maryanne. Mrs. A. B. Smith. 2/27/1819
Smith, Mr. Re: election in 1797? 8/22/1797
Smith, Mr. Member of Vt. General Assembly. 10/24/1800
Smith, Mr. Candidate for governor. 11/2/1801
Smith, Mr. 4/12/1813
Smith, Mr. Postmaster in Rutland. 7/18/1803

428   APPENDIX IV

Smith, Mr. Of Danville. 12/14/1815
Smith, Mr. Of Hartford? 11/7/1818*
Smith, Mr. Hartford sheriff. 2/27/1819
Smith, Mrs. Friend of Bradleys. 6/19/1799
Smith, Mrs. Of Haverhill? 11/3/1796*
Smith, Nathan (Dr.) Prof. at Dartmouth College; friend of WCB. 10/23/1801; 12/7/1801; 9/25/1802; 11/14/1802; 1/16/1803; 3/24/1808; 8/26/1809
Smith, Nicholas. [11/13/1788–7/25/1789]
Smith, Noah. Westminster state's attorney. "He was admitted to the bar of Vermont at Westminster, May 26 1779, with Stephen R. Bradley — these being the first admissions to the bar of Vermont.... Smith [was appointed] State's Attorney within and for the county of Cumberland, *pro tempore*" (Governor and Council Record, vol. 4, 27 May 1779). 6/5/1786*
Smith, Pleney. Vt. Council election [ca. 10/10/1811]
Smith, R.? Of Bellows & Smith? 2/25/1816
Smith, Mr. R. Of Needham. 12/18/1812
Smith, Ralph. Letter to WCB 8/11/1809
Smith, Robert. Secretary of state. 3/26/1811
Smith, Samuel. Writes to SRB 10/8/1812
Smith, Samuel. 2/5/1823; 2/14/1823; 2/25/1823
Smith, <Samuel?>. In suit against James & Thomas Lamb. 3/26/1796*; 3/31/1796*
Smith, William. Deceased. Lands of, in Chester 12/3/1796*; 12/13/1796
Snow, Francis. 2/20/1818
Sparhawk, George K. Brother of Thomas. 8/24/1801
Sparhawk, J. W. Writes to WCB 3/9/1813; 1/17/1814; 4/20/1815
Sparhawk, Thomas. 8/24/1801
Sparkawk, Hubbard (Dr.) 8/26/1809; 11/30/1811
Sparks, Capt. Commanding officer at Fort Pickering. 5/16/1801
Spears, Denming. SRB purchased land from [ca. 1790]
Spencer, Abel. Of Rutland. 7/18/1803
Spencer, Mr. E. Of Westminster. 3/15/1812
Spooner, Alain. Of Windsor. 1/9/1804
Spooner, Alden. ID 2/27/1808; 12/2/1800*; 3/31/1808*; 7/28/1808
Spooner, Alfred. Of Westminster. 3/16/1812; Letter to WCB 11/21/1815
Spooner, Eliakim. Of Westminster; Westminster justice of the peace. 10/6/1794*; 4/1/1802*; 10/30/1810; 12/1810; 3/15/1812; 3/16/1812
Spooner, Eliakim [4/1/1784]
Spooner, Lt. Gov. 1/24/1784
Spooner, Mr. 8/18/1780; 8/22/1797
Spooner, Mr. 4/8/1802*; 8/22/1808
Spooner, Mr. Sued by Mr. and Mrs. Norman. 11/1/1800
Spooner, Mr. Member of Vt. General Assembly. 10/10/1800; 1/30/1804*
Spooner, Paul. 10/20–22/1779; 10/17/1783; [4/1/1784]
Sprague, Elkanah. Of Hartford. 10/14/1780
Squier?, T. [Truman Squires?]. Clerk of Vt. Governor's Council. 9/27/1796
Stanley, Mr. Member of Vt. General Assembly. 10/10/1800; 10/13/1801
Stark, Jedidiah. Of Brattleboro. 6/19/1800*; Debt owed David Goodall 6/20/1800*
Stark, Joel. 10/3/1793
Starkweather, L. Rent owed SRB 3/15/1831
Stearns, Daniel. Of Brattleborough. Patent 2/7/1814
Stearns, Deacon. 9/15/1828
Stearns, Stephen. Of Walpole, N.H. 3/15/1831
Stedman & Gordon. Bill for lumber for SRB's house on Lord Hill in Hartford 6/11/1818*
Stephens, John. SRB purchased land from [ca. 1790]

Sterne, Laurence. Quoted 3/9/1809
Steward, William. 6/4/1779*
Stiles, Elizabeth. Daughter of Ezra. 9/16/1779*
Stiles, Emilia. Daughter of Ezra. 9/16/1779*
Stiles, Ezra. 9/16/1779*; 8/18/1780
Stiles, Ezra, Jr. 9/16/1779*
Stiles, Isaac. Son of Ezra. 9/16/1779*
Stiles, Kezia. Daughter of Ezra. 9/16/1779*
Stiles, Mary. Daughter of Ezra. 9/16/1779*
Stiles, Ruth. Daughter of Ezra. 9/16/1779*
Stillman, George. SRB purchased land from [ca. 1790]
Stinges & Freeland? Writes to WCB 3/11/1812
Stiversant, Petrus. Of N.Y.; owns land in Hartland. 11/15/1800*
Stockwill, Mr. 11/13/1796*
Stoddard, Amos. 3/28/1812
Stoddard, Isaac. Money owed C. Johnson 12/13/1797*
Stone, Abel. SRB purchased land from [ca. 1790]
Stone, Calvin. Tailor for WCB? 11/2/1813
Stone, Col. Debt to Samuel Bayard 7/25/1791; 11/4/1800*
Stone, David. Indenture of 10/6/1784*
Stone, David. Of Walpole. 8/25/1800*; 10/12/1819; 9/15/1828; 3/15/1831
Stone, David. 9/26/1830
Stone & Bellows. 10/12/1819
Storer, Charles. 3/29/1807; 5/26/1807; 6/9/1807; 1/22/1809; 4/12/1813; 6/14/1813*
Storer, Genl. Clement. Of Portsmouth; U.S. representative from N.H. 10/10/1806
Stowe, Mr. 11/15/1810
Street, Amaryllis Atwater (Mrs. Titus). Sister of Mrs. SRB. 2/15/1785*; 10/20/1785*
Strong, Caleb. Governor of Mass. 2/18/1815
Strong, Col. At Wilkinson Ville 5/16/1801
Strong, Ebenezer. 4/20/1804
Strong, James. Of Hudson, N.Y. 11/24/1808*
Strong, John. Of Dorset. 10/14/1780
Strong, Judge. Of Amherst, Mass.; WCB studied law with. 8/5/1800
Strong, Mr. 3/15/1812
Strong, S. Friend of WCB in Deerfield, MA. 12/30/1800; 10/23/1801
Stuyvesant, Peter [Petrus?]. 11/5/1797*; 6/4/1798; 3/20/1800
Stuyvesant, Peter Gerard (son). Represents SRB vs. Coleman. 3/20/1800; 11/25/1800; 5/26/1801*; 10/20/1801*; 12/18/1801*; 11/10/1801*
Sullivan, James. Of Boston. 4/11/1797*
Summers, Luke. SRB purchased land from [ca. 1790]
Sumner, Benjamin. Of Claremont, N.H. 1/19/1803
Sumter, Gen. U.S. senator from South Carolina. 3/6/1810
Sutherland, John. Of Wallingford. 12/24/1800; account with Pearsall 6/6/1803*; 4/2/1805*
Sutherland, John, Jr. Of Wallingford. 12/24/1800; account with Pearsall 6/6/1803*; 4/2/1805*
Sutherland, Mr. Wheat of 1/4/1797*
Swan, Benjamin. Letter to WCB 5/25/1805
Sweetser, William. Sheriff. 11/4/1800*
Swenmore, E. S. Of Boston. 12/14/1812
Tarbox, James. Vt. presidential elector. 11/5/1808
Taylor, John. 5/15/1800*
Taylor, Mr. Member of Vt. General Assembly. 10/13/1801
Taylor, Mrs. Mother-in-law of SRB. Death of 9/22/1809
Taylor, Rev. To vote for WCB 11/21/1812
Taylor, Rev. Assumes Bullen's debts to SRB 1/24/1803

Tele, Joseph. 12/12/1790
Temple, John. SRB purchased land from [ca. 1790]
Temple, Mr. 5/29/1819*
Temple, R. Writes to WCB 7/7/1813; 4/6/1816
Temple, Robert. 4/2/1813
Tennessee lands 1/8/1805
Thatcher, Mr. 11/24/1783; 4/5/1784*
Thayer, William. Letter to WCB 7/1/1810
Theys?, Judge Eleas? [ca. 10/10/1811]
Thomas, Alexander. Letter to WCB 1803
Thomas, John B. Of Kaskaskia, Illinois. 11/18/1810*
Thomas, John H. 2/2/1814
Thomas, Isaiah. Of Worcester. 12/7/1801
Thompson. Of Chester? To evict Bowker 8/31/1802*
Thompson, A. Owns land in Chester. 12/21/1797*
Thompson, John. SRB purchased land from [ca. 1790]
Thompson, William. Money owed C. Johnson 12/13/1797*
Thomson, J. Works on SRB' house on Lord Hill in Hartford 6/11/1818*
Thomson, J. C. 7/7/1813
Thornton, William. ID — 2/7/1814
Thuston, Nathan. [11/13/1788–7/25/1789]
Tichenor, Isaac. [7/31/1783]; 10/17/1783; [4/1/1784]; [10/27/1789]; 1/15/1790*; 2/9/1790; 1/19/1791; 8/1/1803; 11/7/1803; 1/11/1804; 10/28/1805; 3/9/1809; 10/17/1814
Tichenor, Maj. <Levrt. G.?>. Carried letter from D.C. to SRB in Vt. 7/18/1803
Tiffin, Dr. Delivers letter from T. Worthington 10/5/1807*
Tiley [Riley?], Capt. E. Of the schooner *Ruth*. 12/9/1782
Tingey, Como. 12/7/1812
Tingey, Thomas. ID 1/20/1809
Tole?, Capt. Grand juryman. 10/12/1793*
Tolman, Thomas. "[A]t the October session 1784, he was one of the committee appointed to draft a reply to the Governor's speech, the associates being Stephen R. Bradley and Isaac Tichenor" (Governor and Council Record, vol. 3). 10/1784*
Tomlinson, Gideon. 6/3/1812
Tower, Isaac. Accused by John Nott of burning house 10/12/1793*
Town, Dr. Of Westminster. 3/7/1803
Townsend, Isarah. Of Albany. 12/18/1811
Townsend, Micah. Brattleboro, Vt., lawyer.
Tozer, Peter. 12/12/1790
Tracy, Elisha. Of Norwich, Conn. 2/22/18[00?]; 2/22/1808; 3/16/1808; 4/10/1808; 12/15/1808; 2/5/1809; 2/16/1810; 3/22/1810; 1/12/1812
Tracy, Uriah (1755–1807). Representative and senator from Connecticut; major general of Connecticut militia; member, state general assembly 1788–1793, serving as speaker 1793; elected to the 3rd and 4th Congresses and served from March 4, 1793, until his resignation in 1796; elected as a Federalist to the United States Senate to fill a vacancy; reelected in 1801 and 1807, and served from October 13, 1796, until his death; served as president pro tempore of the Senate during the 6th Congress. 12/13&14/1802
Trask, Capt. (J.E.). Friend of J. Ruggles. 8/5/1800; 1/24/1801; 11/14/1801
Trask, James. 5/17/1783*
Treadwell, John. Gov. of Conn. 1809–1811. 7/17/1818*
Treadwell, Mr. 1/8/1810*
Trigg, Mr. 4/1/1808
Tripoli. 2/24/1806*; 2/26/1806; 11/17/1806
Troop, Robert. Vt. land claim 5/26/1793

Troup, Col. Of N.Y. 5/15/1800*
Trumbull, Judge John. 9/17/1820*
Trumbull, Joseph. ID — 6/15/1814*; 11/7/1818*; 11/16/1818*; 12/4/1818*; 2/27/1819; 4/21/1819*
Tuanies?, John. Master of the sloop *Price*. 9/28/1804
Tudor, E. 9/8/1788*
Tudor, Henry Bradley. Grandson of SRB. 9/15/1828; 3/15/1831
Tudor, Henry S. 9/15/1828; 3/15/1831
Tudor, Mary Rowe (1811–1882). Mrs. Henry S. Tudor; youngest daughter of Stephen and Melinda Bradley. 9/15/1828; 3/15/1831
Turner, Mr. 12/7/1812
Turner, Mr. Of Hartford? 8/4/1823*
Turner, T. 4/2/1810*; Writes to WCB 1/7/1814*
Tuthill, John. Writes to WCB 8/22/1808
Tuttle, Mr. 1/29/1809; 8/11/1827
Tyler, B. Of Dartmouth College. 1/24/1826*; 2/16/1828*
Tyler, John. Legal case 3/23/1796*
Tyler, Judge. Vt. 8/7/1801
Tyler, Royall (1757–1826). Graduate of Harvard 1776; served in the Colonial army during the American Revolution and Shay's Rebellion; chief justice of the Vermont Supreme Court, 1807–1813; professor of jurisprudence at the University of Vermont, 1811–1814. 3/23/1796*; 12/13/1797*; 3/9/1809; 3/27/1801*; 10/21/1807; 2/10/1808; 5/4/1810; 11/26/1810; 11/30/1810; 1/27/[1811]; 2/3/1811; [ca. 10/10/1811]; 11/12/1811; 3/16/1812; 11/21/1812; 3/6/1813; 1/15/1814
<Uffoot?>, Samuel. Land formerly owned by, in Concord 1/2/1797*
Underwood, Joseph. [11/13/1788–7/25/1789]
Underwood, Russell. 5/25/1805
Unidentified. Of the Dept. of War Accounting Office. 1/14/1811
Upham, George B. 12/28/1822*; 1/9/1823*
Vanderhoof, Capt. Henry. [4/1/1784]
Van Horne, Augustus. 12/26/1794; 9/17/1795*
Van Rensselaer, Killian Killian. Of Albany. 12/18/1811
Van Zandt, Mrs. 5/28/1812*
Varnum, Joseph Bradley (1750?–1821). Representative and senator from Massachusetts; served in the Revolutionary Army; member, state house of representatives 1780–1785; member, state senate 1786–1795; delegate to the state convention that ratified the Federal Constitution in 1788; elected to the 4th and to the eight succeeding Congresses and served from March 4, 1795, to June 29, 1811, when he resigned, having been elected senator; elected as a Republican to the United States Senate in 1811 to fill a vacancy and served from June 29, 1811, to March 3, 1817; member, state senate 1817–1821. 1/7/1814*
Vaux, Roberts. 2/13/1813
Vermont council election [ca. 10/10/1811]
Verplank, Mr. 7/31/1790
Vincent, Mr. Member of Vt. General Assembly. 10/13/1801
Vose, Roger (1763–1841). Representative from New Hampshire; member of the state senate in 1809, 1810, and 1812; elected as a Federalist to the 13th and 14th Congresses (March 4, 1813–March 3, 1817); member of the state house of representatives in 1818. 1/17/1814; 3/15/1812
Voyage from Calcutta 6/20/1794
Wait, Col. 10/22/1783
Waite, Lt. Friend of J. Ruggles. 8/5/1800
Walbach, Capt. Commanding officer of Fort Constitution. 10/10/1806*; 3/29/1808
Walbridge, Mr. 4/5/1781; 4/6/1781

Walbridge, Mr. Member of Vt. General Assembly. 1/19/1791
Walbridge, Silas. [4/1/1784]
Wales, Aaron. Superintendent of Westminster Meeting House. Permit from 7/3/1799
Wales, Mary. SRB's sister. 9/15/1828
Wales, Mr. Of Westminster. 11/14/1801; 7/30/1813
Walker, Jesse. [4/1/1784]
Walker, William and Jonathan. Of Halifax. 7/1/1802*
Wall, Mr. Re: Mr. Brush's estate 8/13/1790*
Wall, Mrs. Patrick. Widow of New York Tory Crean Brush; mother of Fanny Buchanan. 6/4/1779*
Wallbradge, Col. Ebenezer. [4/1/1784]
Ward, Benjamin. 5/24/1808
Ward, Edmund. SRB purchased land from [ca. 1790]
Ward, Mr. Member of Vermont General Assembly. 1/12/1791*
Ward, William. Mortgage in Newfane 6/29/1789
Ward, Capt. William. [4/1/1784]
Ware, Henry, Jr. Of the American Unitarian Association, Boston. 8/22/1825*
Ware, Jesse. Of Brattleboro. In suit against Ebenezer Clark 6/25/1796*, 8/13/1796*; in suit against Jonathan Nye 8/18/1796*
Ware, Jonathan. 4/20/1804
Warner, Asa. Contract with Pearsall 12/24/1800; account with Pearsall 4/2/1805*
Warner, Daniel. SRB purchased land from [ca. 1790]
Warner, Jacob. Contract with Pearsall 12/24/1800; account with Pearsall 6/6/1803*; 4/2/1805*
Warner, Gen. Jonathan. 6/17/1788*
Warren, Joseph. ID WCB-7/4/1799
Warren, Mr. Regarding land in Chester 12/3/1796*
Warriner, Esqr. Regarding Clark vs. Ware 8/13/1796*
Washburn, Nathaniel W. Money owed Cowles brothers 6/2/1800*; 7/22/1800*
Washington, George (1732-1799). A Virginian, became the commanding general of the Continental Army during the American Revolution; first president of the United States. 1/24/1776; 2/2/1808
Waterman, Asa. Account with Pearsall 6/6/1803*
Waterman, Rev. M. 4/19/1803*
Waters, Constable. 1/24/1784
Waters, Oliver. [4/1/1784]
Watkins, Abner. 3/26/1811
Watkins, Charles. Rent owed SRB 3/15/1831
Watkins, R. Note owed SRB 3/15/1831
Watson, Ebenezer. Hartford printer. 12/4/1774*
Watson, James. Brother of Ebenezer. 12/4/1774*
Wayne, Anthony (1745-1796). Prominent major general in Washington's army during the American Revolution.
Webb, Joshua, Esqr. [11/13/1788-7/25/1789]
Webster, Daniel. 1/17/1814
Wederstramdt, Lt. Re Tripoli 11/17/1806
Weld, Elias. [4/1/1784]
Welles, Ephraim. Letter to Amos Carpenter 11/11/1794
Wellington, Abel. Indenture with 4/9/1818
Wellman, Benjamin. [4/1/1784]
Wells, Joshua. [11/13/1788-7/25/1789]
Wells, Mr. 11/21/1815
Wesson, Isaac. [11/13/1788-7/25/1789]
West, Benjamin. [11/13/1788-7/25/1789]
West, John. 9/29/1788
West, Mr. 6/4/1779*
West, Mr. 5/26/1793
West, Mr. Of Charlestown. 4/30/1785*
Wetherbee, Samuel. Of Concord. 12/14/1815
Wheat, Mr. Of Putney. 6/17/1788*

Wheatley, Mr. Member of Vt. General Assembly. 10/13/1801
Wheaton, Joseph. 9/7/1811
Wheaton, Mrs. Joseph. 9/7/1811
Wheaton, Mr. 11/29/1807
Wheeler, Gideon. SRB purchased land from [ca. 1790]
Wheeler, Capt. Isaac. [4/1/1784]
Wheeler, Samuel. Of Alexandria. 12/30/1811
Wheelock, Eleazer. Recommended by I. Smith 5/26/1807
Wheelock, Dr. John. President of Dartmouth College. 10/23/1801
Wheelock, Mr. Mail carrier in Burlington, Vt. 12/21/1807
Whipple, Commander. Docks brig at Wilkinson Ville 5/16/1801
Whipple, Daniel (deceased). 6/29/1789
Whipple, Mrs. Daniel. 9/4/1789*
White, John. Vt. presidential elector. 11/5/1808
White, Mr. Member of Vt. General Assembly. 9/27/1796
White, Moses. Executor of estate of Moses Hazen. 3/4/1806
White, William. Of Guilford. 1/24/1784
Whitelaw, James. Of Ryegate. 9/27/1802
Whiting, Col. Of Burlington? 11/5/1808
Whiting, Nathan. 3/26/1811
Whitlaw, James, Esqr. 3/27/1802*
Whitlock, Lt. Re: pay of Lt. Joseph Dorr 2/9/1810
Whitney, Esqr. Action against? 8/22/1797
Whitney, Mr. Counsel for Col. John Sargeant. 3/26/1802
Whitney, Mr. 6/19/1800*
Whitney, Wm. R. Clerk of Vt. Gen. Ass. 10/12/1793*, 9/27/1796
Whittelsey, Samuel. 6/24/1822; 8/21/1822; 12/14/1824
Whittelsey, Mrs. Samuel. 6/24/1822
Whittlesey, Chauncey. SRB purchased land from [ca. 1790]
Whittlesey, Charles. SRB purchased land from [ca. 1790]
Whittlesey, Samuel. [ca. 1790]
Wickham, Miss. Daughter of William. 1/24/1788*
Wickham, William. 1/24/1788*
Wickham, Mrs. William. 1/24/1788*
Wickwire, Capt. Jonah. [4/1/1784]
Wier, Catherine. 9/15/1828
Wier (Wires), Charlton. 5/12/1819
Wier, John H. 9/15/1828; indenture with SRB 10/27/1817, 5/12/1819; note owed SRB 3/15/1831
Wilbur, Seprelet. Note owed SRB 3/15/1831
Wilcox, Joseph. Conn. marshal. 3/17/1808*; 12/10/1808*
Wilcox, Mr. 12/4/1818*
Wilder, Benjamin. Of Putney. 11/15/1815
Wilder, Hon. Joseph. Of Lancaster. 12/5/1806
Wilkinson Ville 5/16/1801
Williston, Caleb. Account with Pearsall 6/6/1803*; 4/2/1805*
Wilkins, John? 5/14/1785
Wilkinson, James (1757-1825). Soldier, conspirator; served in the American Revolution under Benedict Arnold and Horatio Gates and joined the Conway Cabal, the group that schemed against Washington. He intrigued with Aaron Burr to establish a separate nation on the western frontier; when the plot was discovered, he ordered Burr's arrest. Leader of the failed expedition to Montreal (1813), Wilkinson left the army in 1815. 11/14/1801; 11/17/1806
Willard, Constable. 1/23/1826*; 3/11/1826

Index of Bradley's Correspondents and Their Letters

Willard, David. Account with SRB 7/24/1784*
Willard, Eli. SRB purchased land from [ca. 1790]
Willard, John. Vt. Marshal. 1/13/1803; 1/19/1810; [ca. 10/10/1811]
Willard, Joseph. 11/12/1800
Willard, Joseph. Deputy sheriff. 7/5/1813
Willard, Margaret. 4/21/1822*; 6/24/1822; 8/21/1822
Willard, Prent. Receipt from 12/11/1789
Williams, Azarias. Of Concord, Vt. 3/27/1802*
Williams, Col. 5/4/1803
Williams, Edward. 9/4/1789*
Williams, Jonathan. 1/23/1808
Williams, Major Leonard. Son of Samuel. 12/26/1811?
Williams, Mr. Member of Vt. General Assembly. 9/27/1796
Williams, Samuel. Selectman of Rutland, Vt. 1/12/1791*; 4/12/1803; 12/26/1811?
Williams, Stephen. Of Springfield. 5/25/1796
Willington, Quincey. 6/3/1808
Willis, Samauel. SRB purchased land from [ca. 1790]
Willougby, Zerah. Vt. Council election [ca. 10/10/1811]
Willoughby, John. SRB purchased land from [ca. 1790]
Wilson, A. Note owed SRB 3/15/1831
Wilson, Benjamin. Son of the Lord Mayor of London. 12/5/1806
Wilson, Jeremiah. Son of Benjamin. 12/5/1806
Wilson, Jonathan. Son of Jeremiah. 12/5/1806
Wilson, Joseph, Esq. 11/1/1800
Wilson, Luke. Of Putney, Vt.; son of Jonathan. 12/5/1806
Wilson, Mr. Former Lord Mayor of London. Estate of 12/5/1806
Wilson, Nathaniel. Son of Benjamin. 12/5/1806
Wilson, Samuel. Account with Pearsall 6/6/1803*; 4/2/1805*
Wing?, D., Jr. Clerk of Vt. General Assembly. 10/5/1804
Wing, David. Vt. secretary of state. 10/31/1803 10/28/1805

Witherell, James. Member of Vt. General Assembly. 10/10/1800; 2/10/1808; 3/24/1808; 7/8/1808
Wolcott, A. Former collector at Middletown. 2/15/1811
Wolcott, Alexander. 5/15/1817*
Wolcott, Oliver, Sr. Gov. of Conn. 1796–1797. 7/17/1818*
Wood, Barnabas. Of Westminster. 3/16/1812
Wood, Capt. Selectman of Rockingham, Vt.
Wood, Mr. Member of Vt. General Assembly. 10/10/1800
Wood, Richard. Of Concord. 5/29/1795*
Woodbridge, Joshua L. 4/23/1787*
Woodbridge, Mr. Ward. Mr. Morgan's agent. 10/8/1818*
Woodbury, Thomas. Money owed C. Johnson 12/13/1797*
Woodleridge? 10/20/1788
Woods, Broadstreet. Bought John Nott's land 10/5/1804
Woodward, Bezaleel. 4/6/1781
Woodward, Judge. Of Hanover, N.H. 8/6/1802
Wooster, David (1710–1777). Maj. general, killed in the battle of Richfield May 27, 1777 (Danbury). Major Stephen R. Bradley served as his aide de camp during this engagement. 7/31/1790; 10/3/1793
Wooster, Thomas. SRB purchased land from [ca. 1790]
Worthington, T. Of Chilicothe. 10/5/1807*
Wosster, Mr. 11/24/1783
Wright, Mr. Member of Vt. General Assembly. 10/13/1801
Wright, Ebenezer. Re: land deeded to Lemuel Cone 12/30/1809*
Wright, Josiah. Vt. Council election [ca. 10/10/1811]
Wright, Peter. [4/1/1784]
Wright, Peter. [11/13/1788–7/25/1789]
Wright, Robert. ID — 2/2/1814

BIBLIOGRAPHY

Principal Collections of Bradley Papers

The Annals of Congress 1790–1813
Contains approximately 150 mentions Stephen Bradley and William Bradley, noting their presence in the Chamber and vote counts. There are very few complete speeches.

*Boston Public Library, Boston, Massachusetts
Contains 3 items, including a printed original copy of "Vermont's Appeal to the Candid and Impartial World."

Duke University Library, Durham, North Carolina
Contains 771 items of personal, military, and political correspondence (Dalton Collection).

Fort Ticonderoga Library, Ticonderoga, New York
Contains 25 letters written by Gen. Ethan Allen to his friend and Lawyer, Stephen Bradley.

The Huntington Library, San Marino, California
Contains 8 letters written by Maj. Gen. William Eaton to Senator Bradley pertaining to the Tripolian War.

Journals of the Continental Congress 1776–1789
Contains 9 references to Stephen Bradley mostly pertaining to his part as an agent to Congress on the subject of statehood.

The Library of Congress, Washington, D.C.
Approximately 450 items in the Henry A. Willard Collection, Series I, II, and III.

*Massachusetts Historical Society, Boston, Massachusetts
Contains 2 items, including a printed original copy of "Vermont's Appeal to the Candid and Impartial World."

National Archives and Records Administration, College Park, Maryland
Contains 30 items concerning the Treaty of Ghent and letters written by William C. Bradley to Secretary of State James Monroe.

National Archives and Records Administration, Washington, D.C.
Contains 4 items concerning Bradley and the 1st Regiment of Vermont Volunteers.

Papers of the Continental Congress
Contains 10 letters concerning Vermont statehood, and 1 pay order to Captain Stephen Bradley.

Schlesinger Library, Radcliffe Institute, Cambridge, Massachusetts
Large number of personal and Bradley correspondence, 1813–1954

Secretary of State, Vermont, Historical Division, Montpelier, Vermont
1. Nye Index: approximately 100 legal papers and petitions.
2. Military papers: approximately 100 Pay Records and Quartermaster Records of the 1st Regiment of Vermont Volunteers and the 8th Brigade.
3. Governor and Council Records (printed): approximately 150 items, mostly letters and commissions. Vols. I, II, and III.

Thomas Jefferson Library, Charlottesville, Virginia
Contains 2 items: both are letters written by Stephen Bradley.

United States Senate Library, Washington, D.C.
Approximately 44 Senate bills introduced by SRB

University of Vermont Bailey/Howe Library, Burlington, Vermont
Approximately 600 items: mostly Senatorial and legal papers. A number of these letters are written by William C. Bradley and his father-in-law, Mark Richards (Lt. Gov. of Vermont).

*Those libraries marked with asterisks contain Bradley items that are printed and/or duplicates of documents found elsewhere.

University of Virginia Alderman Library, Charlottesville, Virginia
Contains references to Bradley in the James Madison Papers. Vol. 15, 346–347 and Vol. 16, 493–494.

Vermont Historical Society, Barre, Vermont
Contains 10 items

Windham County Court House, Newfane, Vermont
Numerous court records concerning William C. Bradley

*Yale University Library, New Haven, Connecticut
Contains 3 items, including an original printed copy of Stephen Bradley's "Astronomical Diary of 1775."

Books

Allen, Ira. *Natural and Political History of the State of Vermont.* London; J.W. Myers, 1798. References to Bradley are on pages 136–147.

Bradley, John C. *Brief Sketches of a Few American Bradleys with Reference to Their English Progenitors.* Press of Hoosick Valley Democrats, 1889. Stephen and William are cited on pages 2–6.

Brant, Irving. *James Madison.* Indianapolis and New York: Bobbs-Merrill, 1950–1961. IV, 419 and 424–25; V, 380; and VI, 233.

Carpenter, Dorr. *Carpenter-Bradley-Graham.* Salt Lake City, Utah: Brigham Young University Press, 2002. Bradley references are on pages 1–14 and 74–141.

Carpenter, Helen Graham. *The Reverend John Graham of Woodbury Connecticut and His Descendants.* Chicago: Monastery Hill Press, 1942. References to Col. Bradley are on page 85.

Crockett, Walter H. *Vermont, the Green Mountain State,* 5 vols. New York: The Century History Co., 1921–23.

Duffy, John J., Samuel B. Hand, and Ralph H. Orth, eds. *The Vermont Encyclopedia.* Hanover, New Hampshire and London: University Press of New England, 2003.

Duncan, Lewis C. *Medical Men in the American Revolution.* War Department, 1931. References to "Bradley's Regiment" are on page 149.

Hall, Benjamin H. *History of Eastern Vermont.* Albany, New York: J. Munsil, 1858. References to Bradley are on pages 341–688.

Keith, Marshall Jones III. *Farmers Against the Crown.* Baltimore, Maryland: Connecticut Coloniel Pub., 2002. References to Bradley are on pages 60 and 61.

Plumer, William. *Memorandum of Proceedings in the United States Senate 1803–1807.* London: Macmillan, 1923. References to Bradley are on pages 15–17, 571, and 637.

Public Papers of Gov. Thomas Chittendon. State Papers of Vermont, Vol. 17 Montpelier, Vermont, Sect. of State Office OCLC 89706, 1963.

Sherman, Michael, Gene Sessions, and P. Jeffrey Potash. *Freedom and Unity: A History of Vermont.* Barre, Vermont: Vermont Historical Society, 2004.

Wilentz, Sean, *The Rise of American Democracy, Jefferson to Lincoln.* New York and London: W.W. Norton, 2005.

Willard, Henry Kellogg. *Willard-Bradley Memoirs.* Privately printed, 1925. References to the Bradleys are on pages 27–69 and 239–257.

Willard, Sara Bradley. *A Tribute of Affection to the Memory of Hon. William C. Bradley.* Boston, Massachusetts: George Rand, 1869.

General Index

Abbey, <Eunce> 364
Abbey, Hezh. 358–59, 359
Abbey, Julia 364
Abbey, Mr. 240–41
accounts 98, 101–2, 102–3, 105–6, 112–13, 118, 120–21, 132, 159–60, 166, 180–81
Adams, Gideon 104
Adams, Jereh 104
Adams, John 38, 41, 217, 266–67
Adams, John Quincy 217, 372–73, 373–74, 374
Alcott, Peter 105, 224
Allen, Ethan 1, 2, 16, 31, 33–36, 53–55, 56–57, 59–60, 90, 106, 107, 108, 113, 114, 116, 117, 118–19, 119, 121–22, 122
Allen, Ethan A. 277
Allen, Heman 338
Allen, Ira 1, 86, 89, 95, 97, 117, 118, 151–52
Allen, Levi 105–6
Allen, Mr. 209
Allen, Zimri E. 338
Alston, Willis 331, 332–33
American flag 2, 16, 162–63
Anderson, John 333
Anderson, Joseph 250–51
Andrews, Stephen 134
Annals of Congress 5, 29
Armsby, Maj. Gideon 104
Armstrong, Capt. Hezikiah 104
Armstrong, John 227–231
Armstrong, Col. Martin 227–231
Arnold, Gen. Benedict 24
Arnold, Mr. 151–52
Ashcroft, Daniel 100–101
Ashley, Thomas 137
Astor, John J. 366
Astronomical Almanac 23
Atkins, Joseph 135
Atkinson, John 357
Atkinson, Mr. 293
Attwater, Esq. 181
Atwater, Capt. 111
Atwater, Major 204
Atwater, Mary Russell 16, 43, 122–23
Atwater, Merab 43
Atwater, Mr. (Reuben or Russel) 115
Atwater, Reuben 16, 43, 93, 96, 108–9, 109, 111, 115, 120, 122–23, 198
Atwater (Attwater), Reuben, Jr. 115, 120, 122–23, 123, 261–62, 273, 274–75, 288, 307, 330, 333
Atwater, Russel 94–95, 96, 98–99, 111, 115, 273
Atwater, Sarah Lamb 261–62, 273, 307, 330, 333
Austin, David 341–42
Austin, Mr. 94–95, 98–99, 292
Averill, Samuel 136
Avery, Samuel 131–32, 139, 187
Avery, Samuel, Jr. 187
Axtill, Joseph 159

Babbet, Thomas 245
Babcock, John 377–80
Babcock, Mr. 289–91
Bacon, Leonard 377–80
Badger, Dr. Jonathan 241, 324–25, 363–64
Badger, Mrs. Jonathan 241
Badger, Widow 363–64
Bailey, Theodorus 191–92
Bailey/How Library (University of Vermont) 6
Bainbridge, Joseph 245
Baker, Samuel 135
Baldwin, Abraham 201
Baldwin, Mr. 205
Baldwin, Simeon 134
Ball, Ebenezer 135
Barbary powers 285, 301
Barber, Caroline 365–66
Barber, Joseph 137
Bard, Isaac 167
Barker, Jonathan 134
Barker, Timothy 134
Barlow, James 136
Barlow, Joel 338–39, 340
Barlow, Samuel 136
Barnes, Stephen 135
Barney, Mr. 301–2
Barns, James 135
Barns, William 135
Barret, John 110–11
Barrett, Thomas 222–23
Barron, Capt. Jas. 236–38
Barron, Samuel 236–38, 240, 242–43, 243, 245
Bartholomew, Joseph 134

Bartlett, Samuel 118
Barton, Lt. Andrew 104
Basset, Mr. 309
Bassett, Mr. 382–83
Bates, Joshua 372–73
Bayard, James A. 382
Bayard, James A., Jr. 382, 382–83
Bayard, Richard H. 382, 382–83
Bayard, Samuel 154
Bayley, Jacob 311
Bayley, John 311
Beach, Abigail Atwater 123
Beach, Elnathan 109, 123
Beardsley, Mr. 179–80
Beasley, Mr. 343
Beckley, John 250–51
Bedle, Samuel Sharp 136
Bellows, Abel 377–80
Bellows, Gen. 185
Bellows, Josiah 43, 377–80
Bellows, Josiah 3rd 377–80, 383–96
Bellows, Rebecca Gratia 377–80, 383–96
Bellows, Samuel 357
Bellows, Sarah Adeline 377–80, 383–96
Bellows, Stella C. Bradley 377–80
Bellows, Stella Louise 377–80, 381, 383–96
Bellows, Stephen R. Bradley 43, 377–80, 383–96
Bellows, Thomas 377–80
Bemis, D. 383–96
Bennet, Benjamin 91–92
Bennet, Nathanial 90–91
Benson, Mr. 208
Biglow, Lawrance 105
Billings, Maj. Samuel 105
Bingham, James H. 277–78
Biscale, <Roodiah> 137
Bishop, Ab. 288–89
Bishop, Mr. 344–45
Bissell, Capt. 183–84
Blackden, Col. 191–92
Blackden, Sarah 191–92
Blake, Dr. Charles 258
Blake, Charles 178–79, 219
Blake, Francis 194–95
Blake, John W. 337
Blake, Jones 337
Blanchard, James 135

Bliss, Mr. 179–80
Bliss, Thomas 138
Bogert, Rudolph 124
Bonaparte, Napoleon 310–11, 341–42, 350–51
bonds 161–62
Bonnycastle, Richard Henry 368
Booth, Benjamin 136
Booth, Reuben 136
Boott, Mary 376
Bostwick, John 135
boundaries 91–92, 140, 141–42, 335
Bowker, Benjamin 222–23
Boyden, Major Josiah 94
Bradle, Samuel L. 134
Bradley, Abraham 15
Bradley, Abraham, Jr. 321, 362, 363
Bradley, Eleanor v, 22
Bradley, Emily 19, 377–80
Bradley, Francis 14, 43
Bradley, Jonathan Dorr 19, 20, 376, 377–80, 381
Bradley, Jonathan Dorr II 20, 21
<Bradley>, Josiah 367, 381
Bradley, Capt. Lemuel 104
Bradley, Louisa 324–25
Bradley, Mary Row viii, 43
Bradley, Mary Rowe 17
Bradley, Melinda Willard 6, 16, 17, 282–83, 301–2, 307, 324–25, 330, 336, 371, 371–72, 375, 377–80, 381, 383–96
Bradley, Merab 319
Bradley, Merab Ann 19, 20, 377–80
Bradley, Merab Atwater 16, 17, 94–95, 109, 109–10, 110
Bradley, Moses 15, 16
<Bradley>, Paulina 368
Bradley, Col. Phillip Burr 24
Bradley, Richards 19, 20, 21
Bradley, Sarah Richards 17, 18, 282, 293, 329, 361–62, 362, 368, 375, 377–80
Bradley, Mrs. S.R. (possibly Sally) 214–15, 217
Bradley, Mrs. S.R. (Gratia Thankful Taylor) 182–83, 183–84, 185–86, 188, 193
Bradley, Stella 16, 43, 193, 202–3, 212–13, 279–81, 282, 282–83, 298, 367, 368
Bradley, Stephen Rowe I 193, 279–81
Bradley, Stephen Rowe II 17
Bradley, Stephen Rowe III 19, 43
Bradley, Walter 344–45
Bradley, William 14, 15
Bradley, William Czar 2, 6, 17, 18, 19, 43, 93, 94–95, 108–9, 111, 115, 120, 122–23, 162, 182–83, 183–84, 188, 207, 207–8, 209–10, 262–64, 276, 279–81, 282, 293, 306, 319, 329, 336, 337, 360, 361–62, 362, 365, 368, 375, 376, 377–80, 381, 383–96
Bradleyvale 213, 255

Bray, Theodorus 136
Breed, Ebenezer 326–28
Brent, Robert 304–5
Brewster, Jacob W. 196
Brewster, Mr. 362
Bridgman, John 89
Bridgeman, Orlando 138
Briggs, Esq. 203
Briggs, J. 383–96
Briggs, Capt. Joseph 104
Brigham, Paul 284
Brown, Ebenezer 224
Brown, Elisha 222–23
Brown, Jabez 158
Brown, Jesse 274–75
Brown, Major Return Bryant 284–85
Brownson, Maj. Gideon 105
Brownson, Isaac 105
Brownson, Timothy 95, 118
Brush, Alexander 104
Brush, Col. 156
Brush, Crean 6, 34, 36, 99, 105–6, 152, 216, 222–23
Buchanan, Fanny 34, 35, 36
Buck, Daniel 271–72
Buell, John H. 182–83, 183–84
Buell, Louisa 183–84
Buell, Sally 182–83, 183–84
Buffum, William 377–80, 381
Bulkley, Capt. Charles 288
Bull, Elias 191
Bull, Lydia 279–81
Bull, George 279–81
Bullen, Joseph 127–30, 190, 205, 213–14
Bullen, Mr. 111
Bundy, James 127–30
Burbeck, Coll 258–59
Burdett, Mr. B. C. 365–66
Burk, Capt. 187
Burk, Mr. E. 336
Burk, <Eliub> 127–30
Burk, Capt. Silas 104
Burr, Aaron 25, 29, 38, 182–83, 191–92
Burr, <Aaron?> 181, 242, 245
Burr, Col. 382–83
Burton, Elisha 224
Butler, Ezra 180
Butler, John 245
Butler, Major 301–2, 363–64
Butler, Mr. 262–64
Butters, Mr. 139

C——m, Mr. 208
Cabell, William H. 287
Cahoon, William 284–85
Calhoon, David 135
Calhoon, James 136
Calhoon, Joseph 135
Calhoun, John C. 372–73
Cameron, Mr. 311–12
Camp, Jonah 135
Campbell, Dr. Alexander 142
Campbell, Edward R. 127–30, 158
Campbell, George Washington 250–51
Campbell, Hugh 245

Campbell, Judge 284–85
Candee & Goodrich 365–66
Caramanli, Hamet (Ahmed) 236–38, 240, 242, 242–43, 250, 262, 268–69, 283–84, 303
Caramanli, Joseph 240
Carleton, Roland 383–96
Carlisle, George 383–96
Carpenter, Abel 180–81
Carpenter, Amos 164
Carpenter, Lt. Col. Benjamin 36, 37
Carpenter, Benjamin 22
Carpenter, Cyrel 101
Carroll, Mr. 382–83
Carter, Dr. 155
Casey, James 357
Chamberlain, Rev. Prof. Joshua 316, 343, 346
Chamberlain, Jason, Jr. 253
Chamberlin, Joshua 167
Chamberlin, William 215–16
Champagny, Jean-Baptiste Nompère de 278–79
Chandler, Thomas 56, 127–30
Chandler, Thomas, Jr. 89
Chapin, Judge 284–85
Chaplin, Mr. 142
Chapman, Mr. 94–95, 98–99
Chase, Dudley 312–313
Chase & Brackett 321
Chauncey, Nathaniel 134
Chenevard, Martha Bull 279–81
Cheney, Samuel 162
Cheshire Volunteers 23
Chipman, Harry 277–78
Chipman, Lemuel 140
Chipman, Mr. 179–80
Chipman, Nathaniel 105, 138, 140, 153, 277–78, 361–62
Chittenden, Martin 340
Chittenden, Mr. 276
Chittenden, Thomas 1, 26, 36, 37, 40, 82–85, 91, 93–94, 120, 151–52, 163, 347–49
Chittendon, Mr. 167
Church, Col. 93–94
Church, Eleazer 100
Church, Col. Timothy 36
Clap (Clapp), Mr. and Mrs. 293
Clapp, Caleb 359–60
Clapp, Mrs. 361–62
Clapperton, Hugh 381
Clark, Capt. Elisha 125–26
Clark, Gershom 139
Clark, Col. Isaac 104–5
Clark, J. 383–96
Clark, Lieut. 266–67
Clark, Mr. 266–67
Clark, Ozias 125–26, 127
Clark, Satterlee 256, 275–76
Clark, Scotto 170–71
Clark, Smith 125–26
Clark, Zadock 135
Clarke, George 169–70, 170
Clason, Isaac 304
Clay, Henry 372–73
Clemson, Capt. 304–5
<Clesson>, Roswell 142

General Index

Clinton, George 37, 38, 347
Cobb, Ebenezer 137
Cobb, Capt. Ezekiel 105
Cobbett, Mr. 332–33
Cochran, Capt. Robert 262–64
Coffeen, John 127–30
Cogsel, Peter 104
Colbert, James 190
Coldwell, Mr. 363–64
Cole, John 138
Coleman, William 40, 179, 181, 224–27
"Colledge Expenses" 48–49
Collins, Micajah 326–28
Collins, Stephen 326–28
Colton, Isaac 103
Comstock, Capt. Daniel 103
Cone, Lemuel 157
Cone, Mr. 111
Constitution: 192–93; adoption 141–42, 143–51
Continental Congress 1, 26, 79–80, 86–87, 87–88, 89
Cook, Jesse 104
Cook, Jonathan 256
Couleler, Joshua 134
Cowdry, Dr. 245
Cowen, James 104
Coxe, Tench 300
Crafts, Samuel C. 179–80
Craige, Capt. 158
Craige, Thomas 127–30
Crane, Seth 136
Crawford, William H. 369, 372–73
<Cris> 96
Croker, John W. 332–33, 334, 343
Crone, Mr. 94–95
Crook, Lt. William 99
Culver, Capt. Daniel 104
Cumberland County 81–82
Custis, Henry 136
Cutbush, Dr. 245
Cuthbert, Mr. 266
Cutin (or Cretin), Silant 222–23

Daggett, David 139
Dana, Mr. 185
Danbury, Battle of (1777) 24, 39
Daniel, Dr. 321
Davis, Francis 105
Davis, Gen. 311
Davis, George 245, 257–58
Davis, Henry 328
Davis, Joseph 136
Davis, Mr. 289–91, 376
Davis, Mr. and Mr. 183–84
Day, Elkanah 127–30
Day, Dr. Sylvester 281, 288
Dayton, Jonathan 201
Dearborn, Henry 209, 214–15, 216, 232, 235, 270–71, 298, 300, 326–28, 329, 352
debts owed SRB 205, 383–96
Decatur, Capt. Stephen 349–50
Dell, Lt. 183–84
Demming, Josiah 316–17
Dennison, George 137
Dennison, Mr. 236–38, 245
Dent, Capt. 240

Dewey, Mr. 216
Dickens, Asbury 331, 332–33, 334, 343, 346
Dickinson, James 321
Dickson, William 250–51
Dinsmoor, Samuel 370, 383–96
Doolittle, Theophilus 135
Dorr, Capt. 361–62
Dorr, Jonathan 181, 293, 298, 300, 305, 306, 309, 310–11, 320, 328–29, 351, 357
Dorr, Mrs. Jonathan 293, 305, 306, 309, 310–11, 320, 328–29, 351
Dorr, Joseph 181, 201, 209–10, 246, 258–59, 310, 304–5
Dorr, Mrs. Joseph 181, 246, 258–59
Dorr, Mrs. 361–62
Dorr, Nathaniel 19, 43, 162
Downing, John 136
Drake, James 134
Drew, Thomas C. 336
Drury, Ebenezer 89
Duane, William 347
Dudley, Medad 134
Dudley, Oliver 135
Duer, Mr. 160–61
<Duncan>, Esqr. 181
DuPonceau, P. S. 218–19
Dutton, Salmon 127–30
Dwight, Chaplain 51
Dwight, Mr. 371

Eastman, Capt. Enoch 104
Eastman, J. 177
Eaton, Lt. 166
Eaton, William 38, 39, 156, 236–38, 240, 242, 243, 245, 250, 257–58, 262, 268–69, 286–87, 303, 304
Eighth Brigade, Vermont Volunteers 27
election 164–65
electors 193–94
Ellery, Mr. 221–22
Elliot, James 194–95, 195–96, 198, 203, 209–10, 215–16, 221–22, 324
Elliot, Mr. 267–68, 330
Elliott, James 185
Ellis, Simeon 137
Ely, Justin 124–25
Enos, Pascal 137
Enos, Roger 137
Enos, Roger, Jr. 137
Epps, Mr. 311–12
Erskine, Gen. Sir William 24

Farnsworth, Commissary General 100–101
Farnsworth, Joseph 105
Farnsworth & Churchill 316
Farwell, Abel 293
Fasset, David 104
Fawcett, Nathan 137
Fay, Col. 168–69
Fay, Elijah 105
Fay, Jonas 58–59, 60, 89, 94, 118, 95

Fay, Joseph 160, 182
Fay, Maj. Joseph 105
Fay, Mr. 301–2
Fay, Nathan 105
Faye, Huldah 298
Fellows, Nathaniel 232
Ferris, Reed 135
First Regiment of Vermont Militia 5, 31, 36
Fisk, Ebenzer 52
Fisk, James 179–80, 284–85
Fisk, Js. 222–23
Fisk, Judge 347–49
Fisk, Miss 375
Fisk, Mr. 94–95, 336
Fisk, Nathan 100, 127–30, 152
Fisk, Solomon 157–58
Fisk, Sgt. Sylvanus 103
Fitch, Russell 314–15, 322, 337
flag see American flag
Flanders, J. 383–96
Fletcher, James 137
Fletcher, Mr. 142
Fletcher, Samuel 36, 93, 94, 97, 100–101, 105
Follert, Martin 105
Foot, Samuel A. 309–10, 323, 325
Foot, Stilman 151–52
Forrest, Thomas 163
Foster, Dan 161–62
Foster, Mr. 323
Fox, James 318
Fr[...], Phinehas 132
Francis, Mr. 298
Frasier (or Fraser), Daniel 172
Freeman, Mr. 127–30
Freeman, Phineas 104
Freeman, Phinehas 125–26
French, Thomas 136
Frost, John 199–200
Frost, Martha 377–80
Fuller, James 104
Fuller, Jonathan 127–30, 222–23
Fulton, Robert 325–26

<Gaas>, Mr. 361–62
Gallatin, Albert 216, 268–69, 314–15, 344–45, 345, 316–17, 350–51
Gallup, Mr. 293
Gallup, Oliver 198
Galusha, Jonas 105, 256, 284–85, 296, 312–13 314–15
Garlick, Heth 136
Garrand, Mr. 345
Geere, Shubal 127–30
General Assembly of Vermont 16, 40
Gerry, Elbridge 344
Ghent Treaty 19
Gibson, Jonathan 159
Gibson, Mr. 301–2
Gilbert, Eliot 179
Gilbert, Mr. 196
Giles, William Branch 289–91
Gilman, Mr. 305
Glover, John I. 155
Glover, Mr. 361–62
Goldsborough, Charles W. 236–38

Goodell, Capt. 166
Goodhue, Ebenezer 164
Goodhue, Joseph 207–8, 256
Goodrich, Adeline Bradley 279–81, 282, 282–83, 298, 365–66, 368, 370, 370–71, 371
Goodrich, Chauncey 81, 289–91
Goodrich, Mary E. 365–66, 367, 371–72, 374, 375, 376, 377–80, 381
Goodrich, Samuel Griswold 43, 282–83, 365–66, 367, 368, 369, 370, 370–71, 371, 371–72, 374, 375, 376, 381
Goodridge, Asael 167
Goodridge, Joseph 376
Gore, Christopher 298–300
Gorham, M. 383–96
Gorham, Mathia 170–71
Gorton, Stephen 195–96
Gould, Stephen 136
Gould, William 90–91
Governor and Council Records 5
Graham, Dr. Andrew 24, 27, 39
Graham, Dr. Chauncy 27, 39, 40
Graham, Col. 191
Graham, Dr. 180
Graham, Mrs. Ennis 132
Graham, Lt. Col. John Andrew 4, 39, 224–27, 232
Graham, Nathan Burr 40
Grammds, Mr. 162
Granger, Gideon 196, 254, 289–91, 318, 347–49
Grant, Charles 137
Grant, John 308–9
Grant, Lieut. 104
Grant, Samuel 377–80
Gray, Edwin 264
Green, Mr. A. 374
Green, Mrs. A. 374
Green, Beriah 137
Green, Capt. Beriah 105
Green, Ebenezer 136
Green, Mr. 314–15
Green, Timothy 86
Green Mountain Boys 16, 26, 34, 36
Greene, Benjamin 142
Griswold, Mr. 288, 309
Griswold, William A. 360
Grosvenor, Thomas Peabody 358
Grout, Hilkiah 130–31, 139

Haithorne, Ebenezer 134
Hall, A. 383–96
Hall, Abel 135
Hall, Atherton, Esqr. 170–71
Hall, Benjamin, 2d 135
Hall, Elihu 135
Hall, Elihu, Jr. 136
Hall, Ezra 383–96
Hall, James 136
Hall, John 135
Hall, John, 5th 136
Hall, Judge 199–200
Hall, Lot, Esqr. 127–30, 167, 262–64
Hall, Mr. 94–95

Hall & Green 368
Hamblet, Hezekiah 134
Hamilton, Alexander 189, 208, 316, 349–50
Hamilton, Col. 169–70
Hanson, Alexander Contee 358
Hanson, Samuel 198, 200
harbors 253, 257
Harding, Seth 235–36
Harrington, C. 115
Harrington, William C. 257, 266–67, 298–300
Harris, Lt. Ebenezer 105
Harris, Theophilus 277–78
Harrison, Samuel 347–49
Harrison, William Henry 330
Harrow, Joseph 104
Hastings, Dr. 204–5, 324–25
Hastings, Seth 253
Hatch, Major 284
Hatch, Mr. 365–66
Hatch, Rufus 284
Hatch, Uriel C. 203, 282–83
Hatch, William C. 181
Hatheway, Simeon 105
Haven, Dr. 340
Haven, Nathaniel A., Jr. 338–39, 340
Hawkins, Benjamin 227–231
Hawley, James 137
Hay, Mr. 179–80
Hayson, Richard 136
Hayward, Stephen 159
Hazen, Charlotte 240–41, 330–31
Hazen, Gen. Moses 240–41, 330–31
Hazen, William 240–41
Heath, Sgt. Phineas 104
<Heileman>, Dr. 207
Helms, William 289
Herman, Lt. Enos 104
Herman, Lt. Simeon 104
Herrington, Theophilus 256
Hickman, Harris H. 333
highway, public 157–58
Hilhouse, Mr. 98–99
Hillhouse, James 289–91
Hinsdale, Jacob 137
Hipkins, Capt. 334
Hitchcock, Lt. 51
Hitchcock, Samuel 140, 151–52
Hodges, Nathan 89
Hodgkins, E. 383–96
Holland, Ephraim 383–96
Holland, N. 377–80
Holland, Nathaniel 383–96
Ho<lt>, Mr. 166
Hopkins, Roswell 58–59, 104, 125–26, 151–52, 167
Holden, James 358–59, 359
Holden, Jonas 159
Holton, Ebenezer 127–30
Holton, Ms. 320
Holton, William 172
Holton, Zoheth 383–96
Hotchkiss, Capt. 94–95, 98–99
Hotchkiss, Mr. F. W. 365–66
Hotchkiss, Lent 98–99
Houghton, Edward 179

Howell, Thomas 135
Howland, Mr. 381
Hubbard, Daniel 135
Hubbard, David 135
Hubbard, John, Jr. 138
Hubbard, Mr. 219–20, 244–45
Hubbard, Prof. 328
Hubble, Elijah 135
Huges, Mr. 262–64
Hughes, Col 189
Hull, Andrew 160
Hull, Andrew, Jr. 286, 311–12, 319, 323
Hull, Mrs. Andrew, Jr. 323
Hull, Betsey 323
Hull, Elizabeth Mary Ann Atwater (Mrs. Andrew) 160
Hull, Gen. 289–91
Hull, Gov. 261–62, 333
Hull, Capt. Isaac 242–43, 243, 245
Hull, Mr. 109, 115, 325
Hull, Mrs. 309–10
<Hull>, Stephen 156
Hull, Gen. William 347–49, 376–77
Hull & Foot 307
Hunnewell, Joseph 137
Hunt, Arad 152–53
Hunt, Col. 105–6
Hunt, Jonathan 125–26
Hunter, Franklin 317
Hunter, Judge William 317
Huntington, Gurdon 189
Huntington, Jonathan 155
Huntington, Josiah 155
Hutchinson, T. 284–85
Hutchinson, Titus 317
Hyde, Ensign Charles 156

Ide, Joseph 170–71
Imlay, W. H. 365–66
independence 57–58, 60–79
Indiana Territory 206
Ingersoll, Jared 218–19
Ives, Abraham, Esqr. 104
Ives, Samuel 134

Jackson, Andrew 372–73
Jacob, Stephen 125–26, 137, 138
Jacobs, Stephen 244–45
Jarvis, Dr. Charles 258–59
Jefferson, Thomas 1, 2, 28, 29, 30, 38, 85, 160, 182–83, 197, 198, 209, 261–62, 256, 257, 266, 266–67, 274, 293, 341–42
Jennison, Daniel A. 377–80
Johns, Mr. 279–81
Johnson, Capt. 266–67
Johnson, D. 383–96
Johnson, Dr. 324–25, 336
Johnson, Lewis 266–67
Johnson, Luis 99
Johnson, Miles 131–32, 139, 159
Johnson, Mr. 160–61, 361–62
Johnson, Moses 167
Johnson, Philemon 134
Johnson, Col. Robert 135
Johnston, Samuel 227–231
Johonnot, Mr. 328

General Index

<Jonah> 96
Jones, Dr. 306–7
Jones, Jabez 340
Jones, Judge 309
Jones, Mr. 321
Jones, Reuben 127–30
judicial system 192–93
Judson, Jonathan 136

Kathan, Lieutenant Daniel 32
Kennedy, William 135
Kent, Seth 135
Keys, Stephen 137, 153
Kidder, O. 139
Kimball, Abraham 134
King, Adonijah 195–96
Kingsbary, Dr. 178–79, 219
Kinsman, William H. 137
Kirby, Ephraim 203–4
Knickerbacor, John 104, 137
Knight, Judge <Elijah> 253, 357
Knight, Samuel 172, 209–10
Knight, Simeon 254–55, 286, 347
Knoulton, Judge 139
Knoulton, Luke 131–32
Knox, Henry 156

Labogh, A. 222
Labogh. Jno. 222
Lake, Elnathan 136
Lamb, Anthony 189
Lamb, Gen. Anthony 261–62
Lamb, Larned 284–85
Lamberton, Allen 104
Lammot, Daniel 219, 221
land, vacant 52, 53, 55–56
land grant 52, 53
land purchases 56, 134–38
Lane, John 127–30
Langdon, <John> 344
Langdon, John 204–5, 306–7
Lansing, Abraham 138
Latten, Thomas 136
Laurie, Rev. James 328
Law, Mr. 185
Law, Thomas 326–28
Law, William 289–91
Lawrence, John 161–62
<Lawrens, Rawsom> 358–59
Lear, Tobias 236–38, 240, 257–58, 268–69, 283–84, 286–87
Leavenworth, Edmund 136
Lee, Maj. Gen. Charles 23, 24, 50
Lee & Haynsworth, Messrs. 306
Leigh, Mr. 246–47
Leigh, Mrs. 246–47
Leppenerell, R. 383–96
Le Roy, Jacob, & Sons 169–70
Levaque, Agustus 340
Lewis, Meriwether 209
Lincoln, Samuel 176–77
Lincoln, Samuel, Jr. 176–77
Lindsey, Thomas 137
Livingston, Edward 218–19
Livingston, Walter 160–61
Livingstone, Widow 377–80
Locklin, Davis 127–30
Locklin, Levi 127–30
Logan, George 201, 382

Loomis, Beriah 222–23
Lord, John G. 104
Lovejoy, Mr. 111
Lovell, Enos 127–30
Lovell, James 262–64
Luce, Elihu 323
Luce, Mr. 293
Lyman, Elias 222
Lyman, John, Jr. 222–23
Lyman, Justice 222
Lyman, Levi 383–96
Lyman, Gen. Phineas 311
Lyman, William 246–47
Lyon, Matthew 89, 90, 151–52, 347–49

<Macheaus>, Paul 125–26
Macon, Mr. 305
Madison, Dolly Paine 326–28, 357
Madison, James 1, 6, 28, 30, 38, 168, 184, 202, 278–79, 287, 295, 301, 326–28, 341–42, 344, 347, 347–49
Maese, Mr. 363–64
Mahumed, <Remed> 236–38
Mansfield, Samuel 135
Marcy, Hadlock 224
Marion, Esqr., Robert 284
Marks, Jonathan 135
Marsh, Daniel 105
Marsh, John 135
Marsh, Mr. 185
Marshall, John 30
Martin, D. 383–96
Marvin, Mr. 125–26, 140
Mason, Jeremiah 134, 338–39, 222–23
Mathers, James 320
Mathews, Mr. 124–25
Matlock, John 295
Matthews, James 103
Mattocks, Samuel 172–73, 173–74
May, Hezekiah 165
May, Mr. 298, 332–33, 336, 368
McClave, John 136
McClung, Maj. 104
McIntosh, Mr. 205
McKean, Jos. B. 218–19
McNeill Esqr, Daniel 190–91
McRae, Alexander 301–2
McWain, Sgt. William 3
Mead, William 137
Mecklenburg, Gen 85
Merrill, Nathaniel 135
Metcalf, R. 195–96
Michigan Territory 247–48, 248–49
Miles, Abner 167
military 216–17
militia 87–88, 108, 154, 155–56
Mills, Mr. 244–45
Minott, Samuel 157, 158
Mississippi Territory 352–55
Mitchal, Isaac 111
Mitchell, Justice 138
Mitchell, Dr. S. L. 326–28
Mitchill, Dr. 240–41
Moffett, Joseph 206–7, 219–20
Montgomery, Mr. 306–7

Monroe, James 168–69, 182, 278–79, 323, 332–33
Moore, <Alphonsus> 186–87
Moore, Col. 306–7
Morgan, Mr. J. 369
Morgan, Johnathan 139, 155, 349–50
Morris, Col. 139
Morris, Gen. 204
Morris, Gen. <Lewis Richard> 221–22
Morris, Gouverneur 194–95
Morris, Lewis Richard 133, 140
Moss, John 136
Mower, Nahum 224
Mullett, Thomas 332–33
Murray, Alexander 268–69

New York–Vermont Boundary Commissioner 29
Nicko[...], Capt. 300
Nicholson, Capt. 268–69
Niles, Nathaniel 151–52, 179–80, 184
Noble, Morgan 135
Norman, Mr. and Mrs. 180
North Carolina 252
Northrop, Amos 50–51
Norton, John 34, 222–23
Nott [Noth], John 37, 174–75, 222–23
Numa, Mr. 221–22
Nutting, Mr. 336

Oak, Seth 90–91
Olcott, Gen. 124–25
Olcott, Elias 127–30
Olcott, Jonathan 155
Olcott, Martha 166
Olin, Gideon 140, 151–52, 180, 215–16
Olin, Judge 184–85
Orentt, Consider 127–30
Osgood, N. 180
Otis, Harrison Gray 293
Otis, Samuel A. 197, 210, 246–47, 250–51

Pa[...], Elijah 132
Packer, Mr. 100–101
Page, Col. 253
Page, William 131
Page, William, Jr. 222–23, 234–35
Paine, Amasa 244–45
Paine, Elijah 125–26, 133, 138, 151–52
Paine, Lieut. 262–64
Paine, Mr. 139, 160–61, 195–96
Panderson, Lemuel 289–91
Parker, Andrew 135
Parker, Dedimus 134
Parker, Lt. Ebenezer 104
Parker, Gamaliel 135
Parker, Isaac 135
Parker, Jacob 134
Parker, Jesse 134
Parker, Timothy 127–30
Parmele, Capt. Alexander 190–91
Parmele, Samuel Davis 190–91, 195

Parsons, Gen. 51
Patten, Nathaniel 118
pay orders 103–5
Payson, Henry 329
Pearsall, Thomas 124, 130–31, 131–32, 139, 155, 157, 161–62, 168–69, 169–70, 179, 182, 246–47
Pees, Judge 289–91
Pell, Elijah 124
<Penniman>, Dr. 314–15
Penniman, Jabez 188, 261, 266, 273–74, 278, 278–79, 319
Penniman, Mrs. Jabez 261, 266, 319
Perham, Lemuel 111
Perkins, Elisha 137
Perkins Library, Duke University 7
Perrin, Abel 381
Perry, Capt. 381
Peters, John T. 317
Phelps, Charles 301
Phillips, John 134
Pickering, Timothy 358, 289–91, 298–300, 373–74, 374
Pike, Capt. 254–55
Pitcher, Ebenezer 138
Plumer, William 7, 30, 31, 257–58, 259, 309, 313–14
Plympton, Joseph 329
Pomeroy, Hen[r]y 127–30
Porter, Asa 167
ports 253, 257
Post, <Justins> 256
Post, Martin 222–23, 234–35
Potter, Dr. 109, 109–110
<Potter>, Mr. 222–23
Powell, Miles 52
Pratt, Samuel 173–74
Preble, Edward 236–38
Prentice, Samuel 219–20
Prentice, Thomas 161–62
Prentiss, Mr. 185
Prescott, Abel 137
Preston, Colburn 89
Preston, <Samuel> 51
Priestley, Joseph 217
<Prire>, Amasa 204
The Prophet 330

Raighter, Col. 266
Rand, Mr. 180
Ranney, Ephraim, Jr. 308–9, 383–96
Ranney, <Waitstill> 318
Rawle, William 218–19
Ray, Joshua 134
Ray, Joshua, Jr. 135
Red(d)ington, George B. 377–80
Reed, Philip 344
Reed, Thomas 136
Reeve, Tapping 1, 23, 372
Rhea, John 250–51
Rhea, Jonathan 289
Rice, Stephen 104
Rice, Thomas 134
Rich, Charles 222–23
Richard, Widow 99
Richards, Mark 6, 17, 18, 162, 177–78, 181, 198, 288, 306, 336, 361–62, 363–64, 368
Richards, <Sheriff Mark> 322
Richards, Mrs. Mark 293
Richards, Sarah (Bradley) 6
Richardson, James 127–30
Rickee, John 127–30
Right, Ebenezer 138
Ripley, Christopher 321, 332, 332–33, 334, 343
Ripley, Eleazar Wheelock 181, 332, 346
Robinson, Col. 93–94
Robinson, David 207
Robinson, Eli 357
Robinson, Elijah 139
Robinson, Jonathan 169, 184–85, 256, 284–85, 298–300, 312–13 314–15
Robinson, Judge 267–68, 273–74, 276
Robinson, Major 151–52
Robinson, Mr. 179–80
Robinson, Moses 26, 31, 33, 35, 36, 58–59, 60, 95, 97, 118, 151–52
Robinson, Nathan 172–73
Robinson, Thomas 318
Rockwood, Cepha L. 318
Rodgers, Capt. 236–38
Rodgers, <Capt. John> 349–50
Rogers, Capt. 361–62
Row, Mary 16
Rowler, Lt. Abner 104
Roy, Silas 139
Royce, L. 282–83
Royce, Mr. 167
Royse, Lydia Bull 279–81, 282, 282–83
Rudd, Joseph 104
Ruggles, Nathaniel 202–3, 212–13, 232, 293, 315, 345
Rush, Benjamin 40, 206
Rush, Richard 340
Russel, John 155
Russell, Joseph 383–96
Rutledge, Mr. 221–22

Sabin, Noah, Jr. 170–71
Sackett, Enoch 105
Sackett, Reuben 105
Safford, David 104
Safford, Jacob 104
Safford, Capt. Joseph 103–4
Safford, Mr. 179–80
Safford, Samuel 137
Sage, Parson 160
St. Cair, Gen. Arthur 363–64
Sanders, Daniel C. 346, 352
Sanford, John 136
Sanford, Oliver 136
Sanford, Seth 136
Sanford, Seth Samuel 136
Sargeant, Eli 195–96
Sargeant, Erastus 137
Sargeant, Col. John 195–96
Sargeant vs. Gorton 195–96
Sawyer, Capt. Jesse 104
Schlesinger Library, Radcliffe College 7
Scott, Nathaniel, & Co. 300
Scott, William 219–20
Seaver, Nathaniel 105
Selden, Esqr. 169
Seley, Benjamin 135
Sessions, Esqr., John 177–78
Seton, Mrs. 212–13
Sharp, Andrew 104
Sharp, Capt. William 104
Shattuck, G. C. (Dr.) 276
Shaw, Dr. 267–68
Shaw, Mr. 312–13
Shaw, Robert Gould 311–12
Shaw, Samuel 284–85, 298–300, 336
Shelden, Asaph 138
Sheldon, Dr. 370
Sheldon, Mr. 179–80, 185
Shepardson, Samuel 284–85
Sheperd, Thomas and John 296–97
<Shepth>, Daniel 127–30
Sherborn, Nathaniel 135
Shipman, Mr. 81
Sikes (Sykes), Col. 196
Sill, R. 51
Simcoe, John Graves 204–5
Skinner, John 371
slavery 41, 232–34, 252, 355–56
Smedley, Mr. 344–45
Smith, Mr. A. B. 365–66
Smith, Cephas, Jr. 180
Smith, Daniel 250–51
Smith, Ephraim 137
Smith, Gen. 382, 382–83
Smith, I. 383–96
Smith, Israel 41, 151–52, 153, 197, 253, 257, 260–61, 284–85, 296, 309, 198, 347–49
Smith, J. 125–26, 125–26
Smith, Jacob 179–80
Smith, James 232
Smith, Joseph 89
Smith, Judge 365–66
Smith, Maryanne 365–66
Smith, Mr. 169, 180, 186–87, 210–11, 360, 365–66
Smith, Nathan (Dr.) 185–86, 188, 276–77, 297
Smith, Nicholas 127–30
Smith, Noah 32, 33
Smith, Mr. R. 351
Smith, Robert 318
Smith, Samuel 347
Smith, Samuel 373, 373–74, 374
Smith, William 167
Snow, Francis 363–64
Sparhawk, George K. 185
Sparhawk, Thomas 185
Sparkawk, Hubbard (Dr.) 297, 324–25
Sparks, Capt. 183–84
Spears, Denming 137
Spencer, Abel 210–11
Spencer, Mr. E. 336
Spooner, Alain 215–16
Spooner, Alden 271–72, 281–82
Spooner, Alfred 337
Spooner, Eliakim 105, 196, 308–9, 336, 337

General Index

Spooner, Lt. Gov. 100–101
Spooner, Mr. 86, 169, 179–80
Spooner, Paul 58–59, 97, 105
Sprague, Elkanah 89
<Squier>, T. [Truman Squires] 167
Stanley, Mr. 179–80, 185
Stark, Joel 161–62
Starkweather, L. 383–96
State Constitutional Convention (1791) 28
Stearns, Deacon 377–80
Stearns, Stephen 383–96
Stephens, John 134
Sterne, Laurence 296
Stiles, Ezra 86
Stillman, George 135
Stoddard, Amos 339
Stone, Abel 138
Stone, Col. 154
Stone, David 369, 377–80, 382, 383–96
Stone & Bellows 369
Storer, Charles 253
Strong, Col. 183–84
Strong, Ebenezer 219–20
Strong, John 89
Strong, Mr. 336
Strong, S. 185–86
Stuyvesant, Peter [Petrus] 172, 179
Stuyvesant, Peter Gerard (son) 179, 181
Summers, Luke 136
Sumner, Benjamin 204–5
Sumter, Gen. 306
Sutherland, John 182
Sutherland, John, Jr. 182
Swenmore, E. S. 350–51

Tarbox, James 284–85
taxes 217–18
Taylor, Mr. 185
Taylor, Mrs. 298
Taylor, Rev. 205
Tele, Joseph 142
Temple, John 136
Tennessee lands 227–231
Thatcher, Mr. 98–99
Thomas, John H. 358
Thomas, Isaiah 188
Thompson, Henry 287
Thompson, John 134
Thuston, Nathan 127–30
Tichenor, Isaac 41, 95, 97, 104–5, 133, 138, 151–52, 212, 214–15, 216, 234–35, 296
Tichenor, Maj. <Levrt. G.> 210–11
Tiley (or Riley), Capt. E. 93
Tingey, Como 349–50
Tingey, Thomas 291
Tomlinson, Gideon 344–45
Town, Dr. 207
Townsend, Isarah 325–26
Townsend, Micah 32
Tozer, Peter 142
Tracy, Elisha 178, 269–70, 274–75, 279, 288, 294, 295–96, 306–7, 329
Tracy, Uriah 201

Trigg, Mr. 277–78
Tripolean War 39, 239
Tripoli 239, 240, 245, 301
Troop, Robert 160–61
Trumbull, Joseph 365–66
<Tuanies>, John 222
Tudor, Henry Bradley 377–80, 383–96
Tudor, Henry S. 377–80, 383–96
Tudor, Mary Rowe 377–80, 383–96
Turner, Mr. 349–50
Tuttle, Mr. 293, 376–77
Twelfth Amendment 2, 29, 38
Tyler, Judge 184–85
Tyler, Royall 296, 256, 267–68, 312–13 314–15, 322, 337

Underwood, Joseph 127–30
unidentified correspondent 310

Vanderhoof, Capt. Henry 104
Van Horne, Augustus 164
Van Rensselaer, Killian Killian 325–26
Vaux, Roberts 355–56
Vermont General Assembly 16, 40
Vermont Historical Society in Barre 7
Vermont Militia, First Regiment 5, 31, 36
Vermont Volunteers, Eighth Brigade 27
"Vermont's Appeal to the Candid and Impartial World" 26
Verplank, Mr. 139
Vincent, Mr. 185
Vose, Roger 336
Voyage from Calcutta 163

Wadsworth, Jeremiah 153
Wait, Col. 97
Walbach, Capt. 277
Walbridge, Mr. 90, 151–52
Walbridge, Silas 104–5
Wales, Aaron 173–74
Wales, Mary 377–80
Walker, Jesse 104–5
Wall, Mrs. Patrick 34, 35
Wallbradge, Col. Ebenezer 104
Ward, Edmund 136
Ward, William 131–32
Ward, Capt. William 105
Ware, Jonathan 219–20
Warner, Daniel 134
Warner, Jacob 182
Warner, Gen. Jonathan 123–24
Washington, George 23, 27, 50, 89, 266–67
Waters, Constable 100–101
Waters, Oliver 104
Watkins, Abner 318
Watkins, Capt. 158
Watkins, Charles 383–96
Watkins, R. 383–96
Wayne, Anthony 39
Webb, Joshua, Esqr. 127–30
Wederstramdt, Lt. 245
Weld, Elias 105

Welles, Ephraim 164
Wellington, Abel 364
Wellman, Benjamin 104
Wells, Joshua 127–30
Wesson, Isaac 127–30
West, Benjamin 127–30
West, John 124–25
West, Mr. 160–61
Wetherbee, Samuel 360
Wheatley, Mr. 185
Wheaton, Joseph 320
Wheaton, Mrs. Joseph 320
Wheaton, Mr. 260–61
Wheeler, Gideon 136
Wheeler, Capt. Isaac 104
Wheeler, Samuel 326–28
Wheelock, Eleazer 253
Wheelock, Dr. John 186
Wheelock, Mr. 261
Whipple, Commander 183–84
Whipple, Daniel 131–32
White, John 284–85
White, Mr. 167
White, Moses 240–41
White, William 100–101
Whitelaw, James 199–200
Whiting, Col. 284–85
Whiting, Nathan 318
Whitlock, Lt. 304–5
Whitney, Esqr. 169
Whitney, Mr. 195–96
Whitney, Wm. R. 167
Whittelsey, Samuel 371, 371–72, 374
Whittelsey, Mrs. Samuel 371
Whittlesey, Chauncey 135
Whittlesey, Charles 135
Whittlesey, Samuel 135
Wickwire, Capt. Jonah 104
Wier, Catherine 377–80
Wier (Wires), Charlton 367–68
Wier, John H. 377–80, 360–61, 367–68, 383–96
Wilbur, Seprelet 383–96
Wilder, Hon. Joseph 246–47
Wilkinson Ville 183–84
Wilkins, <John> 111
Wilkinson, James 245
Willard, Constable 376
Willard, Eli 137
Willard, Henry K. 6, 15, 42
Willard, John 204, 303
Willard, Joseph 180–81, 357
Willard, Margaret 371, 371–72
Willard, Prent 134
Willard, Sarah Bradley Kellogg 6, 44
Willard Bradley Papers (Library of Congress) 6, 7
Williams, Col. 209
Williams, Jonathan 265
Williams, Major Leonard 326–28
Williams, Mr. 167
Williams, Samuel 208, 326–28
Williams, Stephen 166
Willis, Samuel 138
Willoughby, John 134
Wilson, A. 383–96
Wilson, Amy Suter 15

Wilson, Benjamin 246–47
Wilson, Jeremiah 246–47
Wilson, Jonathan 246–47
Wilson, Joseph, Esq. 180
Wilson, Luke 246–47
Wilson, Mr. 246–47
Wilson, Nathaniel 246–47
<Wing>, D., Jr. 222–23
Wing, David 214, 234–35

Witherell, James 179–80, 267–68, 276, 281
Wolcott, A. 316–17
Wood, Barnabas 337
Wood, Mr. 179–80
<Woodleridge> 125–26
Woods, Broadstreet 222–23
Woodward, Bezaleel 90
Woodward, Judge 196

Wooster, David 16, 24, 25, 139, 161–62
Wooster, Thomas 136
Wosster, Mr. 98–99
Wright, Mr. 185
Wright, Peter 105, 127–30
Wright, Robert 358